LAURENTIAN UNIVERSITY

LAURENTIAN UNIVERSITY

A History

LINDA AMBROSE, MATT BRAY, SARA BURKE,
DONALD DENNIE, AND GUY GAUDREAU

Edited by Matt Bray

Published for Laurentian University

By McGill-Queen's University Press
Montreal & Kingston | London | Ithaca

Legal deposit third quarter 2010
Bibliothèque nationale du Québec

Printed in Canada on acid-free paper that is 100% ancient forest free
(100% post-consumer recycled), processed chlorine free

McGill-Queen's University Press acknowledges the support of the
Canada Council for the Arts for our publishing program. We also
acknowledge the financial support of the Government of Canada
through the Book Publishing Industry Development Program
(BPIDP) for our publishing activities.

LIBRARY AND ARCHIVES CANADA CATALOGUING IN PUBLICATION

Laurentian University : a history / Linda Ambrose ... [et al.] ;
edited by Matt Bray.

Issued also in French.
Includes bibliographical references and index.
ISBN 978-0-7735-3772-9

1. Laurentian University of Sudbury – History.   I. Ambrose,
Linda McGuire, 1960–   II. Bray, R. M. (Robert Matthew), 1944–
III. Laurentian University of Sudbury

LE3.L268L38 2010   378.713'133   C2010-901116-3

All reasonable attempts have been made to contact copyright
holders of illustrations and photographs included herein. If you
have additional information to provide regarding copyright and
permissions, please contact the Department of History, Laurentian
University, Sudbury, Ontario, P3E 2C6.

Set in 10/12 Minion with Meta+
Book design & typesetting by Garet Markvoort, zijn digital

DEDICATION

We dedicate this history to all faculty, staff and students at Laurentian University during the past 50 years.

CONTENTS

INTRODUCTION

A product of the post-World War II Baby Boom, Laurentian University of Sudbury/ l'Université Laurentienne de Sudbury, a unique bilingual experiment in post-secondary education, welcomed its first cohort of students in September 1960. Forty-plus years later, it occurred to several Canadianists in the department of history that an institutional history would be an appropriate way of celebrating the university's fiftieth anniversary. No full scale study had been undertaken, although in celebration of Laurentian's 25th anniversary, Gwenda Hallsworth had written a short history, *Le beau risque du savoir: Un bref historique de l'Université Laurentienne / A venture into the realm of higher education: A brief history of Laurentian University*, that focussed on its early years. We did nothing immediately about the idea, but a few weeks later, coincidentally, Vice-President Academic (Anglophone Affairs) Douglas Parker approached us on behalf of then-President Judith Woodsworth with exactly the same idea. Clearly the stars were aligned, and three of us, Linda Ambrose, Sara Burke, and Matt Bray, took up the challenge, joined shortly by our colleagues Guy Gaudreau and Gaétan Gervais. Unfortunately, ill health forced Gaétan to step aside, but we were able to recruit sociologist Donald Dennie, former dean of Social Sciences and Humanities and a student at Laurentian during that first year, to take his place.

Although 2010 then seemed eons away, we knew time would be a factor because in addition to our regular teaching and administrative responsibilities, we all had other research projects that took priority. President Woodsworth appreciated our dilemma and came to our rescue, hiring Charles Levi to spearhead the research phase. Charles' qualifications were excellent. After receiving his doctorate in history from York University in 1998, he served for three years as senior researcher on the University of Toronto History project that in 2002 produced Martin L. Friedland's acclaimed *The University of Toronto: A History*.

Over the course of 2004 and 2005, Charles amassed a large part of the research material on which this history is based. An indefatigable worker, he mined the national and provincial archives in addition to those at Laurentian, scanned newspapers such as the *Sudbury Star* and *Northern Life*, and interviewed a number of individuals prominent in Laurentian's early years, to cite only three of his many research tasks. He also wrote a series of reports on diverse aspects of the university's history that provided valuable context for our individual chapters. While Charles bears no responsibility for how we have utilized the fruits of his labour, our debt to him is enormous.

The list of other groups and individuals to whom the authors are indebted is lengthy. Over the years, Laurentian University (the Office of the President, the Placement Centre Work Study program, the *Vast and Magnificent Land* research fund), and the Ontario Ministry of Northern Development and Mines Summer Jobs Service funded a series of research projects involving the following students who did yeoman service on our behalf: Josée Blanchette, Jennifer Levin Bonder, Kaleigh Bradley, Jennifer Desjardins, Rachel Desjardins, Amélie Dugas, Maya Holson, Andréanne Joly, Brian Kett, Kathleen Labbe, Eric Larocque, Sarah Mac-Dougall, Jason Mercier, Jessica Morrison, Seana Murdock, Sarah Myllymaki, Casey Owens, Jenna Smith, Christina St-Onge, Francine Tisdelle. We are also grateful for the assistance provided by Laurentian University archivist Marthe Brown and her staff, by librarian Nancy Ladouceur, by Mary-Catherine Taylor in Instructional Media and by City of Greater Sudbury archivist Shanna Fraser. We wish to acknowledge, too, the help of organizations such as the Students' General Association and l'Association des étudiantes et étudiants francophones, of the several university departments, administrative and academic, that gave us access to valuable print and photo collections, and of the large number of individuals referenced in the endnotes, sidebars and photo captions.

We must thank as well colleagues and associates, present and past, who served as sounding boards for our interpretive musings, responded to queries about matters of detail, or read and commented upon parts of the draft manuscript. The list includes: Brian Aitken, Stephen Andrews, Stephen Azzi, Peter Beckett, Nelson Belzile, Larry Black, Bruce Burke, Dieter Buse, Jean-Charles Cachon, Ron Chrysler, Danielle Coulombe, Wes Cragg, Leda Culliford, Hermann Falter, Gaétan Gervais, Douglas Hallman, Margaret Kechnie, Andrii Krawchuk, Andrea Levan, Edward Monahan, Douglas Parker, Pat Pickard, Amanda Schweinbenz, Ashley Thomson, Micheline Tremblay, Carl Wallace. Their much-appreciated efforts greatly improved the text, though none is responsible for its content or interpretive approach, these, along with any errors of commission or omission, belonging solely to the authors.

We wish also to acknowledge the patience and dedication of those who transformed our draft manuscript into two published works, one in English and the other in French. Copy editors Jennifer Nault, Sylvie Rodrigue, and Normand Renaud skillfully brought much-needed coherence and consistency to our diverse writing styles, and Frédéric Demers (English to French), and again, Sylvie Rodrigue and Normand Renaud (French to English), adeptly translated the edited texts. Lastly, we owe a debt of gratitude to McGill-Queen's University Press and particularly Philip Cercone, Joan McGilvray, Anna Lensky, and Adrian Galwin for their multifarious efforts to bring the publication of this history to a timely fruition.

On a more personal note, the authors would like to recognize the contributions of one other person to this project. As anyone who works in an academic setting knows, the individual most responsible for the well-being of a department is the secretary, although that title no longer adequately describes the position's critical role, if it ever did. That has certainly been true of the department of history at Laurentian. We have been extremely fortunate that for thirty years Rose-May Démoré has managed the department's affairs with tremendous competence, forbearance, and good humour, creating an atmosphere of cooperation and goodwill that has benefited us all in countless ways.

Apart from two introductory chapters that trace the institution's historical roots in Northern Ontario and examine the immediate circumstances of its founding, we have structured the history of Laurentian University around six principal themes – university governance, academic evolution, bilingualism and biculturalism, students, the faculty association, and the role of women – divided into two categories, evolving structures and developing identities. We realize these are by no means all-inclusive, but believe they collectively encompass the core elements of the Laurentian experience that can be examined in a single volume. No one chronological template perfectly accommodates all of these topics – critical turning points for some do not necessarily coincide with those of others. Still, most fit generally into the three time periods we have adopted for organizational purposes: challenges of the sixties, 1960 to 1972; era of transition, 1972 to 1985; and the modern age, 1985 to the present.

One additional chapter, on federation relations, demands special explanation. At the beginning of the project we were faced with the conundrum of how to handle the associated, but distinctive, histories of Laurentian's three federated denominational institutions, the University of Sudbury, Huntington University, and Thorneloe University. After a good deal of reflection, we decided that because each plans to document its own institutional history, we would limit ourselves to a general chapter on federation relations, recognizing that this underplays their vital place in Laurentian's history. Similarly, our relatively cursory treatment of Laurentian's three original affiliated institutions, Collège universitaire de Hearst, Nipissing University College in North Bay, and Algoma University College in Sault Ste. Marie, the latter two now independent, is explained by their existence from the very beginning, no matter what the legalities, as distinct institutions, each with a separate history.

Cooperative writing projects present special challenges. Historians by their very nature tend to be individualists, bringing to their task particular philosophies and experiences – professional and personal – that shape their interpretations of the past. This is even more so the case when the subject of study is an institution with which the authors have been associated anywhere from ten to fifty years. Complicating the situation is the complexity of Laurentian, a bilingual, multicultural university founded by a tripartite, denominational partnership. Differences of viewpoint inevitably arose between us, though none of a serious nature. As indicated by the fact that authorship of each unit is clearly identified, we addressed this issue by leaving final responsibility for their text to the respective authors. We critiqued each others' drafts, and general editor Matt Bray was responsible for such things as eliminating unnecessary duplication, but we have made no attempt to force our occasionally divergent views into a single interpretative mould. In that sense, the writing of this history reflects the ultimate Laurentian experience of compromise, without which the university would have never come into existence, let alone survived to celebrate its fiftieth anniversary.

PART A | ROOTS

ALPHONSE RAYMOND BUILDING, 1976 | The Alphonse Raymond Building is home to
L'École des sciences de l'éducation

AERIAL VIEW OF THE CAMPUS ATHLETIC FACILITIES | This aerial view showcases the athletic facilities of the Laurentian campus including the 200- and 400-metre outdoor tracks and the Ben Avery Gymnasium which houses the Olympic-sized pool.

BRENDA WALLACE READING ROOM | Students enjoy the sunny space in the Brenda Wallace Reading Room, a 2001 addition to the J.N. Desmarais Library.

J.N. DESMARAIS LIBRARY IN WINTER | Among its holdings, the J.N. Desmarais Library houses a variety of archival materials pertaining to northeastern Ontario.

NORTHERN ONTARIO SCHOOL OF MEDICINE | The first new medical school to be created in Canada in more than thirty years, the Sudbury site of the Northern Ontario School of Medicine opened its doors in 2005, and celebrated the graduation of its charter class in June 2009.

LAURENTIAN BEACH | During the summer months Laurentian's private beach on Lake Nepahwin, staffed with lifeguards, is a popular spot for students, staff and faculty.

TIPI IN FOUNDERS' SQUARE | The tipi in Founders' Square symbolizes Laurentian's tri-cultural identity and its commitment to indigenous students, programs, and communities.

SCHOOL OF EDUCATION BUILDING | Created using sustainable design principles, the new state-of-the-art English Language School of Education building officially opened in 2008.

SCIENCE BUILDINGS AT DUSK | The Fraser building, home to the Faculty of Science and Engineering, the Fraser Auditorium, and Alumni Hall, showcased here against the Sudbury skyline at night.

CAMPUS IN WINTER | This Narnia-like scene evokes some of the beauty of Laurentian's campus in winter.

LAURENTIAN CAMPUS FROM BELL PARK | Familiar to Sudbury residents and tourists alike, this is the view of the campus looking across Ramsey Lake from Bell Park.

SNOWY ROOFTOP VIEW FROM THE STUDENT RESIDENCES, 1976

1 The Origins of Laurentian University

GUY GAUDREAU

The creation of Laurentian University in 1960 did not mark the beginning of university education in Northern Ontario. As early as 1913, Sacred Heart College and later the University of Sudbury had, through their pedagogical practices, established a firm university tradition. In many respects these institutions constituted the origin of Laurentian University. Programs such as mining engineering began with them, and a number of persons who would play a role in the future university such as faculty and board members were already active in them. It is important, therefore, to review the highlights of this prehistory, dominated by a centuries-old religious order that left its mark on Canadian history from the time of New France: the Society of Jesus (la Compagnie de Jésus).

The Founding of a Classical College

The Jesuit presence on the shores of Georgian Bay went back to the early years of New France. After a lengthy absence, the Order resumed missionary activities among the Native communities of Manitoulin Island in 1842, on the urging of Bishop Power of Toronto. Advancing colonization and logging around the Great Lakes and increased contacts with Native peoples prompted the Catholic clergy to establish missions in the area.[1] When the Canadian Pacific Railway constructed its transcontinental line in the early 1880s, it was the Bishop of Peterborough's turn to request religious ministry for the thousands of railroad labourers hard at work in the area.[2] In 1883, consequently, the Jesuits arrived in Sudbury at the same time as the railway company. They immediately founded a mission that soon became a parish. Named Sainte-Anne-des-Pins, the bilingual parish served the Catholic population of a small village whose economic mainstays were still the railway and logging. While constructing the building that would serve as chapel, school and presbytery – work on the first church would not begin until 1887 – Father Hormidas Caron bought a 300 acre parcel of land from Canadian Pacific in anticipation of the future needs of the community. Was a college already foreseen at this point?[3]

Although plans for a classical college (collège classique) were still a far-off dream, it is important to understand the context of the times and the significance of this institution for the Jesuit order. When Father Caron purchased the land in 1886, the Jesuits already operated two classical colleges in French Canada: Collège Sainte-Marie in Montreal, then a bilingual college, and Saint-Boniface College in Winnipeg, which the bishop had placed under their direction a year earlier.[4] In 1886, no college in Ontario offered courses in French, because the two bilingual colleges founded in the middle of the nineteenth century – St. Joseph's in Ottawa, which became a university in 1866, and Assumption in the Detroit area[5] – had ceased to provide French instruction. Only in 1901 would the University of Ottawa become bilingual once again.

A college project slowly began to take shape at the start of the twentieth century. Mining activities that seemed uncertain in the 1890s had by then achieved a measure of stability, as evidenced by the creation in 1902 of the International Nickel Company, an American company, and its investments in the region. Colonization advanced rapidly due to the carefully planned and profitable route chosen for the Canadian Pacific Railway which encouraged the establishment of numerous Catholic parishes based on farming in the Valley north of Sudbury, and in the Nipissing district. The Jesuits played a prominent role in these developments. When in 1904 the Diocese of Sault Ste. Marie was carved out of the Diocese of Peterborough, it had "31,000 parishioners, six secular priests, 30 Jesuit priests and approximately one hundred missions."[6] The strength of the Jesuit presence in the diocese was most probably the reason the new bishop responded favourably to the Jesuit Provincial Superior's request for a college in 1905.[7]

At the time, the possibility of establishing the college in Sault Ste. Marie instead of Sudbury was discussed, but the bishop left the choice of location to the Jesuits. Because of the lack of Jesuit teachers, construction could not begin immediately, so a decision on location was not pressing. From 1910 onward, however, the scales tipped squarely in Sudbury's favour due to its greater Catholic population as compared to Sault Ste. Marie, the higher number of French-Canadian parishes in the area, and the arrival of two other transcontinental railways in the Sudbury district.

In March 1912, the Jesuit Father General in Rome gave the green light to the project. Construction began soon afterwards, and on August 25th Bishop Scollard blessed the cornerstone. This came at a propitious moment as the Sudbury High School had been founded in 1909, and Franco-Sudburian elites were concerned that a number of French-Canadian students were gravitating towards the new English high school. Nonetheless, Bishop Scollard had been quite clear as to the bilingual vocation of the institution to be called 'Sacred Heart College.' And because one of the goals was the training of secular priests, the college was open only to male students.

Scollard, however, had not clearly specified the form that bilingualism would take. His letter to the Jesuit Provincial dated March 31, 1912 seems to indicate that the intention was to offer two complete programs of classical studies, one in French and the other in English. Given the difficulties of providing enough professors, and of space limitations at Sacred Heart College, it was impossible for the president to fulfill the bishop's wishes. "Therefore," according to Thérèse Boutin, "to circumvent the problem, the Jesuits resorted to a somewhat peculiar form of bilingual pedagogy: the professor could, if he so desired, use both languages in the classroom."[8] Because the college faculty came mainly from Quebec and was largely unilingual Francophone, English-language instruction quickly disappeared, and the institution ceased to be bilingual in 1916.

Patriotic considerations were not the only reason the new Jesuit college soon became a bastion of Northern Ontario Francophone aspirations. Then, as now, the law of numbers weighed heavily in such decisions; around 1910, there were 11,000 Anglophone Catholics in the area, and 33,000 Francophone Catholics.[9] By gaining a private religious institution that did not fall under government control in a province in which it was a minority, French Canada in New Ontario could continue to act as if it were the majority, despite the fact that Ontario was then enforcing the sinister Regulation XVII forbidding French as a language of instruction in public schools. But the day would come, near the end of the 1950s, when the community would be forced to come to terms with its minority status, acquiring access to expanded post-secondary education on the majority's terms.

Sacred Heart College

Having established a classical college, French Canadians thereby gained control of a private institution of learning that provided education at the secondary level, namely the first five years of the classical studies program, and at the university level, the last three years of the program. The college offered the most talented elementary school pupils the type of education essential to the training of the community's professional and religious leaders. It also afforded a cultural milieu in which the values of Christianity and of French and Catholic cultures were reproduced and inculcated in youth.

What was the "classics course" (cours classique) and who were the students attending the college? "In the twentieth century," explained Gaétan Gervais, "the classical college was still the dominant form of higher education in French Canada."[10] The classics course required eight years of study, one year having been added to the program in the fall of 1929. The course content was basically identical to that of the other classical colleges in French Canada. The college also offered entrance courses to prepare students whose elementary schooling was deemed inadequate. Instruction was organized as a progression, and the core subjects taught were French, Latin, Greek, mathematics and religion.[11] The program also included extracurricular activities which were considered just as important as formal schooling.

Even though the last three years of the program provided the equivalent of a university education, this did not automatically confer a university diploma. The

SACRED HEART COLLEGE | Founded in 1913, Sacred Heart College, a classical college in the tradition of the Society of Jesus, was the direct antecedent of the University of Sudbury, and, indirectly, of Laurentian University. For nearly a century, it has served the educational needs of the Roman Catholic and French Canadian community in northeastern Ontario and northwestern Quebec.

end point of the program, in fact, was a Bachelor of Arts granted by a university after the student successfully completed his exams. For this reason, it was crucial for Sacred Heart to be affiliated with a recognized university in order to graduate its students. Moreover, this affiliation facilitated the students' passage from college to university. Options for affiliation were of necessity limited, restricted to French or bilingual universities in order to ensure that graduating students could write their final exams successfully.

At first, the college approached the University of Ottawa, Jesuit discussions with the president of that institution starting as early as 1913. Pending an agreement that would inevitably reshape the program, instruction was modelled on the program of Collège Sainte-Marie in Montreal. The affiliation agreement was signed in 1916, forcing Sacred Heart to adjust its program to meet the requirements of the University of Ottawa as the degree-granting institution. Because other Ontario universities recognized the Bachelor of Arts degrees granted by the University of Ottawa, the college had to accommodate them, too. But the Oblates, who controlled the University of Ottawa, did not follow the Jesuit approach to education, or the same program design. Renowned in the field of education, the Jesuits could not easily bow to the Oblate requirements, and dissension finally led to the termination of the affiliation in 1927. A new agreement was then signed with Laval University.

Another problem was how to ensure recognition of diplomas for the handful of graduates who intended to pursue their education at the University of Toronto. While Laval henceforth had a major influence on the college's program, the University of Toronto also had its own entrance requirements. Until 1934, only one of the college's graduates was refused admission there,[12] while eight others were admitted without a problem, four to study law and four to study education. (At the time, to teach at the secondary level, one first had to obtain a BA and complete a teacher training program that was not offered by the Ottawa Teachers' College.) In 1934, however, the University of Toronto refused admission to two college graduates even though they had successfully completed their final exams at Laval. This quickly brought about a reform of the college program, though it still had to meet the Laval requirements. The solution was to reduce the number of hours of Greek instruction in order to offer more mathematics, English and sciences.[13]

While preparing students for bachelor's degrees was the college's primary purpose, it had others as well. In reality, few students actually completed the entire classics course. According to calculations by Josée Valiquette, only about 17 per cent of students who entered the course finished it.[14] The fact that the vast majority interrupted their studies along the way was due neither to failure nor lack of financial resources.[15] It was because the college studies were a means to many ends. For those who intended to teach at the elementary level, the passing of the matriculation examination after Versification (the third year of the classics program) gave direct access to the Ottawa Teachers' College. This explains why in 1950–1951, for example, of the 32 students who passed this examination, only 14 returned to the college the following year.[16]

In this same vein, admission to university programs did not necessarily require the successful completion of the BA exams. Claude Galarneau, an expert in the history of French Canada's classical colleges, states that "departures [from college] occurred mostly after Rhétorique [the sixth year of the program] and those were often the future doctors, lawyers and notaries, who left in order to enter their chosen profession earlier."[17] This was the case at Sacred Heart College as well, because passing the Rhétorique exams brought access to seminaries and universities. As André Bertrand explained, "Jesuit professors at the Collège du Sacré-Cœur generally completed Rhétorique before joining the Jesuit order."[18] In 1950–1951, for example, of the 30 Rhétorique students who passed the exam and obtained their Humanities diploma, only 19 returned to the college.[19]

With regard to the professoriate, faculty members were predominantly Jesuits, either priests or scholastics (in training for the priesthood). Part of this training called the 'regency' lasted three years. During that time, the candidate was required to teach in a college, which explains the presence of scholastics in numbers about equal to that of priests. While a university degree did not matter very much at the time, training in a theological college like Immaculée-Conception in Montreal, whether completed or not, was the rule, one that was broken only when hiring lay teachers in certain specialized subject areas.

Few Jesuits came originally from New Ontario. The vast majority migrated from Quebec to the region which, at the time, was not considered a separate entity, Sudbury, in particular, being considered an integral part of French Canada. Scholastics stayed only a few years at the college, priests rarely more than ten. With the exception of a few individuals, careers were not linked to the college as the institution was part of an educational and ecclesiastical network that required a mobile staff.

Annual student numbers varied. There were about 200 students up until the beginning of the Second World War, and around 300 afterwards. Students came from three regions in roughly equal proportions (about 15 per cent each): northeastern Ontario, southern Ontario and northwestern Quebec, the last being without a college until the early 1940s. About half of the students came from the Sudbury area, among them the day students. For many others, this collegiate institution was not only a place of learning, but also a place of residence where they had to obey strict rules twenty-four hours a day, and where prayer and studies played a central role.

An analysis of the professions chosen by the college's students, without, unfortunately, the benefit of knowing the type or length of their academic pursuits after leaving the college, reveals a state of affairs more complex than generally assumed. The college did not merely produce future priests, doctors and lawyers, the noble professions so highly regarded in French Canada. While 137 classical course graduates did enter these professions, 156 went into teaching, administration, or various other trades and professions.[20] Among non-graduates, declared occupations, as noted in the college's annual yearbooks, indicate an even greater representation of the so-called lesser occupations, among which teachers were a strong contingent, similar to the current situation at Laurentian.

Because the institution was private and denominational, it did not receive grants from the provincial government, but had to depend on contributions from parents and donations from the regional clergy. Financially important, too, was the fact that the teaching staff consisted largely of unpaid priests. Still, even though salaries represented less than 10 per cent of the college's budget – salaries were paid to the few lay professors, to a few servants and as honoraria to consultant doctors and dentists – the college had to find significant revenues to balance their budget, which for 1949–1950 totalled slightly more than $107,000.[21]

According to Gérald Blais, students were drawn from all social classes.[22] An interview with Father Guy Courteau, a former president, suggests that the majority came from families of farmers and labourers.[23] It is difficult to confirm the accuracy of this estimate because student records have not been preserved. According to the only available study, Bertrand's survey of the occupations of the fathers of 283 students in 1962, the families enjoyed mostly modest means, their incomes about the middle class average. Of the occupations surveyed, Bertrand noted that 87 fathers were engaged in commerce (not necessarily as businessmen), while there were 74 miners, 26 labourers, 22 transportation workers, 20 farmers, and 16 mechanics.[24] The student foundation created in 1916 and a system of bursaries created during the Great Depression certainly helped to lessen the burden on families of lesser means, and to attract the brightest elementary school students.

A number of professors and administrators who pursued their careers at Laurentian were alumni of this sound institution of learning. Individuals such as Hugues Albert, Donald Dennie, Gaétan Gervais, Gérard Lafrenière, Ronald Henry, Ronald Perron, and Pascal Sabourin were all educated at the college and brought to their teaching and administrative activities the essence of what they had learned there.

Projects for the Creation of a University

Albert Plante, in a history of Sacred Heart published in 1938, made no mention of transforming the college into a university, although the era would not have been unfavourable for such a development. Perhaps because of uncertainties related to the Depression, however, the project did not fully emerge until 1941 when the Jesuits obtained their Provincial's support for the creation of a university in Sudbury. Stimulated by the war, all economic sectors experienced widespread prosperity, circumstances more conducive to new initiatives in the educational field.

A project of this sort required broad community support, notably from the Order of Jacques-Cartier (Ordre de Jacques-Cartier,) a secret society in French Canada that was very active at the time, and whose political and public arm was l'Association canadienne-française de l'éducation de l'Ontario (ACFEO). The Order's presence in Sudbury has been studied by Pierre Ouellette, who examined the breadth of its interventions not only in education but in the economic sphere as well.[25] J.-Raoul Hurtubise, Liberal Member of Parliament and long-time activist, was a member of the Order, and also of ACFEO's provincial Board of Governors in Ottawa. Although the full history of the Order has yet to be written, we can surmise that both organizations were consulted, since Hurtubise himself presented the request for support to the provincial government, and ACFEO officially supported the project in October 1944.[26]

Strengthened by the endorsement of Sudbury mayor Bill Beaton and of Bob Carlin, the CCF[27] Member of Provincial Parliament for Sudbury, the request quickly became a legislative bill that passed first reading on March 4, 1945. In it, the name 'University of Sudbury' appeared for the first time. The Sudbury Star reported the story in a February 12th article,[28] stating that the college wished to create a 'nondenominational' university, and that Carlin supported the project because a university would make higher learning much more accessible for families of modest means.

The project's nondenominational nature and bilingual character[29] no doubt surprised many, both within the Protestant community[30] and among Irish Catholics and French-Canadians. The proposal, according to the Star, disregarded the Catholic and unilingual Francophone character of the Jesuit college. The nondenominational character, partly factitious, can be explained by the fact that the project envisaged a complex university structure allowing for the coexistence of a nondenominational and bilingual university college – one eligible for public funding – and a university under Jesuit control that would remain Catholic and head up the entire structure. In essence, what was being put forward in an embryonic state was the project of 1960, even though in 1945 the proposal made no specific mention of the structure. To become law, the bill needed to pass another two readings. As Boutin explained:

> On March 4th 1945, the bill passed first reading, but four days later, the three Francophone MPPs at Queen's Park who represented Ottawa area ridings decided to oppose the project. Informed of this change of position, Raoul Hurtubise sent a telegram to the dissidents, warning them that the ACFEO supported this project and that their duty was to do so as well. The crisis was averted. However, before the bill could pass third reading, the minority government of George Drew was defeated on March 22nd 1945 and the project ... was shelved.[31]

The next attempt ended just as disappointingly for the Jesuits. After having been twice tabled in the Ontario Provincial Parliament, in 1946[32] and 1947, the project stalled when the government established the Royal Commission on Education (also known as the Hope Commission), postponing action on the matter. The Jesuits had counted on discussions relating to other proposals to create new universities at that time to help get their project approved. One, for example, called for an Anglophone university in Ottawa to be established on the foundations of Carleton College. In Windsor, Assumption College similarly sought university status.[33] The expansion of the university system in response to the needs of a modern, urbanised economy would accelerate during the 1950s, with 51 acts relating to universities being adopted or amended between 1951 and 1964.[34]

According to Alphonse Raymond, president of Sacred Heart College, the involvement of Liberal MPPs undoubtedly explained the refusal of the Conservative government to support the project, as Premier Drew did not want to provide political capital to his adversaries by agreeing to their request.[35] Despite the support of ACFEO, reiterated in March 1947 in a letter to the premier by president Émile Désormeaux, the Oblates, according to Boutin and Gervais, were most certainly opposed, something that would have brought grist to the mill of opponents to the Jesuits' project. In the eyes of certain influential members of the Protestant community, the officially nondenominational aspect of the project must also have seemed to be a masquerade and a manoeuvre by altogether too intrusive Catholics.

This series of failures at Queen's Park put the university project on the back burner and brought about changes in future strategies. According to some Jesuits who continued to support it, the Sacred Heart College charter adopted by the provincial government in 1914 had already conferred university powers that were still legally valid. This idea had been briefly explored in 1944, but the opinion of lawyers at the time was that even though they appeared to have been quite real, these powers had lapsed[36] and a new charter would therefore be required.

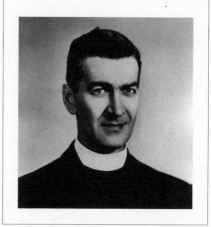

ALPHONSE RAYMOND | Born in Verner, east of Sudbury, Fr. Raymond, a champion of Roman Catholic and French-Canadian rights in northeastern Ontario, was the president of Sacred Heart College from 1952 until 1959, and the first president of the University of Sudbury.

The University of Sudbury

At the suggestion of his predecessor, President Alphonse Raymond, on his arrival in 1953, took up the charter legality question in the hope of finding a way to create a university without the need for a vote at Queen's Park. Several requests to Gaston Vincent, lawyer and president of the provincial ACFEO, went unanswered – once again, Vincent's silence can be attributed to the reticence of the Ottawa Oblates – but at the end of 1955 he finally gave Raymond his legal opinion on the matter. According to Vincent, the charter of 1914 that served as Sacred Heart College's legal constitution did indeed grant the power to "establish ... and maintain faculties, university colleges and other equivalent institutions."[37]

Raymond still had many hurdles to jump, the first of which was to ensure the recognition of the degrees granted by the new university in the making. Laval University and the University of Toronto did not take long to reply positively, but things went quite differently with the University of Ottawa: the reticent Oblates delayed their response until the fall of 1956. Meanwhile, Raymond went to Queen's Park to inform the provincial government of the steps he was taking, in the hope of obtaining government support and, eventually, government financing.

To avoid jeopardizing his chances of obtaining a teachers' college for Sudbury, Raymond initially chose not to reveal anything about other universities' recognition of the Sacred Heart degrees, fearing this might derail the project. On December 15, 1956, however, he sent a press release to the media announcing the college's change of status. In future, the new University of Sudbury would confer its own diplomas, and establish new programs and faculties. Among its priorities would be the creation of a department of continuing education.[38]

The context in which Raymond paid another visit to the Minister of Education in January 1957 is not clear. Bringing with him letters from the three universities that had been consulted, and accompanied by Gaston Vincent and the MPPs for Sudbury and Nickel Belt, Gerry Monaghan and Rhéal Belisle, Raymond met with the Minister of Education, W.J. Dunlop, who, while recognizing the merit of his request, refused to concede that the University of Sudbury enjoyed full university powers. Dunlop therefore suggested a new vote be held in the Legislative Assembly in order to officially name the new Northern Ontario university, and to fully validate its status. On March 30, 1957 the requisite Act passed third reading.[39] The vote carried this time because Monaghan and Bélisle promised their support to other MPPs who needed their support with respect to a similar request from Carleton University.[40] In June 1957, the University of Sudbury held its first graduation ceremony and granted BA degrees to twenty students. The graduation ceremony even attracted the president of Laval University, Bishop Alphonse-Marie Parent.[41]

Raymond had several other projects in mind for the new university. He hoped to offer programs that would cater to the various needs of Northern Ontario in the fields of education, sociology, sciences and even mining engineering and forestry. A school of commerce and a school of music and Gregorian chant were also part of his plan. In an interview with the Sudbury Star on February 14, 1957, he stated that his first step would be to establish a Francophone Faculty of Arts in a building to be erected to the left of the original wing of Sacred Heart College. A bilingual Faculty of Science was to be the second project, on Jogues Street, the site presently occupied by the headquarters of the Catholic School Board of New Ontario (Conseil scolaire catholique du Nouvel-Ontario). The plan was to begin by offering only the first two years of the science program.

Financing for these projects was still an unresolved question. Costs were estimated at $600,000 for the Faculty of Arts, and $1,000,000 for the Faculty of Science. Not surprisingly, Raymond returned to Toronto in the spring of 1957 to meet with Premier Leslie Frost and Minister of Education Dunlop. But he was not the only one to do so. United Church minister Earl Lautenslager had preceded him to promote the cause of a Northern Ontario university that his church wanted to establish.[42]

Raymond and Lautenslager had already tried to come to an agreement on the Northern Ontario university idea, Lautenslager proposing that their churches collaborate on the project. Raymond had declined the offer on the basis that the Jesuits were more competent in this matter, having been actively involved in university education since 1913 and that, in any case, the project provided for bilingual instruction that was already available to both Catholics and non-Catholics.[43] Raymond's refusal to collaborate with the United Church may also be explained in part by the fact that the Jesuit community in Sudbury had reached no consensus on the university idea. Many worried that being surrounded by an Anglophone and Protestant majority would bring about a rapid loss of language and faith for French and Catholic students. Raymond therefore did not have much room to manoeuvre.

The organization of the University of Sudbury structure began in the summer of 1957. Due to a lack of resources, university courses were limited to the arts program, and given at Sacred Heart College in French only. Both facilities and the demand for courses in English were still lacking. Nonetheless, the university admitted its first student, Miss Anita Chevrier, who became Northern Ontario's first university student to take courses given in the region. In 1957, too, the University of Sudbury signed its first affiliation agreement with the Séminaire de Hearst, which would later join Laurentian University.

Although it remained under Jesuit control, the new university established in the spring of 1958 a lay advisory body[44] devoid of significant authority called the Board of Regents. Composed of twelve influential members from various sectors of the community, the board represented an attempt on the university's part to reach out to the entire Sudbury community. Several buildings on Laurentian campus would later be named after members of the board, three of them presidents or vice-presidents of large companies in the area: Ralph D. Parker of Inco, Horace J. Fraser of Falconbridge, and Ben Avery of paper-producing companies in Espanola and Sturgeon Falls. Other members included Timmins businessman Conrad Lavigne and a number of other French-Canadians, including two lawyers, Gaston Vincent and Jean-Noël Desmarais, as well as two judges and a doctor.

In 1958, the University of Sudbury hired Alexandre Boudreau, a man who was certainly the most controversial figure in its history, to offer courses in continuing education. Drawing on his experience in organizing fishermen's co-operatives in the Maritimes, Boudreau prepared courses on unionism in French and English for the workers of Sudbury. Under his influence, some of these workers formed the Northern Workers Adult Education Committee, and took upon themselves the mandate to oust communists from the Mine, Mill union. In 1958, Mine, Mill, representing 18,000 Inco and Falconbridge workers launched a very bitter strike that had lasting effects on the community. The Cold War was in full swing and many people blamed the strike on communist influences. Boudreau's courses were well received, and in 1959 one of his students, Don Gillis, won the union election and became president of Mine, Mill. Three years later, the majority of the Inco workforce voted to change their union's affiliation. After many acrimonious debates, they joined the United Steelworkers of America, a union whose leaders favoured a more pragmatic and generally conciliatory approach.

To some extent, therefore, Boudreau served as the catalyst for those miners who were dissatisfied with the leadership of the Mine, Mill union. Certainly his work was applauded by local elites, company management, and the government, who all welcomed the arrival of a less militant union. On the other hand, many left-leaning workers and intellectuals considered Boudreau a diabolical figure. In their eyes, Boudreau's association with the University of Sudbury tarnished the image both of this institution of learning and of the Catholic Church. The irony in all of this was that the first attempt to create the University of Sudbury fifteen years earlier had been made with the help of Labour Party member Bob Carlin from Mine, Mill.

In order to offer a wider choice of programs, the Jesuits needed more space. For the 1958–1959 school year, therefore, the university leased the Empire Building in downtown Sudbury. The university courses offered there were completely distinct from those at Sacred Heart College. Funds were lacking, so money was borrowed

PRESIDENT ÉMILE BOUVIER, THE UNIVERSITY
OF SUDBURY, 1961 | Appointed in January 1959,
Fr. Bouvier served as president of the University of
Sudbury until the summer of 1960 when he became
the first president of Laurentian University.

or found in other ways. The rent and salaries paid to lay professors, mostly hired to teach the new engineering courses, came partly from the sale of subdivided lots on Brébeuf Street, and partly from the sale of a large parcel of land to the Grey Nuns of the Cross on which they built Notre Dame College.[45] That same year, 1958–1959, courses were offered for the first time to Anglophone students from Sudbury and the surrounding area – an English section of the Bachelor of Arts program as well as engineering courses taught only in English. Among the staff hired to teach engineering was Artin Tombalakian who would have a long career in Laurentian University's school of engineering.

Squaring the Circle

The University of Sudbury could not indefinitely postpone dealing with the question of government funding. As Raymond admitted in his memoir, "we had to face the fact that we would not obtain [government] grants and that running the University of Sudbury without grants was just wishful thinking. We would have stagnated with our small faculty of arts and our two years of engineering."[46] Government assistance, requested by the Jesuits, therefore became the determining factor that shaped the evolving university project examined in detail in the next chapter. A few comments about the contributions made by the Jesuits of Sudbury to that process are necessary.

The Jesuits attempted to reconcile their aspirations – those of a minority in both language and faith – with the interests of a government sensitive to the requests of other religious and linguistic groups. They did not, however, succeed in winning recognition for their historical right of seniority in the sphere of university education in Northern Ontario. In 1959, they did replace President Raymond, seen as too closely linked to ACFEO, with another Jesuit, Émile Bouvier. Bolstered by a mandate directly from the Jesuits' vicar general,[47] Bouvier backed away from the compromises that Raymond and ACFEO were ready to make in a federation in which they would play only a subordinate role.

Even in language matters, the guarantees forced upon, or granted to, Bouvier, to the effect that the equality of the French and English cultures would be assured *as fully as possible*,[48] made many observers wary. One of these was Camille L'Heureux of the Ottawa newspaper *Le Droit*, who, in an editorial published on March 10, 1960 (before Laurentian University was officially established), warned with good reason against the danger of such a stipulation, because "political experience has taught us what this sort of guarantee is worth."

Before concluding, several comments on the history of the Teachers' College of Sudbury, closely related to that of the University of Sudbury, are in order.[49] On the strength of a legal ruling of 1955, the Jesuits lost no time in requesting the establishment of a teachers' college in Sudbury, one that they intended to graft onto their university charter. Despite ACFEO's support for the project, the University of Ottawa, unhappy with the prospect of a new school of education in competition with its own, was able to block the project.

In October 1961, after having had to compromise on the question of Laurentian University, the Jesuit Provincial stated that he was ready to build and manage the required buildings, if need be.[50] The following year, the provincial Throne Speech finally announced the construction of such a school, for which, because of a lack of consensus, the university affiliation remained undetermined.[51] The fight for the control of the Teachers' College was won by the Jesuits, but also by ACFEO, which went so far as to threaten to renege on its promise to award 100 student bursaries should Laurentian become the college's guardian. The government came onside and promised to confer with the president of the University of Sudbury before naming the principal of the Teachers' College. Thus the nomination of the Jesuit Jacques Martineau as principal surprised no one. The college opened its doors in 1963 in rented premises, moved into its current building in 1970 and finally joined with Laurentian University in 1975. Shortly after Alphonse Raymond's death in 1978, the college, which by now was called l'École des sciences de l'éducation, renamed the building after Raymond.

On the strength of their expertise in university education, many Jesuits played a major role in organizing Laurentian in its first years, be it in the library, in the Sciences or in departments such as French and history. When it came to French social and cultural activities, the Jesuits were also very active in transmitting to Laurentian the principles and practices that they followed at Sacred Heart College. They continued lobbying efforts at the provincial level in support of a Teachers' College in Sudbury, despite the objections of the Oblates, with whom they had difficulties from the very foundation of the College. Despite their failure to transform the University of Sudbury into a nondenominational university with government financing, the weakness of the cultural and linguistic guarantees that they man-

UNIVERSITY OF SUDBURY CONVOCATION, 1960 | Convocation of the University of Sudbury in the spring of 1960, the last during its brief tenure as an independent degree-granting institution.

aged to negotiate and the Mine, Mill episode, the presence and the expertise of the Jesuits at the university level in the region since 1913 should be recognized. Without doubt, these are the origins of Laurentian University.

Although they were forced to collaborate as equals with the other two religious groups, and to accept the marginal role that the University of Sudbury would play in the new institution, the Jesuits still held one strong card to play in their discussions with the government. For over four decades their educational efforts had been based in Sudbury, and even though it caused the Jesuits to lose face on so many fundamental aspects of their university project, the government had no choice but to establish the new institution in Sudbury. Had it not been for the Jesuits, it is quite possible that North Bay's strong lobby, active since 1948 and consolidated in 1959 in a nondenominational organization called the Northeastern University Committee, would have succeeded in attracting the new university to their community.

2   The Founding of Laurentian University, 1958–1960

MATT BRAY

In the mid-1950s, the post-war Baby Boom, that aptly named demographic 'Pig in a Python,' portended huge challenges for Ontario's burgeoning university system. Premier Leslie Frost recognized the urgency of the situation, and with his government's assistance, new post-secondary educational institutions emerged in southern Ontario, several, such as the University of Waterloo and the University of Windsor, evolving out of existing denominational colleges. In Northern Ontario too, various communities and groups, denominational and secular, nurtured dreams of a home-grown university.[1]

As discussed earlier, the University of Sudbury had already gone a long way down this path, but one critical barrier remained – religious affiliation barred it from receiving provincial funding. In the autumn of 1958, Sudbury Rector Alphonse Raymond devised a compromise he hoped would overcome this obstacle, but ill-health forced him to resign, leaving to his successor, Fr. Émile Bouvier, the task of broaching the idea to the province. Bouvier outlined the institution's dire financial straits to Minister of Education W.J. Dunlop in January 1959, citing deficits in the range of $150,000 for each of the current and next academic years, and the need for $1.25 million for a new engineering building. To qualify for government funding, the University of Sudbury proposed to transform its advisory Board of Regents into a Board of Governors with control of financial affairs. Dunlop rejected the suggestion. Bouvier also sought grants for the university's engineering program, citing precedents set by the University of Waterloo and the University of Ottawa, but provincial officials ruled that Sudbury's two-year program was neither new nor possessed 'special' features distinguishing it from others in Ontario, the qualifying criteria.[2]

Although ministry officials suggested that a grant to the University of Sudbury might be politically wise, Premier Frost refused to open the Pandora's box of provincial funding for denominational educational institutions as proposed by Fr.

Bouvier. Quite apart from the general principle involved, other groups in Northern Ontario had recently become interested in the question, and political realities dictated their perspectives be considered.[3]

Most notably, in September 1958, the General Council of the United Church of Canada had established a committee on the Church's role in the creation of new universities in Canada. Representing Northern Ontario was Rev. Earl S. Lautenslager of St. Andrew's United Church in Sudbury, a dynamic, determinedly aggressive advocate for Protestantism, the United Church, Northern Ontario, and his community. Thanks to his efforts, in late November 1958, the committee designated Northern Ontario a preferred location for a 'non-Roman university.' Lautenslager immediately invited representatives from the United Church's six northeastern Ontario presbyteries to St. Andrew's in December to discuss the idea.[4]

Several considerations motivated Lautenslager. One, certainly, was the initiative of the University of Sudbury and its implications for Protestantism, and particularly, the United Church, in Northern Ontario. "If we do nothing, the Roman Catholics will close every community to us by occupying it with a proposed college," he wrote in his letter of invitation. Should this happen, he continued rather melodramatically in his address to the December gathering in Sudbury, "I anticipate that we will in due time experience a demand that Northern Ontario become a separate and Roman Catholic dominated province."[5]

Another source of urgency came from within the Northern Ontario ranks of the United Church. Before the National Committee on Universities even met, the North Bay presbytery convoked a meeting of northeastern Ontario presbytery delegates to consider that city's merits as a university site. The initiative, part of a decade-long campaign that had been reinvigorated in 1958 by North Bay and district municipal officials and the city's Chamber of Commerce, culminated in the creation of the Northeastern University Committee (NEUC) in February 1959. A broadly based, non-denominational organization chaired by the local inspector of public schools, J.W. Trussler, the NEUC advocated establishing the university on the foundations of North Bay College (Scollard Hall), the Roman Catholic boy's secondary school administered by the Congregation of the Resurrection, and affiliated with St. Jerome's College in Waterloo. At the presbytery meeting, only the North Bay delegates voted on and approved a motion petitioning the United Church National Committee to endorse the North Bay option. For participants such as Rev. Lautenslager, the secular nature of the initiative rankled. In his presentation to the Sudbury meeting, he commented, "I know of no Chamber of Commerce which has ever founded a university. If ever there was a forlorn hope, it is this one."[6]

The approximately 100 United Church delegates who met in Sudbury on December 10 enthusiastically embraced the university idea, unanimously endorsed the creation of the Northern Ontario University Association (NOUA), and established a thirty-person executive headed by President Lautenslager. A week later in North Bay, the executive approved a constitution defining its goal as: "To found and support in Northern Ontario an institution of higher learning on the university level, United Church and/or Protestant in foundation and control, or at least a Protestant College in a federated University." The constitution assigned to the executive – and by extension, also to the general membership – lobbyist and promotional roles, marshalling support for the university project within the ranks of the United Church and the 'Reformed and Protestant constituency' across Northern Ontario, as well as among government officials, educational authorities and the general public.[7]

To avoid assuming excessive decision-making authority, the executive created an authorizing board, a sort of legislative council composed of the executives and five appointees from each of the participating United Church presbyteries. On critical questions such as location, the purchase of property, and the terms of the federation agreements, the executive could recommend, but the final NOUA decision would fall to the authorizing board. As well, to overcome the difficulties of convening its dispersed membership, the executive delegated many of its powers to a sub-executive of nine. Unfortunately, this arrangement further confused the already overlapping roles of the several involved bodies – the NOUA sub-executive, executive, and authorizing board, the presbyteries, and the national General Assembly of the United Church and its Board of Colleges and Secondary Schools.[8]

Over the next fourteen months, the NOUA addressed three interrelated dimensions of the project. Much of the executive's energy early in 1959 went into a membership campaign designed to demonstrate to Queen's Park the breadth of United Church support for the university idea in northeastern Ontario. As well, Lautenslager explained, a successful drive would strengthen the NOUA's hand in dealing with prospective Roman Catholic partners such as the University of Sudbury. Playing leading roles were Richard Bowdidge, a public relations officer hired in March, and Rev. J.W. Edward (Ed) Newbery, appointed full-time NOUA executive director in July. By December, membership surpassed 12,000, a credible figure. This support laid the groundwork for an associated campaign, fundraising for the construction of a United Church university, tentatively named in March after Silas Huntington, the itinerant preacher whose legendary missionary ramblings in the late-nineteenth century laid the Northern Ontario foundations of the United Church's principal forerunner, Methodism. Although not without its problems, this project also went well, with $1.2 million of the $2 million target pledged by the end of November.[9]

More complicated were questions regarding what kind of post-secondary educational entity Huntington University should be. One possibility, a denominational United Church university, was quickly ruled out because the operating cost inevitably necessitated government funding, and that, as Premier Leslie Frost made clear to a United Church delegation to Queen's Park in early December 1958, would not be forthcoming. Another was affiliation with an existing university, presumably in southern Ontario. The formation of the University of Sudbury, however, had set the opposite precedent, ending Sacred Heart College's connection with Laval University. Just as importantly, the option generated little enthusiasm across Northern Ontario, either within the ranks of the United Church or beyond.[10]

In reality, the university idea captured the Northern Ontario imagination, becoming a symbol of the region's growing demographic and economic importance within the province. In fewer than thirty years, the population to the north and west of the French River had doubled to more than 700,000, and the region's forest and mineral resources contributed far more to the provincial economies – private and public – than conveyed even by this population growth. In northeastern Ontario, communities such as Sault Ste. Marie, Sudbury, and North Bay blossomed into thriving urban centres, their rough-and-ready frontier days long past, no matter what their lingering external reputations. Optimism was endemic in the 1950s, and Earl Lautenslager was by no means alone in thinking that provincial status lay not too far in the region's future. For such people, any formal connection with another university implied a degree of subordination to Old Ontario incompatible with New Ontario's destiny.[11]

By early 1959, Northern Ontario University Association officials had concluded that only a University of Toronto type of non-denominational institution with federated denominational colleges would garner provincial funding, and that the creation of a stand-alone northeastern Ontario university required the cooperation of the several interested groups in the region. Taking the lead in forging this partnership, the NOUA executive first made overtures to the Northeastern University Committee and the University of Sudbury, and then to the Anglican, Presbyterian, and Baptist Churches, though with limited effect in the last two cases.[12]

Initial discussions with the NEUC did not go well. In an April 1959 interview with North Bay's *The Daily Nugget*, Richard Bowdidge complained that the NEUC "is interested only in the promotion of Scollard Hall. It has tied itself to the development of that school and has stated clearly that it does not wish to have anything to do with any University that may be located elsewhere." Complicating negotiations was the Congregation of the Resurrection's insistence that it retain "control of every facet of the life within the School," a proposition unacceptable to Protestant partners. For its part, the NEUC distrusted the NOUA's motivations, suspecting it – not without reason – of being a front for North Bay's regional rival, Sudbury. Not surprisingly, relations between the two cooled, postponing serious negotiations until later in the summer.[13]

As the Bowdidge article implied, at the heart of the differences between the NOUA and the NEUC was the third, and ultimately most critical, aspect of the university question – location. Over the years, eight communities – Cochrane, Timmins, Kirkland Lake, Haileybury, New Liskeard, North Bay, Sudbury, and Sault Ste. Marie – had at various times been touted as sites for a university, although by 1959, none of the first five was realistically in the running. The odds were shorter on the 'Soo,' demographically the second-largest city in the area, but remoteness from the region's population core and main transportation networks made it a long shot.[14]

For the two chief contenders, North Bay and Sudbury, the stakes were high. Each viewed the acquisition of the university as a critical step toward becoming the pre-eminent metropolitan centre in northeastern Ontario. Each had legitimate grounds for its aspirations. Those of North Bay rested on its long-standing position as the 'Gateway to the North,' the hub of a vast transportation network – the Canadian Pacific, Canadian National, and Ontario Northland Railways and Highways 17 and 11 – criss-crossing the area. While demographically only the fourth-largest city in the northeast, North Bay was geographically closer to a greater percentage of the area's population than any other. As home to a provincial Normal School, it already claimed the status of a regional educational centre. A non-industrial community scenically situated on the shores of Lake Nipissing, North Bay had, its proponents argued, "the atmosphere of a university community," a not-so-subtle allusion to its environmental advantages over its chief rival.[15]

Indeed, as events would prove, Sudbury's image as a rough-edged mining community scarred by decades of sulphur fumes stood as a major barrier to its winning the university sweepstakes. Steadfastly ignoring this issue, Sudbury advocates insisted that because their city had already gone a long way toward becoming the predominate metropolitan centre of northeastern Ontario, it was the only logical site for the institution. First and foremost, they argued, its population base of nearly 80,000 people gave it decisive economic and political advantages over all competitors, and especially North Bay, which was less than one-third its size. Three new hospitals appeared in the early 1950s, bringing it to the forefront of health care in the northeast, while the opening of the New Sudbury Shopping Centre later in the decade boosted its commercial centricity. With regard to transportation, the new airport and the recent completion of Highway 69 between Sudbury and Parry Sound creating a road link that complemented existing direct rail ties to Toronto greatly augmented the city's role as entrepôt between northern and southern Ontario.[16]

RALPH D. PARKER | Senior vice-president of the International Nickel Company of Canada, Ralph Parker was instrumental in the founding of Laurentian University, and became the first Chair of the Board of Governors, serving in that capacity until 1965 when he was named Honorary Chair.

Three other factors worked to Sudbury's advantage. First, the city benefited from having the University of Sudbury already in place, a reality that politically could not be ignored by any comprehensive plan to accommodate the post-secondary educational needs of northeastern Ontario. Not all NOUA members accepted this fact, but president Lautenslager did, albeit with reservations about Roman Catholic ambitions in the area. At the association's founding meeting in December, Lautenslager reported having already met with Sudbury rector Raymond. Fr. Raymond had expressed confidence that the province would eventually fund the University of Sudbury as a denominational institution, but Lautenslager believed that when this did not happen, it would federate with the proposed new university. In late March 1959, the NOUA executive formally invited the University of Sudbury to discuss the matter.[17]

Secondly, the same nickel/copper-mining industry responsible for the ecological defacement of the area also strengthened Sudbury's case. At the time, the two major companies, International Nickel and Falconbridge Nickel, accounted for slightly more than 80 per cent of the world's nickel production, giving them, and especially Inco, immense clout at Queen's Park. Regionally the two were also influential, for although in recession in the late 1950s, mining persisted as Sudbury's economic backbone, accounting for nearly 30 per cent of its labour force. Importantly, too, after decades of channelling their local beneficence into social and sports amenities in company towns such as Copper Cliff and Falconbridge, by the late 1950s, Inco and Falconbridge had turned their attention to the broader community issue of post-secondary education.[18]

Various considerations may have motivated the two mining companies to throw their weight behind the Northern Ontario university project. Time, certainly, would affirm that ready access to post-secondary educational facilities offered tangible research and personnel benefits. Favourably disposing Inco and Falconbridge may also have been the anti-communist crusade led by the University of Sudbury's director of extension, Alexandre Boudreau, against their common and relatively new union, the International Union of Mine, Mill and Smelter Workers.[19]

Still, these factors alone do not account for the central role played by Inco's senior vice-president of Canadian operations, Ralph Parker, in the university campaign. Because he had lived in Sudbury for thirty years before moving to Toronto in 1958, Parker took great personal interest in the well-being of the community and particularly its youth, whose future, he believed, depended upon educational opportunity. Already chair of the University of Sudbury's Board of Regents, his association with the NOUA began in February 1959 when he became a 'Distinguished Patron' of the organization. From the outset, he made it clear that his contribution would not merely be honorary, and asked to receive agendas and minutes of all executive meetings. Early on, Parker let his preferences be known – that the university be non-denominational but open to affiliation by all religious groups, and that it be located in Sudbury, an endorsement that obviously boosted the city's fortunes.[20]

Parker's efforts on behalf of the university project may also have owed something to the influence of Premier Leslie Frost. The circumstances of Parker's involvement were later recalled by Harold Bennett, principal emeritus of the University of Toronto's Victoria College and a key player in events leading to the creation of Laurentian:

> In the spring of 1959, Mr. Ralph Parker ... received a telephone call from Mr. Leslie Frost, the Premier of Ontario. He said something like this: "Ralph, old boy, I want you to do me a favour. Get those Sudbury fellows off my back. A man named Lautenslager has organized all the United Church ministers from Muskoka to Moosonee into what he calls the Northern Ontario University Association, and now the Anglicans and the Romans (both French and Irish) are getting into the act. I'd like you to tell them that the Province can't subsidize church-related colleges but that if they can get together behind a non-denominational university, they'll have a deal, especially if there's a bit of nickel money to sweeten the pot."[21]

Bennett's hypothesized account conveys several telling impressions: about the Frost/Parker relationship; about the premier's commitment to a Northern Ontario university; and about another arrow in Sudbury's quiver on the site issue – the possibility of 'a bit of nickel money.'[22]

The third behind-the-scenes factor tipping the scales in Sudbury's favour was Premier Frost himself. In 1948–1949, Frost had served as provincial Minister of Mines, an experience that acquainted him with officials at Inco such as Parker, and generally strengthened his ties to New Ontario. During his tenure as premier (1949–1961), the Northern Ontario economy flourished, both in the resource sectors of mining and forestry and, with the designation of a series of new provincial parks, as a wilderness recreational destination.[23]

By the winter of 1958–1959, Frost's interest in Northern Ontario extended to post-secondary education, stimulated, perhaps, by a recent provincial "Survey of University Expansion and Costs," which revealed that only 5 per cent of Ontario university students came from the North, although the area contained 11 per cent of its population. Several times, he encouraged the Northern Ontario University Association to pursue the project, stressing an alliance with the University of Sudbury. His strongest endorsement came in April 1959 when, in yet another meeting with a NOUA delegation, he spelled out basic ground rules for the new university: "1. No grants will be paid to denominational institutions as such. 2. Grants will be paid to the federated section of a university comprised of two or more denominational institutions. 3. The Premier assumed that Sudbury would be the site of a federated University, but felt that a wider area federation would be an asset."[24]

Given their source, these dicta were compelling. Within two weeks the NOUA executive adopted 'A Tentative Plan for the University of Northern Ontario,' which became the basis of subsequent negotiations. Silent on the subject of location, it called for "a federation of denominational and possible non-denominational residential colleges operating under a non-denominational Board of Governors ... the Board of Governors shall control common faculties and through them, the standards of the University. Denominational colleges would retain responsibility for such subjects as Religious Knowledge and Philosophy."[25]

To facilitate the project, in mid-June Premier Frost offered to convene a meeting of the interested religious groups. This roused the University of Sudbury to action. With the support of Gaston Vincent, president of *l'Association canadienne-française de l'éducation en Ontario* (ACFEO), and of bishops Carter of Sault Ste. Marie, Lévesque of Hearst, and Tessier of Timmins, Bouvier asked the NOUA to appoint two members to sit with two Sudbury representatives on an exploratory committee chaired by Ralph Parker, a logical choice given his connections to both groups. Lautenslager countered by suggesting the membership consist of Parker plus delegates from each of the Roman Catholic, United, and Anglican Churches, a plan that came to fruition in July when Anglican Archbishop W.L. Wright of the Diocese of Algoma agreed to join Bouvier and Harold Bennett, the United Church nominee.[26]

The Parker committee's only meeting took place on September 2 with Edward Higgins, the Sudbury superintendent of public schools, standing in for Archbishop Wright. The opening statement of objectives in the report summarized the NOUA 'Tentative Plan.' Particularly critical was a section designed to "give recognition to the principle of co-operation between the denominations." Clause 1 provided that if the first president was Roman Catholic, the first chair of the Board of Governors must be Protestant, or vice versa. The second prohibited religious tests for faculty or students. The third, ultimately, as the source of Laurentian's bilingual and bicultural mandate, the most important, but in the short-term one of the most contentious, declared "that as far as possible, the principle of the duality of culture and language be implemented" in the federated university. Lastly, the report proposed that if all parties endorsed its recommendations, Parker should chair an implementation committee composed of two representatives from each of the three denominations. All four signed the report.[27]

With the approval of both Bishop Carter of Sault Ste. Marie and the Provincial of the Jesuit Order, the University of Sudbury's Council of Regents endorsed the

Parker report on September 25, and appointed Fr. Bouvier and Sudbury lawyer J.-N. Desmarais to the new implementation committee. The decision caused a rift in Roman Catholic ranks. ACFEO president Vincent angrily resigned from the council, arguing the Jesuits had effectively given up control of the University of Sudbury and betrayed Catholic educational interests in the North.[28]

The NOUA and the Anglican Church of Canada also approved the Parker report, appointing Victoria College's Harold Bennett and Harold Vaughan, secretary of the United Church Board of Colleges and Secondary Schools, and Archbishop Wright and Canon S.M. Craymer to the second committee. Bennett characterized its proceedings as "long and tough," noting that "Dr. Bouvier and Dr. Vaughan took off their dog-collars and tangled with all the vehemence of which only embattled clerics are capable." The first meeting on November 20 resulted in agreement on a number of key points, but at the second a week later, negotiations faltered on two critical issues. One related to the "extent of recognition of duality of culture" in the new federated university. The other arose from a Sudbury organizational chart that in Bennett's view presented the "Protestant Colleges" as merely "Junior Colleges ... dominated by the U. of Sudbury" which claimed a *droit d'aînesse* – right of seniority – by virtue of its Sacred Heart roots. To salvage the situation, Bouvier, Bennett, and Wright formed a special sub-committee to negotiate the items, with success reportedly near at hand by early December.[29]

The efforts of the two Parker committees did not mean that the Northern Ontario University Association abandoned the Northeastern University Committee option. At the same July 1959 meeting that endorsed the Sudbury initiative, the sub-executive resolved to create a joint NOUA–NEUC committee to explore "areas of possible co-operation." Preliminary discussions in August led to a formal meeting of the two groups in North Bay in early November. NEUC chair Trussler explained that along with North Bay College, his committee proposed to seek a provincial charter for a non-denominational university in North Bay, and invited Huntington University to federate with it and locate there. NOUA officials countered by suggesting a 'University-Jr. colleges scheme' involving Huntington, the University of Sudbury, North Bay College, and a Sault Ste. Marie college would better suit the needs of northeastern Ontario. The idea, according to Ed Newbery, "met with no encouragement" from the NEUC. Even so, he reported to the NOUA sub-executive that the NEUC offered "in every way a possible and in many ways an attractive plan," although ironically in light of his later career, his rationale focussed more on what the North Bay alternative avoided; the potentially "grave problems" that could arise in working with the University of Sudbury – "the uncompromising Jesuit attitude evident in other such institutions and particularly ... [its] insistence upon a bilingual curriculum."[30]

By early December, developments on both the University of Sudbury and North Bay fronts had progressed sufficiently to warrant a meeting of the NOUA authorizing board to discuss procedures and federation options. The board first approved the 'Statement of Objectives' in the original Parker report recommended by the NOUA executive, and then adopted for guidance in future discussions the 'principle of co-operation' section of that same document, with one important amendment. In the clause providing that the "principle of the duality of culture and language *be implemented*," it substituted "*be recognized*," diluting it significantly.[31]

The authorizing board also accepted in principle Newbery's report on discussions with the Northeastern University Committee, although information disclosed during the discussion caused a stir. Vaughan and Bennett, it emerged, were both accredited to the United Church's Board of Colleges and Secondary Schools, meaning that the NOUA's negotiations with the University of Sudbury were being conducted at the 'national level,' while those with North Bay were handled 'only at the association level.' To balance the scales, the authorizing board directed the Board of Colleges and Secondary Schools to become directly involved in the NEUC discussions as well. Lastly, it created a 'Fact-Finding' committee composed of one representative from each presbytery to make recommendations on the location of the new university. The committee would meet twice, once at the end of December and again just before the second meeting of the authorizing board in January 1960.[32]

Over the next few weeks, the pace of NOUA–University of Sudbury negotiations accelerated. By late December, tentative agreement had been reached on the two issues confounding the Parker committee, leaving it with only one controversial item: the selection of a name for the new federated university. Bouvier lobbied long and hard for the 'University of Sudbury,' while Vaughan and Bennett pressed for the 'University of Northern Ontario,' Lautenslager's preference, which had been added several months earlier to NOUA letterhead. The compromise, proposed by Ed Newbery, was 'Laurentian University of Sudbury/ l'Université Laurentienne de Sudbury.' Bennett later recalled being surprised by Bouvier's ready acceptance of the name until he discovered that "what I [like Newbery] had thought to be a geographical description suggested to him ... a martyred saint!" Less enthusiastically, Archbishop Wright described it as "as good as can be suggested at the present time."[33]

The executive meeting of the Northern Ontario University Association at St. Andrew's United Church in North Bay on the morning of Friday, January 15, 1960, opened in an atmosphere of high drama. Eighteen men and one woman, as well as an unknown number of authorizing board members who had also been invited, anxiously awaited the presentation of Dr. Vaughan on the two just-completed sets of negotiations. Few anticipated the bombshell that Vaughan dropped on the proceedings. He began by reviewing the negotiations with the University of Sudbury carried out under the auspices of the Parker committee by Bennett and himself, both of whom, he stressed, were not only accredited, but also 'responsible to' the United Church General Council and its Board of Colleges and Secondary Schools. The deliberations had resulted in a 'formula' for a 'free public' institution to be called Laurentian University of Sudbury after the city in which it would be located; to be governed by a Board of Governors and Senate; to have a Faculty of Arts situated in the non-denominational University College, as well as Faculties of Science and Applied Science, all controlled by the Board and Senate; and to have three or more church-related colleges. Both the sub-executive of the United Church Gen-

OFFICIAL ENTRANCE OF THE
LAURENTIAN UNIVERSITY DOWNTOWN
CAMPUS IN THE EMPIRE BLOCK ON
ELGIN STREET, 1960

eral Council and the executive of its Board of Colleges, Vaughan added, "were prepared to recommend United Church participation in this project."[34]

Vaughan then reported briefly on the North Bay option. Ignoring the Northeastern University Committee entirely, he reviewed discussions with the Provincial Superior of the Congregation of the Resurrection who had said the Order did not "contemplate any complete extension into the university field," that is, beyond year one, and was not prepared to provide capital funding, although it might 'participate in' a liberal arts college in North Bay. If a federated university were established at Sudbury, Vaughan predicted, the Congregation would have little choice but to affiliate with it.[35]

Vaughan also emphasized several other points. The province, he believed, would not 'by-pass' the University of Sudbury, given Sacred Heart's several decades of involvement in higher education, nor would it "overlook the density of the French-speaking population" in the Sudbury area. He conceded it would be possible for Huntington University to locate elsewhere than on the main campus of the federated university, but warned that the Board of Colleges and Secondary Schools wanted 'tangible evidence' of the United Church's presence there. Possibly with conscious irony, Vaughan concluded by thanking the NOUA "for the freedom that it had given himself and Dr. Bennett throughout the negotiations," leaving his audience somewhat dumbfounded. As Rev. Dwight Engel of Sudbury later wrote, while delegates had expected to receive guidance, "few suspected that it would be of such a definite and strong nature."[36]

Shortly after Vaughan's presentation, the meeting adjourned so executive members could meet with the Northeastern University Committee as recommended by the fact-finding committee. Little is known about the deliberations, but they must have been awkward. When the NOUA executive reconvened that evening, pro-North Bay members led by treasurer Thomas Palmer went on the offensive, putting forward a motion in opposition to the name 'Laurentian University of Sudbury' and to locating Huntington University in Sudbury if that institution were to come into existence. It failed, nine to six. A resolution directing the executive to prepare a motion along the lines outlined by Vaughan for presentation to the authorizing board, with a vaguely worded addendum recommending the resumption of negotiations with the Congregation of the Resurrection, then passed by a vote of nine to five, but only after lengthy debate and a series of defeated amendments.[37]

Forty-nine delegates from the six United Church presbyteries in northeastern Ontario registered for the second meeting of the authorizing board on the morning of January 16. Vaughan's opening statement bluntly spelled out the view of the higher United Church councils that federation must be with the University of Sudbury in Sudbury, and that Huntington University must be located on the main campus. 'Warm discussion followed,' the minutes pithily recorded. The session then adjourned to permit the fact-finding committee to meet. By a vote of four to two, it adopted a motion proposed by two lay members, one from North Bay and the other from Temiskaming, rejecting federation with the University of Sudbury and calling for further discussions with it, the Congregation of the Resurrection, or any other group prepared to locate the university elsewhere than in Sudbury. Place, not partner, was the sticking point.[38]

According to a Muskoka delegate, when the authorizing board reconvened in the afternoon "all points of view were heard," NOUA president Lautenslager presenting the case for Sudbury, and treasurer Palmer that for North Bay. Fuelling the debate on the first motion to approve a draft bill chartering "a federated Laurentian University of Sudbury ... in which the United Church would be a participant" were the resolutions of the fact-finding committee which explicitly counselled rejection, and that of the NOUA executive, ambiguously supportive. When the allotted time for discussion expired, a standing vote saw the motion pass by the narrowest of margins, twenty-four to twenty-three, with two individuals having either abstained or departed. Not surprisingly, a proposal by Rev. R.B. Hallett of North Bay to make the vote unanimous failed.[39]

Two further resolutions were then debated. The first, an olive branch extended to pro-North Bay delegates, recommended the United Church Board of Colleges and Secondary Schools negotiate "with the Fathers of the Resurrection or any other ... groups interested as to further cooperation." When this passed, the critically important motion locating Huntington University in Sudbury was presented as the first clause of an omnibus resolution. Its other sections proposed establishing a post-secondary educational institution in North Bay in association with any group willing to affiliate with either Huntington or Laurentian, and for two years setting aside 20 per cent of Huntington's capital campaign fund for the project. The motion carried. Huntington University, too, would be in Sudbury.[40]

Two days later, executive secretary Newbery circulated a memorandum to NOUA executive members reflecting on the proceedings in North Bay. It was a

SIGNING THE *LAURENTIAN UNIVERSITY ACT OF INCORPORATION*, MARCH 28, 1960 | From left to right: R.J. Boyer, J.-N. Desmarais, R.D. Parker, J.E. Fullerton, L.J. Côté. R. Béslisle, E. Bouvier, E.S. Lautenslager; seated, Chief Justice Hon. Dana Porter, Administrator.

perceptive if slightly schizophrenic analysis, celebratory about the establishment of Laurentian University of Sudbury and Huntington University, but in turn, defensive, regretful, and mildly indignant about the procedures involved. "It was the majority feeling in the Authorizing Board," Newbery wrote, "that North Bay was in many ways a preferable site for a University and all other things being equal, would certainly have been chosen." But all other things were not equal, he conceded, characterizing the factors presented in Sudbury's favour as "exigencies ... [that] removed the possibility of free selection." The perspective of a half-century confirms Newbery's perception that Laurentian University of Sudbury did not come into existence because of the quixotic decision of one person among forty-seven. By then, forces including the interests of the three founding religious groups, the provincial government, and local industry had effectively usurped the authorizing board's authority, leaving it with little more than the power, fortuitously unexercised, to embarrass the higher United Church councils.[41]

The founding partners of Laurentian University wasted no time setting the required legislative wheels in motion. On January 25, 1960, Ralph Parker, on behalf of a delegation from the University of Sudbury, the Roman Catholic Church, the United Church, and the Church of England, presented the agreement both to the provincial Committee on University Affairs and to Premier Frost, who immediately declared the proposed new university eligible for funding. Two weeks later, the Ontario Provincial Parliament received four private members bills incorporating Laurentian University of Sudbury (non-denominational), Huntington University (United), the University of Sudbury (Roman Catholic) and Lalement University (a stillborn Roman Catholic theological college). In the case of the Laurentian charter, a last-minute snag appeared. The document omitted the critical section regarding the roles of the federated colleges that had been negotiated by Bouvier, Bennett, and Wright. After Vaughan and Bennett protested, the original wording was reinserted, except for a clause creating the non-denominational University College, leaving a thorny issue for settlement another day. On March 28, 1960, Chief Justice Dana Porter, on behalf of the absent Lieutenant-Governor, gave royal assent to the act creating Laurentian University of Sudbury.[42]

Lost in the controversy surrounding the birth of Laurentian University was the history-making enormity of the event, not simply for Northern Ontario, but for the province and even the country. The creation of a non-denominational, bilingual, bicultural, federated university encompassing theologically diverse religious colleges would have been revolutionary anywhere in the Canada of 1960, let alone the reputed backwoods of Northern Ontario. This, after all, was before the only linguistically comparable post-secondary educational institution in Ontario, University of Ottawa, had shed its denominational status; before 'Quiet Revolution' had entered the Canadian lexicon symbolizing the transformation of Québecois society; and before either the Royal Commission on Bilingualism and Biculturalism or the *Official Languages Act* had been conceived. It was a daring, even audacious, experiment in post-secondary education, and it was not surprising that even Laurentian's most enthusiastic supporters experienced occasional twinges of doubt. Still, though not without presenting tremendous challenges, time would affirm the vision of Laurentian's founders.

PART B | EVOLVING STRUCTURES

3 The Challenges of the Sixties, 1960–1972

MATT BRAY

As had been the norm for Canadian universities for many years, the *Laurentian University of Sudbury Act* established a bicameral (Board of Governors, Senate) system of governance. To the board it assigned responsibility for "the government, financial management, and control" of the university. Six of the twenty-four governors were nominated by the province, the rest by the founding Roman Catholic, United, and Anglican Churches. In some respects, the first boards were highly homogenous, drawn from the social, business, and professional elites of northeastern Ontario, especially Sudbury, and predominantly if not exclusively male (Faustina Kelly Cook, the lone female governor during Laurentian's first decade, was appointed only in 1962). In other ways they were calculatedly diverse as religious and linguistic affiliations were critical, given Laurentian's federated character. Fourteen original governors were Protestant, nine Roman Catholic, and one Jewish. Six were Francophone, although the first president, as the *ex officio* twenty-fifth member, added a seventh, as well as a tenth Roman Catholic. Most governors were university educated, but only Dr. Harold Bennett, former principal of the University of Toronto's Victoria College, had expertise in academic administration, giving him special weight in board deliberations.[1]

During the first decade of Laurentian's existence, corporate interests in the Sudbury area played a prominent role in the university's affairs. International Nickel's Ralph Parker headed the Board of Governors until 1965 when he became honorary chair, succeeded by Falconbridge Nickel's Horace Fraser, who held the post until his death four years later. From the outset, the board delegated extensive powers to standing committees, of which the executive was the most important. The first executive consisted of two Anglophone Protestants, one of whom served as chair, Benjamin Avery, vice-chair of the board of K V P Sutherland Paper in Espanola; two Francophone Roman Catholics; a Jewish Anglophone; and board chair Parker and the president, both *ex officio*. Principally via the executive, the board took full responsibility for the management of the university's business and financial affairs, a necessity, as until 1967 Laurentian employed only a single administrative officer in the area variously titled superintendent, bursar, and business officer.

Through the executive, the board also intervened in internal university affairs that were largely academic in nature. At its second meeting in May 1960, for example, the executive, while acknowledging the prerogative of the president could not be 'distributed,' recommended the creation of a presidential advisory committee on appointments composed of three governors (later, in 1965, increased to five) to advise the president with respect to full-time academic appointments, administrative appointments already falling under board purview. The committee was no mere rubber stamp. In May 1961, it assured the board it had "carefully processed and approved" the list of appointees for the coming academic year, and continued to do so until dissolved in 1969.[2]

In contrast to the wide-ranging activities of the board and executive, but in keeping with practice elsewhere, in the early years Senate, responsible for Laurentian's educational policies, seldom involved itself in non-academic matters. This was partly due to its composition. Even after the membership doubled in 1962, the majority of senators were either full- or part-time administrators, hardly disposed to challenging the governance status quo. A contributing factor may have been the unsettled character of the Laurentian faculty. Between 1963 and 1968, faculty numbers quadrupled, and in 1966–1967 alone, half of the teaching complement consisted of new appointees, twenty-four replacing departed faculty. Such rapid growth and high turnover may have inhibited faculty cohesion.[3]

The president headed the university's internal administration with the assistance of a single senior academic administrator, the dean of Arts and Science. During Laurentian's first half-decade, three different men occupied the presidency, an inconstancy that weakened the office's authority and strengthened that of the board. Affecting the situation, too, were the personal attributes of each president and the institutional climate during his tenure.

The Presidency of Fr. Émile Bouvier, 1960–1961

On the recommendation of the original negotiating committee, the Board of Governors appointed Fr. Émile Bouvier, incumbent head of the University of Sudbury, Laurentian's first president. Fluently bilingual, the Roman Catholic Bouvier balanced Parker, the Protestant board chair, as prescribed by the religious duality clause in the first Parker report. Given this exigency and the skeletal nature of its administrative staff, the choice was logical, as the new university needed the leadership of someone with Bouvier's academic stature and administrative experience. After earning his PhD in economics from Georgetown University, Bouvier pursued post-doctoral studies at Harvard where he worked with such noted individuals as Joseph Schumpeter. In 1941 he joined the Faculty of Political Economy at the University of Montreal. There, four years later, he founded la section des relations industrielles, his area of special expertise. Bouvier then moved, in 1951,

HUNTINGTON UNIVERSITY ON LARCH ST., *CIRCA* 1961 | Huntington University purchased its own facility in downtown Sudbury, the old Jackson and Barnard funeral parlour at 83 Larch Street. As the *Sudbury Star* noted wryly in the spring of 1960, 'some structural alterations will be needed.'

to the Ibero-American University of Mexico where he remained until becoming rector of the University of Sudbury in 1958.[4]

From the outset, President Bouvier's relationship with some board members was uneasy. In an era of strongly held sectarian beliefs and linguistic affinities, his Roman Catholic and Francophone roots and University of Sudbury ties raised doubts about his impartiality. Shortly after his appointment, a question arose that heightened these suspicions. At issue was the role of the federated colleges. The matter had supposedly been resolved during the founding negotiations, but the agreed-upon section had been omitted from the first draft of the enabling legislation. Protests from United Church officials resulted only in its partial restoration, leaving undefined the function of the non-denominational University College.[5]

No sooner had the *Laurentian University of Sudbury Act* received royal assent in March 1960 than the issue re-emerged, sparked by an article in Ottawa's *Le Droit*. It asserted that the act prohibited Laurentian from creating "faculties, [and] institutes ... already existing at the University of Sudbury," and that the new university must lease teaching services in these areas from Sudbury. With established departments in arts and sciences, the University of Sudbury would therefore be the principal teaching institution at Laurentian. Huntington (and later Thorneloe, the Anglican federated college) would contribute courses in philosophy and religious studies, the areas specifically assigned to the denominational colleges, while the non-denominational University College would be little more than a conduit for provincial funding to the religious colleges.[6]

Giving weight to *Le Droit*'s claim was the fact that President Bouvier himself endorsed it, both in a presentation to the Sudbury branch of the Société Historique du Nouvel-Ontario in April, and in an address to the National Conference of the Canadian Universities Foundation at Kingston in June. His "Protestant colleagues," he stated in April, had conceded Sudbury's "droit d'aînesse" and agreed that "University College will accept its teaching from the University of Sudbury and will receive grants to pay for this teaching, laboratories and libraries, used by Laurentian." In fact, individuals such as Huntington President Earl Lautenslager, Huntington Principal Ed Newbery, and Edward Higgins, active in Church of England efforts to establish what would shortly become Thorneloe University, vigorously disputed this claim.[7]

The issue festered over the summer of 1960 partly because neither the board nor the executive met, both their chairs, Parker and Avery, being ill. A requirement of the act – that the denominational colleges negotiate federation agreements with Laurentian – precipitated a resolution in late July, when the University of Sudbury drafted a proposal premised on its being the principal teaching college in the federation. Although not opposed to broad teaching roles for all federated colleges, Huntington officials declared the Sudbury proposition "positively unacceptable," and asked "to be assured of the establishment of an active University College under the administration and direction of the Laurentian University of Sudbury." Assuming this could not happen before Laurentian opened its doors, they agreed that in the interim, the two colleges would teach the necessary courses. At least for the time being, the University of Sudbury appeared to have carried the day.[8]

Such would not be the case. When informed that provincial grants depended upon the completion of federation agreements clearly affirming Laurentian's status as a non-denominational institution, the Board of Governors, at its second meeting in late August, appointed a sub-committee including President Bouvier to undertake the task. Though not without difficulty, negotiations with Huntington and the University of Sudbury quickly came to fruition. In an about-face in early September, Bouvier not only recommended to the executive the creation of the non-denominational University College, but also "the advisability of instruction in the Faculty of Arts and Sciences to be given by Laurentian University through University College," meaning the transfer to it of all Sudbury faculty, except those teaching religious studies and philosophy. When forwarding these recommendations to the board, the executive attached a proviso that University College must "continue the system of bilingual instruction followed in the University of Sudbury." To further reassure Roman Catholic and Francophone interests, it nominated Bouvier Principal of University College. Three days later, the board adopted the resolutions and approved parallel federation agreements with the University of Sudbury and Huntington, signed at a public ceremony just two weeks before the beginning of classes.[9]

Apart from clarifying the roles of the federated colleges, the University College issue had other implications for the university's governance. By heightening concerns about President Bouvier's commitment to Laurentian, it widened religious and linguistic fault lines, both between the federated colleges and within board ranks. At the same meeting that approved the federation agreements, the governors appointed Harold Bennett as assistant to President Bouvier, further intruding the board into the internal affairs of the university. When added to his roles as governor, secretary of the board, member of the presidential advisory committee on appointments, and special consultant to, and acting secretary of, the executive, this latest appointment elevated Bennett to the status of a virtual 'shadow' president. From the board perspective, the decision proved fortuitous a year later, when President Bouvier suddenly resigned. The 'shadow' president seamlessly became acting president while an extended search for a permanent successor took place.[10]

Bennett later attributed Bouvier's resignation to the 'substantial deficit' that Laurentian had accrued during his first year in office, but the real reason lay elsewhere. In June 1961, Bouvier dismissed Fr. Yves Ferland, long-serving faculty member at both Sacred Heart College and the University of Sudbury, not only from his position as Laurentian dean of Arts and Science, but from the university. Bouvier accused Ferland of personal insubordination by leading a faculty 'clique' against him, and charged him with professional incompetence, asserting, for example, that Ferland lacked appreciation for the proper 'formation' of students, permitting them such liberties as attending class without white shirts, ties, and jackets. The critical subtext, however, was animosity between the two men, exacerbated earlier in the year when Ferland reportedly informed Fr. Richard, the Provincial Superior of the Jesuit Order, of improprieties on Bouvier's part, for which Bouvier had been reprimanded.[11]

Ferland enjoyed the support of a group of young professors active in the recently established Laurentian University of Sudbury Faculty Association (LUSFA, later LUFA), headed by President Jacques Peltier and Vice-President Kenneth Pryke. Apart from Ferland's personal welfare, they were concerned about the precedent set by the president's unilateral action, given that faculty tenure did not exist at Laurentian. Initially, they followed the counsel of Jesuit colleagues and left the matter to the Order, but when, in early July, Bouvier rebuffed efforts by Fr. Richard to have Ferland reinstated, they invited the executive secretary of the Canadian Association of University Teachers (CAUT), Stewart Reid, to investigate. After meeting with the LUSFA executive and Jesuit representatives, Reid returned to CAUT headquarters in Ottawa with a negative opinion of Bouvier, whom he described as 'authoritarian,' but convinced that Ferland would be reappointed.[12]

That did not happen. Instead, in August, Fr. Richard informed Reid that Ferland had been transferred to l'Université Ste. Marie in Montreal, saying he hoped this would not be interpreted as surrendering to Bouvier in the face of what Richard "agreed was an arbitrary and unjust dismissal." Reid replied that "it must be made clear that Father Bouvier had acted wrongly." Later that same day, Richard authorized Reid to inform Laurentian faculty 'unofficially' that Bouvier would resign shortly. The term of Laurentian's first president thus came to an inauspicious close at the end of September. While brief and early in Laurentian's history, it nevertheless set important precedents with respect to the roles of the board, president, Senate, and faculty association.[13]

To honour the founding president, the Laurentian Board of Governors immediately established a scholarship in his name, and in 1973, l'École des sciences de l'éducation awarded him the Rhéal Bélisle Award in recognition of his role in the college's creation. After leaving Laurentian, Fr. Bouvier became chair of the department of economics at l'Université de Sherbrooke, where he remained until his retirement ten years later. Fr. Bouvier died in 1985.[14]

The Interim Presidency of Dr. Harold Bennett, 1961–1963

Dr. Harold Bennett's acting presidency also impacted the governance system-in-the-making. As suggested by the multiple advisory roles entrusted to him, most governors prized Bennett's experience in academic administration. This did not mean that as president he had free rein in the direction of university affairs, although he was less constrained than others. In January 1962, for example, the executive authorized Bennett and the chair of the finance committee to handle faculty and staff contracts, a function transferred to an ad hoc board committee after his departure. Even so, Bennett was careful not to impinge upon board prerogatives, his governor's hat being the more permanent. As a governor, furthermore, he appreciated the religious and linguistic sensitivities of his fellow board members, and the need for an Anglophone Protestant acting president whose command of French was less than perfect to curry their support.[15]

On balance, Bennett's presidency consolidated the board's supervisory role over internal university affairs. In late 1961, for example, the executive began to examine, in line-by-line detail, all financial transactions, down to the departmental level. Before history could transfer $50 from one departmental pocket to another, or economics purchase a calculator, executive approval had to be sought. In October 1964, when the *Sudbury Star* published the photographs of the members of the executive captioned "These men run the day-to-day affairs of Laurentian," it was not far off the mark – the executive did micromanage important aspects of university life.[16]

Heading the list of challenges faced by the university during Bennett's presidency were funding shortfalls that limited salary increases, program expansion, and the acquisition of essential library materials. Annually, Laurentian experienced deficits covered by special last-minute provincial grants. In its first three years, it received $1.1 million in provincial assistance, an amount one provincial bureaucrat rated, not unfairly, "out of line with the scale and scope of its operations." During this time, Laurentian enrolment remained unexpectedly low, creating, as the dean of Arts and Science noted in early 1963, not only deficits, but an 'overstaffed faculty.'[17]

Another issue that occupied both Bennett's and the board's time and energy was the construction of the new campus on Ramsey Lake Road, officially opened October 8, 1964. At the outset of the site selection process, the board ruled out downtown Sudbury for lack of affordable space and the proper ambience for an educational complex of the grandeur envisioned; besides, the majority of governors preferred a location somewhere in the "general vicinity of the Idylwylde [Golf and Country Club] property." Efforts to purchase the golf course itself very nearly came to fruition in the spring of 1961, but an incipient club membership revolt led by local businessman Ben Merwin caused the board to reconsider the wisdom of alienating some of the most influential members of the community with a fundraising campaign in the offing. Instead, in the autumn of 1961, it selected the more spacious area to the east of the Idylewylde.[18]

Land assembly began immediately. By December 1961, nearly 300 acres had been purchased or expropriated (a special power included in the *Laurentian Act*), with another 250 acquired during the next three years. Simultaneously, University of Toronto architectural historian and planning consultant Thomas Howarth began to design the campus and core buildings. In the spring of 1962, preliminary planning permitted the board to make a number of critical decisions, most importantly, the designation of Phase I of the building program to include the "Library and Podium with foundations provided for later construction of a tower to house a library, Dining and Assembly Halls, Arts Building, Lecture and Class Room Unit, Science I, Athletic Building, Faculty Residences, Roads, Services and Landscaping." Financial constraints eliminated the faculty residences and set back completion of the athletic building, but otherwise, the plan went ahead as outlined. Construction began in earnest early in 1963, and proceeded steadily for the following two years, slowed only by labour stoppages that slightly delayed the opening of the 1964 academic term, and left most buildings usable, but in varied degrees of completion.[19]

A related challenge was Laurentian's first fundraising campaign, a vital task because government policy limited Ontario's contribution to 50 per cent of approved capital costs. In the spring of 1962, with $500,000 in hand from the NICU Foundation (a Falconbridge Nickel agency headed by governor Horace Fraser), the board established a capital funds campaign committee chaired by Ben Avery, and with a goal of $7.5 million, later increased to $9 million. In July, the treasury board confirmed its commitment of $3.5 million in provincial capital funding for Phase I of construction, permitting the canvas to get underway.[20]

The Board of Governors launched the Founders Fund campaign at a dinner hosted by the Sudbury and District Chamber of Commerce in September, 1962, at which the International Nickel Company of Canada announced its donation of $2.5 million, reportedly the single-largest corporate gift to an educational institution in Canada at that time. Over the next fifteen months, contributions, large and small, poured in from corporations – $100,000 from KVP Sutherland Paper, $30,000 from the *Sudbury Star*, $10,000 from Sun Life, $5,000 from Dominion Stores, $5,000 from Labatt's Brewery, $5,000 from the Atkinson Foundation, to cite only a few examples – and from a host of private individuals. By the end of November 1963, the campaign stood only $84,000 short of its goal, a remarkable fundraising feat.[21]

Bennett later described his years as acting Laurentian president as 'among the happiest' of his career crediting the cooperation he received from administrative staff and faculty. From the perspective of university governance, too, these years stood out for their stability, sandwiched between periods of greater, and much greater still, volatility. To a large extent, this was a matter of good fortune, as Bennett's term preceded the revolutionary social forces that shortly engulfed the post-secondary educational world. But it also spoke well of Bennett's administrative abilities because, as his successor would soon discover, heading an institution of Laurentian's religious and linguistic complexity was fraught with pitfalls quite apart from extraneous factors such as mutating governing procedures and practices. At its spring 1971 convocation, Laurentian awarded Bennett an honorary degree in acknowledgement of his multiple contributions to the university during its formative years.[22]

The Turbulent Mullins Years, 1963–1970

Dr. Bennett's acting presidency lasted nearly two years, a surprisingly long time given that the selection of his successor was then solely the prerogative of the Board of Governors, but explicable partly by financial constraints and partly by difficulty in finding appropriate candidates. When Bouvier resigned, the board authorized Horace Fraser to create a 'representative Committee of the Board' to undertake the search. That turned out to be a committee of two. Over the next year, Fraser compiled a list of about fifty names, half of whom, upon closer examination, were deemed to have minimally suitable qualifications. He and board chair Ralph Parker then reduced the number to four, two of whom agreed to stand for the position. The governors interviewed both men, neither Francophone, but both bilingual, in May 1963. The board declared both acceptable, but selected neither because its first choice, Christian Jensen, professor of French at the University of Manitoba, was unavailable until 1964. Instead, it empowered Parker and Fraser to "appoint the one who, in their judgment, can undertake the responsibilities of the Presidency ... on the terms of appointment best suited to the University's needs." In June, Parker offered the position to Stanley G. Mullins, director of English studies at Laval University. Mullins accepted the appointment, effective September 1st.[23]

A man of contrasts whose poetic sensitivities seemed at odds with his authoritarian administrative style, Stanley George Mullins brought to the presidency a variety of strengths including bilingualism, Anglicanism (which, theoretically, gave him a measure of neutrality vis-à-vis the two predominant denominations on campus), a personal attachment to Northern Ontario (his wife, Leatha, came from Sault Ste. Marie, and the family spent summer holidays at their cottage in nearby Thessalon), and, in the words of the *Sudbury Star*, a "sound academic background." Born in Bristol, England, he had been educated in Toronto, where his family moved when he was three. After graduating from Riverdale Collegiate Institute, he earned an honours BA from the University of Toronto, in 1943. He then enlisted in the Canadian Army (Allied Forces) and served for three years in England, Italy, and Northwest Europe, achieving the rank of captain. Upon demobilization, he returned to the University of Toronto, where he obtained an MA in Romance languages in 1948, and then enrolled in doctoral studies in English literature at Laval University. After completing his coursework in 1951, Mullins joined Laval's faculty of English studies, and was named its director in 1958. Although relatively inexperienced in terms of academic administration, his wartime military service and ten years in the Canadian Army (Reserve), highlighted

STANLEY G. MULLINS | President of Laurentian
University, 1963–1970

by his appointment in 1958 as commanding officer of 103 Manning Depot, Quebec, were presumed to compensate for the gap in his curriculum vitae.[24]

President Mullins' term of office, pivotal in the evolution of the university's governance, was easily the most contentious in Laurentian's history. Fundamental to it was the bewildering array of social forces best encapsulated simply as 'the sixties' – the era of exploding student enrolments, expanding post-secondary educational institutions and faculties, student radicalism, changing social and sexual mores, the pill, drug experimentation, the Quiet Revolution in Quebec, Ban-the-Bomb and anti-Vietnam war demonstrations, American draft evaders, the rise of the women's movement, urban unrest – a time of change that tested the patience of the most progressive authority figures. A contributing factor was Mullins himself. For someone accustomed to military command, the challenges thrown up by such an environment proved all the greater – even at Laurentian, peripheral to the mainstream of social upheaval.[25]

The first serious test of Mullins' governing propensities came from an unlikely source, the dean of Arts and Science, Gérard Bourbeau, who had succeeded Ferland in the autumn of 1961. Bourbeau did not have a great deal of administrative experience, but academically, he was well qualified (a PhD in soil mineralogy from the University of Wisconsin), and his military experience – he achieved the rank of major during the war though he did not see overseas service – might have afforded him common ground with the new president. To the contrary, in what was more a case of 'likes repelling,' in February 1964, barely five months after Mullins took office, Bourbeau submitted his resignation to the board. To Mullins he complained about the president's "contemptuous treatment of the office and the person of the Dean." In the resignation letter, Bourbeau cited multiple instances when Mullins had bypassed his office and met personally with science faculty on issues that clearly fell within decanal jurisdiction.[26]

A series of initiatives over the next two months by first an executive subcommittee, then the board, and finally, a board mediation committee, failed to resolve the differences between the two men. The governors went to great lengths to accommodate Bourbeau, endorsing several of his proposals to improve lines of academic and administrative authority within the university, and even proposing to combine the deanship with the new post of vice-president academic. Bourbeau declined the offer. He may have hoped, as rumoured in some Laurentian circles, that Mullins would be forced to resign, opening the presidency to himself. "I was not in agreement with the qualifications of the president who was appointed," he informed the *Sudbury Star*, "he should have been a vice-president of a university." In this 'him or me' confrontation, Bourbeau could not win. No matter how highly it valued Bourbeau – and the concessions it offered suggest this was highly indeed – the board could not remove after only six months a president chosen by its two most influential members. Bourbeau left Laurentian that summer, starting the Mullins presidency off on a sour note.[27]

During the next two years, a confluence of issues led to another crisis in university governance focused on the president. One involved the faculty association's efforts to negotiate a tenure agreement. Prolonged discussions over the winter of 1963–1964 culminated in LUSFA's rejection of the latest proposal, only to have the board adopt it in May on Mullins' assurance that agreement had been reached. New negotiations finally yielded a policy in January 1965, but at the cost of shaken faculty confidence in both the president and the board.[28]

Another issue related to the prickly question of relations between Laurentian and its three federated colleges – the University of Sudbury, Huntington University, and Thorneloe University, established in 1963. Very early on, the colleges viewed President Mullins as an adversary who was determined, as Ed Newbery wrote in July 1964, "to restrict the Church Universities and their Colleges to a minimal place in the University." A year later, Mullins came under scrutiny when the board established a special committee on bilingualism. The committee's existence reflected, first and foremost, dissatisfaction on the part of Francophone governors with Mullins' publicly expressed views about the 'failure' of bilingualism at Laurentian, dissatisfaction that dated from the autumn of 1964. Then, the board public relations committee had recommended that "in 'exterior' expressions which involve the university and from which the public opinion of Laurentian may be influenced ... the President avail himself of the opinion of the public relations committee of the board." If transmitted to Mullins, the directive had little effect.[29]

While the July 1965 report of the special committee on bilingualism acknowledged a high degree of dissatisfaction, especially in the ranks of the federated colleges, with the "day-to-day efficiency in the routine functioning of the University," it never directly criticized Mullins. Behind the scenes, however, negative comments on his presidency by interviewees such as Fr. Rodolphe Tremblay, the University of Sudbury registrar, and board members, such as Robert Campeau and Conrad Lavigne, did not go unnoticed. Revealing was a letter from Huntington president Newbery to Laurentian governor Don James. "Jim Meakes [chair of the special committee] phoned me two nights before our Board of Governors meeting to talk about developments," Newbery wrote. "He asked me point blank if I would cooperate with Mullins *if the report favoured his continuance*." In the end it did. The situation should not be blamed on 'one man,' the report stated, citing uncontrollable 'facts of life,' such as having three presidents in five years and the disruptive impact of the Bourbeau resignation. It even conceded that the board must shoulder a share of the blame, having failed to "define the objects of Laurentian, to clarify the inter-relationship of Laurentian to the federated colleges, and to assist the president to promulgate and carry out a clear, compatible course of action." That may have been true. On the other hand, the idea that the board should become more involved in Laurentian's internal affairs was a serious mis-reading of the shifting sands of university governance in Canada.[30]

By then, forces of change philosophically encapsulated in the 1964 publication of *A Place of Liberty: Essays on the Government of Canadian Universities*, commentaries by prominent Canadian academics such as McGill's Frank Scott calling for a major transformation of the system, were building within Canadian academic circles. By then, too, the Canadian Association of University Teachers and the National Conference of Canadian Universities and Colleges (later, the Association of Universities and Colleges of Canada [AUCC]) had also concluded that the powerful demographic forces of change in post-World War II Canada would impact not only the number and size of post-secondary educational institutions, but also their governance. Accordingly, the two jointly established a commission to undertake "a dispassionate examination and evaluation of the present structure and practices of the government of … universities in Canada."[31]

Heading the inquiry were international educational experts Sir James Duff, ex-vice-chancellor of the University of Durham, and Robert Berdahl, an American political scientist at San Francisco State University. After visiting Canadian campuses of all sizes and complexities (though not Laurentian), Duff and Berdahl submitted their report, *University Government in Canada*, in the spring of 1966. Its endorsement of the two-tiered, bicameral form of university governance, with a Board of Governors primarily responsible for financial affairs and a Senate for academic matters, was hardly surprising; most Canadian universities, like Laurentian, already had such a system. More radical was its assertion that the two spheres of responsibility were not water-tight compartments, that, for example, financial issues often had academic implications requiring the board to involve Senate in decision-making, and its insistence on faculty control of Senate. The report also argued, less forcefully, that on academic questions, Senate must take into account financial implications of primary concern to the board. Senate, it prescribed in one sweeping declaration, must have "specifically the power to make recommendations to the Board on any matter of interest to the university." Other proposals were also revolutionary; that Senate should elect members to the Board of Governors, and vice-versa; that joint board–Senate committees should be responsible for such matters as short- and long-term planning; and that Senate should review the university-wide budget. For those dissatisfied with the status quo, *University Government in Canada* offered both a blueprint of, and justification for, reform.[32]

Contrary to historian Michiel Horn's assertion that the "Duff-Berdahl report had little effect" on Canadian academic governance, it played a critical role at Laurentian where, coming in the wake of the inquiry on bilingualism, it had special relevance. President Mullins drew it to the board's attention, though the governors did not comment on it. As elsewhere, the most enthusiastic reception came from the faculty association. The report's publication coincided with a surge in Laurentian's student enrolment that created an urgent need for faculty. Unfortunately, Sudbury's perceived remoteness and negative environmental image put the university at a disadvantage with respect to hiring and retaining staff. The booming mining economy in the mid-1960s compounded the problem by exacerbating an already serious housing shortage in the community, giving the neophyte faculty association leverage with university authorities.[33]

Specifically, the Duff-Berdahl report prompted LUSFA to reinvigorate a campaign it had launched in the autumn of 1965 to increase the number and ratio of faculty on Senate. Although President Mullins had then promised to address the issue, nothing happened until March 1966, when he proposed the creation of a joint Senate–faculty committee on faculty representation, forestalling a LUSFA motion to this effect. As a consequence of its deliberations, two months later, Senate approved new membership criteria, shifting the balance in faculty's favour. Elections under the new regulations in October produced a decidedly more assertive Senate.[34]

In this context of growing Senate and faculty confidence, the Board of Governors unwittingly precipitated the first skirmish in a four-year battle over the university's governance, when in January 1967 it appointed an ad hoc committee to amend the *Laurentian University of Sudbury Act*. From the governors' perspective, the recommendations developed over the next year were mere housecleaning details – for example, deleting 'of Sudbury' from the university's official title, revising the student Court of Discipline, and providing for the appointment of a chancellor. Procedurally, the committee obtained the approval of the federated colleges in December, and early in 1968, Sudbury MPP Elmer Sopha presented the amendments as a private member's bill to the Ontario legislature. After first reading in March, the bill went to committee.[35]

There, the board's best-laid plans went awry when a student delegation headed by the Students' General Association (SGA) president, Étienne St-Aubin, along with two Huntington University philosophy professors representing the faculty association, Wesley (Wes) Cragg and Garrick (Garry) Clarke, opposed the bill. According to Cragg, the 'general objection' was that its provisions "appeared to centre control of the University … in the hands of the president and the Board of Governors." The interveners also drew attention to an ultimately more decisive flaw, the board's failure to consult with either faculty or students about the proposed changes. The point hit home with government officials who had warned the board that this oversight could scuttle the whole process. After a short debate, the legislative committee voted not to report the bill, stipulating that before its reintroduction, both faculty and students at Laurentian must be consulted.[36]

Prompted by this success, LUFA lobbied Senate to establish a joint committee with the board to study Laurentian's governing practices, and in July 1968, a board–Senate striking committee recommended the creation of a PAC on consul-

tative structures and procedures. Mandated "to study the channels of communication, the consultative structures and procedures, and areas of decision-making
within Laurentian University," the PAC's seven Senate, LUFA, and Students' General Association (SGA) members outweighed its three board and administration
representatives. At its first meeting in October, it elected LUFA representative
Doug Williamson, head of geology, as chair and held a 'wide-ranging and open'
discussion of the university's affairs that concluded with a request for several gov-
ernance-related documents, including the Duff-Berdahl report, for the committee's use. Subsequent meetings also showed promise. A proposal to circulate the
minutes of all governing bodies brought results, even though the board agreed
only to distribute "summaries of its minutes with such reservations as ... [it] may
order."[37]

Student activists at Laurentian did not resort to the extreme measures that
agitated universities across North America during the winter of 1968–1969, but
they did become more insistent in their claim to a place in the governance sun.
In a strategically adept move, in October 1968, the SGA requested that six student
voting positions be added to Senate. Although not without opposition from some
of its members, Senate did so in December.[38]

Faculty power, too, made its presence felt, thanks in part to the PAC on consultative structures and procedures. In February 1969, it circulated a questionnaire
asking senators to evaluate Senate's role within the university. Citing the Duff-
Berdahl declaration that Senate should be able to "make recommendations to the
Board on any matter of interest to the university," the questionnaire identified
nine roles that it might play – review the university operating budget, recommend
administrative appointments, establish policies and procedures concerning faculty employment, participate in the selection of the president, etc. – a philosophical outline of the reform agenda pursued in the next several years. The responses
supported strengthening Senate in all areas.[39]

LUFA also became more proactive, confronting the board over an issue dear to
the hearts of its members, salaries. Until 1965, the board had set salary scales with
little formal input from faculty. That winter it agreed to a faculty presentation, a
procedure more than consultation, but less than negotiation, that continued in
subsequent years. The first overt sign of discord appeared in the fall of 1967 when
President Mullins and the faculty association representatives came away from a
meeting on 1968–1969 salary scales with different versions of what had transpired.
The board resolved the matter by appointing an ad hoc committee of three, including the president, to meet with faculty representatives.[40]

What were now formal negotiations became more disputatious over the 1969–
1970 salary scale. Between December 1968 and April 1969, LUFA rejected three
salary offers from the board negotiation committee. In mid-April, faculty took
the unprecedented step of resolving not to submit final marks or participate in the
university's extension program until a settlement had been reached. A few days
later, the board executive tried a new tack, assigning negotiations, within strict
guidelines, to Laurentian Vice-President Academic Roland Cloutier and comp-

troller Carl Nurmi. They reached a settlement with the LUFA negotiating team, but the board amended it. Faculty voted down the altered version in early May, decrying "the arbitrariness of the procedures." On the other hand, with spring convocation fast approaching, LUFA lifted the moratorium on the submission of student marks.[41]

Over the next few weeks, President Mullins pressed the board's case, circulating a chart among faculty demonstrating that the latest offer brought Laurentian well into line with other Ontario universities. When, as was then the practice, he issued individual contracts to faculty based on this offer, LUFA countered by asking members to turn the unsigned documents over to it. More than eighty did so, to good effect. Two more rounds of negotiations finally smoothed out the last wrinkles, and in late May, a special meeting of the board executive approved the settlement, ending Laurentian's first faculty work stoppage.[42]

Still, the conflict heightened tensions, setting the stage for the next crisis to disrupt Laurentian. In early October 1969, President Mullins informed the academic community that in three weeks he would present a five-year academic plan to the provincial Committee on University Affairs (CUA), and asked for input. Faculty and students were furious at the lateness of this request. On their insistence, the board executive agreed to a 'tripartite' submission – the president on behalf of 'the university,' LUFA, and the SGA – a highly unusual procedure that caused not a little consternation at Queen's Park.[43]

President Mullins presented his quinquennial plan to a special meeting of Senate in mid-October. The Students' General Association dismissed it as 'non-representative' because of inadequate consultation with the academic community. While deploring the absence of long-term planning procedures, LUFA also criticized the substance of the president's proposals. Both at Senate and in its brief to the CUA, it questioned whether the creation of faculties of fine and applied arts, medicine and law had much relevance to Laurentian's immediate academic needs.[44]

As this drama played out, another, even more explosive one was in the making. In September 1969, the PAC on Consultative Structures and Procedures recommended adding seven non-voting members to the board – two from each of Senate, LUFA, and the SGA, and one from the Extension Students' General Association – and four to the finance committee, one from each of these bodies. When the executive considered the matter two days after the embarrassing CUA hearing, it proposed instead naming one member from each association to the board, and none to the finance committee, setting the stage for a confrontation at its meeting on October 31. At the outset, LUFA president Garry Clarke and SGA president Pierre Fortin spoke in support of the four individuals (including student Douglas Los, a future chair of the board) nominated by their associations, as per the PAC on Consultative Structures and Procedures proposal. In thanking them, board chair William Shea noted that the question would be dealt with when it came up on the agenda. Fortin interpreted this as a stalling tactic and so informed about 250 students in the Great Hall. A mass of students crowded into the 11th floor Governors' Lounge singing modified campfire songs such as "Here we sit like birds in the wilderness, waiting for the board to come." Uninvited, Fortin entered the Senate chamber and began to address the board, prompting an adjournment. During the break, Shea met with the students, assuring them their views would receive the 'most serious consideration.'[45]

The student intervention had the desired effect, at least in part. When the issue came up later that afternoon, governors Conrad Lavigne and Judge Anthony Falzetta moved to add seven non-voting members to the board, as per the PAC formula. After an amendment to reduce the number to four failed, the motion passed. With regard to the finance committee, the board followed the executive's advice and took no action. LUFA and SGA nominees immediately took their seats (the two senators did so only in March 1970), establishing a direct channel of communication between these organizations and the board that shortly would prove invaluable. Senate also became more transparent, voting in November to end a long-standing practice by opening its meetings to the general public.[46]

Simultaneously, the faculty association aggressively pursued another reform whose need had been underscored by the CUA fiasco, the creation of a university long-term planning committee. On LUFA's recommendation, the board executive asked Senate to appoint an ad hoc committee to meet with it to discuss the idea. At that meeting in early December, the Senate ad hoc committee on long-term planning, chaired by historian Gilbert Stelter, took the most radical stance to date, proposing in Duff-Berdahl style, a joint board–Senate committee mandated to formulate "the long-range objectives of the university" and to develop a five-year plan "both as to programs … and to budgets, capital, and operation." Key assumptions, the senators acknowledged, were that a Senate budget committee would prepare the annual university (not just academic) budget for submission to the board finance committee, and that the finance committee would include both faculty and students. The executive refused to go along with anything so drastic. Instead, it suggested Senate name a committee of six to meet with the board building and planning committee to coordinate long-term planning. This idea of 'planning' differed so greatly from what Senate had in mind that even President Mullins insisted the executive minutes record his abstention on the vote.[47]

Once broached, the question of a university budget committee including faculty and students could not be easily dismissed. In November, the executive responded to LUFA and SGA petitions on the subject and invited Senate, "as that body on which all university constituencies are represented," to establish an 'academic budget committee' to report to the board executive. Senate promptly created the new standing committee on 'operating budget and academic short-term planning.' The question then arose as to what authority the committee possessed. Senators argued it must be the conduit for all university budgetary submissions to the board finance committee. The executive, while agreeing it had the right to comment 'on any aspect of the operating budget,' refused to concede anything more.[48]

In early 1970, relations between Senate and faculty on one side, and the board, executive, and president on the other, rapidly deteriorated. At a January Senate meeting, the ad hoc committee on long-term planning complained about the board's refusal to accept it as an equal partner, and insisted the building committee was not the appropriate forum. LUFA backed Senate on these issues and had an additional grievance, stalemated salary negotiations, which threatened to become even more divisive than the year before. For its part, the executive reiterated its decision not to add faculty or students to the finance committee, and dug in its heels on long-term planning, insisting the building committee experiment be given a fair trial.[49]

Faculty and Senate frustration with President Mullins also boiled over. In a January 1970 report to the association, Garry Clarke summarized the LUFA perspective: "Since October, President Mullins has become increasingly isolated from the faculty. Attempts of his to dismiss certain faculty members without due process or to deny them tenure have been frustrated by the Association, supported by CAUT. He has not been effective as a channel of communication between faculty and the Board and has been largely by-passed by the Association." Senate also suspected Mullins of failing to communicate its views to the governors, and in February, specifically directed him to do so.[50]

By early March, a 'Mullins must go' campaign, reportedly spearheaded by LUFA president Clarke and senators Wes Cragg and Gil Stelter, gained strength. "The academic senate is under the control of an anti-Mullins caucus," the Globe and Mail stated on March 7, "and copies of the caucus's yet unmoved resolution of no-confidence in Mr. Mullins are passed around the university." A week later, the Sudbury Star commented on 'L'Affaire Mullins' and reported that regrettably, the president, whom it lauded as 'an outstanding administrator,' intended to ask the Board of Governors for a two-year leave of absence. A group of senior faculty members led by Social Work Chair Conn Ashby met with the board executive "in an attempt to inform them of the feeling in the University regarding the role of the President ... to present reasons why a change in the presidency was ... necessary, and to help accomplish this in as civilized manner as possible." LUFA endorsed these initiatives, and demanded an immediate board-Senate presidential search.[51]

The crisis came to a head on March 18 when, 'in the best interest of the University,' the board executive turned down President Mullins' request for a leave of absence commencing July 1970. Senate reacted angrily, the next day passing two non-confidence motions, one in Mullins, the other in the executive for usurping board authority. It also demanded a board-Senate meeting within two weeks to resolve matters, and sent a delegation to lobby the president not to accept the executive's decision on his leave request. Both LUFA and the SGA endorsed these actions.[52]

The absence of President Mullins and board chair Shea from Sudbury during the last week of March put events on hold, heightening tensions. On April 1, the SGA precipitated matters by calling a public meeting of students in the Great Hall to ratify the Senate non-confidence motions. After several hours of discussion – opinion was by no means undivided – student senator Scott Merrifield called for an 'occupation' of the Great Hall foyer. Roughly sixty students took up the challenge, issuing a 'position paper' demanding a public meeting of the board and

Senate no later than April 6. Should it fail to reach an agreement 'satisfactory to Senate' regarding both the presidency and the role of the executive, the students declared, Senate should suspend 'formal academic functions.'[53]

With its two-week deadline to the board fast approaching, Senate, too, ran out of patience. On April 2, it adopted resolutions designed to force the issue, the most critical being a new ultimatum to the board. Asserting that the governors had 'insulted' Senate by failing to meet with it, Senate resolved that if no meeting occurred beforehand, "all academic functions of the university would cease as of 5 o'clock April 3." On the urging of its student members, Senate agreed to keep the library open and provided for the voluntary submission of marks in the absence of final examinations. Because the joint meeting did not take place within the required timeframe, Laurentian's first euphemistically titled 'academic recess' began on April 3.[54]

That evening, Chair Dalton Caswell called a special executive meeting to deal with the crisis. Arguing it would be impossible to convene the full board on such short notice, the executive resolved to ask Senate to appoint six members to meet with it to arrange the joint session. President Mullins, summoned from a meeting in Toronto, then arrived. He reiterated his desire for a two-year leave of absence, but suggested that because of the lateness of his request it not start until July 1971. More importantly, he indicated a willingness to give up the presidency any time after June 1970.[55]

The next day, Senate countered the executive's 'six on six' proposal with the suggestion that its six members meet with the full Senate sitting as a committee of the whole. When the Senate meeting reconvened a couple of hours later, however, fourteen board members appeared. A special ad hoc committee recommended holding the joint board–Senate meeting on April 9, with an *in camera* session to deal with the presidency and an open session on university governance. Both the board representatives and Senate approved the arrangement.[56]

Thursday, April 9, 1970, was a memorable day. An emergency afternoon/early evening meeting of the Board of Governors formulated its positions on the key issues. Non-voting faculty and students actively participated in the debate, which began with presentations by executive and Senate representatives. The ensuing discussion revealed the chief difference between the two sides to be the timing of Mullins' resignation as president, the executive preferring he stay until June 1971 to give Laurentian time to find a replacement. As the board minutes explained, however, 'recent developments' made it 'doubtful' that "such a final year in office would prove to be a happy one either for the President or for the University." The board therefore resolved to undertake a search both for an acting president as of July 1, 1970, and for someone to fill the position on a permanent basis. Later that evening, Shea communicated the decision to the *in camera* joint board–Senate session in the Governors' Lounge.[57]

The anxiously anticipated open meeting in the Great Hall – chaired by Vice-President Cloutier – began at 9:35 p.m. According to the *Sudbury Star*, the crowd was 'not friendly.' Each of the board, Senate, LUFA, and SGA made opening state-

CONSTRUCTION OF THE LAURENTIAN UNIVERSITY GREAT HALL, 1963 | Barely one year after this picture of the future Great Hall was taken, the new Laurentian University campus on Ramsey Lake Road opened.

ments, although only the first offered any degree of suspense. Board Chair Shea defused the situation by announcing that Laurentian would have a new acting president as of July 1, and assured the audience that the search committee would have an equal number of board, faculty, and student representatives. He then outlined the other measures adopted by the board. First, it would add four additional voting members to the finance committee; one elected by Senate, one by LUFA, and two by the SGA. Secondly, it proposed to create a standing committee on long-term planning composed of an equal number of members appointed by the board and Senate. Thirdly, to counter the perception of excessive executive control of the university's affairs, it would hold at least four additional meetings in 1970 (one jointly with Senate), with the possibility of monthly sessions in future academic years.[58]

For obvious reasons, Senate and faculty expressed satisfaction with the outcome of the meeting. The next day, Senate, resolving to "consolidate its gains and move ahead without antagonism," ended the academic recess and adopted measures to ensure convocation took place as scheduled. Students involved in the 'sit-in,' were less pleased, unhappy that decisions about the university's future continued to be made behind closed doors. Nevertheless, they, too, agreed to 'recess' their occupation of the Great Hall foyer.[59]

Understandably, President Mullins – the 'first casualty of the new scheme of things,' in the words of the *Sudbury Star* – took a dimmer view. When presiding over convocation in May, he reportedly participated 'impassively' in handing out degrees to the graduates. In his presidential address he alluded to recent events, thanking 'the loyal few now remaining on faculty' for their support, and calling for evolution, not revolution, in the university's governance. At one point, too, he cryptically referred to 'charlatans and knaves,' a phrase characterized by an anonymous faculty member as 'an arresting piece of terminology.' Prudently, faculty otherwise declined to comment.[60]

Aside from the governance question – a major caveat, to be sure – Mullins' presidency witnessed a remarkable transformation in Laurentian University. Thanks to a new policy adopted in 1965 under which the province not only assumed 85 per cent of the cost of approved projects, but in Laurentian's case applied the formula retroactively to the completed Phase I of construction, for a half decade the university was awash in capital funding. The new campus underwent major changes, particularly because of the eight-storey addition to the R.D. Parker Building, completed in 1969, but also because of a host of other projects begun during this period. Included were the third-floor addition to the classroom building, the Doran Planetarium (with funding assistance from W.J. Doran, president of Doran's Northern Ontario Breweries Limited), Science II, the Horace J. Fraser Building and Auditorium, three residences (University College, Single Students, and Married Students), the extension, including the Olympic-sized pool, to the B.F. Avery Physical Education Building, and l'École des sciences de l'éducation.[61]

During Mullins' presidency, the university's overall financial picture also improved dramatically. The three hundred graduates in the spring of 1970 exceeded the entire student body the year before he took office. During those seven years, enrolment increased six-fold, greatly increasing operating grants, particularly after 1967 when the province adopted a formula funding system based on 'Basic Income Units' (BIUs) tied to student numbers. At that time, too, the Robarts government introduced new grants for 'emerging sectors of universities' and special funding for bilingual instruction.[62]

Finally, Laurentian was academically a very different place at the end of Mullins' term of office. To handle the student influx, its faculty complement quadrupled. As well, it replaced its original general degrees in arts and science with three-year disciplinary degrees; launched a number of four-year honours programs; established five professional schools; and prepared the groundwork for graduate studies. While much of the credit for these accomplishments must go to Mullins' administrative subordinates, such as Vice-President Roland Cloutier, it must be noted that they conformed to an agenda sketched by the president himself in 1964.[63]

Board Chair Shea, therefore, did not simply voice platitudes when, at Mullins' last official board meeting, he acknowledged the president's contributions to Laurentian's growth. In the university's 1969–1970 annual report, Acting President Cloutier also paid tribute to the man with whom he had worked as dean and vice-president for five years, not always amicably. While stressing Mullins' 'total dedication' to Laurentian, Cloutier conceded that neither the president's administrative practices nor vision for the future had found universal favour on campus. "I believe, however," he continued, "that the main grievance held against him was intrinsic to the very nature of the position he was occupying. HE WAS THE PRESIDENT. He was the symbol of authority at a time when society all around the world in general, and in universities in particular, rejects any form of authority." While that was undoubtedly so, it must be added that ultimately President Mullins, like others in his position, embraced too tightly his mantle of authority and failed to gauge either the direction or strength of the governance winds of change.[64]

The measure of an individual, it has been said, is how he or she responds to adversity. On this score Stanley Mullins demonstrated remarkable strength of character. During his leave of absence from Laurentian, he enrolled in a PhD program in English literature at the University of Ottawa, completing the degree in 1982. He returned to the department of English at Laurentian in 1973, a staunch advocate of Canadian literature and Canadian studies when both were still on the cusp of academic respectability. He served as department chair from 1980 to 1983, and was actively involved in the affairs of Thorneloe University, becoming its first director of theatre arts. On his retirement from Laurentian in 1986, Thorneloe awarded him an honorary DS Litt, and named him professor emeritus in 1991. Dr. Mullins resided in Kagawong on Manitoulin Island until his death in 2003.[65]

The Cloutier Denouement, 1970–1972

Most observers looked upon President Mullins' departure as a panacea that would end Laurentian's governance troubles, but that proved not to be the case. One final act remained to be played out. It began in late April 1970 when, as Chair Shea had promised, the board established a presidential search committee composed of a majority of faculty and students headed by a board member, and mandated to seek both an acting president as of July 1 and a permanent appointee. With respect to the former, as per its terms of reference, in early June the committee nominated three internal candidates – Garry Clarke, the LUFA president; Roland Cloutier, the vice-president academic; and Wynn Watson, the director of graduate studies. Senate approved all three and forwarded the names to the board which, not surprisingly, selected Cloutier.[66]

Dr. Roland Cloutier had become dean of Arts and Science in September 1965, the position having been filled by a series of acting deans after Bourbeau's resignation. A professor of general science in the Faculty of Arts at the University of Ottawa, Cloutier's credentials (a PhD from McGill and a long list of publications) were excellent, though he had limited academic administrative experience. Cloutier's decanal performance highly impressed the board, and in the autumn of 1966, it offered him the twin posts of vice-president (academic and student services) and dean, the combination turned down by Bourbeau. Cloutier accepted, but soon realised the workload was too heavy. At his request, in 1967, the executive appointed two part-time assistant deans, one for Arts and one for Science. Even this arrangement proved inadequate, and in the spring of 1969, the university named Classicist Gerald Vallillee acting dean of Arts and Science.[67]

In view of his experience with multiple administrative positions, it was odd that Cloutier chose to retain the vice-presidency along with the acting presidency, especially when it became evident that governance issues had by no means been resolved. One continuing thorny question related to the role of the board executive. In late April, for example, the executive heard presentations from several faculty members who had filed grievances against the university. Even though it ultimately decided these lay outside its jurisdiction, the action elicited objections from Senate, which demanded an explanation for its intervention in 'internal academic problems.' Three weeks later, Senate expanded its critique, urging the board to reconstitute the executive to include faculty and students, and to modify its terms of reference "so that the powers of decision rest with the whole Board."[68]

Equally contentious from the board perspective was the role of Senate. Determined, as Garry Clarke noted, to become "a full partner [with the board] in the making of university policy," Senate broadened its horizons, 'actively reviewing' a wide range of university policies, including appointments. In April, it directed Cloutier to bring all academic appointments to Senate, and created a committee to develop procedures for senior staff appointments. The committee's first report echoed Duff-Berdahl, asserting that "all decisions taken in the entire university community are academic decisions" and therefore subject to Senate review. Accordingly, Senate resolved to make recommendations on "any and all academic and non-academic administrators," and insisted that faculty and students constitute a majority on search committees for both the vice-president and president. While conceding this right with regard to the acting presidency, the board had reservations about recognizing it as a general principle.[69]

In the midst of these diverging viewpoints erupted a new issue that set board and Senate on yet another collision course. 1970–1971 salary negotiations between LUFA and an executive-appointed, nine-person committee (seven governors, Vice-President Cloutier, and Comptroller Nurmi) had stalled, primarily over monetary terms. To break the impasse, in early 1970, LUFA proposed binding arbitration. At first, the executive flatly turned down the idea, but in March, it conceded that if all other avenues became exhausted, arbitration could be invoked 'under specific terms.' It also agreed not to send contract letters to faculty until a settlement had been reached. Intermittent discussions continued over the summer, to little effect.[70]

Just as negotiations picked up in earnest in September, rumours that the executive had approved higher salaries for new appointees than provided in the latest contract offer set off a chain reaction of events. First of all, the board salary negotiating committee threatened to resign on the grounds that its bargaining efforts had been undermined, although it did not do so. In reaction to the apparently impending collapse of talks, LUFA resolved on September 14 to ask the Ministry of University Affairs to mediate the dispute, the request going to Minister Bill Davis three days later.[71]

In the meantime, two board executive actions exacerbated the situation. Under President Cloutier's signature, it sent what the faculty association deemed 'letters of contract' to individual faculty, contrary to the earlier agreement not to do so. Simultaneously, executive Chair Caswell released data to the press about the board offer including information about LUFA president Clarke's personal salary status. Angered by these moves, on September 17, the faculty association wrote a scathing letter to Davis stating that the faculty contracts "were signed by the use of a rubber stamp without his [Cloutier's] knowledge or permission ... [and] were sent in spite of his explicit and strenuous opposition to their issuance in the present context," facts privately confirmed by Cloutier himself. LUFA also issued a press release excoriating the executive's misuse of 'confidential information' and insisting the impasse was due entirely to the executive's refusal to invoke binding arbitration as earlier promised. The next day, LUFA reiterated its appeal to the province to mediate.[72]

On September 20 Senate entered the fray, reaffirming its April motion of non-confidence in the executive, and censuring it for "usurping powers pertaining to the Office of the President" and for 'unethical use of confidential information.' An SGA general meeting in the Great Hall on September 23 went even further, calling for the executive's resignation, its replacement by a new committee that included both faculty and students 'with limited powers of recommendation,' and for a strike if this did not happen. In reply, an 'unofficial' gathering of executive members, minus President Cloutier, issued a press release defending its actions and characterizing the Senate charges as 'hasty and ill-considered.' For its part, on September 25, the board voted confidence in the executive, rejected compulsory arbitration, and directed its salary negotiating committee to continue work.[73]

For Senate this was the proverbial last straw. Three days later, after a lengthy and not always decorous debate, it sanctioned another academic 'recess' commencing October 1, established an ad hoc committee to organize it, and, in a last-ditch effort to avoid following through with it, requested a joint meeting with the board on September 30. The board declined the invitation. After seeking legal counsel, President Cloutier declared the recess beyond the powers of Senate to invoke. He also warned faculty that their participation might constitute 'a dereliction of academic duties' with unspecified job implications. Acting on that same advice a few days later, the executive recommended the board apply for a legal 'injunction or mandamus' ordering Senate to end the recess.[74]

Campus opinion about the recess was more divided than in April, despite Senate efforts such as a public meeting in the Fraser Auditorium on October 1 to rally faculty support. Science faculty in particular questioned its justifiability. On October 2 Science council passed a resolution expressing concern about its impact on students. "While fully appreciating the reasons for calling a recess at this time," the motion read, council "regrets the action and requests Senate to reconsider its position." Initially, about 30 per cent of classes continued to meet, although this percentage fell as attendance dwindled.[75]

Divisions within faculty ranks explained in part why the Laurentian faculty association took a more cautious approach to the recess than might have been expected, given its role in precipitating it. Relevant also was the fact that, contrary to LUFA's original position, organizations such as the Ontario Council of University Faculty Associations and the Canadian Association of University Teachers opposed, on principle, government intervention. Significantly, on October 5, after visits to Laurentian by representatives of the two, LUFA made no mention of provincial mediation, but advised its members to support the recess on the understanding that if no progress occurred, a joint OCUFA–CAUT committee of enquiry should be established.[76]

Meanwhile, the other interested parties – board, Senate, SGA – urged Queen's Park to become involved. At first the idea met opposition, University Affairs deputy-minister E.E. Stewart dismissing it because of "the rather serious precedent that would be established if the Minister … were to intervene." Nevertheless, Minister Davis invited SGA and Senate delegations to Queen's Park. Both presentations, by the SGA on October 6 and Senate the following day, asked for help in resolving not the salary dispute, but the underlying cause of the crisis, the conflict over university governance. Davis gave both a sympathetic hearing, but insisted he could take no action so long as the academic recess remained in effect. Senate got the message. On October 8, "as a gesture of our willingness to assist in a resolution of the University problem," it resolved to end the recess on October 13, after the Thanksgiving break.[77]

The board executive came away from its meeting with Davis on October 14 convinced that he was 'well informed' on the Laurentian situation, and pleased with his determination to resolve the crisis. Members might have been less sanguine had they known about the changed views of Deputy Minister Stewart, which undoubtedly influenced the minister's thinking. In a memo to Davis, Stewart noted 'the relatively inflexible position' of the Laurentian board which "became used [during the Mullins era] to … making decisions on the basis of agreements with the president and find it difficult to understand the current agitation for greater Faculty participation." Contrary to his earlier position, Stewart recommended a 'mediation team' to act as 'Advisors to the President,' the option Davis selected.[78]

In several respects, Davis's candidate to head the inquiry, J.G. (Gerry) Hagey, was an inspired choice. In the late 1950s, Hagey had presided over the transformation of Waterloo College Associate Facilities, the non-denominational branch of Waterloo College, into the University of Waterloo, serving as its first president. His first-hand experience with the trials and tribulations of a young, multi-faculty institution of higher learning would prove invaluable. Just as importantly, he was not a conventional university administrator. After earning a Bachelor of Arts in 1928, Hagey worked for twenty years in public relations with the B.F. Goodrich Company before being named president of his *alma mater*, Waterloo College, in 1953. His academic and corporate experience made him credible to Senate and board alike.[79]

At their first meeting, Hagey informed Davis he preferred to act as a committee of one. He also insisted on a preliminary assessment of the situation before committing himself to the task. Prior to going to Sudbury on November 10, he tactfully circulated on the Laurentian campus a memorandum emphasizing that he had been mandated "to *assist not direct* – you." His meetings with the various constituencies convinced him that the issues in dispute were amenable to resolution. Hagey therefore agreed to act as a consultant on the understanding that the university would not be bound by his recommendations, and only "so long as you [Davis], Laurentian, and I feel that my services are useful."[80]

That turned out to be four busy months. During that time, Hagey met with Laurentian officials, faculty, and students, attended board, Senate and other meetings, and generally assessed governing procedures, all of which provided context for his final report dated March 12, 1971. He also helped to resolve several difficult questions, most notably, the negotiation of a two-year salary settlement. By showing that Laurentian salary scales were comparable to those at Brock, Trent, and Lakehead, he convinced LUFA to lower its expectations, and the board to run a deficit to cover an improved offer. With his counsel, too, the board and Senate agreed on the composition of the presidential search committee, an issue that had delayed the process by several months.[81]

Hagey's final report was a perceptive analysis of Laurentian governance and its evolution that owed a good deal to Duff-Berdahl, and was shaped by the perspective of his fifteen years of presidential experience. In the university's early years as a 'small college' with limited enrolment, faculty, and administrative personnel, he stated, "the Board of Governors not only established policies but did most of its future planning, developed operating and capital budgets, and participated in much of the institution's day-to-day operating procedures." Partly by force of habit, partly because the board lacked awareness of developments elsewhere, this had continued even after Laurentian became a 'multi-faculty' institution in the mid-1960s. Meanwhile, the relatively young, diverse and more idealistic Laurentian faculty, cognizant of the democratic governance practices sweeping university campuses across North America, pressed for greater authority for Senate and the faculty association, swinging the pendulum of change in the opposite direction.[82]

Running through the Hagey report was the conviction that an underdeveloped administrative structure lay at the heart of Laurentian's governance woes. This was not the first time the idea had been presented to the board. In May 1969, the university had engaged Kates, Peat, Marwick, and Company to undertake a study of Laurentian's organization and management practices. The main thrust of its March 1970 report was that "the formal administrative organization is functionally weak and unable to relate effectively to other organizational components." Because of the more pressing concerns at the time, no action had then been taken on its recommendations, but its prescription for a more muscular administration to mediate the competing demands of board, Senate, faculty, and students clearly informed Hagey's thinking.[83]

Hagey offered a number of suggestions to the board. Contrary to Senate's admonition, he counselled it to meet less frequently. "The less they [governors] are involved in the detailed operation of the university," he explained, "the more likely they are to develop a capable administrative organization that will merit the respect of the university faculty and staff." He called on the board to abolish its standing committee on salary negotiations, leaving this task to the administration. Strongly reminiscent of Duff-Berdahl, he advised the governors "to respect the right of Senate, or of any individual or group, to make recommendations to the Board on matters of University policy or procedures for which Board approval is required." Hagey also agreed with Senate that the executive's authority must be limited. The executive should not, he advised, make recommendations to the board in "areas of responsibility of other board standing committees," should pass on recommendations from other committees to the board without comment, and "only act on behalf of the Board when it is directed by the Board to do so."[84]

While clearly supportive of a greater Senate role in university governance, Hagey considered 'administrative over-involvement' to be the bane of its existence as well, criticizing the fact that after Mullins' resignation, the Laurentian Senate had "reached for power to the extent that it is willing to become involved in, and make decisions on, all matters placed before it without regard to whether or not they rightfully fall within ... [its] jurisdiction." As a result, he stated, the too-frequent meetings took too long to cover an agenda devoted too often to issues that, even if they fell within Senate's authority, should be handled by sub-committees. To remedy the situation, he called on Senate to ensure that its standing committees encompassed the full range of Senate business, but no more, and to trust their recommendations. Senate, like the board, he insisted, must set policy, not get bogged down in administrative detail.[85]

Although the Hagey report offered an incisive assessment of Laurentian's governance dilemma, at the time of its release, the university community gave it mixed reviews. Hagey's pointed comments sometimes hit too close to home, perhaps, and for some, his controversial and somewhat gratuitous recommendation to transform the University of Sudbury into a unilingual Francophone college diminished its authority. Still, while it had a less forceful immediate impact than might have been expected, it was by no means without consequence. Rather, the report, and the events which gave rise to it, accelerated a critical shift in roles among the governance entities in the university – board, president, administration, Senate, faculty association, students – that shaped Laurentian's evolution for the next decade and a half.

4 Era of Transition, 1972–1985

MATT BRAY

Well before consultant Hagey submitted his report, the Laurentian Board of Governors embraced several of his recommendations on university governance. In November 1970, for example, it followed his counsel and appointed two senators – one from faculty and one a student – non-voting members of the executive. It also invited Senate and the SGA to nominate representatives to other committees, and elected governors as voting members (changed in 1974 to non-voting 'observers') of Senate. Reform and transparency persisted in subsequent years. In 1972, the board began to circulate executive minutes to non-voting members, and granted membership to the Laurentian University Administrative Staff Association and to "all sections of the University not now represented by the [other staff] associations." Four years later, it allocated a non-voting seat to the Laurentian University Alumni Association, and one to l'Association des étudiant(e)s francophones (AEF) in 1977. Lastly, after developing guidelines for *in camera* sessions, in December 1976, it opened its meetings to the public. Gone was the secrecy that had earlier enveloped board deliberations.[1]

Partly deliberately, partly serendipitously, in the early 1970s the character of the board membership changed in other ways, too. In 1973, three women joined its ranks, two voting and one, a representative of the Laurentian clerical staff, non-voting, ending its status as an exclusively male preserve except for a brief period in the early 1980s. In a 1976 letter to the Ontario Ministry of Colleges and Universities, board chair J.-N. Desmarais noted another significant transformation. "Representation from major business and industry which was perhaps slightly overwhelming in the early days of the University," he wrote, "has dwindled to near nothing." Desmarais was concerned about the impact on Laurentian's fundraising capabilities, but declining corporate involvement in the university's affairs may also have been a factor in the board's relaxation of its hold on the levers of governance during the next decade.[2]

Taking to heart Hagey's views about strengthening the university administration, in November 1970, the board established an ad hoc, joint board–Senate administrative review committee. Hagey chaired the committee's inaugural meeting, which took as its priority the hiring of a vice-president administration and a vice-president academic. On its recommendation, the following January, the board approved the selection of Frederick J. Turner, ex-bursar of Carleton University, as vice-president administration, pro tem. Turner served until 1975 when he was succeeded by Thomas L. (Spike) Hennessy, the former city engineer of Sudbury. In contrast, the academic vice-presidency remained up in the air. With the exception of 1975–1976 when the post was vacant, for most of the 1970s, a succession of pro tem appointees (Hugues Albert, Laurent Larouche, part-time, and Chrysologue Allaire) with special responsibility for Francophone Affairs filled the post. The appointment of a permanent vice-president academic came only in the summer of 1979 in the person of Francis J. (Frank) Turner, the former dean of Social Work at Wilfrid Laurier University. Over the decade, personnel changes also occurred in the other senior management positions at Laurentian – registrar, the directors of continuing education, student services, computer services, and physical plant, and, lastly, comptroller.[3]

In conformity with the Hagey recommendations, the board also reduced its 'over-involvement' in internal university affairs, transferring functions to the Laurentian administration. In April 1971, for example, it disbanded its standing committee on salary negotiations and assigned the task to a team headed by Vice-President Administration Turner. Two years later, the practice had become so entrenched that at a board executive meeting to ratify a memorandum of agreement with LUFA, "the point was made that such agreements ought to come only once to the Executive and Board, not several times in stages." In late 1971, the board also ceased approving specific changes to departmental budgets, and the next year, the executive gave up another power by retroactively approving budget-allocated faculty appointments made by the administration.[4]

The governors also ceded responsibilities to Senate, a body whose enthusiasm for the Hagey report was surprisingly restrained. After discussing it in March 1971, Senate thanked Hagey "for the great amount of work involved in the preparation of the report and for the fairness and clarity with which he treated the issues," and assigned his recommendations to various committees from which little of consequence emerged. Tellingly, Senate paid scant heed to Hagey's warning about the perils of over-stepping its jurisdictional boundaries and intruding into the university's day-to-day administrative affairs. While understandable – these were heady days for Senate, fresh from its triumphs in the confrontations of 1970 – this complicated the realignment of jurisdictions and authority among the several governing bodies.[5]

In order to recast governance at Laurentian in the 'participatory decision-making' mould then sweeping across Canadian post-secondary educational institutions, Senate enhanced its role in a number of areas, four being particularly crucial. One was the adoption of procedures in the spring of 1971 providing for faculty

selection of departmental chairs, school directors, deans, and associate deans, a radical change from the previous top-down appointment process. Another related to planning. In November, Senate created a standing committee on 'academic' long-term planning, and a year later, a special ad hoc academic planning committee of Senate began work on the university's first comprehensive five-year plan. The 1973 publication of "Planning for Tomorrow" firmly secured Senate's place in Laurentian's academic planning schema.[6]

Senate also acquired unprecedented influence over the university budgeting process. The first step came in the summer of 1970 when the ad hoc Senate committee on operating budget and short-term planning prepared, with comptroller Carl Nurmi, the 1970–1971 budget for submission to the board finance committee. Negotiations between the board and Senate later that year transformed the ad hoc committee into a standing Senate committee of the same name. Initially limited to academic budgetary items, in the spring of 1972, Senate empowered the committee to review, "in consultation with the Vice-President, Administration," non-academic allocations as well. Thereafter, Senate became the linchpin in the budgeting process. The Senate committee (including the president, vice-president academic, and comptroller) drew up the budget, keeping the board finance committee apprised of its work, and Senate approved the document before sending it to the board for final adoption. Although not without debate and, on occasion, reluctance, for the next few years the board endorsed the proposed budget with little alteration.[7]

Partly because of its greater budgetary powers, Senate also assumed a pivotal role in personnel matters. In April 1971, for example, it established a committee on appointments and promotions that not only approved new faculty appointments and replacements, but allotted departmental positions. Other Senate committees handled tenure and sabbatical requests, while still others dealt with appeals on these questions and issues such as non-renewal of contracts of non-tenured faculty. Senate by no means simply rubber-stamped the recommendations of these committees; it debated them in detail. One consequence was that Senate meetings became more frequent and lengthier. Another was the diminution of the Laurentian faculty association's involvement in the governing process. While deeming this 'proper,' LUFA President Garry Clarke warned members "it does not necessarily follow that Senate or the academic units ... will use their resources any more rationally or responsibly than the Board or the administration," so the association must play a vital 'watch dog' role.[8]

The Presidency of Edward Monahan, 1972–1977

Senate was able to assert its authority in part because of the lame-duck status of Acting President Roland Cloutier who, caught in the crossfire of events in the autumn of 1970, lost the confidence of faculty. As an ex-president himself, Hagey placed great value on a strong presidency, and on arriving at Laurentian, he facilitated the resumption of the presidential search stalled by the clash between the board and Senate. Unfortunately, procedural ambiguities confused the process.[9]

By April 1971, the presidential search committee composed of representatives of the board, Senate, students, and administration had established a short list of three candidates. Two were external to Laurentian, one internal. Two were Francophone, one Anglophone. All were Roman Catholic. All were men. In early May, the candidates journeyed to Laurentian to meet with the various constituencies, a semi-public 'dog-and-pony show,' as one later recalled. A series of board and Senate meetings then assessed the suitability of each candidate, took non-binding straw votes, and ranked and re-ranked their preferences. Senate deemed all three 'acceptable' with 'a strong preference' for one, while the board favoured another, though not by the 70 per cent majority required by its bylaws. To break the deadlock, the board asked the search committee for a new slate of names. Instead, it recommended the formation of a new committee to undertake another search with an appointment date of July 1972.[10]

Behind the scenes, the parties sought a way out of this procedural embarrassment. While factors such as the candidates' views on university governance came into play, critical, given Laurentian's status as a bilingual institution, was the competency *en français* of the individual most acceptable both to the board and Senate: Brantford, Ontario–native Edward J. Monahan, the associate executive secretary of the Canadian Association of University Teachers. The search committee's 'criteria for judgment' did not designate 'integral bilingualism' as absolutely mandatory, but those heading the list, 'Is the candidate bilingual? Sympathetic to bilingualism?' could not be ignored. In early July, after weeks of backroom bargaining and a new report from the search committee, Senate resolved to approve Monahan's candidacy. In the course of the debate, Wes Cragg emphasized that Monahan 'understands French,' was prepared to learn conversational French, was "sensitive to the French cultural fact," and willing "to devote funds outside of normal formula financing for the advancement of the French cultural fact at Lau-

EDWARD J. MONAHAN | President
of Laurentian University, 1972–1977

rentian." That commitment evidently swayed doubters because in a secret ballot the motion to endorse Monahan passed seventeen to one, with two abstentions. Three weeks later, the board, also noting Monahan's determination to become 'fluently bilingual,' unanimously approved his appointment.[11]

One problem remained. Monahan was not available. In June, after learning that not only had none of the short-listed candidates been chosen but that all three had been excluded from the new search, he had accepted a three-year term as executive assistant to Principal John Deutsch at Queen's University. Although kept informed of later developments, Monahan was still taken aback when on August 1 – his first day at Queen's – Norm Wadge, chair of the board executive, called to offer him the presidency. After meeting with Deutsch, who agreed to release him from Queen's after one year, Monahan accepted the position as of July 1, 1972, an arrangement satisfactory to Laurentian. In the interim, the board reappointed Roland Cloutier as acting president, although ill-health forced him to hand over the duties to Acting Vice-President Hugues Albert in early 1972.[12]

Monahan brought to Laurentian impressive academic credentials, a BA Hons. in philosophy and history, and an MA and PhD in philosophy, all from the University of Toronto, as well as a licentiate in medieval studies from that institution's Pontifical Institute. He began his academic career in 1953 with a three-year appointment as assistant professor of philosophy at Villanova University in Pennsylvania, followed by one year at Xavier University in Cincinnati, Ohio. In 1957, he joined the department of philosophy at St. Francis Xavier University in Nova Scotia, where he remained until 1965 when he began a five-year term with CAUT, one of his tasks being to promote the Duff-Berdahl recommendations. During that time, he became well acquainted with the 'troubled' situation at Laurentian.[13]

Although in retrospect, Monahan characterized his term as Laurentian president as "the most exciting and productive period" of his career, he must on occasion have had second thoughts about the wisdom of his decision. From the outset he faced unprecedented financial challenges – shrinking enrolments, inadequate revenues, and spiralling costs. Small annual deficits covered by special provincial grants had been incurred early in the university's existence, but that changed in the mid-1960s with rapidly growing enrolments and Ontario's adoption of the funding formula, and the allocation of emergent (later supplementary) grants to smaller institutions and bilingual grants to Laurentian and the University of Ottawa. By the early 1970s, Laurentian possessed a reserve fund of more than a half-million dollars, and boundless optimism about future prospects. The province-wide enrolment slump in the autumn of 1971, however, shattered visions of doubled student numbers and new faculties of medicine and law by mid-decade. Instead of the projected increase to approximately 2,400, Laurentian's full-time enrolment dipped below 2,000, creating a revenue shortfall and an operating deficit.[14]

During Monahan's presidency, deficits became the norm. Enrolment stagnated because larger than expected numbers of Northern Ontario students chose universities elsewhere in the province, because of disappointingly low retention rates, and because the bulk of the area's teachers, a major student source in the 1960s, acquired their degrees. The last factor also entailed shifts in students away from the traditional arts and sciences, the areas strongest in terms of faculty, to under-staffed, more expensive professional schools such as commerce. Furthermore, provincial funding failed to keep pace with inflation, and over the decade, per-student funding in Ontario fell below the Canadian provincial average. By the spring of 1974, Laurentian's reserve account was exhausted, forcing the university to fund deficits out of cash flow – not a healthy situation. To be sure, the province responded positively to requests for assistance. As of September 1974, it began to fully fund federated college enrolment, something Laurentian had long demanded, and the following March, it allocated the university a special 'Northern' grant. Still, deficits mounted, threatening to carry the accumulated debt into the realm of unmanageability. Faced in February 1976 with a projected $500,000 shortfall for the coming academic year, Monahan again appealed to Premier Davis. Once more, the province came through. A doubled Northern grant combined with belt-tightening measures produced a balanced budget that provided $100,000 for debt reduction. While bringing immediate relief, the ultimate cost would be high, both for Monahan – whom some in the university community blamed for the faculty and program cuts – and for his successor, who would find provincial authorities considerably less sympathetic to Laurentian's plight.[15]

Against this backdrop, Laurentian's participatory governance practices evolved in trial-and-error fashion. All did not go smoothly. In 1971, for example, two student senators resigned in protest against Senate vacillation and indecision. Although concerned during his first years in office that the system was becoming overly 'populist,' Monahan remained silent, preoccupied with more pressing administrative matters. In a memorandum to Senate in November 1974, however, he cited a number of shortcomings: unworkable Senate procedures for the selection of senior academic administrators; Senate's decision to permit departments to establish their own chair selection procedures that led to a chaotic situation – 63 unit heads over a four-year period, most serving only one year; and the fact that the membership of Senate's twenty standing committees totalled more than 200, a number that tripled when faculty and unit committee personnel were added, and greatly out of proportion to a faculty of 245. Moreover, as Monahan later explained in a 'state of the union' report to the university, both faculty and students had lost enthusiasm for committee work, making it difficult to recruit members and maintain quorum at meetings. Science dean Doug Williamson, otherwise a critic of the administration's cost-cutting measures, concurred, writing, "our insistence on having every imaginable, and some unimaginable, constituency represented on University committees, regardless of relevance or the task to be performed, is not very sensible or practical, and may indeed do little but contribute further to divisiveness and disenchantment with the participatory forms of university governance." Something needed to change.[16]

The board agreed, though more because of the university's budgetary difficulties. In June, 1975, the executive directed the finance committee to modify budget-making procedures to ensure the Senate budget committee produced a balanced budget for 1976–1977. In September, the latter reported that it had done so and that "the [two] Committees have worked out a joint procedure permitting the Finance Committee's involvement in critical stages of the budget-making process," a first tentative step toward greater board budgetary control.[17]

With Monahan's term of office drawing to a close, in December 1975, the board established a joint board–Senate committee to evaluate his performance and weigh the need for a presidential search. The question of university governance occupied a central place in the committee's work. Its survey of the university community revealed considerable sympathy for the president's views about the inefficacy of participatory democracy as practiced at Laurentian. Complaints varied from there being too many committees at too many levels, to the inability of committee members to agree on solutions, to Senate being simply a forum for 'conflicting advocacies,' ignoring the needs of the university as a whole. Proposed solutions varied, but generally involved streamlining the operation of Senate and its committees and/or stronger presidential leadership. The first priority of the report issued in April 1976, therefore, was the creation of a board-Senate committee to examine Laurentian's governance procedures.[18]

This was no sooner proposed than done. The board-Senate ad hoc committee, created to assess and make recommendations to simplify academic administration, and chaired by governor Mary Weaver, came into existence in the summer of 1976; it was mandated to evaluate the "academic administration and its committees and their functioning in order to improve their efficiency and effectiveness." After extensive study, the committee submitted its report in May 1977. Both faculty and administrators, it found, spent too much time on committee work, to the detriment of teaching and research in the former case, and of providing academic leadership in the latter. Reorganization should ensure that faculty have an 'effective voice' in the selection of senior administrative staff, but academic administra-

LANDSCAPE OF THE CAMPUS | By the mid-1970s, Laurentian University had undergone a remarkable physical transformation.

tors, while accountable to faculty, must have authority to devise and implement policy. In an atmosphere of greater mutual trust, the report theorized, the need for many committees would disappear, permitting both parties to carry out their responsibilities more efficiently.[19]

Timing is everything, of course, and that was true of the Weaver report. Although its recommendations on Francophone Affairs eventually bore fruit in 1978 with the creation of the Conseil de l'enseignement en français, whose first director, Gaétan Gervais, became a member of the budget committee in the early 1980s, its impact was otherwise dampened because its release coincided with the announcement that Monahan would leave Laurentian upon the completion of his term in June 1977. Still, by focussing attention on the issue, the joint board–Senate committee on academic administration marked another stage in the evolution of Laurentian's governance.

President Monahan did not originally plan to resign. In November 1975, he advised board chair Desmarais that he was willing to accept an additional three-year term, subject to a performance review as per his letter of appointment. Accordingly, Senate and the board established a joint review committee. Midway through the process, however, the chair of the Council of Ontario Universities (COU), John Evans, president of the University of Toronto, proposed that Monahan become the new COU executive director. On consideration he decided to accept what he later characterized as "a new challenge on a larger playing field," and in late March 1976, informed the Board of Governors of his decision.[20]

As reflected in a LUFA membership survey carried out for his performance review that some at the time assumed to have been a factor in Monahan's resignation – campus opinion about his tenure was divided. Roughly 70 per cent of faculty participated in the poll. On the first question – Should the president be reappointed? – a plurality of respondents said no. On the second – Should a presidential search committee be appointed? – 60 per cent said yes. The final report of the review committee provided a similarly mixed assessment of Monahan's presidency. Beginning with his strengths, it described him as "an excellent administrator who brought administrative stability and functional efficiency out of chaos," something Laurentian sorely needed and a cornerstone of his original mandate from the board and Senate alike. This accomplishment was all the more impressive, it might have added, given the academic vice-presidential vicissitudes that characterized these years. Praiseworthy, too, were his political and academic 'lines of communications' to Queen's Park and its educational bureaucracy, connections that extricated the university from financial dilemmas on several occasions. Finally, the report lauded Monahan's 'consensus' approach to the internal governance of Laurentian that had minimized 'major conflicts' within the institution, an allusion, among other things, to the personnel crises in such units as social work and nursing that occupied a good deal of the president's attention.[21]

On the other hand, that same consensus mode of operation in the guise of insufficiently strong presidential leadership was thought by some to account for weaknesses in Laurentian's participatory democracy. Other critics, especially in the sciences, questioned the academic direction which Monahan proposed to take the university, particularly the orientation toward interdisciplinary studies. Finally, the report noted, some found Monahan's performance wanting on the public relations front. Such people argued that at neither the community nor Northern Ontario regional levels had he represented Laurentian effectively. This criticism was not unwarranted – community relations were not high on Monahan's list of priorities – but then no one either questioned his work ethic or identified what other activities should have been sacrificed to this end. After departing Laurentian, Monahan took that ethic to the Council of Ontario Universities, where he served the Ontario university system with distinction for nearly fifteen years. Upon retirement in 1991, he returned to his academic roots, writing a history of the COU.[22]

President Henry Best, the Affiliated Colleges and the Challenges of Governance, 1977–1984

In contrast to the procedural difficulties that surrounded the appointment of President Monahan, the selection of his successor proceeded with exemplary facility. In April 1976, Senate and the board approved the composition and terms of reference of a presidential search committee headed by board chair Jean-Noël Desmarais and composed of three governors, three senators, two students, and a member of the administration. Over the summer, the committee developed selection criteria that, as became standard practice, specified 'integral bilingualism' as a priority and cast its net far and wide for candidates. It interviewed seven individuals and in late November, ranked Henry B.M. Best at the top of its short list. Two weeks later, the board and Senate both approved the Best nomination.[23]

The son of Dr. Charles Best, associate of Dr. Frederick Banting in the discovery of insulin in the early 1920s and a Laurentian honorary degree recipient in 1971, Henry Best brought to the presidency a wide range of assets. Fluently bilingual, his academic credentials – MA and PhD in history from l'Université Laval – were balanced by administrative experience in both political and university circles. Before undertaking doctoral studies, Best worked in the late 1950s as executive assistant to several federal Conservative cabinet ministers, something, it was hoped, that would stand Laurentian in good stead with Ontario's Davis government. After graduate work at Laval, he joined the faculty of York University in 1964. There, his career followed twin academic and administrative paths – lecturer in Canadian history and director of student services, 1966–1969; associate professor of history, associate dean of Atkinson College; and acting coordinator of Canadian studies, 1971–1973. Lastly, because one of his mandates was to raise Laurentian's community profile, Best was, as *Northern Life*'s Norm Tollinsky wrote, "a bicultural carbon copy of the Sudbury community itself [and] must have been judged a natural for the job."[24]

Because his presidency coincided with Ontario's most prolonged economic downturn since the 1930s, the greatest challenge facing President Best inevitably related to Laurentian's financial situation. The same factors that bedevilled his predecessor – inadequate financing, surging costs, slow enrolment growth (not until the early 1980s would Laurentian's full-time student population surpass 3,000) – rendered the budget-making exercise progressively more difficult. The budget for 1978–1979, the first prepared under his auspices, did not break the uneasy détente between the board and Senate, but its controversial provision for faculty redundancies, mainly in the sciences, did not augur well.[25]

The crisis deepened the following year. In August 1978, Premier Davis appointed Bette Stephenson Minister of Colleges and Universities, a position she would hold for six-and-a-half years. In contrast to her predecessors, Stephenson had little sympathy for the cries of poverty coming from Ontario's universities, especially Laurentian's. Since 1973 its operating grants had doubled, she noted shortly after taking office, yet its enrolment had risen by only 12 per cent. Consequently, the value of its grants per full-time equivalent student had grown by 86 per cent, by far the most in the province. Not surprisingly, when in early 1979 Stephenson announced cuts to Laurentian funding, Best's pleas for reconsideration made little impact.[26]

Meanwhile, the Senate budget committee struggled to prepare a balanced budget for 1979–1980. After months of deliberation it concluded it could not do so without serious academic ramifications. In June 1979, it circulated a draft document that provided for the elimination of four low enrolment, but academically core, departments – philosophy, modern languages, anthropology, and geology. As no doubt intended, this proposal sent shockwaves throughout not only Laurentian, but the entire region. Determined to avoid such draconian measures, Best petitioned both Stephenson and the Minister of Northern Affairs, Leo Bernier, for assistance. Individuals such as Sudbury Regional Chair Doug Frith added their voices to a chorus of support for Laurentian. Not helping the university's cause was the revelation that while few proposed faculty redundancies had actually been implemented, the previous three years had ended with operating surpluses.

HENRY B.M. BEST | President of Laurentian University, 1977 to 1984

The appeals failed, leaving Laurentian in a state of budgetary limbo. Repudiating the idea of excising entire departments, Senate approved a deficit budget that the board rejected, but which in practice served as the university's financial blueprint for the year.[27]

Concerned about the breakdown of Laurentian's budgeting procedures, in August 1979, the Ministry of Colleges and Universities dispatched university affairs officer Peter Wright to Sudbury to assess the situation. Wright attributed Laurentian's problems to a number of factors: the inability of Senate budget-committee members to distinguish between the interests of the university and those of their own division or department; 'unsophisticated' methods of forecasting revenues and expenditures; the lack of a broadly accepted long-range academic plan to guide the budgeting process; and "in part … the Board having delegated many of its powers to the Senate, either consciously or unconsciously."[28]

In response to MCU pressure, in September 1979, the board and Senate established a joint five-person committee headed by President Best "to make proposals for a revision of budgeting procedures." The existing budget committee, the committee's final report noted in early November, was too large and its frequently changing membership lacked expertise and bore no responsibility for its decisions – an unsatisfactory situation. It proposed instead a new university budget committee composed of the vice-president academic, the vice-president administration, and the deans of the faculties, mandated to "report to the President who will present the final budget to Senate, for information purposes, and to the Board … for authorization." Both the board and Senate accepted this recommendation, with one alteration. On Senate's insistence, the board substituted 'consultation' for 'information purposes,' an ambiguous term that the former interpreted as meaning approval and the latter as something less binding. Although Senate argued otherwise, a vital dimension of its authority over budget-making flowed through the administration to the board.[29]

In the short run, the new budgeting procedure did not resolve Laurentian's financial dilemma – only improved province-wide economic conditions and an upsurge in student enrolment in the mid-1980s would finally do so – but it helped to ease tensions within the university. Most importantly, it restored board confidence in the budgetary process. When the new committee proposed a half-million-dollar deficit budget for 1981–1982, for example, the governors acquiesced. That earned the wary cooperation of Senate, which the next year agreed to balance the budget by means of expenditure reductions of $750,000, an order of magnitude it had previously refused to consider.[30]

The financial woes that troubled Best's presidency affected Laurentian in other ways, particularly by precipitating the certification of the Laurentian University Faculty Association as the legal bargaining agent for faculty and librarians. More than anything, this was attributable to cumulative faculty insecurities arising from years of financial uncertainties and from the drastic measures proposed, though not always taken, to deal with them. That it occurred in 1979 in the midst of the worst crisis of the decade and only two-and-a-half years after faculty had formally rejected unionization was certainly no coincidence.[31]

Faculty certification modified various aspects of university governance. In May 1979, in the wake of the faculty vote, for example, the Board of Governors resolved that all staff relations would be considered *in camera*, by voting members only. It also established a staff relations committee composed of voting board members and mandated to act on the board's behalf in the negotiation and administration of collective agreements. The sole exceptions were the board executive's responsibility for the 'overall financial implications' of negotiations and the board's power of final ratification. As well, the staff relations committee circulated minutes only to its members. While explicable by confidentiality exigencies, the more secretive nature of these measures reversed the trend toward openness that had characterized board procedures in recent years.[32]

At the time of certification, LUFA opponents argued that because of the loss of collegiality and "a hardening of the battle lines between 'them' and 'us,'" unionization would diminish faculty's role in the governing of the university. Supporters countered that elsewhere certification not only "preserved the former level of faculty participation in university governance ... [but often] extended faculty participation in management, while clarifying and detailing operational procedures and faculty rights." This debate would continue in future years, but as at other institutions, most immediately, unionization altered the medium of faculty influence on university affairs by shifting governance authority from Senate to the faculty association.[33]

In September 1979, Garry Clarke, both ex-Speaker of Senate and former LUFA president, prepared a memo on "The Role of the Laurentian Senate Under Collective Agreement with Faculty." Although his conclusion that as a result of certification, "Senate, as the typical – and central – institution of collegial government seems bound to wither" was by his own admission, 'too bleak a prognosis,' his analysis was perceptive. Clarke predicted Senate's authority would be compromised by the terms of the collective agreement negotiated by the faculty association, and possibly also by the board taking the opportunity to recapture powers ceded during the previous decade. Senate's three most-vulnerable spheres of responsibility, he stated, were budgeting, appointments and promotion, and academic planning.[34]

Clarke's prognostication proved close to the mark. As already noted, within weeks, control of the budgetary process shifted from Senate to the administration. Shortly thereafter, too, Laurentian's first collective agreement established procedures for appointments and promotions giving the faculty association the power to select half of the new university personnel committee, with Senate naming the other members. Two years later, the board also conceded LUFA's right to appoint the members of the divisional faculty and library personnel committees. With respect to academic planning, a critical step had taken place earlier when, under protest in some cases, the four Senate faculty representatives on the academic planning committee had been replaced by the four deans, transferring authority to administrative hands. Clarke's conclusion that the concept of a "*University* as a self-governing academic community which takes responsibility through the decisions of elected representatives [to Senate] seems to have given way to ... [one] of a public institution which is legally accountable to its (governmental) paymaster, its fee-paying students and its community (through the Board) on the one hand and legally in contract with its employees, academic and other, on the other," was incisive.[35]

The financial and economic crises of the 1970s also affected an external aspect of Laurentian's governance, its relationship with its affiliated colleges. Le Collège universitaire de Hearst had been the first to sign an affiliation agreement in 1963, although its association with the University of Sudbury dating from 1957 meant that it had operated under the Laurentian umbrella since the university's creation. Algoma University College in Sault Ste. Marie was next to enter the fold, in 1965, followed by North Bay's Nipissing University College a year later. Both Algoma and Nipissing commenced classes in 1967.

From virtually the day they opened their doors, Nipissing and Algoma chafed under what they considered Laurentian's heavy-handed strictures on their development, repeatedly appealing to the province for greater independence, preferably full university status. Laurentian, in turn, repeatedly countered that neither economically nor demographically could northeastern Ontario sustain three separate institutions. In the 1970s, two provincially appointed enquiries, the 1972 Wright Commission on Post-Secondary Education in Ontario, and a 1978 Ontario Economic Council-sponsored study by Donald Cameron, *The Northern Dilemma: Public Policy and Post-Secondary Education in Northern Ontario*, recommended disaffiliation for Nipissing and Algoma. Both were ignored because financial and enrolment considerations (in 1976, after a provincial royal commission of investigation, the Davis government placed Algoma in trusteeship) seemed to validate the Laurentian position. Still, this left the province with the conundrum of transforming the Laurentian system into a cost-effective, academically coordinated network under the authority of multiple decentralized governing bodies.[36]

It was President Best's misfortune that Minister of Colleges and Universities Stephenson was doggedly determined to square this circle, forcing him to devote an inordinate amount of time and energy to the question with ultimately little to show for it. Apart from the perennial efforts of the Ontario Council on University Affairs (OCUA) and a 1980 provincial Committee on the Future Role of Universities in Ontario, which considered the question indirectly, three major provincial committees/commissions wrestled with it in the early 1980s. The sequence began in 1981 with an OCUA-appointed committee headed by McMaster University ex-president Arthur N. Bourns, and mandated, in consultation with Best and the heads of the three affiliated universities, to propose structural changes to the Laurentian system. Although only Algoma displayed any degree of enthusiasm for Bourns' plan to create a single multi-campus university (Nipissing and Collège universitaire de Hearst opposed the idea outright, while Laurentian's approval was conditional upon the new university being a highly centralized one, something unacceptable to the other three), Stephenson accepted the OCUA recommendation to proceed with it, and established, in the autumn of 1982, the Committee on University Education in Northeastern Ontario chaired by Harry Parrott, a former MCU minister.[37]

Released in October 1983 after six months of public hearings in five northeastern Ontario communities (Hearst, Sault Ste. Marie, North Bay, Sudbury, and Timmins), the Parrott Committee report fleshed out the Bourns proposal. In classic 'eye-of-the-beholder' style, each institution viewed the multi-campus idea through the refracting lens of its own bias. Laurentian characterized the proposed governance structures as cumbersome, excessively decentralized and insufficiently protective of Francophone interests, and objected to the suggested new name, 'Champlain University.' Nipissing rejected the report on the opposite grounds: that it did not give sufficient authority to the outlying campuses. Hearst, concerned also about the threat to its Francophone character, concurred. Only Algoma again gave the idea relatively unqualified support.[38]

Efforts by Laurentian and its affiliates over the winter of 1983–1984 to devise a common-front response to the Parrott committee report failed. Consequently, in May 1984 the government referred it to the Commission on the Future Development of the Universities of Ontario chaired by Edmond Bovey, ex-president of Northern Central Gas, and with authority to design an action plan for restructuring the entire provincial system. Preparation of the Laurentian submission fell to President Best's successor, John Daniel, who successfully raised 'doubts' about the Parrott committee proposals. In the January 1985 Bovey report, the Champlain University concept receded into the background, replaced by recommendations for a new coordinating council and additional funding for the existing Laurentian system.

The coming to power of the David Peterson Liberals in the wake of the February 1985 provincial election rendered even these proposals passé. The new Minister of Colleges and Universities, Greg Sorbara, eschewed his predecessor's grandiose restructuring schemes, favouring instead a more pragmatic approach, the negotiation of new affiliation agreements giving the colleges greater academic autonomy, which were duly signed in 1986.[39]

The underlying dilemma of the Laurentian system could not be so easily resolved, and the vacillating beat of Laurentian-affiliate relations went on. Algoma came out of trusteeship in 1986, and two years later, it and Nipissing renewed their quests for disaffiliation, though with very different outcomes in the short run. In early 1989, Algoma's continuing financial difficulties prompted the Ministry of Colleges and Universities to impose new strictures on the college, including a provision for Laurentian supervision of its financial affairs, a situation that prevailed for several years. Meanwhile, Nipissing's fortunes went in quite a different direction. In the autumn of 1989, it formally applied to the province for a university charter. The NDP government of Bob Rae elected in 1990 proved receptive to Nipissing's ministrations, and in November 1992, Queen's Park approved a private members' bill establishing it as an independent university. Eventually, Algoma, too, got its wish when in 2008 the McGuinty Liberal government finally granted it full university status.[40]

In contrast to the frustrations of Laurentian-affiliate relations, President Best's efforts to integrate the university into its local milieu proved decidedly more successful, and more rewarding. Over Laurentian's first decade and a half, university-community relations had fluctuated, despite the efforts of the university's biggest local booster, the *Sudbury Star*, which repeatedly trumpeted the university's educational potential, and extolled its economic and cultural values to Sudbury. Yet despite this extensive coverage of all facets of university life, there persisted a discernible distance between Laurentian and the local community, particularly after its move to Ramsey Lake Road in 1964. As *Star* columnist Ian Green noted, "neither a city university nor a suburban one," Laurentian paid a price for "the physical insularity of the campus."[41]

One early effort to overcome this distance, highly successful until financial constraints in the mid-1990s forced the university to withdraw its support, was the joint Laurentian–Sudbury and District Chamber of Commerce Canadian centenary project. The Chamber proposal to purchase the 'Bell Rock' property of Sudbury lumbering entrepreneur, W.J. Bell, and convert the 'Mansion' into a museum and arts centre to be administered by the university first went to the Laurentian board in 1966. The governors were intrigued, but wary, and accepted the offer in principle only after being satisfied that provincial regulations permitted them to use operating funds for this purpose, and the Chamber agreed to conditions limiting the university's financial liability. Even then, negotiation of the formal agreement and site renovations delayed the transfer to Laurentian until 1969. While over the next three decades the university's role in its operation would not be without controversy, the Laurentian University Museum and Arts Centre afforded Sudbury and district a vital cultural dimension the community hitherto lacked.[42]

In the early 1970s, administrative and financial constraints imposed limits on Laurentian's involvement in community affairs, but the Monahan era was by no means a wasteland in this respect. Faculty who came to Laurentian expecting to remain only a short while settled into the community and shifted their research foci to regional matters such as urban development, environmental questions, and First Nations issues. As Science dean Doug Williamson commented in November 1975, "Our geographical location has largely determined that Laurentian is a regional university and has therefore rather special obligations to that region."[43]

Several factors motivated the Board of Governors to place improved university-community relations high on President Best's list of priorities, but none more than the need, in an era of stagnating enrolment, to attract a higher percentage of local students to Laurentian. To this end, during his first year in office, Best invited Laurentian employees to a winter-long series of dinners at his residence at 179 John Street – each attended by a cross-section of Sudburians not directly associated with the university. The dinners were popular both inside and outside university circles, and set a standard of presidential sociability unmatched before or since. Just as important, they put a personal face to the 'gown and town' relationship, burnishing Laurentian's image in the community, and vice-versa.[44]

Early in 1978, the university launched an on-campus initiative with this same objective, a task force on enrolment and community relations. It undertook a variety of projects, many of which had been tried sporadically in the past: broadcasting interviews with Laurentian faculty, students, and administrators on local television (although the 11:15 p.m. Sunday evening viewing time was hardly ideal); liaising with Sudbury Board of Education officials and secondary school personnel; and holding an on-campus 'open house' dedicated to advertising the university's educational strengths and facilities. 'Laurentian Week 1978' also marked the inauguration of the Falconbridge Lectures, a series established by donations from Falconbridge Nickel and its employees to honour the memory of five company officials who died in a plane crash near Barrie, Ontario, in September 1977. For the next three decades, these lectures featured a diversity of world-class scholars and thinkers, such as University of Toronto geophysicist Tuzo Wilson, Canadian astronaut Roberta Bondar, American scientist Linus Pauling, and Canadian jurist Beverley McLaughlin, to name only a few. After its takeover of Falconbridge Nickel in 2006, Xstrata Nickel donated $100,000 to Laurentian, ensuring that the Xstrata Nickel Memorial Lecture Series continued as a vital link between the university and the community at large.[45]

Other developments during the 1970s also fostered closer ties between Laurentian and the community. One was the pivotal role of Laurentian's biology department on the Vegetation Enhancement Technical Advisory Committee, the joint government–university–corporate body created by regional authorities to spearhead the re-greening of Sudbury. Over the next thirty years, the project re-

LAURENTIAN AND THE RE-VEGETATION OF THE SUDBURY BASIN | Nothing better illustrates Laurentian University's impact on the local community than its involvement in the re-greening of Sudbury, a highly successful thirty-plus year initiative that began in the 1970s, and in which the university's department of biology played a central role.

vegetated more than 3,300 hectares of land in the area, transforming the face and image of the community. Similarly, in the spring of 1978, Laurentian hosted, and several faculty including President Best participated in, the 'Sudbury 2001' conference sponsored by the Sudbury Committee, a broadly based community organization dedicated to revitalizing the local economy that suffered massive layoffs in the mining industry.[46]

One Best initiative, the appointment of Elmer McVey, president of the Sudbury and District Labour Council, to the Laurentian Board of Governors improved relations with a segment of the local community not generally involved in the university's affairs, but it drew opposition from some members of the board. On the president's urging, Thorneloe University nominated McVey to one of the Anglican positions, causing several governors to threaten resignation, though none did so. Best later recalled that McVey contributed a great deal to the board's deliberations, especially on issues relating to labour relations, and that he became well-respected by other board members.[47]

Sport, too, brought Laurentian closer to Sudbury, partly through the local support for such nationally acclaimed teams as the Lady Vees, Canadian Intercollegiate Sports women's basketball champions, 1975–1979, and partly because of the state-of-the-art facilities the university provided the community. Three venues stood out. One was the pool complex completed in 1972 and renamed the Olympic (now the Jeno Tihanyi Olympic) Gold Pool in honour of Laurentian graduate Alex Baumann, whose swimming career climaxed at the 1984 Los Angeles Olympics with two gold medals. The all-weather track jointly constructed by the university and the city in 1974 first brought Laurentian an international sporting reputation in 1976 when the German Democratic Republic (East German) track-and-field team utilized it for pre-Olympic training. The Pan American Junior Track and Field Championship hosted by the university in 1980 consolidated that reputation, as did the Canadian Games for the Physically Disabled and the Ontario Summer Games held in August and September 1983, respectively, and the World Junior Track and Field Championships in 1988. Lastly, in late 1980 Laurentian officially opened the Voyageur Vita Par Course, a network of cross-country ski trails that interlinked with those of the local conservation authority, a boon to a community with Sudbury's diverse ethnic composition and climate.[48]

Thanks to initiatives such as these, by the early 1980s, the town-gown relationship had taken a decided turn for the better, reflected in Laurentian's higher enrolment and retention of students from the region. While partly a function of the difficult economic times that kept students closer to home, significant, too, were the facts that increasing numbers of the university's graduates taught in local schools and that children of alumni followed in their parents' footsteps, enhancing the community's sense of ownership of the institution. Laurentian paid tribute to this in 1983 when it celebrated Sudbury's centenary by awarding honorary degrees to five Northern Ontario builders, Sudbury businessmen J.C. McIsaac, Clifford Fielding, and W.B. Plaunt; ninety-three-year old Honorary Citizen of Sudbury, Mary Whalen; and media pioneer J. Conrad Lavigne, of Timmins.[49]

Given that Best's record of community involvement set a precedent that his successors could not disregard, it was fitting that he personally benefited from the warmer Laurentian-community relations. As the board had done earlier with respect to President Monahan, in the spring of 1981, it initiated a presidential review to determine the appropriateness of an extension to Best's term in office. As before, too, the faculty association surveyed its members on the question. According to the LUFA president, Oiva Saarinen, the results were not intended for public consumption, but in mid-April *Northern Life* published a story claiming the existence of a 'dump Best' movement within faculty ranks. In the face of these reports, both the community and the university rallied around the president. *Northern Life* itself editorially praised Best's efforts to integrate the university into the community and called for his reappointment, as did Paul Reid, president of the Sudbury and District Chamber of Commerce. Though divided, the faculty association joined the Board of Governors in censoring *Northern Life*'s reporting of the issue, and in May, the board extended Best's term by two years, to 1984.[50]

Although by no means devoid of the trials and tribulations that characterized his first term, President Best's last years in office witnessed greater administrative stability. To some extent, this was because the increased demands on his time and attention by such matters as affiliate relations necessitated the expansion of the roles of the vice-president academic and the vice-president administration. The former office, filled since 1979 by Frank Turner, became increasingly responsible for internal university affairs, an evolution marked in 1983 by his promotion to the position of executive vice-president. The administrative vice-presidency remained vacant after 'Spike' Hennessy's resignation in 1979. Two years later, however, Ron Chrysler, who had succeeded Carl Nurmi as comptroller in 1978, was named assistant to the president finance and administration, and then in 1983, became vice-president finance and administration, with correspondingly greater authority and responsibilities. This differentiation of tasks freed the president from preoccupation with day-to-day academic and administrative matters and, in combination with the more defined roles of the board, Senate, and faculty association, brought greater clarity to the university's governance.[51]

President Best's association with Laurentian and with Sudbury did not end with his presidency. After a sabbatical leave he returned to the university as a professor in the department of history, serving in that capacity until his retirement in 2000. During these later Sudbury years he remained active in community affairs, the Sudbury Art Gallery and the local farmers' market, to cite only two examples, occupying a good deal of his time and energy. The high regard of the academic and local communities for Dr. Best was reflected in the large memorial service held on the occasion of his untimely death in 2006.

5 The Modern Age, 1985 to the Present

MATT BRAY

From a governance perspective, Laurentian's next twenty-five years unfolded very differently from the first. The maturing and differentiation of roles of the various bodies – board, administration, Senate, faculty association – meant they devoted less attention to the mechanisms of governing and more to the university's core educational mandates, teaching and research, a decidedly progressive development. Governance practices did not stop evolving, but compared to earlier years, change came about incrementally and within the limits of more defined boundaries, some negotiated, others established by precedent. Nor were these decades free of conflict, although increasingly, the 'administration' replaced the board and executive as the focus of discontent on the part of Senate and the faculty association.

The John Daniel Presidency, 1984–1989

As the administration's role grew, the president assumed a correspondingly more central place in the Laurentian hierarchy, setting the governance tone. That certainly was true of John S. Daniel, appointed by the Board of Governors in the spring of 1984 on the recommendation of the now standard joint board–Senate–student selection committee. The British-born, bilingual Daniel had been vice-rector academic at Concordia University from 1980 to 1984, and vice-president for Learning Services at Athabasca University for two years before that. Educated at Oxford (honours, metallurgy, 1965) and l'Université de Paris (doctorate in Physical Sciences, 1969), he taught first in the department of metallurgical engineering at l'Université de Montreal before becoming directeur des Études at Telé-université in Quebec in 1973. As suggested by the Athabasca, Telé-Université, and other appointments, such as his presidency of the International Council for Distance Education, 1982–1985, Daniel had already earned recognition for expertise in the

JOHN S. DANIEL |
President of Laurentian
University, 1984–1989

field. This fit well with Laurentian's educational outreach program which, during his term, stretched not only across Canada, but abroad as well.[1]

Daniel brought to the presidency abundant self-confidence fortified by his senior administrative experience. His on-the-job learning curve was shorter than others, and he did not hesitate to assert the authority of the presidency and the administration. Within months of taking office in July 1984, he submitted a report to Senate critiquing the university budgeting process, faulting it for not providing academic units sufficient lead time to hire new faculty, for not adequately involving the academic planning committee (ACAPLAN), for not clearly defining Senate's role, and for placing the deans and the directeur du conseil de l'enseignement en français in conflict-of-interest positions as both supplicant and arbiter. Daniel then revamped the procedures, limiting the committee membership to the president and vice-presidents, and providing for consultation with academic units, senior academic officers, and ACAPLAN. He also established an eight-month timetable culminating in the submission of the budget to the board in April, though unforeseen contingencies, particularly uncertainty about provincial funding, often played havoc with this schedule. While by no means unchanging (in 1988, for example, the assistant vice-president French language programs was added to the committee), the general framework of these procedures remained in effect for the next quarter-century.[2]

President Daniel challenged Senate on other issues as well. One involved procedures for the appointment of a successor to Vice-President Executive Frank Turner whose term ended June 30, 1984, but whom, at Laurentian's request, stayed over the summer. After canvassing faculty, in September, Daniel informed Senate of his decision to revert the office to that of vice-president academic by transferring responsibility for the faculty collective agreement to a new position on academic staff relations. He also announced the appointment of Angus Gilbert, historian and dean of Social Sciences, as interim vice-president academic, and asked Senate to establish an advisory search committee of board, Senate, and student representatives, chaired by the president. Senate executive did so, but stipulated the committee must "present its preferred candidate to Senate for recommendation and to [the] Board for acceptance."[3]

Although in late March and early April 1985, Senate and the board respectively approved the search committee's nomination of Charles Bélanger, director of institutional research at l'Université de Montréal, from the senators' perspective, procedures had been breached because the board had made the formal offer to Bélanger beforehand, in early March. Daniel's explanation that circumstances had required immediate action and that the failure to first take the matter to Senate had simply been an oversight was supported by his having apprised Senate executive of the appointment on March 8. Still, Senate was not happy and directed its executive to join the board in a review of procedures for the appointment of senior academic administrators. "It is understood," the motion concluded, "that these procedures will reflect the tradition of effective consultation which has been established over the years at this university and that Senate will play a major role in the aforementioned procedures."[4]

The proposal came at a time when the board also sought greater accountability from its senior administrators, both to itself and to the university community. In the autumn of 1985, for example, Daniel and the two vice-presidents presented to the board a review of the past year and outlined objectives for the next year, regular practices thereafter. As well, the governors had second thoughts about their 1980 decision to give the president the power to appoint deans on the advice of a faculty-controlled board–faculty committee. More generally, the devolution of authority to the administration made the board's selection of senior officials all the more critical, offering it an opportunity to influence (at least in theory) the university's academic direction. To this end, it proposed expanding the review to encompass an annual performance evaluation of all senior administrative officers.[5]

The ad hoc committee on procedures for the selection and evaluation of senior academic administrators established by the board in April 1985 therefore had a more limited composition – two senators and three board members – and a broader mandate than envisaged by Senate, to design 'effective procedures' for the appointment, not only of the president and vice-president academic, but also the deans, the chief librarian, and other administrative officers reporting to the vice-president. The committee's final report, submitted to Senate in January 1986 and to the board a month later, did precisely that, delineating procedures involving both Senate and the board that entailed final board approval in all cases. Thereafter, in consultation with Senate and the faculty association, it periodically revised the process to reflect changing university policies on subjects such as bilingualism and employment equity (in 1989) and to cover the promotion of senior academic administrators (in 1994).[6]

The ad hoc committee report did not address the question of annual performance reviews for senior administrators, but in 1986 the board executive adopted recommendations from President Daniel providing for these in all instances except the presidency. Over the year, an informal review process evolved whereby the board chair and other governors met annually with the president to evaluate his performance, and to receive his report on that of the vice-presidents, academic and administration. In 1993, the board executive formalized this procedure, creating an evaluation committee composed of the board chair, vice-chair, executive chair, and past chair. Five years later, the board converted it to a standing senior management compensation committee with added responsibility for compensation issues, further enhancing its oversight of the university's senior administrative personnel.[7]

Undoubtedly strengthening his hand with both the board and Senate during the 1980s was President Daniel's good fortune to take office at a time when Ontario's improving economic prospects permitted the province to loosen the purse strings on funding for post-secondary education. Along with its expanding student population (full-time enrolment rose by one-third between 1984 and 1989, to approximately 4,300), this meant Laurentian's financial picture was rosier than at any time since the late 1960s. Annual grant increases ranged from 7 per cent to 9 per cent, although inflation cut into this, as did periodic changes to the provincial funding formula, such as the Peterson Liberals' 1987 'funding envelopes' intended to control the growth of post-secondary educational expenditures. Even so, by the early 1990s, Laurentian had not only retired its long-standing debt, but accrued a reserve of more than $2 million.[8]

Laurentian's improved financial status was a double-edged sword. On the one hand, it set the stage for difficult contract negotiations between the administration and the university's labour unions, especially the Laurentian University Faculty Association and the Laurentian University Support Staff Association. After more than a decade of restraint and inflationary pressures, these groups were determined to play 'catch up' with respect to salaries, pensions and fringe benefits. They faced a wary administration and board that were not convinced Laurentian was out of the woods, and equally prepared to employ brinkmanship bargaining tactics. As a consequence, the Daniel presidency began with a near walk-out by faculty in the fall of 1984, and experienced two full-scale strikes in 1985, a short one by the Laurentian University Faculty Association in September, and a longer one by the Laurentian University Support Staff Association in October and November. Capping the decade was another LUFA strike that began just before the start of classes in September 1989, and ended in the first week of October. Tellingly, although the usual 'bread-and butter' issues were in play, the faculty association accused not the board or executive, but the administration of bad-faith bargaining and excessive control of university affairs.[9]

On the other hand, Laurentian's more solid financial status and growing student population in the late 1980s both necessitated and permitted the expansion of old and the creation of new academic units and programs, undergraduate and graduate, the hiring, after a period of 'freezes,' of new faculty, and the establishment of a series of research institutes, all of which matured the university academically. These same factors reawakened dreams of a new building phase, the first since the late 1960s.[10]

On this front, the Monahan and Best eras had been exceptionally lean. The Ontario government provided virtually no capital funding to Laurentian, and the uncertain business climate, especially in mining, afforded little opportunity to tap the local private sector. In 1973, the Board of Governors had established a development committee for this purpose, but its major accomplishment was raising $600,000 for the expansion of the engineering program in 1976, and even that had been a struggle despite International Nickel having kick-started the campaign with a $300,000 donation. Nevertheless, in the winter of 1978–1979 the board and Senate endorsed the idea of a major fundraising appeal, its launch to coincide with the celebration of Laurentian's 20th anniversary in 1980. That did not happen. The project repeatedly ran into roadblocks, most notably, the worsening economy that culminated in the early 1980s in Ontario's most severe recession since the Great Depression, and the competing demands for community support, especially that of Inco, from the newly established Science North. The campaign only got underway in 1982 and even then, was restricted in scope, the university community itself contributing nearly half of the $1 million raised during its first year. The external appeal to the broader, corporate world remained in limbo, although behind-the-scenes efforts by President Best and Falconbridge Nickel's Marsh Cooper, a former Laurentian governor, paved the way for a major success in this area. While not publicly announced – Best later recalled Paul Desmarais (president of Power Corporation) asked this not be done until the external campaign was in full swing – in June 1983, the president thanked Desmarais for "l'intérêt que vous continuez de manifester à l'égard de la Laurentienne et de votre souscription pour la nouvelle bibliothèque universitaire."[11]

Very early on, a new library complex had been identified as Laurentian's chief infrastructure priority. The existing facility, spread over five floors in the R.D. Parker Building, had been the subject of complaint by librarians, faculty, and students before the 'tower' had even been constructed. Cost inefficient, because of the need to staff multiple exits at all times, and user unfriendly, it lacked proper environmental controls, and by the early 1980s was quickly running out of space. In autumn 1984, when President Daniel proposed the board rejuvenate the fundraising campaign in the context of Laurentian's 25th anniversary, the new library again headed the list of projects, along with a student centre, another badly needed campus facility.[12]

Once again, events, this time political in nature, postponed the best-laid plans. Reduced to minority status in the spring, 1985 provincial election, the Progressive Conservative government of Frank Miller suffered defeat at Queen's Park in June, ceding power to the Liberals led by David Peterson with the support of the New Democrat Party. The policy of the new minority government (and also of its majority Liberal successor elected in 1987) of decentralizing provincial services particularly benefited Sudbury, leading to the transfer of the Ministry of Northern Development and Mines to the city in 1990, and, two years later, the opening on the Laurentian campus of the Willet Green Miller Centre, a massive provincial mining and minerals research complex. Equally important, the unsettled political climate (the 1985 Liberal–NDP 'accord' had a two-year time limit) provided a window of opportunity for a new appeal to the province for capital assistance.[13]

Over the winter of 1986–1987, planning for a new Laurentian University development campaign accelerated under the leadership of retired Inco executive James

Grassby. In May, the campaign received a boost when Minister of Colleges and Universities Greg Sorbara, citing the needs of the provincial facilities to be transferred to Sudbury, announced the Peterson government would contribute two-thirds of the cost of the new library, which, combined with in-hand pledges from previous campaigns, left only $5 million of the $15.5 million goal to be raised. This materialized in rapid fashion, surpassing the campaign target eighteen months ahead of schedule, thanks to a $1 million donation from Paul Desmarais's Power Corporation, $1 million from the Desmarais family itself, $1 million from International Nickel, $300,000 from Falconbridge Nickel, and a plethora of smaller, but still substantial, gifts from regional and local businesses and individuals.[14]

Construction of the new Laurentian University Library began in the summer of 1988 and took eighteen months, with the shift to the new location in February 1990. Named in honour of J.-N. Desmarais, a founding member of the Laurentian Board of Governors, its official opening coincided with spring convocation that year. The board also hoped to start work immediately on the student centre, but a series of setbacks – student dissatisfaction with the size and design of the original plan to extend the third floor of the Parker Building, financial constraints – delayed completion of the project until 1992. Except for the Health Sciences Education Resource Centre whose funding was promised by the out-going Peterson government in 1990, but which was not finished until 1993, this was Laurentian's last major capital project of the decade.[15]

One of the most controversial initiatives of the Daniel presidency, but for those involved one of the most exciting, was l'Université Canadienne en France (UCF). As explained to the board in June 1986, the plan was to establish "an intensive one-year program in France for Canadian undergraduate students recruited in roughly equal proportions from English language and French language universities ... based largely on second-year courses in Humanities and Languages and ... designed to equip future leaders in different areas of Canadian life with bilingual competency and understanding." A joint effort with Sam Blyth, president of Blyth and Company, a Toronto student travel firm, and modelled on his Lycée Canadien, a senior matriculation program for Ontario secondary students in St. Jean Cap Ferrat outside Nice, UCF was to be located in nearby Villefranche-sur-Mer. Negotiations with Blyth, responsible for the infrastructure of the new campus, led to board approval in February 1987, although not without lengthy discussions about its financial viability. Simultaneously, Senate approved commencement in September 1987 of the academic program designed by a faculty committee chaired by project coordinator and dean of Humanities, Douglas Parker, who became UCF's first director, serving until 1992, when he was succeeded by Walter Schwager, former dean of Social Sciences.[16]

Hindsight suggests the 'Villefranche' initiative would have stood a better chance of success had its launch been delayed a year. On the other hand, the extremely positive response to the UCF concept from other Canadian universities, the source of the majority of the 200 students who enrolled in the autumn of 1987, boded well. As Parker later explained to board chair Alan Querney, however, the first term yielded a variety of complaints that resulted in the departure of 15 per cent of the students that Christmas. In part, these departures arose out of unrealistic expect-ations about UCF's capacity to 'magically' cultivate French-language fluency, but most related to the shortcomings of the unfinished campus – unsatisfactory and distant hotel accommodations instead of on-site student residences, an expensive shuttle bus service, and the discomfort of 'cold and dark' classrooms due to an inadequate electrical generator compounded by two months of 'torrential' rain. The situation greatly improved in the second term, but UCF's reputation suffered, hurting recruitment in subsequent years.[17]

While at first few at Laurentian questioned the bilingual, bicultural objectives of l'Université Canadienne en France, its fluctuating, disproportionately Anglo-phone, enrolment began to generate debate about the appropriateness of a small, regionally mandated Ontario university operating a campus in France that did not primarily cater to its own students. Not helping the UCF cause was the autumn 1989 departure from Laurentian of its staunchest ally, President Daniel. Still, an academic review initiated by Acting President Bélanger recommended in Octo-ber 1990 that the arrangement with Blyth be renewed, citing the quality of UCF's academic program, the value of the student experience, and the credit it brought to the university. In November, consequently, Senate narrowly voted in favour of its continuation and, after lengthy negotiations, Laurentian signed a new five-year agreement with Blyth effective July 1992.[18]

Because a budgetary analysis had stated that UCF did not then 'represent a net loss of revenue for the university,' the review committee did not address financial issues, but its report noted that "if this assumption of economic self-sufficiency were to prove to be unwarranted ... UCF would need to be evaluated ... in terms of its net cost." Unfortunately, barely had the ink dried on the new Blyth contract when another enrolment decline in the fall of 1991, the first in a series, coupled with provincial funding restraints, invoked this caveat. A 1992 ACAPLAN review affirmed the 'sound academic programme' offered by UCF, but Laurentian's worsening financial picture forced the administration to renegotiate the Blyth contract to minimize the university's liability in 1994. A year later, new provincial funding cuts occasioned another round of negotiations that resulted in UCF's early closure in July 1996. Laurentian's overseas venture, characterized by President Ross Paul shortly after taking office as one that "adds flair and contributes to ... [the university's] image of being outward-looking and imaginative in meeting the educational needs of Canadians," came to an end.[19]

President Daniel's departure from Laurentian in 1990 should not have taken anyone by surprise even though in late 1987, after a review of his performance by the board executive acting as an evaluation committee, the governors had approved his five-year reappointment, the first full term renewal in the univer-sity's history. A measure of the board's high regard for Daniel, this also reflected the strong endorsement of Senate, and the support of 60 per cent of the faculty polled by LUFA, a notoriously fastidious group. The writing appeared on the wall six months later when the board granted his request for a ten-month study leave to enrol in the program of national and international studies for senior execu-tives at the National Defence College in Kingston. Three months into the leave,

Daniel resigned the presidency, effective July 1990. The explanation came shortly with the announcement of his selection as vice-chancellor of the United Kingdom Open University, a post he held for eleven years and in the midst of which he received a knighthood for contributions to higher education in Great Britain. Sir John Daniel then served as the UNESCO assistant director-general for education from 2001 to 2004, and thereafter headed the Vancouver-based Commonwealth of Learning, an organization dedicated to the "development and sharing of open learning/distance education knowledge, resources and technologies" in the British Commonwealth.[20]

In late 1988, Daniel had given a 'state of the university' presentation to Laurentian faculty that, in retrospect, had all the characteristics of a farewell. He began by defining the presidential role as two-pronged – internally to "ensure that the institution is well-run and to maximize the quality of the resources and services available to teaching and research," and externally to "gain the support of governments, the schools and the wider community for what you [faculty] are doing." He then evaluated the past four-and-a-half years in these terms, finding, not surprisingly, but not unfairly, that the university had made major strides. Greater credibility with the province, he argued, had benefited Laurentian financially, enabling it to increase the number of student-courses *en français* by 38 per cent; to expand its distance education outreach via the establishment of the Contact North Network; and to develop research facilities related to Northern Ontario such as the Geomechanics Institute. Academically, Daniel noted, Laurentian had matured in other ways, too, citing the fact that during his tenure the number of full professors had doubled, enhancing its potential for post-graduate studies, and that while it had strengthened its administrative 'team,' its administrative costs were lower than any other Ontario university. Finally, he stated that relations between the university and its community had improved, quoting an Organization of Economic and Cultural Development study that emphasized Laurentian's pivotal role in Sudbury's recovery from the devastating recession of the early 1980s. In the presentation, Daniel emphasized these accomplishments were due to the combined efforts of the board, administration, and faculty. That was certainly the case, but his leadership also contributed to the university's success, a fact recognized by Laurentian when it awarded him an honorary Doctor of Laws in 2006.[21]

The Presidency of Ross Paul, 1991–1997

In the autumn of 1988, the Board of Governors, Senate, and LUFA approved President Daniel's recommendation of Academic Vice-President Charles Bélanger as acting president for 1989–1990. The selection of Bélanger's replacement was less straightforward. In the end the office was split, with director of graduate studies Lloyd Reed becoming acting vice-president programmes and research, and Dean of Social Sciences Michael Dewson acting vice-president faculty affairs.[22]

President Daniel's resignation modified these plans. The board immediately established a board–Senate presidential search committee, although the actual

ROSS H. PAUL | President of
Laurentian University, 1991–1997

selection process began only in early 1990. In April, it became evident that the committee had difficulty finding a suitable candidate when the board executive discussed contingency plans should no selection be made by June 30. That proved to be the case – no candidate received the necessary 70 per cent support from the committee – so in August the board and Senate directed it to renew the search, with a deadline of December 31. With the aid of a different 'head-hunting' agency, the second search proceeded expeditiously, and in January 1991, the committee recommended the appointment of Ross H. Paul. Both the board and Senate quickly approved the nomination.[23]

Daniel's resignation also affected the interim administrative arrangements. In June 1990, the board executive asked Bélanger to continue as acting president until the selection of a new president. He agreed to do so, and recommended the acting vice-presidential appointments of Reed and Dewson also be extended. Complicating the situation, Bélanger notified the board that he would not serve the last year of his academic vice-presidency, postponed to 1991–1992. It therefore established an academic vice-presidential search committee which, constituted late in 1990, made rapid headway. The following February, Senate and the board approved the nomination of Paul Cappon, associate professor of sociology at McGill University and director of the Centre for Aids Studies at the Montreal General Hospital, for a five-year term, creating the unusual situation of the university's two senior academic administrators taking office at the same time.[24]

In several ways, President Paul's academic credentials and administrative experience paralleled those of this predecessor. A graduate of Bishops's University in Quebec (BA economics and mathematics), he earned an MA in educational administration from McGill and a doctorate in comparative education from the University of London, with expertise in distance education. Like Daniel, too, Paul brought to the presidency administrative skills honed in Quebec and Alberta. After a stint as dean of Arts at Montreal's Dawson College, he became academic vice-president at Athabasca University, holding the position for ten years until appointed acting president there in 1990–1991.[25]

On the other hand, from its outset the Paul presidency differed markedly from that of Daniel. Reflecting on it shortly before leaving Laurentian, Paul acknowledged that one of its greatest challenges had been the 'deep cutbacks' in provincial funding in the later years of his term. If anything, that understated the case. While always critical, to a greater extent than usual, provincial funding policy defined the flow and ebb of these years. They began with the Rae government's introduction of 'corridor funding' – the setting of enrolment minimums and maximums for each institution – designed to control provincial expenditures by discouraging uncontrolled growth at large universities while smaller institutions had excess student capacity. For Laurentian, the idea worked well in the first half of the 1990s, its full-time enrolment climbing to nearly 5,500 in 1994–1995. From an overall financial perspective, however, the growth had a downside. By exceeding its corridor minimum, Laurentian (except for increased tuition fees) did not garner the larger provincial grants yielded by the old system, funds which might have buffered it against the coming financial storms.[26]

Other factors over which Laurentian had no control also counterbalanced the positive effects of enrolment growth, notably rising inflation and ballooning government debt, both provincial and federal, which ultimately resulted in the most drastic financial cuts in the university's history to date. The incisions began slowly, with a warning by the provincial NDP government in late 1991 that increases would be limited to 2 per cent or less for the next three years. In fact, those projections were overly optimistic. In December 1992, the province announced that 1993–1994 grants would fall, not increase, and that those for the following year would return to 1992–1993 levels.[27]

And then came bad news. In the spring of 1993, the Rae government introduced the 'social contract,' a plan to reduce the provincial budget by $6 billion, one-third coming from public sector allocations. As opposed to the promised increase, 1993–1994 grants fell by 8.5 per cent, apart from the provincially legislated 'social contract' reductions in employee salaries, with further cuts in each of the next two years. Laurentian coped by increasing tuition fees (35 per cent over three years), by eliminating a series of varsity sports (women's indoor and field hockey, men's and women's curling) in 1993–1994, and by cancelling eight low-enrolment programs in 1995–1996.[28]

And then came worse news. On the heels of the March 1995 Chrétien Liberal budget which called for huge cuts in federal transfers to the provinces, the June 8 Ontario election brought to power the Mike Harris Progressive Conservatives, committed to a 'Common Sense Revolution' to set the province's financial house in order. Exacerbating the situation, after fifteen years of steady growth, 1995–1996 brought a decline in Laurentian's full-time enrolment, the first of a five-year series. On top of everything else, the full financial impact hit just as the 'social contract' ended and employee associations expected long-denied pay increases. 1996–1997 was a veritable *annus horribilis*. Full-time enrolment declined by 400, bringing Laurentian dangerously close to its corridor minimum below which its grants would be reduced. Budgetary cuts mounted to $7 million. To meet the university budget committee's mandate to produce a balanced 'base budget,' officials increased tuition fees by a massive 20 per cent and introduced an early leaving assistance plan. Sixty-five Laurentian employees including twenty-five faculty members took up the offer, generating long-term savings, but producing a board-sanctioned 'one-time expenditures' deficit of $2.3 million to be eliminated over the next five years. The consolidation of several administrative departments, faculty reduction via non-renewal of term contracts and non-replacement of retirees, closure of l'Université Canadienne en France a year ahead of schedule, and elimination of financial support for the Laurentian University Museum and Arts Centre rounded out the major cost-saving measures. During President Paul's first term, Laurentian's financial profile changed greatly. Overall revenues declined by 9.3 per cent. Government grants fell from 77 per cent to 66 per cent of total revenues while tuition income increased from 18 per cent to 29 per cent. The faculty complement decreased by 7.7 per cent while 13 per cent of other positions disappeared.[29]

These trials and tribulations inevitably affected university governance, though less so than during the comparable period of the 1970s. While attributable in part to the university's greater maturity – the product of time and experience – and in part to the 'same lifeboat' circumstances shared by all university sectors, credit must also be given to President Paul. By his own estimation a pragmatic administrator, his inclination toward cooperation rather than confrontation helped to round the rough edges of governance relations. This was especially notable with respect to labour issues. Despite the multiple funding cuts and the deleterious effects of the Rae government's 'social contract' on all employees, Laurentian was remarkably free of strife during his presidency.[30]

These trying times focused attention on one key aspect of university governance, administrative 'accountability,' both internal and external. A report prepared in 1993 by an 'Independent Study Group' on behalf of the Canadian Association of University Teachers entitled 'Governance and Accountability' expressed concern about excessive administrative authority, and stressed academic self-government and an enhanced role for Senate. Another report that same year of special relevance to Ontario universities was the product of the provincial government's Task Force on University Accountability. A wide-ranging examination of university governance, it also emphasized the multi-directional nature of accountability by university authorities. In this context, the Laurentian board, on President Paul's urging, took steps in the winter of 1994–1995 to strengthen ties with Senate, initiating a series of discussions between their two executives.[31]

The joint meeting in March 1995 addressed three critical issues. With regard to the academic review process, the governors argued and Senate representatives agreed that the board must be kept fully informed because academic programming often had implications either financially or for the collective agreements that required board action. The second topic, restructuring of the Board and Senate, arose directly out of the Task Force on Accountability report. A Ministry of Education and Training (MET) guideline ensuing from the study called for the Board of Governors at Ontario universities to grant full voting rights to representatives of faculty, staff, and students. This presented a problem because the *Laurentian Act* specifically excluded faculty and staff from holding voting positions on the board, though not students who, in 1986, had been allocated one of the non-denomin-ationally designated positions. It also directly impacted Senate because in April 1994, in line with other MET directives, a board ad hoc committee on restructur-ing proposed new procedures that shifted primary responsibility for the appoint-ment of faculty representatives to the faculty association. While agreeing that Senate must continue to play a role in the selection process, the governors offered no suggestions about how this might be done. In fact, the point became moot in 1996 when the new Harris government abandoned restructuring plans, leaving the status quo intact.[32]

Another Task Force on University Accountability proposal underlay the third major issue debated at the March 1995 joint executives meeting, the role of Senate in the budgeting process. The task force not only insisted that budgetary prepara-tions be done "in an open manner involving broad consultation with the major internal constituencies, in particular the senate," but suggested Senate receive in-year updates showing actual results as compared to budget estimates. While Lau-rentian governors and senators generally agreed on the need for closer 'linking of academic and financial plans,' specific procedures of the sort recommended by the task force did not materialize until September 1997 when, on the basis of a letter of understanding between the administration and LUFA signed during contract negotiations, Senate established the Laurentian University Accounts Committee.[33]

Elected by Senate, the accounts committee consisted of a majority of faculty members including the LUFA president or his/her designate with a mandate "to review the expenditures of the University for the previous year." To that end, it had access both to Laurentian's annual audited financial statements and to reports submitted to the board finance committee comparing actual expenditures to the budgetary figures, and could request additional information from university officials. Lastly, it could make recommendations to the board finance commit-tee, forwarding them along with the finance committee responses to Senate for information.[34]

By providing a mechanism for Senate, and especially faculty, to monitor the university's financial affairs on an ongoing basis, the accounts committee, which became operational in 1999, marked a shift in Laurentian's governance balance. Its reports to Senate, while affirming the integrity of the university auditing process, regularly criticized the accounting system's failure to provide "adequate, under-standable information in a user-friendly way." They also expressed concerns about budgetary procedures – inconsistency, lack of transparency, frequent lateness, 'confusing' reporting of expenditures, insufficient review of administrative costs, and inadequate linkage to the university's strategic academic priorities. Succes-sive accounts committees became increasingly frustrated because their proposals to remedy these ills, while acknowledged and on occasion even endorsed by the board and/or administration, were seldom implemented. From Senate and faculty association perspectives, therefore, while the account committee's efforts shed additional light on the university's financial affairs, significantly greater board–administration financial accountability did not materialize.[35]

Laurentian's bleak financial picture inevitably affected building and construction plans. Whereas in the mid-1990s, the province provided limited funds for renovations to the Parker Building and the reconstruction of Founders Square, the university's major project, a new student residence, was repeatedly deferred because of financing difficulties. On the related fundraising front, the news was somewhat better. In the spring of 1996, the Harris government announced the Ontario Students Opportunities Trust Fund (OSOTF), a program that matched, dollar for dollar, funds given for student bursaries before March 31, 1997. In October the board approved a new fundraising campaign with the ambitious objective of raising $10 million in the next six months.[36]

Chaired by Gordon Gray, president of Rio Algom Limited, the internal Laurentian community phase of the 'Coming of Age: Building Laurentian's Future' capital campaign kicked off with great fanfare in January 1997, President Paul setting an example by making a large personal donation. Highlighted by a $1-million gift from the Baxter and Alma Ricard Foundation, this phase was immensely successful, the $5.5 million subscribed at the provincial deadline doubled by OSOTF matching grants. Paul immediately announced the next phase of the campaign would be launched in September with the aim of reaching $15 million. Without the provincial incentive, this proved more challenging, but the university celebrated its accomplishment by unveiling the 'Donor Wall' in the J.N. Desmarais Library in June 2000.[37]

On the positive side of the ledger, too, the Paul presidency brought a significant enhancement of the First Nations profile on campus. As discussed elsewhere, thanks to the efforts of Ed Newbery, in the early 1970s the University of Sudbury had become the home of Native studies at Laurentian. As the range and numbers of First Nations programs and students grew, the need for Laurentian itself to accommodate them administratively became more urgent. A first step came during the Daniel presidency when the university's new Native human services program established a mechanism to report annually to the Robinson-Huron First Nations Assembly, the forerunner of the Laurentian University Native Education Council (LUNEC) created by President Paul in 1991 in conformity with provincial Ministry of Colleges and Universities guidelines. Mandated to advise the office of the president "on all aspects of academic and support programmes targeted for Aboriginal students at Laurentian University," LUNEC consisted of representatives of a broad range of First Nations organizations in Ontario. On its recommendation in the spring of 1993, the university hired the first Native student counsellor.[38]

In the autumn of 1993, Senate and the Board of Governors transformed the Laurentian University Native Education Council from a presidential advisory committee (PAC) into a legally constituted entity designated, in the words of the former, "to make recommendations about issues affecting the Aboriginal student population and the general Aboriginal community." During the next fifteen years, it worked diligently not only to expand program and course offerings (the four-year honours program in Native studies, the Aboriginal legal education certificate), but to advance the position of First Nations in the university's administrative hierarchy. So, too, did the Native Students' Association. In 1999, for example, when President Watters proposed the creation of dual Francophone and Anglophone vice-presidents academic, Senate passed an amendment moved by a First Nations student providing for a third vice-president responsible for Aboriginal affairs, though it was not then implemented. Still, in recognition of the ever-increasing First Nations presence on campus (by 2009, Aboriginal students were estimated to make up 10 per cent of the Anglophone student population, and 14 per cent of the Francophone), Laurentian designated its mission as bilingual and tricultural. Administratively, that translated in 2009 into the creation of the new position of associate vice president indigenous programs, responsible for Native student affairs and recruitment, Native academic programming and research, and Native outreach.[39]

With the exception of one discordant note, the 'Coming of Age' campaign represented a high water mark in President Paul's presidency. Popular and well-respected within both Laurentian and the Sudbury community, his request for a renewal had been readily approved by the board and Senate in December 1995. Barely had his second term begun, however, when in July 1997 he submitted his resignation, effective six months later, in order to assume the presidency of the University of Windsor. The sour note came just before his departure when rumours circulated on campus that the board had awarded Paul a special honorarium, part of which had been earmarked as his personal contribution to the fundraising campaign. A few senators felt strongly enough about the issue to move a motion at the December 1997 Senate meeting encouraging the president 'to do the honourable thing' and give up the honorarium. The motion received little support, suggesting the incident did not seriously diminish Paul's standing, a conclusion borne out by the warm public farewell accorded him by the university community. After leaving Laurentian, Paul served for two terms as president of the University of Windsor, retiring in 2008.[40]

The Watters Presidency, 1998–2001

Upon receipt of President Paul's resignation, the board executive established a presidential search committee in July 1997, with serious recruitment efforts commencing in October, too late for a candidate to be found before his departure. In December, therefore, the board appointed as interim president Geoffrey Tesson, sociologist and former dean of Social Sciences who had been named vice-president academic in 1996, only the second permanent internal appointee since the position had been created in 1967. With the assistance of a professional consulting agency, the search proceeded quickly, and the following February, the committee presented the name of Jean R. Watters to Senate and the board for confirmation. Both approved his nomination to a five-year term commencing August 1998.[41]

The first Francophone to be selected as president since Fr. Émile Bouvier nearly forty years before, Watters was viewed by some in the university community with

JEAN R. WATTERS | President of Laurentian
University, 1998–2001

scepticism, not because of his academic credentials, which were quite conventional, but because his administrative profile was not. Québecois by birth and early education, in the 1970s he earned both a BA and MA in education from the University of Calgary, and then completed his doctorate in that field at l'Université de Montreal in 1984, specializing in adult education. Watters' administrative experience was equally pan-Canadian. In the 1980s, he became director of the bureau de l'éducation des adultes at l'Université de Sherbrooke, and in the early 1990s he headed an Edmonton-based consulting firm specializing in strategic planning and research. Most immediately relevant, he came to Laurentian not from the university sector but after four years as founding president of Collège Boréal, Sudbury's Francophone college of applied arts and technology.[42]

Both benefitting and suffering from being a somewhat known quantity, Watters' presidency began in an environment of mixed uncertainties, which his first presentations to the university community in September 1998 did little to dispel. His declaration to the board executive and Senate after only one month in office that his goal was to make Laurentian "the most innovative university in Ontario within five years" struck some as out of touch with political and financial realities. As at other Ontario post-secondary educational institutions, red ink continued to wash Laurentian ledgers, the product of declining enrolment (in 1997–1998 the worst-case scenario materialized when full-time student numbers fell to 4,100, below the university's corridor minimum, though, fortunately, the province did not invoke a financial penalty), frozen provincial funding, and debt reduction commitments. That situation persisted throughout the Watters years. Annually, officials went through agonizing cost-cutting exercises encompassing all facets of university life, not the most ideal of circumstances for bold new initiatives. [43]

Watters' comments to Senate in September 1998 that "in his view, the question is not if there will be a Francophone University [in Ontario], but rather when and where that Francophone University will be [located]" also unsettled the university community, raising hopes in some and fears in others about the ultimate objective of his then-unspecified restructuring plans. Neither was warranted. In terms of governance, the changes introduced early in 1999 extended the principles of bicameralism, already functioning, in part, at the departmental and decanal levels, to the senior administration. Despite Laurentian's nearly forty-year history as a bilingual institution, the idea stirred up a good deal of controversy, the board executive, for example, narrowly adopting the April motion to establish the new positions of vice-president academic (Anglophone Affairs) and vice-president academic (Francophone Affairs) by a rare recorded vote. After the requisite searches, in June 1999, Senate and the board executive approved the nominations of Douglas Parker, professor of English and ex-director of l'Université Canadienne en France, to the former position, and André Roberge, associate vice-president (Francophone Affairs), to the latter.[44]

By relieving him of responsibility for Laurentian's day-to-day administrative affairs, the dual vice-presidencies permitted Watters, as he explained to the board, to focus on 'external' duties such as government relations and serving on such committees as the Association of Universities and Colleges of Canada Task Force on Learning Technology and the provincial Task Force on Learning Technology. In this respect, he took a more 'hands-off' approach to internal affairs than his predecessors. He chose, for example, not to chair the budget committee, entrusting this to Vice-President Administration Ron Chrysler, although responsibility for the presentation of the final document to the board and Senate remained his. The days when presidents such as Monahan effectively served as their own vice-president academic with respect to the internal governance of the university had long passed.[45]

This did not mean that Watters played no internal role, because during his presidency several major initiatives were launched, one in particular bearing his imprimatur. As suggested by his external committee work, Watters was an early and ardent advocate of the educational potential of the new communications technology. A cornerstone of his plan to make Laurentian a leader in innovation was to effect a 'wireless' revolution on campus, a measure of far-sightedness fully appreciated by the technologically uninitiated only in retrospect. In its early phases he also supported, in the face of resistance from some board members, efforts to establish a Northern Ontario medical school. Similarly, he encouraged Anglophone Vice-President Parker and the management team in their ultimately successful quest for an English-stream Bachelor of Education program. Lastly, it was on Watters' watch that Laurentian entered into an agreement to offer joint Bachelor of Arts and commerce degree programs with Georgian College in Barrie, Ontario. That these projects took flight when Laurentian was still very much in the financial doldrums stands to his credit.[46]

Originally, President Watters had received a much warmer welcome from the Board of Governors than from the academic community at large. Over time, however, his relations with some members of the board became strained. Increasingly, governors complained about what they considered Watters' propensity to announce new projects too hastily or without adequate consultation with the board and/or the university community. The matter came to a head in the spring of 2000 when the board executive proposed a series of 'recommendations' designed to "assist Dr. Watters with meeting the Board's expectations." Watters objected to what he considered board infringement on 'operational matters,' which he argued fell under 'management's jurisdiction.' Nevertheless, after debate, the motion carried. Without strong support from the university community at large, his situation became increasingly untenable, and a year later, he submitted his resignation, effective July 1, 2001, to become president of the Technical University of British Columbia, an institution more in tune with his personal interests and expertise.[47]

The Woodsworth Years, 2002–2008

On the recommendation of the executive, in June 2001, the Laurentian Board of Governors named Herman Falter acting president. A member of the department of chemistry, Falter had served in a variety of administrative positions over the years, most recently as acting vice-president academic during the interregnum between the Paul and Watters presidencies. Complicating the situation was the resignation of Vice-President Academic (Francophone Affairs) Roberge to become president of l'Université Ste-Anne in Nova Scotia. The board struck a search committee for this position and nominated Gratien Allaire, the former associate vice-president (Francophone Affairs), to act in the interim. That turned out to be more than a year because early in 2002 the board decided to 'pause' the search until the arrival of the new president. Consequently, the new vice-president academic (Francophone Affairs), Harley d'Entremont, ex-president of l'Université Ste-Anne, took office only in January 2003.[48]

The joint board–Senate–student search committee for the new president established in June 2001 immediately got down to work, and in mid-December brought forward the name of Judith Weisz Woodsworth. A milestone in Laurentian's history, Senate and the Board of Governors quickly approved the nomination of the university's first female president. Born in Paris, France, Woodsworth grew up in Winnipeg, but began her post-secondary education at McGill University where she earned a BA in French and philosophy. Then came a Licence ès Lettres from l'Université de Strasbourg followed by a PhD in French literature, again at McGill. Between 1974 and 1980, Woodsworth taught French language and literature, first at the University of Toronto and then at the University of Western Ontario's Huron College, and worked as a translator with the National Defence Section of the Translation Bureau. She then joined the Département d'études françaises at Concordia University in Montreal, where, during the next seventeen years, she held a number of administrative positions, including chair of the department. In 1997, Mount Saint Vincent University in Halifax appointed her to a five-year term as vice-president academic.[49]

Much like her predecessor in the 1980s, John Daniel, Woodsworth had the good fortune to assume the presidency at a time when the financial storm clouds that for the previous decade had hovered over Ontario's universities, and particularly Laurentian, began to lift. In November 2001, the Board of Governors had resolved that not only must there be no deficit but that the university's 2002–2003 budget must provide for debt reduction – a daunting challenge. By the spring of 2002, however,

JUDITH W. WOODSWORTH | President of
Laurentian University, 2002–2008

several unexpected windfalls including a provincial sales tax refund of approximately $1.7 million had improved the situation dramatically. The good news continued after Woodsworth took office. That autumn, the provincial government announced a 50 per cent increase to Laurentian's Northern grant. Then, too, the university experienced an enrolment spurt because unexpected numbers of Ontario secondary students 'fast-tracked' to avoid the 'double cohort' tide coming a year later when both the final Grade 13 and the first Grade 12 Ontario secondary-school graduating classes flooded the post-secondary educational system.[50]

The impact on Laurentian of the double cohort, a miniature demographic 'Pig in a Python' of the sort that brought the university into existence in the first place, was immediate. First-year applications for 2003–2004 listing Laurentian as their first choice rose by 101 per cent, and that autumn total enrolment grew by 21 per cent, the highest in the Ontario system. The explosion of students continued for the next three years. In 2006–2007, total Laurentian enrolment surpassed 9,100, a 44 per cent increase over 2002–2003 and double the provincial growth average. Funding underwent an equally extraordinary rise. By 2006–2007, total university revenues (excluding the federated colleges) had climbed to $131 million, 39 per cent more than in 2002–2003. Gone was the $1-million plus accumulated deficit, replaced by a nearly $1.5-million surplus. The university's future never seemed more promising.[51]

In May 2003, when presenting the 2003–2004 budget to Senate, President Woodsworth noted that the revenues generated by the double cohort would enable the university for the first time in a decade "to consider net additions to … expenditures." Reduced to its simplest terms, this meant developing new academic programs and research facilities, hiring new personnel, particularly faculty, and accommodating the space needs of the growing staff and student populations. With the greater financial resources at their disposal, Laurentian authorities proceeded with vigour on all fronts. Between 2002 and 2006, the faculty complement grew by 27 per cent, a startling contrast to the hiring inactivity of the previous decade. After an extensive strategic planning exercise launched by the Board of

Governors on Woodsworth's arrival, the period brought several major academic initiatives, some such as the Northern Ontario School of Medicine and the English-language concurrent Bachelor of Education previously in the planning stages, and others such as the series of PhD programs, which were entirely new. Finally, the university's research profile soared, with funding quadrupling to $38 million between 2003 and 2006, and with the creation in 2007 of the Centre for Excellence in Mining Innovation, a major factor in Laurentian's number-one ranking in Canada for research income growth that year.[52]

The Achilles' heel of this remarkable expansion was the cost, both for personnel and for new building construction. In 1999, the Harris government had introduced a 'SuperBuild' infrastructure program, nearly three-quarters of a billion of which it allocated to the university sector. The program provided supplemental funding for the construction of the Brenda Wallace Reading Room and Computer Centre, the 2001 extension to the Laurentian University Library initiated by a donation from the Wallace and Fielding families in memory of the wife of former board chair James Wallace. Because of its declining enrolment and limited space requirements, Laurentian did not otherwise fare well in the SuperBuild competition. And just when the university's needs spiralled, the new McGuinty Liberal government discontinued the program, forcing Laurentian to 'self-finance' projects such as the new West Residence, the School of Education Building, and the Ben Avery Athletic expansion, all long-term financial commitments.[53]

As had happened several times before in the university's history, therefore, Laurentian's prosperity was fleeting, coming to an abrupt halt in 2007–2008. A contributing factor was a small enrolment decline due to the graduation of the double cohort the previous year, but the main culprits were large increases in the salaries and benefits and operating expenses categories, 33 per cent in the latter case, that produced a $1.4-million deficit, with budgetary projections for 2008–2009 in a much higher range. As in the past, the university budget committee faced this challenge by instituting a thorough review of expenditures. Its 2008–2009 report, littered with 'cuts,' 'reductions,' and 'freezes' in faculty positions, contingency accounts and staffing, to name only a few, called for the elimination of more than $6 million in spending, belt-tightening with a vengeance.[54]

More bad news followed. Few at Laurentian – or elsewhere – anticipated the global economic crisis in the autumn of 2008, an untimely development from every conceivable perspective. It inevitably affected Laurentian's ambitious 'The Next 50 Campaign,' launched in January to fundraise $50 million in celebration of the university's Golden Anniversary in 2010. Chaired by Scott McDonald, a Laurentian commerce graduate and executive vice-president of human resources and sustainability at Vale Inco, the campaign's 'flagship' project was the construction on the Robertson Cottage site of the Vale Inco Living with Lakes Centre, the future home of Laurentian's Cooperative Freshwater Ecology Unit. In the tradition of its predecessor, Inco, Canada, Vale Inco kicked off the campaign with a commitment of $4.5 million. Thanks also to large contributions from other sources such as the Ministry of Training, Colleges and Universities ($5 million), Industry Canada ($5.152 million), FEDNOR ($2.475 million), the Northern Ontario Heritage

Fund Corporation ($2 million), by May 2009, Laurentian had raised the full $20 million for the project, an incredible feat given the devastating economic collapse of the previous eight months. And, albeit at a slower pace, The Next 50 Campaign soldiered on.[55]

Laurentian did so, however, without the benefit of Woodsworth's presidential stewardship. She tendered her resignation to the board in early February 2008, and shortly afterward, Concordia University announced her appointment as president and vice-chancellor commencing August 1. Despite the university's financial reversals at the time of her departure, Woodsworth's presidential term witnessed a remarkable transformation, whether measured in terms of student enrolment, of new academic programs (undergraduate and, especially, graduate) and of research funding and institutes, or of infrastructure. While fate, in the guise of the double-cohort and Ontario's greatly improved economic climate, played a part, President Woodsworth's consultative, but decisive, management style and student-centred focus deserved a share of the credit for these achievements, which elevated Laurentian's status in the Canadian university world to unprecedented heights.

A New Era Begins: The Presidency of Dominic Giroux, 2009–

In April 2008, the board executive established a presidential search committee to seek a replacement for Woodsworth, and appointed Robert Bourgeois as interim president. Reflecting changing views about the role of the presidency, perhaps, Bourgeois's nomination was intriguing. Traditionally, acting presidents had been drawn from the academic stream, whereas he was Laurentian's vice-president administration, having succeeded Ron Chrysler who retired in 2006 after twenty-three years in the position. Traditionally, too, acting presidents had a long association with the university, as with Geoffrey Tesson in 1997 and Herman Falter in 2001, something Bourgeois obviously did not have. Relevant here was the fact that the two other logical candidates for the post, the longer-serving vice-presidents academic, Francophone and Anglophone Affairs, shortly announced they would not seek a renewal of their appointments, with the former, Harley d'Entremont, leaving the university in August 2008, and the latter, Susan Silverton, the following summer. Laurentian, clearly, would embark on its second half century with a very different senior administrative team.

Events also suggested the university's second half century would begin with a very different administrative philosophy. In December 2008, the Board of Governors and Senate approved the unanimous recommendation of the presidential search committee, Dominic Giroux. Holding a BA and a BEd from the University of Ottawa and an MBA from the Hautes Études Commerciales in Montreal, Giroux came to Laurentian as out-going assistant deputy minister in the Ministry of Education and the Ministry of Training, Colleges and Universities of Ontario. Before that he had been chief financial officer of two Francophone school divisions, one in eastern Ontario and the other in southern Ontario. Impressively, in 2008, he received two leadership awards, one in education from the University of

DOMINIC GIROUX | President of
Laurentian University, 2009–

Ottawa and the other from the Montreal business community. While unconventional from a Laurentian historical perspective (he was the first president not to have previously held a university appointment, and the first since Stanley Mullins not to have a doctorate), Giroux's credentials and experience reflected views in some quarters about the changing nature of university leadership. Academia, went this line of thinking, did not necessarily produce the best qualified individuals to head up a post-secondary educational institution. Indeed, earlier in 2008, the University of Ottawa had set an example, naming as president and vice-chancellor Allan Rock, an Ottawa alumnus (BA, LLB) but better known as a cabinet minister in the Liberal Chrétien government in the 1990s.[56]

While traditionalists look askance at this development, it may be that this is the logical next step in the evolution of university governance. As even smaller post-secondary educational institutions like Laurentian grew in size and complexity, they evolved into major corporate entities (Laurentian's total budget in 2007–2008, for example, was nearly $150 million) with the need for business and managerial expertise apart from the office of the vice-president administration. Simultaneously, the Laurentian Board of Governors, while becoming more broadly representative of the community, also became less business oriented – again in 2007–2008, only a handful of its voting members came from the corporate world – and less able to provide that expertise. At the same time, the roles of senior administrative officials became more specialized. Vice-presidents academic assumed ever greater authority over the institution's internal academic affairs, while the president dealt increasingly with such external matters as relations with government, fundraising, public relations, and alumni affairs. Though only the next half century will tell, the appointment of an individual with President Giroux's particular administrative qualifications may very well have marked another turning point in the ongoing saga of university governance, at Laurentian and elsewhere.

6 Facing Hard Facts: The Establishment of Basic Academic Programs, 1960–1985

DONALD DENNIE

Universities generally have two main mandates: teaching students in undergraduate, master's, and PhD courses and programs, and undertaking research which is intended to fuel the knowledge that forms the basis of education. While these two fundamental raisons d'être vary according to time period, culture, and priority, they continue to be the cornerstone of any university. This was certainly the case for Laurentian University. During its first twenty-five years, Laurentian was primarily an educational institution for undergraduate programs, focused on offering a university education to the population of northeastern Ontario. In the mid-1980s, Laurentian began placing more emphasis on research.

This chapter tells Laurentian's story by describing the development of academic programs since 1960, and briefly outlining the bureaucratic structures that have accompanied their evolution. It will then analyze the growth of research, made possible through research centres, grant programs, and administrative and regulatory frameworks that Laurentian established in order to support and promote this essential function. On the whole, it can be said that both academic programs and research have evolved from a general to a specialized focus over the course of Laurentian's history.

Academic programs have been designed to address the needs of the student population, mostly based on their numbers and in conjunction with the evolution of various disciplines. Of necessity, they have also reflected the university's financial position. In its first decades when the university conferred mainly bachelor degrees and certificates, this was particularly so at the undergraduate level as compared to the graduate and post-graduate offerings which have greatly expanded over the past twenty years.

The bachelor's is the first university degree awarded to students who have received a high school diploma and who meet the criteria set out by each individual university. This degree can be a Bachelor of Arts, a Bachelor of Science or

THE OLD LAURENTIAN LIBRARY IN DOWNTOWN SUDBURY | Chief Librarian Fr. Filion explains Laurentian's card catalogue system to fellow chief librarians Bruce Peel, from the University of Alberta, and Peter Russell, from the University of Toronto.

a bachelor's degree in one of various professional disciplines, for example social services or nursing. At Laurentian, the criteria for and structure of the bachelor's degree have changed over the years.

Undergraduate Studies, 1960–1985

Laurentian University welcomed its first student cohort in September 1960. Since it had mostly inherited the University of Sudbury's programs and courses, at first the university focused on the Arts and Science programs, in addition to offering three professional programs.

In its first year of operations, 1960–1961, Laurentian was a federation comprised of the University of Sudbury College (a Catholic institution managed by Jesuit Fathers), Huntington University College (a United Church institution), and University College, a nondenominational institution. Thorneloe, the third federated college (an Anglican Church institution), joined the federation in 1963. Within this federation, academic programs were shared as follows: the two denominational institutions were mainly responsible for philosophy and religious studies programs and University College was responsible for all other programs.[1]

Like University College, the University of Sudbury offered its programs both in French and in English.[2] Huntington and Thorneloe programs were only taught in English. This is still the case today.

The first student cohort could choose among the following programs: Bachelor of Arts (programs offered in French: littérature française, histoire, philosophie, économie, politique, biologie, chimie, physique and mathématiques; as well programs offered in English: English, French, political economics, history, philosophy, biology, chemistry, physics and mathematics); a one-year engineering program; a Bachelor of Commerce offered in English, and a Bachelor of Science in nursing.

The BA program with options, which attracted the greatest number of students, offered a "liberal arts" instruction as follows:

> Its fundamental mission was to train the elites on whom rests a civiliza-
> tion's progress. It is a university's undertaking to prepare men who are able
> to occupy leadership positions and serve society by leading it to achieve its
> full potential and its perfection. Thus it must actively take part in the main-
> tenance and development of human knowledge through scientific research
> and in-depth studies. It must promote and guide the intellectual, spiritual
> and social progress of the faculty and students. It must collaborate with civil
> and religious powers and institutions. Furthermore, Laurentian University
> believes in the trandescendence of spiritual, moral and human values. At the
> apex of the values hierarchy, it holds the supernatural values transmitted by
> the Christian Revelation.[3]

This general orientation, inherited from the University of Sudbury, was based on a curriculum that ensured all students were exposed to a range of disciplines aimed at furthering their mindset in the tradition of liberal arts as they were developed in western civilization.[4]

However, this philosophy would alter radically over the first few years of Laurentian's history, since it had been founded at a time when Canadian and Quebec universities were undergoing profound changes.

> From 1955 onward, Canadian universities were completely transformed from
> what had usually been, with only one or two exceptions, small, struggling
> undergraduate institutions into large, diverse institutions with wide ranges
> of undergraduate and professional programs and, in most instances, an
> impressive array of graduate programs.[5]

Quebec universities would also undergo a transformation starting in the 1960s, when the newly elected Liberal government completely overhauled the education system. The structure of classical colleges, champions of a liberal education, was dismantled. The few classical colleges in French Ontario also began dis-
appearing during this decade.[6] Stanley Mullins, president of Laurentian Univer-
sity at the time, recognized that this development was fundamentally changing the institution:

> If the years immediately preceding 1967–1968 left any doubt concerning the
> role of the university in society, events of the past year have removed such
> doubt. The university is not only in the modern world, it is – in its present
> form – at the service of contemporary society. Newman's concept, cher-
> ished though it may be by many dedicated to the liberal arts, is as dead as
> nineteenth-century liberalism. Knowledge has progressed too rapidly, the
> demands of an egalitarian society have been too pressing, the needs of a
> world harnessed to the force of technology have been too omnivorous.[7]

Faced with the rapid evolution of how university training was configured, Laurentian needed to keep in step by adapting its own teaching philosophy and altering its programs and structures.

Consequently, in 1963, the university president asked Senate to begin reorganizing courses. He believed that courses should be grouped in divisions, which would make them easier to manage and provide a better framework for programs. He also thought that courses and programs should be organized based on the model used in American universities.[8] In 1963–1964, Laurentian University, through committees and sub-committees, launched a program review process to reframe the way that programs were organized and to bring them more in line with the other Canadian universities by introducing specialized divisions for each discipline.

This change from general programs (which required students to take mandatory courses, such as French, English, philosophy and religious studies) to programs based on a disciplinary specialization, and from a religious orientation to a secular one, was also in step with the alteration taking place in the profile of faculty members. In the first years, Laurentian professors were not only educated in liberal arts, but came from various religious orders. Recruiting new secular professors, in order to offer an increasing number of courses, brought a new vision to program development and its framework. In fact, the acting dean of Arts and Science at the time noted that the academic year 1963–1964 was a productive one with regard to revising curriculum and programs, and that these changes reflected the predominance of secular professors in the faculty.

As was the case in other institutions, the revision and transition to a disciplinary specialization inevitably brought about the restructuring of the Faculty of Arts and Science. This restructuring was also taking place in other universities, even the most well-known, like the University of Western Ontario in London. As Howard Clark recounts in *Growth and Governance of Canadian Universities*:

> In 1957 pressures for the breakup of the historic Faculty of Arts and Science were already evident. The actual separation into distinct faculties of Arts and Science occurred several years later after a period of often acrimonious debate between the two sides. In the late 1960s, I was fascinated to see the same course of events, and to hear the same arguments, as the single Faculty of Arts and Science at the University of Western Ontario split into three separate faculties of Arts, Social Sciences and Science. Remarkably the same process, with the same arguments pro and con, occurred while I was president of Dalhousie, leading in this case to the formation of a Faculty of Arts and Social Sciences and a Faculty of Science.[9]

At Laurentian University, these changes first brought about the implementation of four-year programs (honours programs in English, *programmes de spécialisation* in French), starting in 1966–1967. Prior to creating these faculties, assistant deans had been named in 1967 for programs in Science, Humanities and Social Sciences, and, in the early 1970s, for the Professional Schools programs. In 1975, the Faculty of Arts and Science was restructured into three faculties: Humanities,

Social Sciences, and Science, and the Faculty of Professional Schools was also created to house the professional programs.[10]

Each of the four faculties was then assigned various disciplines and programs, which were diverse in their nature. Well-established disciplines fell under Humanities and Science. The other two faculties consisted of relatively new disciplines, or ones that were new to Canadian universities (Social Sciences), or that were of a professional and applied nature (Professional Schools). The introduction of these last two – Social Sciences and Professional Schools – at Laurentian and elsewhere, met with strong resistance from traditional disciplines.

Specialized Divisions for Each Discipline

From its very beginning, a type of linguistic specialization established itself at Laurentian, and brought with it trouble and political conflicts, especially in the 1970s and 1980s (as Guy Gaudreau recounts elsewhere in this book). While the various BA programs were offered in French and English for the most part, the Professional School programs were only offered in English, except for a handful of courses taught in French. Furthermore, the programs offered by the Faculty of Science were mainly in English, especially from the 1970s onward.

The division of the Arts into two faculties – Humanities and Social Sciences – was mainly the result of the incredible growth of Social Sciences programs in the 1960s, but it also came about because these two groups embraced very different theoretical paradigms, especially in terms of methodology. Humanities were based on a series of disciplines (English, Français, philosophy, religious studies, classical studies and modern languages) whose objective was to study languages and texts – literary, philosophical or religious – spanning from antiquity to modern times. Over time, other disciplines, resting on other ancient artistic and creative forms (theatre, music) or more contemporary ones (communication) were added to this foundation. Basically, this range of disciplines and programs was similar to the offerings of other universities. What made it more distinctive and complex was the distribution of programs within the University College.

During its first twenty years, University College was responsible for teaching the English, French, Français and philosophy programs (in collaboration with the federated colleges) as well as modern languages. Originally, the English program taught mainly English literature (more specifically British literature) along with some language courses (composition) which were mandatory for students in other disciplines. During the 1970s, courses in Canadian literature and American literature were added to the curriculum as well as a course on women's literature and one on film. These offerings would take on more importance during the 1980s. At the end of the 1960s, students were no longer required to take English courses, and this had a huge impact on the number of course registrations in this program.

The Français program was similar to the English one, offering courses in composition and grammar, and particularly French literature courses. In 1970, a few students protested the orientation of the program, which they claimed was too

STUDENTS IN A LANGUAGE
LAB IN THE 1970S

European, and demanded that the university offer courses on Franco-Ontarian culture, literature and language. In a letter to the secretary of Senate, a lecturer in another department (Pierre Bélanger, of the department of sociology) stated that the program offered by the French department constituted cultural colonialism, which perpetuated the cultural alienation of Franco-Ontarians.[11] As Georges Bélanger explained :

> The first step occurred in the early 1970s, when a group of mostly Franco-Ontarian students indicated their dissatisfaction and stated that they disagreed with the contents of literature programs and courses offered by the university's French department. To protest, they used a "sit-down strike" method. They demanded that the university offer more courses on French-Canadian and Quebec literatures. This first very radical demonstration provoked the authorities to the point that they had to make extensive changes to the program.
>
> Notwithstanding the means – a sit-down strike – which was still very popular at the time, and notwithstanding the nationalist and separatist wave coming from Quebec and sweeping through all of French Canada, this demonstration, which had a strong cultural impact, spoke effectively to the claims and feelings of Franco-Ontarian students: in the midst of a deep identity crisis, they wanted, first and foremost, here and now, to study French-Canadian and Quebec authors and works. They were stating their refusal, and inability, to recognize themselves exclusively in French literature courses, and were issuing a demand similar to that of Quebec students only a short time before.[12]

One course in French-language Canadian literature had been offered since 1963, but in 1976 the department created courses in Franco-Ontarian and French-Canadian literature and culture. It also introduced linguistics courses. Furthermore, it offered the Français program, as of 1962–1963, for Anglophone students who wanted to further their knowledge of French language and literature. This program was originally offered within the modern languages program but was subsequently moved to the French department

Modern languages offered a huge assortment of language and literature courses during Laurentian University's first twenty years. In addition to the French courses, it offered courses in Spanish, Italian and Russian, and for a few years in the 1970s, Ukrainian and Finnish courses.

University College and the three federated colleges shared the philosophy program, creating the need for a joint department in 1964. However, Huntington and Thorneloe stopped offering courses in philosophy at the end of the 1960s and these professors joined the faculty of University College. As of 1970, the joint department consisted only of University College and University of Sudbury, the former offering courses in English only and the latter in both French and English. During the first decade, the program included courses in ancient, medieval and contemporary philosophy. In the 1970s, it also began to give specialized courses such as: philosophy and arts, philosophy of education, philosophy of science, etc. As for the English program, the fact that students were no longer required to take mandatory courses in philosophy as of 1969 had a considerable impact on the number of registrations.

The religious studies program was a joint effort between the three federated colleges: University of Sudbury, Huntington and Thorneloe. At first, this program mainly focused on the Bible and religion. In the 1970s, it was split in three: Judeo-Christian tradition, world religions and contemporary religious issues.

In the 1970s, two programs based on the traditions and cultures of the founding people of Ontario were added to the (joint) religious studies and philosophy programs: Native studies[13] (which was first called "Indian-Esquimo"[14] and then "Amerindian-Esquimo"[15]) and folklore.

The Native studies program was created to address a renewed interest, at the political and academic levels, in First Nations peoples. The political activism of certain Native groups, mainly in the United States, contributed to this renewed interest. In Canada, the White Paper, published in 1969 by Pierre Elliot Trudeau's Liberal government, had reopened the controversy surrounding the fate of indigenous communities in Canada. The purpose of this draft legislation was to eliminate the laws and bureaucracy controlling the status of Natives and guarantee them greater equality within Canadian society. A general outcry from Natives and several non-Natives ensued and the government withdrew the bill in 1971.[16]

Edward Newbery, professor with the University of Sudbury's department of religious studies – and Huntington University's president from 1963 to 1968 – pushed to revive an interest in an interdisciplinary program in Native studies. This was premised on the fact that the future of "Indian" communities depended on a psycho-spiritual renewal, since culture, society and civilization were born out of faith. After having identified and restated the results of the confrontation between European colonizers and First Nations people, Professor Newbery believed that

J.W. EDWARD NEWBERY | Ed Newbery's association with Laurentian began with his appointment as executive director of the Northern Ontario University Association in 1959, and continued when he became first principal and then president of Huntington University. His longest tenure, however, was with the department of Native studies at the University of Sudbury founded in the 1970s.

it was time to restore the spirit and attitude of Native people towards nature, and reawaken a proactive and productive role in ecology and conservation.[17]

In 1971, the program's rationale and objectives were presented to Senate in a document entitled: "An Interdepartmental Programme in Amerindian-Eskimo studies. Rationale." This read in part:

> The programme is intended to acquaint students as fully as possible with the situation of, especially Canada's, native people. This includes their pre-Colombian life, their confrontation by in-coming Europeans and the consequence of this, the treaties, the reservation system, the Indian Act and its revisions, the problems of integration, acculturation, assimilation, native rights, identity and education, language, the secret of the people's endurance and their renaissance, the present worth of their ancient insights in the light of modern problems sociological and ecological, twentieth century aspirations and the non-Indian role in respect to these.
>
> It is a study which is related to several disciplines in the university and the hope is to draw upon these for a programme which is broad in its coverage, expert in its handling and integrated in its bearing upon the Indian's future.[18]

Originally, this interdisciplinary program consisted of courses from the sociology, religious studies, history, English, philosophy, anthropology, geography and political science programs.

During a forum on Native studies programs organized at Trent University in Peterborough in 1973, the program offered by the University of Sudbury was criticized for not having sufficient Amerindian content and for depending on the goodwill of participating departments.[19] In addition to the problems identified during the forum, there were also divergent visions about its nature and objectives. For its pioneers, the program had an experiential function, as stated in Professor Newbery's document. But colleagues from the other disciplines, in Social Sciences in particular, argued that the program needed to be more "academic." For example, the three professors in the program of anthropology submitted a critique of the program to the Senate program committee, stating that, in their opinion, it needed to be revised based on more solid research, planning and organization done by experts who were familiar with the post-secondary needs of the region's First Nations people.[20]

Based on these and other comments, President Monahan appointed an external committee to assess the program. The committee submitted its report in November 1975.[21] It recommended that the program be maintained, its courses be overhauled, one or two professors be hired, and an ad hoc planning committee appointed to develop the program and the administrative structure. The authors of the report noted the divergent visions for this program – the experiential and religious vision, and the more academic vision based on research and academic criteria – and recommended an approach that combined both.

In 1976, the ad hoc committee submitted its report. It recommended a program focused on indigenous content: Ojibway and Cree language courses, and courses on various aspects of Amerindian culture, education, identity and religion. These courses would have the course code NATI and the program would no longer be interdisciplinary. Lastly, the report recommended the program be integrated into the Faculty of Humanities, and that it be an academic and administrative entity within the University of Sudbury.[22] Laurentian University's Senate approved these changes in 1976 and the program has essentially stayed the same until now, at least in regard to the combination of Ojibway and Cree language courses, and the various aspects of First Nations cultures.

Beginning in 1975, the University of Sudbury also offered a folklore program.[23] There were six 3-credit courses, which constituted a continuation or minor. Folklore is the science of a country's traditions, customs and folk art, in this case, French Canada. The program was linked to the Centre franco-ontarien de folklore directed by Father Germain Lemieux, S.J., who had launched his research program in 1948.

Huntington University College inaugurated its general and specialized music program, offering courses in music history, music appreciation, and music theory in addition to performance courses.[24] Thorneloe University College gradually became responsible for the classical studies program during this period. Courses in Greek and Latin were offered, as well as those on Greek and Roman authors. In 1960, Latin, which until then held a place of honour in the classical college curriculum, lost significant prominence to the point that members at a Senate meeting in 1961[25] indicated surprise at its absence from the curriculum. The following quotation reflects the liberal arts philosophy at the time: "It was stated that it could not be seen how a BA degree could be given if Latin were not included among the compulsory subjects for all students since this subject was considered an essential element of culture." A continuation program in Latin language and literature was established in 1963, and a concentration program in 1969.[26] Thorneloe began offering courses (sufficient for a continuation) in women's studies in 1978.[27]

When Laurentian University was established in 1960, there were fewer courses and programs in the Faculty of Social Sciences than in Humanities. The growth of the Social Sciences throughout the 1960s and 1970s paralleled that recorded in other Canadian and Quebec universities. In his report to the Committee on University Affairs in 1969, the president noted the imbalance between the two Arts divisions.

> Within the Faculty of Arts and Science, disquiet is experienced because of the growing imbalance between Humanities and Social Science programmes. During the last two years … some Humanities courses have lost more than half their enrolment. One must be on guard here against the notion that students, who were formerly compelled to take Humanities courses, now follow their real interests in shifting to Social Sciences. The problem is of much greater complexity than that. Under the old curriculum, the Humanities flourished in all years; and this fact indicates that students, when once exposed to the great themes in history, philosophy, language and literature at university level, continue to follow these programs after all direction or compulsion (an ugly word) had lapsed.[28]

The split between Humanities and Social Sciences, which occurred gradually in the 1960s, was therefore a result of the growth in student registrations in Social Science programs, but was also due to the fact that the Social Sciences focused more on theory and methods than did the Humanities.

During its first year, Laurentian started offering courses in some Social Sciences disciplines, including history, geography (English only), economics and political science (offered jointly at the time) as well as in psychology and sociology (the latter two being offered through the philosophy program).

From the beginning, the history program – in addition to the economics program – was likely the most complete. This reflected the prior development of this discipline within the University of Sudbury. It offered courses in medieval and contemporary history, as well as on the history of Canada, England and the United States. In 1965, the program was split into two main branches: Europe and North America, since the Middle Ages.[29] The program also offered courses in other fields, such as ancient and medieval Europe, Asia, China, Japan, Latin America and methodology or historiography.

Since the University of Sudbury had also developed an economics program, it offered many courses to start with: theory, economic history of Canada, currency, the banking system and finance. In the 1970s, it added courses in economic development for Canada and microeconomics. At the time, these courses were also used by the commerce program (as they continue to be today).

STUDENTS IN
READING ROOM OF
THE LAURENTIAN
UNIVERSITY LIBRARY
IN THE FEDERAL
BUILDING ON LARCH
STREET, 1961

The political science program, which started in combination with economics in 1964, became independent in 1967, and evolved quickly in the 1960s and 1970s with four specializations: Canadian government, international relations, comparative politics and public administration.

The geography program, which was integrated with the geology program from 1962 to 1970 and which initially offered only four courses, also expanded rapidly. In the 1970s, it had courses in cartography, population, regional geographies, Canadian geography as well as urban, political and economic geography. These courses were eventually grouped into two specializations: physical geography and human geography.

It was undoubtedly the psychology program that experienced the most impressive growth over the years. Starting with one course offered within the philosophy program, it attained the status of department in 1962 (even though it was combined with the sociology program in 1964). It rapidly became the program with the greatest number of students in the Faculty of Social Sciences, and in Arts in general, as evidenced by two reports submitted to the executive committee of the Board of Governors. The first, in 1962, mentioned that Laurentian had to rent a special classroom (remember that the university's premises were then still located downtown) to accommodate the unexpected number of students (90) in the psychology courses offered in the summer of 1962, as well as hire an assistant for marking assignments.[30] The second report, submitted by the dean in 1963, stated that the number of professors for 1963–1964 would not suffice, and even more so in 1964–1965 if the projected numbers of students opting for a concentration in the field were accurate.[31] The course offerings increased quickly (in addition to methodology and theory, there were courses on development, motivation and affectivity, personality, learning, psychopathology and knowledge) and were organized into two main branches: experimental and clinical. Many of these same courses still compose the core of the program.[32]

The sociology program, which would become independent from the psychology program in 1969, was a topic of debate among the federated colleges and University College as early as 1962. In April of that year, the dean of Arts and Science wrote to President Bennett:

> It seems to me that Sociology is certainly among those academic sciences which should not be taught by the denominational colleges. Otherwise it could become exposed to denomination biases which are incompatible with the discipline itself ... So far officials of the University of Sudbury have expressed their interest in teaching social work or catholic social teachings. But I am very much against teaching the science of sociology in the federated colleges for the reason that, as has been alleged, it is apparently a controversial subject.[33]

The issue was resolved in the fall of 1962, when the federated colleges decided to stop teaching sociology because of financial reasons. Dean Bourbeau explained:

> Dr. Bennett and I concur in restoring the responsibility for the teaching of Sociology to the University College in 1963–1964 under the Department of Psychology and under the leadership of a competent Canadian sociologist holding a PhD in Sociology. The end in view is to inaugurate in due course a Department of Sociology in University College.[34]

The sociology program also developed quickly, especially in the 1970s. It focused on family, socialization, criminology, sociology of law and Canadian society, in addition to the traditional theory and quantitative methods courses. Even in the early days, the department's meetings were a forum for lively debate between supporters of quantitative methods (statistics) and qualitative methods.

The concentration in the anthropology program was inaugurated in 1972;[35] it was combined with the sociology program, for which it became a continuation. The three professors in the program (one Francophone and two Anglophones) offered courses to introduce students to the important fields of the discipline: physics/biology, socioculture, linguistics, and archaeology.

In 1971, Social Science professors started discussing the idea of setting up an interdisciplinary program in Canadian studies.[36] These discussions occurred in the context of renewed interest in Canadian nationalism (especially in English Canada) following several events (including Canada's centennial year in 1967 and Quebec's nationalist outburst in the 1960s), and publications on the status of teaching about Canada in schools. As Stan McMullin wrote:

> In 1968, inspired by the Centennial celebrations, A.B. Hodgetts published *What Culture? What Heritage?* Hodgetts examined the teaching of Canada

in hundreds of schools and concluded: "We are teaching a bland, unrealistic consensus version of our past; a dry-as-dust chronological story of uninterrupted political and economic progress told without the controversy that is an inherent part of history."[37]

The Canadian studies program was created in 1971 with courses commencing in September 1972.[38] In addition to the fundamental courses (CANA) in Canadian studies, which were shared by several professors, the program drew upon courses from various disciplines including economics, English, Français, geography, history, political science, religious studies, sociology and anthropology.

This interdisciplinary structure of the program gave rise to budgetary problems as early as 1975. In a letter to the program's coordinator, President Monahan stated that the program must be integrated with each participating department's respective programs so as to be an integral part of the professors' workloads.

> This has not occurred for a variety of reasons. As a result, the programme continues to depend on overload payments to provide academic support. Given the small enrolment in the courses which are peculiar to the programme, it is questionable whether the University should maintain the programme. The Budget Committee is inclined to judge that, unless the academic needs of the programme can be met from within the regular course assignments of the faculty in the participating departments, i.e. without overloads, the programme in its present form should be abandoned.[39]

The coordinating committee replied that it was too early to judge the success of the CANA 1000 courses, especially since neither the course nor the program had been advertised at that point. Furthermore, there was high demand in the Sudbury region for this type of program, especially since the Ministry of Education had decided, in 1974, to offer a Canadian studies program in secondary schools. Lastly, this BA program was deemed necessary to serve as a foundation to a proposed master's program in Canadian studies.[40] The program continued and two other courses (CANA 2000 and CANA 3000) were added in the following years. However, the budgetary question remained, and issues about the program's structure and quality were continually raised in the 1980s and the 1990s.

The law and justice program[41] was the second interdisciplinary program created in the Faculty of Social Sciences during this period. It originally offered courses in sociology, philosophy, political science and psychology. The program was the brain child of professors in philosophy, designed to counter the considerable drop in enrolment in their courses after Senate's decision to eliminate their mandatory status. With the help of criminology professors, they created a program that was not technically in Law – thus a non-vocational program – but, rather, that was inspired from the liberal arts, by combining moral aspects (individual and collective rights) and legal aspects. It was the first program of its kind in Canada, and very popular with students. Over the years, the program created its own courses with a JURI designation, gradually ceasing to be dependent on other departments for course offerings.

The establishment of the Faculty of Professional Schools, and especially the creation of the schools themselves at the end of the 1960s caused considerable controversy within the university. In a 1969 letter to the associate dean of Science, the chair of biology indicated the need to establish priorities for the university's development. According to him, the growth had been cautiously managed to date:

> But now, clouding this careful growth, we find that we have become encrusted with a layer of partially academic units. In some cases these units seem to be more responsible to some outside professional organizations than to the university. This alone must make the academic worth of these units suspect.[42]

Vice-President Academic Cloutier addressed the controversy in the president's report submitted to the Board of Governors:

> Some difficulty has been experienced in coordinating the work of the main academic unit, the Faculty of Arts and Science, and that of the newly created Professional Schools. In reviewing the situation, one is tempted to explain the opposition between the academic unit and the professional ones as a "lonely child reaction." Laurentian University, since its inception, had been exclusively a one unit institution. With the establishment of the Professional Schools, several problems became evident to the members of the Faculty of Arts and Science namely: the relative status of a Director of a Professional School and that of a Dean of a Faculty, the relative value of a professional degree and that of a traditional academic one, finally the relative budgetary priority given to the Professional Schools with respect to the Departments of the Faculty of Arts and Science.[43]

In his report to the Ontario Council on University Affairs, President Mullins also mentioned the strained relations between the Faculty of Arts and Science and the Professional Schools:

> Members of this Faculty feel that the establishment of professional units, many of which have commitments to professional organizations, to industry, and to government, weakens the traditional concept of a university: devotion to truth and learning, a philosophy that sees in knowledge its own power.[44]

This apprehension, prevalent for many years, was in response to the creation of three new professional programs at Laurentian: a four-year Bachelor of Science in physical and health education, a four-year Bachelor of Science in social work (English only) in 1967–1968,[45] as well as bachelor 's degree in the science of languages, designed to train translators and interpreters in 1968–1969.[46]

In its first year, Laurentian had offered three professional programs: business administration, engineering, and nursing. The business administration program (which would later become the commerce program and the school of commerce) was the only one able to offer courses and a degree without interruption, in accounting and business management. In 1972–1973, the school of commerce, in collaboration with the school of physical education, launched a new program: Bachelor of Commerce in sports administration (SPAD).[47] From the start, this limited enrolment program was extremely popular, mainly because it was one of the only programs of its kind in Canada. Offered only in English, it combined courses in commerce and physical education, and attracted students from all across Canada.

Created in 1958, the engineering program was limited to one year of study in 1960 because there were not enough laboratories in the university's downtown location to meet the requirements of the Association of Professional Engineers of Ontario. Once the new campus was functional, in 1966–1967, the university offered (in English only), a two-year program with specialties in four areas: chemical engineering, civil engineering, metallurgic engineering and mining or geological engineering.[48]

As soon as the engineering program was re-established, it was faced with another crisis (the first of many throughout its history). In 1971, the *Ring of Iron*[49] report recommended the program's closure (more specifically, it recommended that Laurentian stop admitting first-year students in September 1971), alleging that engineering programs offered by other universities in southern Ontario were sufficient to meet demand. Laurentian launched a lobbying campaign in defence of the program aimed at the province's university presidents and at the Committee of Deans of Engineering of Ontario Universities. The campaign was a success, and the university continued to offer the two-year program. Engineering chair Artin Tombalakian reported:

> I am happy to report that with the support of key members of the Committee including the Dean of Engineering of the University of Toronto we were able to protect and secure the maintenance of the two-year engineering program at Laurentian University.[50]

The program continued to expand in the 1970s. In 1971–1972, it began to offer a specialization in mechanical engineering.[51] In 1973–1974, a two-year program in chemical, civil or mechanical engineering, and a three-year program in mining engineering or ore processing were added.[52] Finally, in September 1977, a four-year program in mining engineering and ore processing began, made possible by a fundraising campaign aimed at the mining industry, that provided funds raised to purchase laboratory equipment.[53] It should be noted that this initiative

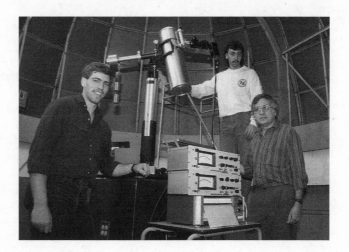

THE DORAN
PLANETARIUM IN
THE EARLY 1970S

by the engineering program met with some opposition from within the university, mostly for financial reasons, but partly for others. The department of geology, which was then considering creating a mining geology program, was particularly unhappy about it.

The Bachelor of Science nursing program, created in 1960, was suspended in 1963. The university president informed Senate that the Board of Governors had done so because the local nurses' association was hesitant about recognizing a degree from an institution that did not have qualified staff.[54] In 1965, the *Royal Commission on Health Services Report* (better known as the "Hall Report" for its president, Judge Emmett Hall) recommended the creation of a school of nursing at Laurentian University,[55] and the president appointed an ad hoc committee to study the question. Armed with a request from both local nursing schools for the creation of a school of nursing at Laurentian, the university president asked the Assistant Minister of Academic Affairs to authorize its creation.[56] In May 1965, the request was granted. The program was approved by Senate and the Board of Governors in 1966,[57] and following approval by the College of Nurses of Ontario, the first students were admitted in September 1967.

Like the school of engineering, the school of nursing has also experienced some controversy over the years. In the early 1970s, the Kergin-Turner report recommended its closure based on an assessment of the program. As Wendy Gerhard later noted:

In the early 1970s, the programme was reviewed and serious concern about the programme was expressed by the nursing profession, by the Ontario Region of the Canadian Association of University Schools of Nursing and by the College of Nurses. Indeed, there was a recommendation that reached the Senate that the School of Nursing be closed. As a result of strong community input, the programme was not closed, but serious measures were taken to change the programme ... in the fall of 1972, 73 or 74 there was a decision taken not to admit a first-year class.[58]

Following the revisions made by the university, the school began to admit students once again in September 1975.

According to Roland Cloutier, Acting President, the social work program was created to address the needs of social workers in Northern Ontario. He indicated this in his annual report to the Committee on University Affairs in 1970, where he stated that the creation of such a program reflected Laurentian's regional mission.

It is the shortage of competent social workers in this north-eastern part of Ontario which has forced us to introduce a four-year programme in Social Work. At the risk of seeming facetious, let it be said that it takes more than natural kindness and an easy smile to qualify as an efficient member of a social agency. Social Work is a science which rests heavily on the classical human disciplines. It is a science different from all other sciences because of its multi-discipline approach.[59]

According to Cloutier, the program had to be offered in both languages to address the bilingual nature of northeastern Ontario. He hoped that courses could be offered in French within a short period of time, as soon as professors and resources would become available. It took a while, but by the end of the 1970s courses were offered in French.

The need for translators and interpreters, not only in Northern Ontario but country-wide, justified the creation of a program in the science of languages. The federal government's adoption of the French-language Services Act in 1968 had resulted in an increased level of bilingualism within the federal public service, which also heightened the need for qualified translators and interpreters.

For Francophones, 1975–1976 was an important year as it marked the inauguration of the French teacher training program, l'École des sciences de l'éducation. This school was the result of the integration of l'École normale de Sudbury with Laurentian University on July 1, 1975. L'École des sciences de l'éducation offered a one-year program leading to a teaching certificate for French-language students who wished to teach in Francophone elementary schools and classes in Ontario.[60] As explained in the Laurentian University Gazette:

L'École Normale de Sudbury was created in 1963, when it was granted a charter by the Government of Ontario that would allow it to serve the Francophone population of Northern Ontario. As early as 1965, it was anticipated that it would be brought into a closer relationship with Laurentian University. In 1970–1971, Senate created an ad hoc committee to study the integration of the École Normale. At its meeting on July 14, 1973, Senate formed the committee that submitted the integration project that was approved at its meeting on March 21, 1974.[61]

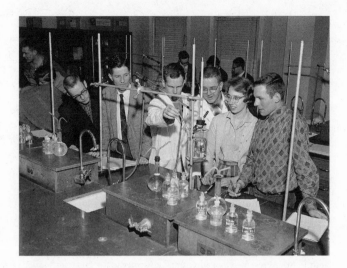

STUDENTS IN A
CHEMISTRY LAB,
1961

A Bachelor of Arts in education[62] was also created for students who wanted a general preparation (especially in psychology) before receiving their teaching certificate. English students could pursue their BEd at Nipissing College in North Bay which had been affiliated with Laurentian University since 1967.[63]

Science programs grouped more logically into a single faculty both because of their limited enrolment and their natural affinities, The several science disciplines were more clearly defined by their learning objectives (nature in general, organic or inorganic, at micro and macro levels) and by research methods (experience and observation, except for mathematics, which was on a more intellectual and abstract level), hence their boundaries were fairly well-defined compared to the Arts and Professional Schools. During the course of their evolution, however, those boundaries became less concrete.

> Despite borderline cases, the science departments constitute a natural entity traditionally interlocking in their way of thinking, methodology, content, in the very often very specialized equipment and facilities they use and share.[64]

For example, the biology program offered courses in zoology, botany, anatomy and physiology. The program also gradually started giving courses in ecology (plants, animals, insects, dry soils), an area in which it now specializes. It also offered a course in freshwater biology. By the 1970s, the program had already earned recognition for its work on the reclamation of barren industrial lands, which became one of the department's strengths and was reflected in its courses and research.[65] Moreover, the environmental issue was integrated into courses and research projects in other areas of biology and in other scientific disciplines.

The chemistry program studied the physical, organic and inorganic properties of matter. Biochemistry (which studies chemical reactions in biological environ-

TABLE 6.1 | PROGRAM REGISTRATIONS, 1961–1978

Program	1961–1962	1965–1966	1969–1970	1973–1974	1978–1979
Arts	61.5	77.3	60.3	40.0	30.6
Sciences	26.7	13.8	13.9	11.5	8.9
Professional Schools					
Commerce	7.8	5.4	8.3	12.1	19.8
SPAD				2.2	5.2
Engineering	3.9	3.5	2.3	2.3	6.2
Nursing			1.9	2.3	5.6
Physical Education			7.5	12.2	9.7
Social Services			3.8	6.4	6.0
Translation			1.9	10.8	7.9

Source: Brief Presented by Laurentian University to the Ontario Council on University Affairs, May 17, 1979.

ments, such as cells, or with biological objects, such as proteins) became increasingly important to the point of initiating a four-year program in 1978–1979.[66] Students were also able to take combined specialized programs in biology-chemistry, chemistry-physics, chemistry-geology and physics-geology.[67]

The mathematics department taught calculus, algebra and geometry. Computer courses began to be developed in 1970. As for physics, its courses revolved around the fundamental elements of the discipline such as mechanics (movement), electromagnetism, thermodynamics and quantum mechanics. The Institute of Astronomy, founded in 1967–1968, offered its first courses in 1968–1969 and gradually increased its courses offerings[68] as part of the physics program. In the 1970s, the department was renamed the department of physics and astronomy. The construction of the Doran Planetarium in the late 1960s contributed to a heightened popularity of this subject, both at the university and in the region.

Geology was added to these four disciplines in 1961–1962, offering only a few courses. At first, it was combined with the geography program, but then it became a separate department in 1967. This program, which was not taught in all universities, continues to thrive because it is linked with Sudbury's unique geological features and its mining industry. As Science dean Doug Williamson commented:

> It should first be recognized that Laurentian University enjoys an unrivalled geological setting, strategically located close to the junction between the Archaean, Huronian and Grenville geological provinces, with the Sudbury Nickel Irruptive straddling the contact, and providing the setting for one of the world's largest concentrations of copper-nickel sulphites.

Given these unique natural advantages, in addition to our location at the heart of a vast mineral industry … we should spare no effort to capitalize on such a favourable situation.[69]

Courses in mineralogy, petrology, mine exploration and ore depositions reflected this relationship with the environment. In the 1970s, the program gradually moved to earth sciences, an area that became very important after 1980.

In summary, these disciplines, with broad learning objectives, were developed from Laurentian's already-existing base. By the dawn of its third decade, the relative weight of these programs, measured by the number of registrations,had changed drastically, as shown in table 6.1.

With the creation of the professional school programs, mainly at the end of the 1960s, the academic profile of Laurentian University changed considerably. Arts in general lost half of their students, and Science two-thirds. This realignment of the student distribution, combined with the financial difficulties faced by the university, created tensions both between faculties and among professors.

Extension Courses

During its first year, Laurentian established a division for "extension courses" which it had inherited from the University of Sudbury, a service the latter had established in the late 1950s.[70] Through these extension courses, the university fulfilled its mission to offer courses and programs to northeastern Ontario residents, allowing students who were 21 years old or older and had not completed their Grade 12 to register for university courses offered through this division, with the approval of the dean of Arts and Science. The university calendar in 1960–1961 described the extension courses as follows:

In addition to regular courses offered by the schools and faculties, the university wishes to help Northern Ontario residents cultivate their mind by offering a variety of complementary courses inspired by the region's intellectual needs: evening courses, intensive seminars, social training courses for workers, miners and farmers.

The faculty of Arts and Science also offers evening classes for adults wishing to obtain a bachelor in the long term. This degree is equivalent to a bachelor obtained through "extension courses" in other Ontario universities.

Furthermore, the Centre for Folk Culture offers, for various professional classes, special courses in civics and public administration, as well as in accounting, management and industrial relations.[71]

In 1960, extension courses were given either on campus during summer and winter, or by television. In 1958, the local television station (CKSO, predecessor to the CTV station) had offered to broadcast courses for the University of Sudbury.

In 1960, Laurentian continued this practice. A press release announcing that two courses would be offered that year stated that "It is the first venture of its nature, although modest, in the history of Canadian universities."[72] The two courses were economics (offered in English by professors Lucien Michaud, Cedric Rabin and Jacques Peltier) and Français (offered by André Girouard). These courses were broadcast twice a week, Wednesday and Saturday mornings, and students could meet with their professors in person once a month on campus.

Extension courses became available by videotape in the mid-1960s. Also during this time courses began to be offered in various northeastern Ontario communities including: Timmins, Elliot Lake, New Liskeard, Kirkland Lake, Englehart, Cobalt, Sturgeon Falls, and even in those further south like Bracebridge and Parry Sound. Full-time and part-time professors at Laurentian travelled to these locations every other weekend to offer courses for three hours on Friday evening and three hours on Saturday morning. A team of administrators also travelled to these communities during the course registration period. Most of the students registered in these courses were elementary and secondary school teachers working towards their BA in order to improve their academic qualifications. According to new Ontario Ministry of Education requirements, students admitted to the Teachers' College or l'École normale had to have a BA.

As these statistics attest, the courses proved to be very popular: From 1970 to 1984, "a total of 10,745 off campus courses were taken, 7,715 (71.8 percent) of them by women."[73] According to Mawhiney and Paul, from 1970 to 1994, 5,761 students – of which three quarters were also women – received their BAs through distance courses.

In 1974–1975, this branch of the university's operations was renamed the Centre for Continuing Education.[74] During this period, the Centre also started giving "multimedia" courses, meaning television, audio and correspondence courses, as well as in-class courses with professors.

Graduate Studies, 1960–1985

Master's programs represented the first graduate degrees in the university system. To be admissible, students must generally have completed a four-year honours degree in a given discipline.

Graduate programs can only be offered by a university after a rather long evaluation process, one which in Ontario requires the seal of approval of the Ontario Council of Graduate Studies.[75] The Council ensures that the program curriculum is appropriate and especially that professors teaching the courses have the required qualifications, including a strong research and publication portfolio and the capacity to supervise theses. Furthermore, the Council regularly (normally about every seven years) reviews the programs to ensure that they continue to meet the requirements and maintain an acceptable level of quality.

Laurentian began planning and creating master's programs relatively early in its history. As early as the spring of 1967, President Mullins stated that one of Senate's main tasks in the coming year would be to plan the inauguration of master's programs. At the April meeting that same year, he declared that graduate studies planning had to begin immediately.[76] Senate subsequently established the school of graduate studies in 1968,[77] and Graduate Council was created in 1972.[78]

In May 1968, the vice-president academic held meetings with departments who had expressed an interest in establishing master's programs. In total, twelve departments participated in the meetings, indicating widespread interest in graduate studies.

> [Of these] nine departments indicated positive interest. These were: Biology, Chemistry, English, Français, Geology, History, Mathematics, Philosophy and Physics. The Departments of Classical Studies, Economics and Psychology preferred to wait a few years.[79]

Almost every department seemed to want to submit a request for a master's program to the graduate council. Other documents suggest that in addition to the previously mentioned departments those of chemistry, engineering, political science and sociology were also interested. A Laurentian report to the Ontario Council on University Affairs in 1970 included the personal reflections of the director of graduate studies who noted that eighteen master's programs were planned between 1969 and 1974, in addition to a possible PhD program in psychology.[80]

Biology, chemistry, geology and physics (the latter would become applied physics in the early 1980s and then return to its original name in 2007) were the first disciplines to get approval for Master of Science programs (MSc), as of 1970–1971.[81] In his 1970 annual report, the president wrote:

> Programmes in four departments were approved by the Ontario Council of Graduate Studies: Biology, Chemistry, Geology and Physics … only Biology and Physics accepted graduate students in September 1969.
> Two graduate programmes (French, Philosophy) were not approved.
> One (Mathematics) is now in the process of reappraisals. Briefs are being prepared by the Departments of History and English with appraisals to be conducted in 1970–71.[82]

This situation angered some programs in Humanities and Social Sciences. Four departments – English, Français, history and philosophy – met to discuss their respective situation concerning graduate studies. They believed they were at an unfair disadvantage with respect to space and library resources compared with the Sciences. They also complained about the lack of guidance from the administration concerning the development of master's programs. While not wanting to cause conflict between Arts and Science, they repeated their intention to pursue the approval process for their programs, provided the university confirmed its support. Lastly, they asked the administration to define a specific policy for the university as a whole:

Finally, a general policy is required for a framework within which our own problems and those of the university as a whole can be planned. The creation of a graduate structure is therefore seen as a matter of urgency.[83]

Both the school of graduate studies created in 1968, and Graduate Council, established in 1972, were designed to provide such a structure for these emerging fields of study.

In general, negative assessments given to departments related to lack of space, and lack of library and teaching resources. In certain cases, the direction or specialization of the program was considered too vague or too narrow. For example, the Graduate Council's evaluation committee decided not to approve the history program in October 1971 for three reasons: i) the orientation (European history and history of North Ontario) was too narrow; ii) library resources were inadequate; iii) teaching resources were insufficient (more specifically, professors did not have the necessary qualifications for the proposed specialization areas).[84] The department was given the opportunity to respond to this negative assessment, and following a meeting with the evaluation committee in April 1972, the program was approved.

The mathematics program had a similar experience. The evaluation committee criticized the program for being too broad and lacking library resources. Still, it was approved by Graduate Council in 1970 (and by Senate in 1972 after a delay), but before it could admit its first students, the Ontario government imposed an embargo on funding of new graduate programs. In a letter to the acting president in March 1971, the Minister of Colleges and Universities stated that the new directives were aimed at balancing registrations in master's programs with society's actual needs and demands.[85] The president responded that such a decision would seriously affect the university's programs, even leading to the cancellation of some. The minister replied that the embargo only applied to programs with no registrations for the 1970–1971 academic year.[86]

These new directives were part of a re-evaluation of graduate programs in Ontario, by the Ontario Council of Graduate Studies at the end of the 1960s following the creation of the Advisory Committee on Academic Programmes (ACAP). According to Howard C. Clark, one of the first members of this advisory committee, the committee's objective was as follows:

The creation of ACAP and the work it undertook were bitterly resented in many of the universities. After much acrimonious discussion, the committee developed a process in which all the supporting documentation for a provincial set of graduate programs (for example, in chemistry or sociology) would be placed in the hands of a group of international consultants who would visit all programs, engage in any other consultation thought necessary, and develop a report containing recommendations on the future of each program. On the basis of this, ACAP would develop its own report for submission to the COU [Council of Ontario Universities].

... the work of ACAP did curb the ambitions of all universities and prevented the introduction of a flood of ill-conceived and hastily devised graduate programs ... it was the work of ACAP that eventually led to the fairly rigorous and continuing quality assessment of all Ontario graduate programs now conducted through the Ontario Council of Graduate Studies.[87]

Further to the embargo imposed on the funding of new graduate programs, the government also demanded that five-year plans be submitted and approved by ACAP. Consequently, in 1972 the university prepared a five-year plan.[88] After having reiterated the need for graduate studies to stimulate research, the report stressed the need to develop programs in all areas in order to eliminate animosity on the part of departments, and of programs offered only in French, that did not have a graduate program. It recommended the continuation of existing programs in biology, chemistry, geology and physics, and the implementation of already-approved programs in mathematics (although it did recommend that the program be both theoretical and applied), and in English,[89] as well as the implementation of the history[90] program, then under evaluation. The last, which specialized in nineteenth-century social history in Europe and North America, was the first to be offered in both French and English. The report also recommended the creation of a master's program in physical education for 1973 and psychology for 1974, noting that these two were ready for evaluation. Programs in sociology and political science were recommended for 1975, and in commerce for 1976.

In May 1972, ACAP advised Laurentian that it was unable to approve the five-year plan, mainly for financial, but also for academic, reasons:

In short, ACAP's tentative view of the enrolment prospects causes one to question Laurentian's financial ability to provide staff, student stipends, and extra library funds for all the proposed programmes. ACAP is inclined to believe that a small number of programmes might be more viable, particularly if they were of a kind not readily available elsewhere in the province.[91]

In general, the provincial committee was more interested in the proposal for a program such as Nordic studies, since it was not offered elsewhere in the province, something that became one of its leitmotifs especially with regard to small universities. After noting that the history and English programs were related because they covered the same period, the committee suggested that Laurentian study the possibility of developing a master's program in Humanities which would group English, history and Français. ACAP also indicated that it could not support programs in psychology, sociology or political science, as these were already being offered elsewhere. It also suggested that it would not support the proposed programs in physical education and commerce, as these were not central disciplines.

Faced with this reality, the director of graduate studies stated that, based on a difficult financial period and ACAP's refusal, "there is little doubt that graduate planning at this university must be reviewed and reshaped to fit the present

JACK PORTER AND LUCILLE DENNIE | Registrar of Laurentian University from 1975 to 1996, Jack Porter also was the highly successful coach of the men's hockey team, the Voyageurs, in the late 1960s and early 1970s, and again in the 1980s.

and future resources."[92] For this reason, he asked all departments with existing graduate programs or in the course of developing them to rethink their programs to take into account teaching resources, student registrations and professors' qualifications.

In the meantime, Senate's academic planning committee (ACAPLAN) prepared a development plan for undergraduate and graduate programs, which it submitted to Senate in May 1973.[93] The report stated that BA programs had to be of high quality, and recommended the creation of interdisciplinary programs in earth sciences, Humanities, Canadian studies and outdoor education. At the graduate level, it recommended new interdisciplinary programs in earth sciences, Canadian studies, and child and development studies. The rationale was that financial and human resources for these programs could be pooled within several departments and schools. It also recommended the creation of programs for which there was an identifiable need and a substantial demand.

Echoing what the ACAPLAN report had recommended, the school of graduate studies submitted a new five-year plan (1974–1979)[94] based on the following central idea:

> In summary, this proposal is the result of a long (sometimes painful) process
> of maturing during which we have profited of the expert advice of many
> individuals and groups, not the least of which has been ACAP. We are confi-
> dent that we are presenting now a five-year plan which is within the capabil-
> ities of our human and financial resources which will serve with high qual-
> ity programmes an important cross-section of our northern population.

The plan recommended that programs in biology, history and geology be continued and that programs in chemistry, English and physics should admit students in September 1974, on the condition that they submit proposals for establishing joint programs with other departments. (It was suggested, for example, that the English program be integrated into a Canadian studies program.) Furthermore, it recommended cancelling the mathematics program. Its most important recommendation, however, was the creation of four interdisciplinary programs: earth sciences, Canadian studies, child and development studies, and science.

The provincial committee approved this new five-year plan in 1974.[95] It stated that the English program would have to stop admitting students once the new master's program in Canadian studies was approved, if and when that happened. The chemistry and physics programs would also have to stop admitting students once a new interdisciplinary science program was approved, if and when that happened. The committee added that, should the proposed programs not be approved, the university would then have to decide if the English, chemistry and physics programs could continue as independent programs (with ACAP reserving the right of approval). As it was, the creation of the proposed Canadian studies program was not possible before 1978, and the science program was never created, so the university and ACAP permitted the three programs to continue.[96] Physics was redefined as applied physics. The mathematics program never came to be as the university followed up on its five-year plan and cancelled this program during its first year of operation.

Beyond the five-year plan, Laurentian launched three collaborative projects with other universities in the mid-1970s. The first was a master's program in Français offered jointly with the University of Ottawa.[97] This program only lasted a few years, and in 1984 a report on the state of Laurentian's graduate studies declared it moribund and discontinued it. The report emphasized that a master's program in Français was needed to serve the region's Francophone population, but that the department's faculty did not have the strength to support the program on its own.[98] The second was a collaboration with the Ontario Institute of Studies in Education (OISE) which permitted the teaching of certain OISE courses in Sudbury as well as its use of certain Laurentian courses as electives. A third collaborative program was proposed for commerce. The university negotiated an agreement with York University permitting the first year of its MBA program to be taught at Laurentian. However, the freeze on graduate programs in small universities at the time prevented this project from being implemented. Despite this, commerce was eventually able to develop a master's degree in business administration.[99]

The only interdisciplinary program identified in the five-year plan to be implemented was child and development studies. The program was developed out of discussions among the three participating programs – sociology, psychology, and physical education. It was assessed and approved at the end of the 1970s, and admitted its first students in 1980–1981. The objective of this program was "to offer students an integrated perspective of human development, from conception to early adult life."[100] Taught in both English and French by professors in the three disciplines, it was renamed "human development" and added a science stream (MSc) to accompany the MA version in 1997–1998. Throughout these developments, the program's objective remained consistent: "to give students an integrated perspective in human development."[101]

From 1960 to 1980, Laurentian had great ambitions for developing graduate programs. In the early 1970s however, these ambitions met with bureaucratic and financial realities that seriously limited the number and scope of programs. Some at Laurentian suspected that these barriers were put in place intentionally, in order to curb the growth of smaller universities,and to benefit the more established, larger institutions. This view was clearly articulated in a presentation to the Ontario Council on University Affairs in 1977, when Laurentian stated that:

> The system approach over the past few years, in particular the Five-Year
> Plan, has imposed on us, in common with other 'emerging' universities,
> levels of constraint and scrutiny to which the majority of universities have
> not been subject and which have had the effect of preventing Laurentian
> from consolidating and stabilizing its graduate programme. The freeze has
> imposed a fresh constraint at a time when some hope of such consolidation
> and stabilization seemed at last possible. Universities with established pro-
> grammes, operating within a much greater overall budget and total range of
> programmes, have a degree of flexibility in adapting their finances and plans
> to cope with sudden changes in procedure or financing. A small univer-
> sity which is still in the process of establishing its minimum graduate and
> research basis has no such flexibility; the impact of the freeze is necessarily
> immediate and severe.[102]

One year later, the report presented to the Committee took up the same argument, using a different tone. It concluded as follows:

> George Orwell once pointed out that anyone had the right to dine at the
> Ritz, all that was needed was the money. If we follow the metaphor –
> (and we recall that the prototype for an Appraisal brief was for a PhD in
> Gastronomy) – we find ourselves being cast for the role of Lazarus, looking
> south to the tables of Dives.[103]

Research from 1960–1985: A Simple and Isolated Activity

Research is and has always been an essential academic activity, one that has progressively become more expected of all university professors. At Laurentian, however, research did not always have the same priority that it does today. To understand the evolution of research at Laurentian, we must start by distinguishing between two periods: the first, from 1960 to 1984, and the second, from 1985 to present. The research performed by professors at Laurentian during its first twenty-five years was much less complex than it is today. It also tended to be an isolated activity, whereas today it is more of a collective or team effort.

Until 1984, very few rules governed research. A professor could perform either contractual or applied research, or fundamental or theoretical research. In the case of contractual or applied research, the professor would secure funding from a community agency or an industry (for this reason, the mining industry proved to be very important at Laurentian). The research objective would be largely determined and defined by the sponsor. For fundamental or theoretical research, the professor would perform research to test a hypothesis (in natural or Social Sciences) or to develop greater understanding of an event or historical figure, or a literary or musical creation, for example. In general, the researcher would have to request funding from a foundation or from the National Research Council of Canada, the Canada Council for the Arts or the Medical Research Council, which were the main granting agencies in the country.

Where research was concerned, there was from the very beginning a clear distinction between the Sciences and the Arts, a distinction summarized in a report submitted to the Committee on University Affairs in 1968.

Departmental reports show nearly all members of the teaching staff busily occupied in their chosen niche. All our scientists enjoy supporting grants from outside agencies and produce results accordingly. In the Arts faculty, Research is a more personal enterprise and hence difficult to assess. Not infrequently a scholar's life work will be comprised in a single book not published until after his retirement; while all too often, prodding from university administrations results in an unhealthy eagerness to publish no matter what. Assessment of the Arts teacher will continue to be based on his scholarly reputation among colleagues and pupils rather than on a quantitative analysis of works in print.[104]

Existing sources did not allow reliable tracking of research done by Laurentian professors during that period, though some information can be found in the president's annual reports submitted to the Board of Governors. For example, Professor Jean Havel of political science was responsible for the first book published by Laurentian University Press about his research on policy in the Sudbury region.[105] Several biology professors began researching the water quality in lakes in the region, and also launched the re-vegetation project in the area. The president's report in 1966–1967 indicated that Science professors received grants from the National Research Council of Canada totalling $40,700 for that year.[106]

But generally, research was a challenge for a university of Laurentian's size. In his address to faculty in September 1974, President Edward J. Monahan highlighted the challenges and accomplishments in research. "As an institute of university education, Laurentian is responsible for performing research and we need to be constantly involved in this field," he stated.[107] According to him, Laurentian faced many obstacles: i) faculty members were relatively young and focused on finishing their PhDs and thus Laurentian did not have the same resources as long-standing universities; ii) the funding system for Ontario universities benefited, to a greater extent, established universities with many graduate programs, especially doctoral programs, for which they could receive increased grants, enabling them to build research facilities; and iii) Laurentian did not receive support or endowments from the private sector.

Despite this, the university was successful in obtaining several research grants, especially in the Faculty of Science from the National Research Council. These grants totalled $1,250,000 in 1974, which allowed the funding of individual projects, the hiring of research assistants and the purchase of necessary equipment. Researchers also received grants from the Council for the Arts, the Medical Research Council and the Defense Research Board, in addition to funds for contract research.

Laurentian also received an annual grant of $25,000 from the National Research Council (NRC) which the president allocated, at his discretion, to professors doing research in the NRC's area of authority. In 1974–1975, Laurentian also began to receive an annual grant from the Council for the Arts to facilitate research projects in Humanities and Social Sciences.

President Monahan also mentioned that the university had created a research fund that would be increased by $25,000 per year, until it reached 1 per cent of the university's annual budget. He referred to a proposal that Senate had adopted on September 23, 1973, and which read as follows:

> That Senate approve the creation of a research fund which would come out of general operating revenue. The fund would total $25,000 the first year and would be increased by $25,000 every year, until the annual allocation reaches 1% of the University's general operating revenue. The funds would be administered by the President, as advised by the research committee.[108]

This advisory research committee, created by Senate, was mandated to maintain a complete list of current research projects at Laurentian, to encourage shared use of resources, and to facilitate the exchange of information; as such, it was to inform members of the university community about the research needs of groups in the region. Senate recommended that Laurentian hire a research coordinator and that "Nordic studies be part of the research topics at Laurentian University." In his remarks, the president indicated that the university did not have the necessary resources to create an Office of Research. He did support Senate's recommendation on Nordic studies, declaring that he hoped more professors would do research on problems relating to "our region and the North."

In the early 1980s, the dean of Social Sciences, describing his faculty's situation, also affirmed the importance of research at Laurentian, without mentioning specific research projects. Thus, at the time, research was considered an essential element of Laurentian's mission. Unfortunately, the means of accomplishing this on a large scale were not yet available. The Sciences had a certain advantage, especially because of the National Research Council of Canada, established in 1916 under the name Honorary Advisory Council for Scientific and Industrial

Research, in order to help secondary industry, to encourage scientific research and to advise government on scientific issues. Part of its mandate was to give grants to universities for scientific research.[109]

For the Arts, the situation was more complex. Not only were there fewer funds available, but small universities had particular difficulty getting funding. The financial challenges faced by Laurentian University in the 1970s also inhibited the development of a research infrastructure (space, equipment, research centres, graduate studies) which would have allowed researchers to access funding. In addition, in the Arts there was no common orientation, with research being done mostly on an individual basis.[110]

The creation of the Canada Council for the Arts in 1957 had enabled some professors in the Arts to receive research grants. But it was mostly the creation of two research councils at the federal level, in 1978, that contributed to the promotion of research in Canadian universities, including Laurentian. Since their inception, the Natural Sciences and Engineering Research Council (NSERC) and the Social Sciences and Humanities Research Council (SSHRC) have proved to be major grant sources in these two grand domains of knowledge.[111] At Laurentian, Science and Engineering professors received many grants for research in their respective disciplines. Professors in other faculties were relatively less successful in obtaining subventions, especially from the Social Sciences and Humanities Research Council whose budget was considerably smaller than that of NSERC.

Research was mainly an individual activity during this period. Nonetheless, several research institutes were created, facilitating the carrying out of collective projects. The first was the Sudbury Cardio-Thoracic Foundation. The experimental section of this foundation was established on Laurentian's campus in 1965. The objective of this research unit was to provide facilities for studying and treating clinical disorders related to the circulatory and pulmonary systems. It was linked to the Sudbury Hospital Board.[112] Because this research was performed on animals, an animal facility was established in 1969. At a later date, research conditions in this facility were deemed unsatisfactory and a separate building was constructed in 1981, linked to the Science building, to allow scientific research on animals.[113]

The Institute of Astronomy was created in 1967–1968 to give courses in astronomy but also to manage a planetarium that shortly afterwards opened to the region's public. As of 1968, the institute had two telescopes, one of which had been supplied by NASA to track satellites.

The Institute for Research in Fine Particles was founded in July 1969, "as an interdisciplinary agency offering graduate studies and also means for research in the area of microparticulate physics and techniques."[114] This institute represented the research section of the master's of physics program (along with the Institute of Astronomy, it merged with the department of physics in 1973 to become the department of physics and astronomy).

In 1976, six Franco-Ontarian professors from various disciplines formed the Institut franco-ontarien (IFO), aimed at promoting research, producing publica-

TABLE 6.2 | AMOUNTS OF RESEARCH GRANTS BY FACULTY, 1980–1986

Faculty	Amount received $	Percentage of total	Number of recipients
Humanities (1981–1986)			
University College	165,005	2	8
Federated colleges	99,635	1	
Social Sciences	818,666	9	9
Child and Development Studies program (1980–1985)	429,276	5	
Professional Schools (1980–1985)	1,248,614	13	9
Science and Engineering (1981–1986)	6,520,129	70	63
Total	9,281,325 ·	100	89

tions, and gathering documentation on the Franco-Ontarian population. On the twenty-fifth anniversary of its creation, the *Revue du Nouvel-Ontario* published a retrospective work of the accomplishments and raison d'être of the Institut franco-ontarien.

> The Institut franco-ontarien was created because its founders felt a need to understand in greater depth the franco-ontarian community, to document this knowledge and to share it.
>   The Institut was established to promote research, produce publications and gather documentation on the various aspects of the Franco-Ontarian population.[115]

In 1978 the institute launched the *Revue du Nouvel-Ontario* to promote and publish works presenting research on the Franco-Ontarian population. It also organized symposiums on Franco-Ontarian realities and undertook applied and theoretical research on French Ontario.

Another journal, *Revue de l'Université Laurentienne/Laurentian University Review,* launched in 1967, permitted both Anglophone and Francophone professors to publish their research in areas as diverse as Humanities, Social Sciences and Science. It gave priority to articles with an interdisciplinary orientation, and to those on Canadian studies. This review ceased publication in 1987 after having lost its grant from the Social Sciences and Humanities Research Council the year before.

In 1984, the Centre in Mining and Mineral Exploration Research (CIMMER)[116] was established on the basis of a federal grant of $1.5 million. In creating this centre, the Faculty of Science and Engineering capitalized on Laurentian's unique location, which is at the heart of one of the most important mining complexes in the world. Dedicated to interdisciplinary research and development related to mineral exploration and mining, CIMMER brought together researchers from many Arts and Science disciplines. More specifically, it attempted to gather research related to the mining sector from various university departments, and to give direction to this research. It also coordinated the use of facilities and fundraising activities to support interdisciplinary research efforts related to the mining sector.[117] Since then, CIMMER has been responsible for the creation of both the Geomechanics Research Centre (GRC) and the Mineral Exploration Research Centre (MERC). Efforts to create a school of mining, however, have not yet come to fruition.

The 1986 report submitted by the Laurentian University task force on academic priorities discussed rather eloquently the disparity between faculties in obtaining research grants. This task force was mandated to make recommendations to the university, through Senate, regarding priorities set by Laurentian in the areas of research and academic programs. The report stated there was an almost total lack of data on research, and that existing data was dispersed and hard to find. The task force surveyed professors in all disciplines in order to determine the amount of research grants received from 1980 to 1986 by faculty. The results are reproduced in table 6.2.[118]

One can conclude that most of the projects in this short period were geared more toward applied research. For example, in the Sciences, almost $5 million came from sources other than NSERC. In the other three faculties, funds were mainly provided by SSHRC, either through direct funds or through funds given to the university for internal allocation.

By the mid-1980s, a culture of research was clearly present in the natural sciences. One of the major priorities in 1985 of the new administrative team, headed by President John Daniel and Vice-President Academic Charles Bélanger, would be to develop measures and policies that would stimulate such a culture among all sectors of the university.

7 Building on Past Achievements: Research and Graduate Studies, 1985 to the Present

DONALD DENNIE

Undergraduate Studies: Building on Past Achievements

In the third decade of its history, Laurentian University was building on what it had achieved over the previous two, at both the undergraduate and graduate levels. Programs had become more specialized and new professors had joined the faculty, bringing new and different viewpoints and orientations. Research, which had begun to take on a more prominent role, added to the corpus of knowledge disseminated in the academic programs and contributed to the creation of graduate and post-graduate programs. At the outset, we will explore the consequent development of the bachelor programs.

In 1980, the Faculty of Science welcomed a new – yet former – program: the school of engineering. After serious disagreements that occurred in 1978 between the president's office and the school's administration (and part of its faculty), it had been taken under supervision. A decision had to be made: either close the school or merge it with the Faculty of Science. After many lively discussions and numerous meetings, the Science Academic Council approved a merger, a decision that was shortly thereafter confirmed by Senate;[1] thus was born the new Faculty of Science and Engineering.

No sooner had the merger been implemented than the school of engineering underwent a review of its accreditation. At first, because of the confusion within the school, the renewal was denied, but shortly afterwards, once changes had been made to the teaching staff, it was granted. Assured of its survival, the school modified its program in the early 1990s. In 2000, when the school again risked losing its accreditation, the president established the presidential advisory committee on engineering (PACE) to study the situation and recommend solutions. Among the committee's recommendations were that the bachelor program be revised and a doctoral program be established.[2] Starting in 2002–2003, the school, with Sen-

STUDENTS RUNNING
THE REGISTRATION
GAUNTLET IN 1992

ate's blessing, introduced the following bachelor program: a common first year and two four-year programs, one in engineering and the other in chemical engineering with options in environmental engineering and extractive metallurgy.[3] In the other five programs, greater specialization gradually evolved, mainly in the environmental, ecological and medical fields.

For its part, the chemistry department added the biochemistry program and became the biochemistry department. In 1986, the changes was explained:

> Because chemistry is a mature and central science, the complex and varied knowledge base of the discipline is enormous and increases almost exponentially almost every year. The net effect of this expansion has been to spawn off from the central discipline any sub-disciplines which, in many cases, such as biochemistry, have become recognized disciplines themselves.[4]

Later, in 1999, the department created certificates in environmental and medical chemistry.[5]

The computer science program, which had been expanding since the 1980s, was attached to the mathematics program. At the end of the 1970s, the dean of Science had informed the vice-president academic and research that, because of financial considerations, any future development in mathematics would most likely be in this area.[6] In 1984, two autonomous programs, a BSc and a BA were created in mathematics and computer science respectively,[7] and in 2000, the BSc in computer science was converted to a BCosc.

Over time, geology gradually became defined as earth sciences, to the point that a BSc in this field was created in 1981.[8] This specialization became stronger with the development of two programs. That in environmental earth science (BSc), in collaboration with biology, physics, chemistry and geography,[9] was created to study the complexity of the natural environment and the effects of human activity on the earth's natural systems. The earth sciences program[10] (BA) was offered in collaboration with geography, and aimed to provide a balanced understanding of the natural environment. This program also had developed concentrations in mining geology and solid earth science which were eliminated in 1996 following an ACAPLAN review of academic programs.

As early as 1991, the geology department decided that this reorientation in focus signalled it was time to change its name to the department of earth sciences. The dean of the Faculty of Science and Engineering, Reid Keays, justified the change as follows:

> There are at least two dozen Geology departments in universities across Canada and around the world that have evolved in departments of Earth Sciences over the last twenty years in order to support broader undergraduate programmes and encourage modern research directions.[11]

While the geography department initially opposed the change, claiming it would cause confusion with the previously established earth sciences program, it eventually dropped its objections and Senate approved it in 1995. Over the next fifteen years, earth sciences also began to specialize in the area of mineral deposits, having formed closer ties with the mining industry.

The physics program began to specialize in the biomedical field by creating a biomedical option in 1996, and joining with the Michener Institute in Toronto to establish a radiation therapy program.[12] Several faculty members also participated, and still do, in the Sudbury Neutrino Observatory (SNO) project. As discussed below, SNO has gained international recognition since its establishment in 1990.

From 1997 onward, biology developed biomedical, ecological and zoological options.[13] In 2004, the forensic biology option became an independent program called forensic science.[14] It combined biology and chemistry courses with its own in forensic science.

According to Rizwan Haq, former dean of the Faculty of Science and Engineering, the Science programs' increased specialization was attributable to two factors. Firstly, all Science disciplines had seen a phenomenal growth in their body of knowledge, which had led, as we have seen in the case of chemistry, to the creation of numerous sub-disciplines. Secondly, Science disciplines at Laurentian focused on the regional environment, which explains their involvement in the areas of environment, ecology and medicine, the last being linked to the establishment of the Northeastern Ontario Regional Cancer Centre in Sudbury as well as the Northern Ontario School of Medicine.

In addition to this specialisation, the boundaries between Science disciplines, relatively watertight fifty years ago, had blurred, leading in many cases to greater interdisciplinary interaction. According to Haq, it was necessary for these boundaries to become less rigid to facilitate finding solutions to the common problems which transcended disciplines.

On the topic of interdisciplinary programs, behavioural neuroscience[15] and liberal science[16] must be mentioned. In the latter, students take a minimum of nine courses in the natural sciences from at least three departments; at least one course in two of the following departments: chemistry, mathematics and computer science, physics or astronomy; two continuations in different departments; and one elective in the Humanities or Social Sciences; and five other electives, two of which must be outside of the Sciences.

In the Humanities, four new programs – theatre arts,[17] fine arts,[18] communication studies[19] and communication publique[20] – were inaugurated by Thorneloe, Huntington and the University of Sudbury respectively. Theatre arts and fine arts were articulated programs, the first between Laurentian and Cambrian College, the second between Cambrian (music and theatre production), Huntington College (music), Thorneloe (theatre arts) and Laurentian. The articulation agreements stipulated that students had to take courses at both Cambrian and Laurentian. The communication studies program was also an articulated program between Cambrian and Huntington, in which the first three years were offered at Huntington and the fourth at Cambrian. Students registered in the program specialize in journalism, public relations or advertising. The University of Sudbury program, communication publique, was offered only at Laurentian, and consisted of two sections, journalism and public relations.

When Huntington College announced during the 2004–2005 academic year that it would be forced to eliminate the music program, both the Sudbury and the Laurentian communities reacted strongly. Senate meetings held in December 2004 and January 2005[21] were especially stormy. But the controversy subsided when President Judith Woodsworth announced that Laurentian would assume responsibility for the program. Negotiations ensued between Laurentian and Huntington and, in June 2006,[22] Senate established a music department that would eventually be located in the new English School of Education building, constructed in 2008.

Existing Humanities programs have also been modified. The English program was divided into four streams: literature, drama, rhetoric and film.[23] In Français, a cinematographic studies program was introduced at the end of the 1980s, but ACAPLAN had recommended its elimination in 1995. In both programs, a predominantly female faculty resulted in the development of new courses focused more on women's contribution to literary and artistic creation. A new specialized program in modern languages was created in 1992, and the German and Russian language programs were eliminated in 1995.[24]

Social Sciences inaugurated the following interdisciplinary programs: labour and trade union studies,[25] sports psychology, which combined courses in physical education and psychology,[26] and études de la santé (health studies) offered only in French.[27] Labour studies, taught in English only, combined courses in sociology, economics, commerce, law and justice, political science and women's studies. This program proposed not only to initiate students to the world of work and unions, but also to revive the history of union and labour history in the Sudbury region, which had been very eventful throughout the twentieth century. Études de la santé

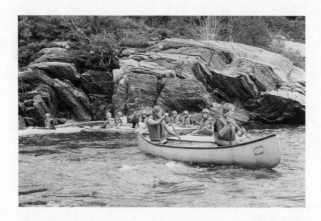

SCHOOL OF HUMAN
MOVEMENT STUDENTS
PRACTICE THEIR
CANOEING PROWESS

offered courses in sociologie, science politique, sciences infirmières, économie, folklore and histoire.

Existing programs were also modified. The history department added courses on northeastern Ontario as well as on Franco-Ontario in general, and began welcoming women to its faculty during the 1990s. Because of these changes, ACA-PLAN suggested in 2002 that the department launch a program review to integrate new opportunities presented by the faculty's expertise in the areas of social history, including the history of gender, Franco-Ontario and French Canada.

The anthropology program obtained administrative autonomy at the end of the 1990s, and full departmental status in the early 2000s. To its early specializations it added medical anthropology and forensic anthropology; the latter, with its biology option, contributing to the creation of the forensic science program in 2004.

The Faculty of Professional Schools launched three new programs and redefined the physical and health education program. The three new programs were: études du mouvement coopératif in 1981–1982, a general BA, offered only in French, which became, in 1986–1987, an honours BComm in administration des cooperatives,[28] kinesiology (honours BSc),[29] and Native human services, a social work program added to the school's English and French roster.[30] The objective of this honours BA, which constituted the second set of courses aimed at Native students at Laurentian but was also available to non-Natives, was to train social workers to work with both Native and non-Native communities. The physical and health education program added three new specialized programs in 1986–1987: health promotion, kinesiology (BSc) and outdoor education.[31]

In collaboration with the universities of McMaster and Ryerson, Laurentian developed a midwifery program which conferred a bachelor of health sciences degree in the subject in 1993–1994.[32] Then, at the decade's end, the arts d'expression program was launched so that Francophone students could obtain a diploma in theatre and cultural production.[33] Senate had approved this program at its June 17, 1999 meeting following a theatrical demonstration put on by students taking courses in the field.

Throughout the years, Laurentian not only created programs, it also made the controversial decisions to eliminate several, including Canadian studies and the school of translators and interpreters. The interdisciplinary Canadian studies program consisted of three CANA-designated courses, and a collection of offerings from other Humanities and Social Sciences disciplines. In 1988, following an external review of the program, ACAPLAN had recommended it be eliminated, stating that there was no collective commitment from the departments involved to it. Although enrolment in the first-year course was adequate, such was not the case for second and third-year courses. Furthermore, ACAPLAN had concerns about the program's overall quality.[34]

Both Thorneloe and Huntington Colleges offered to assume responsibility for the Canadian studies program, but Laurentian refused, the vice-president academic at the time stating that these offers represented only letters of intent and not concrete propositions.[35] In any event, the Senate motion of December 1988 to eliminate the program was defeated. At the following meeting on January 19, 1989, President Daniel told members in response to a question that Laurentian had definitely set aside the proposals made by the federated colleges. However, only the first-year CANA course was offered in 1989 which led to a program overhaul in 1991.[36] Senate voted to eliminate the program in 1996 following ACAPLAN's revision of programs.

. One of the oldest schools at Laurentian, the school of translators and interpreters, stopped admitting new students in 2002. This had been preceded, in 1998, by the transfer of programs and courses to the département d'études françaises.[37]

During Laurentian's fifth decade, two major programs were created. The first was the Northern Ontario School of Medicine, administered jointly by Laurentian University and Lakehead University in Thunder Bay. Although the school had only one dean, its courses, mainly in English, were offered in their entirety on both campuses. Practical instruction also takes place in numerous other rural and urban communities in Northern Ontario, in Native, Francophone and Anglophone settings. The school welcomed its first student cohort in September 2005 and its first graduation ceremony took place in the spring of 2009. One of the school's main objectives is to train doctors to practice in Northern Ontario. This was the first school of medicine to be created in Canada in thirty years.[38] Born in the digital age, it has developed an innovative, partly electronically-delivered curriculum.

Since its foundation, Laurentian had dreamed of establishing a school of medicine. In 1969 and 1970, in its report to the Ontario Council on University Affairs, Laurentian Acting President Cloutier had discussed the need for establishing such a school:

In health matters, it is accepted that the concept of regionalisation requires, in each region, a Health Sciences Center and its contained Medical School, both to train the broad spectrum of Health-Care Personnel and to be involved in service to, and research into problems peculiar to the particular

region. The Ontario Council of Health in its report recommends this solution to the Hall Commission's broader recommendations regarding the Regional Organization of Health Care.[39]

Cloutier also commented that the health sciences centres, including schools of medicine, were spread like precious jewels along Ontario's border, but that central and northern regions, with their issues relating to geography, environment and demographics, were completely deprived of them. He mentioned that the Sudbury region's health professionals strongly supported the idea of a school of medicine and of a health sciences centre at Laurentian. A petition supporting such a school had been circulated throughout Northern Ontario.[40]

In the early 1970s, the provincial government established directives for the creation of new medical schools which provided for a satellite teaching centre for Laurentian. In its report to Ontario Council on University Affairs in 1973, President Monahan stated that "recent decisions not to proceed with the establishment of the proposed satellite teaching centre are deplored since this means that the long needed improvement in regional medical educational facilities has once again been delayed." The president obviously realized that Laurentian would not see such a school in the near or even the distant future, because he indicated in his 1975 report that Laurentian did not have immediate plans to add other professional schools, in medicine, law or dentistry.

The idea of having a school of medicine at Laurentian was revisited in 1999 when the university administration decided that health sciences were a priority and named a director of health initiatives.[41] Supported by the McKendry report,[42] the project for a northern school of medicine was approved by the provincial government. It is interesting to note that both the McKendry report and lobbying done by both northern universities reverted to the same argument used in the early 1970s, that such a school would train doctors who would be more likely to set up practice in the North after graduating. Senate approved the school of medicine program on April 19, 2005.

At the end of the 1990s, Laurentian had also explored the possibility of establishing a BEd program offered only in English, at first jointly with Lakehead University, and later with Nipissing University. In the end it decided to undertake the project on its own.

The creation of a bachelor's degree in teaching (BEd) in English was approved by Senate in January 2003,[43] and was accredited by the Ontario College of Teachers in May 2003.[44] This was an important decision for educating Anglophone teachers in Sudbury, and it resulted in a significant increase in enrolment. Contrary to the consecutive program offered by l'École des sciences de l'éducation, which admits students after their BA or BSc, the English BEd program is a five-year concurrent program, where students study simultaneously in a BA or BSc discipline and in education. Only the fifth year is entirely devoted to studies in education. The first student cohort was admitted in 2003 and graduated in 2008.[45]

The e-business program was launched in 2002[46] for students interested in both computer science and business administration. This was an interdisciplinary program that combined courses mainly in computer science and commerce.

Lastly, at the end of the 2000s Laurentian began to explore the idea of establishing a school of architecture. This proposition garnered financial support from the City of Greater Sudbury's municipal council. In June 2009, the Laurentian Board of Governors and Senate approved the creation of a school of architecture in principle, and the Northern Ontario Heritage Fund provided $700,000 for project development, a hopeful sign that the proposal will quickly come to fruition.

The Relative Weighting of Programs

Table 7.1 shows program registrations between 1985 and 2007. Table 6.1 illustrated that the relative weight of programs from 1961 to 1978 had largely changed in favour of Professional Schools, and at the expense of Arts and Science. Table 7.1 reveals that this weight shifted again as of the early 1980s. Arts in general accounted for approximately 50 per cent of total registrations, which meant the pendulum had swung back towards this sector. Sciences also regained ground. The Professional Schools have maintained a good proportion of enrolments; the creation of an English-language teachers' college in 2002 and of the Faculty of Management in 2005 increased this proportion, which had gradually decreased from 1990 onward.

Certificates and Diplomas

Especially during the 1980s, Laurentian developed a series of certificate and diploma programs in various fields. A program leading to a certificate consists of a series of coherent undergraduate courses which are generally first, second and third-year courses. Thirty credits are required to obtain a certificate, and these can all be counted toward a bachelor's degree, but not towards another certificate or

TABLE 7.1 | PROGRAM REGISTRATIONS, 1985–2007

Faculty	1985–1986		1990–1991		1996–1997		2002–2003		2007–2008	
	N	%	N	%	N	%	N	%	N	%
Arts*	1,112	34	2,273	51	1,991	46				
Humanities	–	–	–	–			388	7	778	10
Social Sciences	–	–	–	–			1,263	21	1,426	18
Arts general**	–	–	–	–	–	–	1,335	22	1,553	19
Science and Engineering	530	16	559	12	841	19	630	11	731	9
Science general**	–	–	–	–	–	–	493	8	410	5
Professional Schools	1,645	50	1,656	37	1,541	35	1,823	31	2,338	28
Administration									911	11
Total	3,287	100	4,488	100	4,373	100	5,932	100	8,147	100

Sources: Statistical report on registrations, 1986, 1991, 1997, Registrar's Office; Registrations, 2002, 2007, Institutional Research Office.

*Statistical reports from the Registrar's Office do not make a distinction between Humanities and Social Sciences, grouping them in the Arts category.

**Students are registered in Humanities, Social Sciences or Science programs but have not yet declared a concentration; this category only starts appearing in reports in 2002.

diploma. (The university had launched its first certificate, for bilingualism, at the end of the 1960s when the requirement for a second language was eliminated. This became the certificate in bilingualism in 1973–1974, obtained by passing an oral and written examination.)[47]

A diploma is a series of coherent courses, the majority of which are fourth-year courses. It also requires thirty credits. Thesis courses can be counted toward another degree, but not another diploma. The diploma mostly interests students who already have a three-year general bachelor and want to obtain the equivalent of a fourth year in the same discipline. Since university regulations do not allow students to obtain two degrees (general and honours) in the same discipline, the diploma enables them to obtain the equivalent of the second degree. Mature students who are particularly capable of taking a program due to their experience may also be admitted for a diploma. In general, certificates are interdisciplinary while diplomas are concentrated in one discipline.

The Centre for Continuing Education focused on correspondence courses with the inauguration of its Envision program in 1987–1988.[48] Furthermore, following the establishment of Contact North in 1987, the Centre began to give courses by teleconference. Since the 1990s, too, many courses have become available online, a trend that keeps growing.

Since the 1960s, Laurentian also has offered its programs at the affiliated universities, Nipissing (North Bay), Algoma (Sault Ste. Marie) and Hearst. The first

---

UNIVERSITÉ DE HEARST

In 1953, Bishop Louis Levesque founded the Petit Séminaire de Hearst. At the time, Ontario still did not allow publicly funded French or bilingual secondary schools. To pursue their education at the secondary level, Francophones had to attend either English high schools or denominational bilingual private schools. Given this situation, only a privileged few pursued their education beyond the elementary level. By providing his diocese with a "Petit Séminaire," the Bishop of Hearst's intention was to ensure that young men in Northern Ontario had an opportunity to obtain a secondary-level education, thus following in his diocese the tradition of Catholic education in Ontario.

In September 1953, the Petit Séminaire de Hearst welcomed its first 35 students. The curriculum for their education was modelled on that used in Quebec's "collèges classiques." Shortly thereafter its founder, along with one of his main collaborators, Reverend Maurice Saulnier, decided to modify the curriculum to make it compatible with that taught in secondary schools in Ontario. In 1957, an affiliation agreement, which made possible the first university-level program, was signed with the University of Sudbury. That same year, construction began on a new building which the Hearst campus still occupies today. To finance his educational pursuits, Bishop Levesque regularly called upon the generosity of the population of the diocese. From 1957 to 1959, a diocesan fund-raising campaign collected over $345,000, a sum that represented about 50% of the building costs. In 1959 the Petit Séminaire de Hearst was incorporated as a non-profit corporation under the name Collège de Hearst.

At the turn of the next decade, the young educational institution received a growing number of students at the secondary and post-secondary levels, and prepared to offer courses in new university disciplines. In 1961, its first seven graduates obtained their university degrees. Because the Collège did not have a university charter, diplomas were conferred first by the University of Sudbury and then by Laurentian. In December of 1963, agreements were signed that marked the beginning of a long and fruitful affiliation with the newly created Laurentian

---

University. Several months earlier, the first group of female students had entered the pre-university program, which was equivalent to grade 13. Their arrival forever changed the face of the institution. Since then, almost 75 per cent of all its diplomas have been conferred on women.

With the advent of publicly funded French-language secondary schools, Collège de Hearst ceased to offer secondary level education, and the boarding school closed its doors in 1970. These changes compelled the institution to partially revise and reformulate its mission. The Board of Governors and the faculty became secularized, in part due to returning young professionals who had been educated at the Collège itself. Among them was a young professor of sociology, Raymond Tremblay. He was the first lay person to hold the positions of director of studies and then president, and he has been at the helm of the institution ever since.

In 1971, Ontario recognized the institution as a public university, qualifying it for 100 per cent financing by the province. A year later, the institution became the Collège universitaire de Hearst and increased its part-time programs, which over the following years would allow teachers from across the region to pursue their education. The faculty travelled to many different communities, and taught evening courses to these part-time students. When the Kapuskasing campus opened in 1976, services to this dispersed clientele increased further.

Despite this vitality, the Collège universitaire de Hearst's financial situation remained fragile. The part-time student population, comprised mainly of elementary-level teachers, declined as this group obtained their diplomas. In 1978, a financial crisis threatened the very existence of the institution. Numerous discussions with government officials convinced them that the province's smallest university – and its only French-language university – must be saved. An extraordinary grant of $200,000 in 1980 permitted it to survive and to continue, not without difficulty, its mission, and to diversify its services, leading to the creation of the Timmins campus in 1988.

In 1995, government cutbacks forced the Collège to declare another financial emergency, which brought about the elimination of some programs and a number of staff positions. The institution survived thanks to salary reductions and increased workloads agreed to by the personnel. Opting to increase rather than reduce its services, the institution decided to strike out on a new path and introduced full-time programs at Kapuskasing and Timmins. Until then, only the Hearst campus had offered this option. By expanding its regional mandate, it succeeded in increasing student enrolment. Furthermore, in order to distinguish itself from newly created French-language community colleges in Ontario, it adopted a new business name: Université de Hearst.

With over 1,000 graduates, l'Université de Hearst has, for almost 60 years, contributed to the educational, cultural and economic life of its region. Its success is due first and foremost to the unwavering support of the Diocese of Hearst, and of the population of northeastern Ontario.

two have since become independent institutions. Nipissing was granted its charter in 1992 and Algoma gained its independence in 2008. L'Université de Hearst continues to be affiliated with Laurentian, and is the only entirely French university institution in Ontario.

Throughout the years, Laurentian has offered programs jointly with other institutions, occasionally private ones, for example l'Université canadienne en France, but mostly public ones, such as the colleges of applied arts and technologies. In 1987–1988, Laurentian established l'Université canadienne en France which was jointly administered by the university and Blyth & Company, a Toronto travel company. The *Laurentian University Calendar* explained: "This is a program designed for Anglophone and Francophone students in all provinces to spend a year in the South of France while continuing to obtain university credits recognized in Canada."[49] The overseas campus offered mainly a one year program, with courses in literature, music, history, classical studies and languages. Every year, l'Université canadienne en France set a theme around which the courses focused.

In 2001, the Faculty of Humanities and Social Sciences began a partnership with Georgian College, in Simcoe county, where several of its programs were offered, in English only, to students in the region. This partnership has grown from 54 students and three programs in 2001 to over 1,000 full-time students in 2010 who can obtain their BA in eight disciplines, as well as a bachelor of business administration, and the beginning of the social work program.

When the provincial government implemented changes requiring nurses to obtain a university degree to practice their profession in the early 2000s, Laurentian initiated a nursing program, in English, given jointly with three colleges of arts and technologies: St. Lawrence (Cornwall), Northern (Timmins) and Sault (Sault Ste. Marie).[50] In 2002 Laurentian also joined with the Michener Institute in Toronto to offer a BSc in radiation therapy,[51] and in 2006, the school of social work signed an agreement with Université Sainte-Anne in Nova Scotia to offer its entire bachelor's program via its online program.[52]

Graduate Studies since 1985

Since the early 1980s, Laurentian has created a dozen new graduate programs. However, it did suspend one – English – in December 1983, following a negative assessment from Ontario Council of Graduate Studies (OCGS). The Council had concluded that the program needed major improvements and called for student registration to stop immediately. The assessment was based on the fact that the program had inadequate faculty resources, and also that faculty members did not have sufficiently strong research and publications portfolios. The university appealed this assessment, noting that the program satisfied regional needs and that the initial specialization, Victorian literature, imposed by OCGS had become too narrow considering the evolution of professors' research interests.[53] The vice-president academic and research decided to cease admitting students in the program "until such time as we have made a firm decision on our future intention re this programme." He also indicated that the program would not be restarted without positive a re-evaluation.[54] In 1980, the geology MSc also experienced low enrolment and was threatened with closure, largely for financial reasons. It was able to continue when the situation with the program turned around.

Laurentian established a number of new graduate programs between 1980 and 2000, in four faculties. In Science, a master's in mining engineering, inaugurated in 1988–1989 in collaboration with Queen's University, enabled students who were registered in graduate studies at Laurentian to complete the majority of the degree requirements at Laurentian. This partnership ended in 1995–1996 when the school of engineering established its own programs in mineral resources:[55] a master's program in engineering, which required courses and an industrial project; and one in applied sciences, which required courses and a thesis. These interdisciplinary programs were established after consultation with local industry, and admitted full-time and part-time students with degrees in engineering or science. L'École des sciences de l'éducation began offering a master's of education (MEd) jointly with the University of Ottawa in 1988–1989,[56] but this ended in 1992–1993 because of administrative problems and a requirement that was too demanding for students, that they live in residence at the University of Ottawa.

Professional Schools began offering a master's of business administration (MBA) in 1986–1987.[57] The school of social work welcomed its first Francophone students in the maîtrise en service social (MSS) program in 1992–1993,[58] and the Anglophone students in the master's of social work (MSW) in 1996–1997.[59] These two programs were offered part-time, and students – most of whom worked full time – participated in intensive four-day sessions every six weeks. In 2008, after the program had been revised, the OCGS authorized the school to admit full-time students.

The master's program in orthophonie, offered jointly with University of Ottawa, was launched in 1994–1995.[60] Its objective was to "train professionals able to work in French in Ontario." Candidates needed knowledge of the basic principles of psychology and linguistics, and received highly specialized training in the field of communications disorders.[61] Contrary to other programs offered jointly, students taking courses at Laurentian received their degree from this university. In 2000, citing difficulty recruiting qualified professors, Laurentian stopped offering this program at the graduate level.

The Faculty of Social Sciences and Humanities introduced two new master's programs in the mid-1990s. In the Social Sciences, the department of sociology began offering its MA program in 1994–1995.[62] This program was completely bilingual and specialized in applied social research. The Humanities inaugurated an interdisciplinary master's program in 1996–1997.[63] The philosophy underpinning the Interdisciplinary Master of Arts in Humanities: Interpretation and Values was described as follows:

Inquiry into how our interpretation and values shape the world around us and how we are shaped by the interpretation and values of others is traditionally the province of the humanities and is expressed through textual study: liberal, critical, philosophical and religious. Our programme is designed to stress the commonalities between our various humanities disciplines."[64]

Planning for this Humanities initiative had begun in May 1990 after several professors expressed to the dean an interest in creating such an interdisciplinary program.[65] For ten years, this program was offered jointly with the federated colleges but in 2006, University College took over full responsibility while relying on the contribution of several professors from the federated colleges.

Since 2000, five graduate programs have been created: the online program in business administration, the nursing program (MSCN),[66] the graduate diploma in science communication,[67] the master's of human kinetics[68] and the master's in psychology.[69] The mathematics department recently submitted for evaluation a graduate program with a specialization in computational science, a field combining computer science and mathematics.

Doctoral Programs

The doctorate, or PhD, represents the second level of graduate studies. To obtain a doctoral program, a university must go through a very rigorous examination process, both within the university and by OCGS. As well, the doctoral program, like the master's, is subjected to a very strict OCGS evaluation every seven years. To obtain the Council's authorization to offer a doctoral program, a department or faculty must have faculty members who are qualified, and possess an acceptable research and publication portfolio, as well experience supervising theses.

According to former director of graduate studies Lloyd Reed, in the 1980s the provincial government had forbidden Laurentian and other universities of similar size from developing doctoral programs[70] for which they would have received provincial funding. This restriction remained in place until around 1999–2000. According to the dean of graduate studies, Paul Colilli, Laurentian had various reasons for launching such programs when the government lifted the embargo. First of all, the faculty's research profile had improved considerably, and Laurentian wanted both to enhance its research environment and to augment revenues. Also, the federal government launched its research chair and innovation fund programs during the same period to encourage Canadian universities, regardless of their size, to undertake research. Enrolment was undoubtedly destined to increase because of the double cohort, and the provincial government wanted to accommodate all students who wished to pursue graduate studies. Thus the Liberal government created a fund for expanding graduate studies programs. Finally, it was the university's thinking that such programs in strategic fields would be beneficial as far as sources of financing were concerned, whether from industry or government. For all of these reasons, Laurentian decided to establish a series of post-graduate, mostly doctoral, programs.

After the government lifted this restriction in 2000, Laurentian created six doctoral programs; four in Science, one in the Professional Schools and one in

LAURENTIAN UNIVERSITY'S FIRST STUDENT EVER TO EARN A PHD, IN BIOMOLECULAR SCIENCES, RYAN MAILLOUX, POSES AT CONVOCATION IN JUNE 2008

Humanities/Social Science. (Previously, Laurentian's only other involvement in doctoral studies had been a joint PhD program with University of Ottawa in clinical psychology inaugurated in 1992–1993.[71]) These doctorate programs are: boreal ecology[72] (biology), bio-molecular sciences,[73] natural resources engineering,[74] mineral deposits and Precambrian geology,[75] rural and northern health,[76] and sciences humaines/human studies.[77] It is anticipated that a seventh doctorate program, in material science – an interdisciplinary program based on engineering and chemistry – will be approved in 2010.

The boreal ecology program, offered in English only, defines its objective as "the study of all aquatic and terrestrial aspects of boreal ecosystems (genetic, physiological, morphological, behavioural and ecological) at micro- and macro-habitat scales with emphasis on structural systems, impacts of disturbance, restoration and species sustainability and conservation." The biology department had previously tried to establish a joint doctoral program with Guelph University in 1993. According to the letter of agreement proposed between the two universities, this program would have allowed Laurentian professors who possessed the requisite qualifications to offer courses and supervise students in Guelph's doctoral program. Laurentian professors would have been named adjunct professors and could have taught courses in either Sudbury or Guelph. Students registered in the Guelph program could have done their research in Sudbury as well.[78]

ACAPLAN refused to approve this joint program, however, concerned about its financial implications, particularly the cost of the additional resources required. Furthermore, the program would not attract additional students at Laurentian, since they would be registered at Guelph University. Lastly, "ACAPLAN members asked why such a doctoral program is not proposed for Laurentian."[79]

Students in the bio-molecular sciences program are prepared for careers in academic teaching, in research, or in the biotechnological, pharmaceutical or biomedical industries. This program involves the participation of faculty from the biology, chemistry and biochemistry, and physics departments, the school of human kinetics, the Northern Ontario School of Medicine, and also of the staff of the Northeastern Ontario Regional Cancer Centre and the Sudbury Regional Hospital.

The natural resources engineering program specializes in the fields of mining engineering, robotics, automation and advanced technologies. It follows up on a program that Laurentian had tried to establish jointly with Queen's University. Both this program and that on mineral deposits are designed to take advantage of the geographical location of the Sudbury region for their studies and research. The geology department, like the biology department, also had previously considered the creation of a doctoral program in collaboration with other universities; first with Ottawa and Carleton universities in 1996 and then with the University of Western Ontario in 1997. In both cases, nothing came of the discussions. According to the dean of Science and Engineering at the time, talks with Ottawa and Carleton fell through because the project had received lukewarm support from the departments in both Ottawa and Sudbury. However, as soon as the provincial restriction on doctoral programs was lifted, Laurentian was able to use the documentation prepared during the discussions to propose its own program.

The rural and northern health program corresponds closely to the objectives set out in Laurentian's strategic plan, the university having identified that sector as one of its priorities. As an interdisciplinary program, it is also relates directly to the Northern Ontario School of Medicine which specializes in training doctors for rural and northern areas.

Lastly, the sciences humaines/human studies program, the only fully bilingual PhD program, is focused on one fundamental theme: human development.

> The main field of the doctoral program in human studies is human development. Its object is the human being as a social being and as a unique being; interdisciplinarity is both its tool for analysis and its means of study, interdisciplinarity drawing from traditional disciplines in Humanities and Social Sciences in order to create new knowledge and a new paradigm called interdisciplinarity.[80]

Francophone students are trained in four fields: cognition and communication, regional and cultural studies, Franco-Ontarian and Francophone studies, and health. Anglophone students can specialize in one of five fields: human development, critique of gender relations and sexuality, regional and cultural studies, interpretation of values and ethics in politics, and health. Previous attempts in the 1990s to set up a doctoral program in human development did not come to fruition because of a lack of faculty qualified to teach at this level. Laurentian conferred its first doctoral degrees in the program shortly before its fiftieth anniversary.

Research: 1985 to Today

When President Daniel took office in July 1984, he wasted no time showing his true colours with respect to research. In an interview with *Northern Life*, Daniel stated that one of his chief priorities would be to build research capacity at Laurentian. Echoing former President Monahan, he indicated the university should focus primarily on the field of research on northern resources. It would be difficult, he admitted, but Laurentian had to begin systematically developing its research infrastructure.[81]

During its mandate, the Daniel-Bélanger administration was responsible for the following developments: establishing a new research office, which in 1986 combined with the school of graduate studies to became the school of graduate studies and research; hiring an assistant to the director whose responsibility was to assist professors with grant applications; and publishing the *Research Bulletin* at Laurentian which, from 1990 to 1999, apprised research chairs of available research grants. The administration also enunciated a policy on procedures for the creation and financing of research centres and institutes that was approved by Senate.[82] It inaugurated a policy on administrative fees related to research, establishing the Laurentian University Research Fund (LURF) which provides modest grants to researchers to enable them to begin research projects.

Since this policy was adopted, the number of research centres at Laurentian has not stopped multiplying. In 1985, the university had three research institutes or centres: the Institute for Research on Microparticules, the Institut franco-ontarien and the Centre in Mining and Mineral Exploration Research (CIMMER). Today, Laurentian has close to twenty, supporting numerous fundamental and applied research projects in various disciplines.[83]

The Centre for Excellence in Mining Innovation (CEMI) is a coalition of institutes and universities working in the main research fields deemed relevant and important to the mining industry. Created on the initiative of the Ontario Mineral Industry Cluster Council to capitalize on the vast mining-related infrastructure already in place in the region, CEMI has elevated the City of Greater Sudbury to the rank of internationally renowned research communities by enabling it to compete successfully in the competitive field of mining sector–related research. The centre focuses on mineral exploration, deep mining, integrated mine engineering, automation and telerobotics, as well as environment and land reclamation.

The Cooperative Freshwater Ecology Unit (CFEU), founded in 1989 under the direction of John Gunn, provides research opportunities in the fields of restoration ecology, environmental science, and aquatic resource management, for undergraduate and graduate students, and provides an educational program that benefits students, government, and the general public. The centre's current areas of study include climate change, endangered fish species rehabilitation, zooplankton and fish community interactions in acid-stressed lakes. As Laurentian's next fifty years begin, CFEU prepares to move into its new home, the Vale Inco Living With Lakes Centre constructed on the site of the Robertson cottage, the signature project of the university's fundraising campaign.

The goal of the Centre in Mining Materials Research (CIMMR), affiliated with the department of earth sciences, is to promote and enhance interdisciplinary materials science research and education and its relations with all aspects of the mining and mineral industries. Major areas of focus by faculty working under the aegis of the centre include: advanced materials for optimizing mining processes and environmental controls, characterization of mining materials, separation science, and mineral process engineering.

The Centre for Research in Human Development (CRHD), established in 1987 under the leadership of John Lewko, the director of the child and development program, is an interdisciplinary research centre that supports a range of basic and applied research activities across several academic units. Major research initiatives within the centre include: the well-being of seniors; environmental ethics and decision-making; transition from school to work; Native youth; youth at risk; in-body changes during growth; development of emotions; neuropsychological development; social-relational development; and family and socialization.

The Northern Health Human Resources Research Unit created in 1992 under the direction of Ray Pong and transformed in 1997 into the Centre for Rural and Northern Health Research (CRaNHR) is a joint research centre based at Laurentian University and Lakehead University. The centre conducts interdisciplinary research on population health, health workforce and healthcare issues, with a view to achieving a better understanding of health conditions, particularly in rural and northern areas. Researchers associated with the centre conduct studies on the management, organization and effectiveness of rural and northern health services, as well as on the training, distribution and utilization of healthcare providers.

The Elliot Lake Research Field Station (ELRFS) was established in 1992 to support research into the effects of low-level radioactivity on the environment resulting from regional uranium mine waste tailings in the region of Elliot Lake. The laboratory currently provides a wide range of inorganic and radionuclide analytical services to private industry in support of soil/manure/plant/animal tissue analysis, wastewater treatment plant operations, and environmental effects monitoring and research.

The Geomechanics Research Centre (GRC), created in 1987 and headed by Peter Kaiser, is engaged in applied research in the field of rock mechanics and ground control. Current research, in cooperation with the Canadian mining industry, includes: support of mining excavation in hard rock; mechanized rock excavation; support of bursting ground; geomechanics of deep mining; risk-cost benefit analysis; and use of micro-seismic observations for mine design.

Established in 1976, the Institut franco-ontarien's objectives are to produce research and publications, organize colloquia and conferences and gather documentation on various aspects of the Franco-Ontarian population. Research projects sponsored by the Institut are mainly focused on education, health, the elderly, and culture and society.

The Institute of Northern Ontario Research and Development (INORD) which came into existence in 1987, is the centre at Laurentian specializing in social and economic research on northeastern Ontario. Its website carries articles, research papers and presentations relevant to regional issues. INORD's aim is to promote research cooperation between social science faculty, and public, private and voluntary sector groups in northeastern Ontario.

SUDBURY NEUTRINO OBSERVATORY, 1997 | Since the mid-1980s, scientists in Laurentian's physics department have been key members of the Sudbury Neutrino Observatory – a unique detector of neutrinos from our Sun – located 2 kilometres underground at the Vale Inco Creighton Mine. SNO's results have confirmed new properties for solar neutrinos and received world-wide recognition.

The Laurentian University Mining Automation Laboratory (LUMAL), a joint school of engineering and Inco venture created in 1993, aims to enhance and support teaching in mining automation/robotics and in the application of new technologies in the mining sector. It seeks to provide research expertise in mining automation and to develop strong industrial links with Canadian companies focusing on new mining technologies.

The Mineral Exploration Research Centre (MERC) has several objectives which include promoting collaborative university-government-industry research on mineral deposits and Precambrian geology, pursuing a fundamental understanding of mineral deposits and their geological settings, aiding the Canadian mining industry in the discovery of ore deposits and training geologists in mineral exploration research techniques. The Mining Innovation, Rehabilitation and Applied Research Corporation (MIRARCO), established in 1998, is a not-for-profit applied research and technical service company formed through collaboration between Laurentian University and the private and public sectors. MIRARCO promotes mining innovation and provides a bridge between researchers and industry.

The Sudbury Neutrino Observatory (SNO), the Canadian-led international scientific project situated two kilometres underground in Inco's Creighton mine, is commonly referred to as "Canada's eye on the universe." Established in 1990, the observatory has become a permanent, first-class facility for underground scientific research where an international team of over 130 researchers, working to understand how nuclear fusion operates in the sun, have found new properties of neutrinos that change the laws of physics at the most elemental level.

The Institute for Sport Marketing (ISM) was established in 2001 with funding from a variety of private corporations and sports organizations. It analyzes Canadian sport, recreation and physical activity funding. In 2006, Laurentian also inaugurated the Branch Research Data Center at the J.N. Desmarais Library where researchers, especially in the Social Sciences, can consult Statistics Canada data on campus.[84]

Two new research centres, the Centre for Research in Occupational Safety and Health (CROSH) and the Centre for Research in Social Justice and Policy (CRSJP) were created in 2008. CROSH brings together researchers from various disciplines – human kinetics and human development. The CRSJP unites researchers from many disciplines.

This veritable explosion of research centres at Laurentian is closely linked to the expansion of the mining industry in the Sudbury region since the 1990s. A third of these centres are closely connected to the mining industry, whether through financing or cooperative efforts. These centres also have important ties to the development of graduate studies programs in Science, Professional Schools, Humanities and Social Sciences.

Over the past ten years at least, the field of health, which is obviously closely related to the school of medicine, has become a major source of financing for research. The creation of the Canadian Institutes of Health Research in 2000, in accordance with a federal law that came into effect on June 7, 2000,[85] was definitely a factor in the numerous research projects launched in this field at Laurentian.

Strategic Planning and Infrastructure

Because research activities had grown so greatly since 1985, Laurentian thought it wise to develop strategic plans for research, and expand its infrastructure to manage them. The university had elaborated strategic plans since 1972 to give direction to its development in the academic sector,[86] but it was only in 2000[87] that it adopted one focused solely on research. Senate adopted a modified version of this plan in 2004.[88] It defines five key areas of research: i) mineral resources; ii) environmental sciences; iii) regional economic, political, social and cultural development; iv) health; and v) underground sciences. In all of these areas, emphasis is on both fundamental and applied, problem-solving research undertaken in close cooperation with industrial and public sector partners in the region. These five research areas complement and overlap each other, and are closely linked, first and foremost, to the Greater Sudbury region, and then to Northern Ontario. The objective of the strategic plan was to orient research and graduate studies curriculum in these areas in order to achieve international research recognition, and also to provide guidelines for resource allocation within the university.

The Canada Research Chairs program is part of this resource allocation. Established in 2000 by the federal government, the purpose of this program was to create research chairs in Canadian universities to enable the development of international research excellence in the fields of natural sciences, engineering, health sciences and human sciences. It was launched with the objective to create 2,000 research professorships in Canadian universities.[89] Laurentian University was granted a total of seven research chairs in April 2000;[90] this allocation, which is periodically adjusted, depends on the research grant totals received by the university's researchers from national granting agencies. Gustavo Arteca, of the chemistry and biochemistry department, was the first recipient of a research chair at

Laurentian. Presently, on the eve of its fiftieth anniversary, the university has seven chairs.[91]

As can be seen, research grew exponentially at Laurentian after 1985, particularly in the early 2000s. The university administration became increasingly conscious that the infrastructure set up in 1986 to provide a framework for these activities was no longer adequate. The research office, which was integrated with the school of graduate studies, was unable to direct and manage this facet of university life. Consequently, in 2003, Vice-President Academic (Anglophone Affairs) Douglas Parker announced to Senate that a new position, that of associate vice-president research, was being created in order to ensure the continued progress and growth in the field of research.[92] According to Parker, this position was mandated to assume and ensure leadership in research and to manage research activity at Laurentian. "Furthermore, the associate vice-president, research, will promote and support research done by faculty members, manage all research contracts and grants from granting councils (NSERC, SSHRC, CIHR) as well as be responsible for the administrative supervision of research centres. This person will also be responsible for Laurentian's Canada Research Chairs, for the research office and for the office responsible for matters of intellectual property."[93] The creation of this position would allow the office of the dean of graduate studies to focus only on the development and administration of graduate and post-graduate programs. In addition, this meant that the Graduate Studies and Research Council was no longer responsible for research. In September 2004, Liette Vasseur took up her post as associate vice-president research. When Vasseur left Laurentian in the summer of 2009, another administrative shuffle combined responsibility for graduate studies and research into one office, that of vice-president research and graduate studies.

In 2004, the university also established the Research Council, whose mandate was to make recommendations to Senate or, when appropriate, through Senate committees, about anything concerning research. The council was also responsible for encouraging and facilitating research, developing and maintaining appropriate research program directives, facilitating new research program developments and making recommendations on long term research planning.[94] In January 2005, Senate changed the name of this council to the Research, Development and Creativity Council,[95] to reflect faculty members' activities in these three important areas of university life. This nomenclature recognized the importance of Humanities which is more focused on creativity, for example, in the areas of literature and theatre. This new council is mandated to make recommendations pertaining not only to research, but also to development and creativity.

Consequently, the Research, Development and Creativity Office, directed by the associate vice-president and governed by the Council, has multiple responsibilities and duties. In addition to those listed above – research centres, Canada Research Chairs, LURF, advice and assistance for grant applications, research promotion – the office is also increasingly responsible for managing many policies, internal (developed and approved at Laurentian) as well as external (developed and adopted mostly by government and ministry agencies). Over the past few years, these policies have reshaped considerably the way research is done, not only at Laurentian but in all the universities and research establishments in Canada.

Research Grants

Changes brought to the research infrastructure since 1985 have definitely had an impact on the amount of research grants received by Laurentian faculty. These grants totalled more than $9 million between 1980 and 1986, and then more than doubled from 1989 to 1994. In addition to these external grants, faculty members received internal funds for research projects. From 1989 to 1994, the overall amount of these grants was worth $1,087,527, of which 6 per cent was allocated to Humanities, 22 per cent to Professional Schools, 53 per cent to Science and Engineering, and 19 per cent to Social Sciences.

According to former director of graduate studies and research Dieter Buse, this research portfolio measured by external grants received was very good by comparison with small- or medium-sized universities. The amounts received from contracts outweighed those from granting councils such as NSERC or SSHRC. However, the criteria used to judge research should not be limited to dollar amounts or to the number of publications. With respect to publications, these criteria must also take into consideration quality, as measured by the number of publications in periodicals of national and international reputation. This last criterion was one area where Laurentian faculty did need improvement.[96]

The total funds received to finance research projects represented a major sign of improvement at Laurentian. According to the associate vice-president research, "recently, Research Infosource, which annually ranks the 50 best Canadian universities, has ranked Laurentian first for growth in research funding, including private, sponsored and public funding." The university had received a total of $38,600,000 in research funding, which represented an increase of 133 per cent over 2005 when it had received $16,600,000.[97] This research funding came from four major sources: provincial government (26.4 per cent), industry (10.3 per cent), federal government (27.4 per cent) and three granting councils (36 per cent).[98] It is obvious that the establishment of research centres and graduate studies programs and structures have had a highly positive impact on research activities at Laurentian over the past twenty-five years.

Conclusion

These chapters endeavoured to provide a summary of the development and evolution of academic and research programs at Laurentian University from its foundation in 1960 to the present. It is obvious that these two important fields are fundamental underpinnings of university life, and that they have gone through significant changes over the past fifty years – and will most certainly go through several more in the future.

Between 1960 and 1985, approximately, Laurentian focused on program development, starting with bachelor's, or undergraduate programs, and then, at the end of the 1960s, master's, or graduate programs. Since 1985, the university has been more systematic in developing its graduate programs, especially, more recently, at the doctoral level. It has also vastly improved its achievements in research.[99]

Over the next few years, the challenge for Laurentian will be to ensure the continuance of a healthy balance between teaching and research, the two pillars of the university's mission. This debate is currently taking place in several universities and involves two opposite visions for research and teaching roles. Some people claim that teaching and research must go hand in hand, that each enriches the other. Partisans of mutual enrichment generally expressed themselves as such in 1978. As President Best's brief to the Ontario Council on University Affairs then stated:

> In preparing a submission on the role and importance of research ... in a small university, such as Laurentian, I am assuming that the central justification for its pursuit is two fold: firstly, to augment knowledge and secondly, to enhance the quality of university education. Fundamental research is the base from which all significant advances of knowledge are made, whether the contributions arise from individual scholarship or large-scale research undertakings; it is essential for the vitality of academic institutions. Even in a small university ... our essential but modest involvement in scientific research plays a vital role in awakening in our students the creative and imaginative response, without which learning cannot flourish.[100]

Others, on the contrary, claim that this mutual enrichment is a myth, that both activities are mutually exclusive. Stuart Smith, who had presided over the Commission of Inquiry on Canadian University Education on behalf of the Association of Universities and Colleges of Canada, took up this position in 1991, as follows:

> Smith discussed growing professorial preference for research over teaching and a related desire to teach specialized courses. He argues that teaching and research were activities that competed for scarce time and resources. In so doing he challenged dominant ideas about teaching and research ... His view was that universities' fundamental obligation is teaching and that research is secondary to teaching.[101]

As Laurentian increasingly becomes oriented more toward research and graduate studies, this debate on undergraduate teaching will be become more pronounced. It is one that very much needs to take place.

PART C | DEVELOPING IDENTITIES

8   The Berkeley of Sudbury: Finding a Voice, 1960–1972

SARA BURKE

"Welcome to the Berkeley of Sudbury."
(SGA president's address to first-year students, September 1970)

In the fall of 1960, restaurants in downtown Sudbury began to notice an unusual number of young people coming in during the lunch hour. The newcomers, mostly clean-cut, well-behaved young men, were the first students to attend Laurentian University. The new university opened on September 19, 1960, with enthusiasm, but little physical presence – no dining hall, residence, student centre, or athletic facilities – and students attended their classes in a range of unlikely buildings scattered throughout the area. This makeshift accommodation disguised a far-reaching ambition: to bring together young Canadians of different languages and denominations, French and English, Catholic and Protestant, into one undergraduate body. The first students at Laurentian were participating in what the *Sudbury Star* announced impressively to be "the greatest experiment ever to be undertaken in Canadian higher education."[1] During the university's formative years, Laurentian students were successful in meeting the challenges of this experiment, establishing their space on the new campus in 1964, creating the first student association, newspaper and yearbook, and most importantly, fighting for and winning a voice in the upper levels of university governance. Swept up by the radical student movement of the late sixties, undergraduates in Sudbury emerged from the first decade with a distinct sense of themselves, proud of their place in the new university, and confident in their ability to change the future.

Drawing largely on the population of Sudbury and Northern Ontario, Laurentian's enrolment grew steadily throughout the 1960s, yet the overall percentage of Francophone students declined sharply after the first five years, and continued to drop. In 1960–1961, the total enrolment was 185, 52 per cent of whom were Francophone. Five years later, enrolment had risen to 901, with only 14.6 per cent Francophone. By 1969–1970, the total number of students was 1,773, but only 12.5 per cent were Francophone.[2] Relations on campus between French and English students were often strained, and the issue of bilingualism became a central point of debate throughout the 1960s and 1970s. A key factor in student activism, however, was the ability of Laurentian's two student populations to join together to form an effective campaign for the advancement of undergraduate interests.

On a tour of the early downtown campus, a *Globe and Mail* reporter remarked humorously on the university's motley assortment of buildings, concluding that "Laurentian lives in town."[3] The university occupied space on Larch, Elgin, Lisgar, and Durham Streets, including the Northern Ontario and DeMarco buildings. Although all the buildings were hastily adapted to fit their new purpose, Huntington College undoubtedly occupied the oddest space, having offices over a pool hall on Durham Street and classes in a former funeral home on Larch. One professor who taught at Huntington in 1961 recalls that the foot lockers for women students were six feet deep, and that the "study room for the men was white tiles, very bright lights in the ceiling, and a drain in the floor."[4] The University of Sudbury, housing the office of the first president, Fr. Émile Bouvier, was located in the Empire Building on Elgin Street. The largest space – ironically in view of the fact that it had the lowest enrolment – was given to the facilities and library of the non-denominational University College, which used 5,000 square feet of Sudbury's federal building on Lisgar Street.[5]

With no residential accommodation, students lived in boarding houses and private homes across the city. Of the 185 full-time students who registered in the fall of 1960, the University of Sudbury had the largest number, 135, while 36 were enrolled at Huntington and 14 at University College. The majority of students were in first year, with 85 in second or third year, most having previously attended the University of Sudbury. From the beginning, Laurentian also attracted a large number of part-time students who took evening courses to work toward their degree, and non-degree adult learners who enrolled in extension courses in mathematics, electricity, co-operatives, and leadership.[6] A precursor of the university's future role in Native education, as early as 1962, the extension department offered courses for adults from nearby First Nations communities.[7]

Although conscious of their university's raw newness, Laurentian students were quick to introduce the same institutions that characterized more established universities in the post-war period. In 1960, the existing students' council for the University of Sudbury expanded its jurisdiction to form the Students' General Association of Laurentian University (SGA). The new SGA occupied office space on the third floor of the DeMarco building; one half contained desks for the members of the executive, and the other doubled as a social centre and a meeting room. The SGA included students from both official language groups, and the executive consisted of a president and two vice-presidents, one Francophone and one Anglophone. The SGA's first constitution, ratified in 1965, was also bilingual, and had been developed using models from both English- and French-Canadian universities, including Ottawa, Toronto, McGill, Laval, and Montreal. While all students voted for the president, the two vice-presidents were elected only by their own language group.[8] From its inception, the SGA pushed for a greater level of self-government, demanding control over the association's finances, and a tribunal to preside over student discipline. In the yearbook, the *Laurentiana*, produced by the association in 1963, the SGA president stated: "We must ask that where students' interests are concerned, that we must be heard, we must ask that we be consulted, we must ask that our ideas be taken into account."[9]

At the time Laurentian was established, undergraduates at Canadian universities were closely regulated, and university presidents and deans took it as their responsibility to act *in loco parentis* when monitoring students' moral and social behaviour. Administrators assumed that all young people, and especially young women, needed constant supervision to prevent misconduct such as premarital sex, drinking, gambling, or vandalism. Rules in university residences were stringent, requiring students to sign in and out, respect curfews, restrict their visiting hours, and, for women, attend all social events suitably chaperoned.[10] University students were there not only to learn, but to have their characters formed along lines suitable for future leadership roles in society.

Among the officers of Laurentian's first administration, rooted in the Jesuit educational tradition of Sacred Heart College, this assumption was perhaps more strongly pronounced than at Canada's larger universities, many of which, by 1960, had already begun to ease the rules for student behaviour. Fr. Bouvier, Laurentian's first president and incumbent head of the University of Sudbury, had been critical of Fr. Ferland, the first dean of Arts and Sciences, for laxity in the regulation of student dress, insisting that male students attend class wearing white shirts, ties, and jackets. Even after Bouvier's departure, however, the Laurentian Faculty Council followed a strict student dress code, emphatically declaring in 1962: "Coats and ties are required. Windbreakers and open shirts are not to be tolerated."[11] Sober dress was particularly stressed during convocation ceremonies at the Sudbury High School auditorium, where men were instructed to wear "a suit dark in colour with a tie of appropriate colour," while young ladies were to "wear dresses of a light colour (preferably white) with light coloured shoes."[12] In the classroom, students were forbidden to smoke, eat, or drink, and were required to observe the rules of courtesy "by punctual attendance and proper decorum."[13]

The first dean of men, Maurice Regimbal, was appointed in 1960, with the responsibility of supervising all student activities. The board executive decided against appointing a separate dean of women on the grounds that each college would be hiring deans of residence following the move to the new campus. Regimbal's title soon was changed to dean of students to reflect the co-educational nature of his job. In spite of the SGA's request for more control over student discipline, the university established a Court of Discipline, consisting entirely of administrative officers.

In these early years, female students at Laurentian represented a minority of the undergraduate population, and their social roles remained traditional. In 1966, for example, male students outnumbered female students by nearly four to one: the full-time enrolment was 1,111 students, of whom 850 were male and 261 female.[14] The executive of the Students' General Association and the staff of the student newspaper, *Lambda*, were almost entirely male, and in all public matters, the voice of the student body at Laurentian was dominated by young men. Fr. Bouvier had set the tone in his presidential message of 1960: "Laurentian is born, a new student

STUDENTS DEMONSTRATING THE DRESS CODE, 1965 | While other campuses in Canada had eased restrictions about student dress codes by the 1960s, Laurentian's first president insisted that men should wear white shirts, ties, and jackets to attend classes.

body is born, a new spirit is born and a new generation of men is born. The Laurentian men."[15]

Even as the undergraduates as a whole became politicized at the end of the decade, female students continued to play a secondary role in university governance throughout this period. The "coed" image projected by the media both on and off campus reinforced the view, common since the 1920s, that most young women attended university to achieve social rather than academic goals. To supplement the annual frosh, homecoming, and carnival queen competitions, *Lambda* instituted a weekly item called "Wench of the Week" (or "Poulette de la Semaine" as it appeared in *Le Lambda*), displaying photos of attractive young coeds caught off-guard by the staff photographer.[16]

The views of early Laurentian students toward sex and marriage roles were conservative. Inspired by the recently publicized Kinsey report on human sexuality, *Lambda* conducted its own "sex survey" in November 1963. The question, "Do you approve of pre-marital sex relations?" received a positive response from 48 per cent of the males and 20 per cent of the females. This decisively "no" reaction to the question of pre-marital sex, particularly from the women, led *Lambda* to wonder whether Laurentian students could boast a higher level of morality, or in fact could instead be considered prudes.[17]

Sports formed an increasingly central part of student identity at Laurentian. In 1962, dean of students Maurice Regimbal was appointed the first director of athletics. The earliest intramural sports available for student participation were football, hockey, basketball, volleyball, badminton, tennis, curling, and golf. Before the completion of the first phase of the physical education building on the new campus in April 1965, Laurentian athletes had to make use of different facilities in the city: the YMCA, Sudbury Arena, Sudbury High School, and Lockerby Composite School. Regimbal's office, appropriately, was located in rented rooms above the DeMarco sports store on Elgin Street.[18] Beginning in the spring of 1962, the university held an annual sports banquet to honour the top intercollegiate and intramural athletes.

Laurentian's intercollegiate sports teams needed a unique nickname, and after two years of debate, the name Voyageurs was unveiled at the annual dinner in March 1964. Other suggestions had been Micmacs, Laurentian Shield, Couriers, Sabres, Cavaliers, and Meteors. Voyageurs was selected because it conveyed a sense of Northern Ontario's history and culture, and, perhaps most importantly, because it required no translation. For the university president, Stanley Mullins, the choice also was idealistic. He explained at the banquet that the name "has an extra meaning for us, not only for the connotation of blazing trails into the unknown, but also because the voyageurs depended so entirely on one another for their progress and their well-being."[19] The new nickname was not accepted immediately, as some students complained that 'Voyageur' did not denote an athletic team. Equally controversial were the crest and the bright gold blazers designed for the Voyageur varsity teams. The crest – a bearded, touque-wearing Voyageur – was unveiled as the official Laurentian athletic symbol at the annual banquet in 1965 to an unreceptive audience. Still, by the spring of 1965, the *Sudbury Star* was able to report that Laurentian students were now proud of their nickname, and most had come around to thinking that the eye-catching gold blazers were at least distinctive. The "shaveless hero" crest, however, had to wait longer for full acceptance.

In April 1965, the new athletics building – later named the Benjamin Avery Physical Education Centre – was officially opened. The controversial Voyageur crest, in spite of its negative reception a few weeks before, was painted prominently in the centre of the new gymnasium floor.[20] Work was still underway on the playing fields and tennis courts, which were ready for use the following year. Due to financial constraints, the full range of planned athletic facilities, including the outdoor track and the addition housing the Olympic-sized pool, were not completed until 1974.[21]

Maurice Regimbal recognized the importance of athletics in creating a sense of collegiate spirit among students at the nascent university, as well as encouraging good community relations. In November 1963, he organized Laurentian's first pep rally preceding a varsity hockey game at the Sudbury arena which featured the enthusiasm of Laurentian's newly-formed pep band and cheerleading squad. Apart from the cheerleaders, who attended all the home games for the hockey and basketball teams, and often did the decorating for athletic dances, interest in varsity games among students fell off dramatically after the first year.[22]

In the first decade of sport at Laurentian, men's hockey emerged as its strongest team, winning the Ontario Intercollegiate Athletic Association (OIAA) championships every year from 1963–1964 to 1970–1971. The men's volleyball and basket-

VOYAGEUR HOCKEY – OVER THE BOARDS | In the 1960s, men's hockey at Laurentian established itself as the strongest varsity team of the decade, winning the Ontario Intercollegiate Athletic Association (OIAA) championships every year from 1963–1964 to 1970–1971.

ball teams also quickly put Laurentian sports on the provincial map, achieving the distinction of winning both OIAA championships in 1962–1963. In 1969–1970, the men's basketball team again won the OIAA championship, and the following year, in 1970–1971, men's volleyball regained the provincial championship. Compared to hockey, volleyball and basketball, men's soccer initially got off to a slow start until the arrival of Greg Zorbas as player/coach in 1969. Under Zorbas' rigorous training, the team gained its first OIAA championship in 1969–1970, and for the next two years.[23]

Laurentian students eagerly anticipated the university's move to the new Ramsey Lake Road campus in the fall of 1964. During the first four years, students had found it difficult to establish the variety of student activities, clubs, or societies normally associated with undergraduate culture. In particular, lacking designated student space or communal areas, students tended to be isolated within their individual colleges, rarely coming into contact with others outside of class. The colleges hosted regular dances for students and their dates at Halloween and Christmas, or special theme nights such as Huntington's "Beatnik Party," held in December 1962 at "The Morgue."[24] Beginning in the spring of 1961, students participated in an annual formal banquet and graduation ball, held initially at the Cassio Hotel's Venetian Room and then in the Great Hall after the move to the new campus. Student leaders complained about their cramped downtown office space, and looked forward to the move to the new campus. "Next year," *Lambda* wrote excitedly in January 1964, "we become a university in every sense of the word. We doff the garb of a second-rate, disjointed institution, and assume a physical aspect fully indicative of what must be the most important cultural concern in the North."[25]

STUDENTS IN THE BOWLING ALLEY | Moving to the new Ramsey Lake Road campus in 1964, students quickly and aptly nicknamed the first-floor hallway of the Arts building 'the bowling alley.'

On the first day of classes, October 8, 1964, the students were thrilled by their new "dazzling, mud-infested campus."[26] The SGA was allocated a suite of rooms on the second floor of the Library (later the Parker) building consisting of a main lobby area, lounge and two small offices, one for the president and the other shared by the two vice-presidents. The university attracted a record enrolment of almost 300 new students, and with a total student population of only 556, the first-year students – adorned in the mandatory blue beanies of frosh week – greatly outnumbered returning sophomores and seniors as they congregated in the Arts building corridor instantly nicknamed "the bowling alley."[27]

Students could now eat together, either ordering a full meal in the formal dining room in the Great Hall (although they could not sit at the 'High Table' reserved for senior administrators and faculty), or a quick soup and sandwich downstairs in the cafeteria. Both were run by the franchise Versafoods, which provided food services to universities across Canada. In 1964, students could purchase a full dinner of roast turkey, coffee, and dessert for under a dollar. Laurentian students, however, were used to a far greater selection in the downtown restaurants, and during the first few weeks complained repeatedly that the cafeteria prices were too high.[28] These early protests established what would prove to be an enduring grievance among the students over the quality and price of cafeteria food. In 1966, students protested again, this time against President Mullins' decision to restrict seating in the dining hall to those purchasing a full meal, and two years later, the students organized a boycott of the cafeteria to demand higher quality and lower prices.[29] Plans for a separate student centre – ambitiously named the Campus Centre – were underway by 1967, but were delayed and then eventually shelved in favour of adding an extension to the third floor of the Parker building, something that did not happen until the 1990s.

FIRST-YEAR STUDENT PARTICIPATING IN FROSH WEEK, 1962 | During frosh week first-year students were subjected to various humiliating demands from senior students, which they obeyed to avoid the consequence of appearing in kangaroo court. Note the distinctive 'beanie' hat that all frosh were required to wear.

Once firmly established on the new campus, Laurentian students were able to fully develop the traditions of undergraduate life. Each fall they were welcomed back to the university with banquets and dances. The homecoming weekend in October, featuring a hockey or football game, ended with the crowning of a new homecoming queen. Winter brought ice sculptures and dances at the carnival festival, and the crowning of the carnival queen. The students formed clubs and associations to encourage social interaction, such as the drama society, the chess club, and the curling league, as well as program-based groups like the history society, which was started in 1965 to promote student life within the department.

Prominent among the original student activities at Laurentian was frosh week, a foundation of undergraduate culture inherited from nineteenth-century men's universities such as Toronto and McGill, when first-year students were ushered into the university by ritualized forms of humiliation. Throughout the 1960s, both frosh and freshettes were required to identify themselves by wearing bright blue hats and outrageous clothing, and to head downtown to shine shoes, provide cigarettes and gum for senior students on demand, and, if very unlucky or rebellious, undergo the trials of kangaroo court. "This is the time of year when Sudbury more closely resembles a university town, than the nickel mining city," the *Sudbury Star* commented in September 1966.[30] The penalties dealt out by kangaroo court could include, for male students, being put into the stocks and having the letter "L" shaved onto their scalps; for female students, being roughly shampooed with mustard. The highlight of the week was the crowning of yet another pageant winner, the Laurentian Frosh Queen, at the frosh dance usually held at the Mine, Mill Hall.[31]

As at most universities, the regulation of student behaviour fell mainly to the residences. During the downtown years, supervision had been difficult because students lived independently in boarding houses and private residences. The construction of student residences on the new campus allowed university administrators a much closer view of student interaction and behaviour. The first student residences opened at Thorneloe and Huntington in 1964, followed by those of the University of Sudbury in 1966 and University College in 1970. During the early 1970s, the single students and married student residences were added to the complex. The University of Sudbury had the strictest rules regulating contact between male and female students, and it appointed a dean of women to monitor the behaviour of female students living in residence.[32]

At Huntington, a residence council was established to preside over questions of student conduct and the operation of the residences. Visiting privileges were restricted to students in second year or higher, or over twenty-one years of age, and guests were only allowed to enter rooms during specific posted visiting hours, and after they signed the guest book. While infringements such as repeated excessive noise or disregard for visiting hours were dealt with by the student-run house committee, any action concerning expulsion had to be referred to the residence council.[33] Residence rules were more stringent for women than for men. At Huntington, for example, the dean of residence in 1965, Dr. Mary Hinde, declared that female students were limited to one late date a week. "Does this rule apply to the men? – No," she explained nonchalantly. "For this purpose the two residences are separate."[34] In all the residences, sexual activity was strictly forbidden. At the University of Sudbury, this included married couples, as two students discovered in 1969, when they were asked to leave the residence after their marriage, even though they each maintained separate rooms.[35] For all Laurentian students, serious charges of misconduct were brought before the university court of discipline, on which there was no student representation.

As the percentage of French-speaking students declined during the decade, the issue of preserving bilingualism and biculturalism became a lightning rod for activism among Francophone undergraduates. Early in the university's history, these students took on an increasingly political role within the larger student body over the issue of French-language rights, on campus and beyond. In 1964, students organized l'Association des étudiants Canadiens-Français du nord-Ontario, and petitioned the Royal Commission on Bilingualism and Biculturalism for French high schools in Ontario. Over the next few years, their activism within the university took different forms: protesting the fact that student cards were issued in English only, campaigning for bilingual signs on campus, and creating a biweekly French program, "Votre Université vous parle," on local television.[36] In 1965, following the report of a special committee on bilingualism, the Board of Governors approved a number of recommendations designed to strengthen bilingualism at the university, including the appointment of a director "to encourage participation by students in activities which cross language lines and tend to bridge the cultural gulf."[37] Due to financial reasons, however, this position was never created.

Tensions over the issue of bilingualism were deeply embedded in the foundations of the new university, and uneasy relations between Francophone and Anglophone students shaped undergraduate culture at Laurentian during its early

years. "Do the French agitators at Laurentian fail to realize that their cause is not only hopeless but also fruitless?" one Anglophone student wrote in 1962. "Do they not see that this extreme Pro-French feeling has to die out at Laurentian if Laurentian is to exist united[?]"[38]

Until 1965, *Lambda* was published bilingually, with contributions printed in either French or English, a compromise that neither language group found satisfactory. English-speaking students objected to what they saw as the disproportionate amount of French content promoted by a "Pro-Français" editorial staff, while Francophone students protested the increasing dominance of English in all aspects of university life. In 1965, the newspaper began publishing two separately edited versions, *Lambda* and *Le Lambda*. *Le Lambda* immediately adopted an editorial position critical of the university administration, and advocating more complete bilingualism at Laurentian.[39] On the other hand, in March 1966, a *Lambda* editorial criticized the activism of Francophone students, accusing them of "passionate fanaticism" in their campaign to ensure bilingual signs on washroom doors. "It is going to take a lot of extremely hard and long work by every single member of the French section to preserve their language and culture at Laurentian," the editorial concluded pessimistically. "I must be honest. I feel that the task set before the French of Northern Ontario is impossible."[40]

Until the late sixties, the language issue overshadowed other student concerns. Apart from references to the Quiet Revolution in Quebec, Francophone campus politics focused on the internal bilingualism question, and were slow to reflect a sustained interest in political issues beyond the university such as the civil rights movement or the Vietnam War. Similarly, among English-speaking students, only a small minority exhibited the larger concerns beginning to mobilize their counterparts at other universities. After a lecture on apartheid in South Africa received a poor turnout in January 1965, one student wrote in *Lambda* that the parochial view of French-English relationships had produced a group of ostriches with their heads in the sand, so engrossed by petty arguments over the signs on washroom doors that they were unaware of the crucial problems facing the world. "Laurentian University is too great to be contained within the smallness of its bilingual problem," the article stated. "We need to be made acutely aware of what lies outside our narrow boundaries."[41] Yet the issue of Francophone rights could also strike an early chord of sympathy with English-speaking students who wished to break from British colonial attitudes and pursue a more independent Canadian nationalism. At a Halloween dance held at the International Hotel in November 1962, for example, a group of French and English students remained seated during the playing of "God Save the Queen," and then stood up to sing "O Canada" together, unaccompanied by the orchestra, while the musicians packed up their instruments.[42]

The first issue to spark widespread support and unite all students was not apartheid or university governance, but the creation of a more autonomous social space on campus, specifically, a student pub. In 1967, the SGA began a campaign to establish a privately run pub for students on campus, to be named the Nag's Head. Far from promoting student alcoholism, *Lambda* argued, a campus pub would reduce drinking by discouraging students from attending commercial beer halls and hotels in Sudbury. The plan received the backing of faculty members and local businessmen who formed a committee to promote the project with the Board of Governors. In the fall, the SGA president distributed a letter to all faculty members, urging them to participate in an upcoming student rally on behalf of the pub: "There is a definite need at Laurentian for a congenial atmosphere where students may associate with their peers and where faculty and students may 'relax, talk, sing and find pleasure in good company.'"[43] In November, more than 700 students rallied at Memorial Park in downtown Sudbury to indicate their support for the Nag's Head. The board tentatively approved the idea, and initially proposed that the pub be located in the new campus centre, then in the early planning stages.[44] The building of a separate campus centre, however, was delayed and eventually shelved, and the Nag's Head was never opened. Instead of a privately run pub, after 1971, the SGA began operating its own pub on campus, the Cul de Sac, later named the Voyageur.

Following the Nag's Head demonstrations, the SGA adopted a more overtly political role, and Laurentian students, English- and French-speaking, began to identify their own concerns with those of the international student movement that was sweeping through North American and European universities. As other historians have documented, the Canadian student movement prompted activist groups on many campuses to challenge the *in loco parentis* authority of administrators and demand greater student representation within the governing structure of their universities. Student activists often recognized themselves as participants in national or global movements for social change, and their insistence on a voice within their own universities was accompanied by a growing sense of responsibility to respond to injustice in society.[45]

STUDENTS IN NAG'S HEAD DEMONSTRATION, 1967 | In the fall of 1967, 700 students marched in a downtown demonstration to insist upon the creation of a proposed campus pub, to be named 'Nag's Head.' That proposal did not materialize because of delays in the construction of student centre, but since 1971 the SGA has operated its own pub on campus, originally called the Cul de Sac, then the Voyageur, and later still, The Pub Downunder.

During the first decade of its existence, Laurentian was managed closely by the Board of Governors, and most of the daily administrative details came under the direct supervision of the board executive and the president. This administrative structure marginalized not only students, but also faculty and other levels of the administration. As students began to articulate their demands for representation and consultation in university governance, they found faculty to be useful allies in their campaign against the university Senate.[46]

In 1968, the SGA initiated the first in a series of student protests that, in concert with the activities of Senate and the Laurentian University Faculty Association, would culminate in a major revamping of the university's governance. In March 1968, the Board of Governors attempted to amend the *Laurentian University Act* via a private members bill in the Ontario legislature. Although the amendments were housekeeping matters, the board had not consulted with Senate, the faculty, or students, and the SGA launched a protest against what it termed "this closed-shop type of decision-making."[47] In particular, the students objected to the fact that changes were proposed to the membership of the court of discipline without adding student representation. The SGA organized a student rally, prepared a brief, and sent a delegation to present it in Toronto at Queen's Park. In the bilingual brief to the government, the SGA stated: "It is indeed regretful and frustrating that the three major bodies within the University, namely the Administration, the Faculty, and the S.G.A.L.U., are only able to function *alongside* each other and not *together* in a cohesive manner for the betterment of the University."[48] After a two-hour debate, the parliamentary committee voted not to report the bill, and instructed the board not to bring it back without the appropriate consultation process having been done.

Clearly annoyed by the students' actions, President Mullins informed *The Thorne*, a student newspaper at Thorneloe, that the SGA should have communicated their grievances with the administration before going to the legislature. "Laurentian's image suffered from the resulting publicity," Mullins told *The Thorne*.[49] In the summer of 1968, the board reluctantly acceded to Senate's demands to launch an inquiry into university governance, and created the presidential advisory committee (PAC) on consultative structures and procedures.[50]

The students' success in turning back the board's amendments in 1968 represented a general politicization of undergraduate culture at Laurentian, diminished French-English differences, and coincided with a radicalization of the student movement across the country. Marked by militant student protests in France, Italy, West Germany, and Czechoslovakia, as well as in the United States, the winter of 1968–1969 witnessed student unrest at universities all across Canada.[51] In November 1968, a student occupation of four floors of the administration building at Simon Fraser University in Burnaby, British Columbia, was broken up by the RCMP, who entered the building in the early hours of the morning and made 114 arrests. There was also controversy at the Regina campus of the University of Saskatchewan. Following the publication of an allegedly obscene picture in the student newspaper, the *Carillon*, the administration attempted to censor the newspaper. At a mass meeting in January 1969, Regina students voted to censure the Board of Governors, and in February, a group of them disrupted a board meeting and harassed members attempting to leave. Also in January at l'Université de Moncton in New Brunswick, resurgent Acadian nationalism prompted Francophone students to boycott classes and occupy a university building. That same month, students at Sir George Williams University in Montreal occupied the faculty club and computer centre for nearly two weeks. Angered by the board's delay in responding to charges of racism against a faculty member, the students eventually vandalized the cafeteria and set fire to the computer centre, causing nearly $2 million in damage.[52]

Throughout the winter, these and other such tumultuous events were reported eagerly in the pages of *Lambda* and *Le Lambda*.[53] Student leaders at Laurentian adopted the rhetoric that characterized the movement across the continent; urging young people to be self-aware, and to link their own personal fulfillment to the larger goals of social change.[54] "This is the year of Student Power," a *Lambda* editorial announced in the September 1968 issue. "The tools for improving Laurentian are at hand. It is now up to us, students, faculty and administration to take these tools in hand and create the ideal academic community." In the same issue, the SGA encouraged students to take action for reform. Citing the success at Queen's Park in March, SGA President Etienne St-Aubin predicted a new political orientation for the student association. "[W]e are trying to create a dynamic, aggressive, democratic and positive SGA," he wrote. "The days of the SGA as another department in this university, as a glorified Student Services Corporation are hopefully numbered."[55]

In October, the SGA sent two delegates to attend the Canadian Union of Students (CUS) congress in Guelph. In an interview with the *Sudbury Star*, St-Aubin stressed that the student movement was committed to achieving university reform, but only through non-violent means. "Student power is human power," he reassured the *Star*.[56] That fall, the SGA also sent a letter to faculty members inviting them to communicate openly with the students on equal terms. The letter stated: "[W]e're maybe naïve enough or optimistic enough to think that things *can* be changed, knowing full well that things *must* be changed."[57] The mood that winter was aptly caught by *Lambda*'s self-effacing headline in November: "This University Belongs to the Student! Dig It. But Don't Worry Mullins, He Doesn't Have the Guts to Take it."[58]

Although cooperating with their Anglophone colleagues, for many Francophone students, the issue of university governance was inseparable from their central concern over the survival of French culture at Laurentian. As a more broadly based student movement began to emerge over the winter, Francophone students worked to direct the new activism of the SGA toward the cause of Franco-Ontarian rights. In October 1968, a group of them prepared a brief for the Board of Governors, in which they leveled scathing criticisms of the current state of bilingualism, and demanded immediate steps to increase French enrolment and preserve the use of the French language within the university administration.[59] Although criticized by some Anglophone students, the brief was endorsed by the editors of both *Lambda* and *Le Lambda,* and the SGA president made a personal appeal for unity on the issue. "The topic of bilingualism at Laurentian University is one that arouses deep emotions and reactions," St-Aubin wrote in *Lambda* in November. "These emotions usually lead to words and acts of hatred and bigotry, mainly because of the heritage of hatred and bigotry that many individuals possess."[60] A few days later, SGA council passed a motion supporting the brief in principle to "insure the survival of bilingualism at Laurentian University."[61]

The students again exercised their new political strength in December 1968. After nearly a year of lobbying, the SGA was informed that students would be given six seats on Senate, and two seats on the Committee on Bilingualism.[62] By the end of term, it seemed that Laurentian students had successfully gained a voice in university governance without any of the disruption that had characterized the student movements at Moncton, Regina, or Simon Fraser. "[R]eform should and can be instituted through civilized discussions and improved communications," one student told *Lambda*. "If reforms such as those called for in the S.G.A. Brief to the Presidential Advisory Committee are instituted then Laurentian can boast, and boast proudly, in having achieved its 'quiet revolution'!"[63] This hopeful attitude would be short-lived.

Buoyed by their achievements over the previous winter, the students at Laurentian had underestimated the resiliency of the existing governing structure. Faced with demands for change, the board's primary response was to maintain the status quo. During the winter of 1969–1970, the students again confronted the administration, and student activism at Laurentian became more radical. The first incident occurred in October 1969 when students and faculty joined together to criticize a brief prepared by the president, Stanley Mullins, submitted to the Provincial Committee on University Affairs. Claiming that Mullins' brief had been written without consultation with department heads, faculty, or students, the SGA organized an "awareness day teach-in" on Monday, October 20, to discuss university problems. The mass teach-in attracted a huge crowd of more than 1,200 students, so the meeting had to be moved from a lecture hall to the cafeteria. Mullins did not attend the teach-in, and after several hours of waiting for the president to arrive, about 200 students climbed the stairs to his eleventh-floor office and chanted angrily for his appearance. The events of what *Lambda* termed "Wake-up Monday," ended only after Mullins came out of his office and agreed to answer the many questions directed at him by both students and faculty.[64]

The following week, another large crowd of students gathered, this time to confront the governors over the question of student representation on the board. The presidential advisory committee, appointed the year before to inquire into university governance, had recommended that seven non-voting members be added to the Board of Governors, including two elected by the SGA and one Extension Students' General Association representative (ESGA). The board executive rejected this proposal, and offered instead to appoint only four new members – including one SGA representative – to the board. On October 31, at a meeting of the full board, about 250 students again occupied the lounge outside, disrupting the proceedings with loud chanting and clapping. The president of SGA addressed the crowd, telling the students: "We have to affirm to the board of governors that we want a democratic university. We want a voice at all levels."[65] Late in the day, after the crowd had dwindled, the meeting recessed and the chairman announced that the board had approved the original proposal to appoint seven new members as non-voting observers, including the three student representatives.[66]

The culmination of student radicalism at Laurentian occurred in April 1970, when students staged a ten-day occupation of the Great Hall, and the Senate, sympathetic to their demands, effectively shut down the business of the university. As Matt Bray has discussed in a previous chapter, over the winter of 1969–1970, a group of faculty and students on Senate systematically began to oppose the president on a number of issues, and in January, they had started a campaign to force Mullins' dismissal, circulating a resolution of non-confidence around the university.[67] The board executive took a firm stand against the growing pressure to remove Mullins, and at its meeting on March 18, adopted two motions that outraged Senate: first, to reject a Senate appeal to add faculty and students to the finance committee; and second, to reject the president's request for a leave of absence.[68]

Senate responded quickly. At a meeting the following day, it passed one vote of non-confidence in Mullins, and another in the executive.[69] The SGA followed this lead, passing their own resolution expressing non-confidence in the president and the Board of Governors: "Be it resolved that we now question their competence in the administration of the University, in view of their failing effectiveness in the present situation. We no longer have confidence in this body and now hope that further action be taken by the Department of University Affairs."[70] The SGA forwarded this resolution to the provincial government.[71]

The tense situation erupted on April 1, 1970, when the students held a mass meeting in the cafeteria to protest the actions of the board. After the meeting unanimously resolved to support Senate, the editor of *Lambda* suddenly announced that he was tired of the bureaucracy, and called for a sit-in in the lobby outside the cafeteria. As he left, followed by about 20 students, the SGA president pledged his support, and the sit-in began. On April 2, Senate took the extreme measure of formally endorsing the student occupation of the building, giving the board an ultimatum that if it did not agree to a joint meeting with Senate to seek a solution to the situation, Senate would call an academic recess and suspend all academic activities the following day. The students appealed for support to the community, and student leaders consulted union officials in Sudbury. That same morning, the students started picketing businesses owned by members of the board executive, and distributed copies of their position paper to workers at the entrance to Inco plants. On the evening of April 3, Senate went ahead with its threat, called an academic recess, and closed down the university.[72] "In a situation believed unprecedented in Canadian university history," the Toronto *Globe and Mail* reported, "the students and the faculty of Laurentian are allied against the board and the president, Stanley Mullins."[73]

The conflict was now at an impasse, with the board executive and president on one side, and the Senate, students, and faculty on the other. Final exams were suspended, students dragged sleeping bags and pillows into the cafeteria lobby, and the academic work of the university ground to a halt. Speaking on behalf of the students, the editor of *Lambda* told the *Globe and Mail* that they would continue the occupation until the board confirmed Mullins' resignation, established a presidential search committee with student and faculty members, and made a commitment that the university's governing structure would be reformed.[74] The board backed down, and agreed to hold an open joint meeting with Senate to discuss the crisis. Following several days of negotiations, the board and Senate reached an agreement, and Senate called off the recess on April 10. After ten days, the students gathered up their cushions and sleeping bags and ended their occupation of the lobby.[75] The board voted to accept President Mullins' offer to resign effective July 1, 1970.

In sharp contrast to the occupations at Simon Fraser and Sir George Williams universities, throughout the ten day sit-in at Laurentian, the police had not intervened. Within the community, the students' protest struck a chord in keeping with Sudbury's tradition of labour activism. Union members supported the students'

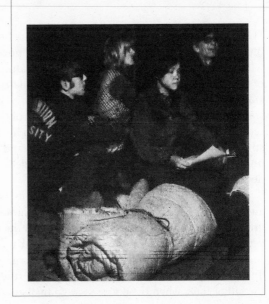

STUDENT SIT-IN IN THE
GREAT HALL, 1970

picket of local businesses owned by board members, Copper Cliff Dairies and
A&W donated food to the students occupying the lobby, and the mayor allowed
his car to be used to distribute leaflets.[76] The students and Senate gained a significant victory: Mullins resigned, the board agreed to add student representation to
the finance committee, and to give students, through Senate, representation on
the search committee for a new president.[77] During an orientation assembly that
September, the SGA president proudly welcomed the new first-year students to
"the Berkeley of Sudbury," alluding to the Berkeley campus in California, then the
epicenter of student radicalism in the United States.[78]

Laurentian's crisis in governance was not yet over, however, and in the fall of
1970, students had one final showdown with the administration. Following the success of the sit-in during the spring, the returning Laurentian students continued to
demonstrate their unity and politicization. After salary negotiations broke down
between the board executive and faculty, on September 23, the SGA held a mass
meeting of students and endorsed a Senate motion censuring the board. By October 1, Senate had declared the situation intolerable and, once again invoked an academic recess, shutting down the normal work of the university.[79] Although some
faculty attempted to continue teaching, the majority of students supported Senate
and boycotted classes. On October 6, four busloads of Laurentian students travelled to Queen's Park, where the SGA president presented to the Minister of Education, William Davis, a brief outlining the problems at Laurentian, and a petition
calling for government mediation.[80]

After meeting with Davis on October 7, Senate passed a motion at his request
ending the recess as of October 13, its minutes recording "a gesture of our willingness to assist in a resolution of the University problem."[81] Davis then appointed

J.G. Hagey, president emeritus of the University of Waterloo, to undertake an inquiry into the situation on behalf of the government.[82] Over the following winter, Hagey made several extended visits to the campus, meeting with members of the board and with representatives from Senate, the faculty association, and the students. In his report, submitted in March 1971, Hagey supported the concept of shifting administrative power from the Board of Governors to a Senate that represented the interests of faculty and students. In his introductory comments, Hagey stressed that the relations between students and governing bodies in Ontario's universities had changed, that students were demanding and obtaining a voice in developing university plans and policies.[83]

The period of radicalization at the end of the sixties temporarily united French and English students in a cause that became of primary importance to both groups: gaining a political role for students in the governing structure of the university. During the early stages of the student movement at Laurentian, French-speaking students provided leadership by drawing on their tradition of activism. Their success in mobilizing the Anglophone student body was demonstrated in the fall of 1968, when the entire SGA council endorsed the brief on bilingualism. For Francophone students, the issue of university governance was linked closely to their concern for the protection of French culture and language among the growing Anglophone majority. As a more broadly based movement developed over the winter of 1968, Francophone students took the initiative and allied the new radicalism of the SGA to their ongoing campaign for Franco-Ontarian rights.

In the decades to follow, the unity of the radical years could not be sustained in the face of ingrained differences that existed within the student body. While Laurentian students felt the impact of the student movement across Europe and North America, their politicization ultimately served to intensify their own unique sense of place. In 1971, the yearbook *Laurentiana* was renamed *Slag*, and dedicated to the class of 1971: "To those under the shadow of the slagheaps, to those in the north, of Laurentian and the future, a toast."[84]

9   We Know Who We Are: Exploring New Identities, 1972–1985

SARA BURKE

"We know who we are ... but who are they?"
(Cartoon, *Lambda*, September 1970)

A student cartoon published in *Lambda* in September 1970 depicted a juxtaposition of two very different figures: On one side, captioned "Us," is a young man, wearing jeans, vest, and beads, his face obscured by his tangled hair and beard; on the other side under the caption "Them," is a middle-aged man in a business suit and striped tie, his expression one of baffled frustration. The subtitle reads: "We know who we are ... but who are they?"[1] The Laurentian students who emerged from the protests of the sixties bore little resemblance to the clean-cut young men and women attending classes a decade earlier. Many students now rejected the sober, conservative images they associated with their parents; grew their hair, wore brightly coloured tie-dyed shirts and faded jeans, and listened to the new psychedelic music associated with the more permissive counterculture. This physical transformation, however, marked only part of the change that set the new generation of students apart from their predecessors. Of perhaps greater significance were the altered perceptions of the students themselves, both in relation to the university administration and to each other.

Earlier, while students had tried to circumvent university regulations, they still accepted these rules as a necessary part of the university's role *in loco parentis*. By the late 1960s, Laurentian students had begun to question the very foundation of this power. The student movement that sparked campaigns for university governance reform weakened the principle of *in loco parentis* and had a corrosive effect on students' attitudes toward figures of authority.[2] In 1968, a *Lambda* editorial angrily attacked the residence rules, which, as the newspaper pointed out, were particularly restrictive for women. "Girls in residence pay top rates for rooms," the editorial claimed, "and yet are treated like two year olds. Sign out, sign in – don't miss curfew or you catch hell and lose the rest of your late nights for the week. Childish!"[3]

Many Canadian students were no longer prepared to tolerate what they viewed as antiquated attitudes regulating sexual conduct, and some began to participate

US
We know who
we are ...

THEM
... but who
are they ?

University government.
what is happening at Laurentian

US ... AND THEM | As the
1970s dawned, student culture at
Laurentian began to reflect a new
climate of opinion that questioned
administrators' rights to restrict
the conduct of students and argued
that the university should abolish
the last vestiges of its "parental"
role in the discipline and conduct of
students.

in the more sexually permissive youth culture, defined by sex, drugs, and rock and roll.[4] For a period of time, both the newspaper and yearbook became openly provocative in their language, sexual content, and references to drug use, as though the student editors were deliberately goading the university administration into imposing censorship. Yet Laurentian officials refrained from interfering with the student press, perhaps unwilling to provoke storms of student protest. In 1968, for example, Vice-President Roland Cloutier defended *Lambda* from the board's charges that it printed "indecencies," arguing that a self-correcting system would be more effective with the editorial board than overt interference.[5]

The first indication of a drug culture among Laurentian students had come in the winter of 1967, when an article published in *Le Lambda* stated that a group of about twenty students regularly smoked marijuana, and that at one time or another, almost half the student population had tried it, usually procuring it in the Yorkville district of Toronto. President Mullins reassured the media that there was less drug use of any type by Laurentian students than by students elsewhere, but he nevertheless ordered the dean of students to look into the situation. The RCMP also started an investigation into *Le Lambda*'s report.[6]

As at other universities across North America, over the next decade, pot smoking became a common aspect of student culture at Laurentian. In a meeting in 1976, the SGA council discussed the degree to which pot was smoked openly at the Voyageur Pub, expressing concern that the pub "will one night be busted and then closed." After a long discussion about the ineffectiveness of student security, the SGA recommended that students should go outside the pub to smoke pot.[7]

The attitudes of Laurentian students mirrored those in other Canadian institutions, as a new climate of opinion began to question administrators' rights to restrict the conduct of university students. At the end of sixties, the government had appointed the Commission on Post-Secondary Education in Ontario to assess all aspects of the province's burgeoning university system. Reporting to the Davis government in 1972, the Commission made a wide range of suggestions, including Recommendation 58, which proposed that all vestiges of *in loco parentis* be abolished.[8] At Laurentian, however, university officials were still willing to enforce rules regarding student conduct, particularly in the residences. In their challenge to regulations, as in their earlier attack on university governance, the students found important allies among the faculty on Senate. In March 1972, the University of Sudbury started court action to evict three students from residence after two men were found having coffee in a woman's room at 3:00 in the afternoon. Refusing to move out of their rooms, the students received support from the SGA, which promised to underwrite all their legal expenses. Groups of students carrying placards reading, "Watch where you drink your coffee," picketed outside the University of Sudbury. Senate came down strongly in favour of the students, passing a motion deploring the recourse to legal proceedings and the lack of adequate internal procedures for resolving such conflicts. Senate then took the opportunity to endorse the Commission's Recommendation 58, condemning the practice of *in loco parentis*, and passed a further resolution urging the abolition of the 'motherhood' role by institutions in the discipline and supervision of student conduct.[9]

This new policy was confirmed in 1974, when the executive committee reported to Senate that it had decided against striking a student disciplinary review committee on the grounds that "the present policy of the University ... is not to act *in loco parentis* but to treat students as adults and hence responsible for their actions before the law."[10] Conforming to the new policy, the new single students and married student residences, which opened in the fall of 1973, had few rules, and students were expected to govern their own behaviour and interactions. Each floor of each wing had a don, a designated senior student whose main function, *Lambda* explained, "is to give inhabitants someone to go to if something goes wrong in their apartment."[11] The final end of *in loco parentis* came in 1980, when changes to the provincial *Landlord-Tenant Act* extended the same rights to students living in university residences as regular tenants in Ontario.[12]

An anti-authoritarian attitude also prompted students to reassess their behaviour toward one another, and to question some of the established traditions of student culture that now seemed liable to exploitation or abuse. Not surprisingly, one of the first targets of this new sensitivity was the ritual initiation of first-year students. In September 1969, the proceedings of kangaroo court were interrupted when a group of sympathetic upper-year students – described as "long-haired hippies" by *Lambda* – came in and sat down with the frosh, singing loudly and refusing to leave.[13] The following year, the SGA abandoned the traditional frosh week activities, banning kangaroo court and blue beanies in favour of an orientation program aimed at treating first-year students as equals.[14] In January 1973, the

SGA reformed the traditional beauty contest for the Winter Carnival to reflect changing sensibilities among students. Instead of electing a carnival queen, judges were asked to select a Mr. and Miss. Carnival pair, assessed "on the basis of their congeniality, their ability to communicate, meet people and be sociable." One of the questions asked of the participants was: "Do you think women should be treated on an equal basis with men?"[15]

For students at Laurentian, the sit-ins, pickets, and mass meetings of 1969 and 1970 represented the high point of effective politicization, and they entered the new decade with a defined role in university governance. This role was solidified in November 1970, when the Board of Governors appointed one student senator a non-voting member of the executive committee, at the heart of university government. It was not until 1986, however, that Laurentian students achieved voting representation on the board itself.[16]

Yet during the 1970s, political activism among students as a whole began to decline. In 1971, two student representatives resigned their seats on Senate, characterizing the behaviour of other senators as fractious and indecisive. The following year, *Lambda* announced that only nine nominations had been received for thirty-three vacant positions on various university committees. "Senate, with its elaborate committee system is a bulky, time-consuming organization," the SGA president told incoming students in September 1974. "However it is the supreme decision-making body here at Laurentian for all academic matters. At present, student input is nil."[17] The university president agreed. In his report of October 1975, Edward Monahan noted that most students felt no commitment at all to serve on university committees, and many student seats remained vacant throughout the year. Where former students fought for representation at this level, he claimed, their successors had "a somewhat more serious approach to study and less interest in participating in the governance of the university."[18]

Historians have argued that the youth movement of the sixties only temporarily disguised the older divisions of class, race, ethnicity, and gender, as the following decade witnessed significant challenges to constituted authority, from movements for Quebec nationalism, women's rights, and Aboriginal rights.[19] University students at Laurentian and elsewhere during the 1970s and 1980s did not become less political in temperament; rather, they started to identify themselves more specifically along lines defined by language, experience, culture, gender, and sexual orientation. Instead of one undergraduate association, there were three: the Students' General Association (SGA); the Association of Laurentian Part-time Students (ALPS), formed in 1969; and the Association des étudiant(e)s francophones (AEF), created in 1974. In addition, in 1978, the graduate students of Laurentian established the Graduate Students' Association (GSA). As well, various groups of students began to recognize their collective minority status, and to form clubs to articulate needs not adequately represented by the larger associations; these included the Women's Liberation Group (1969), the International Students' Organization (1972), the Native Students' Club (1973), and the community of gay and lesbian students (1977).[20]

Following the achievements of the student movement in gaining representation in governance in 1971, Francophone students returned the focus of their activism to securing French-language rights both within and beyond the university. In the fall of 1972, French-speaking students began producing a newspaper, *Réaction*, which, along with *Lambda,* was partially funded by the SGA. The burden of supporting two official student publications, however, put a strain on the finances of the SGA and sparked repeated clashes among the students on the editorial boards.[21] The next year, Francophone students formed an association separate from the SGA, La Maison des Francophones, to serve the needs of French-speaking students at Laurentian. In the fall of 1974, the separation became official when Francophone students held a referendum and voted in favour of the creation of an independent student association. While the SGA continued – in theory – to be a bilingual organization representing all students at Laurentian, French-speaking students formally established the separate Association des étudiant(e)s francophones. *Réaction* ceased publication after 1980, but in 1987, Francophone students revived their separate newspaper, renamed *l'Orignal déchaîné.*[22]

Adopting the tactics that had been so successful in the protests of the late sixties, Francophone students began a campaign to strengthen French rights and gain political recognition apart from the SGA.[23] They achieved some success in 1977 when the Board of Governors recognized the split among the students, and created another non-voting seat for a representative of l'AEF, alongside that of the SGA. In 1976, the SGA had allocated one of its six student Senate positions to l'AEF, and shortly afterwards, another to a representative from ALPS. Together l'AEF and the SGA formed a joint committee to run the student pub, negotiating such issues as the amount of time designated to playing French or bilingual music.[24]

Having gained a distinct and formally recognized voice in university governance, Francophone students turned their focus toward the goal of enhancing services for French-speaking students at Laurentian. In 1979, in an effort to create a nucleus for services spread throughout campus, Francophone students asked the administration to trade the existing offices of l'AEF and *Réaction*, and their lounge and cloakroom, for space on the third floor of the classroom building. When this request was refused, activists disrupted the use of the elevator in the Parker building, and for three days, occupied the eleventh floor, which housed the Governors' Lounge, the Senate chamber, and president's office.[25]

SGA members were critical of what they viewed as l'AEF's audacious demands and outdated militancy. "If nothing else, occupying the administration tower brings back visions of the good, old days of the students' movement," the SGA president wrote in *Lambda.* "It went well with Woodstock, the peace movement and Jimmy Hendrix. Unfortunately the time for this phase of our lives has come and gone."[26] Yet the tactics of l'AEF proved to be effective. University President Henry Best promised to meet with Francophone student leaders to discuss more suitable office space, and to create a better physical focus on campus for Francophone activities, but refused to allow the occupation to continue after the study break, claiming that outsiders were aggravating the situation. Following negotia-

NATIVE STUDIES |
The Native studies
program, founded in 1971,
was one of the first formal
initiatives acknowledging
the tri-cultural nature of the
Laurentian community.

tions with the administration two weeks later, the students were granted their original wish to centralize all French-language student services, as well as French courses for translation students, on the third floor of the classroom building.[27] "It was a victory for bilingualism," the president of l'AEF stated.[28]

This sense of victory was fleeting. As Guy Gaudreau discusses more fully, Francophone students became increasingly critical of Laurentian's bilingual policy, and frustrated by the limited range of French courses available. In particular, they protested the fact that the physical education and commerce departments did not offer any courses in French, that the Science Faculty and Professional Schools offered only a bare minimum, and that even Social Science and Humanities courses offered in French could be cancelled from one year to the next. By 1980, a group of Francophone faculty, students, administrators, and community representatives had formed a task force for a Franco-Ontarian University, and had started compiling statistical information to define the status of Francophone students at Laurentian. Their ultimate goal – eventually deemed financially impossible by the provincial government – was to establish a French university in Northern Ontario, either as a separate, new complex or an autonomous university within Laurentian. The student leaders of l'AEF threw their full support behind this campaign, arguing that French as a language of common usage was overshadowed by English at Laurentian, and that the bilingual policy was a failure. The Francophone university idea continued to be debated over the following decade, prompting concern among some Anglophone students that the existence of a separate French institution would inevitably drain resources and enrolments from Laurentian. In 1991, the SGA council formally declared its opposition to the establishment of a French university.[29]

Native students were another group to seek a distinct identity on campus during the 1970s. Following the release of *The White Paper* in 1969, in which the Trudeau government announced its intention to repeal the *Indian Act*, the Native nationalist movement gained force and focused attention on Aboriginal rights and the struggles of Canada's First Nations.[30] During the previous decade, the university had offered extension courses for adults from nearby Native communities, but made no attempt to accommodate Aboriginal students within the larger student population until the establishment of the department of Amerindian studies in 1971.[31]

Interest in Native studies had been fueled by the 1968 Hall-Dennis Report on Ontario's education system, which harshly criticized the existing state of federally run education for Native children and recommended the transfer, with community participation, of all federal schools on Native reserves to local school boards. The Report also suggested that at least one Ontario university set up a special institute for Canadian Indian studies. In response, Edward Newbery, the ex-president of Huntington University and a professor of religious studies at the University of Sudbury, started a seminar study group on North American Indian culture that evolved into the Institute of Indian Studies in 1970.[32] Out of this, in turn, came in 1971, the University of Sudbury's Interdepartmental Program in Amerindian-Esquimo Studies, which four years later, transformed into the department of Native studies – the first of its kind in Canada.

In 1970, the Institute of Indian Studies initiated a study of the Ojibway language, and employed six young Native people to visit First Nations communities and tape-record interviews with elders.[33] The Amerindian studies program then offered credit courses in Ojibwa, taught by Stella Kinoshameg at the University of Sudbury in the regular academic year, and on Manitoulin Island during the summer. In 1973, Native students received financial aid to pursue university education when the Donner Foundation awarded a $17,000 grant to assist Amerindian studies. Newbery, as head of the program, arranged for half of the grant to be used to support research scholarships for students studying Native languages. The following year, $7,000 in scholarships went to Native students who were attending Laurentian and conducting research on the problems of language transcription.[34]

In the early 1980s, the department enrolled students in courses on and off campus, including classes for First Nations men and women in prison in fifteen provincial and federal institutions. The latter had been facilitated by a further grant of $75,000 from the Donner Foundation in 1980 to the Native studies department to support its educational program for Native people in prison, and to provide bursaries for working students to continue to study at the university level. The goals of the program were to strengthen Native life and to offer training to future leaders by providing courses in the history, culture, and concerns of the First Nations.[35]

The first Native Students' Club at Laurentian was formed in November 1973 with a charter membership of eight Native students. Its goals were "to better orientate Native students to life at Laurentian [and] to act as a system of mutual self-support." The club also welcomed non-Native associate members, usually, but not exclusively, students in the Native studies program. Assigned space at the University of Sudbury for meetings, studying, and social activities, the club organized such events as skating parties and film viewings about Native life, and distributed a Native newspaper, *Akwesesne Notes*, on campus. In April 1975, the club sponsored a Native powwow at Laurentian.[36]

Female students also claimed a separate identity on campus. As Linda Ambrose explains later, the impact of Canada's second-wave women's movement was increasingly evident throughout the 1970s and 1980s at Laurentian. During the late 1960s, *Lambda* had reported sporadically on such controversial developments as the Pill being prescribed to female students at Western, but in general, the rise of the women's movement remained undocumented in its pages.[37]

In October 1969, Laurentian's first women's liberation meeting was held when a small group of female students got together to assess "where women are today." Topics discussed included the commercialization and degradation of women's bodies, inequality in marriage, and birth control. Significantly, the women talked about their lack of voice; how the current student movement at Laurentian had, in fact, been dominated by men. Analyzing the recent burst of activism – the teach-in, occupation of the governors' lounge, and the SGA mass meeting – the female students noted that only one or two women had ever spoken. "For one thing, women have been forced into accepting an inferior attitude – that is, to feel that their opinions are not really worth expressing."[38]

Female students recognized that their lives were very different from those of men at Laurentian, and in the 1970s, the university slowly began to respond to their concerns. In 1973, it created the presidential advisory committee (PAC) on the status of women, and in 1978, Thorneloe University founded the women's studies program. Four years later, Laurentian officials approved the university's first sexual harassment policy, and the SGA endorsed the PAC's proposal to establish a women's centre on campus to deal with harassment issues. In March 1984, *Lambda* devoted a special issue to International Women's Day, including articles on such issues as sexual harassment by professors, birth control, feminism, pornography, and women's work. That year, the women's centre was launched on Student Street in the Single Students residence, but the initiative lost momentum when its supporters graduated. It did not establish a permanent presence on campus until May 1994, when it reopened in the new student centre on the third floor of the Parker building.[39]

Gay and lesbian students at Laurentian first began to organize during the 1970s, but their efforts to raise awareness about gay rights encountered considerable hostility from the larger student population. The first gay student group in Canada had been founded at the University of Toronto in 1969, and during the early 1970s, the Canadian gay rights movement held its first public demonstrations.[40] In January 1972, *Lambda* quietly announced an upcoming conference hosted by the York University Homophile Association entitled "Sexuality and Human Rights," and invited interested persons at Laurentian to contact the organizers.[41] In 1977, at a meeting held at Laurentian, the Ontario Federation of Students (OFS) passed a resolution affirming its support for the gay movement and endorsing a thirteen-point program put forward by the Coalition for Gay Rights in Ontario. "[G]ay women and men as a group have suffered great injustice in our society and continue to be the objects of destructive sex-role attitudes and the victims of sexism and homophobia," the resolution stated. "[G]ay people have organized with the aim of overcoming oppression as gays, the attainment of equal civil rights being a first step towards this aim." Although the resolution obviously had been supported by a group of students from Laurentian, the president of the SGA distanced himself from the proceedings, telling the *Sudbury Star* that the report would damage the credibility of the OFS, and that he knew of no "gay clubs" at Laurentian.[42]

Lambda remained virtually silent on gay issues throughout the 1970s, but the newspaper gained a more critical perspective in the early 1980s, and a series of controversial articles appeared dealing with feminism, pornography, and gay rights. Even so, in 1983, after reprinting an article from Montreal criticizing homophobia at Bishop's University, the *Lambda* editor felt it necessary to defend her decision to publish material on gay rights: "As with any other minority, being subjected to violence, repression and misunderstanding, it is a responsibility of *Lambda* to inform its readers about important developments."[43] In 1985 and 1986, *Lambda* consciously risked a backlash from "a particular sector of our readership" by devoting entire issues to gay and lesbian topics. Urging students to confront homophobia, an editorial argued that society had to recognize the rights of gays and lesbians to come out of the closet "without fear of mental, emotional or physical abuse."[44]

During the early 1990s, members of the gay, lesbian, and bisexual community of Laurentian pushed the student associations and newspapers to recognize, educate, and raise awareness about homophobia. In 1993, the newly-formed Association of Gays and Lesbians of Laurentian – later Pride@LU – started a regular column in *Lambda*, "Out and About Gay," to encourage open discussion about being gay in today's society, and by the next year it had a membership of about 40. Following the example of other universities, in the spring of 1995, the Laurentian Counselling and Resource Centre organized "Jeans Day," encouraging all members of the university community to wear jeans to challenge discrimination and show their support for equity for gay, lesbians, and bisexuals on campus.[45] A flyer announcing a meeting in November 1995, called the *Gay and Lesbian News*, conveyed the same message: "Who are we ... [?] Brothers, sisters, students, aunts, uncles, classmates, teachers, friends, neighbours, athletes, non-athletes!, mothers, fathers."[46]

The campaigns of Laurentian students to create a more tolerant environment were waged against a backdrop of growing financial restraint and meager accommodation on campus. During the early 1970s, declining enrolments produced revenue shortfalls and operating deficits.[47] The decline continued throughout the decade, and it was not until the early 1980s, when the full-time student population rose above 3,000, that Laurentian began a gradual recovery. With the realization that retention rates were low, and that many northern students were choosing to go to other universities, the SGA repeatedly pressed the administration to provide improved facilities for students. In particular, the lack of a student centre – promised since the early 1960s – became a growing issue. In the late 1960s, plans had been drawn up for a Campus Centre to house the proposed Nag's Head Pub, as well

STUDENT PEP RALLY

as social space and offices for the SGA and *Lambda*. The project had been delayed, and then dropped outright from the five-year plan announced in the summer of 1970. Instead of a separate centre, students were promised temporary space in the new addition to the Parker building.[48]

The SGA was determined to improve student services, and after months of intensive lobbying, in September 1971, it gained control of a former second-floor cafeteria known as Cafe Robot. Two or three nights a week, Cafe Robot became the home to a temporary pub, the Cul de Sac (later named the Voyageur), and students used the space during the day as a lounge, lunch room, card room, and study hall. That same month, the SGA opened an on-campus store, La Boutede, also on the second floor of the Parker building, which sold confectionary items as well as record albums and campus crested clothing.[49] La Boutede initially promised to be a money-maker, yielding a net profit of $4,300 in its first three months, but soon both the store and the pub struggled to break even, most of the proceeds going into salaries and operating costs. In 1975, the SGA negotiated a permanent license with the Liquor Control Board of Ontario, allowing the association to put the venture on firmer footing, hire a manager, and move to larger, permanent quarters in the lower cafeteria, located downstairs from the Great Hall.[50]

In the fall of 1973, the opening of the new student residence complex containing the Single Students and the Married Students residences provided an opportunity to designate additional space for students' recreational and social activities. Student Street, located on the ground level of the Single Students building, housed a grocery store, a clothing store, and a restaurant, and the administration announced plans to provide space for recreational facilities, such as card rooms, and to relocate the SGA and *Lambda* offices from the library tower to a new build-

GRADUATION,
CIRCA 1972 |
Convocation ceremony
at the Sudbury arena

ing.[51] In 1982, the SGA committed its membership to contributing to the "Lauren-tian Fund," a student levy of an additional $20 per year, per student, for the next five years to help pay for student bursaries and for the construction of the Campus Centre building. In the end, the plan for a separate building was scrapped, and a centre for students would not materialize until the extension to the third floor of the Parker building was completed in 1992.[52]

The fall of 1971 marked a turning point for Voyageur athletics when Laurentian became a member of the newly formed Ontario University Athletic Association (OUAA), joining fifteen universities from Ontario and Quebec. The new league provided the Voyageurs with tougher competition. In the old Ontario Intercollegi-ate Athletic Association, Laurentian teams had played against those from other small, provincial universities such as Waterloo Lutheran (now Wilfrid Laurier); after 1971 the teams competed in a loop that included the universities of York, Toronto, Carleton, Ottawa, and Queen's. In a *Sudbury Star* article from March 1971, Maurice Regimbal, the athletics director, confided his apprehension that the Laurentian teams might have a "rocky road" in front of them in the new league.[53]

Laurentian athletes responded to the challenge, however, and the 1970s and 1980s proved to be extraordinary decades in Voyageur history. Laurentian teams repeatedly won provincial championships: men's soccer (nine times between 1970 and 1990); men's alpine ski (1971–1972); women's field hockey (1971–1972); women's basketball (eight times between 1974 and 1990, including a five-year winning streak from 1974 to 1979); men's volleyball (1976–1977); men's Nordic skiing (seven times between 1977 and 1990, including a six-year winning streak between 1977 and 1984); and men's curling (1988–1989). In 1971–1972, following its provincial title, the men's soccer team won Laurentian's first national Canadian Interuniversity Athletic Union (CIAU) championship. [54]

SOCCER ACTION VS McGILL | Greg Zorbas arrived at Laurentian as player-coach of men's soccer in 1969, and the team began rigorous training which led to the capture of their first OIAA championship in 1969–1970. The team held that title again for the next two years.

This national championship did much to raise the profile of Laurentian's athletes, both within and beyond the university. In 1972, after receiving little support from students throughout the season and the playoffs, the triumph of the soccer Vees was witnessed only by a small crowd of spectators at the final game. In a year marked by dour news of rising tuition and student debt, *Lambda*'s account of the win conveyed a new sense of pride that soon characterized its sports coverage generally: "Laurentian's courageous bid for Canadian Championship glory, ended victoriously last Saturday at home with a 4-1 score board win over the Montreal Loyola Warriors ... Though each demonstrated skill and technique, the number one team, the Vees, managed to continually move the game into patterns of play more advantageous to them and were rewarded by the fluid motion of the game and clever passing of the offensive drives."[55] The repeated success of the Voyageur teams throughout the 1970s gained them a loyal following among Laurentian students.

In contrast to the handful of spectators who watched their championship win in 1972, over 1,000 people cheered the soccer Vees on to victory in their final game against Waterloo during the provincial OUAA championships in the 1981–1982 season.[56] When the team won the CIAU finals in the 1983–1984 season, defeating McGill 2-1 in the last minute of double overtime, Laurentian fans again were out in full force. "I'll never forget the fans swarming on the field, the snow on the ground," manager Alex McGregor remembered years later. "It was probably the gutsiest team I have ever seen in terms of hard work, desire, and the Voyageur spirit."[57]

By the early 1980s, Laurentian had established a reputation for excellence in a number of sports, particularly women's basketball, men's Nordic skiing, and men's soccer. In 1982, Sandy Knox, the coordinator of intercollegiate sports, was asked by *Lambda* to explain how the Voyageur teams could compete at such a high level in spite of the university's comparatively small enrolment. Knox commented that Laurentian did not have a large variety of sports, and they were able to put more emphasis on the sports in which they did participate. "We have many high calibre coaches and we do a lot of recruiting," she stated, adding, "We put special emphasis on Northern Ontario athletes."[58]

Although provision for women's sports such as tennis and badminton had existed since 1962, there were no competitive women's intercollegiate athletic teams until 1968, when Laurentian joined the Ontario-Quebec Women's Conference of Intercollegiate Athletics (OQWCIA), and after 1971, the Ontario Women's Intercollegiate Athletic Association (OWIAA). Rooted in the nineteenth-century traditions of older men's universities such as McGill and Queen's, intercollegiate athletics were oriented toward male sports, and emphasized the importance of competition in physical education for men. By the late 1960s, however, the new women's movement was challenging male dominance in sport, as in other aspects of Canadian society.[59]

A critical key to boosting women's athletics had been the appointment of Pat Pickard as director of women's programs in athletics in the spring of 1967. Believing in the benefits of a competitive physical culture for women, Pickard had persisted in getting the university to fund an intercollegiate program for women, first introducing volleyball, and then establishing what would be one of the strongest components of Laurentian's athletic program, the Lady Vees basketball team. She had many obstacles to overcome, particularly the fact that women's sports were generally considered secondary in importance to men's. In 1967, for example, Pickard had been unable to get the money to send the varsity women's volleyball team to a tournament at Carleton, even though the men's hockey team had travelled to Windsor.[60] Her efforts on behalf of women's athletics received a strong endorsement during the visit of Canadian Olympic track star Abby Hoffman, who gave a public lecture to Laurentian students in March 1972. Female athletes, Hoffman claimed, were not encouraged to excel, and were placed in a subordinate position, reflected in the fact they got the hand-me-downs from men's sports.[61] By the 1970s, Pickard had succeeded in securing equal resources and facilities for the women's program, and in 1977, she was appointed Laurentian's director of athletics, one of the first female directors in Canada.[62]

Women's basketball at Laurentian followed a remarkable trajectory, rapidly moving from an intramural sport in 1967 to the number-one ranked women's team in Canadian intercollegiate competition. From 1974–1975 to 1978–1979 the team won both the provincial (OWIAA) and the national Canadian Women's Intercollegiate Athletic Union (CWIAU) championships.[63] The "Bronze Baby," the nickname for the trophy awarded to the best women's university basketball team in Canada, spent five years in Sudbury.[64] Following an eastern division contest in

WOMEN VEES WIN NATIONAL CHAMPION-SHIP, 1975 | From 1974–1975 to 1978–1979, the Lady Vees 1975 basketball team won both the provincial (OWIAA) and the national (CWIAU) championships. The "Bronze Baby," the nickname for the trophy awarded to the best women's basketball team in Canada, spent five years at Laurentian.

which Laurentian defeated the University of Toronto 74-14 in January 1977, the coach of the Toronto team complained to the media that the Lady Vees were not healthy for the league because of their domination in Ontario. "We agree with the statement that it's 'harder to play against good players,'" Pickard responded. "However we believe also that it is difficult if not impossible to improve when playing against weak players."[65] The next year, when the team again won the national championship, coach Norm Vickery commented: "When you're used to winning, it's harder to lose. Pride becomes involved because the girls try harder when they fall behind. These girls just refused to accept the idea of losing."[66] In a statement to Senate in 1986, the university confirmed its commitment to women's athletics as one of the key principles of the department of interuniversity athletics: "Equality of opportunity shall exist for men and women in all aspects of the interuniversity athletic program."[67]

In the early 1970s, Laurentian's athletic facilities were upgraded to include an Olympic-size swimming pool and an all-weather surface outdoor track, enabling the athletic program to gain international recognition in other sports over the following decade. The swimming pool, the largest in Northern Ontario, opened for use in 1972 in the newly constructed addition to the Benjamin Avery Physical Education building. This facility brought the Laurentian Swim Club into existence. One of the first children to enroll in the Swim Club was Alex Baumann, then nine years old, who would go on to train at Laurentian with coach Jeno Tihanyi. In 1984, Baumann brought glory to Laurentian and to Sudbury when he won two gold medals and established world records in the 200- and 400-metre individual medley events in swimming at the Los Angeles Olympics. Following the Olympics, Baumann returned to Laurentian to finish his degree in political science, while continuing to compete with the varsity swim team.[68]

UPCOMING VARSITY EVENTS, 1978 | This 1978 announcement of upcoming games testifies to the growing popularity of varsity sports.

The second upgrade, the outdoor track completed in 1974, was constructed jointly by the university and the city of Sudbury. The track had an artificial, all-weather surface and regulation throwing circles, making it at that time one of the best in Canada. In the summer of 1976, fifty members of the East German Olympic track team came to Laurentian for their pre-Olympic training in order to avoid athlete overcrowding at the Montreal Olympic site. With these new facilities in place, Laurentian hosted a variety of large sporting events, including the Junior Pan American Games in 1979, the Junior Pan American Track and Field Championship in 1980, the Canadian Games for the Physically Disabled, the Ontario Summer Games in 1983, and the second annual World Junior Games in 1988. During the late 1980s, Nordic skiing at Laurentian was enhanced with the creation of the Voyageur Vita Par Course, a network of cross-country ski trails connected to those of the conservation authority.[69]

While Laurentian athletes achieved success in spite of limited budgets, the rising cost of university education began to affect a growing number of students. During the 1970s and 1980s, students supported various efforts of the Ontario Federation of Students (OFS) to limit fee increases, if not reduce them. In October 1972, Laurentian students participated in an OFS referendum, voting in favour of a provincial tuition strike if the government refused to retract new policies affecting tuition and student loans. When the SGA council went ahead with the January fees boycott "as a political act," Senate showed its support by waiving the normal rule forbidding students who failed to pay their second-term fees from attending lectures. Urged by the SGA council and *Lambda* to "withhold your fees," in January 1973, more than one-third of Laurentian students joined in the province-wide OFS strike and refused to pay their tuition. Sit-ins and office occupations occurred at a number of Ontario universities, including Western and York. At Laurentian, student activists held a one-day moratorium on classes and took over the elevators and occupied the tenth-floor lobby outside the treasury offices in the Parker building.[70]

After this first province-wide action, the OFS boycott became, for a number of years, a regular second-term event. In February 1977, for example, the SGA, in conjunction with the OFS, participated in a one-day moratorium in which students across the province boycotted classes and picketed Manpower offices in opposition to the $100 increase in tuition fees slated for the next year. In October 1977, too, a large gathering of students representing the SGA, ALPS, and l'AEF confronted Harry Parrott, the Ontario Minister of Colleges and Universities, over the issue of proposed changes to the Ontario Student Assistance Program, particularly the increased minimum contribution and the system of accumulating interest on student loans. In 1978, the majority of Laurentian students opted to have a voice at the federal level to protect post-secondary education, voting in a SGA referendum in favour of joining the National Union of Students.[71]

Annual protests of tuition hikes continued into the 1980s, providing a point of common interest among the otherwise disparate student groups on campus. In March 1980, French and English students from the SGA and l'AEF put aside their differences over space and representation to stage a joint occupation of the eleventh floor of the library tower in protest against a major increase in tuition fees. Following the example of Francophone students at the University of Ottawa, l'AEF officially joined the Ontario Federation of Students in 1986.[72] This collaborative approach to protest between the SGA and l'AEF continued into the next decades, as the burden of rising tuition became a central challenge facing all Canadian students in the late-twentieth century.

10   This Ain't Berkeley: Students in the Modern Age, 1985 to the Present

SARA BURKE

"Let's face it, the 60's are over and this ain't Berkeley."
(*Lambda* editorial, February 1995.)

After the splintering of activism in the 1970s, Laurentian students became more aware of the complexities of the issues, more sensitive to the possibility of dissent within the undergraduate body, and more skeptical that social change could be brought about by enthusiastic idealism. The full- and part-time student population was large – exceeding 5,000 after 1986 – and increasingly diverse. In 1986, the *Lambda* editorial staff was amused to find a back issue from 1968 displaying an upraised fist and the slogan, "This University Belongs to the Student! Dig it." The *Lambda* editor reprinted the page, with an accompanying editorial that was partly nostalgic and partly condescending about the innocent idealism of the sixties' student movement. Commenting on the modern "do-gooders," the editor wrote: "It is my hope that a new activism can be created among the students of our generation. An activism based more on equality, justice and freedom and less on image and opportunism."[1] These brave words disguised what proved to be an uneasiness shared by many students to commit wholeheartedly to any political or ideological cause.

University governance continued to suffer from a lack of interest among students, and student seats on university committees routinely fell vacant.[2] From the late 1980s onward, students tended to be preoccupied increasingly with the burden of student debt, the demands of working, which many more of them were forced to do, and the anxiety of planning for the future. Compared to their predecessors, Laurentian students were attracted to humanitarian issues that were more international in scope, including the campaigns of Amnesty International on behalf of political prisoners, the end of apartheid in South Africa, the spread of AIDS, and the refugee sponsorship program run by the World University Service of Canada.[3] Issues closer to home, however, seemed to be much more problematic, exposing fractures within the undergraduate body.

During the first Laurentian University Faculty Association (LUFA) strike in September 1985, the SGA executive made the controversial decision to support the

LAISSEZ-NOUS NOTRE BIBLIOTHÈQUE, *CIRCA* 1989 | Physical education students protested the amalgamation of library holdings from across the campus into one central facility because of the distance from the Ben Avery Gymnasium.

faculty on the grounds that underpaid professors would eventually leave, and thus lower the quality of education at Laurentian.[4] Shortly after the faculty settled, the Laurentian University Staff Association (LUSA) went on strike. Throughout the thirty-day strike, the SGA council was indecisive, and this indecision was mirrored by divisions among the students themselves. In a student opinion survey about the LUSA strike in November 1985, 25 per cent supported LUSA, 15 per cent supported the administration, and the remaining 60 per cent were neutral or uncertain. After an acrimonious debate, the SGA council passed a motion to take a neutral stance on the LUSA strike. Francophone students in l'AEF, in contrast, supported the strikers' demands for equal pay for work of equal value, and for a fair job evaluation program.[5]

The second LUFA strike, which took place in September 1989, sparked an even more intense and divisive reaction from the students. The SGA organized an information rally in the Great Hall, attended by over 1,500 students. After an angry confrontation, the meeting broke up when half of the students marched to the picket lines to confront LUFA members, while another large group rallied outside the library tower with a petition to the president demanding an end to the strike. A second student rally demanding a resolution was held a few days later, with representatives from both l'AEF and the SGA, followed by a march of students from Laurentian to downtown Sudbury.[6]

A boost in student enrolment during the mid-1980s led to the first new building phase since the early 1970s. The most urgent need for students was a new library building. The old library in the Parker building was completely inadequate; the space was far too small to house the volume of materials required by Laurentian's expanding programs; and collections for physical education, education, and science were scattered throughout the campus. With most of the study space given over to the collections, the reading areas were overcrowded and noisy. As Chief Librarian Andrzej Mrozewski pointed out to *Lambda* in 1985, the Parker building lacked such necessities as reinforced floors, a centralized surveillance system, and a temperature controlled environment. Construction of a new, designated library building began in 1988, and the J.N. Desmarais Library opened in February 1990. An addition to the library, the Brenda Wallace Reading Room and Computer Centre, was constructed in 2001, providing students with an elegant room for quiet studying, as well as a computer lab for learning and research.[7]

The second, but perhaps equally urgent, need from the students' point of view, was the long-promised Campus Centre. Initially conceived as part of the five-year building plan in 1970, the construction of the centre had been repeatedly delayed and redirected. When serious planning for a student centre finally began in the mid-1980s, the student associations expressed discontent with its relatively small size. In 1989, members of the SGA voted in a referendum to increase the student levy and pay an additional $15 toward the building fund to allow an enlargement of the projected space. After a revised plan was adopted that allowed for a larger, more student-oriented space, the new student centre in the extension to the third floor of the Parker building was finally constructed, opening in February 1992. Offices that had previously been scattered throughout the campus were moved into the Centre, including the four student associations, the SGA, ALPS, GSA, and l'AEF, the campus radio station, and the two student newspapers, *Lambda* and *l'Orignal Déchaîné*. Space also was provided for clubs, games, meetings, and socializing, and for an expanded student services complex.[8] During the next two decades, the university further improved student facilities, opening the new West Residence building in 2006, and expanding the Benjamin Avery Physical Education complex in 2009.

While facilities at Laurentian during the 1980s improved only slowly, in the fall of 1987, a few Laurentian students were given a more exotic option to take courses far away from Sudbury's wintry campus, at Villefranche near Nice in the south of France.[9] When the project was announced, Laurentian students questioned the administration's decision to spend money on an expensive opportunity for "rich kids," at a time when a new library and student centre were urgently needed. "If all the time, effort and money that has been put into Villefranche was put into projects at Laurentian there might be some improvements here," *Lambda* complained in 1987.[10] *Lambda* and the student associations remained hostile to Villefranche throughout its duration, maintaining that the project drained resources from the Sudbury campus and benefited only a minority of Laurentian students. In 1990, for example, *Lambda* commented: "There seems to be no doubt that UCF is a publicly funded 'private' university for privileged anglophone students."[11]

Student culture in the 1970s had been anti-authoritarian, and the rejection of the universities' role *in loco parentis* on most Canadian campuses had allowed students to throw off outdated restrictions and adopt a more experimental approach to drugs, alcohol, and sexual activity. By the mid-1980s, however, students at Laurentian and elsewhere were experiencing some of the negative consequences of this culture, and both administrators and student associations began to seek a middle ground, navigating between permissiveness and regulation. In a national survey

"OKAY! OKAY! I SEE YOU'RE FULLY QUALIFIED FOR THE JOB"

CARTOON OF FEMALE SECURITY OFFICER, 1983 | As Laurentian began to implement policies on sexual harassment and gender equity in the 1980s, the idea of women working as campus security officers still seemed radical to some.

conducted for the Addiction Research Foundation in the fall of 1988, researchers concluded that a quarter of the total sample of Ontario university students were heavy drinkers, consuming more than 28 drinks per week. Laurentian had a higher percentage (14 per cent versus 11 per cent) of students classified as hard drinkers, and Laurentian's statistics revealed a greater frequency of alcohol-related problems, such as drinking and driving, experiencing a hangover, and missing class as a result of drinking.[12] A study of Laurentian students conducted over ten years later in the fall of 1999 revealed that little had changed regarding students' drinking habits. The majority of the students surveyed said that they had twelve or more drinks per week, and 57 per cent reported being injured as a result of drinking.[13]

The old position of dean of students had disappeared in the early 1970s, and it was not until 1985 that Laurentian appointed the first coordinator of student services, Padraig Blenkinsop, reporting directly to the president. Unlike his predecessor, Maurice Regimbal, who had been responsible for supervising the students' conduct, Blenkinsop's primary roles were to encourage clubs and societies, coordinate services, and facilitate communication among the university's student associations.[14]

Over the years, conditions at the six student residences – Sudbury, Thorneloe, Huntington, Married Students, Single Students, and University College – had steadily deteriorated. In addition to cracked windows and stained carpets, the laissez-faire environment of the 1970s had created a residence lifestyle in which vandalism, noise, and wild parties went largely unchecked, and the student-run resident student councils had few resources to deal with the problems that arose. By the mid-1980s, University College in particular had become known as the party residence, with a tradition of practical jokes that pitted floor against floor and usually involved vandalizing the washrooms (smearing honey on the toilet seats was a favourite prank). "One of the major concerns in U.C. is the negative image projected," the student representative from UC told *Lambda* in 1985. "It is believed that once students move in, they actually conform to the make-up of the residence; the legend is kept alive."[15]

Following the example of other Ontario universities, in 1986 Blenkinsop attempted to implement, with little apparent success, the Campus Alcohol Policies and Education (CAPE) program, which taught students about the dangers of drinking and encouraged moderation with alcohol. Enlisting the support of Olympic athlete and political science student Alex Baumann, the CAPE committee launched an education program that included workshops, a non-alcoholic beverage competition, and distribution of literature to first-year students. In spite of participation from the SGA, ALPS, and l'AEF, Laurentian students responded negatively to the program. "The hardest thing will be trying to get students to give it a chance," the SGA vice-president admitted at the end of the program's first year.[16] By the early 1990s, this initiative had evolved into the Alcohol Awareness Week Committee, which designated a week every October to host a series of activities, such as a spaghetti supper, aimed to educate students about drinking responsibly.

In 1987, Blenkinsop made a second attempt to influence student behaviour. The council on student life, consisting of nine students and nine staff members, was designed to serve as a parliament of student services on campus. Its goal was to establish a series of sub-committees on aspects of student life such as space, student rights, housing, and student activities, and to seek solutions and make recommendations on a wide spectrum of issues relating to student services. However, once the sub-committees were set up, Blenkinsop found it difficult to get the committees to meet, and little progress was made. A step forward came in 1992, when the opening of the new student centre enabled the university to centralize and enlarge services for students, and the second floor became home to the Counselling and Resource Centre, Native Student Services, Special Needs, Student Awards Office, and the Off-Campus Housing Office.[17]

As part of a larger restructuring plan, in 1994, the university transferred Student Services into the academic stream and appointed a new director, John Gonder, who reported to the vice-president academic rather than to the president. Gonder's first task was to conduct a survey of Laurentian students and prepare a report recommending the future direction of Student Services based on student needs. Issued in 1995, the *Focus on Students Report* made a wide variety of recommendations designed to enhance student experience, regulate excessive behaviour, and establish appropriate protocols to protect the rights of students. After two years of discussion between members of the administration and the student associations, in 1998, Senate approved a revised non-academic Code of Student Conduct, and a new Charter of Student Rights and Responsibilities. Although not quite a return to the paternal attitude of *in loco parentis*, the code was an attempt to reinstate the authority of the university and reduce the degree of student self-government.

CITY TRANSIT BUS | The location of the campus away from downtown meant a daily commute either by car or city transit for off-campus students.

The code ensured that the composition of the disciplinary bodies was weighted in favour of members of the administration, rather than students. Under it, students accused of misconduct, such as offenses involving drinking, would be tried before a judiciary panel consisting of two students, and three members selected from faculty, staff, and the administration. An appeals panel was established to allow for a review of the judiciary panel's decisions, but it, too, had only minority student representation.[18]

Native students continued to expand their presence at Laurentian. By the 1980s, the Native Students Club had evolved first into the Native Studies Student Association, and then, in 1994, into the Native Students' Association (NSA), to meet the needs of all First Nation students enrolled at Laurentian.[19] The association had about 60 student members in 1985, and an organized council that planned social and cultural activities, such as sponsoring speakers on Native issues, hosting powwows and conferences, and holding get-togethers and bingo nights in their space at the University of Sudbury. The NSA also took on a political role, advocating for the rights of Native students and expressing a perspective distinct from that of the larger student associations. During the second LUFA strike in 1989, for example, the NSA issued a press release stating the concern that Native students at Laurentian would lose their financial support from the Department of Indian Affairs if the strike continued.[20]

Gerry Trudeau, president of the NSA and a student senator in 1987, believed that Native students at Laurentian needed to establish connections with other

Native student associations in Ontario and beyond. Trudeau became the national commissioner of indigenous affairs for the Canadian Federation of Students, and launched a campaign to form a national organization to unite Native student associations across Canada. In the fall of 1990, the NSA hosted a conference, "Rebuilding Our Nations," at the University of Sudbury, which included a political forum, attended by Ovide Mercredi and Elijah Harper, an educational forum on the events at Kahnawake the previous summer, and various sessions on Native self-government, economic development, and social issues.[21]

Native students participated in a sit-in at the Sudbury offices of the Department of Indian Affairs in 1991 to protest the federal government's capping of funds for Native post-secondary education. "Post-secondary education is an aboriginal and treaty right," the president of the NSA explained in *Lambda*. "The capping of funds is a direct violation of agreements between the federal government and Native people."[22] Acknowledging the importance of First Nations students in the university's cultural makeup, in the fall of 1991, the Laurentian University Native Education Council (LUNEC) was formed to advise the president and senior administration on all issues affecting Aboriginal students. Membership on LUNEC included voting representation from First Nations in Ontario, as well as non-voting representation from the NSA, and faculty from Native studies and Native human services.[23]

The NSA and Native Student Services began to sponsor an annual Native Awareness Week, beginning in 1995, in which a range of activities – including films, workshops, and a powwow – were featured to sensitize non-Native students and faculty to the concerns and issues facing First Nations people. Both Elijah Harper and Ovide Mercredi returned to Laurentian on several occasions: Harper came in 1992 to speak at a traditional Native dinner organized by the NSA, and in 1999, he gave the keynote address for Native Awareness Week; Mercredi returned in 1997 to launch Native Awareness Week, and then serve as special adjunct professor at the University of Sudbury in 1998, when he presented four public lectures on Aboriginal politics. Recognizing that many students of Aboriginal ancestry needed to be encouraged to self-identify, the NSA and Native Student Services also began organizing special orientation events in September for incoming students and their families.[24] "The fact is that being an 'Indian' is not a certain look or talk," a Native contributor reminded *Lambda* readers. "We are here among you, trying to survive and succeed just like you."[25]

During the early 1990s, decreasing enrolment, and the growing deficits of the provincial and federal governments led to deep cuts in provincial funding, forcing the university to increase tuition, cancel programs, and delay building plans. As Matt Bray describes, in the spring of 1993, the provincial government introduced the "Social Contract," a plan to reduce the budget by cutting public sector funding. Over the next few years, Laurentian experienced the most drastic financial reductions in its history. With provincial funding frozen, plans for a new student residence were put on hold – the West Residence would not open until 2007 – and tuition fees increased 35 per cent over three years.[26]

CAREER DAY | The bowling alley regularly becomes the site for various displays and information fairs, providing students with direction as they apply for graduate programs and career opportunities.

The soaring cost of university education in the 1990s again became a unifying issue, bringing students together to protest a common cause. The modest social and economic background of the majority of Laurentian students made them particularly vulnerable to the increased financial burden. In a comparative survey of first-year students at universities across Canada conducted in the fall of 1988, it was revealed that Laurentian students came from less affluent families, were more dependent for financial support on employment and state assistance, and were far more likely to come from families where neither parent completed high school.[27]

Beginning in the late 1980s, the SGA and l'AEF regularly cooperated to orchestrate Laurentian's participation in provincial and national events protesting rising tuition costs and government under-funding: the Day of Action every January organized by the Canadian Federation of Students, and, every March, the Week of Action sponsored by Ontario Federation of Students.[28] In an effort to bridge the two student populations, in 1986, the SGA created the position of director of bilingual affairs, and began to sponsor an annual Bilingual Week of Action every February, in which campus bilingualism was promoted through guest speakers, French and English entertainment, social activities, and films. *Lambda* also returned to its earlier practice of publishing a French-language section.[29]

During the dark days of the "Social Contract" in the mid-1990s, the student associations organized a particularly sustained protest. In May 1994, the president of the SGA wrote to Jack Porter, secretary of Senate, objecting to the proposal that faculty take their Rae Days during the first week of January 1995, delaying the beginning of classes in the second term. As part of the National Students' Day of Action in January 1995, the SGA and l'AEF organized a student strike involving a march to downtown Sudbury, picketing, and a boycott of classes, to draw attention to the damaging effect of continuing cutbacks in funding and increased fees on university education.[30] Drawing over 600 students throughout the day, the student strike at Laurentian was described by the media as the third-largest protest in the province, after those in Toronto and Ottawa. Responding to a *Sudbury Star* criticism that the student protest had fizzled out early, the editor of *Lambda* defended the level of student commitment at Laurentian, noting dryly: "Let's face it, the 60's are over and this ain't Berkeley."[31]

The financial cutbacks of the 1990s had a significant impact on Laurentian athletics. The success of the interuniversity program over the past two decades had been premised on the strategy that resources not be spread too thinly, and that only a limited number of successful teams be supported. As Sandy Knox had explained in 1982, this strategy had allowed the Voyageur program to excel in spite of Laurentian's small size and remote location. The athletic directors also recognized the importance of fan support; the Lady Vees basketball and men's soccer teams had an enthusiastic and loyal fan base, but others, such as the women's field hockey or men's cross-country running teams, were virtually unknown to most Laurentian students.

In 1993–1994, the directors of the athletics program were faced with major cuts, and they made the difficult decision to preserve funding for the nationally recognized Vees teams by sacrificing less successful sports: women's indoor and field hockey, and men's and women's curling. Men's hockey was put under review to determine whether it could become self-sufficient.[32] The alpine ski program had already been cut, in 1989. At that time, athletic director Peter Ennis had defended the decision on the grounds that the sport had been in a difficult position: the students had been forced to self-coach, drive to events in their own cars and make their own arrangements, and money had not been available to upgrade the program to full varsity sports status. Ennis had stated: "If Laurentian, which is currently reviewing all its sports programs for the next two years, had the money, it would be placed either into the other programs or used to add another female team."[33]

The university created a sports marketing position to explore external funding initiatives, and, by 1995, community sponsors had been secured for nine varsity teams. Beginning in 1995–1996, women's soccer was added as a varsity sport. At the end of the decade, the athletics program was again reviewed, and in 2000, the university announced it would focus its resources on the eight interuniversity teams deemed most likely to attain national recognition: men's basketball, women's basketball, men's swimming, women's swimming, men's soccer, women's soccer, men's Nordic skiing, and women's Nordic skiing. The teams cut were men's volleyball, men's and women's cross-country running, men's and women's track and field, and, most controversially, men's hockey. Although the decision to eliminate hockey was regretted by many Voyageur fans, the team had been unsuccessful in its efforts to foster significant support among the students, and unable to compete with the Sudbury Wolves for interest within the community.[34]

In spite of the cutbacks, Laurentian teams continued to be highly competitive in Ontario's interuniversity leagues. The 1990s got off to a strong start when the Lady Vees basketball team won the OWIAA and the CIAU championships in 1990–1991, and the men's Nordic skiers won the OUAA championship in both 1990–1991 and

MODEL PARLIAMENT | Professor Rand Dyck and student Daniel Charbonneau, of the department of political science, organized the first model parliament in 1993. Since 1998 the annual event has been held at the House of Commons in Ottawa.

1991–1992. In 1991, the soccer field was improved, and new stands constructed for the large numbers of Vees' fans. The soccer Voyageurs continued to be one of the strongest university teams, securing the provincial championship in 1991–1992 and 1994–1995. The Lady Vees also stood out in women's basketball throughout the decade, taking the provincial title five times, in 1991–1992, 1992–1993, 1994–1995, 1997–1998, and 1999–2000. Men's basketball gained strength at the end of the 1990s, winning provincially in 1997–1998 and again in 1999–2000. The women's Nordic skiing team distinguished itself as well, winning the provincial championship in 1991–1992, 1994–1995, 1995–1996, 1998–1999, and 2002–2003.[35]

Fans of the Voyageurs, nicknamed the Pot Bangers, turned out for home games in full force, faces painted and pots in hand to make as much noise as possible. When the men's basketball team won the provincial Wilson Cup against McMaster in March 2000, the television commentator stated that the LU Pot Bangers were the noisiest and most enthusiastic fans in the Ontario University Athletics (OUA).[36] As one fan pointed out in a letter to *Lambda*, Laurentian's success in athletics was entirely out of proportion to its size, location, and funding. "Laurentian has a growing, beautiful, proud spirit," the letter stated, "and more and more it is being demonstrated to the rest of Canada's Universities by its most dynamic manifestation – the Laurentian Sports Machine."[37]

THE VOYAGEUR MASCOT

Until the financial retrenchment at the end of the decade, the 2000s represented a period of growth for Laurentian. In 2003, the double cohort of secondary school graduates boosted the total enrolment by 21 per cent, and the surge of students continued for the next three years. The enrolment increase was matched by an expansion of programs at both the undergraduate and graduate level, and the establishment of the Laurentian at Georgian program in Barrie and Orillia after 2001. In sharp contrast to the early years, by 2009, female students represented the majority of the undergraduate population. Between 1986 and 2007, women on average accounted for 60 per cent of all undergraduates, and in 2007, the number of female students reached a high of 5,510 out of a total enrolment of 8,147, or 67 per cent of the total undergraduate body. By comparison, the percentage of Francophone students declined steadily after 1986; it then represented 20 per cent of the total student population, but only 17 per cent in 2007.[38]

Native students at Laurentian moved from a hidden minority into recognition as one of the three main groups in the cultural composition of the university. In 2007, the number of Native students at Laurentian was estimated at 650, representing about 8 per cent of the total undergraduate population.[39] In symbolic acknowledgment of this shift, in the summer of 1998, the red-and-white Anishinabek flag was added to the display of flags hanging in the student centre. Along with the Canadian and Ontario flags, the Anishinabek flag is now flown prominently next to the green-and-white Franco-Ontarian flag, itself born of the activism of Laurentian students and faculty.[40]

Laurentian has always had a diverse student population. Founded as an experiment in bringing together young people in the North of both French and English heritage, over the past fifty years, the university has redefined its cultural makeup to recognize the importance of First Nations students. During the first stage of Laurentian's development in the 1960s, students joined together to establish their voice in the hierarchy of the university, adopting the activist tactics of the student movement to campaign for improved facilities and increased autonomy. This period of unity could not be sustained during the divisive decades that followed, and the 1970s saw a splintering of activism as students formed new communities based on gender, language, culture, sexual orientation, or experience. The anti-authoritarian culture of this second stage eroded the university's traditional assumption of *in loco parentis*, and responsibility for student conduct shifted to student self-government. After the mid-1980s, Laurentian students became more skeptical about activism and more aware of dissent; many issues exposed fractures among the different constituents on campus. The more permissive student culture that emerged in the 1980s led to concerns from students and administrators that the overall quality of student life had declined, and the university's recent history has been characterized by efforts to create a more inclusive and tolerant campus.

The history of Laurentian is part of the larger social history of education in Canada, and in many ways, Laurentian students have followed a pattern similar to those attending other universities in the post-war period. In facing the test of diversity, however, the experience of students at Laurentian has been unique. The complexity of a bilingual, tricultural northern university continues to represent, as the *Sudbury Star* predicted in 1960, a challenging experiment in higher education.

11 From Optimism to Disillusion, 1960 to 1971

GUY GAUDREAU

Writing the history of French-language education and bilingualism at Laurentian in a few dozen pages is a huge challenge since there is so much to say. At Laurentian, thousands of Franco-Ontarian students have acquired a profession, developed their talents and gained an appreciation for learning. Rare are those who do not have excellent memories of their stay here. Many graduates who went on to get a master's or doctoral degree elsewhere have reported that their preparation had been more than adequate, and that they never felt disadvantaged compared to students from larger universities. It must be acknowledged that, on the whole, the professors who provided French education did their work well.

Furthermore, if we compare the two first decades to today, undeniable progress has been made, be it at the administrative level, which has become truly bilingual, or in the program offerings, which are much more varied today than in the past. Reasons to rejoice abound and should be recognized.

What is perhaps most striking in this history that must neglect so many facts are the roles played by individuals in Laurentian's evolution. Though external politics, in Ottawa, Toronto or Quebec, have had a structural influence on Laurentian's destiny, we must also recognize the role of internal forces that resulted from the arrival and departure of many individuals: presidents, administrators, professors and others. The historian is often wary of the hero's role in the story of humanity, but one must admit that a president or a professor can make a difference and accelerate the course of history or, conversely, force persons of the best intentions to make distressing retreats.

If individuals were able to play important roles, it is because the functioning of the university encouraged them to do so, by offering administrators standard contracts for five years which, though renewable in principle, were rarely renewed in practice. This means that almost every year the university experiences the arrival and departure of individuals in administrative positions. Such uncertainty threatens the institution's continuity. Situations arise where two administrators work well together, but when the senior-level member leaves, files cease to move forward because mutual confidence and cooperation no longer exist. There have been many such cases. The personalities of individuals, much like the positions of power, remain a key element of a university's operations. It may be regrettable, but it is the way things are. A newly arrived president like John Daniel can easily shake everything up and leave his mark on history by changing its course.

It should not come as a surprise that the following pages recall many conflicts, fed not only by changing administrative personnel, but by the very nature of a university; a world of ideas peopled by specialists in their fields who are ready to fight tooth and nail to defend their positions. In this sense, a university is truly a battlefield of ideas and principles, one generally not obvious to the student body and the general community. The development of critical thought is something we practice day to day. In fact, a fundamental principle of university life is academic freedom, which necessarily entails freedom of opinion. These freedoms sanction and even encourage dissent and dispute. In the western world, universities are certainly the institutions that best tolerate dissidence. And Laurentian can be proud of its record on this point. Diverging opinions have certainly been one of the forces at play in Laurentian's dynamics.

The evolution broadly sketched here is divided into three periods that coincide with those adopted in other parts of this book. Two turning points emerge: the early 1970s and the middle of the 1980s. They serve as markers for this history told in a critical perspective that spares no one, not even the author of this article who is far from universally admired.

From Optimism to Disillusion, 1960–1971

Legal Constitution

Despite the historical precedent established when, in 1960, the provincial government provided financing for a university for French-language programs,[1] it would be difficult to find in the legal documents that created Laurentian University a precise definition of the terms governing the practice of bilingualism and the position of French-language programs. Article 4, clause I of Chapter 151 of the Statutes of Ontario, the law that created Laurentian University, written in English, confers these powers:

> 4(1)(a) to establish and maintain, *in either or both* of the French and English languages, such faculties, schools, institutes, departments and chairs as determined by the Board ...
> ...
> 4(1)(c) to establish a college of the University within the Faculty of Arts and Science to be known as University College, which college shall give instruction *in either or both* of the French and English languages in such subjects ...

The legislators did not venture onto this terrain, leaving it to Laurentian's governors and senators, namely, the majority, to define the terms. This would contribute to making French education and bilingualism a story filled with ups and downs. But one aspect of the Statute should be noted in particular: programs were expected to be asymmetrical because there was no obligation to provide the same programs in English and in French.

One of the reasons at the time for this asymmetry was that few believed that the Franco-Ontarian minority – the name "French-Canadian" would still be in use for a few years – would require programs such as medicine, law or commerce.[2] In fact, the question of legal studies had been raised at the very beginning, at a meeting of the Board of Governors on September 10, 1960. For the vast majority of the board – but not for a French-Canadian like Judge Albert Saint-Aubin – it seemed obvious that a law program would never be offered in French in Ontario. Yet fifteen years later, common law was being taught in French at the University of Ottawa!

Robert Campeau, a board member and businessman, who would some time later become famous for a short-lived but spectacular foray into high finance, had indeed attempted at that September 1960 meeting to introduce an amendment requiring the new institution to guarantee that French instruction would be maintained, at the very least. According to his proposal, failure to observe this commitment would result in recourse to the courts. However, Campeau's point of view did not win the approval of the board, which followed the recommendation of the lawyer hired by Laurentian to the effect that this amendment would change the initial agreement between the University of Sudbury and Laurentian University.[3]

For the Jesuits of the University of Sudbury who, as discussed in the first part of this book, adhered to the project of a bilingual university, the matter was more or less beyond discussion. In 1957, they had already transformed their former Sacred Heart College, a unilingual French-language institution since 1916, into the University of Sudbury, an institution that from 1958 onward offered courses in French and English. Certainly, not all Jesuits in the region had warmly accepted this change,[4] and some had lent their support to the provincial ACFEO and the Sudbury regional ACFEO in their lobbying for a French, non-bilingual university. Like many minorities, the French-Canadian community in Ontario was divided, which made it easier for the majority to find allies in favour of its project for a bilingual university.

According to Donald Dennie, who examined the history of bilingualism at Laurentian in a well documented thirty-page report,[5] the university calendars in this period are quite revealing. Though there was some ambiguity about intentions, for our part, we are struck by the statement of the university's cultural mission, which seems to be a response to the disappointed proponents of a homogenous Francophone university.

The University has pledged itself to the maintenance and promotion of both the English and the French languages and cultures, inside as well as outside

TABLE 11.1 | LAURENTIAN'S STUDENT POPULATION BY LINGUISTIC GROUP, 1960–1969

Academic Year	Francophones		Anglophones	
	Total	%	Total	%
1960–1961	95	52	88	48
1961–1962	89	35	166	65
1962–1963	64	24	200	76
1963–1964	85	23	276	77
1964–1965	120	22	436	78
1965–1966	132	15	769	85
1966–1967	174	15	956	85
1967–1968	180	14	1,084	86
1968–1969	258	17	1,242	83
1969–1970	215	12	1,558	88
1970–1971	263	13	1,829	87
1971–1972	259	13	1,764	87
1972–1973	235	12	1,623	88

Source: "Presentation to the Committee of University Affairs," November 1973, 29.

the classrooms. The bilingual nature of the University expresses the belief of Canadians of vision and goodwill that the prevailing tendency in the shaping of our civilization ought to be toward unity rather than toward segregation. The University itself aims to be a place where theories and techniques of cooperation between cultures can be put to the test and taught to the future leaders of Canadian communities.[6]

While the student population during the university's first academic year guaranteed equality between the two linguistic groups, this equilibrium was immediately lost in 1961–1962 when French-Canadian students represented only a third of the population, and the year after that, as table 11.1 indicates, they composed only one quarter. Their severe minority status, which remains to this day, would no doubt be one of the most enduring features of Laurentian's history.

This distribution of the student population provides a fairly precise, yet underestimated indication of the number of courses offered. During the winter session of 1966, for example, 99 courses were offered in English and 33 (25 per cent) in French. In 1970–1971, the proportion of French-language instruction fell below 20 per cent and remained at this level. According to President Monahan, in a document written in 1976,[7] the reason for the increase in the total student population during the second half of the 1960s and the diminishing proportion of the Francophone student population was the introduction of new programs offered in English only in the Professional Schools (nursing, education, physical education and social work). The school of translation, also newly created, did not manage to

offset this influx of new Anglophone students. Another consideration, undoubtedly, was the fact that until 1968 there were no provincially funded French secondary schools, a situation which forced Franco-Ontarian students to attend bilingual schools where a number of them pursued their education in English.

Initially, Laurentian was expected to receive a percentage of Franco-Ontarian students similar to their demographic presence in the region, namely about one third. President Mullins, in his address to the graduating class of 1969, showed that he certainly was aware of this moral commitment to the Franco-Ontarian community and admitted to having failed in this area.[8] Mullins must assume a portion of the responsibility for this failure, for having advocated, along with the Anglophone majority of the country, a façade of bilingualism built on good intentions in which simple awareness of the other group's language would suffice. The wish he expressed at the start of his mandate in 1963, to make Laurentian a bilingual institution, did not come to fruition, although he had then identified the beginning of a solution, calling for students to progress to the point where they could not only take second-language courses, but also courses in their field of study taught in the other language.[9] At that time, Mullins could count on the fact that students were required to take a course in a language other than their mother tongue in order to graduate, although this requirement would be eliminated in the mid-1960s – with his tacit approval, obviously – when it was decided that a course in another modern or ancient language could be substituted for one in French.[10]

The linguistic imbalance that appeared during Laurentian's early years soon provoked reactions and revealed problems in its operations as far as bilingualism was concerned. It led G.A. Bourbeau of the Faculty of Arts and Science, the only dean in place at that time, to submit in the fall of 1963 a very critical report on the last twelve months of his mandate, in which he pointed out numerous problems in the university's operations, as discussed in a preceding chapter. Among

ANDRÉ GIROUARD | A Jesuit and professor of French literature at Laurentian who had originally joined the University of Sudbury in 1958, André Girouard was, in the 1960s and 1970s, unquestionably the leader of the university's Francophone community.

the secondary issues that he presented as irritants was the fact that Laurentian had authorized the nomination of unilingual Anglophones as department heads. "The appointment of non-bilingual departmental chairmen in Laurentian University has established a precedent which denies to a French speaking professor the right to express his views and to make his requests in the language of his choice."[11] These critical assessments of the university's structure were so serious that they led the dean to resign on June 30, 1964, thus depriving Franco-Ontarians of a strong voice at the upper administrative level.

In the fall of 1963, the media in Sudbury paid scant attention to the issue of bilingualism. The mood was optimistic, the main preoccupation was the construction of the campus, then in full swing, and glowing reports appeared about the grants and donations being made to bring the campus to life on the shore of Ramsey Lake. The French cause would have to wait for better days to be heard.

But the signs of trouble were unmistakable. For example, in December 1962, Tom Bertrim, an Anglophone student upset by the recriminations of militant Francophone students, published a cry from the heart asking the pro-French movement to rally to create a climate of unity on the university campus. The title of his article published in the December 1962 issue of *Lambda* was very explicit: "The Français-Anglais Split … at Laurentian." It must be understood that over the course of the 1960s, some militant students began to demand bilingualism, for example, on tickets to events, signs on bathroom doors and in the promotional material produced by Laurentian's bilingual student association. This quickly led to the organization of events held in French only.

Another sign of trouble appeared in December 1963: the creation of l'Association des étudiants de langue française du Nord de l'Ontario, known by its acronym ADELFNO.[12] This association, whose facilitator was the Jesuit André Girouard, a professor in the French department, would continue its activities for some years, rallying students from Laurentian and private secondary schools in order to increase French-Canadian participation in the university. Even though inadequate preparation of students in Anglophone public secondary schools had led Laurentian to create in 1963 a program called "l'année préliminaire," Girouard maintained that a movement was needed to demand publicly funded French secondary schools, which would in turn produce more Grade 13 graduates. As a means to this end, a survey was distributed in all schools and a petition organized for parents and students across Northern Ontario. When the Laurendeau-Dunton Commission on Bilingualism and Biculturalism invited groups to submit memorandums, ADELFNO responded immediately. At its third annual conference, in December 1965,[13] it invited Vice-President Cloutier to address the assembly, an indication that the association was to some extent recognized by Laurentian.

The Era of Bilingualism Committees

Campeau reignited the debate on bilingualism in the fall of 1964 by demanding true bilingualism. Senate, in its meeting on November 26, 1964, decided to strike a committee – the first in a long series – "in order to study, with regard to educational policy, the academic implications of bilingualism at Laurentian University."[14] The report was expected on September 30, 1965, but had still not been submitted as of February 25, 1966, because the committee had not yet met, suggesting a certain lack of concern.

This may have been the context in which the Board of Governors revisited the question. One of the governors, Jim Meakes, proprietor of the *Sudbury Star*, raised the question of Laurentian's bilingualism, and this led the board to recommend the creation of another committee with a mandate to report within six weeks,[15] the report to be submitted to the board's executive "for the better attainment of this goal, particularly in respect of maintaining in the administration of the University an equitable recognition of the two founding races."[16] This committee would produce the Meakes report, discussed in a previous chapter, which dealt with biculturalism and not just bilingualism, thus echoing the proceedings of the Laurendeau-Dunton Commission which that same year had published a preliminary report widely circulated by media. It was therefore not surprising that among the recommendations of the Meakes Report, besides the creation of an office of vice-president to be filled by a French-Canadian and the nomination of a French-Canadian dean, was the creation of a permanent committee on bilingualism "mandated to study the academic repercussions of bilingualism."[17] But this mandate, as President Monahan later admitted, would never be clarified in operational terms,[18] leading many to believe that the committee was in fact simply a means of letting irresolvable and controversial issues stagnate. As Dennie ironically noted, "the era of advisory committees on bilingualism" had begun.

These administrative changes had little effect. President Mullins recognized this the following year in a speech to the annual meeting of the Canadian Alliance held at Laurentian. "President Mullins Says Bilingualism a Failure at Laurentian," read the title of an article published in the *Sudbury Star* on May 24, 1966. Though it would be necessary to require students to take language and literature courses in the other language to ensure bilingualism, Mullins admitted a few months later that this sort of bilingualism would result in fewer student registrations, making the idea impracticable. [19]

When Timmins businessman Conrad Lavigne, a promoter of the French language and culture at the table of the Board of Governors, was reappointed as a governor in 1966, he took advantage of the opportunity to ask the Minister of Education at the time, Bill Davis, for clarifications about the true nature of bilingualism at Laurentian. Should it be a completely bilingual institution as Premier Robarts had declared in a speech in 1965, or should it be a university where, as recognized by President Mullins, Franco-Ontarians could take courses in French?[20] The Minister's answer shed light on the dominant sentiment of the Anglophone majority:

> It was the intention, I believe, to provide for the students whose first language was either French or English to receive instruction in their own language in so far as this was practicable. I believe also that the University had as an objective the maintenance and promotion of both the English and French languages and cultures both inside as well as outside the classrooms. Again, however, I believe the latter objective has to be pursued in the light of practicability, since considerations of availability of staff, financial resources and the like must be taken into account.[21]

Only beginning in 1966 were the costs of bilingualism introduced progressively into the debate, thus complicating the issue. Mullins alluded to this, indicating that the low number of Francophone student registrations did not compensate for the higher costs that bilingualism entailed.[22] For Monahan, his successor, there was no doubt that the first grants for bilingualism awarded by the government, in 1967, represented major progress. But this new government funding, a largely improvised measure, would add to the debate questions of appropriate use and transparency of those funds. Here was Monahan's point of view on the matter:

> But the Grant was calculated on the concept of incremental costs, a concept that was not accepted at Laurentian as appropriate in the light of its particular circumstances – a small institution undertaking to provide French-language courses and programmes to a Franco-Ontarian community that was seriously disadvantaged economically, socially and culturally as well as educationally. More significantly, there was no clear statement of the

government's objectives re bilingualism. Not only was there no agreement on the rationale for calculating the size of the Bilingual Grant; there was no clear statement of bilingual objectives and priorities.[23]

The Interventions of the French Department and a Favourable Political Context

While the forces working in favour of the French fact at Laurentian at the Board of Governors level were Campeau and Lavigne, among the faculty the most active professors were members of the French department, as illustrated by a number of events that occurred between 1968 and 1971.

In the fall of 1968, student activism reached new heights in the western world, and while at Laurentian the student movement had been until then led by Francophone students, the only ones able to function in both languages, the French section of the Students' General Association (SGA) called a meeting on October 25th to which faculty were invited. This meeting followed the presentation by the SGA to the Board of Governors, one week earlier, of a brief calling for true bilingualism. The *Sudbury Star* reported on this intervention in an article entitled "Students Request Changes to Restore 'Lost Bilingualism' at Laurentian University."[24]

The students called this meeting, the minutes of which were written in French and later translated and conserved in this version, to add weight to their demand and to increase their support.[25] The document indicates the presence of many professors in the French department who moved and seconded motions. Of the five professors whose presence can be ascertained, three came from the French department, the Jesuit André Girouard and the professors Michel Bideau and Léandre Page.[26] Their motions, in essence, called for French programs in the Professional Schools, a minimum and "normal" level of registrations for Francophone students, corresponding to one third of the student body – as opposed to 14 per cent – bilingual secretaries and the creation of an ombudsman instead of a Bilingualism Committee without any significant power. This last request, however, went unheeded.

An examination of the considerations raised in the brief reveals the impact of Quebec's sovereignty movement. In fact, reported in the *Sudbury Star*, "One conclusion reached in the brief is that Laurentian is a decisive factor in either national bilingualism or an independent Quebec."[27] It was not surprising that the Quebecois cause had repercussions at Laurentian and that students and professors wanted to surf this big wave. All of Canada, including the country's new Prime Minister Trudeau elected in June 1968, was more or less in reactive mode to the aspirations of the Quebec independence movement.

The call for bilingual secretaries was in fact a demand for the application of the hiring policy adopted in 1961 which was obviously not being respected. The reaction of the Board of Governors, stated in the minutes of the meeting on November 29, 1968, showed that there was no will to apply this hiring policy, and that the best course for the moment was nothing more than pious hope, an attitude that sadly

UNIVERSITY OF SUDBURY, 1967 | The recently completed University of Sudbury in the foreground stood, in 1967, in marked contrast to the rest of the campus which was still very much a work-in-progress.

would become all too typical of Laurentian: "That all applicants for academic and non-academic positions at Laurentian University should be willing to work in and be sympathetic toward a bilingual environment." Only several years later would a more forceful hiring policy be adopted.

As for the objective of having a student body which would be one-third French speaking, the governors stated, without providing an explanation, that in their view this was already the case. The president, in a Senate meeting on December 12, 1968, explained the administration's point of view on this thorny issue which remains current even today. Mullins argued that students registered at l'École des sciences de l'éducation, at that point not yet affiliated with Laurentian University, made the percentage rise to 30 per cent because 170 more students should be added to the 289 Francophone students, as compared to the 1,243 Anglophone students[28].

On the question of opening the Professional Schools to new French programs, the board appeared more welcoming, decreeing: "That all professional schools and new faculties be officially designated as bilingual, and that the French-speaking professors be provided as far as possible wherever the numbers of French-speaking participants warrant."[29] In so doing, it was simply following the policy in effect across Ontario's education system.

To come into effect, this resolution adopted by the Board of Governors still needed to be passed by Senate, the body with authority over programs. That would take another year because this same resolution was passed in December 1969,[30] Senate this time responding to a new demand coming directly from the faculty of the French department.

In this instance as well, the context provided by Canadian politics no doubt explains the success of these pro-French demands at Laurentian. In 1969, Canada's *Official Languages Act* was finally adopted. Not only did this federal law make the majority more aware of the legitimate demands for better French services at Laurentian, but it gave more weight to the pressures exerted by the likes of Laurentian professor Girouard and governor Lavigne.[31]

A group of fifteen professors from the French department signed a manifesto delivered to the administration[32] in October, demanding that the principle of bilingualism be applied to all official documents produced by Laurentian University. The manifesto arose from a meeting at which they had voted that "all official documents written in English only be returned to their sender and in no way be taken into account."[33] Lavigne sent this manifesto to the Board of Governors, who entered it into the minutes of their meeting on October 31st. His observation as president of the Bilingualism Committee was eloquently derogatory:

> May I state at the outset that we have no cause for alarm. The situation of
> Bilingualism and Biculturalism at Laurentian is no worse. It is only as bad as
> it has ever been. From observations of some members of the B. & B. commit-
> tee and checking over my 300 pages of notes and minutes of the 1965 special
> committee looking into Laurentian's mandate, I find little has changed since
> the special inquiry ... The B. & B. Aspect of Laurentian is dependent on the
> 85% majority for survival.[34]

At this meeting, Lavigne also demanded a redefinition of the powers, the composition and the functioning of the Bilingualism Committee, which would be introduced gradually six months later when it was decided, firstly, to make it a joint committee of Senate and the Board of Governors. But was this a sign that he had been too critical? In any case, he would not preside over this committee again. Though it seemed that the wishes of the Timmins businessman were finally being answered, it must be noted that this joint committee arose in the context of a power struggle between Senate and the Board of Governors as to the definition of their respective roles.

Later, the Committee addressed the financial aspects of bilingualism and sought to acquire new responsibilities in this area, showing firmer will in its interventions. The minutes of its meeting in December 1970 reported that:

> the direct costs of bilingualism for the current year are approximately
> $375,000; this amount does not include many supplementary costs. Accord-
> ing to the numbers provided, it would seem that every Francophone student

who registers at Laurentian robs the place of an Anglophone student: for this reason, we do not take into account the $132,000 attributed to the number of Francophone students registered at Laurentian. In any case, it is obvious that it is very difficult to find out how the bilingualism budget is administered.[35]

These statements are revealing in several respects. Whether the amounts discussed were exact or not, no one at the time seemed to know what the financial ramifications of bilingualism were, and, most importantly, certain administrators seemed convinced that bilingualism was a millstone around their necks, despite it being at the very heart of the idea of creating Laurentian University, which certainly indicates mistrust and much incomprehension.

In January 1971, the Board of Governors recommended that 20 per cent of the grant obtained by Laurentian in 1971–1972 for its French programs and services be administered by the Committee. At this same meeting, a request made by la Maison française was discussed and it was decided to give its facilitator, the militant professor Girouard, a small budget of $2,250 to finish the winter season and cover costs incurred over the summer.

Another Jesuit in the same department, Fernand Dorais, created a commotion worthy of the front page of the *Sudbury Star* in September 1971.[36] At the meeting of Senate that month, he noisily tendered his resignation as a senator and immediately wrote a document in which he justified his action on the grounds that he lacked the competence this body required:

> Mr. F. Dorais suddenly came to the stinging realization that, when he addressed the Senate in French, his position could have no impact on the two thirds of the members of the Senate who, not knowing French, could not understand the meaning or the importance of Mr. Dorais' intervention. For all practical considerations, it was as if Mr. Dorais had not spoken at all.[37]

Because of his poor command of English, he could only abstain on Senate votes, which in his opinion exacerbated his incapacity to be a member of this body. Although he reversed his decision after being pressed to do so, Dorais had underscored in very forceful terms the imbalance in mutual comprehension that remains to this day between Anglophones and Francophones. Since he could not rebuke the Anglophone majority for their desire to participate fully in meetings where exchanges were in both languages even though they did not speak French, all he could do was to withdraw from their proceedings to make them aware of the unease that such situations always create for the minority participant.

La Maison française

What was "la Maison française?" It was a project led by Girouard – that name again – whose intent was to regroup in one physical space a number of Francophone socio-cultural activities that could benefit from the presence of a facilita-

A STUDENT SING-SONG | Note the early posters of *La Nuit sur l'Étang* on the wall.

tor. This was not a new idea. According to its advocate,[38] such houses existed in many Ontario universities where a few floors in certain residences were reserved for those who wished to learn French. As Girouard explained to the Joint Committee on Bilingualism in November 1970:

> The language of communication in the French House must be French. A number of cultural activities are provided to foster exchanges. The purpose of this House is to create a meeting place between Anglophones and Francophones. The facilitator should be a full-time employee living in residence and acting as an intellectual guide for students. The residence is in the University of Sudbury, but it is hoped that a new building with a residence on the upper floor will be built.[39]

Though a new building to serve this Maison would never be constructed, and despite the failed attempt to create one in the Huntington residence, the activities of la Maison française had a certain measure of success. Assembling and coordinating existing clubs such as the student newspaper, the film club, the writers' club and the student theatre group la Troupe universitaire[40] was a natural mandate for la Maison française. Administering grants awarded by the Joint Committee on Bilingualism and the SGA was another aspect of its mandate.[41]

Despite its merits, la Maison française did not yet represent a turning point in the history of the Francophone community at Laurentian University. The principal factor of change came from elsewhere, from the obligation imposed on the university, then having serious internal problems, to revise its governance. This led to the Hagey report that has already been discussed in another section of this book. While the Francophone community stagnated and even regressed on the political level, it was alive with an unprecedented cultural effervescence that has even been described as a "cultural revolution."

The Hagey Report

We need not review the origins of this report, but to conclude this first part of the history of the French community and bilingualism, we will discuss one of its recommendations, namely the proposal to create a French college inside Laurentian University. Though this recommendation would never be implemented, the discussions about this idea and the resistance it provoked provide an excellent testimony to the thinking that prevailed at that time. Quoted here is the third recommendation of the report:

> That consideration be given to establishing a French College within Laurentian University. The college should be under the direction of a principal who would report to the president of the university.
> Following are some of the reasons for this proposal:
> a) A truly bilingual university is impractical. It is reliably reported that even Ottawa University is finding this to be a fact.
> b) People do not like to be forced into accepting either French or English even though they may be quite willing to do so voluntarily.
> c) English speaking as well as French speaking students should be able to enrol in the French College where they will be identified as making an effort to become bilingual.
> d) By having its own principal, there will be a senior officer of the university whose major responsibility will be the promotion of the French language and culture.
> e) Although the students enrolled in the French College would be at liberty to attend any of the university lectures for which they qualify, a separate French College would likely help to make more of the university courses available in French than there are at the present.
> ...
> In spite of the strong feeling that Laurentian should be a bilingual university, the fact is that it is not bilingual and most probably never will be. However, there is every possibility that a strong French College within the university would increase the interests of all Laurentian's students in bilingualism and biculturalism.[42]

This recommendation, which logically advocated regrouping French-language programs and nominating a person who would be responsible for their development, would nonetheless be categorically rejected by the Board of Governors in

April 1971 after deftly mandating the Joint Committee on Bilingualism to examine the proposal and submit its own recommendation. Hagey's proposal had visibly annoyed the eight Francophone members of the Joint Committee who stated that they had not been consulted on this matter, and suggested that should the proposal be implemented, it would create a ghetto. Basically, the model provided by York University's Glendon College did not apply to the Northern Ontario situation.

In fact, Hagey had not even received the necessary support from Francophones. On this issue, Dennie, in the previously mentioned report, certainly exaggerated the enthusiasm that this appealing idea had raised in them. Along with the president of the University of Sudbury,[43] the eight members of the Joint Committee including governor Lavigne opposed the idea. A reading of the Board of Governors' minutes reveals that at this same meeting the governors turned down a request from Francophone students dissatisfied with the bilingual *Lambda* who wanted financing for their own recently-launched newspaper, *Réaction*. Once again, the governors rejected a proposal to separate the Francophone community from the majority, just as the Maison française would never physically come into existence.[44] At a time when Quebec separatism was going strong, perhaps such proposals smacked too much of independence!

12 Claiming a Space, 1971 to 1984

GUY GAUDREAU

From the Troupe universitaire to the Théâtre du Nouvel-Ontario

Let us render unto Caesar that which is Caesar's. While in the midst of a financial crisis in the early 1970s, Laurentian University served as the cradle for several Franco-Ontarian cultural activities that would quickly become widely recognized across Ontario and even beyond. La Troupe universitaire, the student theatre group in existence since 1961 and the inheritor of Sacred Heart College's long theatrical tradition, changed its orientation in 1969 under the notable influence of professor Dorais.[1] A collective endeavour inspired by the counter-cultural movement in fashion at the time, it evolved over the course of the 1969–1970 academic year.[2] The experiment was repeated the following year, with new members who arrived in the fall; Pierre Bélanger, a graduate of Sacred Heart College who became director of la Troupe while he was a lecturer in the sociology department, and new students, notably André Paiement, Gaston Tremblay and Robert Paquette.[3]

Originally from Ontario's Temiskaming region and not much older than his young baby-boomer students, Bélanger defined a vision of the theatre which was at odds with traditional theatre, and probably inspired by the practice of a young author from Montreal, Michel Tremblay:

1   Express in a realistic manner the life of the people of Sudbury and the "New-Ontario" region. "It's not a matter of bringing theatre to the streets, but rather of bringing the streets to the stage."
2   Use a creative process that would allow for the expression of people's reality in the here and now, namely collective creation.
3   Incorporate many different media in a production.[4]

This vision produced a cult phenomenon in the history of theatre in French Ontario, *Moé, j'viens du Nord, 'stie!,* a production whose reputation is probably overblown. The play was first presented on campus on February 1, 1971. It enjoyed real success, and so it was decided, as customary for la Troupe, to take it on the road across Northern Ontario. This, too, met with success, inspiring some members of the group, André Paiement among them, to develop theatre productions outside the context of Laurentian. Their idea turned into a summer project that benefited from the Ontario program sponsored by the Youth and Leisure section of the Ministry of Education. Thus was born Théâtre du Nouvel-Ontario as a professional theatre group in 1971.

Without having the title, professors Girouard and Bélanger were certainly natural *animateurs* of the project. At this point in the 1970s, grass-roots promotion of cultural activities was on everyone's mind in the western world. In 1969, the *Saint-Denis Report* on cultural life in Ontario had called for this type of leadership across all of Northern Ontario. The regional section of l'Association canadienne-française de l'Ontario had hired a duly mandated facilitator whose salary was covered by grants from the Secretariat of State starting in January 1970.[5] Governments viewed this type of facilitation as a way to reach out to the electorate by validating its culture.[6] Public authorities also saw these facilitators as indispensable agents for change; their social and cultural activities helped draw the people closer to the seats of power that minorities, pacifists and protesters were assailing.

Though there were no investments in new programs, Hugues Albert, vice-president academic and research, hired a Francophone *animateur* in 1972. He was fortunate in recruiting the talented, yet discrete, Yvan Rancourt whose essential role across in the Northern Ontario Francophone community is a story that must someday be told. Originally from Quebec's Abitibi region, he had arrived on campus a year earlier to assume duties as an accounts controller for the Students' General Association. He already knew the students and, as he himself said in an interview in the winter of 1996, he "listened to what people were dreaming and to what made people dream."

Franco-Parole: The Birth of La Nuit sur l'Étang and
Prise de parole Publishing House

Thanks to a bilingualism grant provided by the Ontario government, Laurentian had in 1972–1973 a budget of $540,000 to serve the needs of the university's Franco-Ontarian community.[7] *Le service d'animation* received $20,000 of these funds.[8] Ideas were abundant and the need to express them urgently felt.

On March 15–16, 1973, Rancourt, Dorais and a group of students organized a symposium entitled *Franco-Parole* whose purpose was to reflect on the future of Laurentian. For the opening day, the student newspaper *Réaction* published a 144-page document that served as the event's program. "Ten years after its creation, it's time to reconsider this institution."[9] About one hundred participants carefully examined all aspects and services at Laurentian as a basis for preparing a series of recommendations.

The most concrete result of this symposium was undeniably the first *Nuit sur l'Étang* (a music festival presenting a concert program of Francophone musical artists) which became an annual event celebrated at Laurentian for the next 25 years. A book of poetry entitled *Lignes-Signes*, produced with Rancourt's support was also published. This publication gave birth to Prise de parole, a publishing house whose reputation is today firmly established.

When questioned about his role and his contribution as a facilitator for such projects, Rancourt gave this explanation:

> When you're a facilitator, you're not a leader and you shouldn't try to put forward your own aspirations because that won't work: as soon as you're gone, everything collapses ... The bad part of being a facilitator is that you end up losing your job, because people take charge of themselves and decide they don't need you anymore. If they reach that point, it's probably because you've accomplished your mandate![10]

Not all the facilitators who worked at Laurentian understood their role in this way. It might even be said that on the whole their relations with the student movement during the 1970s were fairly strained. As Gaétan Gervais recalled in an interview in 1996, the facilitators were paid by the vice-president but really worked for the students who considered themselves to be the real boss. And when facilitators sometimes took on the role of spokesperson, they were accused of usurping the place of elected students. All in all, such arrangements could not easily be harmonious.

The Birth of l'AEF and of the Franco-Ontarian Flag

A few years earlier, Franco-Ontarian students had created their own student newspaper and were no longer content to be represented by the SGA, a bilingual association, even though it had a Francophone section that in the past had monopolized the association's key positions. The good relations between Franco-Ontarian and Anglo-Ontarian students that Rancourt had observed at the SGA on his arrival were by 1973 a thing of the past. "Because the position of vice-president, francophone affairs [in the SGA], had become increasingly marginalized, the person elected to this position, Thérèse Boutin, noisily tendered her resignation."[11]

In a meeting to discuss the reorganization of la Maison française held on March 6, 1974 and attended by students and professors, the idea of forming an independent student association with the proposed name "la Maison des francophones" was first put forward. One of the people responsible for organizing the meeting was Dorais who replaced Girouard in this leadership role partly because the latter's health problems temporarily put him on the sidelines. Discussion of the reorganization of la Maison française reflected the fact that the Francophone community profile had rapidly evolved of late, and also that a new structure had appeared in Laurentian's administration, namely the Francophone Affairs committee, whose mandate went much farther than simply coordinating socio-cultural activities (which by then had become the mandate of la Maison française). As well, a year earlier, the administration had made encouraging promises to the university's

Francophone community (in the report "Planning for Tomorrow," a discussion of which follows).

Another key element in understanding the events leading to the creation of l'Association des étudiant(e)s francophones (AEF) was raised by Richard Théoret in an interview he gave with respect to a project tracing the history of the Franco-Ontarian flag.[12] As the editor of *Réaction* and the first vice-president of l'AEF, he was a close observer of events in this period. According to him, 1974 witnessed the arrival of a generation of students quite different from those of the 1960s, many of whom had been educated in English or bilingual secondary schools. For the new generation of students who attended French secondary schools, having a unilingual student association of their own seemed the more normal state of affairs.

In the eyes of its supporters, la Maison des francophones was to become a "clearing house of all Francophone student organizations and events on the campus of Laurentian University."[13] While one advantage of the existing SGA model was that individual students did not have to identify and clearly choose a linguistic affiliation, the new approach would be quite different. As was generally known – and is the case still today – a certain number of Franco-Ontarian students did not concern themselves with Francophone activities and political representation on campus, preferring to blend into the Anglophone mainstream. Offering a French-language student association in parallel with the existing nominally bilingual association would produce no consensus on campus.

To launch the project, an election was organized at the end of April to establish the first 'central committee.' Of all the students whose mother tongue was French, 58% participated in the vote, which left an important minority of students who, at least tacitly, either did not approve of the project, or had no interest in it. While believing that they had secured a legitimate mandate, the members of the central committee knew that they needed to do more, and garner broader support. At its first meeting on June 14, 1974, "le Comité central de la Maison des francophones" – the name sounded somewhat left-leaning – decided to change its name to something with a more popular appeal. They chose "Canayens de l'Université Laurentienne, Ontario-Nord" (an approximate translation would be "Canucks of Laurentian University, Ontario North"). The resulting acronym, CULON, which sounded like 'long butt,' was vaguely indecent. Dorais' influence could be suspected here!

One cannot but draw a line between the ADELFNO and CULON, organizations that both loudly and clearly proclaimed their allegiance not to Sudbury, but to Northern Ontario. The idea that Laurentian's Francophone community had a regional dimension was very much current at that time. For example, readers of the French student newspaper *Réaction* followed the battle for a French-language high school in 1971 and 1972. The regional dimension was also front and centre in the name of the renowned group CANO: its acronym meant "Artists' Cooperative of Northern Ontario." Evidently, the small Franco-Ontarian minority was striving to broaden its base of legitimacy by promoting its regional dimension.

Since "money forms the sinews of war," CULON formally asked the SGA to hand over the dues – $27 per student – that it had collected from students. Faced

RAISING THE FRANCO-ONTARIAN FLAG, 1975 | The Franco-Ontarian flag is hoisted in front of the University of Sudbury for the first time, on September 25, 1975. One of the co-designers, student Michel Dupuis, stands at the foot of the flagpole while the other, the young history professor Gaétan Gervais, preferring to remain in the crowd, may be seen on the right of the photograph.

with the SGA's refusal, which, understandably, undermined its legitimacy, and under pressure from the administration, CULON decided to hold a referendum in the fall, the question now being whether an autonomous French student association was in fact desired.

Four hundred and thirty students who had declared French as their mother tongue were invited to vote in this referendum on October 7 and 8. Participation was heavier than in April, with 320 students casting a ballot, a participation rate of 74 per cent. With a slim majority of 56.5 per cent l'Association des étudiant(e)s francophones was born,[14] whereupon CULON enthusiastically dissolved.

In this chronicle of the defining period in the history of Laurentian's Francophone community, a few comments must be made about the creation of the Franco-Ontarian flag in 1975. This story has been told elsewhere, so suffice it to say that Laurentian was the birthplace of this symbol that is now recognized everywhere in the wider Francophone community. The flag, designed by the young history professor, Gaétan Gervais, and his student, Michel Dupuis, was raised for the first time on a flagpole at the University of Sudbury – not at Laurentian – on September 25, 1975. This initiative was not widely noticed outside of the campus, but over the years, it became a powerful symbol of identity around which consensus is now complete. As well, it provided a fitting conclusion to four vibrant years in the history of Laurentian's Francophone community, though not for the issue of French-language education at Laurentian, which remained very fragile.

Planning for Tomorrow

The arrival of a new president in the summer of 1972 combined with the university's financial crisis over a number of years to usher in a new era, forcing the administration to reflect on the future of the institution, and prepare its first development plan. The university's Academic Planning Committee naturally took the leadership role in this endeavour, which occupied all of the 1972–1973 academic year. In April 1973, the Committee submitted 20 proposals to the Senate, the objective being to debate them and approve the final report by the last meeting in June.[15] The report was entitled "Planning for Tomorrow – Pour la planification de notre avenir."

The content of these recommendations certainly challenged Laurentian's Francophone community. Besides the unrealistic objective of expecting 'all personnel' to have a good knowledge of their second language within five years, meaning minimum-level bilingual proficiency, the Committee recommended, notably, increasing the number of courses offered in French and the number of bursaries for bilingual students, as well as striking a new committee on Francophone Affairs which would coordinate the revision and development of French programs.[16] The creation of this committee, more or less the ancestor of the current Conseil des programmes en français, was finally approved by the Senate in December 1973. It immediately went to work under the leadership of the vice-president academic and research, Hugues Albert, suggesting that it was the administration's representation in the university's Francophone community, rather than vice-versa.

The creation of this committee relegated the Joint Committee on Bilingualism, which to this point had been the Francophone community's foremost administrative body, to a secondary level. In comparison, the new Senate committee had a very broad mandate: "All the rights and interests of Francophones from three points of view, administrative, academic and socio-cultural, are the responsibility of the Francophone Affairs Committee." It could study all questions pertinent to the Francophone community and had the right to review the preparation of budgets attributed to Francophone programs and activities. While promoting the cultural expression of the Franco-Ontarian fact, it would ensure that policies affecting Francophones were put into practice. All in all, it was quite a program!

Among the debates sparked by the adoption of "Planning for Tomorrow," of particular interest was undoubtedly the one on biculturalism that occurred in June 1973. The idea of bilingualism was not a major issue, but biculturalism was quite another matter. According to the *Sudbury Star* on June 22nd,[17] many senators wanted to eliminate all reference to this concept, preferring the vision of Pierre Elliot Trudeau who had proposed multiculturalism – into which French Canada was merged – in order to respect all cultural communities present in Canada. Despite Wes Cragg's forcefully expressed point of view that Canadians were necessarily either Anglophone or Francophone, this debate signalled a turning point when biculturalism, seen as too exclusive, was dealt a mortal blow.

A TYPICAL DAY IN THE
BOWLING ALLEY

Many other recommendations in this report concerned the Francophone community. Briefly, the list included: 1) bilingualism would thereafter be indicated as an asset in all job postings for professors and administrators; 2) the ability to teach in both languages would be a criterion for promotion; 3) personnel in a position of contact with the public would be fully bilingual, not just minimally so; 4) graduate programs in French would be developed; and 5) the number of French books in the library would increase with an acquisitions program developed to meet this goal.

The origins of these laudable propositions were not simply internal to Laurentian; they also emerged from the provincial level where two commissions of inquiry in 1972 had underlined the need to do more for bilingual university programs and services, and to acknowledge the additional costs involved. The Symons commission, whose mandate was to examine French-language secondary education, made a troubling observation about the weakness of French-language programming in this 1972 statement: "[T]he Ontario university system does not yet offer to Franco-Ontarians the opportunity to study in their own tongue the range and variety of courses which it has long been possible for English-speaking university students to take in their tongue in the province of Québec."[18]

Similar observations came from the Wright commission on post-secondary education in Ontario in December 1972, when it proposed fifteen recommendations concerning, in particular, "better programmes in the fields of health sciences ... as well as education, commerce and continuing education."[19] Even library resources were identified as a matter of concern.

Obviously, governmental authorities were aware of the repercussions on Canadian unity of the treatment of the Franco-Ontarian minority.[20] Laurentian was prepared to do its part. That is why, in 1974, following a report submitted by the Francophone Affairs committee, Senate took further steps and adopted a policy aimed at ensuring full bilingualism among administrative personnel. More than thirty administrative positions were designated as requiring integral bilingualism, including those of president, vice-president, dean and registrar. Senate went even further in decreeing "that the position of Chairmen of Departments or Directors of Schools offering programs in French or planning to do so be designated as a position requiring integral bilingualism."[21] All this, theoretically, was a major advance.[22]

However, as President Monahan later admitted:

> All of these recommendations were adopted by Senate, but not all of them have been implemented. Indeed, one can judge fairly that very few of these proposals, and only the least significant ... All faculty and administrative postings are now listed as bilingual preferred. Some academic units have taken seriously the request to seek actively for bilingual faculty; but some have not. And bilingual faculty in many disciplines, especially those in which the University has been hiring, are still difficult to find. A number of recent appointees to senior administrative positions have been integrally bilingual, but not all. Only two of the four Deans named in 1974 possessed this capability. And recent appointees to the offices of Vice-President (Administration) and Registrar lacked this capability. Other University officers whose positions pre-date 1973, including the President, have yet to meet fully this requirement.
>
> Second-language training for staff was expanded, with mixed results. A number of academic units have developed plans to expand their French-language offerings; but again these have been the exceptions to the norm. With the University facing retrenchment and resources at a premium almost everywhere, there has been little incentive to undertake to develop new programmes of any kind. French-language programmes have been no exception.
>
> Despite the adoption of an internal plan intended to strengthen the University's commitment to bilingualism, the implementation of this plan has been largely thwarted by the shortage of the financial resources necessary to render it operational.[23]

No doubt, financial difficulties partly explained the university's inability to make good on its promises to its French community. Though Queen's Park recognized the need to offer more to Franco-Ontarians, it did not, according to Monahan, adjust its grants to reflect this. But these difficulties obviously did not explain everything. The decision to hire or nominate a unilingual candidate for a position designated as bilingual cannot easily be justified in terms of financial constraints. The example provided by non-bilingual persons at the highest administrative positions could have no other effect than to encourage blatant disregard for the policy. From another perspective, it is apparent that these years when French programs made little or no progress clearly contrasted with the encouraging progress on the cultural level, and even on that of political autonomy.

During this time, the Francophone Affairs committee was not idle. Arguably, it lacked a true chair because the university vice-president who assumed the position was serving only in an acting capacity while the search for a permanent appointee continued. In its quest for a new legitimacy, the committee, through its secretary, Benoît Cazabon, convened an assembly of Francophone professors and administrators on February 7th to discuss this question. Though similar meetings had taken place in the past, it could be said that this one is in fact the birth of l'Assemblée des professeurs francophones that was officially created the following year, in April 1976. This body of Francophone professors remains active today, despite its unofficial status, and will be discussed in further detail later.

Thirty professors attended this meeting which unanimously adopted two motions. One affirmed the necessity of nominating a vice-president academic and research who was a Francophone by virtue of mother tongue and culture, and called for the position to be left vacant until the right candidate was found. The second identified six other positions at upper administrative levels that required obligatory full bilingualism, and insisted that if no competent candidate could be found internally, external candidates should be recruited.

The letter sent by the committee to governors, senators and the president on February 11th was perfectly clear. It expressed concern over the upcoming nomination of two vice-presidents, four deans and the director of graduate studies. Disappointed by the system of exceptions put in place to bypass the rules for nominations, and worried about the composition of the committees, the Francophone Affairs committee demanded that full bilingualism be not just a criterion of competence, but a condition *sine qua non*. Nothing, however, came from such efforts, not even from the letter of protest issued by l'AEF on April 22, 1975 following the nomination of two unilingual Anglophones: dean of Sciences Douglas Williamson and Vice-President Administration Thomas Hennessy.

The Francophone Presence at the Department Level: An Overview

To understand the evolution of French and bilingualism at Laurentian, the state of affairs at the department level must also be examined. A report prepared by the Academic Planning Committee in April 1975[24] provided a complete statistical account, thanks to a survey sent to all units at Laurentian and its federated universities. Table 12.1 shows the results.

If this table can be believed, almost two thirds of all professors, 87 in total, mastered both official languages, while 51 were unilingual. This surprising result was due in particular to the solid performance of the department of sociology, which at that time was the university's most bilingual department, producing more than its share of deans. The nine professors in the school of translation, the ten professors of religious studies, as well as the ten colleagues at the French department who were not as bilingual as the table suggests, also weighed heavily in the totals.

The real cause for dismay was the number of Francophone programs offered, which can only be described as paltry. None in the Sciences! In the Professional Schools, the scene was dismal. In some cases, there were competent professors who could have taught courses in French, but who were assigned to the English

Department or School	Fully bilingual professors	Minimally bilingual professors	Francophone programs
English	2	3	Not applicable
Astronomy	2	0	None
Biology	2	3	None
Chemistry	2	2	None
Commerce	0	3	None
Physical Education	1	3	None
Classical Studies	1	0	Not applicable
Français	10	1	3-, 4-year and master's (part time)
Engineering	0	0	None
Geography	3	0	3-year
Geology	0	2	None
History	5	7	3-, 4-year
Modern Languages	5	2	Not applicable
Mathematics	3	4	None
Philosophy	4	2	3-year
Psychology	5	6	3-, 4-year
Physics	2	3	None
Economics	3	1	Continuation
Nursing	1	0	None
Political Science	2	4	3-, 4-year
Religious Studies	10	0	3-year
Social Work	2	3	None
Sociology and anthropology	13	2	3-, 4-year (socio.) 3-year (anth.)
Translation	9	0	3-, 4-year
Total	87	51	

* L'École des sciences de l'éducation is not included.

programs. In the Sciences, nine professors were able to teach in French, but they were spread out among six departments. Consequently, few courses in this faculty were taught in French, only four in 1974–1975. As for master's programs, only the French department offered one, and it was part-time.

Let us pursue our analysis by reference to the distressing findings that Gaétan Gervais presented in a report written in April 1976, along with recommendations that the Bilingualism Committee later submitted, once again unsuccessfully.[25] The Gervais report entitled 'For a Reform of the Programs in French at Laurentian University' had been prepared as a discussion paper for a meeting of the Assembly of Francophone professors at the request of the Francophone Affairs and Bilingualism Committees. No document differed more strikingly from the mass of material submitted to the Senate than this one, which the Administration later translated into English.

To regroup Francophone professors who were too dispersed to offer coherent programs designed for the Franco-Ontarian clientele, the report proposed the creation of seven homogenous Francophone teaching units. Like so many other recommendations, this one never came to fruition because Francophone professors at that time, like today, clearly preferred to be grouped together on the basis of their disciplines, not linguistically, thereby demonstrating strong solidarity with their Anglophone colleagues in their respective departments. Nonetheless, the thinking around this report allowed a more in-depth examination of the realities of the situation that prevailed at the time in the various departments and schools with regard to French programs.

According to Gervais, the weakness of the resources provided for courses taught in French should not have been an impediment to rethinking the model established to serve the Anglophone majority. "Despite the small number of French speaking professors and students, we are forced to live within structures that are slavish imitations of the English models. Thus, the lack of global planning and the dissipation of knowledge (a dissipation which corresponds to the needs of the English-speaking majority) forces French-speaking professors to offer only fragments of programmes."[26] This observation led him to call for the creation of a position of vice-president responsible for French programs, something that would happen later. Anglophone colleagues considered it completely normal for their vision of the programs to be applied to the minority as well, and represented, for all, the royal road to knowledge. To this way of thinking, structuring programs specifically for the Franco-Ontarian community was virtually going against nature.

According to Gervais, a major weakness of French programs was the limited choice of courses. A bachelor's degree taught by three professors could not equal in quality one offered by eight faculty. Not surprisingly, Franco-Ontarian students had to take half of their courses in English. Few Franco-Ontarian students studied at Laurentian because many of them went to Ottawa where they could truly study in French.

Inspired by the Gervais report and worried about the way grants for bilingualism were being used, given that they were not attributed specifically to French-language programs, l'AEF waded into the debate with a manifesto on bilingualism submitted to Senate. The Association presented three proposals, some of which are still very pertinent today.

1   That the Academic Senate of Laurentian University, in its internal organization, be split into two chambers (one Anglophone, one Francophone) and that these two chambers exercise power jointly over the Senate.
2   That the grants for bilingualism be managed by the Bilingualism and Biculturalism Committee with the Francophone Affairs Committee, under the direction of the vice-president, academic.

3   That Francophone courses no longer be parallel to Anglophone courses, in
    order to allow for the autonomous development of Francophone programs
    at Laurentian University.

The demand for a bicameral Senate, heavy with consequences, was not l'AEF's
alone. It had first been formulated by the Francophone Affairs committee and sent
to the Senate in March 1976. The reply had come from the Senate's secretary, the
unilingual Jack Porter, who had skated around the question by requesting a definition of the concrete modalities of bicameralism.[27] The demand also stemmed
from the efforts of the citizens' committee of ACFO de Sudbury, which had
requested, as early as 1971, the creation of two independent sections in the university, one French, one English, not just for academic matters, but for services,
administration and finances as well.[28] The surprise victory of the Parti Québécois
in November 1976 and the sudden fear that Canada would split in two, in our view,
effectively buried this idea for a long time, though it occasionally resurfaced.

The Institut franco-ontarien and the Conseil de l'enseignement en français

Although there were fewer than ten Franco-Ontarian professors among Laurentian's faculty in 1977, under the impetus of Cazabon, Dennie and Gervais, they
formed a research group devoted to Franco-Ontarian questions and invited colleagues from other Ontario universities to join. Thus was born the Institut franco-
ontarien (IFO), the purpose of which was to reflect on different Franco-Ontarian
realities, past and present. The Institute's first director was Benoît Cazabon. A
scholarly journal that published only articles written in French, under the direction of Donald Dennie, was established a year later. La Revue du Nouvel-Ontario
was a rival to the research journal that the University had created ten years earlier, the Laurentian University Review/Revue de l'Université Laurentienne. The
latter publication had attempted to address the Franco-Ontarian community in
1971 by publishing its first edition devoted to "the Francophone fact in Northern
Ontario,"[29] and by stating that its mandate was "to promote the universal vocation of the French language and French literature." In order to meet this wider
goal, the review published articles that were diverse in nature, their only common
denominator being the fact that they were written in French. The bilingual review's
orientation no doubt explained the desire to create another scholarly publication
with a specifically Franco-Ontarian mandate. As stated in the introduction to the
first edition of la Revue du Nouvel-Ontario:

> The revue also intends to pursue another one of the Institute's objectives,
> namely to help stimulate the Franco-Ontarian community. From its begin-
> nings, the Institute wished to go beyond strictly academic pursuits and play
> a facilitating role in community-based activities by making research find-
> ings known through publications and participating in the initiatives of
> community groups.[30]

FRENCH DEPARTMENT
PROFESSORS JACQUES
BERGER AND PASCAL
SABOURIN BROWSE
THE *REVUE DU NOUVEL-
ONTARIO* AND OTHER
FRANCOPHONE
JOURNALS

Another stage in the struggle to ensure the development of the Francophone community on campus succeeded in 1978 by taking advantage, once again, of an opportunity that arose from a reconsideration of the university's governance necessitated by its modest growth and need for reform. A joint committee of the Senate and the Board of Governors had been struck for this purpose in 1976. After seven months of weekly meetings, the committee produced the Weaver report[31] in 1977.

Specifically on the Francophone question, the committee observed that the vice-president academic and research, who held final responsibility in these matters ever since the creation of the Francophone Affairs committee, was overloaded with various files, and did not have the time to meet his obligations relating to Francophone Affairs. A new solution was required, and a year would be needed to have it approved by the Senate, due mainly to the Academic Planning Committee's in-depth examination of the Weaver report. Finally, September 1978 witnessed the creation of the Conseil de l'enseignement en français (CEF) and of the position of directeur des programmes en français (director of French programs), the council's coordinator.

Had it not been for the interventions of the Assembly of Francophone professors and the Francophone Affairs committee, the university's administration might not have come up with such a solution. In fact, since 1976, as a show of protest against the slow pace of desired reforms, the members of the Francophone Affairs committee had followed an "empty chair" strategy, thus paralysing it while concentrating their efforts in the newly created assembly of professors. This was the body that had already proposed the creation of the CEF in 1976[32] and that had said it was prepared to wait for the recommendations of the Weaver committee.

TWO STUDENTS READ
THE FRANCOPHONE
STUDENT NEWSPAPER
RÉACTION IN THE
EARLY 1980S

Thereafter, the Francophone Affairs committee had formally proposed its creation in 1977,[33] but then it had to wait for the planning committee's recommendations.

Many meetings were required to establish the CEF – there were eleven between October 24 and December 18 – because the project started virtually from scratch. The council's operation was very collegial, as indicated by the fact that its secretary, Justin Lévesque, professor of social work, not its director, signed the minutes. From the outset the CEF worked closely with the assembly. On March 22, 1979, for example, the CEF decided, as if this was the natural course of things, "that a general assembly of Francophone professors will be held on Friday, April 6th 1979."[34]

This advance marked the most important break with the past for Laurentian's Francophone community up to that point. Most notably, a director chosen by elected members in the various faculties and services had been entrusted with the council's leadership position. "Members of the Council," the *Laurentian University Gazette* explained, "proceeded to choose the Director of the C.E.F. after consultation with the Assembly of Francophone professors."[35] Consultation with the Assembly provided the CEF director with a solid base of legitimacy. Girouard, who had recovered from his health problems, was chosen unanimously, and was partially relieved of his teaching duties so that he could devote himself to these responsibilities. Instead of representing the administration before the community and drawing its legitimacy from the administration, the Council had become the voice of the aspirations of the community and could also depend on the Assembly to act as a pressure group. Because he could deal with these questions almost full-time and count on the input of persons from all areas of the university, the director was in a position to work for progress in the area of French-language programs.

Among the accomplishments of the CEF and its director Girouard was the études coopératives program adopted by the Senate in 1981 and implemented in the winter of 1982. That, at least, was the achievement emphasized in the university's annual report for 1981 published to highlight Laurentian's 20th anniversary.[36]

Girouard also wanted his communications studies program to be implemented, but "the Ministry of Colleges and Universities' freeze on new programmes ... abruptly put an end to [it]."[37] However, the failure that no doubt stung him the most during his mandate which ended June 30, 1981 was his effort to transform the CEF into a true faculty,[38] and to turn his position into a full deanship with all attendant powers such as a seat on the budget committee, and the authority to hire professors. In fact, control over funds related to French-language education, many times demanded, notably in October 1979, always met with Senate refusal.[39] As for hiring – even of Francophone professors for which he had in fact written the grant applications submitted to the Council for Franco-Ontarian Education – the procedure was completely beyond his control. This great defender of Laurentian's Francophone community expressed his point of view thusly:

> Nominated by Senate and therefore answering to Senate, the members
> of the Bilingualism and Francophone Affairs Committee represent the
> Francophone community only in a broad sense, since their mandate does
> not stem from this community, and the weight of their recommendations
> was weakened by the absence of any authorized consultative procedure. It
> is therefore not surprising that the Bilingualism Committee is in a state of
> hibernation and that the Francophone Affairs Committee had decided to
> be totally inactive in the two years preceding the creation of the Conseil de
> l'enseignement en français. In comparison to other committees, this Council has the advantage of being the official representative of the Francophone
> sector in the Senate and its recommendations have the same weight as those
> of a faculty council. However, this power to present recommendations is
> weakened by the power granted to faculty councils who can pass judgment
> on the CEF's projects, as if its members were not quite members of a true
> council. Even more serious is the absence of any right regarding the budgetary aspect of French-language programmes: the deans of traditional faculties continue to approve budgets and hire professors for its programmes
> over which they have no jurisdiction, or will continue to refuse to establish
> French-language courses and programmes for budgetary reasons.[40]

Given these circumstances and again in poor health, Girouard, not surprisingly, refused a second mandate, and the university established a selection committee in March 1981 to choose his successor. Divided over the issue of a French faculty, the Assembly of Francophone professors nonetheless remained convinced of the need to acquire more powers from the administration for the CEF. For this reason, the "empty chair" strategy was once again applied; the nomination process to replace the CEF's director was boycotted, and no candidates were proposed.

This manoeuvre produced results. In August 1981, Gaétan Gervais was finally designated as Girouard's replacement and President Best granted him a seat on the budget committee as well as full administrative authority over 5 per cent of the bilingualism grant.[41] In exchange, the CEF promised to drop its demand for a French faculty, to Girouard's displeasure, for a good while.

For Gervais, as for Girouard, the basis of his legitimacy clearly stemmed from the Franco-Ontarian community and not from the administration, even if, in contrast to Girouard, he owed his nomination to the latter. The administration no doubt understood it was important that "the Council [be] directed by a high-level academic administrator appointed by the University."[42] Gervais, whose mandate was renewed for five years at summer's end in 1983, nevertheless intended to pursue his activities in close collaboration with the Assembly, a conception of the role of CEF director that would lead to pitched battles with certain colleagues and administrators.

The CEF had been asked to develop for the spring of 1982 a three-year plan "dealing with the development of the Francophone component of academic programmes,"[43] and under Gervais' direction, it took aim at the school of commerce, "where registrations are the highest in the entire University."[44] According to Gervais, "it seems unacceptable ... that it persists in being completely unilingual."[45] The development of a French-language commerce program was certainly Gervais' most decisive success as director. Although today its existence seems quite normal, at the time the idea of offering an education in French in this discipline made no sense for many Anglophone professors in the school. It was well known that the language of business was not the language of Molière! However, a French-language program in this discipline was not a new idea because it had been put forward by the Francophone Affairs committee as early as 1974.[46] To a certain extent, this development represents a psychological tipping point because, thereafter, French-language programs could be proposed in any area.

Besides intellectual barriers – often the hardest to overcome – another fundamental obstacle appeared when French-language programs were introduced in a department or school: the weakening of the English-language program because the new French course offerings were often not accompanied by essential new resources. Only with additional grants, applied for by the CEF, could new French-language programs be mounted. That remained the case for the next fifteen years, during which time French-language programs were established in the Professional Schools and in the Sciences.

For the school of commerce, thanks to Gervais' persistence, Laurentian finally obtained funding from governmental authorities in 1983 to create three positions funded by the Council for Franco-Ontario Education (CFOE). These CFOE positions eliminated the last objections raised by the school, which to this point had opposed the hiring of the first professor despite Senate's request in a motion going back to the fall of 1982.[47] However, the establishment of a French-language commerce program starting in the 1983–1984 academic year took its toll on Gervais' health, forcing him to take a leave from December 1983 until the May of the following year.

Meanwhile, in October 1982, the provincial government had created another committee to study the university situation in northeastern Ontario. "Known as the Parrott committee, it submitted its report in [October] 1983 and recommended

PRESIDENT BEST
PROPOSES A TOAST
TO LAURENTIAN'S
FRANCOPHONE
COMMUNITY

a fundamental restructuring of Laurentian's university system."[48] The report, proposing a fusion of Laurentian's several colleges and universities, remained a dead letter because of the various campuses' objections to losing their autonomy. However, in response to the government's desire for better coordination among northeastern Ontario's four university institutions, Laurentian proposed including representatives of the Collège de Hearst on the CEF. Moreover, President Best found a skilful way to counter the traditional demands that the CEF and the ACFO had presented to the Parrott committee a few months earlier. As Best confided to the chair of the Board of Governors:

> I would like to add that the possibility of a bicameral Senate, a Faculty or a
> French college (… none of these ideas are new) had also been considered,
> but the general view was that the CEF is now working quite well and there is
> every reason to believe that we would obtain vastly improved results if this
> body assumed more extensive responsibilities.[49]

In essence, the CEF had demonstrated such effectiveness that nothing more was required!

Best's departure in 1984 brought about the arrival of a new team of administrators who would impose their vision for Laurentian's development. Before proceeding to this third period in Laurentian's history, one last episode should be recalled, namely the laborious decision, made in 1983, to give students the choice of writing their papers and exams in the language of their choice.

The story began in September 1981 when the dean of Professional Schools asked the vice-president to clarify the university's rule that permitted students to use the language of their choice in their written communications. Up until this point, the rule had never caused trouble, but things took another turn when Franco-

Ontárian students who had to take courses in English insidiously asked to submit their work in French, given the absence of French programs in the Professional Schools. The issue raised by their request became a veritable hot potato, and it was obvious that the answer would have political repercussions. Vice-President Frank Turner passed the question on to the secretary of the Senate, who in turn forwarded it to the Joint Committee on Bilingualism in October 1981. No reply having been forthcoming, the question was once again addressed to the same committee in February 1982, again in March, and once more in December. The answer finally arrived in May 1983, after twenty months! It established the rule that remains in effect to this day: a student may submit a paper or an exam in the language of his or her choice, and the professor is responsible for its evaluation and decides on the best course of action to do so.[50]

13   Don't Worry, Be Happy!
1984 to the Present

GUY GAUDREAU

The third phase of the history of Laurentian's Francophone community unfolded with new leadership in place. André Girouard retired in 1986, and Gaétan Gervais took a leave of absence the following year. The Assemblée des professeurs francophones, which to this point had worked closely with both of them, now found itself somewhat disorganized and in need of new spokespersons, a role that the new professor of commerce, Jean-Charles Cachon, could not fulfill alone.

Francophone issues were no longer raised by professors and students, as to this point had been the case, but by the administration whose hand was forced by political and judicial considerations. By appropriating the issue, administrators could define its legitimacy in their own way and on their own terms. The political context began to change in the middle of the 1980s with the new federal *Charter of Rights and Freedoms* which afforded protection to official-language minorities and had legal implications for the educational system, and when the Ontario government adopted Bill 8, the *French Language Services Act*, in 1987.

From Director to Vice-president

Back with a renewed five-year mandate in 1983 after returning from sick leave, Gaétan Gervais continued to pursue, with the support of the CEF, the development of new programs, especially in the Professional Schools, namely nursing, physical education and social work. However, the arrival of President John Daniel in 1984 changed the relationship, which to then had been harmonious, between the CEF and the other administrators. Shortly after taking office, Daniel reconfigured the budget committee, excluding Gervais and the deans from this crucial decision-making body. A portend of tense relations to come, this decision, followed in 1985 by the nomination of a new vice-president, Charles Bélanger, to whom Gervais was answerable, eventually led the latter to move to Toronto in

1987 to work on assignment for the Ministry of Colleges and Universities. It must be noted that Gervais's departure was not forced upon him by the administration because, despite his often unwavering dissension, it almost always displayed openness towards his ideas, as it did towards those of others who opposed it.

One of the battles that Gervais did bring to a successful conclusion involved the library, where the purchase of French books and periodicals did not meet expectations. In the interests of French programs, and because Franco-Ontarian students had every right to study works in their mother tongue, greater efforts were needed to ensure that more resources were ordered in French. In October 1983, Gervais had asked the chief librarian to provide information on the budgets for the acquisition of books in French. Despite repeated requests, not the slightest progress on the issue was made. In January 1985, therefore, Gervais addressed twelve questions to the president on this matter.[1] He also copied them to the secretary of Senate, with the request that answers be provided at the upcoming monthly meeting. By making the issue public, and at the risk of making new enemies, Gervais forced the chief librarian to be accountable.

From the point of view of the chief librarian and of those responsible for science programs, whose periodicals, almost exclusively in English, took up the lion's share of the purchasing budget, a book was a book, without regard to language. And because basic textbooks were available only in English, given limited resources, the best that could be done was to aim for the highest cost effectiveness. When Senate saw how few funds were specifically budgeted for French books, however, it established a year later a special advisory committee for the library's French-language collection with Gervais as chair. He ultimately presented a report to the Senate on April 18, 1986, in which he recommended the creation of a catch-up fund and a formula for budget-sharing that would ensure the purchase of a certain proportion of French books and periodicals.[2]

The creation of the position of assistant vice-president of French programs and services to replace that of the director of French programs was recommended by the Joint Committee on Bilingualism, after nine meetings held between November 1986 and May 1987. Senate approved the recommendation in January 1988. After having rejected a French faculty, a French college and a bicameral Senate, its members had decided that this new position would ensure a better response to future challenges.[3] In fact, several major political developments had caused the rethinking of this question. In addition to Bill 8, the *French Language Services Act*, the Churchill report had underscored the lower level of educational achievement among Franco-Ontarians. Of great significance, too, was the establishment of autonomous French-language school boards in Ontario, the first of which appeared in 1988. As is well known, these school boards were the consequence of successful judicial challenges based on the *Charter of Rights and Freedoms* adopted in 1982.

Unable to work harmoniously with Bélanger, Gervais left his position in the summer of 1987. Six months were needed to redefine the position and find the right candidate, in the person of Dyane Adam. New to Laurentian as a professor

DYANE ADAM | Named assistant vice-president of French programs and services in June 1988, Dyane Adam was the first woman to hold an upper-level administrative position at Laurentian. In this role she proved adept at walking a tightrope between serving the administration to whom she owed her first loyalties, and demonstrating sensitivity to the needs of the Francophone university community and staunchly defending the rights of women.

of psychology in the summer of 1987, she was appointed assistant vice-president of French programs and services in January 1988.[4] As the first woman to occupy an upper-level administrative position, she started off her position on June 1st, 1988 with a disquieting feminist speech. She had a seat at the budget committee and, as had been agreed, coordinated the Conseil de l'enseignement en français.

Being so new to the institution, Adam did not have the same relationship or the same partnership with the Assembly of Francophone professors. In contrast to that of Girouard and Gervais, her legitimacy of necessity came from the administration, even more so because she did not yet personally know the Francophone faculty. Adam nonetheless made progress on various dossiers, holding evening gatherings and numerous informal meetings, calming fears and frustrations in some quarters, and fostering exchanges. She had strong consensus-building skills and undeniable political instincts, as her later appointment as Commissioner of Official Languages would confirm.

In a general sense, Adam benefited to a great extent from the work done by Gervais. In the fall of 1988, President Daniel recognized this when he stated that the number of courses offered in French had risen by 34 per cent since 1984, and that registrations of French students had risen by 38 per cent, in comparison to a slim 9 per cent for the Anglophones students during the same period. In the words of the president, "you are all aware of the main reason for these encouraging changes. It is the implementation of new programmes, in particular in the Professional Schools."[5]

Over the course of her five-year mandate, Adam focused on the development of French-language science programs, with the assistance of generous financial support from the Government of Ontario's program for CFOE positions. When, at the end of the 1980s, Ontario changed its funding policy for these positions and transformed its program of one-time, one-year grants into recurring and renewable grants, Laurentian was guaranteed ongoing financing for positions that would probably not have been created through the good will of the Laurentian majority alone.

The arrival of about fifteen new colleagues in the Sciences progressively transformed the Francophone faculty, due to the fact that in their professional practice everything is done in English, that being the universal language of communication, but one that nonetheless drains the fragile cultural identity of Franco-Ontarians. In addition, new professors both in the Sciences and in other disciplines were unlikely to be Franco-Ontarian because few Franco-Ontario sons and daughters earned doctoral degrees. When the departure of its traditional leaders is added to the picture, it is not hard to understand why the Assembly of Francophone professors lost much of its political sensibilities. Most newcomers need time – when they are in fact able to do so – to comprehend the importance of the political issues affecting minority communities.

By the early 1990s, therefore, the Assembly of Francophone professors had been transformed and relegated to a secondary role. Overshadowed by the formally sanctioned CEF whose mandate and functioning were tied closely to Senate, the Assembly included many individuals won over by Adam's management style. Not surprisingly, the Assembly, led somewhat maladroitly by Yvan Morais and the author of this chapter, turned to social activities, organizing welcoming parties for new professors in the autumn and, after Adam's departure in 1993, organizing the annual Souper de la francophonie, an event that she and Raoul Étongué-Mayer had initiated in 1990. The future of Laurentian's Francophone community was being decided elsewhere, in the offices of the vice-presidents, from which other compromise solutions would emerge in time, but also from within Sudbury's Francophone community which, in 1989, was preparing to do battle for a French university.

Attempts to Institute Bicameralism

The departure of Gaétan Gervais in 1987 undoubtedly facilitated the creation of the position of assistant vice-president in the fall of that year. The administration would certainly have had more difficulty taking this step if it had to deal with the generally more combative director of the CEF. His leaving also permitted the Joint Committee on Bilingualism to get back into harness and to pursue its evaluation of Laurentian's administrative structure, this time in a political context that was particularly favourable to Ontario's Francophone community.

> The Joint Committee on Bilingualism has been attempting for over two
> years [since 1987] to revise the present administrative structures so that
> they will take into account the new developments and particular needs with
> respect to French language teaching at Laurentian. As an institution apply-
> ing for designation under Bill 8 on French language services, the criteria for

designation, i.e. accessibility, availability, permanency, and quality of services, as well as an effective francophone representation at all decision levels, are also part of the background for this exercise.[6]

The first results of the committee's deliberations were presented by the president in January 1989, just before the creation of Ontario's first Francophone college, la Cité collégiale, was announced. Was this a coincidence? We think not. Daniel's proposal put out for discussion at the time was the creation of a Francophone teaching faculty. The proposition, which did not take into account the obstacles that the idea had encountered during Girouard's time, circulated only briefly. On February 17th, Dean Michael Dewson informed the president that he had twice met with his faculty – the first was with the Francophone professors only – and that their reactions were unfavourable.[7] Given that the president's plan would have had the greatest impact on the Faculty of Social Sciences, another solution would have to be sought.

Five models for the management of Francophone programs were subsequently developed by the joint committee in its search for a solution. Besides a revised plan for a Francophone faculty, other proposals were the collegial, modular and bicameral models, plus one that combined the modular and departmental models. The characteristics of each need not be discussed here; only the bicameral model – as originally presented by the administration – attracted support, notably from the Assembly of Francophone professors, support that was sufficiently broadly based to warrant a trial over a period of a few years.

A sounding of all Francophone professors on campus confirmed the choice of the so-called bicameralism option. Approximately forty professors, however, signed a petition demanding a form of bicameralism in which the autonomy of the Francophone sector would be much more pronounced in comparison to the original proposal (providing for a vice-president of Francophone Affairs, parity between Francophones and Anglophones at all administrative levels, etc.). Re-examined during 1992–1993, this administrative restructuring plan was first the subject of a report approved by the Senate in 1993;[8] then of a second entitled "Governance of the Laurentian Francophone Community: Three Options," submitted in the spring of 1998; and finally of that called "Recommendations to the president on modifications to the administrative structure" submitted in 1999, whose major component would be approved that same year, completing the administrative reorganization undertaken for the benefit of Laurentian's Francophone community.

A striking aspect revealed by the analysis of the documents pertaining to bicameralism written during the 1990s was the conscious effort to drastically dilute the concept of bicameralism. For example: "'Bicameral model' or 'bicameral option' is a poor choice of terms. The University cannot function efficiently in a model involving two bodies at the Faculty level or higher, and it should not attempt to do so."[9] Stripped of its true meaning, the expression nevertheless continued in usage, overshadowing the more precise wording that the authors of these reports had proposed, namely 'the administration of programs by the linguistic group,' as Senate had approved in June 1993, or another more recent expression, 'adapted bicameralism.'[10]

This semantic masquerade did not occur innocently. It went hand in hand with a determination not to displease anyone or the majority, and to accommodate situations that were necessarily quite different in various departments and schools. The terms that best summarize this timid revision of the administrative structure are pragmatism and mutual respect at the department and school levels. Thus, there was no question of imposing bicameralism in areas where the Francophones had not succeeded in obtaining control over their programs. "Senate also adopted bicameralism in principle, for schools and departments to implement at their pleasure."[11]

The bicameralism discussed during this era, inverted and optional, was light-years away from the idea of two bodies with parity status demanded by some since the middle of the 1970s. For them, the true meaning of bicameralism demanded its application where ultimate authority lay, to Senate. It was therefore not surprising that such a timid approach resulted in nothing more than minor reforms, as evidenced by the positions of program coordinator and vice-dean.

Let us begin with the vice-deanship introduced in the fall of 1990. Although assistant deanships existed previously, the position entailed dealing with specific secondary tasks in order to provide relief to the deans. Starting in 1990, this function was disguised with the title of vice-dean, and each faculty was allocated two of them, one for French programs and one for English. Both would be primarily responsible for advising students. "Matters of the administration of the Collective Agreement will ultimately of course remain the responsibility of the Dean."[12]

As for the program coordinators – these already existed in some schools in 1990 and they have become more widespread since – these are not recognized by the collective agreement. Even meetings of a Francophone program in a department or a school had no administrative weight because the only administrative body officially recognized and deemed competent was the department and its chair. Some program coordinators had a reduced teaching load, but most held this position informally and without compensation, so they in fact appeared to be unofficial coordinators.

As stated in the 1993 report, one of the fundamental principles of this management model approved by the Senate was "to guarantee that each linguistic group will play a dominant role in the development and management of academic programmes in their respective language, and in the choice of teaching personnel."[13] Such autonomy was, however, difficult to institute in practice because the department remained the sovereign body. Generally only the adoption and modification of courses in an existing program could be decided by the linguistic group in parallel French and English structures, starting in 1999.

Still, there were some good moments in 1997 for those who desired Francophones to take greater control over programming, particularly because of the efforts of the vice-president of Francophone Affairs, Gratien Allaire, who had arrived in the summer of 1993 as Adam's replacement. In the Social Sciences, sev-

OFFICIAL LAUNCH OF
AN ISSUE OF *REVUE
DU NOUVEL-ONTARIO*,
CIRCA 1984

eral French programs were organized. In history, for example, professors involved with the teaching of courses in French held their first meeting in January of that year. Coordination at the faculty level resulted in several French courses being recognized by more than one program, thus providing more varied offerings to students. In the fall of 1997, there was even the creation of a Francophone chamber alongside an Anglophone chamber in the Social Science faculty council. These duplicate faculty bodies continued to exist for a few years, but then lapsed as new council members replaced old around the table.

More concretely, at the departmental and school levels various academic units experienced the so-called bicameralism very differently. A few adopted parallel structures, with both a Francophone and an Anglophone committee that worked well and ensured full autonomy for French-language programs. This was the case in social work and the school of physical education. On the other hand, in many departments, everything was dealt with in English in order to avoid the kind of frustrations Dorais had experienced in the early 1970s. In some other departments, discussions occurred in both languages. Retirements could quickly transform the situation, whether the retiring members were unilingual or bilingual.

Before concluding this section on the place occupied by the Francophone community in Laurentian's administrative structures, a few words must be said about the position of vice-president of Francophone Affairs, a position that evolved greatly over twenty years, and marked considerable progress. To begin with, the arrival of Dyane Adam had, to a certain degree, facilitated the transformation of the position of director of the CEF into the position of assistant vice-president of Francophone Affairs, a title that her successor, Gratien Allaire, inherited. Dyane Adam had worked efficiently with Bélanger, the vice-president academic and research, and the same can be said about Allaire's work with Vice-President Geoffrey Tesson, whose open-mindedness towards the need for autonomy for Francophones merits special mention. So no one was really surprised when Allaire was promoted with the title of associate – not assistant – vice-president of Francophone Affairs.

Despite Tesson's support, Allaire was not reappointed to this position, and this led to the arrival in 1998 of a new associate vice-president of Francophone Affairs who, this time, was recruited internally. André Roberge was a professor in the department of physics. In March 1999, following recommendations made by Tesson, Roberge and Ron Smith, the Senate decreed that the functions of the vice-president academic and research would, for the first time, be entrusted to two title holders with parity status, one for Francophone Affairs and one for Anglophone Affairs. At last, what Gervais had wished for in 1976 became a reality.

On February 8, 2002, however, Acting President Hermann Falter announced that the selection committee for the new Francophone vice-president – Roberge had left for l'Université Sainte-Anne – had dissolved, and that it would resume the search only after the arrival of the newly appointed president, Judith Woodsworth. Many Francophone professors feared that the position would be eliminated for reasons of administrative efficiency. These rumours, founded or unfounded, caused the Assembly of Francophone professors and its president (the author of these lines) to again man the barricades. Several emails, a resolution approved almost unanimously by the Assembly on April 5th asking that the position be maintained, as well as an intervention by the incoming president, brought about the resumption of the recruitment committee's activities. In January 2003, the committee recommended the appointment of Harley d'Entremont, who in contrast with his predecessors, was given a second term in 2007.

A French University in Ontario

With so many sources of disappointment for Francophones, it was not surprising that on a number of occasions the idea of a French university in Ontario was discussed. Two particular episodes provide a gauge of the state of mind of the university community. The first occurred in 1980. Various bodies had then pressed the government to recognize the need for such a post-secondary institution, notably l'AEF and the Council for Franco-Ontarian Education. The youth organization, Direction-Jeunesse, even hired a researcher to collect data on the status of Francophones at Laurentian. The Comité d'action pour une université française en Ontario, CAUFO, was subsequently created, with Serge Dignard as its president and members such as André Girouard of the CEF, Georges Bélanger of the French department, Raymond Lallier of l'École des sciences de l'éducation, Roger Bernard of the Collège universitaire de Hearst, as well as the president of the University of Sudbury, Lucien Michaud.

It must be said that the low number of programs offered in French at that time explained many frustrations and worked in favour of the demand for a French university. A second argument was the comparatively advantageous situation of Quebec's Anglophone community. As Dignard explained in an interview with the *Sudbury Star,* "if Québec's English-speaking minority were forced into bilingual institutions, they would be screaming murder."[14]

Another factor, perhaps even more important, was the issue of transparency in the administration of the bilingualism grants received by Laurentian. When

CAUFO made its position known, Minister H.K. Fisher of Colleges and Universities received a very revealing memo on the subject from Deputy Minister B.A. Wilson on July 2nd 1980. It stated:

> the University has never made public its disposition of bilingualism grants and detailed expenditure on programs in French.
>
> This lack of public accountability may have created the feeling among Franco-Ontarian students and faculty that the bilingualism grant was not used wholly to fund courses in French. The feeling of powerlessness to improve the program and course offerings at the University could be the origin of the demand for a separate institution.[15]

After sending one of his public servants, Claude Lacombe, to Sudbury and Hearst for meetings with members of the CAUFO,[16] the Minister took no further action on this project, which was considered unrealistic and not a reflection of the wishes of Franco-Ontarian students who, according to Deputy Minister Wilson, preferred to study in a bilingual institution.

Though the idea continued to be discussed through the 1980s – witness the 1985 special edition of the *Revue du Nouvel-Ontario* devoted to the topic of a French university in Ontario[17] – it gained a higher profile when it began to be taken up not just by convinced academics, but by the general public as well. In February 1989, Hector-L. Bertrand, editor of *Le Voyageur*, supported the idea of a French university when commenting on President Daniel's project to create a French faculty. The editorial read: "The only efficient solution to the current problem is the creation of a French public university in Sudbury that would serve all of French Ontario. Ottawa has just recently obtained a French post-secondary college. Sudbury must now demand a totally French public university."[18] The position could not be more clearly stated.

Over the next twelve months, newspapers reported many declarations on the virtues of bilingualism and a French university. The political context clearly had changed thanks to the *French Language Services Act* and the judicial impact of the *Charter of Rights and Freedoms*, developments that also encouraged Northern Ontarians to demand a unilingual French community college. There was also the Meech Lake Accord, still in the news because, although it had been signed in April 1987, it needed approval by all ten Canadian provinces before June 23rd 1990 in order to recognize Quebec as a distinct society.

These three measures, of direct and indirect benefit to the Franco-Ontarian cause, were nonetheless disturbing to a certain segment of the Anglophone population.[19] This gave President Daniel the opportunity to respond to Bertrand's editorial the next day. He defended Laurentian's bilingualism as the best solution to counter extremists such as Jack Andrew, who had brought his anti-bilingualism campaign to a crowd of 900 at Sudbury's Grand Theatre, and Billie Christiansen, the candidate for the anti-bilingualism Confederation of Regions Party defeated in the November 1988 federal elections, who stridently voiced her displeasure at

THE OFFICIAL
OPENING OF THE J.N.
DESMARAIS LIBRARY
BY PAUL DESMARAIS
IN JUNE 1990

having lost her job at Laurentian for lack of fluency in both official languages.[20] Astutely, the president used the extremism of certain Anglophones as a bogeyman to promote a more moderate position in line with his administration. Two months later, Daniel went further in a letter to the *Sudbury Star*:

> But the country is now debating the Meech Lake Accord and we at Lauren-tian are developing new organizational arrangements. Perhaps we shall call them the Ramsey Lake Accord!
>
> ...
>
> Like Canada, of course, Laurentian experiences separatist forces that would split it up ... I believe that northern Ontario will lose something valu-able if the separatist forces win the day ... Canada has chosen neither to assimilate its minorities in a melting pot like the U.S.A., nor to promote sep-arate development like South Africa, so a bilingual university makes sense in a region like Northeastern Ontario.[21]

That same year, a number of university members formed a group to promote the idea of a French university. Called la Société des universitaires de langue fran-çaise de l'Ontario (SULFO), one of its spokespersons on campus was Jean-Charles Cachon. In the fall of 1989, he convened a meeting of the Assembly of Franco-phone professors, and attempted to rally the professors in attendance around the project. The author of this chapter, then a newly arrived professor, was not con-vinced, nor was the majority of the other colleagues in attendance, most of whom were also newcomers. One argument against this project was the fear of creating a small, second-rate university that would be more of a ghetto than a place of intel-lectual growth.

Although the project did not find fertile ground inside Laurentian's walls, it was better received in the outside world when, for example, SULFO responded to state-ments by the president[22] to the effect that the critical mass of students required for such a project had not yet been attained.[23] *Le Voyageur*'s editor could always be counted on to promote the project and to denounce its opponents, who, in his opinion, were not only Anglophones "but all too often a small number of Francophones who come from outside our province."[24] In this same edition of *Le Voyageur*, SULFO published a two-page insert that rebutted the nine main objections voiced by opponents of a French university.[25] This insert, which enjoyed some success, was a reproduction of a text published earlier by the student newspaper *L'Orignal déchaîné*, founded in 1987 by Normand Renaud, an outspoken lecturer, and Bruno Gaudette, a history student. Though officially a statement by SULFO, it had in fact been drafted by Renaud who had become a strong advocate for the idea of a French university in Ontario.

Several attempts were made to reignite the debate, but the project gradually died down on the university scene. The first six months of 1990 brought a period of linguistic tensions that no doubt discouraged the exchange of ideas. February 1990 saw the sad episode when the Sault Ste. Marie municipal council passed its 'English-only' resolution, and June witnessed the death of the Meech Lake Accord. It seemed no longer an appropriate time for concessions to Francophones, and even less so one to set a precedent for Ontario. The Franco-Ontarian community therefore turned its sights on a less controversial project, the creation of a second French-language college for Northern Ontario.

The State of Laurentian's Francophone Community in 2007

To conclude this historical account, we now examine the current situation of Laurentian's Francophone community, beginning with the annual trends in student enrolment as well as the state of bilingualism and French programs offered by Laurentian and its federated universities, in comparison to the related picture 35 years earlier. Firstly, table 13.1 reproduces recent data on registrations as published in the registrar's official annual statistics.

In the early 1970s, the administration was uncomfortable with the fact that the Franco-Ontarian community counted for less than a third of registrations, a level then considered to be its rightful share. So it is surprising that today no one speaks out against the fact that the Francophone student body is now an even smaller minority, a state of affairs not accounted for by the growing assimilation of the Francophone population. After a few years during which the percentage hovered around 25 per cent, thanks to the creation of new French programs in the Sciences and the Professional Schools, the level has now once again dropped under 20 per cent. The relatively recent presence of a contingent of international students who almost exclusively enter English programs would be a convenient explanation if the nature of the recruitment efforts were not called into question.

Certainly, one could use the mother tongue of students as the criterion for measurement in order to give more weight to the Franco-Ontarian presence on campus. In fact, occasionally the administration does so to demonstrate the place occupied by the Francophone community, as in a brochure the university

TABLE 13.1 | THE EVOLUTION OF THE NUMBER LAURENTIAN'S
UNDERGRADUATE AND GRADUATE STUDENTS, FULL-TIME AND PART-TIME,
ACCORDING TO THE LANGUAGE OF THE PROGRAMS,* FOR SELECTED YEARS

Year	French Undergrad.	Master's and PhD	TOTAL	English Undergrad.	Master's and PhD	TOTAL
1986–87	1,074	19	1,093	4,264	223	4,487
	(20%)	(8%)	(20%)	(80%)	(92%)	(80%)
1988–89	1,418	16	1,496	4,732	172	6,338
	(23%)	(9%)	(23%)	(77%)	(91%)	(77%)
1990–91	1,951	18	1,969	5,306	158	5,464
	(27%)	(10%)	(26%)	(73%)	(90%)	(74%)
1993–94	1,707	72	1,779	5,745	192	5,937
	(23%)	(27%)	(23%)	(77%)	(73%)	(77%)
1997–98	1,243	96	1,339	4,548	250	4,798
	(21%)	(28%)	(22%)	(79%)	(72%)	(78%)
2000–01	1,173	54	1,227	4,321	271	4,592
	(21%)	(17%)	(21%)	(79%)	(83%)	(79%)
2003–04	1,466	53	1,519	5,755	351	6,106
	(20%)	(13%)	(20%)	(80%)	(87%)	(80%)
2006–07	1,555	41	1,596	6,987	517	7,504
	(18%)	(7%)	(18%)	(82%)	(93%)	(82%)
2007–08	1,476	59	1,535	6,671	586	7,257
	(18%)	(9%)	(17%)	(82%)	(91%)	(83%)

* The main language of a program is a criterion that overestimates the weight of Francophone
registrations, because Francophone students often take some courses in English even though they
are registered in a French-language program, to benefit from better course availability. Students in
English programs practically never take French courses.

published in 1993–1994 entitled 'La présence francophone à l'Université Laurentienne. Les réalisations concrètes.'[26] When this criterion is used, the proportion of
Francophones in 1991–1992 was 29 per cent instead of 24 per cent (as per the main
language of programs), not a negligible difference. But the mother tongue factor
does not take into account subsequent assimilation at the elementary and secondary school levels and even at Laurentian – by reason of the unavailability of certain
programs – and more importantly, it in no way alters the trend observed over the
past years.

The extremely poor results observed at the graduate level, a growth sector
for the university, have some bearing on the situation, as well as the creation in
2003 of the very popular English program in education. The scarcity of Franco-
Ontarian students at the graduate level needs to be examined and its causes discovered. One might wonder if the very asymmetrical aspect of program offerings
in French is responsible, as was the case with undergraduate programs over the

course of Laurentian's first two decades. As stated in the university's official website in the fall of 2007, there were 14 master's and PhD programs offered in English only, compared to 7 bilingual programs that can be taken entirely in French.

It could be said that professors in the Sciences sector are largely responsible for this deplorable situation. Bound to the language of Shakespeare in their research activities and wishing in all good faith to offer what they consider best for their students, they have not realized that a number of them owe their employment to the presence of a Franco-Ontarian community that could rightly expect more from them, even though it does seem to request it loudly. Unconcerned with the political dimension of programming, their concern is to train the best chemists or biologists according to the needs of the market in Ontario or North America, thereby scrupulously abiding by universities' rules of the game.

But is it their role to deal with the political dimension of program offerings in a bilingual university? When they requested graduate programs, they did so in good faith by not insisting on bilingual programs, for fear of asking for too many resources and thus risking that their request be turned down. If they can be excused for not taking the political dimension into account, the same cannot be said of the vice-presidency of Francophone Affairs, a position where political calculations are a daily concern. Since Adam's tenure, the holders of this title have been answerable to the institution and to its primary function which is expansion, rather than to the Franco-Ontarian community to which they nonetheless owe their existence. On the whole, they have adjusted their mandate to the absolute requirement of solidarity with their Anglophone colleagues in administration.

Returning now to program offerings in French, exactly what has been offered during the last fifteen years? Let us make a count. There have been few new undergraduate programs. One can point to the communication publique program offered at the University of Sudbury, the arts d'expression program, and the orthophonie program which had a difficult debut, evolving from a master's program into an undergraduate program. As for programs offered in both languages, one can add midwifery, and that accounts for all of the gains. But programs were also lost, like translation and cinema studies, as well as courses in anthropology. This tally is modest in comparison with the costly, unilingual school of medicine and the Anglophone education program.

Blaming the administration alone would be far too simplistic because one must also recognize the paralyzing apathy of the Francophone faculty members, even in the Social Sciences and the Humanities where academics were traditionally more militant. Existing programs are deemed to be sufficient. Lacking skilled leadership for some time now, and dominated, for reasons well known, by the presence of colleagues who come mostly from Quebec, Francophone faculty members go about their business as if they were performing their duties in a majority environment. Don't worry, be happy.

Moving forward in this quest for reasons to rejoice, we come to table 13.2, which presents a review of programs actually being offered in French in the fall of 2007 along with a categorisation of the state of bilingualism among faculty members.

TABLE 13.2 | AN ESTIMATION OF BILINGUALISM AMONG FACULTY MEMBERS
AND FRENCH PROGRAM OFFERINGS IN VARIOUS DEPARTMENTS AND SCHOOLS
IN THE FALL OF 2007*

Department, School or Faculty	Bilingual professors	Professors acquiring bilingualism	French programs
English	2	10	Not applicable
Anthropology	0	4	None
Arts d'expression	3	0	3-, 4-year
Biology	7	10	3-, 4-year
Chemistry and Biochemistry	14	5	3-, 4-year
Commerce*	16	16	4-year
Communication publique	2	0	3-, 4-year
Law and Justice	4	3	3-, 4-year
Classical Studies	3	0	None
Women's Studies	0	2	None
Folklore and Ethnology	1	0	3-year
Français and Orthophonie	10	3 (+2 upcoming)	3-, 4-year
Engineering	2	15	None
Geography	6	6	3-, 4-year
History	9	6	3-, 4-year and master's
Modern Languages*	5	2	Not applicable
Mathematics and Computer Science*	9	10	3-, 4-year
Philosophy	7	4	3-, 4-year
Psychology	6	10	3-, 4-year and master's
Physics	7	3	3-, 4-year
Midwifery	0	1	4-year
Physical Education	14	12	4-year and master's
Economics*	5	8	3-, 4-year
Education	9	3	3-year, Initial training
Nursing	9	19	4-year
Liberal Science	1	0	Continuation
Political Science	8	3	3-, 4-year
Religious Studies	4	4	3-, 4-year
Earth Sciences	2	13	None
Social Work*	10	9	3-, 4-year and master's
Sociology	10	8	3-, 4-year and master's
Theatre	0	2	None
TOTAL	177	193	

* This estimate is based on consultations with faculty members and secretaries in these various academic units. It does not count the vice-president and the president, but includes the dean in office in his or her faculty, who is then counted with the department to which he or she is related. Only full-time professors on campus or on sabbatical leave were counted, whether they were permanent or not. We recognize that this criterion puts a program such as midwifery at a disadvantage.

MICHEL DUPUIS AND
GAÉTAN GERVAIS AT THE
CEREMONY HONOURING
THE 30TH ANNIVERSARY
OF THE FRANCO-
ONTARIAN FLAG, 2005

If French programs are insufficient in number, the problem does not lie in the selection of faculty members. The proportion of professors who communicate in both languages on a regular basis – the definition of bilingualism used for this survey – certainly seems adequate because it accounts for more than 40 per cent of all faculty members. A solid contingent of Francophone professors is definitely present in all areas of the campus.

In light of the weakness of Francophone registrations, and even when the number of students per course is taken into account, table 13.2 leads to the unavoidable conclusion that a significant number of Francophone professors teach courses in English on a regular basis. This is true not only in master's and doctoral programs, but also at the undergraduate level.

Many reasons explain this situation. Certain bilingual candidates were hired for English positions in departments that offered both programs, as was the case in chemistry, for example. Sometimes, the department hired such candidates even when it had no French program, as was the situation in earth sciences or in classical studies. In bilingual departments, professors are often tempted to offer the same course in both languages to avoid course preparation, to allow more time for research or because limited resources sometimes force departments to give a professor an English course for which there are numerous registrations instead of a French course with few. And teaching a course with two students instead of fifteen is rarely an encouraging proposition. If the dean or the vice-president does not play the role of watchdog, however, the Français program may be affected, whereas the idea that a program can draw on a high number of bilingual professors is seen as excellent because it permits students to be exposed to a greater variety of professors. Unfortunately, we are convinced that a potential for the communication of knowledge in French is thus diverted to benefit the majority!

Thanks to the quality of their research and publications, a criterion of utmost importance for the Ministry of Colleges and University when attributing graduate programs, Francophone professors participate in all of the programs the university offers in English – with the few French courses sometimes made available – to such an extent that these programs would fail without their contribution. Should not the Franco-Ontarian community, ever a weaker complainant, benefit from them in turn?

Despite all of this, progress since 1975 has been impressive. The variety of French undergraduate programs is not complete, but compares very favourably to what was offered 35 years ago. The Sciences offer many complete programs, as do the Professional Schools. In certain social science departments, a student can even take an undergraduate program and a master's program in French if he or she so desires, without heading off to Ottawa. Besides the programs listed in table 13.2, there are also two programs where personnel are shared by different academic units. This is the case for the master's program in human development and the new doctoral program in human studies, both offered in French and English.

Though Laurentian offers the Franco-Ontarian community a glass that still seems half empty, and though it has been offered only and always after repeated requests, we must recognize at this time of the celebration of Laurentian's fiftieth anniversary that the glass is also half full. Of course, our collective thirst is greater, but we must acknowledge that the content of the glass satisfies most of us.

14 "In a Man's World": The Early Years, 1960–1972

LINDA AMBROSE

As Laurentian struggled through the structural and political puzzles of launching a bilingual university in Northern Ontario, waves of feminist issues were sweeping the country. Yet in Sudbury, and at Laurentian during its earliest years specifically, the presence of women in the whole enterprise was somewhat muted. Indeed, in 1965, one university research report noted that "Sudbury is a city of men. For every 100 women, there are 107 men, compared to a ratio of 101 men to every 100 women for both Ontario and Canada."[1] Despite that demographic imbalance between the sexes, as the 1970s dawned, there were indications that change was coming to Laurentian and the initial pattern of women sitting quietly on the sidelines of the new university, content to make an occasional donation or to serve tea at special events, was coming to an end.

When the university began in 1960, it was firmly rooted in the then-familiar postwar pattern of gender relations with very separate roles for men and women. However, the history of women at Laurentian mirrors the patterns in Canadian society at large, and the outcomes of the women's movement and of changing provincial and federal policies about women's place in society, the workplace, and higher education that began to be felt across the country translated into issues leading to policy changes and practical implementations on the campus at Laurentian.

As early as 1961, CAUT, the Canadian Association of University Teachers, passed a "Policy Statement on Equal Opportunity for Women Faculty Members" which stated:

> The Canadian Association of University Teachers is of the opinion that, in accordance with the principle of equal pay for work of equal value, there should be no discrimination based upon sex among faculty members, with regard to pay, status or work-load. Women who are appointed to the teaching staff of a Canadian university are expected to have the same opportunities as similarly qualified men.[2]

On most campuses across the country, including Laurentian, it would be at least a decade and often longer before the principle of equality for women would guide policies and actions. The history of that evolution is not a tale of unhindered progress, but rather one of conflict and change. Often the developments came about reluctantly and met with much resistance.

From a twenty-first century vantage point, it is surprising to see how much change has occurred, and how recently some of it was implemented. While most would agree that universities are still not utopian worlds of equality for all, completely free from discrimination of any kind, at the same time, one has to admit that in the realm of gender politics, a great deal of progress has been made across the country in general, and at Laurentian in particular. Laurentian now has policies in place to guard against harassment (sexual and otherwise), to insist on equity in pay and working conditions, and to prevent discrimination in access to scholarships, bursaries, and day care.

Examples of this progress abound. Indeed, at the time of this writing, Laurentian's first female president (Judith Woodsworth) ended her term of leadership in July 2008, and a woman was chairing the Board of Governors and overseeing the selection of the next president (Carolyn Sinclair, current chair since 2007, is the second female Board of Governors chair; Maureen Lacroix being the first from 2001–2004). Several women were occupying senior administrative positions including Susan Silverton, vice-president academic (Anglophone Affairs); Liette Vasseur, associate vice-president research; Denise Ouellette, university secretary; Anne-Marie Mawhiney, dean of the Faculty of Professional Schools; and Huguette Blanco, acting dean of the Faculty of Management). Among faculty, women make up approximately 36 per cent of the total number of professors, a proportion still well short of half, but one that has doubled since the early 1970s. With approximately three dozen departments, programs, and schools at LU, fourteen (39 per cent) have female chairs or directors.[3] On a percentage basis, female undergraduate students at Laurentian in 2007 outnumbered their male peers 67 to 33.[4]

These facts seem to describe an entirely different school than the Laurentian of fifty years earlier. The battles fought over women's issues in the 1970s and 1980s, and the policies and practices put in place during the 1980s and 1990s account for the transformation that took place. Attention to the larger provincial and national context serves to explain why Laurentian was driven to undergo this evolution. Even though women are currently quite prominent as leaders at Laurentian, their individual positions of power are tenuous. As they step down to take up other opportunities, watchful consideration of the place of women at Laurentian must continue into the future so that the elusive quest for real equality between the sexes can be realized.

"In a Man's World": The Early Years, 1960–1972

Throughout the sixties, women sometimes made local headlines in connection with the new university, but they usually did so in one of two ways: as supporters or as exceptional women. Most often, their supporting roles were either as benefactors of the new institution or as dutiful wives of the men who managed and taught at the university. The other media depiction of women at Laurentian was as exceptional individuals, either as female students who graduated from the new university (albeit vastly outnumbered by their male peers), or even more rarely, as female professors taking up the job of teaching "in a man's world."[5] Female professors usually made headlines for their very presence; whenever a woman was hired to teach at Laurentian, it was newsworthy. Some were even featured for their pioneering roles as they carved out academic careers for themselves. Another group of women, far less likely to be noticed at all, were the female staff members whose quiet work behind the scenes as secretaries and clerks allowed the whole enterprise to continue operating.

Indeed, attempting to trace women's presence at Laurentian in the earliest years is not easy because sources are at best quite fragmentary. However, by looking carefully into the archival records of university governance and administration one is able to piece together a picture of women's experiences at the university in its first decade. To paint the picture of women's roles at Laurentian in the early years, press accounts also serve us well, although they most often highlighted women whose achievements were regarded as exceptional. Again, this mirrors the larger trends in Canadian society where attention was paid to women who were noteworthy, what historians of women have come to call the "women worthies," the "firsts" to break into all-male spheres by virtue of their own achievements.

An example of one woman who played a key supporting role, yet one behind the scenes, was Elizabeth M. Granger Bennett, married to Laurentian's second president, who was the object of media attention when, in December 1961, the *Sudbury Star* described her as "a charming personality, with a delightful sense of humor, a quiet composure and quick wit." But the newspaper hastened to add that "she is far more than that ... she is a 'brain' as well."[6] In fact, the president's wife held three degrees: a BA from Victoria College, University of Toronto, and an MA and PhD from the University of Wisconsin, where she achieved "top scholastic standing." Mrs. Bennett had taught modern languages and was a professor of French on three different campuses before coming to Sudbury. The newspaper was actually celebrating the fact that Elizabeth Bennett had recently won the Ryerson Fiction Award for 1960 for her third novel, *Short of the Glory*. Journalist Betty Meakes explained that although the plot, set in New France in the 1690s, made it "remote from us in time and custom," yet the book's message was quite contemporary. That message, she wrote, was, "How people of different languages and regions can learn to live together in friendship, and to appreciate each other's distinctive approach to life." With her academic background and her obvious sensitivity to issues of language and culture, no doubt Elizabeth Bennett was an important ally and advisor to her husband Harold Bennett, as he gained the respect of his fellow administrators and board members, in part because of his sensitivity to religious and linguistic differences. Indeed, the president's wife might have made a fine university president herself, but it would be more than forty years before Laurentian would welcome a woman to that role. In the 1960s, women such as Elizabeth Ben-

IODE MEMBERS DONATE UNIVERSITY MACE | Women made significant contributions to the university in the founding years through their community organizations. The university mace, a gift from a local chapter of the IODE, was constructed using local copper and nickel, and adorned with gold studs.

nett were still celebrated more for their "warmth and personality" than for their leadership or administrative potential.

Another example of women taking up supporting roles as wives of university officials made news in the *Sudbury Star* two years later when it was reported that President Mullins was to head a tour of the new campus for "members of the Board and their wives." While women were included in the tour and the reception afterward, there was no mistaking the gendered division of roles. When the tour group returned for a reception downtown, it was "the wives of the administration officers" who were to serve refreshments.[7] At special events held on the campus, refreshments were also sometimes served by the university's female staff members. When an "informal afternoon tea" was held in the library in the spring of 1963 to thank the donors of books and reference works, it was Mrs. George McEwan, the secretary to the chief librarian, who acted as hostess for the afternoon, "assisted by members of the library staff."[8]

Yet women did more for the university in those early days than merely host social occasions or accompany their husbands for photo opportunities. By the mid-twentieth century, Canadian women's organizations were continuing to make significant contributions to a variety of charitable causes and institutions, as they had done since the late-nineteenth century in the context of church groups and social clubs. In Sudbury, benevolent women, particularly those who had attended postsecondary institutions themselves, stepped forward to assist the fledgling northern university in a variety of ways. By the spring of 1964, the University Women's Club of Sudbury had established a Laurentian project committee and they sent a letter offering "to present a ceremonial mace to the University, if such a gift would be acceptable." When the Laurentian executive committee discussed this offer at their April 15, 1964 meeting, they agreed that they were indeed, "interested in the proposal and would be happy to discuss design and other details if the club should decide to make a firm offer."[9]

Women in the community continued to make such offers, with donations of various items, including books for the library and funding for the establishment of scholarships.[10] Another women's group that made significant donations to the university in this period was the Imperial Order Daughters of the Empire, which gave gifts of money and donated the flag and flagpole for the new campus. After the move to the present campus, the local University Women's Club continued its close relationship with the school, attracting as many as eighty CFUW members to a meeting in the fall of September 1966, when Mrs. Mullins hosted the group at the president's new residence on John Street.[11] On that occasion, the club planned to sponsor the performance of an opera, presumably as a fundraiser that would benefit Laurentian directly through the group's continued donations.

While involvement in the form of charitable donations from women's groups in the Sudbury community was probably the most often reported, it was by no means the most direct experience of women with the university. Women who worked on the campus form an important part of the story. Grace Hartman, one of the earliest university employees, was no stranger to the Sudbury community. Hartman, a former school trustee and local alderman who would go on to serve as the first female mayor of Sudbury in 1967, inquired about employment possibilities as the university anticipated its move to the new campus.[12] She wrote a letter indicating that "when the University decided to appoint a Dean of Women," as Hartman assumed it would, she "would appreciate being considered for the position." The executive committee replied to her inquiry indicating that they were impressed with her qualifications, but it was not clear that a university dean of women would be necessary, given the fact that the federated colleges would be staffing their own residences, including hiring deans of residence for men and for women. But Hartman was a good candidate for a university employee, and rather than reject her application, the executive committee decided to place her anyway. Instead of the job she first suggested, Hartman was hired to work in the extension division as assistant director. It is interesting to note that when she worked out the terms of her employment, she also negotiated the very title of her job. As the archival record reveals, "Mrs. Grace Hartman has agreed to accept appointment for the session 1964–1965 for full-time service at the salary proposed, but would prefer the title of assistant director rather than assistant to the director." More than simply semantics, Hartman's early insistence on a job title that indicated a sharing of power rather than a subservient role foreshadowed the push for employment equity and pay equity measures that were almost twenty years away for most women at Laurentian.

Student experiences are more fully explored in another part of this book, but it is significant to note that the earliest media accounts of female students are provided in photographic evidence. The *Sudbury Star* published the graduation photographs of the classes of 1964, 1965, and 1966, in which the proportion of women seemed to hover consistently around 25 per cent of the total graduates.[13] While

HUNTINGTON UNIVER-
SITY STUDENTS, 1960 |
In the early years male
students outnumbered
females by a ratio of 4 to 1
but women at Laurentian,
as elsewhere, tended to
cluster in Arts programs.
Note that these students at
Huntington wore academic
robes to class.

such a source gives an indication of the statistical proportion of female students on campus, one must turn elsewhere to get a sense of the gendered nature of student experience. Life in the university residences provides an important glimpse at the experiences of female students.

Reminiscent of the earliest years of co-educational experience from decades earlier, different standards of conduct were applied to women living in residence than those imposed on men. In a document dealing with "terms of reference for dons," Huntington outlined various policies that presumably applied to both sexes, such as "voluntary total abstinence" from alcohol; "gambling to be discouraged"; and "entertaining between men and women only on the ground floor, not in rooms." However, when it came to curfews, stricter guidelines were applied to women than to men. In a memo dated January 18, 1965, Mary Hinde, the dean of residence at Huntington, explained that: "From now on *late dates* (after midnight Sun – Thurs., after 1:30 Fri and Sat) are *to be kept down to one a week* ... Does this rule apply to the men? – no; for this purpose the two residences are separate."[14]

This "special treatment" for female students can be explained variously. At one level, it was simply an extension of conservative values that were established much earlier in the century as co-education emerged and women were regarded as being in need of protection. But even past mid-century, the fact that women were treated differently from men at Huntington, a church college residence, does not seem completely surprising, given the values held by members of the church community. Moreover, although these differing standards for the sexes seem strange to twenty-first century readers, they were still widely shared views, and particularly in Sudbury. A survey conducted in 1972 by the Laurentian school of social work found that 63 per cent of 1,956 Sudbury respondents would say "the place of women is in the home."[15] Although attitudes might have been more liberal among the university community than the local population at large, the parents of local

SANDY KNOX, HUMAN KINETICS, AND PAT PICKARD, ATHLETICS | These two faculty members worked tirelessly to promote intercollegiate athletics programs for women, arguing that adequate resources were crucial to the success of the teams.

university students probably felt entirely comfortable with the deferential curfews and restrictions on women students.

Female students were not the only group of women receiving special attention at Laurentian. Women who arrived as teachers on university campuses in the 1960s could expect to draw attention because of their relatively small number. Pat Pickard was appointed director of women's programmes in athletics in the spring of 1967, the only woman among eight faculty hired that spring.[16] The *Sudbury Star* reported on campus hirings in the late summer and fall of 1968. Each new professor, male or female, was routinely introduced in the pages of the local paper, with a brief description of their expertise and background. Browsing through press clippings about faculty hiring only serves to reinforce the fact that the majority of the new faculty members were men.

When one (unnamed) female professor arrived in Sudbury to start her teaching career in 1964, her reaction to the local landscape became a news item. A taxi driver, who drove the woman into town from the Sudbury Junction CNR stop, reported that his passenger was not impressed with the environment. "'It's rocks, rocks, rocks, nothing but rocks,' she exclaimed to the driver and he told us that the newcomer was ready to turn around and go right back to wherever she had come from!"[17] The driver assured the new professor that the new university campus was quite picturesque, and that she "couldn't find anything better."[18] Other voices echoed the attractions of Sudbury, not just its natural beauty, but also the ethnic diversity, cultural events (concerts, art shows, and Canadian Club meetings), and sporting opportunities for golf and sailing. In reaction to a less-than-flattering report about Laurentian's isolated location published by a Toronto newspaper in the summer of 1965, local columnist Robert Evans defensively retorted that Sudbury was "one of the most cosmopolitan cities in all [of] Canada, and don't you forget it!"[19] Women were surely not the only ones to react to Sudbury's isolated location and barren landscape in the 1960s, and when the reaction of that one unnamed female professor to her new surroundings was recorded in the local newspaper, no doubt she spoke on behalf of many other new arrivals.

Staff appointments were not always featured as prominently in the local newspaper as faculty ones, but in October 1968, a headline proclaimed "Two Women, Three Men Gain Laurentian Posts." The men who were hired filled these positions: a translator, a counselling officer, and a junior programmer. The two women, both university graduates, were Jean Baxter, who became editor of publications and assistant to the registrar, and Marlene Cholette, who was hired as an analyst programmer in computer services.[20]

Despite the conservative attitudes revealed in the residence rules, the community survey, and the fact that women's appointments were considered particularly newsworthy, there were rumblings that things were about to change in the 1970s. As the new decade approached, it was clear that women's issues were about to take a much more prominent place in the life of the campus.

One of the earliest issues to surface was daycare, which came up for discussion in the fall of 1968 when the faculty association created a committee to study the feasibility of establishing a nursery for the children of staff and students. If women with young children were going to fully participate, either as students, teachers, or staff on the campus, then child care provisions were necessary. But the feasibility report, received in April 1969, was not encouraging. According to the study, creating a Day Nursery (the term that was current in the postwar years for a daycare) was estimated to be $75,000, and even that price would provide spaces for only thirty to thirty-five children.[21] It would be another five years before the dream of such a facility would become a reality. But by raising the issue and exploring the costs associated, the question of daycare was placed on the agenda. Indeed, this was right in step with the Royal Commission on the Status of Women in Canada, which conducted hearings and received briefs in these same years. In its 1970 report, the Royal Commission concluded that, "The time is past when society can refuse to provide community child services in the hope of dissuading mothers from leaving their children and going to work. We are faced with a situation that demands immediate action."[22]

As the second wave of the women's movement unfolded in various ways throughout Canadian society, raising consciousness about women's questions was an important first step toward change. Questions continued to be asked as the ripple effect of feminist issues washed over the Laurentian campus, in the heart of a hard rock mining country. But when water washes over rock for long enough, it does eventually bring about change, even in the hardest places. Arising from the problems identified by the Royal Commission, legislative changes at the provincial level began to have such an impact on campuses throughout Ontario including Laurentian. One issue that came to light in the spring of 1971 was women's eligibility for the Laurentian University Pension Plan. According to the existing plan, "All male employees shall be eligible to join the Plan after completion of one year of

UNIVERSITY STAFF REVIEWING FILING SYSTEM | In the early years, the university was a highly gendered workplace and from the beginning women have dominated the secretarial and clerical jobs, making their indispensible, though often under-appreciated contributions to keep the whole university functioning.

service and all other female employees shall be eligible to join the Plan after completion of three years of service." That blatant case of sexual discrimination had to be corrected, thanks to a new piece of legislation, the *Women's Equal Employment Opportunity Act*, passed at Queen's Park on June 26, 1970. To comply with that new law, Laurentian's executive committee voted on March 26, 1971, to change the policy to "All other employees shall be eligible to join the Plan after completion of one year of service."[23] This was just the first of many instances to come where Laurentian would have to realign its employment practices to keep in step with the feminist advances that were coming into law. But the changes came slowly over the next twenty years, and this early example about pensions was only a foreshadowing of things to come as women working at Laurentian began to claim their place as full and equal participants in the university.

The fact that such unfair practices existed and needed to be reversed was a reflection of a larger social problem. To draw attention to the issues of social justice that women routinely faced, and to call for change, academic study about the role of women proved to be an important catalyst. At Laurentian, feminist inquiry began to emerge, and one of the earliest forays into this fledgling field came in the form of courses that simply added women to the curriculum, such as a course in the sociology department entitled "Women in Society." Senate adopted a recommendation from the Academic Planning Council at its March 1972 meeting that such a course should be offered. A full-fledged women's studies program was still several years in the future, but these courses, devoted to women's place in society, were among the first signs that some academic attention was being paid to women, even if only to ask, "What about the women? What were the women doing?"

Another event that added focus to feminist issues at Laurentian was the visit of Abby Hoffman, Canadian Olympian in track and field, who was a guest on the campus in March 1972. In a speech delivered on that occasion, Hoffman blamed economic restraint for the lack of female athletes, but she went on to say that the problem was deeper than simple economics or lack of funding for sport. The problem, she argued, was pervasive in Canadian society-at-large, because "women are cultured not to excel in sports, but instead to look for husbands."[24] Hoffman's remark made local headlines, and her visit was yet another part of the ongoing consciousness-raising process at work on the Laurentian campus, which had a cumulative effect as the times were changing. Laurentian was about to change as well, somewhat reluctantly perhaps, but change it would.

15 "Decidedly No Cause for Rejoicing": Identifying Women's Situation, 1972–1985

LINDA AMBROSE

The period from 1972 to 1985 saw significant gains in tackling women's issues at Laurentian, although most progress came in the form of identifying problems rather than solving them. Concrete outcomes and actual changes would come later, resting for the most part on the foundations established during this critical period. Like the rest of the country, women in Northern Ontario had looked with anticipation to the 1970 *Report of the Royal Commission on the Status of Women in Canada*, which documented women's realities and firmly established a case for claims that men's and women's experiences of living and working in this country were worlds apart. In the years following the publication of the Royal Commission's report, wide-reaching initiatives were introduced in many different areas of society to try to redress the problems. However, what soon became evident for academia, as for many other sectors, was the fact that such changes would come slowly and incrementally.

Arising from the questions that the Royal Commission brought to light, one of the very earliest efforts to document the situation of women at Laurentian was undertaken in 1973, through the efforts of LUFA's status of women committee. This committee, chaired by Kathryn Molohon of the sociology and anthropology department, was convened to compile data about women at Laurentian. As the minutes of the February 22, 1973, meeting explain, "Both OCUFA and CAUT have been active in gathering information regarding the status of academic women, and in working toward the correction of 'academic inequities' between male and female faculty. In late January 1973, the Executive of the Laurentian University Faculty Association reconvened [sic] a Committee on the Status of Women. This was done in response to requests by both OCUFA and the CAUT for information and activities regarding the status of academic women at Laurentian."[1]

The LUFA committee on the status of women collected data on women at Laurentian and their findings record the distribution of women in four types of pos-

JOHANNE RIOUX AND THE INSTRUCTIONAL MEDIA TEAM PROVIDE TECHNOLOGY AND COMMUNICATIONS SUPPORT TO FACULTY, STAFF AND STUDENTS.

itions: administrative staff (who had their own association and negotiated with the vice-president administration for salaries and benefits), secretarial staff (who had a separate association from LUFA and also negotiated with the vice-president administration for salaries and benefits), library staff (who negotiated as part of LUFA for salaries and benefits with the vice-president academic), and faculty. The total number of women in all four categories during 1972–1973 was 184. Among the administrative staff, there were sixty-six total employees with fifteen women and fifty-five men. The secretarial staff showed a very different proportion. With 126 total workers, 122 were female secretaries, but only four were male clerks. The report noted that none of the male clerks was among the highest paid secretarial staff. In the library, there were ten professional librarians (five men and five women), six total major support staff (one woman was office supervisor of all chief librarian's library staff, including secretaries, student help, etc.; five technicians included four women and one male.) At the time, there were 233 faculty members, including deans. Of these, thirty-seven were women, including part-time faculty. By rank, the thirty-seven female faculty included: three instructors, fifteen lecturers, fourteen assistant professors, three associate professors, and two full professors (both in the school of nursing).

These statistics closely mirror the findings of the Royal Commission on the Status of Women, which revealed in its 1970 report that when it came to academics, "the number of men was 'roughly six times greater than the number of women,' and that the women were concentrated in the lower ranks."[2] Historian Mary Kinnear demonstrated that this participation pattern for academic women had not changed very much since the 1920s, and argued that "informal barriers, hiring and promotion criteria maintained by the university and a shared consensus on the part of women and men about appropriate behaviour for women served to minimize women's participation in the profession."[3]

On the Laurentian campus, that reality was no different. Despite the inequities revealed by the LUFA statistics, when asked by the Committee on University Affairs (CUA) to comment on whether Laurentian had a policy of equal opportun-

TABLE 15.1 | ACADEMIC AND SUPPORT STAFF AT LAURENTIAN UNIVERSITY, 1972–1973

Category of work	Total workers	Male workers	Female workers	Women as percentage of category
Administrative staff	66	51	15	22.7%
Secretarial staff	126	4	122	96.8%
Library	16	6	10	62.5%
Faculty	233	196	37	15.9%

Source: LUA, PO63, IV, 44 "Laurentian University Faculty Association Committee on the Status of Women," February 22, 1973.

TABLE 15.2 | WOMEN FACULTY AT LAURENTIAN BY RANK, 1972–1973

Rank	Women faculty	Percentage of total women at Laurentian
Full professor	2	5.4%
Associate professor	3	8.1%
Assistant professor	14	37.8%
Lecturer	15	40.5%
Instructor	3	8.1%
Total	37	100.0%

Source: LUA, PO63, IV, 44 "Laurentian University Faculty Association Committee on the Status of Women," February 22, 1973.

ity for both employees and students regarding gender, the university affirmed that it did have such a policy. In a November 1973 report to CUA, Laurentian replied to a series of questions that had been posed, including this question: "Do you have a policy on the hiring, remuneration, and promotion of women in all fields of employment in your institution?" Although no specific policy was cited, Laurentian's reply was that "The University operates on a policy of equal opportunity for men and women, which policy includes appointments, salary, and promotion." Interestingly, however, there was no offer to produce the text of the policy, as the university volunteered to do when asked about issues such as tenure and sabbaticals. When asked "Do you have a policy on equal opportunity for women in admissions to all programmes?" Laurentian's answer was "The same equal opportunity policy covers admission to all academic programs."[4] Again, there was no offer to produce the policy.

In reality, there was no formal policy on equality for women, and Laurentian, like so many other campuses, did not directly address issues of gender equality at all. The University of Alberta was more honest in its response when its 1975 "Report on Academic Women," revealed that "The Senate Task Force on the Status

WOMEN STUDYING IN UNIVERSITY COLLEGE RESIDENCE | Although some residences' original policies established different rules for women than for men on issues such as curfew and visitors, by the 1970s those gender distinctions came to an end.

of Women, after more than one year's study, has concluded that discrimination against academic women on the basis of sex does exist at the University of Alberta."[5] The difference was, of course, that the Alberta study was conducted by a task force on the status of women, while Laurentian's answer was a denial on the part of senior administrators that any problem existed. While this could be interpreted as a "cover up" it may be more accurate to understand the university's responses as a simple lack of consciousness. Rather than a conspiracy to "keep women down" at Laurentian, it was more that there was no conscious effort to enable women to thrive. In fact, the new northern university, like so much of Canadian society, had simply not thought about whether there were inherent inequities in the way that it operated.

However, a 1980 status of women report at Laurentian drew the sobering conclusion that when it came to women's issues,

the situation ... at Laurentian University does not differ in any appreciable degree from that at other universities. And although this is decidedly no cause for rejoicing, we may take comfort from the observation that at least our predicament is neither unique nor aberrant.[6]

In other words, women at Laurentian were no better off, but probably no worse off than women on other campuses. Still the report established that there was definite room for improvement at Laurentian. The period from 1972 to 1985 was a time to gauge and report upon the problems, many of which would only see concrete measures taken sometime later.

To paint a picture of the situation province-wide, it is important to note that around the same time that LUFA compiled its statistics on women in 1973, the Ontario government's Ministry of Colleges and Universities initiated a study on the status of women in Ontario universities in 1974–1975. To collect the data and collaborate on the findings, each university appointed one person to serve

NURSING STUDENTS |
Following the approval of
the College of Nurses of
Ontario, the first nursing
students were admitted
in September 1967.

as spokesperson. The findings were published in a 1975 report entitled *Women in Ontario Universities*. Distinguishing Laurentian from all the other universities was the fact that it was the only school to appoint a man rather than a woman to serve as its spokesperson for the study. Five years later, Laurentian's presidential advisory committee (PAC) on the status of women asked rhetorically, "Does this humorous note in our history indicate that Laurentian has a problem recognizing and acknowledging the status of women in its community?"[7] To academic women dealing with the realities of life at Laurentian, the situation was anything but funny.

While one might take some consolation in the fact that Laurentian's statistics about female participation were in step with realities in other parts of the country, that very fact could also be used to justify existing conditions. As the 1975 "Report on Academic Women" from the University of Alberta argued, it was not enough to compare one campus to another, nor even to resign oneself to the fact that such imbalances existed throughout society:

One way of rationalizing the injustices is to say, "The University is just like the rest of society!" Such an attitude, however, does not reflect the University's traditional justification of itself as a community of scholars and does not take seriously the privileged position the University enjoys. The University is a highly protected environment supported by the rest of the community. Like few other institutions, it has been given the opportunity to create a human community where persons are valued. Surely, then, the University has the responsibility to embody human dignity within its environment. If it cannot deal with what is happening to persons, then who can?[8]

One of the ways that the university could begin to deal with questions surrounding women's issues was to address them directly through its classroom offerings. Laurentian did so by introducing a women's studies program in 1978. As the local newspaper explained, the program was "aimed at providing solid academic knowledge to meet the inquiries of those (male and female) who have had their consciousness raised by the women's movement."[9] The new program was clearly a product of the times, as it made an effort to bring an academic understanding to the issues that the women's movement had brought to the forefront. The program consisted of four courses, of which students would take three: the compulsory introductory course WOMN 1000E "Women in Modern Society"; and any two of SOCI 2600E "Male and Female in Contemporary Society"; ENGL 2700E "Women in Literature;" and RLST 2390E "Women and Religion."[10] Although it would be more than ten years before a student could graduate with a degree in women's studies, these initial course offerings were an important first step in recognizing the academic legitimacy of studying women's issues.[11]

There were other positive signs for women at Laurentian, though it would be a gross exaggeration to suggest that equality existed. Three women joined the Board of Governors in 1973, although only two of them, Sara Speigel and Eleanor Copeland, were voting members. The third woman, Billie Christiansen, secretary to Laurentian President Ed Monahan, occupied a non-voting position as representative of the Laurentian clerical staff.[12] By 1980, the statistics about female participation on the twenty-four-member board were not encouraging because during the first twenty years of the university's history "only six women ha[d] been appointed to the Board of Governors of Laurentian University as voting members." Moreover, by 1984, with the resignation of Sister Leona Spencer, who had served since 1980, the board once again reverted to being an all-male entity.[13] When it came to establishing a female presence on the board, it seemed to be a case of one step forward and two steps back.[14]

The prospects were no more promising on the daycare front and here it was not only the administration, but the faculty association itself, that could not seem to find the resources to support such an initiative. Six years after the idea of creating a campus day nursery was first raised, the daycare facility on campus celebrated its official opening in 1974 with funding from the Ministry of Community and Social Services. Given the findings of the feasibility study, which concluded that the costs would be prohibitive, the executive committee had agreed to leave the idea of creating a daycare in the hands of the university's administrative staff. Although faculty delegations made repeated appeals to both the administration and the faculty association for funding, the requests fell on deaf ears. In October 1974, LUFA still maintained that it had no money to give to the Laurentian Child and Family Centre, and a committee composed of faculty and students reported this refusal, pointing out that while "all other universities give support, only LU does not."[15] By 1980, the daycare centre on the campus existed as "a private, incorporated, co-operative, bilingual day-care centre" serving children from both the university community and the community at large. Of parents who used the daycare, 55 per cent were community members, 32 per cent students, 11 per cent staff, and 2 per cent faculty.[16]

Beyond female representation on the board and the lack of resources for a central women's issue such as daycare, women were doing no better when it came to salary levels and rank. Dorothy Zaborszky, assistant professor in the English

DOROTHY ZABORSZKY AND
MARGARET KECHNIE |
Dorothy Zaborszky (left)
and Margaret Kechnie gave
leadership to the presidential
advisory committee on the
status of women, each of them
authoring important reports
that called upon the university
to take appropriate measures
to ensure equity for women as
students, staff, administrators,
and faculty.

department and a tireless champion of women's rights on campus, confronted the administration in 1974 when she suspected that women were being appointed at lower ranks and salaries than their male peers. She pointed to the case of one new female colleague who was appointed at a much lower salary step than a male peer, even though the woman had a PhD, recent publications, and years of experience. Zaborszky concluded, "What we have, really, is blatant discrimination on the basis of sex." Rejecting these claims as "totally unjustified and unfounded," Vice-President Hugues Albert replied, "As you well know, we cannot make any comparison between different sectors of the University." He went on to note that although the female colleague in question could have requested a general review of her salary, she had not done so. Chances are quite high, however, that the woman in question did not know that she could have made such a request because in the days before unionization, new faculty members were not well informed about their right to negotiate starting salaries, particularly not women.

Eight years later, statistical evidence bore witness to Zaborszky's suspicions about gender differences in pay when the *Sudbury Star* reported that among 208 male faculty members and 48 female faculty members, the average male professor's salary at Laurentian was more than $5,500 higher than the average female faculty salary.[17] Incidents such as these, in the days before unionization and before any talk of pay equity or employment equity, only served to strengthen the case of feminists such as Zaborszky who suspected that when the university claimed it had a policy of "equal opportunity" for its female employees and students, regardless of gender, the whole story was not being told.

But before that story could be told, the situation had to be documented and widely accepted attitudes had to be challenged. If change was to occur, then the case had to be made that discrimination on the basis of sex was indeed widespread and systemic, even if it was not done consciously. Following the province's lead on its study of the status of women across university campuses, President Monahan created the PAC on the status of women in June 1975. The terms of reference given to that committee were:

To review the status of women at Laurentian University in their various roles as members of faculty, administration, academic support staff and the student body, and to recommend on all relevant matters so as to insure that all women members of the University community receive fair and equitable treatment in every aspect of the University's operations.[18]

Similar studies were underway at most Canadian campuses in this period, and reactions to these investigations varied, as one academic noted, from "suspicion to rather sceptical tolerance."[19] At Laurentian, the PAC produced a preliminary report in August 1976, but a full-fledged report did not appear until four years later after President Henry Best reactivated the PAC on the status of women in 1979.[20] The PAC that wrote the 1980 report was chaired by Dorothy Zaborszky. The other committee members included commerce professor, Bernadette Schell; one member of the Board of Governors, Eleanor Copeland; one representative of the Laurentian Support Staff Association, Elaine Dupuis; one administrator, Jean Baxter; and two students, Aniela Brown (part-time student) and Lorna Williams, who replaced Sonya Popovich (full-time student).

The twelve-page report was more comprehensive than the one conducted by LUFA seven years earlier, because it not only included statistical information, but made recommendations about how to translate "ideas into practical realities."[21] This report also expressed impatience with the lack of progress for women at Laurentian. Striking a provocative note, the report contrasted the situation of women on the campus with that of Francophones, arguing that: "Although the relative percentage of Francophones is probably smaller than that of women, significant overtures have been made to them by the university administration, and this we heartily endorse. At the same time, we note that we have seen no such overtures made to women."[22] As Guy Gaudreau illustrates elsewhere in this book, the overtures to Francophones came as the result of a great deal of protest, struggle, and evolution; women at Laurentian, however, had not yet made the same kind of concerted effort to have their voices heard. By drawing this parallel between the situation of women and that of Francophones, Zaborszky and her committee were consciously signalling that the battles over the status of women at Laurentian were about to become much more political. In the same academic year that the report was published, the Laurentian Faculty Association was undergoing the process of union certification and Zaborszky and her committee were hopeful that the new collective agreement with its non-discrimination clause would "have a beneficial effect on the situation of women faculty (as indeed on all others)."[23]

The 1980 report included twenty recommendations that provided a measure by which to assess how the administration was doing in its efforts to foster an environment of fair and equitable treatment for women. There were six general recommendations, and several specific recommendations, with one relating to full-time students; four to part-time students; two to faculty; three to support staff; two to administrative staff; one to daycare; and one to the Board of Governors. The lone recommendation concerning full-time students was "that all forms of discrimination toward women studying at Laurentian University be strongly discouraged and eliminated."[24] This recommendation was wide-sweeping and general, and as a result, very difficult to measure. The lack of more specific initiatives might be traced to what the committee noted in its report as a frustration that among full-time students there seemed to be a great deal of indifference toward women's issues.

The situation of part-time students was a different story. In 1977–1978 women represented 58 per cent of the students in Canada enrolled in part-time studies, but women studying part-time at Laurentian exceeded that number significantly, accounting for 64 per cent of all part-time students in 1977–1978 and 68.3 per cent in 1979–1980. Yet there were areas where women were extremely underrepresented. For example, only 0.9 per cent of science students were women and there were no women at all in the school of engineering. The report's recommendations for part-time students were quite specific, calling on the administration to investigate why these sectors of the university failed to attract women and to provide academic counselling specific to women's concerns during hours that accommodated working women. Financial assistance in the form of awards and government assistance to women studying part-time were also recommended, as was the creation of a co-operative daycare venture for part-time students.

The recommendations concerning faculty dealt with two items. First, the university was asked to make "special efforts to seek qualified women candidates for senior administrative posts." The second, relating to faculty recruitment, asked the university to advertise all positions in *CAUT Bulletin, University Affairs,* and where appropriate, in professional journals. The ads should "clearly state that the position is open to both men and women," and all hiring committees should include women in their membership whenever possible.[25] These recommendations were measurable and on June 19, 1980, the university Senate ratified them.[26] One could now see clearly whether or not the university was abiding by this new recommendation simply by reviewing the published advertisements of faculty positions and the composition of its hiring committees. Yet while it was easy to publish gender-inclusive ads, it proved much more difficult to actually hire enough women for the positions. Solutions about how to make university teaching and research positions more accessible to women proved to be elusive, and the specific policy measures that would address this problem were still several years away.

Recommendations dealing with support staff and administrative staff also proved difficult to achieve. Indeed, with aims that included making "an effort to remove the stigma undervaluing skills attached to women's jobs in general," and "a review of any tendency to underestimate the value of work performed by women," the report pointed to perceptions, attitudes, and values that were deeply embedded within society. Correcting these would require much more than a simple majority vote in the Senate. Yet the fact that the 1980 report raised such concerns is highly

LAURENTIAN
STUDENTS,
CIRCA 1960S

significant. Indeed, the kinds of problems that the PAC identified in its report set the agenda for the next decade as the university community took up the complicated and important task of creating greater equality through measures such as pay equity, employment equity, and affirmative action. It would take approximately ten years before these problems would be consistently addressed through university policy initiatives, but the fact that the report raised them and called for change was an important catalyst in that process.

Within two years of the publication of the report, LUFA roundly criticized President Best for the lack of progress for women on his watch. In 1982, Zaborszky and Lloyd Wagner, representing LUFA, claimed that Best had failed to implement the recommendations brought forward in the 1980 PAC "Status of Women Report." Moreover, they alleged that Best had even refused to provide funds to send a representative to the CAUT conference on the status of women although LUFA had agreed to share the expenses equally.[27] While funding a representative to the CAUT conference would have been relatively easy, many of the twenty recommendations involved changes of policies and processes (not to mention attitudes), that would take several years to evolve.

When the university administration was slow to move on implementing the kind of changes that the 1980 report called for, some women decided to take matters into their own hands to challenge and change the sexist assumptions they lived with everyday. In March 1981, Doris Parker, a secretary in Laurentian's computer services office, made history when she refused to serve coffee to her boss, claiming that it was not part of her job description. For that refusal, Parker was threatened with dismissal,[28] but the staff association took up Parker's cause and the case went to arbitration. Parker, a twelve-year employee of the university, had been asked to serve coffee at meetings. Her boss reportedly told the labour arbitration board investigating the matter that he believed "his status is enhanced when a secretary asks his guests if they want coffee."[29] Laurentian's director of personnel told the *Sudbury Star* that normally secretaries did this without protest.[30] But

Parker stood her ground and made national headlines when the *Globe and Mail* declared on July 31, 1981: "A secretary is not a waitress: arbitrator rules in coffee case." Deciding in Parker's favour, the labour adjudicator pointed out that there was no mention of coffee service being part of secretarial work in the collective agreement, and given the fact that "times and attitudes have changed," women should not be expected to perform this work.[31]

Within a year after the coffee case, another major development took place on the campus, this time in the form of a policy initiative for all women. At its May 20, 1982 meeting, Senate adopted the university's first ever sexual harassment policy. Administrator Jean Baxter spoke on behalf of the PAC on the status of women, explaining to the local media that "Ontario's new Human Rights Code attempts to legislate against sexual harassment in the workplace, and what the [Laurentian] committee has done is construct a policy that applies specifically to people in a university setting."[32] According to Baxter, Laurentian was one of the first universities in Canada to adopt such a policy, and the policy's dual function was "to discourage sexual harassment and set up the necessary procedures so that victims of sexual harassment can seek redress."[33] One important feature of the policy was a clear definition of what constituted sexual harassment. The working definition was:

> Any unwanted, sexually oriented, verbal and/or physical advances made
> by a person who knows or ought to know that such attention is unwanted,
> constitute sexual harassment when: a) such conduct has the purpose or
> effect of interfering with an individual's work, study, or academic perform-
> ance and/or creating a negative psychological and emotional environment
> for work, study, and academic performance. b) submission to such conduct
> is made either explicitly or implicitly a term or condition of an individual's
> employment, education, academic status or academic accreditation. c) sub-

mission to or rejection of such conduct by an individual is used as the basis for decisions regarding educational or academic status and/or academic accreditation.[34]

Not everyone welcomed the new anti-harassment initiatives. In the spring of 1984, Janet Sabourin, then chair of the PAC on the status of women, explained to LUFA President Lloyd Wagner that while policies "cannot hope to change people's attitudes – only control behaviour," she hoped that LUFA would endorse the policy because it provided "an avenue for complaint and a mechanism whereby such complaints can be dealt with fairly." Moreover, Sabourin pointed out that "the fundamental objective in proceeding with a complaint is to put a stop to offensive behaviour" rather than to take punitive action. Because she feared that LUFA might hesitate to endorse a policy that would lead to members launching complaints against fellow members, Sabourin encouraged Wagner to give his support to the policy. She pointed out to him, however, that while her committee anticipated LUFA's support, they did not require it. Sabourin told the LUFA president, that should he decide not to endorse the policy, she and her committee would like to know the union's reasons. "Do spare us the argument, however," she insisted, "that should this policy be implemented, we would have a dozen harassment complaints on our hands."[35] There is no doubt that the same people who cheered for Doris Parker when she refused to serve the coffee, cheered again when they realized that now women at Laurentian actually had a formal policy to which they could turn to identify and label inappropriate behaviours directed toward them because of their sex.

16 Policies and Practices for Equity and Equality, 1985 to the Present

LINDA AMBROSE

The introduction of the sexual harassment policy was only the first of many initiatives put in place during the 1980s in order to move closer to the elusive goal of equality for women on the Laurentian campus. Where the period from 1972 to 1985 was dominated by studies designed to document the problems women encountered, the next ten years witnessed the creation of policies to redress those problems. Again, these initiatives were part of a larger context of change happening throughout the country and the province of Ontario specifically. The importance of those legislative changes should not be underestimated; they provided the impetus for Laurentian to take action on women's issues.

The statistical reality of women's presence at Laurentian in the mid-1980s showed some improvement from the situation documented by the LUFA study more than ten years earlier. Of the 231 teaching faculty in 1985–1986, 55, or 21 per cent were women. While there was some slight movement of women upward through the ranks among the full-time professors, (there were fifteen female associate professors now, compared to only three in the previous study), the pattern was still the familiar one: Women were clustered in the lower ranks with only four at the rank of full professor, and twenty-one, almost half of all the women, at the level of assistant professor. Forty-three per cent of the forty lecturers were women, as were two of the four instructors. The grim reality of the mid-1980s was that while there were few new hirings, even at the lowest levels, women were in short supply (see table 16.1).

Women occupied the office of "Chairman or Director" in only four departments and schools out of nineteen across campus. There were only three other women in administrative positions in 1985–1986 including the dean of Professional Schools and one of the two assistants to the president.[1] Of the 252 full-time, non-academic staff at Laurentian, 146 (57.9 per cent) were women, by far the majority of whom (106 of the 146) worked at clerical jobs, where they represented 92.2 per cent of

TABLE 16.1 | WOMEN FACULTY AT LAURENTIAN BY RANK, 1985–1986

Rank	Women faculty	Percentage of total women at Laurentian
Full professor	4	7.3%
Associate professor	15	27.3%
Assistant professor	21	38.2%
Lecturer	13	23.6%
Instructor	2	3.6%
Total	55	100.0%

Source: Margaret Kechnie and Patricia C. Hennessy, *The Challenge for Laurentian: Employment Equity.* Sudbury, Ontario: Laurentian University, 1987. Table 2, p. 41

the workforce in that category. Of the remaining forty women, two were in upper management, nine in middle management, three were supervisors, twenty-one were semiprofessionals and technicians, and five were semi-skilled manual workers.[2] Among the student population, there were 3,329 full-time undergraduate students in 1986–1987, 53.4 per cent were women, as were 40 per cent of the 100 graduate students.[3] In the decision-making bodies of the university, one woman (of twenty-four total members) served on the Board of Governors; thirteen women (of sixty-four total members) served on Senate; and only five women chaired any of twenty-four university-level committees.[4] With the exception of the student enrolments, these numbers do not paint a positive picture for women.

Twenty-five years after its founding, as an employer, Laurentian still had a long way to go when it came to equity for women. Aware that there was work to be done in this area, in December 1985 the Board of Governors passed the following resolution:

> Laurentian University supports the principle of employment equity for women and agrees to develop policies which ensure that the opportunities for appointment, promotion, and the conditions of service for academic, administrative and support staff are equal for women and men.[5]

To ensure that progress was made in this area, it agreed at the same meeting, to conduct a study that would "identify any possible inequities at Laurentian University" and "recommend suitable guidelines and procedures to prevent such inequities and to eliminate inequities should they exist."[6] To accomplish this task, social work professor Anne-Marie Mawhiney was named the first employment equity coordinator, mandated to apply for government funds to conduct a campus-wide study.[7] When the funds were secured, however, Professor Mawhiney was on sabbatical, so Margaret Kechnie, professor of women's studies at Thorneloe College, and Patricia C. Hennessy, manager of academic staff relations, were appointed coordinators of the employment equity project. With funding from the Ministry

MAUREEN LACROIX | Maureen Lacroix, member of the Board of Governors from 1996 to 2009, was the first woman to chair the board, from 2001 to 2003.

of Colleges and Universities Ontario Women's Directorate, Kechnie and Hennessy hired Andrea Levan to conduct extensive research about women. On the basis of this research they prepared an employment equity report that was published in 1987, suitably entitled "The Challenge for Laurentian: Employment Equity."

Part of the challenge of improving the situation for women was educating the Laurentian community about what employment equity actually meant and what it would take to achieve it at Laurentian. Employment equity is defined as:

> A comprehensive program designed to overcome discrimination in employ-ment experienced by members of equity groups. The goal is to give equity groups access to all jobs, re-evaluate traditional jobs and improve equity groups' overall economic situation. An employment equity plan is designed to eliminate barriers that create discriminatory practices and denies access to all jobs to members of a designated group and to address past discrimina-tory practices.[8]

The four designated groups that employment equity targeted were: women, aboriginal people, disabled people, and visible minorities.[9] While the focus of this chapter is solely on women, that limited view does in fact reflect the reality of what happened at Laurentian because the employment equity initiatives recom-mended in 1987 did not deal with the other three designated groups. Justification for that narrow focus rested on the fact that the province of Ontario took that same approach, recognizing that "women's participation at all levels of the educational system was essential if the cycle of underrepresentation was ever to be broken in the larger employment world."[10] More than twenty years later, at Laurentian and beyond, there is still a great deal of work that remains to be done around equity issues for aboriginal people, disabled people, and visible minorities.

LUSU STRATEGY SESSION | In the context of changing legislation around pay equity and employment equity, the staff union (LUSU formerly LUSA) was vigilant in its efforts to protect its members, leading to a three-week strike during the academic year 1985–1986.

Because the purpose of employment equity legislation was to ensure equal opportunities and equal access to employment, employment equity plans pay particular attention to hiring procedures and practices. The Laurentian report made this its focus. Echoing the ideas that had been raised in the 1980 report on the status of women at Laurentian about the wording for job advertisements and the need to seek out qualified women for senior positions, the employment equity report went on to make some very specific recommendations for a five-year and a ten-year plan. One of those recommendations was "that certain priority departments receive particular attention and action in the first five years of this program. These priority departments are social work, biology, chemistry, commerce, and mathematics and computer science and history."[11] These units achieved "priority status" by having the dubious distinction of having no women faculty members.[12]

When it came to non-academic personnel, the employment equity report found that patterns of employment at Laurentian were in keeping with those in "the larger employment world and at other universities" in terms of the jobs typically performed by men and those typically performed by women. For example, 72.6 per cent of the non-academic women working on campus were in clerical jobs, and women occupied 92 per cent of all clerical jobs. At the same time, "of 35 employees working in the physical plant, one (a secretary) [was] a woman. Of thirty working in the library, only four [were] men."[13] In view of those findings, the report identified what it called "two distinct problems," namely that women were "underrepresented in management and supervisory positions" and that women were "virtually absent from key sectors of the non-academic work force, especially those jobs which have been traditionally performed by men."[14] One of the consequences of these problems was that women's salaries reflected a clustering at the lower end of the pay scale.[15] That issue of low pay for female workers would become the next issue driving change for women at Laurentian.

In 1987 the province of Ontario introduced the *Act to Provide for Pay Equity*, the stated purpose of which was "to redress systemic gender discrimination in compensation for work performed by employees in female job classes." Compared to measures aimed at ensuring equal pay for work of equal value, this pay equity legislation went further because it was "a proactive piece of legislation that applies to the public sector as well as private sector employers with more than 10 employees."[16] Growing out of the initiatives sparked by human rights legislation, pay equity captured some of the same concerns that had been raised by the PAC status of women report in 1980, particularly those concerning the "undervaluing of skills attached to women's jobs" and the fact that wages for women with training "in secretarial, office and other administrative skills [should] be on par with those of skilled positions for men."[17] Those twin concerns about undervaluing the skills of women and underpaying them in relation to men were precisely what pay equity was designed to address.

Although it is based on the principle of equal pay for work of equal value, pay equity was more far reaching because it was not a complaints-based process, but rather a "job-to-job" comparison. Rather than dealing with the idea that men and women doing the same job should receive the same pay, pay equity compares jobs traditionally performed by women to those traditionally performed by men, assessing the value of the work to the organization, and ensuring that jobs of equal value to the organization are rewarded equally.[18] The *Pay Equity Act* precipitated a campus-wide initiative to study women's jobs at Laurentian in an effort to establish the "value" of that work for the university as a whole. The process of assigning "value" to each job was a complex one that took into account several factors, including the skill, effort, responsibility, and working conditions attached to each position. Pay equity was not a performance review of individual workers, but rather a reconsideration of the value of the work being performed to the organization as a whole. The idea behind this initiative was to correct the undervaluing that had commonly been attached to jobs traditionally performed by women.

After the province passed its legislation, employers such as Laurentian had no choice but to comply and create a pay equity plan, which had to be in place by January 1, 1990. However, in this instance, Laurentian was actually ahead of the legislation. The process had not been an easy one because in the fall of 1985, the members of the Laurentian University Staff Association (LUSA) walked off their jobs to protest what they regarded as unfair pay scales and an arbitrary system of evaluating jobs. The strike lasted three weeks, and had the desired effect. On July 1, 1986, after a process of negotiation with LUSA, the university and the union agreed upon a system for joint job evaluation. As the published handbook explained, the plan "which has been developed is a point factor system that provides for the formal and systematic comparison of positions in order to determine the worth of one job relative to another."[19] Each of the non-academic jobs on campus was scored on a scale that measured four areas including working conditions, job complexity, level of responsibility, and competence in areas such as numeracy, language, experience, and education and training. The joint job evaluation system assigned point scores to fourteen different criteria within these categories, and depending on the job's score, the level of pay was assigned. Having undertaken this exercise,

CAMPUS SAFETY MEASURES |
While Laurentian was one of the first universities in Canada to adopt a policy on sexual harassment (1982), it was not until 1989 that the first Sexual Harassment Education and Complaints Chair, Norma McCrae-Ward, was hired. Under her watch a system of security measures were put in place to improve safety on campus.

and having created a system to maintain and reevaluate it on an ongoing basis, the university was well placed to respond to the pay equity legislation and its demand for a pay equity plan.

In compliance with the *Pay Equity Act*, on December 22, 1989, in anticipation of the January 1, 1990 deadline, Laurentian posted its pay equity plan. In preparing the plan, the university and the staff union worked together, and the document assured authorities that "both sides were aware of pay equity issues and ensured the new system addressed these issues." Laurentian and the union agreed that the joint job evaluation system they had developed three years earlier was "gender bias free" and that the factors and points system that had been developed satisfied both parties that pay equity was now in place.[20]

The joint job evaluation exercise and the pay equity review at Laurentian resulted in substantial pay adjustments in 1985, 1986, and 1987 for a number of women among the staff and administration, particularly secretarial workers. Because of the progress already accomplished under the joint job evaluation system, the pay equity plan, which was posted at the end of 1989 dealing with 175 employees, did not result in any pay equity adjustments. Once again, the authors of Laurentian's 1980 report on the status of women must have felt vindicated to see the fulfillment of something which had seemed so elusive and difficult to define when they proposed it almost ten years earlier.

The year 1989 was an eventful one for a number of women's issues at Laurentian in addition to pay equity. On the positive side, it was then that Norma McCrae-Ward was hired as the first sexual harassment education and complaints chair, and a full-fledged women's studies program was formally launched. Yet there were problems that persisted and questions that needed to be raised, such as why there was no woman on the presidential search committee that had been struck that year. In the same month that the pay equity plan was signed off and the women's studies program was launched, the university community in Sudbury joined in shock with the rest of the country as the media reported the horrible news that fourteen young female engineering students had been massacred in Montreal at l'École Polytechnique. It was a sobering reminder that although institutions of higher education in Canada were making some progress on women's issues, there were still very real concerns to be addressed. For individuals lulled into a false sense of security that women's issues on campus were settled, the horror of the Montreal Massacre served to reawaken a sense of urgency, not just for campus security issues, but for women's issues in general.[21]

That revived awareness meant that the activities of the PAC on the status of women were still extremely important despite the gains already made. An analysis of the PAC during this period shows that the committee's role was evolving. From its founding in 1975, the PAC had conducted studies and made recommendations that would eventually result in legislative and policy changes, but after some of those measures were in place, the committee became more of a watchdog group, serving as a resource for women on campus by providing information and support for individuals. In the 1990s and after, the PAC expanded this role, serving not only the campus, but the broader community as well. Involvement with the highly successful events such as annual LEAF breakfasts, in support of the national charitable organization Women's Legal Education and Action Fund, and work with the downtown women's centre are two examples of how the PAC took on outreach work. That work was possible because women on campus now operated more from a position of security. By this time, female faculty and staff could look to their respective unions for support on questions of equity and fair treatment. Issues such as equitable pay were no longer matters to be taken up with the PAC, but with the chief negotiators and union stewards.[22] The other way in which the PAC evolved was that while faculty members were dominant in the earliest years, by the late 1980s and 1990s, staff and administrative workers have become more prominent in lending leadership to the committee.

One reflection of the new role that the PAC on the status of women assumed is the annual Celebrate Women event, held in conjunction with International Women's Day every March. The PAC created a system of awards to acknowledge the achievements of outstanding women connected with the university. As the *Laurentian University Gazette* reported, "The Status of Women Committee holds this event every year to celebrate the achievements of women associated with Laurentian University, whether they are students, faculty, staff or members of the Board of Governors. The intent is to present, to the community, women whose achievements have advanced the status of women and who stand out because of ability, determination and courage."[23] Identifying role models and mentors for other women was another important outcome of these awards.

Beyond the annual celebration, the functions of this committee are varied, including enhancing and supporting the working and learning environment of women of the Laurentian community and carrying out research related to

UNIVERSITY WOMEN'S CENTRE OPENED, 1994 | Janice Porter (left) and Sue Vanstone on the occasion of the opening of the university women's centre in 1994.

the status of women at Laurentian University; raising community awareness of women's issues in general, specifically within the Sudbury community in order to support, participate in, and take a leadership role when appropriate; communicating the activities and accomplishments of the committee both with and outside the university; providing input in the development of pertinent policies; and advising and advocating on issues of women equity.[24] These wide-reaching functions provide evidence that the focus of this committee has evolved from the specific battles fought in the 1970s and 1980s to broader concerns over equity and safety on campus.

Employment equity policies were put to the test in the 1990s as the school of engineering went about the process of hiring new faculty members. Doug Goldsack, dean of Sciences and Engineering, wrote to the chairs of science departments and the director of the school of engineering in the spring of 1992 to remind them that "with a faculty of over 70, only 3 of which are females, we need to redress some of this imbalance."[25] The Sciences and Engineering faculty was about to hire nine new faculty members and Goldsack urged his colleagues to abide by the employment equity guidelines. Revealing that he intended to ask for weekly updates on the hiring searches, he added, "I see no reason why some of these positions cannot be filled by females this time around and will be actively encouraging you to seek out suitable candidates over the next few months."[26] In the school of engineering, only 15 of the 115 students were female and there was some consensus in the community that female role models for women would be important.

When the school of engineering finally hired two women in the spring of 1993, a controversy arose because of an unsigned letter that appeared in the pages of the local newspapers, indicating that the school of engineering was hypocritical to celebrate the women's arrival at Laurentian because the school of engineering was "forced" by administration to recruit females.[27] Exactly who was protesting the hirings is unclear since the director of the school of engineering, Anis Farah, supported them; in fact while he pointed out the statistical difficulty of hiring female engineers because of the small pool of qualified women, and the extremely small percentages of female faculty in engineering programs at other Ontario universities (2 per cent at Western, 4 per cent at Toronto, 2.7 per cent at Waterloo, and none at Lakehead), he informed the vice-president academic that "when Laurentian hires one female faculty in Engineering, our ratio will be 6% which will put us among the highest percentages [in the province]."[28] The case of the school of engineering underlines the complexity involved in achieving employment equity across the university because of the variation that existed in female participation among different disciplines. The low participation rates of women as students and as faculty in science and engineering programs is still an issue, not only at Laurentian, but across the country.

Even with all the advances, including policies and measures in place to prevent discrimination against women in the areas of pay levels, access to employment opportunities, and harassment, the problems did not disappear. Indeed, countless women's stories testify that sometimes those very policies created more animosity and overt challenges to women taking their places in the academy because the policies themselves and the increasing presence of women were chipping away at the male bastion of power over Canadian campuses. Examples from across the country abound and there is every reason to believe that the experiences of women at Laurentian were no exception. A genre of literature emerged in the 1990s that documented Canadian women's experiences in the academy. Examples include Paula J. Caplan's *Lifting a Ton of Feathers: A Woman's Guide to Surviving in the Academic World* (1994) in which two Laurentian professors, Mercedes Steedman and Mary Powell, participated; The Chilly Collective's *Breaking Anonymity: The Chilly Climate for Women Faculty* (1995); and Elena Hannah, Linda Paul, and Swani Vethamany-Globus's *Women in the Canadian Academic Tundra: Challenging the Chill* (2002). Each of these books is informed by the individual experiences of academic women which clearly demonstrate that the problems and challenges for women did not end with the introduction of harassment policies or equity initiatives.

The fact that these published accounts are based on individual stories is significant. As the second wave of the feminist movement swept across the country, its shared mantra was that "the personal is political," and more than twenty-five years later, these individual stories still testify to that fact. While the specifics of the stories vary, the themes resonate with most academic women who have experienced the challenges of living out their lives as women and as academics. The qualitative evidence contained in stories comes from a different type of inquiry than the quantitative studies that dominated the 1970s, but the message remains the same: There is still a long way to go in creating real and lasting equality for women. In part, one can conclude that it was the creation of policies such as Laurentian's on harassment, pay equity, and employment equity, and the victories of women such as Doris Parker that gave women the courage to speak up and tell their own stories.

	Total number	Male	Female.	Female percent
All full-time	416	268	148	35.6%
Full professor	102	83	19	18.6%
Associate professor	123	83	40	32.5%
Assistant professor	149	84	65	43.6%
Lecturer	35	14	21	60.0%
Part-time	84	51	33	40.7%

Source: Data compiled by Lee-Ann Fielding, LUFA Executive Officer, 2008.

While the stories also reveal that progress has been made, current statistics show that in terms of equal participation, academic women at Laurentian still have a long way to go. Data compiled by LUFA in 2008 reveal that of 416 full-time faculty members, 148 (35.6 per cent) are women. Upon closer examination though, it becomes evident that the number of women faculty decreases as the rank increases. That is, only 18.6 per cent of the full professors at Laurentian are women, while 32.5 per cent of associate professors, 43.6 per cent of assistant professors, and 60 per cent of lecturers (the lowest paid among faculty) are women (see table 16.2). While the proportion of women in the upper ranks has increased since 1985, the familiar pyramidal structure of women clustered at the lowest levels still persists.

Optimists say the glass is half full; pessimists say it is half empty and someone has quipped that an objective observer will notice that "the glass is bigger than it needs to be." When it comes to the progress of women at Laurentian University, some will say that much has been accomplished. Others will say that the progress is slow and discouraging. On one point all can agree: the university is a tricky place in which to measure the status of women. While female students presently outnumber their male peers by a ratio of almost two to one, the ratio is reversed when it comes to female faculty, who represent slightly more than one-third of the total number of teaching staff. Meanwhile, the departments and programs of the university function because of the behind-the-scenes work of countless women who continue to occupy jobs that have traditionally been done by women, and without whom the entire enterprise would grind to a halt. For women at Laurentian, is the glass half full, half empty, or are gender politics at universities just more complicated than they need to be?

17   Confrontation, Détente and Accommodation, 1960–2010

MATT BRAY

Although defined by the agreements signed between Laurentian and the University of Sudbury and Huntington University in September 1960, and Thorneloe University in January 1963, for much of Laurentian's first decade, federation relations were adversarial, the devil being both in differences of principle and in details of implementation. Because their affiliated churches founded Laurentian and nominated three-quarters of its Board of Governors, the federated universities, in a manner analogous to the 'provincial rights' arguments put forward by individuals such as Premier Oliver Mowat of Ontario in late nineteenth-century Canada, insisted their status was at least equal to that of the main institution. Laurentian authorities, in contrast, subscribed more to Prime Minister John A. Macdonald's centralist view, arguing that the colleges, by virtue of their more limited responsibilities, occupied a subordinate position on the federation scale.[1]

While these conflicting perspectives existed during the short-lived Bouvier presidency, religious and linguistic differences within federation ranks blurred the lines of demarcation. The University of Sudbury had little reason to challenge an institution whose character, academic and administrative, had, until recently, been its own in all essential features. For Huntington, the case was different. Principal (later president) Ed Newbery deplored the colleges' restricted role and pressed for a greater federated presence on such university bodies as Senate. He also stood apart from his Sudbury counterpart, Rector Oscar Boily, in suspecting Bouvier of manipulating appointments "to keep the administration and academic control of the university in Roman Catholic hands."[2]

The situation changed when Harold Bennett became acting president in late 1961. He by no means rejected the centralist interpretation of the Laurentian federation – in 1963, Bennett proposed a distinction be made between the federated universities' governing role and their teaching role as colleges – but because of his Victoria College, University of Toronto, background, he better appreciated

THE UNIVERSITY
OF SUDBURY

their viewpoint, and particularly their financial dilemma. Although the founding churches had opted for the federation model so their colleges would be eligible for provincial support, government policy severely limited their funding. During the winter of 1962–1963, the board, on Bennett's recommendation, raised their share of grants and lowered Laurentian's administrative charges, increasing college revenues significantly. The colleges responded in kind. In 1961, Huntington had taken umbrage at a Laurentian suggestion that the federated colleges "concentrate on residences and on [student] social affairs." A year later, the three federated universities informed Laurentian that they were prepared to assume initial responsibility for residences and dining facilities on the new Ramsey Lake Road campus.[3]

While the Bennett presidency ameliorated relations between Laurentian and the federated universities, that of President Mullins had the opposite effect. Within months of Mullins taking office, Huntington's Newbery complained that the new president had "the apparent intention of confining the *federating* denominations to a role, as [University of Sudbury Rector] Father Matte says, of 'playing catechism' in a few rooms on the campus." Then, too, Matte sought former Huntington president Earl Lautenschlager's help in his struggle with Mullins, and even considered withdrawing Sudbury from the federation. Such collegial cooperation diminished sectarian differences between the colleges, Newbery commenting to an associate on "the friendliness and grace of individual Jesuits" at the University of Sudbury with whom he worked, although he remained distrustful of "their 'Empire-Building' methods as an order."[4]

In 1963, a dispute over fundraising – a matter of special importance to the federated universities because they did not qualify for provincial capital assistance – further united the three against Laurentian. Both the University of Sudbury and Huntington had already carried out campaigns, the latter under the auspices of the Northern Ontario University Association. When the Laurentian Founders' Fund canvas began, all three federated institutions agreed to delay new efforts until its goal had been met. With that end in sight in July, Laurentian informed them it would receive requests for approval of their campaigns, a stipulation in the federation agreements designed to avoid competing appeals. The colleges had never been happy with this provision, either with the understanding that they would focus primarily on 'non-industrial' sources of funding, such as parishes and congregations, or with having to go 'cap in hand' to Laurentian for permission. No requests were forthcoming.[5]

Relations worsened during the winter of 1963–1964. Neither the University of Sudbury nor Huntington submitted permission requests until December, although both had been fundraising for several weeks. After "considerable discussion," the Laurentian board authorized them "to conduct a campaign for capital funds beyond the limits of the jurisdiction ... under its federation agreement," but with the proviso that appeals to those who had already contributed to the Founders' Fund must explain that a second gift would be welcomed, but not expected. The University of Sudbury's Board of Regents found this restriction so offensive that in early February its chair, Senator Rhéal Bélisle, called for a joint meeting of the Laurentian and Sudbury executives to "eliminate the unpleasantness of the past few weeks." At that meeting, the Laurentian board agreed to delete the offending text. More importantly, in March, it created a presidential advisory committee (PAC) on federation relations "to consider any questions regarding federation relationships which the respective members of the federation wish to raise."[6]

While welcoming this initiative, from the federated university perspective, the proposed composition of the PAC on federation relations was unsatisfactory. In addition to the board chair and the board secretary, who acted as 'convenor,' it would consist of three persons, one named by each of the federated institutions. The catch was that they had to select their candidates from the list of Laurentian governors nominated by their respective churches, and experience had shown that the first loyalty of such individuals did not necessarily lie with the college. Acknowledging this concern, the board expanded the committee's membership to include the heads of the three federated universities.[7]

The PAC on federation relations got off to a promising start. Prompted by a joint submission from the University of Sudbury and Huntington, in the autumn of 1964 it launched a study on 'federality,' and on the committee's urging in early 1965, Laurentian halved the administrative charges to the colleges. Still, President Mullins remained a worry. In May 1965, he presented an aggressively centralist interpretation of the federation to the Montessori Club of Sudbury. Laurentian, he asserted, "does not at present control the voting shares in its own company," that is, nominate a majority of its own board members, yet its Act clearly gave it superior powers. Only Laurentian could receive provincial funding, he stressed, and only Laurentian could establish new faculties, schools, and institutes, or admit the federation and affiliation of other colleges. "We [Laurentian and the federated colleges] are partners," Mullins concluded, "although not equal partners in the carrying out of the intentions of the founders of this institution."[8]

HUNTINGTON UNIVERSITY DURING ITS LATER CONSTRUCTION PHASE

The timing of the Montessori speech, only days after the Laurentian board had established a special committee on bilingualism chaired by *Sudbury Star* publisher James Meakes, suggests Mullins (and probably some governors) wanted federation relations added to the committee's agenda. Certainly, that is what happened, with the issue quickly assuming a major place in the committee's deliberations. One of its three day-long hearings involved only representatives of the federated universities, many of whom complained, sometimes bitterly, about their shabby treatment by President Mullins.[9]

The sections of the special committee's July 1965 report dealing with federation relations greatly disappointed the federated institutions. Stating that 'honest differences' existed between Mullins and 'others' about the colleges' role in the university, the report somewhat pejoratively asserted that the colleges viewed Laurentian as "a 'creature' of Sudbury, Huntington, and Thorneloe Universities, conceived in a marriage of convenience, brought on by their mutual interest in securing financial assistance from the government of the Province of Ontario, not otherwise available to them in their single state." In contrast, Mullins' entire Montessori speech was appended and his core arguments summarized in the text. Tellingly, too, apart from proposing that the PAC on Federation Relations be transformed into a board standing committee, something the governors did immediately, its recommendations simply called for more study and greater efforts by all parties to improve relations.[10]

One other balloon floated by the Meakes committee also signalled bias on the issue of federation relations. With respect to appointment procedures for the Laurentian Board of Governors, the report stated "there does not appear to be a legal obligation for the board to elect only those persons nominated by the churches." Political considerations, however, took priority over this legality. During the winter of 1965–1966, the board proposed to amend its bylaws reducing the number of governors nominated by each federated university from six to three. The provincial government agreed to the idea providing the founding churches approved. Only the Board of Colleges of the United Church of Canada did so. Both the University of Sudbury's Board of Regents and Archbishop Wright on behalf of the Anglican Diocese of Algoma demurred, throwing a monkey wrench into Laurentian's efforts to gain control of its voting shares, to use Mullins' terminology.[11]

For the federated universities, a step backward came in early 1966 when the Laurentian board sought the views of the Ministry of University Affairs on the appropriate financial arrangements between the university and the colleges. In a May meeting with Laurentian governors Parker, Fraser, and Bennett at Queen's Park, Minister William Davis took a decidedly anti-federation college stance. Denominational post-secondary educational institutions, Davis stated, would not in the foreseeable future be eligible for direct provincial assistance, nor did they qualify for recently announced funding for undergraduate residences. He also informed the delegation that the Robarts government was 'dissatisfied' with the Laurentian policy of sharing its government of Canada grant with the federated colleges on a 50/50 basis instead of using the provincial formula for tuition fees. Because the federal Liberal government had declared its intention of allocating this funding to the provinces rather than directly to individual universities, this did not bode well for the colleges. At an August meeting with Laurentian's executive and federation relations committees and church representatives, Davis reiterated these views, and also stated that the province was willing to amend the *Laurentian Act* to reduce the number of governors appointed by the federated universities. However, the governance storm then gathering within Laurentian put the latter issue on a backburner for nearly two decades.[12]

In May 1967, the pendulum swung back in the colleges' favour when the Laurentian governors approved a "Statement on Relationships between Laurentian University and its Federated Universities," developed by the committee on federation relations. Assertively pro-federated university, the ten-point document declared that "the Colleges contributed by the church-related Universities ... are integral units of the Federated University," have a teaching function not limited to philosophy and religious studies, and play a critical role in the administrative and student life of the university. Furthermore, the Laurentian board resolved that the document be presented as a joint brief to Minister of University Affairs Davis by President Mullins and the heads of the three federated universities.[13]

Thereafter, federation relations came more to the forefront of the Laurentian board thinking. As chair of the federation relations committee, Dalton Caswell, explained in October, 1968, the committee met once a month, giving the federation partners the chance "to openly discuss any subject which may concern the Colleges or the University as a whole." Subjects for consideration ranged from matters of principle, such as the teaching programs for the federated institutions, to more practical concerns, such as timetables, use of classroom space, and on-campus nursing services, to name only a few.[14]

ST. MARK'S CHAPEL AT THORNELOE UNIVERSITY | The only freestanding chapel on campus, St. Mark's was constructed in 1968 with funding from the Fielding family of Sudbury.

Unfortunately, the federated universities' deteriorating financial circumstances negated the gains from these new consultative procedures. With limited provincial assistance, they were dependent on their church affiliations both for operating subsidies and for capital funding to construct administrative buildings, classrooms, and residences. When the latter proved insufficient, they had no choice but to mortgage their properties, the additional costs of which, as President Newbery noted in 1967, inflated annual operating deficits. Exacerbating the situation, that year Laurentian acceded to provincial wishes and revised its method of sharing federal grants with the colleges, although the province partially offset federated losses by funding their students at 50 per cent of the non-denominational rate under the new 'formula' system.[15]

Though by no means immune to the financial pressures of the day, the University of Sudbury, with the weight of the Jesuit Order behind it, emerged from the financial challenges of these years with its teaching programs intact. Huntington and Thorneloe did not fare so well. Demoralized both by having to negotiate "through the unsympathetic attitudes of university and state," and by his inability to convince the Board of Regents to take seriously Mullins' efforts to 'neutralize the College,' Newbery resigned the Huntington presidency in February 1968. (A year later, he moved to the University of Sudbury where he founded the Amerindian – later Native – Studies program.) The situation worsened. In addition to the financial dilemma, faculty and student discontent with the Huntington board and its governance practices that mirrored developments on the main campus, roiled the institution. In September, the regents established a committee for revision and renewal to examine the college's affairs. One finding, that Huntington had been forced to use capital funds to cover operating deficits, was particularly worrisome. To reduce its financial commitments, in the spring of 1969, Huntington transferred its philosophy program and faculty (including Garry Clarke and Wes

Cragg, both prominent in Laurentian's governance reform movement) to University College, limiting its teaching role to courses in religious studies.[16]

While Huntington's fear of becoming a mere dormitory on campus very nearly materialized, a worse fate threatened Thorneloe – its demise as a denominational institution and the sale of its facilities to Laurentian University. As a delegation explained to the Laurentian board executive in March 1969, Thorneloe's problem was a $375,000 mortgage. Despite revenues from student residences, it annually incurred deficits that threatened to swell if, as rumoured might happen (and in fact did), the Anglican Diocese of Algoma reduced its subvention. Thorneloe therefore offered to transfer all properties, excluding St. Mark's Chapel, to Laurentian, in return for the university taking over the mortgage. It also stipulated that Laurentian must retain the name 'Thorneloe College' and endeavour 'so far as possible and desirable' to perpetuate "the traditions, customs, hopes, and aspirations with which Thorneloe College is now endowed."[17]

Although agreeing to the arrangement, the board executive quickly discovered this was not easily done because it required an amendment to the *Laurentian Act*. In the adversarial climate of the winter of 1969–1970, opposition from various groups within the university community, especially the Laurentian University Faculty Association, thwarted efforts to do so, and in December, the Thorneloe board released Laurentian from its commitment to take over the college. To cut expenditures, Thorneloe authorities then went one step further than Huntington, eliminating both philosophy and religious studies programs for the 1970–1971 academic year, although it maintained a series of continuing education courses in the latter discipline.[18]

For the federated universities, the challenges of the late 1960s fundamentally altered both perceptions about their place in the Laurentian system, and the reality. No longer could they convincingly argue that the federation was a partnership of equals in terms of authority, if not role. The financially lean years of the early 1970s reinforced this fact, particularly for Huntington and Thorneloe, making survival on a reduced scale the more realistic objective. To assist the federated universities, Laurentian petitioned the Davis government to fund their students on the same basis as those in non-denominational institutions. In the autumn of 1972, a glimmer of hope appeared when President Monahan and the heads of the three federated universities met with the committee on university affairs to discuss the matter. The meeting eventually bore fruit. A year later, the Minister of Colleges and Universities announced that, as of September 1974, church-affiliated institutions would be put on an equal funding footing with others. The doubled grants not only greatly helped the federated universities, but permitted Laurentian to restore the administrative fees charged to the colleges to real-cost levels. Monahan estimated that in the first year, Laurentian's revenues from this source would increase six-fold.[19]

Apart from the increased revenues, the federated universities also benefited because the change in the provincial funding policy altered Laurentian attitudes about their teaching role in the university. With their students fully funded, unique

"HE SAID WOULD YOU LIKE SOME MORE CHAMPAGNE, **NOT** THAT HE LIKES THE NAME CHAMPLAIN"

NORTHERN LIFE'S PERCEP-
TIVE AND WITTY TAKE
ON THE PARROTT COM-
MISSION RECOMMENDA-
TION ABOUT RENAMING
LAURENTIAN 'CHAMPLAIN
UNIVERSITY'

federated university programs posed less of a threat to Laurentian offerings, and in December 1974, the federation relations committee recommended the colleges, "be encouraged to expand their academic commitments within the University." Over the next three decades, each did so, both by rebuilding and expanding their joint programs in religious studies and philosophy, and by moving into areas not directly competitive with Laurentian: folklore (later folklore et ethnologie) and Amerindian (later Native) studies at the University of Sudbury, women's studies and classical studies at Thorneloe, and music (with Cambrian College) at Huntington in the 1970s; theatre arts at Thorneloe; and ethics (with Laurentian and the University of Sudbury) at Huntington in the 1980s; gerontology at Huntington in the 1990s; interarts (with Laurentian and Cambrian College) at Thorneloe, communication studies (with Laurentian and Cambrian College) at Huntington, and communication publique (with Laurentian and Cambrian) at the University of Sudbury in the 2000s. While spiritual matters continued to be of prime concern to the federated universities, this program expansion, along with their well-established student residence responsibilities, guaranteed that they did not simply 'play catechism' on campus.[20]

Larger enrolments and increased funding from their expanded teaching functions also eased the federated universities' financial burdens and diminished tensions with Laurentian. Still, differences periodically arose when the university revised revenue-sharing arrangements or raised fees for administrative services, as happened in the late 1970s. During the 1980s, federation relations were relatively harmonious, as reflected in the 1986 decision of the three founding churches to reduce the number of their nominees to the Laurentian Board of Governors from six to five.[21]

In the early 1990s, federation issues again came to the forefront. The 1992 final report of the Laurentian strategic planning committee, prompted in part by on-campus concerns about competition for students from the colleges, recommended, 'in a spirit of cooperation,' a review of the federation agreements. The heads of the four institutions took up the idea and established a presidents' commission on federation relations. Chaired by Laurentian governor Jim Smith, the commission included the four presidents and one member of the Board of Governors/Regents and one faculty member from each of the four universities. Commencing in October 1992, it carried out comprehensive studies on the federation relationship centred on three main themes: academics, finance, and governance. Its report, submitted a year later, "Laurentian University: A Collaborative Federation," recommended ways to enhance the collaborative governance character of the Laurentian federation, but still ensure uniformity of academic appointments and standards across the institutional spectrum via such mechanisms as a federation management committee and a federation academic committee. With respect to governance, too, in March 1994, the Laurentian board altered the composition of its federated relations committee by adding one board/Regent member from each of the federated colleges, in line with a commission recommendation. Finally, in the wake of the presidents' commission (and partly on the initiative of Laurentian's ad hoc committee on board restructuring then also at work), the federated colleges agreed to reduce the number of their appointees to the Laurentian board from five to four.[22]

The reforms of the mid-1990s shaped the unfolding of federation relations during the next decade and a half. With both formal (the Board of Governors federation relations committee, the federation management committee, the federation academic committee) and informal (ad hoc meetings of the institutional presidents, registrars, etc.) consultative mechanisms in place to address a broad spectrum of issues of common concern – funding, enrolment, security, pensions, student support services, etc. – relations between Laurentian and the three federated universities took on a more settled, equitable character. This did not mean these years were conflict-free. As in the past, both the degree of attention paid to federation issues, and the nature of the relationship at any given time, depended upon variables such as the personalities of key individuals, especially at the presidential level, the financial situation, and the enrolment picture. Still, in contrast to the volatility of the 1960s and the quiescence of the second phase of the next two decades, the modern era of federation relations since the 1990s has been characterized by greater mutual understanding and cooperation. As Andrii Krawchuk, president of the University of Sudbury, wrote in 2009: "Over and above our institutional autonomy and distinctiveness, our federation remains first and foremost a relationship – a community of institutions."[23]

18 The Early Years, 1960–1972

LINDA AMBROSE

When Laurentian University opened its doors in downtown Sudbury for the 1960–1961 academic year, there were thirty-four full-time faculty members and twenty-four part-time instructors on the payroll.[1] The following year, twenty-three of the full-time faculty continued, six resigned, and five went on leave to further their studies. Fourteen new full-time faculty members were recruited in 1961–1962 and nine more were appointed in 1962–1963, while five left and six went on leave. In other words, although the overall numbers were small, proportionately a great deal of movement occurred with faculty coming and going. That earliest period was followed by several years of rapid expansion and continuing high turnover. Then the growth slowed and eventually gave way to a period of little turnover in the following decades. In the late 1970s and early 1980s, declining enrolments halted the growth of post-secondary institutions, and caused university teachers at Laurentian University and elsewhere to seek job security through unionization and collective bargaining. Economic conditions and demographic realities meant that there was very little new hiring at Canadian universities throughout the late 1980s and early 1990s.

By 2008, Laurentian University employed more than twelve times the original number of full-time faculty (416) and more than three times the original number of part-time instructors (84).[2] In recent years, there has again been a high degree of faculty renewal with long-serving faculty members retiring, replaced by newly minted PhDs with active research programs and aspirations to teach in graduate programs. This "changing of the guard" has altered Laurentian's institutional culture, meaning that individuals who now seek to build academic careers in Sudbury have a very different experience from their predecessors of thirty or forty years ago. These chapters trace the evolution of that changing experience for faculty members who have taught students, conducted research, and served their community as professors at Laurentian University from its earliest days until the present. Particular attention is given to unionization because labour relations

"List of Faculty Teaching at Laurentian University, 1960–61"
When the university opened its doors in 1960, there was no formal mechanism for collective bargaining, and therefore each one of the thirty-one faculty members negotiated the terms of his employment directly with the president.

Professors
Bouvier, E., S.J., PhD, Georgetown-Harvard, Economics
Cadieux, L., S.J., PhD, Laval, History
Ferland, Y., S.J., BA, Lic. En Science, Montreal, Mathematics
L'Archeveque, A., MD, Biology (Visiting Professor)
Leclaire, R., S.J., PhD, Georgetown, Physics

Associate Professors
Robillard, F., S.J., MSc, Montreal, Physics

Assistant Professors
Allaire, C., S.J., MA, Montreal, Chemistry
Almazan, V., MA, Strasbourg, Languages
Dupas, A., S.J., MA, Loyola, English and French Studies
Girouard, A., S.J., BA, Montreal, French Literature
Scanlon, P., MA, Wisconsin, English

between the university and the Laurentian University Faculty Association have been at the core of the faculty experience throughout the institution's history.

In Laurentian's early years, all university teachers were hired on ten-month appointments, and annually, each faculty member directly renegotiated the terms of his or her own employment with the president of the university.[3] The president then recommended to the Board of Governors the contract details of salary and rank for individual faculty members. In 1960, faculty salaries ranged from $3,000 to $10,000 depending on experience and qualifications. Of the original thirty-four full-time faculty members, only four had doctoral degrees, four had master's degrees, and the rest had bachelor's degrees though many were working toward obtaining their master's.[4] Those who commanded the highest salaries (seven individuals were paid $7,500 or more in 1960–1961) had PhDs, extensive teaching experience, and/or additional administrative responsibilities as dean or department chairs.[5]

The individual nature of these arrangements meant that a great deal of power was concentrated in the hands of the president, leaving room for much arbitrary decision-making. None of what are now considered standard conditions of aca-

Stingel, R., MA, Toronto, English (Visiting Assistant Professor)
Szelle, L., LLD, Budapest, Political Science, History
Tombalakian, A., PhD, Toronto, Chemistry

Lecturers
Barrera, M., MA, Mexico, Spanish
Brodeur, L., BA, Manitoba, French Literature
Carrier, Y., S.J., MSc, Fordham, Biology
Devriendt, A., Dip., Mons and Colorado School of Mines, Engineering
Gueneau, J., S.J., MA, Paris, Mathematics
Kampouris, J., Business Administration, Sociology
Kwei, A., MA, Toronto, Physics
Lafleur, P., BA, Montreal, French
Lemieux, C., S.J., MA, Laval, History
Michaud, L., S.J., BA, Laval, Economics
Pare, L., MA, Fordham, Philosophy
Peltier, J., BA, Ottawa, Economics
Pezet, J., BA, Laval, Extension Department
Pryke, K., MA, Duke, History
Rabin, C., BSc, South Carolina, Economics
Shea, J., BA, London, Sociology
Sirtori, A., Lic.es Lettres, Milan, Languages
Vachet, A., MA, Ottawa, Philosophy

demic life were in place: There was no policy for tenure, no procedure for granting sabbatical leaves, and no standardized system of appointment or progress-through-the-ranks. Within the first decade of the university's existence, efforts to ensure some semblance of job security and standardized working conditions became major goals of faculty members.

The bilingual Laurentian University Faculty Association (LUFA) was established during the first year of the university's existence, although it would not be certified as a union until 1979. From the 1960s however, LUFA negotiated with the Board of Governors on behalf of its members as provided by the objectives defined within its constitution: "1) to promote the welfare of the Faculty, and of the University; 2) to protect the freedom of teaching, thought and research within the University and to improve their quality; 3) to cooperate with other bodies whose interests may be similar; and 4) to deal with all other matters considered to be in the interests of the Association or of its members."[6] Given the initial, arbitrary practices of the board and president to fix salaries, recommend promotions, and offer and renew contracts, it is clear that faculty members needed to work together to protect their collective interests.

INDIGENOUS LEARNERS TAKE EXTENSION COURSE, 1962 | With a commitment to life-long learning, as early as 1962 Laurentian was offering extension courses at various sites throughout northern communities to adult learners.

LUFA archives reveal that in 1960–1961, twenty-seven members paid the $10 annual membership dues, and the association disbursed $178.15 on social activities, the Laurentian Theatre Guild, condolences, bank service charges, and stationary. Two years later, the annual membership fee increased to $15 annually and LUFA paid $240 to join the Canadian Association of University Teachers (CAUT).[7] Membership in the national association was important, as it allowed Laurentian faculty members to keep apprised of developments that were occurring on other campuses regarding matters such as tenure, sabbaticals, and pensions. Indeed, at this time, academics across the country entered into a period of greater activism in an effort to protect their professional interests. The sudden and largely unplanned expansion of Ontario's post-secondary institutions in the 1960s resulted in the rapid growth of ad hoc procedures for all manner of faculty issues. Dissatisfaction over how staffing issues were handled led faculty across Canada to new levels of activism that eventually would lead to unionization.[8]

As discussed elsewhere, questions concerning faculty members in this period did not simply relate to remuneration or job security. Also at stake were issues about the level of participation in and influence of faculty members on institutional decision-making. In his 1976 article, "Modes of University Government,"[9] W.M. Sibley traced three periods of university governance: the Age of Authority (up to the 1960s), the Age of Participation (late 1960s to 1970s), and the Adversary Age (1970s and after). All of these were clearly on display at Laurentian, although sometimes it seemed that there was much crossover between these periods as the university administration continued to act in a very authoritarian manner, while faculty demanded and won the right to greater participation in institutional decision-making and university governance. At the same time, the level of conflict increased, and it became clear that Laurentian was entering a long and protracted period of adversarial relations between its faculty association and the administration. Debates about faculty representation at the level of Senate and board decisions are discussed elsewhere in this book, but it is important to bear in mind here that it was within that same context around the years of the Duff-Berdahl report (1966) that LUFA, like other faculty associations across the country, struggled to establish standard policies and procedures for such matters as the granting of tenure and sabbaticals and acceptable grounds for dismissal; issues that today's academics have come to take for granted. The story that unfolded at Laurentian was typical of the kinds of questions that were being raised on campuses throughout Ontario and across the country.

In Sudbury, while these larger issues about the principles of fair remuneration, basic job security, and adequate representation in decision-making were important to faculty, there were also even more immediate and pragmatic issues to be considered: one of the most pressing was faculty housing. Laurentian faced a major challenge in trying to attract faculty members because of the housing crisis in Sudbury. On May 31, 1961, President Bouvier reported that "five Ph.D. applicants have turned down Laurentian University for several reasons, especially because of lack of residential facilities."[10] In meeting this challenge, the university considered several different solutions, including an elaborate plan to build a faculty housing complex on the new Ramsey Lake Road campus, a plan that had to be abandoned for financial reasons. Instead, the board opted to "study the feasibility of making second mortgage loans to members of the faculty to assist them in the purchase or construction of residential housing for themselves."[11] The board modelled this procedure on existing practices at the University of Toronto, where bank loans for faculty mortgages were guaranteed by the university itself. By the following year, Laurentian's board adopted a bylaw with a process to approve second mortgages for its employees who wished to make such arrangements.[12]

While financial assistance for housing was an important initiative, it did not address the immediate crisis that new faculty members faced upon their arrival in Sudbury: there simply was no place to live. Few houses were for sale and rental accommodation was at a premium; as a result, Laurentian made a foray into real estate. In the spring of 1967, the board authorized the "Staff Reception Committee in consultation with the Comptroller" to reserve up to twenty apartments or houses in Sudbury, as they became available over the summer months, and to pay rent on these units in order to hold them for the fifty-one new faculty arriving to take up new positions that fall. In August, the executive received a report that the following premises had been acquired: "Caswell Apartment Building: 3 units Net Cost $367.50; Benvenuto Apartment Block 1 unit Net Cost $50.00; Commodore Apartment Block 3 units Net Cost $176.25; Lakeshore Apartment Block 1 unit Net Cost nil; McVittie Residence – vacant in July and August $350.00. Rent of three furnished residences used to accommodate new faculty arrivals over a short period while satisfactory quarters were being sought: $1,270.00; Total $2,213.75.

RANDOLPH APARTMENT BUILDING | As the number of faculty members expanded rapidly after the move to the new campus, local housing shortages were acute and so in 1967 the university purchased the Randolph Apartment building in downtown Sudbury to ease the situation. The arrangement was short-lived, as the administration sold the building in 1972.

The President stated that this service by the University to new members of the staff had been greatly appreciated."[13]

This list of properties, however, did not provide enough housing for the growth projected to take place. Consequently, in June 1967 the university entered into its biggest and most controversial real-estate venture, the purchase of an apartment building in downtown Sudbury at the corner of Cedar and Drinkwater Streets, known as the Randolph Towers. Laurentian agreed to pay $235,000 (with $75,000 down payment and 7 per cent mortgage on the balance) for the building, which was deemed to be "in good condition, requiring only minor renovations to provide 23 housing units."[14] It seemed to be a very logical move and a convenient location for university personnel. What no one had anticipated, however, was the public's 'violent reaction and severe criticism' that ensued. It order for the university to take ownership and begin the preparations for faculty and staff occupancy late that summer, the existing tenants were given only one month's notice to vacate their apartments.

According to the *Sudbury Star,* "a proportion, even a preponderance, of the residents ... are widows or retired persons which made the situation seem doubly hard. The general impression built up that Laurentian University president Professor Stanley Mullins and the university's Board of Governors must be a group of hard-hearted individuals."[15] Indeed, based on that perception, a group of dislocated tenants decided to take their protest directly to Queen's Park. In a letter to Premier Robarts, they explained that:

We find it incomprehensible and unbelievable that our local University, representing three Christian churches of our community ... would entertain for a moment, taking over a complete apartment block in a manner that would result in the occupants being deprived of their homes on such scanty notice. It makes us wonder if the purchase of the apartment building by Laurentian University, and the manner in which the present tenants would be required to vacate, has been given all necessary consideration ... We, the undersigned, encouraged the building of a University in this community and many assisted by donations and other means and never, at any time, gave any thought that in so doing it might one day result in ... twenty-two or so family occupants forced to vacate and look for alternative accommodation in an already chaotic real estate situation in this neighbourhood.[16]

Commenting on the letter of protest, Premier Robarts captured the essence of the situation when he wrote to Bill Davis, who held the dual portfolios of Minister of Education and Minister of University Affairs, saying, "The shortness of such notice does not make good public relations for this institution."[17]

Davis reported back to the premier that while Laurentian was desperate for housing space, it had completely botched the public relations considerations around refitting the building for faculty use. In an effort to save face and smooth community relations, the university met with the majority of tenants and in the end, all of the tenants found alternate accommodation, except one elderly resident who was allowed to stay in the building. Davis reported in early September that he had spoken to President Mullins about the matter, and that "Mr. Mullins notes that the University is conscious of the need for good public relations and states that the whole affair has now quieted down and that no real problem exists."[18] While that problem seemed to be in abeyance, the premier was further briefed to the effect that "The main theme of this acquisition of an apartment building by the University has been a lack of planning. This lack of long-term planning is also evident in their potential development for student housing."[19] Five years after the Randolph Towers public relations fiasco, the university sold the building, citing financial reasons, including low rents and high maintenance costs.[20]

To be fair to President Mullins, managing Laurentian's rapid growth in this period was no easy task. The growth could be measured in many ways, the most visible being the new campus under construction, but there were also new programs being established. Clearly, the new campus and the new courses were all created to serve the ever-increasing number of students flocking to Laurentian. Within a decade of its founding, the student population had climbed to 2,100 students, more than ten times the 185 full-time students enrolled in the fall of 1960.[21] More students required more teachers, of course, and in the later 1960s the local newspaper explained "the staff at Laurentian University is shooting up like the seven-storey tower over the library building."[22]

By the fall of 1967, Laurentian had 140 full-time professors and lecturers, and a total of 475 employees.[23] As faculty ranks expanded, so too did the strength of

EARLY TEACHING TECHNOLOGY | To meet the challenge of providing university education throughout the region, Laurentian began early to incorporate technologies for distance education into classroom teaching.

their demands. Universities across the country competed for limited numbers of scholars to fill the ever-expanding ranks of the professoriate, often looking outside the country. In January 1969, Laurentian had 164 faculty members, 86 of whom were 'of foreign birth.' The common perception was that most non-Canadian faculty members came from the United States, but the situation at Laurentian showed a very different reality. Of the eighty-six members who were not born in Canada, only eight were American. As the *Sudbury Star* reported, "England and France have the largest representation with 18 and 11 respectively. India ranks third with nine; then the U.S.; West Germany, five; Pakistan four and Belgium and the United Arab Republic three each. There are faculty contingents from 26 foreign countries at Laurentian."[24]

As the university administration struggled through this dizzying period of growth, LUFA was making important strides in protecting the interests of faculty members. In 1963, negotiations began between the faculty association and the Board of Governors to create an employment policy that would spell out how faculty would join the permanent teaching staff, how they would move through the ranks, how much they would teach, and under what terms they could take leaves. These issues were hard fought and a long period of negotiations ensued. At the spring convocation in May 1964, some confusion arose when President Mullins prematurely announced that an agreement on faculty appointment, promotion, tenure, teaching load, and leave had been agreed upon. LUFA was alarmed by that announcement, because although they had seen a draft document, they did not agree with all of its content, and therefore they successfully took steps to continue negotiations with the board over the matter.[25] The final agreement came several months later, when both parties gave their support for the document entitled "Revised University Regulation 64-1 (December 31, 1964) Policy on Appointments, Tenure, Promotion, Teaching Load and Leave."[26] While the policy preserved the existing practice that appointments were made by the Board of Governors on the recommendation of the president, it also spelled out how faculty would transfer from undergoing annual contract renewals to becoming permanent staff after a period of probation that varied according to academic rank. The policy made provision for the termination of faculty members, but it stipulated that this would be done "only on the grounds of immorality, misconduct in office, or incompetency or dereliction of academic duties."[27] Those conditions for dismissal were open to interpretation and the final decision about appointment still rested with the board, but the adoption of this policy was historic because it was one of the earliest policies of tenure to be developed in the country.[28]

Also included in the document were provisions for several other pressing issues, including promotion through the ranks, which was to be granted by the board on the approval of the president and with the recommendation of the department chair and the dean of the faculty. Teaching loads were set at nine hours of instruction per week, with recognition that for the sciences, this would include laboratory supervision. Department chairs could recommend a reduced teaching load in order to promote research, and members with administrative duties were granted reduced teaching loads with the approval of the dean and the president. Other major advances for faculty included the provision for leaves of absence for those who wanted to work on advanced degrees, carry out research, "or pursue any other professional undertaking approved by the Dean and the President ... Such leave must be in the best interests of the University."[29] Sabbatical leaves were also addressed in the policy, although an early draft of the policy declared, "Until such time as more uniformity exists in Canadian Universities, no policy regarding sabbatical leave will be established at Laurentian University of Sudbury."[30] By the time it was approved by LUFA in January 1965, significant progress had been made and the final wording read: 'The University recognizes the desirability of granting sabbatical leave for research or study purposes. For the present, each case will be given individual consideration."[31]

LUFA had achieved significant progress with the creation of this policy because it identified the major issues and set out the terms of faculty employment, and while those terms would be refined and renegotiated in the years to come, it was a major development that Laurentian faculty now had a written policy addressing standard procedures for appointment, tenure, promotion, workload, and leave. These questions were not settled for all time, but with the creation of this employment policy document, at least the issues were identified and from that point forward, LUFA would be vigilantly working to protect the interests of its members. Only five years after its founding, this meant that among Canadian academic institutions, Laurentian was in the vanguard of labour relations.

In addition to all of these issues, there was the question of money. In the fall of 1965, the LUFA committee on salary, pensions and fringe benefits completed its list of recommendations, explaining that the report was 'neither final nor exhaustive' because, as Joseph Chung, chair of the committee, explained, "Some of the vital problems have not been explored and do need careful studies. On the other hand, the Committee feels that the recommendations contained in this report are the minimum requirements for reasonably healthy progress of Laurentian and that they should be immediately brought to the attention of the Administration."[32]

The report was based on the idea that Laurentian University's administration must bear three objectives in mind when setting faculty salaries: "1) to attract qualified people from other professions; 2) to attract qualified people from other universities; and 3) especially to retain those faculty members who are already at Laurentian." In order to accomplish those goals, the committee compared the salaries of Laurentian faculty to two other groups and concluded that the administration would need to substantially increase the remuneration paid to faculty members. The first comparison group was Sudbury high school teachers. The committee found that Laurentian professors with the same years of teaching experience were paid from 13 per cent to 24 per cent less than local secondary school teachers, with the salary discrepancy increasing as experience levels rose. The second comparison group was other Ontario university teachers, and here the committee found that Laurentian salaries for full and associate professors lagged behind the provincial average by 6.9 per cent and 7.6 per cent, respectively.[33]

Anticipating the administration's rebuttal to these figures, the report argued that "the experience of Laurentian academic staff is by no means more limited than their colleagues elsewhere in the Province. Nor is their professional competence poorer than [the] competence of university teachers at other universities." Indeed, in the committee's opinion, Laurentian faculty needed to be compensated for "several detrimental regional factors which are absent at other Ontario universities." Moreover, the report made the case that university teachers in Canada had "failed to share equitably [in] the nation's growing prosperity." As proof, the report offered this statistic: "Over the period from 1937/38 to 1963/64 ... while the income of an average Canadian rose by 412 per cent, the typical salary of university professors increased by no more than 266 per cent." Using these calculations, the committee concluded that "if the academic salary had increased as fast as the average Canadian's income, it would have amounted to $16,440 in 1963/64 as against the actual figure of $9,103 in the same year."[34] Constructing arguments that ranged from local comparisons with school board employees, to provincial comparisons with other Ontario universities, and even to the average national income outside academia, the authors of the report hoped to convince the Laurentian administration that professors in Sudbury were woefully underpaid.

The debate did not go away, nor did levels of pay for faculty improve very much during the 1960s. Indeed, on July 31, 1970, Garry Clarke, president of LUFA, informed F.B. Lavoie, the chair of the salary negotiations committee of the Board of Governors, that the faculty association and the administration were a long way from successfully negotiating a settlement on the question of faculty salaries, and that outside intervention might be necessary to settle the matter. Clarke was convinced that what divided the two sides were 'matters of fact, not matters of opinion.' Specifically, he pointed out that "the Board apparently believes that professors of comparable qualifications are paid more at Laurentian than at any

BRIAN KAYE, FINE PARTICLE RESEARCH LAB | One of the benefits of the new campus was the space it provided for research facilities, such as those occupied by Professor Brian Kaye for his Fine Particle Research Lab.

other university in Ontario," while "the Faculty, on the other hand, believes that professors of comparable qualifications are paid among the lowest salaries in the province, and when account is taken of the cost of living, substantially less than at other emergent universities."[35] Given that impasse, LUFA suggested that the matter should be referred to arbitration.

In the summer when Clarke made that suggestion, the Laurentian community was still recovering from the turmoil that had occurred in spring of that year. In April 1970, after a vote of non-confidence in the university president, and a great deal of media coverage (including coverage on the front page of the *Globe and Mail*) over the Senate-supported, week-long student "sit-in," President Mullins had been forced to resign. Yet, just as the fall term was beginning, and Acting President Roland Cloutier had taken over, it was clear that there was even more conflict on the horizon. While the April protest captured a great deal of attention because of the unprecedented alliance between student protestors and Senate members, it took place just as classes had ended so was of little consequence to actual university operations, but in mid-September, the *Sudbury Star* reported that "Laurentian Teachers Threatening Strike Over Salary Dispute."[36] This time it seemed that the protest might have even greater impact than the events of the past spring because classes had just begun for the fall semester. The sides were quite far apart as the Laurentian executive committee claimed that the salary offer they were making represented a 13.49 per cent increase, while the faculty association claimed it only amounted to 7 per cent.

Technically, the faculty could not 'strike' since they were not yet unionized. Instead, Senate declared a 'recess,' which lasted from September 30 to October 13 and involved the suspension of classes across the campus, although many science professors refused to participate and continued to teach their classes. While the breakdown of salary negotiations precipitated the recess, the larger issue was conflict over university governance as LUFA president Garry Clarke asserted in early October, "Legislators [elsewhere] are much more liberal than the board of governors here." Professor Don Wallace concurred by saying that, "We feel the conflict is much broader than salaries now and can't be settled just by settling salaries."[37]

It is interesting to note that just as the 'recess' was beginning, a general meeting was held on the campus to debate the wisdom of turning the recess into a full-fledged strike. Weir Reid, the executive secretary of the Mine, Mill and Smelter Workers Union Local 596, was among those who attended a public meeting on the question, and several students called for faculty to "have the guts to call a strike."[38] Meanwhile, others reasoned that "the strike weapon is less viable for university teachers than for almost any other group" because, for example, when local miners went on strike, Professor Don Wallace reasoned, "at least they know they are hurting Inco. I don't think a strike [by professors] would hurt the board of governors at all."[39] Moreover, it was not clear that strike action on the part of Laurentian faculty would do anything to advance the outstanding issues around greater faculty participation in decisions regarding salary, tenure, and sabbaticals. The divided opinion about striking and even about whether or not to unionize would be revisited at Laurentian in the next period of its history.

After the recess ended in mid-October with the intervention of the provincial government, ex-president of Waterloo, J.G. Hagey, was appointed to mediate the various questions troubling Laurentian, including the outstanding issue of salary negotiations. In the course of these discussions, it came to light that Laurentian was in dire financial circumstances with a deficit budget forecast.[40] With Hagey's assistance, LUFA and the Board of Governors negotiated a two-year agreement resolving what Hagey characterized as "a major cause of controversy between faculty and board during the crisis."[41] Both sides agreed that the new salary scales were "established on a basis that compares favourably with those at other Ontario universities." Anticipating that higher enrolments would continue into the following year and that new faculty would be hired, there was agreement that "the revised salary scales will help Laurentian to attract these new professors."[42] In hindsight, it seems that the optimism of that press release was somewhat overstated because although the salary issue was temporarily settled, the coming decade would see some significant debates around what the most effective mechanisms might be to continue to guarantee faculty members' best interests.

19   Consolidation, Certification, 1972–1985

LINDA AMBROSE

Like many other campuses across the country, Laurentian experienced a period of unprecedented growth during the decade of the 1960s that led, among other things, to the headline-making conflicts of 1970. A study commissioned by the Association of Universities and Colleges of Canada described the national situation this way:

> The outstanding feature of the Canadian university system in the 1960s was its explosive growth, in numbers of institutions, students and teachers, and in the amount of provincial and federal money poured into the system. Qualified teachers were hard to come by in many fields, and the price paid for their services rose sharply and steadily. Accompanying the growth of the 1960s were some developments that led to restlessness among faculty members.[1]

"Restlessness" among faculty at Laurentian continued to develop during the next fifteen years as LUFA moved toward certification and members debated the implications of what it would mean to become unionized.

The fact that professors at Laurentian and across Canada began to consider organizing into labour unions was very much a product of the times. After such rapid expansion in the 1960s, and the historic clashes over university governance, Laurentian University, like so many other campuses, found itself in what Sibley has described as "the Adversary Age," the same period that Owen D. Carrigan calls "the Age of Unionism." Carrigan explains the context of the times:

> Suddenly, in the early Seventies, static or even declining enrolments and financial stringencies brought expansion to an end. The job market tightened, and the climate of austerity that now prevailed in the universities

clashed with still rising faculty expectations. An atmosphere of insecurity and apprehension developed. In their time of trouble, professors took the same recourse that so many of their blue-collar fellow citizens had taken in similar circumstances – the formation of unions.[2]

Laurentian was definitely among the campuses that experienced the drop in enrolment, with the resultant financial stringencies, but at the same time, other complaints surfaced that were typical of the times and the atmosphere. Individuals who wanted to challenge the way they were treated by the administration had to take individual legal action. And some did so.

There were several instances in the 1970s of faculty members who complained about the way that they were treated with regard to various issues, including the perceived injustice of denying tenure to faculty members and then rehiring them to do further contract work with no promise of permanency;[3] the suspicion (at least in one infamous case, well-founded suspicion) that some faculty members were hired without a thorough process of verifying their academic qualifications;[4] and the unilateral decision of the president to remove the director of engineering from his role and attempt to dismiss him from the university.[5] At the same time, when husbands and wives were both employed at the university, it seemed like acceptable budgetary logic to pay the woman less because of the man's financial stability.[6]

In one case in 1974, Bud Germa, the MPP for Sudbury, wrote to James Auld, the Minister of Colleges and Universities, on behalf of a former instructor at Laurentian, asking for a public inquiry into the administrative practices at the university. Germa told Auld, "I also am aware of various other disgruntled faculty members presently on staff. You will recall approximately one month ago another Professor from this University discussed with you personally his dissatisfaction with the operation of this university. I am also sure that you are aware of other complaints which have been registered against this Institution."[7] Such direct appeals to the government on behalf of individual faculty members reveal the nature of the problems that academic staff members were facing. As previously noted, the university and the faculty association were already engaged in a form of collective bargaining over several issues even without formal union status, yet there was no formal legal recourse that could be taken by LUFA on behalf of individual members when they were caught up in situations that were perceived to be based on unfair and arbitrary decision making.

Advocates of unionization were convinced that formal certification under the *Ontario Labour Relations Act* would provide better protection for LUFA members. As Carrigan explains, "One problem of great concern on many university campuses was the lack of clearly defined procedures, especially in key areas such as promotion, tenure, and arbitration. Some faculty felt that their careers were protected by nothing more than the whim and caprice of Boards and administrators. In uncertain times, this was simply not sufficient assurance."[8] Others argued that LUFA was already doing a fine job of representing its members, and there was no

ARTS BUILDING CLASSROOM | A typical classroom setting in the Arts building. Note the small class size, something that Laurentian has worked to maintain.

need for the association to seek certification. Meanwhile, on some campuses, university administrators felt threatened by the increasing demands and faculty associations' moves toward gaining greater bargaining power backed by legal recourse. According to Carrigan, "Board members and administrators concluded that faculty expectations had become unreasonable. They argued that there would soon be no effective authority in the university and that total chaos would result."[9]

The question of whether or not to unionize was more complicated than just moving beyond entrenched views representing pro- and anti-union positions. Some faculty members were convinced that as enrolments fell and university deficits mounted, the only way to guarantee their jobs and protect themselves from the possibility of cuts to faculty positions was through the bargaining power offered through unionization. Others were not so sure, and they argued that because LUFA members already had job security with the existing policy on tenure, unionizing was neither necessary nor wise. One of the most outspoken opponents of certification was Garry Clarke, who had served as LUFA president from 1968–1971. He wrote a memorandum entitled 'The Role of the Laurentian Senate Under Collective Agreement with Faculty,' in which he expressed the fear that after LUFA unionized, the university might "preempt or qualify the procedures or the decision of Senate," and that the board could be expected to begin "resuming powers under the Act which have been exercised in the last 10 years by Senate."[10]

The anti-union argument that Clarke and others were making is an interesting one, and quite specific to academia. The concern was that by unionizing, faculty members' status as professionals would be denigrated, and they would be regarded as labourers, under contract, with the university administrators as their 'bosses.' At stake were the recent victories which granted faculty members greater representation in university governance. All this would be lost, the naysayers argued, if professors were to become 'mere employees' of the university rather than partners and full participants in the decision-making structures.

GARRY CLARKE, LUFA PRESIDENT | Providing leadership to the faculty association through the tumultuous period when faculty members successfully gained greater representation in university decision-making, Garry Clarke was one of many LUFA members who worried that certification might jeopardize those hard-fought gains.

More than just traditionalists chafing at the thought of a different model, the reluctant faculty members had a number of fears which, according to D.D. Carter, of the Faculty of Law at Queen's University, included:

> union organizers disrupting collegial relationships; a closed shop being imposed upon the university community; a highly formalized employment relationship replacing the traditional university-faculty relationship; union solidarity replacing academic excellence; the strike and picket line replacing rational discussion; and government and union interference in the adminis-tration of the universities.[11]

The same fears were on the minds of Laurentian faculty members whose oppos-ition to unionization was so strong that they declined the opportunity to meet and discuss the possibility.

That lack of support for unionization was clearly displayed at a general meet-ing of LUFA on October 19, 1976, when a vote was taken to determine whether or not the association should proceed toward certification as a collective bargaining unit. Although there were almost 250 academic staff members, the decision to begin exploring the process of moving toward certification was carried with the following results: twenty-seven in favour, seven opposed, and one abstention.[12] This number of voters represented little more than 10 per cent of the membership of LUFA at the time, and the low participation rate is evidence that the majority seemed quite satisfied with the collective bargaining efforts that LUFA had man-aged to accomplish up this point, even without formal union status. In a writ-ten memorandum, forty-eight faculty members expressed their collective view, arguing:

On job security, we have a policy which is the product of consultation between Senate, the Faculty Association and the Administration. When established, it was in many respects the first and the finest in Canada. It may be that it now needs review. But again no one has shown *how* present policy and procedure is inadequate, *what* alternatives would be preferable, or *why* we need a union to negotiate improvements.[13]

Yet despite the poor attendance at the meeting, it is clear that the effort to move toward certification was launched that day, even though the pro-union camp was vastly outnumbered by LUFA members who were happy with the existing consultation process. Given that inauspicious beginning, it would be misleading to say that the road toward certification at Laurentian was either a straight or smooth one. In November 1976, a membership vote was held on the certification question and 124 ballots were returned, with 99 voting yes and 25 voting no. The voter turnout was still quite low, representing less than half of the LUFA membership, and therefore the result was not considered sufficient to approve certification. A second vote was scheduled for the following month, and on December 8, 1976, the result was quite different: 199 total votes were cast with only 72 voting yes to certification, 119 voting no, and 8 spoiled ballots – a clear defeat. According to the report published in the *Laurentian University Gazette*, 287 ballots were distributed, meaning that 88 members (almost one-third of eligible voters) chose not to cast a ballot at all.

The forty-eight faculty who had authored the 'Open Letter on Faculty Certification,' must have felt vindicated because their arguments had won the day as they successfully persuaded their colleagues to oppose the idea. They argued that "a LUFA union would negotiate with the Board of Governors conditions of service which for several years have been recognized *de facto* as within the jurisdiction of Senate: appointments, promotions, tenure, redundancy, and so on. The faculty would thus be offering the Board an opportunity and an invitation to intervene in areas which have for six years been determined through self-government."[14] Opponents to unionization had won the day, but the debate was not over.

After the unsuccessful attempt at certification in 1976, three significant developments took place which began to sway faculty opinion on the certification question. First, there was a change in the LUFA leadership. After Lloyd Wagner's term as LUFA president ended in 1976, Wes Cragg took up the position from 1976–1978, followed by Roy Kari from 1978–1979, and Hermann Falter from 1979–1980. All three were well-respected faculty members with doctorates and under their leadership, LUFA rallied to make a second effort to achieve certification and negotiate its first collective agreement with the administration. Second, and even more importantly, there was bleak economic news with which to contend. In the fall of 1977, the new university president, Henry Best, reported to the Board of Governors that enrolment was down by 225 full-time students, a number that represented a drop of close to 10 per cent. It was a bad omen and a sign of things to come as falling enrolments in an ailing economy would mean tighter budgets. This gave way to the third factor that ultimately swayed opinion: rising concerns over job security for faculty members. Indeed, the practice of reducing faculty numbers (even by dismissing tenured faculty members) in order to balance budgets was being widely discussed across the country during this period, and the 1979 CAUT *Handbook* contained a whole section entitled 'Guidelines Concerning Reductions in Academic Appointments for Budgetary Reasons.'[15] In part, the guidelines established that "in matters of financial exigency, the academic staff association or union should act as the watch dog over the interests of its members."[16] The new LUFA leadership realized that declining enrolments and fiscal restraint might actually lead Laurentian to declare 'financial exigency' and if this happened, the threat of cutting faculty positions was very real, despite the strong policy on tenure which had been negotiated some years before. The new fiscal context provided reason enough for LUFA to revisit the certification question, and for several individuals, including Wes Cragg and Hermann Falter, to reverse their personal positions on the question of certification.[17]

In the spring of 1978, a certification organizing committee was struck and Roy Kari arranged to meet with CAUT officials to discuss strategies and procedures. That fall, in advance of a meeting of the LUFA membership scheduled for October 13, Kari circulated a memorandum to the members addressing the concerns about certification.[18] His memo contained two appendices: 'Some Suggested Advantages of Collective Bargaining,' which raised ten items, including efficiency, equality of power, legal force, impasse resolution, communication, understanding the university, individual problems, definition of policy, rights guarantee, and competitive power; and 'Possible Negative Consequences of Collective Bargaining,' which addressed fifteen items, including costs, flexibility, job actions, union power, bureaucracy, power shifts, adversary relationship, demands on faculty, students, funding problems, diversity, faculty rights, loss of current unspecified rights, outside arbitration, and seniority. Kari planned to address these concerns at the October meeting, allotting five minutes of discussion time to each item. Such a short discussion period must have been less than satisfactory in the minds of those who still opposed certification, but the format ensured that a wide range of issues would be addressed. That meeting was the first step in an ongoing process that continued for several weeks, as LUFA leaders who now favoured certification met one-on-one with their colleagues trying to convince the previously undecided or opposed to accept the urgency of the new rationale for certification.

Exactly one month later, on November 13, 1978, Kari communicated to faculty members that "an absolute majority of faculty have signed [union] membership forms, but [recruitment] will continue for another week."[19] At the end of the month, Ashley Thomson, LUFA secretary, reported to faculty members on behalf of the LUFA certification organizing committee that 61 per cent of full-time teaching faculty and librarians had voted for certification and that Kari was taking formal steps to ask the Ontario Labour Relations Board (OLRB) to hear the LUFA application.[20]

SIGNING THE COLLECTIVE AGREEMENT, 1980 | While faculty and administration had practiced collective bargaining with positive results even before the faculty association was formally certified as a union, concerns about job security tipped faculty opinion in favour of unionization by the late 1970s. In the fall of 1980 the signing of the first collective agreement after certification was a milestone for faculty labour relations at Laurentian.

There were several delays in the process throughout the winter and spring of 1979. At least one faculty member questioned whether 'fair notice' had been given of an OLRB hearing in December, since he claimed that he only heard about it the day before it took place; the same person alleged that LUFA had practiced 'coercion and intimidation' in getting members, but when the OLRB arranged a February hearing to hear the complaint, the professor in question withdrew his charges. In the end, the OLRB called for a certification vote to be held in early April. The question that appeared on the ballot was: 'In your employment relations with Laurentian University of Sudbury, do you wish to be represented by Laurentian University Faculty Association?' Fewer than 200 LUFA members voted (only 188 ballots were cast), and the result was: 107 yes, 81 no. Further challenges arose as one member questioned the validity of the vote on April 4, because the official notification of the vote was only distributed in English and he claimed that the question was incorrect and unclear. Objections notwithstanding, the OLRB granted certification to LUFA on July 9, 1979.

Though the battle had been a hard-fought one, this victory for LUFA's certification organizing committee was really only the beginning of a great deal more hard work and protracted negotiations between the faculty association and the administration. After the announcement of the positive vote for certification, the faculty association and the administration got down to work on the creation of the

SWIM COACH JENO TIHANYI AND
OLYMPIC GOLD MEDALIST ALEX
BAUMANN

new collective agreement, a process that took almost a year and a half. Although the two sides were not starting from scratch, now that the members were officially unionized, none of the previous agreements that LUFA had negotiated with the administration were binding and everything was up for discussion. In that context, the stakes were high for both sides, and there was a dogged determination by both parties to ensure that the agreement they were creating would be very carefully constructed.

For leadership on the issues of how to proceed in establishing collective bargaining and how to write a collective agreement, faculty associations across the country, including LUFA, looked to CAUT, which described itself in the 1970s as 'a lobbying agent for faculty members.'[21] As political scientist Howard Clark explains, in response to faculty fears in the 1970s:

> CAUT quickly put in place guidelines for collective bargaining, developed
> model clauses for collective agreements (all of which favoured the transfer
> of authority and power to faculty), and as a national organization provided
> not only information but also personnel, legal advice, and support to local
> faculty associations engaged in bargaining with their boards. It was an
> aggressive and impressive strategy, especially since its main thrust was not
> necessarily monetary; the focus was very much on securing legal protection
> for the participatory governance that had so recently been gained.[22]

Commenting on the role that CAUT played, and the tone that it struck in the 1970s, Carrigan explained that "while in many ways the CAUT guidelines were marked improvements on the procedures operative in some institutions, the vigor, and even abrasiveness, with which the campaign was sometimes carried on aroused strong resentment among university Boards and Administrations. This helped to sharpen the conflict on many campuses."[23]

At Laurentian, the 1979 negotiations were not really marked by a high degree of conflict, but some resentment did surface on the part of President Best, in response to CAUT's involvement in the process. Donald C. Savage, the executive secretary of CAUT, vigilant about the newest member of the rapidly growing family of certified faculty associations, observed the developments at Laurentian with great interest and a certain degree of impatience. At the end of October 1979, he wrote a memorandum to all Laurentian faculty members in which he lamented the slow progress of the negotiations and offered scathing criticisms of President Best's leadership.[24] Best responded with his own memorandum to the faculty in which he accused Savage of committing "the most flagrant example of grossly improper interference in the internal affairs of a university that I have seen in this country."[25] Clearly, the gloves were off between these two, with Best calling Savage's memo 'shocking,' and 'crassly unprofessional,' accusing the executive secretary of 'incredible impropriety' as he attempted to 'create anonymous adversaries' out of Laurentian colleagues who were serving in administrative capacities. The president reminded faculty members that administrators were not "'threatening aliens' parachuted in from outside," but rather fellow faculty members who "may well return to full-time teaching and become members of the bargaining unit" when their administrative roles ended. He assured the faculty that he firmly believed "that the leaders of the Faculty Association and the members of the academic administration of Laurentian University [were] men and women of good will who bring sincerity and ability in the search for 'lucem et veritatem' in the present negotiations."[26]

True to Best's expectations, the in-house negotiations were conducted in good faith by both parties and the two sides managed to draft a collective agreement sixteen months after LUFA's certification. The Laurentian Board of Governors approved that first contract on November 27, 1980.[27] While there was celebration on both sides that a deal had been reached, the fact that LUFA was now certified did not solve all the problems and Laurentian was about to experience a period of labour relations that closely resembled what Sibley characterized as 'adversarial.' Henry Best left the president's office in 1984 to take up full-time teaching duties as a professor in the history department, and his successor, John Daniel, was the one who would clash with the unionized faculty association as the pathway to settlements became more quarrelsome and confrontational, leading the faculty association to resort to its newfound legal right to strike.

20 From the Strikes and Social Contract, to Growth and Expansion, 1985 to the Present

LINDA AMBROSE

When the front page of the first issue of the student newspaper *Lambda* declared in September 1985 that "for the first time in the university's 25 year history, Laurentian students were faced with a strike by their professors,"[1] it was an accurate, although debated, headline. Technically, it was the first strike, but as noted, it was not the first labour disruption. Long-serving academic staff could clearly recall their memories of the 1970 'recesses,' and no doubt many people drew parallels between the two occasions when classes for students were interrupted early in the fall term. This time around, however, many things were different from the way they had been fifteen years before. First of all, this was a legal strike action taken by LUFA members, the first of its kind since certification. A second major difference was the duration: While the 1970 incident lasted several weeks, this strike would be resolved in less than a week's time, with classes resuming on September 16, 1985. The third major difference was the issues at stake. While the 1970 recess was prompted by a breakdown in salary negotiations, that issue was only the tip of the iceberg as faculty protested to ensure their voices were heard on a range of issues around university governance. This time, money was the one and only issue because the 1985 strike was all about salary levels.

The LUFA negotiating team originally asked for a 40 per cent increase in faculty salaries, claiming that that was how far faculty salaries had to increase in order to reach parity with the rest of the province. The administration immediately countered that "a comparison of the provincial salary average of all the Ontario universities with the average salary at Laurentian is not an appropriate way to evaluate salaries at universities."[2] Mike Dewson, the university's chief negotiator, argued that because Laurentian had fewer professors in the top ranks of the pay scales, (ie. fewer full professors than the older universities), it was reasonable that the average Laurentian salary would be lower than the provincial average. In addition, the administration insisted that a more realistic measure would be to compare Laurentian to other small universities including Brock, Lakehead, Trent, and Wil-

PROFESSORS ON STRIKE, 1985 | Laurentian faculty members exercised their legal right to strike when they walked off the job in September 1985 in a dispute centering on salary levels; the strike was resolved in less than one week.

frid Laurier. Given that pool, administrators argued that Laurentian faculty were actually the second-highest paid of the five schools. Based on that logic, the university had offered a wage increase of 3.85 per cent in a one-year deal. Obviously, the two sides were worlds apart.

The strike officially began on Monday, September 9, 1985, just days after "more than 150 of the 251 members of [LUFA] attended a contract discussion and voted 88 per cent to reject the university's last contract offer."[3] The negotiations, which had been ongoing throughout the summer, had resolved a number of issues around the assessment of faculty members' performance, academic workload, appointment and renewal, sabbatical leaves, merit increments, stipends for department chairmen/directors, and grievance and arbitration. But the one area where they simply could not come to an agreement was the proposed salary grid.[4]

The striking professors received support from the Sudbury & District Labour Council, and a photograph of the picket line, published in *Lambda*, shows a group of eight strikers wearing sandwich-board signs declaring, "Faculty on Legal Strike."[5] Both sides told the press that they were concerned about student reaction to the strike, hoping that it would not prove too disruptive to the new academic year. Kit Lefroy, LUFA's external vice-president, reported that faculty members were "especially concerned about the students. A short term effect is that it will be a terrible inconvenience for them."[6] The inconvenience did prove to be short-lived, as classes resumed the following Monday.

Faculty members voted to accept a settlement even though many were 'openly dissatisfied with management's contract offer.'[7] The offer consisted of a 15 per cent pay increase over two years. President Daniel reported that 'both sides are displeased with the contract,' but he pointed out that LUFA had given up more than the administration because faculty negotiators had moved quite far from their original demand of a 40 per cent increase. While the settlement represented some concession for the faculty demands, it still kept LUFA quite far from its goal of provincial parity. Lefroy pointed to lingering bitterness about the administration's staunch refusal to even consider parity, and he recounted that in order to reach a settlement: "We bent (on parity). But I suspect if that ever becomes an issue again, there won't be any bending." He continued by predicting that highly qualified faculty 'will begin to leave this place' and the result would be a lower quality of education at Laurentian.[8] An editorial in the local paper retorted two days later by pointing out that perhaps professors did not have as much leverage in the current academic job market as they imagined:

> [There is no] law that says a professor or anyone else has to stay in a job that is inadequately rewarded. But those who go looking will find the employment market somewhat limited in the university field, just as it is for lesser mortals. Not even a Ph.D. is a guarantee of a salary cheque these days.[9]

The strike had ended, but it would be inaccurate to say that the problems were resolved. On the day that classes began after the strike, President Daniel told the press: "We don't kid ourselves ... administration realizes the frustrations from the week-long labor dispute will linger."[10] But frustration among faculty was not the only issue that the university was facing. What is not clear is whether Daniel saw the next dispute on the horizon: just a few weeks later, non-academic staff walked off their jobs in a strike that lasted for three weeks. By all estimates, it was a difficult year to be president of Laurentian, and a student editorialist captured the concerns of many constituencies when he wrote:

> there are many students who have given up on Laurentian. Two strikes in one term alienated a lot of people who believed they were getting a quality education, and as a result, the city of Sudbury and the university are both losers. There are still many problems to solve at Laurentian and I hope that Dr. Daniel can create a better atmosphere for the most important part of any learning institution – the students.[11]

Two years later, when a new contract for faculty was approved so that the salary issue was settled for another two years, Daniel announced his intention to seek reappointment for another term as president, which would begin July 1, 1989. To that end, LUFA conducted a survey among its members, and while the results showed that 'the faculty are pleased with Dr. Daniel's request,' at the same time, there was a large number of very negative comments. Bernadette Schell and Pierre Simoni wrote to the Board of Governors on behalf of LUFA to explain the faculty's reservations. They noted that "while there is always an element of faculty discontent no matter who the administrators are, or their effectiveness, the list of negative comments and the numbers [in the LUFA survey] are serious enough to require concerted effort by Dr. Daniel and the Board in order to effect a turnaround."[12] The specific concerns that Schell and Simoni identified were "Dr. Daniel's management style which seems to preclude informing Faculty of major policy decisions until they have been taken." As a result of this communication model, faculty shared a certain 'suspicion and wariness' which caused resentment about the increased amount of committee work that faculty members were being called upon to perform, particularly since there was a shared perception that given the

LUFA BARGAINING SESSION | The level of Laurentian faculty salaries was the one issue that continually resurfaced during bargaining sessions through the 1980s and 1990s, as LUFA negotiating teams bargained diligently in an effort to reach wage parity with other Ontario universities.

president's management style, these committees were 'called upon to arrive at predetermined conclusions.'[13] In addition, they pointed to the situation around Laurentian's campus in France, 'Villefranche,' which they argued "has demonstrated the need of exercising control over the President's decisions," because faculty members feared that "resources have been diverted from essential and underfunded services such as the library" in order to fund the overseas experiment.[14]

Faculty feelings of discontent and suspicion about management and misdirected spending galvanized when it came time to negotiate salaries again in 1989. President John Daniel was on a study leave that fall, and Acting President Charles Bélanger was left to manage the tense situation that emerged. Bélanger told the press in September 1989 that "the last two years have yielded the highest number of students in Laurentian since it opened in 1960." According to the *Sudbury Star,* there were 4,282 full-time students, (a 7 per cent increase over the previous fall), and as many as 4,000 part-time students.[15] While the acting president worried about jeopardizing those enrolment statistics, professors wondered why this growth was not being reflected in their own salaries, which were failing to keep pace with provincial counterparts.

As the contract talks approached the eleventh hour, Jean-Charles Cachon, LUFA's spokesperson, explained to the media that there were two critical issues at stake: the first was "the university's demand for control over a professor's tenure, dismissal and renewal in the case of contract employees, and promotion." On these questions, LUFA wanted to maintain grievance rights. "The second contentious issue," Cachon simply stated, "is money." Once again faculty members raised the issue of wage parity with other universities in Ontario. The faculty association explained that Laurentian's professors were ranked 13 out of 15 Ontario universities in terms of salary levels. Realizing that the administration would once again argue that a more appropriate comparison would be small universities of a similar size and age, LUFA hoped to preempt that line of argument by pointing out that Laurentian professors earned 15 per cent less than their peers at Lakehead.[16] When LUFA called for salary increases of 13 and 11 per cent in a two-year agreement, the university countered with an offer of 9 and 8.5 per cent. That final offer was rejected by 76 per cent of LUFA's members, and professors took to the picket lines on Monday, September 11, 1989, in Laurentian's second strike in fewer than five years.[17]

Two weeks into the strike, talks broke off and were suspended for five days when the two sides failed to reach an agreement after a mediator was called in. The long duration of the strike was not something either side had predicted, and while an unresolved labour dispute is never easy to endure, in hindsight, many faculty members recall their days on the picket line with fondness because of the relationships that were fostered between colleagues. Indeed, the 'solidarity' on the picket lines resulted in some life-long friendships between people from different faculties who had never had much occasion to interact before, but first met during the strike because they happened to be assigned to the same picket line duties.

Meanwhile, headlines declared that student reactions to the strike were mixed. While some called it 'frosh week two,' others expressed anger about the fact that they had already paid tuition, but could not begin their classes.[18] In the third week of the strike, Native students expressed concern over the fact that the strike might mean they would lose their financial support from the Department of Indian Affairs because they were not fulfilling one of the conditions of their funding eligibility: proof that they were attending classes. A press release from the Native Students' Association said "funding pays for food, accommodation, transportation and other necessities. The possibility of losing sponsorship limits parents' ability to provide for their children."[19] For students who were themselves parents, the loss of that funding might also mean that they would lose subsidized daycare spaces, which would jeopardize their ability to study after the strike ended.[20]

When talks finally resumed on September 29, the provincial mediator imposed a news blackout.[21] Just a few days later, this was the much-anticipated headline: "Laurentian Professors Vote 77 per cent to Accept Contract."[22] The details of the salary settlement were: a 6.5 per cent increase retroactive to July 1, 1989; another 1 per cent on January 1, 1990; 6 per cent on July 1, 1990; another 2 per cent on January 1, 1991; and in the third year, depending upon inflation and cost-of-living allowances, a raise between 7 and 9 per cent. In addition, each LUFA member received a $1,000 signing bonus. These financial gains brought Laurentian faculty closer to parity with their peers at Lakehead University in Thunder Bay, which became the point of reference for LUFA negotiators. As welcome as the salary increases were, Jean Charles Cachon told the *Sudbury Star* that it was on the question of grievances that faculty had won their real victory because the new agreement spelled out that eight out of nine promotion committee members would now be faculty members. He explained, "Before, the president made all the decisions. It was not grievable except in cases of extreme discrimination. Now all cases are grievable."[23]

While John Daniel was technically still the president of Laurentian during the academic year 1989–1990, he was absent from the campus for the duration of the strike because he was on leave for the last year of his term in office. Just one month after the end of the strike, he announced his resignation from Laurentian to become vice-chancellor of the Open University in Britain. It seemed a perfect fit for him, not only because it was a return to his homeland and to a campus where

STUDENTS PROTEST 1989 FACULTY STRIKE | For the second time in less than five years, Laurentian faculty went on strike in the fall of 1989, and as the month of September slipped away, students worried that a long strike might jeopardize their academic year. The final settlement was announced on October 3, 1989 and classes resumed shortly afterward.

he had previously spent time as a visiting lecturer, but also because Daniel was a champion of distance education, and he described the Open University as an institution that "caters to working adults who want to continue their education and study at home."[24] While Daniel's term as president was riddled with a great deal of conflict over labour relations, there were also some very positive achievements at Laurentian under his leadership such as the new construction on campus valued at $60 million, including the new J.N. Desmarais Library and plans for the new student centre. Reflecting on his performance as president, Daniel said he was proud of the fact that "Laurentian ha[d] become a much more credible university," under his watch, something he said could be measured "by the fact that the number of students increased by one-third" since his arrival, and by the fact that "we've hired some very good faculty."[25]

In fact, the number of faculty had increased and then declined again during Daniel's term in office. By 1988, the number of professors had grown to 324, but in the aftermath of the strike by the time Daniel left, the faculty complement hovered around 300 members in total. Although student enrolments were increasing overall, there would not be a significant increase in faculty numbers until the late 1990s when faculty numbers would surpass 350 for the first time in Laurentian's history.

The sluggish pattern of faculty hiring in the early 1990s can be explained largely by the state of the Ontario economy. When Bob Rae made political history in October 1990 by becoming the first NDP provincial premier ever elected east of Manitoba, Ontario was in the throes of an economic recession and the new government faced a provincial deficit that was quickly spiralling out of control. Projecting a deficit of $9.7 billion for 1991–1992, Rae's government first tried to spend its way to recovery before turning to a series of measures that came to be known as the "Social Contract." In his memoirs, Rae quipped that these strategies left him in "the unenviable position where the left felt my brain had been captured by Bay Street, and Bay Street thought I was some kind of Maoist."[26]

Rae explained that in implementing the "Social Contract", beginning in 1993, his objective was "to get public-sector management and their unions to address the need for savings, and to achieve these savings without big reductions in service to the public or unemployment among public-sector workers."[27] As historian Peter A. Baskerville explains:

> The Social Contract was certainly novel. At its heart were savings gener-
> ated by requiring public-sector workers to take as many as 12 unpaid 'holi-
> days' per year. Rather than simply impose budget cuts, Rae's government
> promised that workers and their employers would negotiate 'voluntary'
> agreements.[28]

The unpaid 'holidays' quickly came to be referred to as 'Rae Days' and all public sector workers earning more than $30,000 per year were required to work out with their employers how they would fulfill this requirement.

For faculty members at Laurentian, the "Social Contract" resulted in a particularly bitter solution. Not only were the unpaid days required of each LUFA member, resulting in a series of salary deductions taken in installments from monthly paycheques, but wages were frozen at 1993 levels for a period of three years. In its spring 1994 newsletter, LUFA pointed out to its membership that while "many universities in Ontario kept PTR [progress-through-the-ranks] increases running in spite of the Social Contract," Laurentian did not, and as a result, "our salaries ... are falling behind the rest of the province at an alarming rate."[29] Roy Kari echoed that concern when he shared with LUFA members what the LUFA Social Contract Negotiating Committee had tried to impress upon the university administration, "that LUFA's demands for payment of an increment were modest, realistic, and necessary."[30] Indeed, Kari reminded LUFA members that their average salaries were the lowest in the province, that the low value of Laurentian's PTR increments meant that younger faculty could never hope to attain future salaries comparable to what older faculty were receiving; and that the non-payment of the increment through the duration of the "Social Contract" would have a serious negative affect on younger faculty for the remainder of their working lives and would reduce the pensions of faculty whose retirements were imminent.[31]

Indeed the "Social Contract" was a bitter pill for all Ontario public service workers to swallow, but LUFA members felt particularly aggrieved because of lingering resentments about salary levels below provincial parity over which they had already fought repeatedly. Now the outlook was even bleaker because the prospect of ever catching up seemed even more remote. At the same time, controversy arose over how faculty members would fulfill the required 'Rae Days.' Faculty members argued that it was important for them to take the required days off during the teaching term so that the public would be aware of the impact. While the administration argued that LUFA members should stagger their 'Rae Days' by making individual decisions about which classes to cancel, LUFA President Wendy Jerome argued that it made much more sense to make a collective decision so that the disruption for students would be predictable, and have less impact. She requested, for example, that the four days of unpaid leave might be taken at the end of the Christmas break, meaning that the start of classes was delayed for a few days in early January 1995.[32] This seemed like a logical solution, and one that appealed to both students and faculty alike, as it simply meant an extended Christmas vacation and more time for family activities.

When the director of personnel circulated a memo to all employees in early February 1996 that the last social contract deductions would be taken that month and that "effective March 1, 1996 all salaries return to the pre-Social Contract level," it was welcome news.[33] Yet there was little else to celebrate. Indeed, the legacy of the "Social Contract" did leave Laurentian faculty with an even greater salary gap, further behind the provincial average than before, and with a lingering bitterness about having been denied even the modest PTR increments that would address the cost of living during the "Social Contract". This legacy was revisited for the next ten years during every negotiation session and as a result, the administration conceded to several salary adjustments during the negotiations of 2002 and 2005. At the same time, however, other universities also received salary adjustments, and so the catch-up game continued.

Interesting trends emerge when one looks at historical data from the past twenty years about the growth of Laurentian's faculty complement and student population (see figure 19.1). In the early- and mid-1990s, while the "Social Contract" was in effect, student enrolments reached higher levels than ever before.

With almost 8,000 students from 1992 to 1994, some faculties and programs faced larger classes than they had ever had to manage, and at the same time faculty were asked to take the required 'Rae Days' and accompanying pay cuts. This led to questions about workload among LUFA members, and a move toward renegotiating the expectations around the number of courses one would be expected to teach. The high enrolments were not sustained through the late 1990s, when numbers once again fell, dipping below 6,000 students from 1998 through to 2001.

The downward trend was reversed soon after that, and as figure 19.1 demonstrates, enrolments steadily increased through the early 2000s, increasing from 5,968 students in 2001–2002 to an all-time high of 9,100 students in 2006–2007.

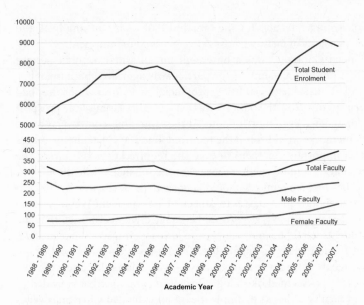

FIGURE 19.1 | Student Enrolment and Faculty Hiring Trends, 1988–2008[34]

There are several explanations for that growth, including the 'double cohort' that occurred when the province of Ontario eliminated the fifth year of high school, consisting of OAC (Ontario Academic Credits), or Grade 13, as it was commonly called. In 2003, the provincial university system was swamped with double the number of first-year applicants and enrolment numbers at Laurentian reflect that provincial trend. But the double cohort only explains in part the growth of Laurentian as enrolment continued to climb through the coming years, and did not fall as sharply as predicted with the graduation of the Class of 2006. Adding to the overall growth were new initiatives at Laurentian including the introduction of a new school of education, which offered a concurrent BEd degree in the English language, the articulation agreements that Laurentian entered into with community colleges, the expansion of graduate programs, and the creation of the 'Laurentian at Georgian' program, providing students in Barrie and Orillia, Ontario with the opportunity to begin (and in some cases complete) their university studies in Simcoe County, thus boosting Laurentian's student population numbers. All of this expansion in student numbers was very positive for the university's fiscal health, but it added pressure to the workload of faculty members (particularly chairs of departments with programs at Georgian), and it presented a plethora of questions about relations between the two campuses. By 2008, there were close to 1,200 students enrolled in programs offered through the partnership with Georgian College and that rapid growth left all parties somewhat dizzied by the programs' unpredicted popularity. At the time of writing, LUFA had begun to express formally its dissatisfaction with the many unanswered concerns about how the 'Laurentian at Georgian' initiative was unfolding for faculty members.

An additional pressure on faculty in the period after 2000 was the growing emphasis on the importance of research as a measure of faculty success. Indeed, as new colleagues began to be hired in the late 1990s to replace those who were taking retirement, search committees were surprised to see the calibre of applicants. Because there had been so little hiring during the previous decade, and because there was a growing pressure on academics to 'publish or perish,' when new positions did begin to open up, the applicants presented themselves with impressive lists of credentials. Most applicants had completed PhDs, peer-reviewed publications, post-doctoral funding, and/or research grants to their credit, and thus, the new hires signalled that they were equipped to help bring Laurentian into the twenty-first century and help to build the reputation of the university in the areas of research and graduate teaching.

While Laurentian was originally founded as a university mainly known for its undergraduate teaching, over the past decade, its reputation for graduate studies and research has been enhanced. With the creation of the new medical school and the introduction of six new doctoral programs since 2004, Laurentian's profile is changing. In the fall of 2007, the Research, Development and Creativity Office (RDC) celebrated the accomplishments of its researchers. According to a November 2007 press release from RDC, Laurentian's impressive research reputation was indeed cause for celebration because of its "faculty and students who have obtained national and provincial public grants for research. To date, more than 130 Laurentian researchers were funded and their research projects were awarded a total of $5,345,529 in public funding in 2007. Research activities cover a broad spectrum across the sciences, health, engineering, social sciences and humanities."[35] Liette Vasseur, associate vice-president research, was pleased to highlight these achievements because, as she explained, "We have all the reasons to celebrate our recent successes in research and are very proud of our professors, who are among the top scientists in the country. They are contributing to the development of new discoveries that will have a lasting impact on the region, its economy and our reputation."[36]

That focus on research success was central to President Woodsworth's strategic goal of enhancing the university's reputation and it was exactly the kind of thing that public and private funding sources wanted to hear, but it became a source of controversy among LUFA members. Some faculty expressed concern that such a preoccupation with measurable research outcomes might be coming at the expense of attention paid to undergraduate teaching. At one level this was simply part of a larger, ongoing conversation among Canadian academics about the relationship between teaching and research where moderate voices concluded that the two pursuits were not mutually exclusive, but symbiotic and complementary. While that balanced conclusion seemed obvious to the majority of colleagues, there is no question that such a strong emphasis on research outputs presented a significant new set of expectations and pressures that academics at Laurentian (and elsewhere) had not encountered in earlier decades.

As Laurentian University approaches its fiftieth anniversary, the challenges that faculty now face are a far cry from the struggles of their predecessors almost fifty

SHEILA COTE-MEEK | In 2006 Professor Sheila Cote-Meek from Native human services was appointed to the newly created position of director academic (Native Affairs), and in 2010 she became associate vice-president (Indigenous Programs).

years earlier. Laurentian University at fifty years of age has evolved from a strictly undergraduate teaching institution to one that now offers a wide range of master's and PhD programs. In 2007–2008 Laurentian's student population included 8,147 undergraduate students and 633 graduate students, while faculty members numbered almost 393 in the same year. Laurentian faculty members are actively involved in all three aspects of the academic enterprise: teaching, researching, and serving the community through academic involvements, both on and off the campus. As they do so, LUFA continues to protect their interests.

Long-serving faculty members at Laurentian University have certainly seen a myriad of changes from the earliest days of the downtown campus to the ongoing development of the Ramsey Lake Road property. That evolution has been shaped over the years by the constantly changing contexts of provincial politics and shifting academic priorities. From the mid-1960s on, LUFA proved quite successful at negotiating important polices concerning faculty appointments, tenure and dismissal, and sabbatical and study leaves for its members. After nineteen years of struggle, negotiation, and accommodation, in 1979, faculty members unionized to protect their interests and meet the emerging challenges of economic restraint and declining enrolment. In many ways, the story of faculty experiences at Laurentian mirror those in other parts of Ontario and across the country, and the history of labour relations between LUFA and the university administration echoes themes that are common to other post-secondary institutions.

As the face of post-secondary education in Ontario has changed dramatically over the past fifty years, so too has Laurentian changed. The history of Laurentian's faculty members, and particularly of their faculty association and labour activism, is one of change, challenge, and development. From a fledgling university scattered throughout the downtown, where each professor personally negotiated his own terms of employment with the president, to a full service university with unionized faculty members, graduate programs, research funding, and nearly 40,000 alumni who have passed through their classes, it is clear that Laurentian's faculty members have come a long way from their modest beginnings.

CONCLUSION

From a variety of perspectives relating both to evolving structures and to developing identities, the history of Laurentian University/l'Université Laurentienne divides into three parts: the challenges of the sixties, an era of transition, and the modern age. That was first and foremost true of university governance. Established just before the onset of the social and political turmoil that swept across North America in the mid-1960s, Laurentian structures and practices reflected traditional views about the hierarchical nature of post-secondary educational governance. As elsewhere in Canada, authority in the new university reposed in the Board of Governors and, to a lesser extent with respect to internal academic affairs, in the office of the president. Organizations representative of faculty and students – Senate, the faculty association, the Students' General Association – lacked both power and strategies to acquire it.[1]

Mirroring events around the world, the upheaval of the later 1960s at Laurentian that culminated first in the resignation of President Stanley Mullins in the spring of 1970, and then in the Hagey report a year later, precipitated a major shift of authority away from the board and president to Senate, faculty and students. While the pendulum did not swing quite as far as decried in 1970 by J.A. Corry in *Farewell the Ivory Tower* – "much of the substance of power has been taken out of the president's office and away from the board of governors," he wrote, "the members of the academic staff now have what has been taken out, and they have nearly a veto on the use of what is left" – it did significantly enhance the influence of faculty, especially via Senate, on Laurentian decision-making.[2]

The second phase in Laurentian's governance trajectory, a period of transition from the early seventies to the mid-eighties, entailed a readjustment of the multi-polar governing relationships that focused on an expanded, more powerful administrative structure. In the process the pendulum swung back to the governors, though only in part. A significant share of the recaptured authority stayed in the hands of the president and administration which thereafter mediated the competing demands of the several governing constituencies, including the board. Conversely, Senate gradually lost the dominant place in university affairs that it occupied in the 1970s, partly to the administration but also to the faculty association after its certification as a legal bargaining agent in 1979.

The Daniel presidency in the mid-1980s marked the consolidation of Laurentian governance. If not at its beginning, by its end the roles and responsibilities of each of the major governing components were clearly demarcated. This did not mean that thereafter Laurentian governance underwent no change, or was free of conflict. Whether the Board of Governors, the presidency, Senate or the faculty association, the functioning of an institution depends very much on the individual, or key individuals, of which it is composed. Over the next two and a half decades, character interacted with circumstance to nudge power first in one direction and then the other. The shifts, however, occurred within defined limits and did not fundamentally alter the university's governing balance.

The history of relations between Laurentian and the three federated universities also divides into three distinct periods. The first era – as in the case of university governance, essentially the extended 1960s – was both the most volatile and the most critical in shaping the relationship. At its outset, the federated institutions viewed their collective authority as equal to that of Laurentian by virtue of their critical roles in its founding. This interpretation met with opposition from Laurentian officials, however, and the financial crises that particularly engulfed Thorneloe and Huntington in the late 1960s and early 1970s rendered it untenable. A major turning point in the federated universities' fortunes occurred in the mid-1970s when the province of Ontario began to fully fund the students of denominational institutions, enabling them, over the next two decades, to expand into new teaching areas and gain greater financial stability. After a period of relative quiescence, federation relations again came to the fore in the early 1990s. In response to renewed concerns on the part of both Laurentian and the federated universities, the presidents' commission on federation relations recommended a series of formal mechanisms to enhance the collaborative governance character of the federation. In concert with informal consultative practices already in place, these mechanisms inaugurated the modern era of greater cooperation and mutual understanding.

One other aspect of Laurentian's governance evolution also demands comment. During the university's half-century of existence, no president or vice-president academic served two full terms in office. Only the vice-presidency finance and administration had a significant degree of stability, Ron Chrysler holding the position for nearly a quarter-century. Furthermore, no permanent president and only five permanent vice-presidents academic (Roland Cloutier, Geoffrey Tesson, Douglas Parker, Andre Roberge, Patrice Sawyer) came from within Laurentian ranks.

The explanation for these anomalies, exceptional in the Canadian university setting, can only be conjecture, but the two cannot be unrelated. One reason may be that a 'messiah' factor – the quest for a saviour of the institution's often precarious fortunes be they financial or academic – seems to have dominated searches for senior administrative personnel. That certainly would account for why so few nominees came from within the university. In a small community like Laurentian, especially in its early years but even in the modern era, faculty and staff knew well each other's strengths, weaknesses and idiosyncrasies, a familiarity that impaired the prospects of internal candidates. 'Better the devil you don't know' seems commonly to have been the aphorism in play. Then, as invariably happened, if the selected individuals failed to live up to expectations, or if the university's challenges proved too daunting, or if more attractive prospects elsewhere presented themselves, they departed, most having earned a reputation for administrative competence. While Laurentian has been generally very well served by its senior administrative personnel, one cannot but wonder about the costs of this frequent changing of the guard in terms of continuity and implementation of the university's unique educational mandate.

The development of academic programs was also a three-part story. When Laurentian was founded in 1960, one of its first challenges was to establish and offer academic programs for northeastern Ontario. It initially met this challenge by continuing the programs that the University of Sudbury had offered since 1958: a general BA, Arts and Science options and a few so-called professional programs. In short order, however, it redefined its programs, just as many other Canadian universities did as well. Laurentian began to offer four-year honours degrees in the mid-1960s, and by the end of the decade it had established professional schools of social work and physical education. Near the end of the 1960s as well, it had established its first graduate programs, mostly in the Sciences. This redefinition of programs also brought about the division of the Faculty of Arts and Science in 1975, thus creating four faculties: Humanities, Social Sciences, Sciences and Professional Schools.

In 1972, new funding and academic criteria introduced by Ontario's Ministry of University Affairs essentially forced Laurentian to invest more time and energy in planning the development of its undergraduate and graduate programs. It also placed a greater emphasis on research, although this mainly remained the solitary endeavour of particular professors. By the early 1980s, most of its programs, especially at the undergraduate level, were relatively well established. In the Professional Schools, the school of engineering was integrated with the Faculty of Science, and a school of education was established for the training of Francophone teachers.

The arrival of a new president in 1984 brought major changes, especially in the area of research. Laurentian began to structure this essential part of university life to a greater degree, by adopting policies for funding and establishing institutes and research centres. In the last twenty-five years, the number of these centres has grown and the funds obtained from funding councils, foundations or government sources have increased substantially. Along with these research activities, Laurentian has also established many graduate programs. Since 2000, six new doctoral programs have been created and many master's programs as well. The Northern Ontario School of Medicine, associated with Laurentian and Lakehead universities, has also given the institution a new profile.

For students, the complexity of Laurentian's bilingual and tricultural experience has presented a significant challenge. Founded as an experiment in bringing together young people in the North of both French and English heritage, over the past fifty years the university's cultural makeup has been redefined by the growing importance of First Nations students. During the first stage of Laurentian's development in the 1960s, students encountered the divisions created by differences of language and religion. They also faced the daunting task of establishing the institutions of undergraduate culture – student government, a newspaper, a yearbook, clubs and societies, interuniversity athletics – as the new university literally was constructed around them. Nevertheless, the first period up to 1972 was one of considerable success, as students overcame their differences and joined together to establish their voice in the hierarchy of the university, adopting the activist tactics of the international students' movement to campaign for improved facilities and increased autonomy.

This unity could not be sustained during the difficult decades that followed, however, and the second period between 1972 and 1985 saw a splintering of activism as students formed new communities based on gender, language, culture, sexual orientation, or experience. No longer comfortable with the idea that they could be represented by one organization, Laurentian students established a variety of associations, groups, and societies that better reflected their diverse needs. Furthermore, many undergraduates considered themselves free from traditional forms of authority. The anti-authoritarian culture of this second stage eroded the university's role of *in loco parentis*, and responsibility for student conduct shifted almost entirely to personal and collective self-regulation.

During the modern era, from 1985 to the present, Laurentian students became more sceptical about activism and more conscious of dissent; consequently, various issues such as the LUFA strikes exposed fractures among the different constituents on campus. Many students increasingly were burdened by the need to juggle the responsibilities of family, school and work, and student debt became a significant concern. In the larger and more divided student population, the rising cost of higher education was one of the few causes capable of mobilizing the entire undergraduate body. The more permissive culture that emerged in the 1980s led to apprehension among students and administrators that the overall quality of student life had declined, particularly within the residences. The modern period has been characterized by ongoing efforts to create a balance between university regulation and student self-government, and to ensure a more inclusive and tolerant campus. In these three periods, as well, Laurentian students steadily consolidated their physical presence in the university; moving from makeshift lodging in stores, office buildings and even a funeral home in downtown Sudbury; to the raw accommodations of their "dazzling, mud-infested" new campus; to winning their long-fought campaigns for a student pub, space for events and recreation, and finally to a designated student centre.

Like students, Laurentian faculty members have experienced profound change over the past fifty years. Imagine a meeting between a group of the original Laurentian University faculty who taught at the various downtown locations in the fall of 1960 and a group of newly hired professors beginning their academic teaching careers in 2010. The realities of the two groups would be worlds apart in many important ways. Not only would their experiences of teaching be vastly different, but their expectations about employment conditions and the protection afforded them by their faculty association would be unrecognizable to the other group.

In the earliest days, each faculty member negotiated individually with the president and/or a board committee the terms of his or her employment contract, and then the Board of Governors ratified the agreement. By the mid-1960s, collective bargaining was in place and the Laurentian University Faculty Association made historic agreements with the administration about tenure, workload, and leaves of absence. These were impressive developments, well ahead of many other campuses across the country, and those policies, coupled with the hard-fought battles of 1970 over greater involvement of faculty members in the decision-making processes of the university, led the majority of its members to conclude in the mid-1970s that the transformation of LUFA into a legally constituted bargaining agent would not be necessary.

As enrolment growth slowed both at Laurentian and across the country during the 1970s, it became clear that faculty jobs might be in jeopardy as universities tried desperately to balance their budgets. Alarmed by the possibility that even tenured faculty might not enjoy guaranteed job security, LUFA, on the advice of the Canadian Association of University Teachers, urged its members to consider union certification. While the idea was at first rejected by a majority of colleagues who feared unionization would jeopardize faculty involvement in university decision-making, in the end the pragmatism of job security won the day, and LUFA was certified in 1979. During the next ten years, faculty members exercised their legal right to strike on two occasions (1985 and 1989), as they continued to fight for wage parity with their colleagues at other campuses across the province. The 1990s brought new challenges as LUFA weathered the storm of the social contract's "Rae Days" and fluctuating enrolment trends.

Entering the twenty-first century, Laurentian was well on the way to changing from a primarily undergraduate teaching institution into a research university with an increasing number of graduate programs and a complex set of articulation agreements with other institutions. Growing enrolments coupled with new expectations about faculty research productivity meant that faculty members faced new challenges quite unlike the experiences of their colleagues just a few decades earlier. Indeed, if the new generation of LUFA members could sit with their predecessors and compare notes on their experiences of teaching, research and service at Laurentian University, both parties might wonder if they were actually talking about the same institution.

Laurentian's history is one of undeniable progress on many levels: the faculty's contribution to university governance, the development of new programs and graduate studies, students' increased role in decision-making processes. These are all reasons to rejoice and to recognize a fundamental trend in our history, a course of development that certainly justifies the celebration of this 50th anniversary. Nonetheless, in regard to French-language education, it must be recognized that the evolution has been much less magnificent, in the sense that Laurentian's development has been two-tiered, with a fast track for the Anglophone majority and long periods of running on the spot for the Franco-Ontarian minority, for whom the clearest advances were achieved in the past, roughly between 1983 and 1993. Since then, there has been nothing to compare with the situation currently enjoyed by the majority, which attracts a larger and more diverse clientele with its new schools of medicine and education.

That being the case, it should be remembered that the two periods when Laurentian broke with this trend – the early 1970s and the middle of the 1980s – had a critical impact on the progress of French-language education. The need for fundamental administrative reforms as indicated in the Hagey report and "Planning for Tomorrow" was recognized in 1973 with the creation of Laurentian's first homogenous Francophone administrative body, the Francophone Affairs committee, from which all subsequent developments originated, such as the Direction de l'enseignement en français and the position of vice-president (Francophone Affairs). In this same period, in great part thanks to the Service d'animation and a few professors who were in touch with the community, Laurentian produced three of French Ontario's leading institutions, namely le Théâtre du Nouvel-Ontario, la Nuit sur l'Étang and the publishing house Prise de parole.

The other period that broke with the trend was the mid-1980s, a time of major renewal in the ranks of the personnel. Laurentian's Francophone community lost its two foremost leaders in quick succession when André Girouard retired in 1986 and Gaétan Gervais left for Toronto in 1987 because he was unable to work with the new administration established by President Daniel who had arrived in 1984, followed by Vice-President Bélanger a year later. As well, the political and constitutional contexts in Canada and Ontario contributed to a change of course for French-language education. The judicial repercussions of the *Charter of Rights and Freedoms* generated high hopes for Franco-Ontario, which still lacked a self-governing educational system. The decision to create the first French school boards and the adoption of the *French Language Services Act* in 1987 resulted in significant new funding for the development of university programs offered in French, and this increased the number of Francophone students at Laurentian to about one quarter of the enrolment around 1990. Since then, their number has declined and a leader to stop this trend has not emerged. This 50th anniversary is not a happy one for those who believe that the Franco-Ontarian community should comprise one third of the student population at Laurentian according to the original agreement.

Just as for Francophones, the experience at Laurentian for women has not been one of uninterrupted progress. In the earliest days of the university's history, women were definitely part of the story, but their presence is difficult to trace because they were not equally represented in the student body, the faculty cohort, the university administration, or the university board. When women did break into these ranks in increasing numbers, they often made headlines simply by their presence. The one place where women were well represented was the very place where their work was undervalued, namely in staff positions as secretaries and clerks. Searching the early press accounts, one finds women in graduation pictures where they comprised less than one in four of the graduating class, in reports of new faculty members being hired where women were noteworthy for their entry into the male world of teaching, and in the charitable work of women in the community who raised money for university projects or agreed to host (often by serving tea) or accompany their husbands to official university functions. As the 1960s drew to a close, questions about the status of women were coming into focus across Canada as public attention turned to a wide range of subjects where inequities between the sexes were so common that they had previously gone unnoticed.

From 1972 to 1985, attention to the question of the status of women was premised on the idea that women at Laurentian were no better off, yet probably no worse off, than those on other campuses across the country. That realization did not lead to a laissez-faire acceptance of the status quo, but instead prompted a series of studies to explore the reality of women's experiences. These statistical analyses provided data for making comparisons between women and men, but also for comparing Laurentian with other universities. Under the direction of the presidential advisory committee on the status of women, the reports took on the mandate of not only documenting problems, but suggesting solutions. Issues including access to day care, pay equity, employment equity, and sexual harassment were identified and measurable goals to redress these problems were proposed.

During the past twenty-five years, policies were implemented and women at Laurentian have benefited from a variety of measures designed to ensure equity and protection. The participation of female students has steadily grown until now they represent two-thirds of the student body, the number of faculty women has increased from 16 per cent to 36 per cent of the total teaching staff, and Laurentian has welcomed one female president, while two different women have chaired the Board of Governors. Yet it has not been a story of unhindered progress, and as administrators come and go, the representation of women in the highest ranks of the decision makers is still far from half. Progress has been made, but there is still much room for improvement.

In a 1962 address to the University Women's Club of Sudbury, dean of Arts and Science Gérard Bourbeau, taking 'Laurentian as Canada writ small' as his theme, commented optimistically that "Laurentian University can be considered a fulfillment of the B[ritish] N[orth] A[merica] act in the sense that it involves a federation of denominational colleges into one bilingual and bi-cultural academic entity."[3] As on the national scene, translating this vision into structures and practices broadly acceptable to the university's various linguistic, cultural and federated constituencies has proven no easy task. As President John Daniel wrote in 1989, "All the tensions of Canada are present in the network of campuses, study centres and isolated learners that constitute Laurentian University. On the Ramsey Lake campus we teach and work in two languages ... We live and breathe the challenges of federal-provincial relations as ... [the] colleges or campuses try to live together in harmony within Laurentian."[4]

Such tensions and challenges, viewed by some as detrimental to the university's development, have also been a source of strength. They have contributed to the intellectual thrust and parry vital to the advancement of knowledge, the core of the post-secondary educational mandate. Just as importantly, they have bred a tolerance of ideas, opinions and cultures different from one's own, a quid pro quo essential to the continuing existence of a diverse and complex institution such as Laurentian, and indispensable to society at large. Lastly, the resulting intellectual milieu, always stimulating if sometimes frustrating, has benefited Laurentian faculty, staff and students alike, broadening horizons and opening new worlds not only to study but to conquer.

Whether because of these tensions and challenges or in spite of them, as this history details, during its half-century Laurentian has had many tangible achievements to its credit. The university began as a tiny entity offering three-year bachelor degrees in a narrow range of arts and science disciplines to a student population of a few hundred. Fifty years later it has become a bilingual, tricultural, multi-faculty and multi-degree (bachelor, bachelor honours, master's, doctoral) granting institution with a total enrolment in excess of 9,000, with a wide range of disciplinary, professional and interdisciplinary programs, and with a broad research focus that in many areas is national and international in scope and recognition. During its fifty years, Laurentian has graduated more than 40,000 students, the great majority of whom came from Northern Ontario, and its alumni are scattered around the region, across Canada and throughout the world.

In other important ways, Laurentian University has also well served Northern Ontario, and particularly the City of Greater Sudbury, playing a major role in ameliorating the impact of the post-1970 decline of the mining industry as a local employer, and in the community's remarkable environmental, social and cultural transformation during that period. In the autumn of 1965, the *Toronto Daily Star* in what was otherwise a rather unflattering portrait of the new university and its community predicted that this might happen. "Today," the *Star* wrote, "Laurentian is a bleak place when held up to the cultural wealth of its southern sisters, but there are indications its potential is as rich as the mother lode of ore beneath it."[5] That very much turned out to be so.

NOTES

Chapter One

1 For the context of the renewed interest in missions in Canada during this period, see in particular the introduction to the work of Fernand Ouellet and René Dionne, *Journal du père Dominique du Ranquet, s.j. 1843* (Sudbury: Société historique du Nouvel-Ontario, 2000), 266 pp.

2 Albert Plante, *Vingt-cinq ans de vie française. Le Collège de Sudbury* (Montréal: 1938), 16.

3 Robert Toupin, "Le rôle des jésuites dans l'enseignement classique et universitaire de la région de Sudbury," *Revue de l'Université Laurentienne/Laurentian University Review* 3, 4 (1971): 73.

4 Guy Gaudreau and Michel Verrette, "Évolution des effectifs étudiants au Collège de Saint-Boniface, 1885–1967," *Cahiers franco-canadiens de l'Ouest* 6, 1 (1994): 89.

5 Gaétan Gervais, "L'enseignement supérieur en Ontario français (1848–1965)," *Revue du Nouvel-Ontario* 7 (1985): 27–34.

6 Thérèse Boutin, "L'Université de Sudbury," 1982, typewritten manuscript, 3. (Translated from the original French.)

7 Plante, *Vingt-cinq ans*, 33.

8 Boutin, "L'Université de Sudbury," 5. (Translated from the original French.)

9 Ed. Lecompte, "Les Jésuites au Canada au XIXe siècle," tome II, Livre XVIII, manuscript preserved in the Provincial Archives of the Society of Jesus, quoted by Plante, *Vingt-cinq ans*, 50.

10 Gervais, "L'enseignement supérieur," 34. (Translated from the original French.)

11 André Bertrand, *L'éducation classique au Collège du Sacré-Cœur* (Sudbury: Société historique du Nouvel-Ontario, 1988), 20.

12 Bertrand, *L'éducation classique*, 16.

13 Plante, *Vingt-cinq ans*, 136.

14 Josée Anne Valiquette, "L'évolution des effectifs étudiants du Collège du Sacré-Cœur, 1913–1960," Laurentian University, department of history, fourth-year research paper, 1993, 19.

15 Plante identifies this factor as the most common reason for leaving college. See *Vingt-cinq ans*, 81.

16 Bertrand, *L'éducation classique*, 29.

17 Claude Galarneau, *Les collèges classiques au Canada français (1620–1970)* (Montreal: Fides, 1978), 148. (Translated from the original French.)

18 Bertrand, *L'éducation classique*, 33. (Translated from the original French.)

19 Bertrand, *L'éducation classique*, 33.

20 See appendices 6 and 7 in Valiquette's research paper.

21 Bertrand, *L'éducation classique*, 43–4.

22 Gérald Blais, "Le Collège du Sacré-Cœur, Sudbury, Ontario," MA, Université d'Ottawa, 1968, 93 pp.

23 Blais, "Le Collège," 69, quoted by Bertrand, *L'éducation classique*, 30.

24 Bertrand, *L'éducation classique*, 30.

25 Pierre Ouellette, "Éducation et économie, 1927–1965," in Guy Gaudreau, ed., *Bâtir sur le roc* (Sudbury, Prise de parole and SHNO, 1994), 67–74.

26 Boutin, "L'Université de Sudbury," 11.

27 CCF: Co-operative Commonwealth Federation, now the New Democratic Party.

28 "Sacred Heart seeking status of university," *Sudbury Star*, February 12, 1945, 5.

29 "Studies suited to area slated for university," *Sudbury Star*, March 13, 1945, 7.

30 See the article "Un cri de rage. Un cri de race." published in *L'Ami du Peuple*, February 22, 1945, 5, a report on the outraged reaction of a reader of the *Sudbury Star* which had published this letter a few days earlier.

31 Boutin, "L'Université de Sudbury," 12. (Translated from the original French.)

32 See in particular two articles from the *Sudbury Star* dated March 21, 1946, "University of Sudbury bill is held over," 1, and March 22, 1946, "Premier sends university bill back to committee," 1–2.

33 "State Sudbury logical site for university," *Sudbury Star*, April 30, 1946, 1.

34 Gervais, "L'enseignement supérieur," 21.

35 Alphonse Raymond, "Origines universitaires à Sudbury," *Revue de l'Université Laurentienne/Laurentian University Review* 3, 4 (1971): 68.

36 Alphonse Raymond, *1914–1978. Mes souvenirs recueillis, transcrits et annotés par Huguette Parent, s.c.o.* (Ottawa: Centre franco-ontarien de ressources pédagogiques, 1996), 91.

37 Gervais, "L'enseignement supérieur," 40. (Translated from the original French.)

38 "Jesuit Order extended charter of Sacred Heart," *Sudbury Star*, December 17, 1956, 1 and 3.

39 Raymond, "Origines universitaires," 69.

40 Raymond, *1914–1978*, 98–9.

41 Boutin, "L'Université de Sudbury," 19.

42 Raymond, "Origines universitaires," 69.

43 Raymond, *1914–1978*, 99.

44 "Sudbury University names 12-man board of regents," *Sudbury Star*, May 8, 1958, 20.

45 Raymond, *1914–1978*, 109–10.

46 Raymond, *1914–1978*, 118. (Translated from the original French.)

47 Thèrese Boutin's interview with Émile Bouvier in Montreal in August 1981; see Boutin, "L'Université de Sudbury," 25.

48 Boutin, "L'Université de Sudbury," 28. (Translated from the original French.)

49 For further details, see Pierre A. Riopel, "La fondation de l'École normale de Sudbury (1957–1963)," *Revue du Nouvel-Ontario* 33 (2008): 95–132.

50 Letter from University President Oscar Boily to Roger Charbonneau, ACFEO, October 2, 1961, Collège du Sacré-Cœur archives (quoted by Boutin, "L'Université de Sudbury," 38).

51 Riopel, "La fondation de l'École normale," 125–7.

Chapter Two

1 Paul Axelrod, *Scholars and Dollars: Politics, Economics, and the Universities of Ontario 1945–1980* (Toronto: University of Toronto Press, 1982), 54; Edward J. Monahan, *Collective Autonomy: A History of the Council of Ontario Universities, 1962–2000* (Waterloo: Wilfrid

Laurier University Press, 2004), 4–5; Roger Graham, *Old Man Ontario: Leslie M. Frost* (Toronto: University of Toronto Press, 1990), 387; Émile Bouvier, "L'Université Laurentienne de Sudbury," *Relations* (May 1960): 120. See also Edward F. Sheffield, "The Post-War Surge in Post-Secondary Education, 1945–1969," in J. Donald Wilson, Robert M. Stamp, and Louis-Philippe Audet, eds, *Canadian Education: A History* (Scarborough: Prentice-Hall of Canada, 1970); Doug Owram, *Born at the Right Time* (Toronto: University of Toronto Press, 1996); and David Foot, *Boom, Bust & Echo* (Toronto: Macfarlane Walker and Ross, 1996).

2 Émile Bouvier, "L'Université Laurentienne de Sudbury," Archives of Ontario (hereafter AO), RG3-23, box 186, file 279G, "Sudbury, University of, Sacred Heart College," F.A. Farrell to Hon. L.M. Frost, February 26, 1959; ibid., RG2-217, box 4, "Laurentian University of Sudbury 1959," Bouvier to Dunlop, January 23, 1959 (2 letters); ibid., C.F. Cannon, Chief Director of Education, to Dunlop, February 2, 1959; ibid., RG3-23, box 186, file "Sudbury University of, Sacred Heart," R.A. Farrell to Leslie Frost, February 26, 1959.

3 Ibid.

4 Laurentian University Archives (hereafter LUA), P109, II, A, 1, 11, Lautenslager to Brother in the United Church Ministry in Northern Ontario, November 27, 1958. Emphasis in the original. See also AO, RG2-217, box 5, "Northeastern University North Bay," Rev. Dr. E.S. Lautenslager, "A Statement on the 'Northern Ontario University' and the Responsibility of the United Church of Canada," January 9, 1959; Richard Bowdidge, "Murray's coffee played its role," *Sudbury Star*, November 24, 1984. See also Richard Bowdidge, "Honorary degree for Ed Newbery much deserved," *Sudbury Star*, June 14, 1986.

5 LUA, P109, II, A, 1, 11, Lautenslager to Brother in the United Church Ministry in Northern Ontario, November 27, 1958; ibid., Lautenslager presentation at St. Andrew's Church, Sudbury, December 10, 1958.

6 Ibid., Resumé of NOUA Minutes, 1958–1960, November 1958; ibid., II, A, 4, 1, "The University Problem in Northern Ontario and the Part Being Played by the Northeastern University Committee in Solving that Problem"; ibid., II, A, 1, 11, Lautenslager presentation, December 10, 1958.

7 Dwight Engel, "The Founding of Huntington University," BD thesis, Emmanuel College, University of Toronto, 1961, 24–6. Engel, it should be noted, brought a unique perspective to the subject because he served on the authorizing board. LUA, P109, II, A, 1, 11, Resumé of NOUA Minutes, 1958–1960, "Dec. 17"; AO, RG2-217, box 5, Proposed Constitution of Northern Ontario University Association; LUA, P109, II, A, 1, 3, "The Northern Ontario University Association Constitution," March 20, 1959.

8 AO, RG2-217, box 5, Proposed Constitution of Northern Ontario University Association; LUA, P109, II, A, 1, 1, NOUA Sub-Executive Minutes, May 11, 1959; Engel, 30.

9 LUA, P109, II, A, 1, 3, Lautenslager to "Dear Brother in the Northern Ontario Ministry," February 27, 1959; ibid., II, A, 1, 11, Resumé of NOUA Minutes, 1958–1960, "Mar. 17"; ibid., II, A, 1, 1, Brief for members of the Authorizing Board, "A University for 'Northern Ontario' (N.O.U.A. answers to some questions which have been asked recently)," December 5, 1959; Brian Aitken, "Huntington, Silas," *Dictionary of Canadian Biography*, vol. 13, 495–6; Engel, 35–43; Richard Bowdidge, "An eye on everything," *Sudbury Star*, September 26, 1980.

10 LUA, P109, II, A, 1, 11, Lautenslager presentation at St. Andrew's Church, Sudbury, December 10, 1958; AO, RG2-217, Department of Education University Files, box 5, "Northeastern University North Bay, 1959–61," Rev. Dr. E.S. Lautenslager, "A Statement on the 'Northern Ontario University' and the Responsibility of the United Church of Canada," January 9, 1959.

11 Carl Wallace and Ashley Thomson, eds, *Sudbury: Rail Town to Regional Capital* (Toronto: Dundurn Press, 1993), 168–214; Carl Wallace, "Introduction," *Laurentian University Review*

(hereafter *LUR*) 17 (1985); Oiva Saarinen, "Municipal Government in Northern Ontario: An Overview," *LUR* 17 (1985): 2; Gordon Brock, *The Province of Northern Ontario* (Cobalt, ON: Highway Book Shop, 1978), passim.

12 LUA, P109, II, A, 1, 3, Lautenslager to "Dear Brother in the Northern Ontario Ministry," February 27, 1959; ibid., II, A, 1, 5, NOUA Executive Minutes, December 17, 1958; ibid., II, A, 1, 1, NOUA Executive Minutes, March 10, 1959; ibid., II, A, 1, 11, NOUA Sub-Executive Minutes, May 25, 1959.

13 *The Daily Nugget* (North Bay), April 21, 1959; LUA, P109, II, A, 1, 11, Resumé of NOUA Minutes, 1958–1960, January 29, 1959, February 12, 1959, March 5, 1959, April 21, 1959; ibid., II, A, 4, 1, "The University Problem in Northern Ontario and the Part Being Played by the Northeastern University Committee in Solving that Problem"; ibid., II, A, 1, 1, Minutes of the Authorizing Board, December 5, 1959; Engel, 47–8.

14 LUA, P109, II, 4, 2, "On the position and aims of the Northern Ontario University Association," undated, *circa* January 1959; "Haileybury seeking north university," *Toronto Star*, October 21, 1959; *Financial Post*, August 8, 1959; LUA, P109, II, A, 2, 3, "J.W.E. Summary of the Fact-Finding Committee," December 30, 1959.

15 Ibid., II, A, 4, 1, "The University Problem in Northern Ontario and the Part Being Played by the Northeastern University Committee in Solving that Problem." Many of these same claims had been made a decade earlier during a previous campaign for a university. See AO, RG3-17, Office of the Premier, box 462, "University for Northern Ontario," North Bay Board of Trade to Hon. George Drew, January 15, 1948.

16 Oiva Saarinen, "The 1950s," in Wallace and Thomson, 196–9.

17 LUA, P109, II, A, 1, 11, Lautenslager presentation, December 10, 1958; ibid., Resumé of NOUA Minutes, 1958–1960, March 25, 1959.

18 Saarinen, 193. In 1960 Inco produced 69 per cent of the world's nickel as compared to Falconbridge's 12 per cent. See F.B. Howard-White, *Nickel: An Historical Review* (Toronto: Longmans Canada Limited, 1963), 221–6.

19 See Mike Solski and John Smaller, *Mine Mill: The History of the International Union of Mine, Mill and Smelter Workers in Canada Since 1895* (Ottawa: Steel Rail Publishing, 1985), 137–8; LUA, P109, 49, 2, 11, Boudreau to J.K. Stern, American Institute of Co-operation, November 28, 1958; *Toronto Telegram*, June 2, 1960.

20 LUA, P109, II, A, 1, 3, Lautenslager to "Dear Brother in the Northern Ontario Ministry," February 27, 1959; ibid., II, A, 1, 11, Resumé of NOUA Minutes, 1958–1960, April 7, 1959, April 23, 1959; ibid., II, A, 1, 7, Sub-Executive Minutes, "Report of interview with Mr. R. Parker," April 23, 1959.

21 Ibid., PO77, Harold Bennett fonds, file 1, "Convocation Address at Laurentian University, May 29, 1971."

22 See "An eye on everything," *Sudbury Star*, September 26, 1980, in which Richard Bowdidge also credits Frost for Parker's involvement.

23 Richard S. Lambert and Paul Pross, *Renewing Nature's Wealth* (Toronto: Ontario Department of Lands and Forests, 1967), 476–99.

24 Axelrod, *Scholars and Dollars*, 88–9; *Sudbury Star*, May 13, 1961; LUA, P109, II, A, 1, 11, Lautenslager presentation, December 10, 1958; ibid., II, A, 1, 1, Frost to Hillyer, April 16, 1959; ibid., II, A, 1, 12, NOUA Sub-Executive Minutes, May 11, 1959, Report of Interview with Frost, April 29, 1959.

25 Ibid., II, A, 1, 1, "A Tentative Plan"; Richard Bowdidge, "University issue is an old theme," *Sudbury Star*, February 19, 1983.

26 LUA, P109, II, A, 1, 11, Resumé of NOUA Minutes, 1958–1960, June 12, 1959; ibid., II, A, 1, 12, NOUA Sub-Executive Minutes, May 11, 1959, June 18, 1959, July 20, 1959.

27 Ibid., "Report Submitted by the Special Committee called by Invitation of the University of Sudbury under the Chairmanship of Mr. R.D. Parker, September 2, 1959"; ibid., PO77, Harold Bennett fonds, file 1, "Convocation Address at Laurentian University, May 29, 1971." On September 29th the Executive adopted a slightly revised version of the opening three paragraphs of the Parker report as the formal "Statement of Objectives" of the NOUA. See ibid., P109, II, A, 1, 5, NOUA Executive Minutes, September 29, 1959.

28 Thérèse Boutin, unpublished manuscript, "L'Université de Sudbury," 1982, 29; Pierre Ouellette, "Education et économie, 1927–1965," in Guy Gaudreau, ed., Bâtir sur le roc (Sudbury: Prise de parole and SHNO, 1994), 86–7.

29 LUA, P109, II, A, 1, 11, NOUA Sub-Executive Minutes, September 10, 1959; ibid., PO77, Harold Bennett fonds, file 1, "Convocation Address at Laurentian University, May 29, 1971"; Engel, 51–2; LUA, P109, II, A, 1, 7, NOUA Sub-Executive Minutes, November 30, 1959; ibid., II, A, 1, 1, Minutes of the Authorizing Board, December 5, 1959.

30 Ibid., July 20, 1959. See also ibid., II, A, 2, 4, Form letter, post–July 20, 1959 signed by Lautenslager, Newbery and Palmer to members of Sudbury Presbytery "Re: Special Meeting of Presbytery"; ibid., II, A, 1, 1, "Report of an informal meeting of available members of the Northeastern University Committee and of the Northern Ontario University Association," August 24, 1959; ibid., II, A, 1, 11, Sub-Committee Minutes, September 10, 1959; ibid., II, A, 1, 8, "Northern Ontario University Association and Northeastern University Association [sic] Discussions, November 10, 1959"; ibid., II, A, 1, 7, NOUA Sub-Executive Minutes, November 30, 1959.

31 Ibid., II, A, 1, 1, Lautenslager to Rev. E. Robertson, Blind River, October 17, 1959; ibid., Minutes of the Authorizing Board of the Northern Ontario University Association, December 5, 1959.

32 Ibid. At the next meeting of the executive committee on January 15, 1960, Vaughan himself acknowledged this was the case. See ibid., II, A, 1, 5, NOUA Executive Minutes, January 15, 1960.

33 Ibid., Lautenslager to E. Robertson, October 17, 1959; ibid., PO77, Harold Bennett fonds, file 1, "Convocation Address at Laurentian University, May 29, 1971"; "Pick 'Laurentian' for north's new university," Sudbury Star, January 18, 1960. See also LUA, Charles Levi interview with Ed and Rena Newbery, June 3, 2004.

34 Ibid., P109, II, A, 1, 5, NOUA Executive Minutes, January 15, 1960.

35 Ibid.

36 Ibid.; ibid., III, A, 3, T.M. Palmer to Newbery, April 10, 1960; Engel, 66.

37 LUA, P109, II, A, 1, 5, NOUA Executive Minutes, January 15, 1960.

38 Ibid., Minutes of the Second Meeting of the Authorizing Board, January 16, 1960; ibid., Minutes of the Fact-Finding Committee of the Authorizing Board, January 16, 1960; "Sudbury group stalled formation of North Bay university," The Daily Nugget (North Bay), June 7, 1984.

39 Gordon Aiken, Looking Out On the 20th Century, vol. 2 (Orillia, ON: RO Publications, 1993), 618. According to Aiken, after recount, a subsequent secret ballot vote favoured Sudbury by two or three, although this was not recorded in the minutes. LUA, P109, II, A, 1, 1, Minutes of the Second Meeting of the Authorizing Board, January 16, 1960.

40 Ibid.

41 Ibid., J.W.E. Newbery, "Another Big Step Forward A University in the North," June 18, 1960.

42 Ibid., III, A, 3, Newbery to Rev. T.E. Floyd Honey, Board of Overseas Missions, February 25, 1960; Sudbury Star, January 26, 1960; Globe and Mail, February 11, 1960; LUA, P109, II, A, 1, 5, NOUA Executive Minutes, March 4, 1960; Sudbury Star, March 29, 1960.

Chapter Three

1 Glen A. Jones, Paul Goyan and Theresa Shanahan, "University Governance in Canadian Higher Education," *Tertiary Education and Management* 7, 2 (2001): 136; Glen A. Jones, Paul Goyan and Theresa Shanahan, "The Academic Senate and University Governance in Canada," *Canadian Journal of Higher Education* 34, 2 (2004): 38; *Laurentian University of Sudbury Act*, ch. 151, 1960; Laurentian University Board of Governors' Minutes (hereafter Board Minutes), May 7, 1960; AO, RG32, 1, 1, Acc.12230/1, box M6, Rhéal Belisle to Leslie Frost, March 2, 1960; ibid., John Robarts to G.W. Reid, May 10, 1960; *Sudbury Star*, September 21, 1960.

2 Laurentian University Executive Committee Minutes (hereafter Executive Minutes), May 18, 1960; Board Minutes, May 30, 1961, May 25, 1964, October 31, 1969.

3 Jones, Goyan and Shanahan, 137–8; *Laurentian University of Sudbury Act*, 151, 18, 1960.

4 *Sudbury Star*, October 8, 1964; "Necrologie Rev. Père Émile Bouvier," *Laurentian University Gazette*, March 27, 1985; Board Minutes, May 7, 1960; www.125.umontreal.ca/Pionniers/Bouvier.html, "Émile Bouvier (1906–1985)."

5 Executive Minutes, July 14, 1960, August 18, 1960; LUA, P109, III, A, 3, Newbery to Rev. T.E. Floyd Honey, Board of Overseas Missions, February 25, 1960; ibid., II, A, 1, 5, NOUA Executive Minutes, March 4, 1960.

6 Roger Poirier, "Sanction royale au bill de l'université Laurentienne," *Le Droit* (Ottawa), March 29, 1960, 18, translation by author. See also *L'Ami du Peuple*, March 31, 1960, and Émile Bouvier, "L'Université Laurentienne de Sudbury," *Relations* (May 1960).

7 Executive Minutes, May 18, 1960. See also LUA, II, B, 3, 2, "News Releases," Rev. Father Émile Bouvier, S.J., "The Creation of New Universities The Laurentian University of Sudbury," June 2, 1960; "An 'abnormal birth' for 4 universities Bouvier at Kingston," *Sudbury Star*, June 2, 1960; AO, RG2-217, Department of Education University Files, 1943–1964, box 4, "Laurentian University of Sudbury, 1960," Bouvier address to the Société historique du Nouvel-Ontario, April 19, 1960, translated by the department; ibid., J.W.E. Newbery to C.F. Cannon, Director of Education and others, April 19, 1960; LUA, P109, file I, 4, Earl Lautenschlager to D.P. Best, June 27, 1960; AO, RG32, 1, 1, Department of University Affairs, Acc.18006, box M374, E.G. Higgins to C.F. Cannon, June 28, 1960; LUA, P109, I, 4, Lautenslager to D.P. Best, June 27, 1960, June 28, 1960.

8 Ibid., II, B, 1, 2, Minutes of Huntington Senate, August 3, 1960; ibid., Draft federation memorandum, August 11, 1960; ibid., I, 4, Lautenslager to A.B.B. Moore, August 16, 1960; *Sudbury Star*, September 2, 1960.

9 Board Minutes, August 25, 1960, August 18, 1960; *Sudbury Star*, September 2, 1960; Board Minutes, September 7, 1960, September 10, 1960; *Sudbury Star*, September 12, 1960; LUA, F64, 3, "Archives University Administration," Laurentian University Annual Report, 1960–1961.

10 Ibid., P109, II, B, 1, 1, Newbery to Avery, August 29, 1961; Board Minutes, September 10, 1960; *Sudbury Star*, September 21, 1960.

11 LUA, PO77, Harold Bennett fonds, file 1, "Convocation Address at Laurentian University, May 29, 1971"; Kenneth Pryke, personal diary, June 23, 1961, June 24, 1961.

12 National Archives of Canada (hereafter NAC), MG28, I208, Jacques Peltier, president, Kenneth Pryke, vice-president, Léo Paré, member of the executive, André Vachet, member of the executive, Laurentian University of Sudbury Faculty Association, to J.H. Stewart Reid, executive secretary, Canadian Association of University Teachers, July 5, 1961; ibid., Reid to Gordon Turner, July 14, 1961; ibid., Reid's notes on his visit to Laurentian Univer-

sity, July 10 and 11, 1961; LUA, Charles Levi interview with Kenneth Pryke, February 19, 2005. Reid, it should be noted, was particularly sensitive to Ferland's situation, having in the late 1950s resigned from the United College in Winnipeg over what he considered the unjust dismissal of his colleague, Harry Crowe. While Crowe was reinstated, Reid was not, at which point he became the first full-time national secretary of the CAUT. See Michiel Horn, "Unionization and the Canadian University: Historical and Personal Observations," *Interchange* 25, 1 (1994): 41.

13 NAC, MG28, I208, Reid's notes, "Visit to my office Friday, August 4, 1961 by Father Boily and Father Richard, Provincial of the Order, at 11:30 a.m."; Executive Minutes, September 25, 1961, January 31, 1962; Board Minutes, February 22, 1962, May 28, 1962.

14 Ibid., February 22, 1962; *Sudbury Star*, May 12, 1973.

15 Executive Minutes, October 18, 1961; Board Minutes, December 11, 1961.

16 Executive Minutes, November 29, 1961; "These men run the day-to-day affairs of Laurentian," *Sudbury Star*, October 8, 1964.

17 AO, RG44, Ministry of Finance Policy Planning Division, "Laurentian University 1960–1966," D.L. James, Finance Committee, Laurentian University, to John Robarts, Minister of Education, November 23, 1960; LUA, PO77, Harold Bennett fonds, file 1, "Convocation Address at Laurentian University, May 29, 1971"; Board Minutes, October 26, 1961; letter to editor from Arnold McKee, Department of Economics, *Sudbury Star*, May 29, 1962; Laurentian University, Office of the Registrar, Senate Minutes (hereafter Senate Minutes), October 30, 1961; AO, RG2-217, box 4, "Comments from Department of Economics on Laurentian University budget submission, 1961–1962"; ibid., RG6-44, Ministry of Finance Policy Planning Division Subject Files, Laurentian University 1960–1966, Report, 1963–64; LUA, F65, 4, Dean Bourbeau to Stewart Reid, CAUT, February 13, 1963.

18 Ibid., I, 31, 3, Klemens Dembek, "Preliminary Study," May 2, 1960; ibid., Report by George C. Tate, Real Estate Committee, July 21, 1960; Executive Minutes, December 3, 1960; *Sudbury Star*, January 19, 1961, February 8, 1961, February 15, 1961; Executive Minutes, February 22, 1961; *Sudbury Star*, March 28, 1961. See also The Historical Committee of Idylwylde Golf and Country Club, *Idylwylde's First Fifty Years 1922–1972* (Toronto: Canadian Yearbook Services, 1972); Executive Minutes, April 5, 1961, July 14, 1961; LUA, L8, 2, 1961, Bemi and Murray, Architects, "Report on the selection of a site for Laurentian University, Sudbury, Ontario"; Board Minutes, October 26, 1961; *Sudbury Star*, October 28, 1961.

19 LUA, I, 30, 4, University Solicitors, Cassels, Brock, Des Brisay and Guthrie to R.D. Parker, October 18, 1963; ibid., I, 31, 3, "Real Estate Committee, 1961–1965," Cassels, Brock, Des Brisay and Guthrie to H. Lemire, January 12, 1965; *Sudbury Star*, December 15, 1961, October 8, 1961; Board Minutes, May 28, 1962.

20 Ibid., January 18, 1961, December 11, 1961; *Sudbury Star*, December 12, 1961, December 30, 1961, February 23, 1962; Board Minutes, May 28, 1962; Executive Minutes, June 27, 1962; AO, RG2-217, box 6, "Laurentian University, Sudbury," J.R. McCarthy to Chief Director, July 12, 1962; *Sudbury Star*, August 3, 1962, September 14, 1962; Board Minutes, September 14, 1962.

21 *Sudbury Star*, September 14, 1962, September 15, 1962, March 25, 1963, April 17, 1963, July 30, 1963, August 21, 1963, October 8, 1964; Board Minutes, December 9, 1963.

22 LUA, PO77, Harold Bennett fonds, file 1, "Convocation Address at Laurentian University, May 29, 1971."

23 In November 1961 the faculty association had asked to participate in the selection process but this had been refused. See LUA, PO63, II, A, 1, 1, Report of meeting between the Executive Committee and the President, November 20, 1961. Board Minutes, October 26, 1961, and Appendix III, May 18, 1963; LUA, PO77, "Laurentian University Presidential Prospects,

1963," Don James to R.D. Parker, June 5, 1963; Board Minutes, Appendix V, June 30, 1963, R.D. Parker to Professor S.G. Mullins, June 14, 1963; ibid., Appendix I, July 30, 1963, S.G. Mullins to R.D. Parker, June 20, 1963.

24 Tragically, the Thessalon family cottage would be the site of a parent's worst nightmare when in August 1965, President Mullins' youngest son, five-year-old John Frederick, drowned there. See the *Sudbury Star*, August 30, 1965. Ibid., July 9, 1963; *The Northern Ontario Record*, July 20, 1963; LUA, PO77, "Laurentian University Presidential Prospects, 1963," Horace J. Fraser to the Board of Governors, Curriculum Vitae of Stanley George Mullins, May 18, 1963.

25 See, for example, Douglas Owram, *Born at the Right Time*; Cyril Levitt, *Children of Privilege: Student Revolt in the Sixties: A Study of Student Movements in Canada, the US and West Germany* (Toronto: University of Toronto Press, 1984); Myrna Kostash, *Long Way from Home: The Story of the Sixties Generation in Canada* (Toronto: Lorimer Press, 1980); John Kettle, *The Big Generation* (Toronto: McClelland and Stewart, 1980); Tim Reid and Julyan Reid, *Student Power and the Canadian Campus* (Toronto: Peter Martin Associates, 1969).

26 LUA, I, 30, 4, "Board Correspondence," Bourbeau to Mullins, February 4, 1964; ibid., Bourbeau to the Board of Governors, February 4, 1964.

27 Board Minutes, Appendix I, G.A. Bourbeau to H. Bennett, March 4, 1964; ibid., March 11, 1964; Executive Minutes, April 15, 1964; *Sudbury Star*, May 22, 1964; *Globe and Mail*, May 23, 1964. See also Board Minutes, Appendix, April 27, 1964, J.R. Meakes to R.D. Parker, April 27, 1964, in which Meakes, the chair of the ad hoc committee, stressed that at no time did the committee discuss with Bourbeau "any aspect of tenure or qualification for the presidency of Laurentian University – neither did the Dean indicate to this committee any circumstances which would have to do with 'accepting candidacy to the office of the president of Laurentian.'"

28 Ibid., May 18, 1963; LUA, PO63, IV, 13, 2, Resolution of LUFSA General Meeting, April 16, 1964; Board Minutes, May 25, 1964; LUA, PO63, IV, 13, 2, University Regulation 64-1, May 25, 1964, "Policy on Appointments, Tenure, Promotion, Teaching Load and Leave"; LUA, I, 30, 4, Jean Havel, LUSFA, to Board, May 26, 1964; ibid., Mullins to Board, May 28, 1964; ibid., PO63, II, A, 1, 1, Berg to Mullins, January 11, 1965. See also Bourbeau's comments on Mullins' convocation address as reported in the *Globe and Mail*, May 27, 1964.

29 LUA, III, A, 1, 3, Newbery to Rev. Dr. J.S. Bonnell, July 24, 1964; ibid., I, 30, 4, Minutes of the Public Relations Committee, October 19, 1964.

30 Ibid., "The Report of the Special Committee of the Board of Governors of Laurentian University," 5–7; ibid., "Synopsis of Comments at June 3rd Meeting"; ibid., Rodolphe Tremblay, S.J., registrar, University of Sudbury, to J.R. Meakes, June 3, 1965; ibid., Robert Campeau and Conrad Lavigne, "Laurentian University and its Related Problems"; ibid., Robert Campeau to H.J. Fraser, May 26, 1965; ibid., III, A, 1, 1, Ed Newbery to Don James, July 13, 1965, emphasis added.

31 George Whalley, ed., *A Place of Liberty: Essays on the Government of Canadian Universities* (Toronto: Clarke-Irwin, 1964). Interestingly, Laurentian philosophy professor and activist Garry Clarke was a scion of the publishing family involved. James Duff and Robert Berdahl, *University Government in Canada* (Toronto: University of Toronto Press, 1966), 3. See also LUA, PO63, IV, 49, Canadian Association of University Teachers, "Proposal to the Canada Council for support of a survey of Canadian university government," December 1960.

32 Ibid., IV, 4, Press Release, "Study of University Government," September 11, 1964; *University Government in Canada*, 32; Jones, Goyan and Shanahan, "The Academic Senate and

University Governance in Canada," 137–8. See also Donald C. Rowat, "The Duff-Berdahl Report," *CAUT Bulletin* 14, 4 (1966), and Peter Cameron, "The Duff-Berdahl Report. Will the Patient Live?" *CAUT Bulletin* 15, 2 (1966).

33 Horn, "Unionisation and the Canadian University," 44; P.B. Waite, *The Lives of Dalhousie University*, vol. 2, *1925–1980 The Old College Transformed* (Montreal: McGill-Queen's University Press, 1998), 249–50; H.B. Neatby, *Creating Carleton: The Shaping of a University* (Montreal: McGill-Queen's University Press, 2002), 153–4; LUA, Laurentian University President's Report, 1965–1966, 1; ibid., F62, 2, J.R. Mapstone to Roland Farrant, September 14, 1967; LUA, Charles Levi interview with Dr. Laurent Larouche, April 21, 2005. Laurentian also faced competition from newly established Lakehead University in Fort William which at precisely this time also experienced a massive growth in students, forcing it to hire an additional 42 faculty members. See H.S. Braun, *A Northern Vision: The Development of Lakehead University* (Thunder Bay: Lakehead University Press, 1987), 93.

34 Senate Minutes, November 15, 1965; LUA, PO63, II, A, 1, 1, Griggs to LUSFA Executive, March 11, 1966; ibid., Griggs to Nicholson, March 21, 1966; ibid., V, B, 2, LUSFA Minutes, March 28, 1966; ibid., Griggs to M. Fortier, March 28, 1966; ibid., II, A, 1, 2, Report of Joint Committee of Senate and Faculty Association on Faculty Representation on Senate, April 28, 1966; Senate Minutes, April 28, 1966, May 17, 1966, October 6, 1966; LUA, V, B, 2, LUSFA Minutes, October 20, 1966.

35 Board Minutes, "Report to the Board of Governors of the Special Committee ... on desirable amendments to the Laurentian University of Sudbury Act, 1960," May 17, 1967; ibid., May 25, 1967; LUA, PO62, II, B, 2, Wesley Cragg, "Report on Representation of the Faculty Association before the Private Bills Committee of the Ontario Legislature on March 21st, 1968, with regard to Bill Pr. 47 (An Act Respecting Laurentian University of Sudbury)," March 28, 1968.

36 Ibid.; AO, RG32, 1, 1, Acc.13856, box M297, E.E. Stewart to W.C. Alcombrack, Office of the Legislative Counsel, Dept of the Attorney-General, December 1967; ibid., RG32, 1, 1, Acc.13856, box M297, LUSFA draft proposal, March 21, 1968; ibid., RG32, 1, 1, Acc.13856, box M297, E.E. Stewart to Minister, March 22, 1968; *Sudbury Star*, March 22, 1968, March 25, 1968; Étienne St-Aubin, "S.G.A. Presidential Report," in *The Thorne*, published by the Thorneloe University Students' Association, *circa* March 30, 1968; J.W.E. Newbery, "Regarding Huntington College and the Bill to amend the Laurentian University Act," April 2, 1968, personal files of Wesley Cragg.

37 LUA, PO63, II, B, 2, LUSFA resolution moved by A.W. Cragg, seconded by M. Perrault, March 28, 1968; Senate Minutes, Notice of Motion, March 27, 1968; ibid., April 29, 1968; Board Minutes, May 31, 1968; Executive Minutes, September 18, 1968; AO, PO63, IV, 28, Presidential Advisory Committee on Consultative Structures and Procedures, Minutes, 16 October, 1968, November 7, 1968; Board Minutes, October 18, 1968; LUA, PO63, IV, 28, Mullins to Williamson, December 4, 1968; Board Minutes, November 29, 1968.

38 Senate Minutes, December 12, 1968, January 23, 1969. The SGA had previously petitioned Senate on the matter of student representation early in 1966 but in March withdrew the request "for the time being." See Senate Minutes, March 24, 1966.

39 Executive Minutes, April 16, 1969; LUA, PO63, IV, 28, Presidential Advisory Committee to Members of Senate, February 20, 1968; ibid., Williamson to various individuals, March 27, 1969.

40 Ibid., II, A, 4, J.R. Winter, LUSFA treasurer, to E.J. Monahan, associate executive secretary, CAUT, October 18, 1965; ibid., A, 1, 1, J. Berg to Stanley Mullins, October 20, 1965; Executive Minutes, November 17, 1965; Board Minutes, November 19, 1965; Executive Minutes, January 19, 1966; LUA, PO63, IV, 34, President Mullins version, and Wynn Watson, LUFA

President, version, Minutes, August 15, 1967; Board Minutes, October 27, 1967; LUA, PO63, II, A, 1, 2, Mullins to Cloutier, November 15, 1967; Executive Minutes, December 13, 1967; LUA, PO63, II, A, 1, 2, Gerry Vallillee, LUFA president, to colleagues, January 12, 1968.

41 Executive Minutes, November 20, 1968; LUA, PO63, V, 2c, LUFA Minutes, December 11, 1968; Executive Minutes, December 18, 1968; LUA, PO63, V, 2c, LUFA Minutes, December 19, 1968; Executive Minutes, February 19, 1969, March 19, 1969, April 16, 1969; LUA, PO63, V, 2c, LUFA Minutes, April 17, 1969; Executive Minutes, April 22, 1969, May 6, 1969; LUA, PO63, V, 2c, LUFA Minutes, May 9, 1969.

42 Ibid., F68, 1, Mullins to Academic Staff Members, May 9, 1969; ibid., Laurentian University Faculty Association Salary Negotiations Bulletin No. 5, May 14, 1969; ibid., PO63, V, 2c, LUFA Minutes, May 21, 1969; Executive Minutes, May 29, 1969.

43 LUA, PO63, II, B, 2, Mullins to Clarke, October 3, 1968; ibid., Clarke to Mullins, October 22, 1969; ibid., "Timetable of Recent Events," Faculty Association to Board of Governors, October 31, 1969; Sudbury Star, October 18, 1969, October 20, 1969, October 21, 1969; AO, RG32, 1, 1, Acc.14105/3, box AOH3, J.S. Bancroft to E.E. Stewart, October 15, 1969. While the Mullins memorandum was dated October 3, the Faculty Association did not receive it until October 7.

44 LUA, PO63, II, B, 2, "Appendix," LUFA to the Board of Governors, October 31, 1969; ibid., IV, 28, G.I. Clarke to president Mullins, October 22, 1969; Sudbury Star, October 18, 1969, October 20, 1969, October 21, 1969.

45 LUA, 49, 2, PAC on Consultative Structures and Procedures, Minutes, September 10, 1969; Executive Minutes, October 22, 1969; Board Minutes, October 31, 1969; Sudbury Star, October 31, 1969, November 1, 1969.

46 Board Minutes, October 31, 1969; Senate Minutes, November 20, 1969, November 27, 1969.

47 LUA, PO63, II, B, 2, Clarke to Dr. H. Bennett, Secretary, Board of Governors, October 30, 1969; ibid., LUFA to the Board of Governors, October 31, 1969; Board Minutes, October 31, 1969; Executive Minutes, November 14, 1969; Senate Minutes, November 20, 1969, November 27, 1969; LUA, PO63, II, B, 2, "A Proposal to the Executive Committee of the Board of Governors on Long-Range Planning, December 10, 1969" by the ad hoc Senate Committee created November 27th and meeting on December 3, 1969; Executive Minutes, December 10, 1969, January 23, 1970.

48 Ibid., May 21, 1969, November 14, 1969; Senate Minutes, November 20, 1969, November 27, 1969; Executive Minutes, January 23, 1970.

49 Senate Minutes, January 20, 1970; LUA, PO63, V, 2d, LUFA Minutes, January 20, 1970; Executive Minutes, January 23, 1970, February 19, 1970.

50 LUA, PO63, V, 2d, "President's Report"; LUFA Minutes, January 20, 1970; Senate Minutes, February 19, 1970; Sudbury Star, March 14, 1970.

51 Ibid.; Globe and Mail, March 7, 1970; Sudbury Star, March 14, 1970; LUA, PO63, V, 2d, LUFA Minutes, March 16, 1970.

52 Sudbury Star, March 19, 1970; Executive Minutes, March 18, 1970; Senate Minutes, March 19, 1970; LUA, F68, 1, D.H. Williamson memorandum, April 6, 1970; ibid., PO63, V, 2d, LUFA Minutes, March 24, 1970; ibid., LUFA endorsement of the Senate lack of confidence motions, March 24, 1970; Sudbury Star, March 20, 1970.

53 Ibid., March 31, 1970, April 2, 1970; Globe and Mail, April 2, 1970; Sudbury Star, April 3, 1970; LUA, F68, 1, "Position Paper of Students engaged in Occupation at Laurentian University," April 2, 1970 (12:40 a.m.); Sudbury Star, April 3, 1970, April 4, 1970, April 6, 1970.

54 Senate Minutes, April 2, 1970.

55 Executive Minutes, April 3/4, 1970; Board Minutes, Special Meeting, April 9, 1970.

56 Senate Minutes, April 2, 1970, April 4, 1970, April 6, 1970, April 8, 1970, April 9, 1970, April 10, 1970; *Sudbury Star*, April 4, 1970; *Globe and Mail*, April 6, 1970.

57 Board Minutes, April 9, 1970.

58 Senate Minutes, April 9, 1970; Board Minutes, April 9, 1970; *Sudbury Star*, April 9, 1970, April 10, 1970; LUA, PO63, II, A, 1.3, G.I. Clarke, president, LUFA, to Douglas Wright, chairman, Committee on University Affairs, April 17, 1970.

59 NAC, CAUT Papers, box 200, file 2, G.I. Clarke to Dr. Alwyn Berland, Executive Secretary, CAUT, April 16, 1970; Senate Minutes, April 10, 1970; *Sudbury Star*, April 10, 1970, April 13, 1970.

60 Ibid., April 10, 1970, May 30, 1970, June 1, 1970; Senate Minutes, April 10, 1970.

61 Board Minutes, November 19, 1965, May 19, 1966.

62 University of Toronto Archives (hereafter UTA), B72-0021, 019, Mullins to all members of Faculty, June 6, 1967; Neatby, *Creating Carleton*, 108–13.

63 LUA, F47, 2, Mullins to R.B. Willis, Presidents' Research Committee, University of Western Ontario, September 8, 1964.

64 Board Minutes, June 26, 1970; LUA, Presidential Report, 1969–1970, 1–2. Emphasis in the original.

65 *Laurentian University Gazette*, June 18, 1986.

66 Board Minutes, April 24, 1970; Executive Minutes, May 20, 1970, June 10, 1970; Senate Minutes, May 21, 1970, June 1, 1970; Board Minutes, June 26, 1970.

67 Ibid., January 22, 1965; Executive Minutes, August 4, 1965; Board Minutes, May 19, 1966; Executive Minutes, November 23, 1966; *Sudbury Star*, December 12, 1966; Executive Minutes, May 17, 1967, August 23, 1967, October 16, 1968, November 20, 1968, April 16, 1969, June 18, 1969.

68 Ibid., August 19, 1970, April 30, 1970; Senate Minutes, April 30, 1970, May 21, 1970.

69 LUA, PO63, V, 2d, LUFA Minutes, May 6, 1970; Senate Minutes, April 30, 1970, May 21, 1970.

70 Executive Minutes, September 19, 1969, October 2, 1969, December 20, 1969; LUA, PO63, V, 2d, LUFA Minutes, January 20, 1970; Executive Minutes, January 23, 1970; LUA, PO63, II, B, 2, Dalton Caswell, chairman, Executive Committee, to B.F. Lavoie, chairman, Board Salary Negotiation Committee, February 4, 1970; ibid., II, A, 1, 3, Clarke to Caswell, February 18, 1970; Executive Minutes, February 19, 1970, March 18, 1970, April 30, 1970; LUA, PO63, V, 2d, LUFA Minutes, May 6, 1970; ibid., II, A, 3, David Pearson, secretary, LUFA, to the Board of Governors, May 7, 1970; Executive Minutes, May 20, 1970, June 11, 1970, June 25, 1970; Board Minutes, June 26, 1970.

71 *Sudbury Star*, September 15, 1970; LUA, PO63, VI, E, 1, Roland Cloutier memorandum, September 15, 1970; Senate Minutes, September 20, 1970; LUA, PO63, V, 2d, LUFA Minutes, September 14, 1970.

72 Ibid., VI, E, 1, LUFA memorandum, September 15, 1970; ibid., II, A, 1, 3, G.I. Clarke to Hon W.G. Davis, September 29, 1970; *Sudbury Star*, September 15, 1970, September 16, 1970; AO, RG32, 1, 1, Acc.18006, G.I. Clarke to William Davis, September 17, 1970; LUA, PO63, VI, E.1, Roland Cloutier memorandum, September 15, 1970; ibid., IV, 5, LUFA press release, September 17, 1970; ibid., II, A, 1, 3, G.I. Clarke to Hon W.G. Davis, September 29, 1970.

73 Senate Minutes, September 20, 1970; Board Minutes, September 25, 1970; Senate Minutes, September 24, 1970; *Sudbury Star*, September 24, 1970; Board Minutes, September 25, 1970. On September 15, 1970, Cloutier wrote an affidavit affirming the LUFA claim.

74 *Sudbury Star*, September 29, 1970; Senate Minutes, September 28, 1970; LUA, PO63, II, A, 1, 3, G.I. Clarke to Hon W.G. Davis, September 29, 1970; ibid., VI, E, 1, Cloutier to all members

of Senate and all members of the university community, September 30, 1970; *Sudbury Star*, September 30, 1970.

75 Ibid., October 1, 1970, October 2, 1970; LUA, G7, Minutes of Faculty Council, Science Section, October 2, 1970.

76 Executive Minutes, October 7, 1970; *Sudbury Star*, October 3, 1970; AO, RG32, 1, 1, Acc.18006, E.E. Stewart to Minister, October 5, 1970; LUA, PO63, VI, E, 1, LUFA Minutes, October 5, 1970.

77 *Sudbury Star*, October 3, 1970; Senate Minutes, October 5, 1970; Board Minutes, October 5, 1970; Senate Minutes, October 8, 1970; AO, RG32, 1, 1, Acc.18006, Memorandum from E.E. Stewart to file, October 1, 1970; LUA, PO63, VI, E.1, SGA "Brief to the Members of the Ontario Legislature with regards to the crisis at Laurentian University," October 6, 1970; *Sudbury Star*, October 6, 1970, October 7, 1970; *Globe and Mail*, October 7, 1970; Senate Minutes, October 8, 1970; *Sudbury Star*, October 8, 1970, October 9, 1970; *Toronto Daily Star*, October 9, 1970.

78 Executive Minutes, October 28, 1970; AO, RG32, 1, 1, Acc.18006, E.E. Stewart to Minister, October 5, 1970.

79 Axelrod, *Scholars and Dollars*, 59–60; Executive Minutes, October 28, 1970; Board Minutes, October 30, 1970.

80 NAC, RG28, I208, box 128, file 31, CAUT phone log, Garry Clarke to "AB," October 20, 1970; University of Waterloo Library (hereafter UWL), Hagey Papers, A79-0030/231, Hagey to Charles Hanly, executive vice-chairman, OCUFA, November 20, 1971; Senate Minutes, October 29, 1970; LUA, I, 36, 3, Summaries of meetings between J.G. Hagey and representatives of the SGA, November 11, 1970; ibid, J.G. Hagey and Senate, November 12, 1970; ibid., J.G. Hagey and the Board of Governors, November 12, 1970; *Sudbury Star*, November 12, 1970, November 13, 1970; Board Minutes, October 30, 1970; UWL, Hagey Papers, A79-0030/231, Hagey Memorandum to Laurentian University, undated (pre-November 10, 1970); ibid., Hagey to Davis, November 16, 1970.

81 LUA, F65, 1, J.G. Hagey, "Consultant's Report to Laurentian University," March 12, 1971, 1; Senate Minutes, Correspondence, J.G. Hagey, Report to Senate, November 19, 1970; Executive Minutes, November 25, 1970; Board Minutes, Appendix II, January 29, 1971, "Agreement between Faculty Association Salary Negotiating Committee and Board's Salary Negotiating Committee, December 16, 1970"; Board Minutes, November 27, 1970, January 29, 1971; LUA, F65, 1, J.G. Hagey, "Consultant's Report to Laurentian University," March 12, 1971, 2.

82 Ibid., 5–6; *Sudbury Star*, March 23, 1971.

83 Board Minutes, November 29, 1968, May 30, 1969; LUA, F61, 1, Report of Peat Marwick organisational review, 1970, in "Dean's Office," box 37; ibid., 61, 1, Report of the ad hoc administrative review committee, January 19, 1971.

84 Ibid., J.G. Hagey, "Consultant's Report to Laurentian University," March 12, 1971, 6–9; Executive Minutes, April 22, 1971; Board Minutes, April 28, 1971; LUA, F65, 1, J.G. Hagey, "Consultant's Report to Laurentian University," March 12, 1971, 2, 8–9.

85 Ibid., 5–6, 10–13.

Chapter Four

1 Board Minutes, November 27, 1970; Executive Minutes, February 12, 1974, January 21, 1972, February 22, 1972, April 18, 1972, January 6, 1976; Board Minutes, December 10, 1976.

2 *Sudbury Star,* February 3, 1973; AO, RG32, 1, 1, Acc.18996, box 389, Jean-Noël Desmarais to Harry Parrott, January 27, 1976.

3 Laurentian University, Office of the Registrar, Senate Briefs (hereafter Senate Briefs), 1970–1971, Report of the ad hoc Administrative Review Committee meetings of December 1, 1970, January 19, 1971; Board Minutes, November 27, 1970, January 29, 1971; Executive Minutes, May 12, 1972; Board Minutes, April 28, 1971; Senate Minutes, April 17, 1975; Board Minutes, May 30, 1975; *Sudbury Star,* June 4, 1975; Edward J. Monahan, "The Test of a Presidency," unpublished draft mss, in possession of the author, 322; Senate Minutes, May 17, 1979; Board Minutes, May 25, 1979; *Laurentian University Gazette* (August–September 1979); LUA, Charles Levi interview with Edward Monahan, May 5, 2005. President Monahan later recalled that his experience at Queen's University, where at the time the deans reported directly to the principal and the vice-president academic was "a relatively minor player," led him not to press the vice-president academic question at Laurentian. Edward Monahan to Matt Bray, December 1, 2008.

4 Board Minutes, April 30, 1971; Executive Minutes, October 26, 1971, June 5, 1973, April 18, 1972.

5 Senate Minutes, March 25, 1971.

6 Jones, Goyan and Shanahan, "The Academic Senate and University Governance in Canada," 39; Senate Minutes, May 13, 1971; Board Minutes, April 9, 1970, June 26, 1970; Senate Minutes, July 13, 1970, November 11, 1971; Board Minutes, January 26, 1973; *Sudbury Star,* April 3, 1973, April 4, 1973.

7 Board Minutes, June 26, 1970, December 7, 1973; AO, RG32, 1, 1, Acc.18925, RC4, P.J. Wright, to B.A. Wilson, assistant deputy minister, MCU, August 15, 1979.

8 Senate Minutes, April 30, 1971; ibid., January 13, 1972, February 24, 1972, October 26, 1972, February 14, 1974; LUA, PO63, V, 2d, Laurentian University Faculty Association, President's Report, May 6, 1970.

9 Board Minutes, April 24, 1970, September 24, 1970, October 28, 1970; Senate Minutes, October 22, 1970.

10 Board Minutes, April 30, 1971; *Sudbury Star,* May 3, 1971; Monahan memoirs, 303; Senate Minutes, May 5, 1971, May 20, 1971; Board Minutes, May 7, 1971, May 21, 1971, June 25, 1971.

11 Ibid., April 30, 1971, Appendix II, Report of the Laurentian University Presidential Search Committee, April 28, 1971; Senate Minutes, July 7, 1971; Board Minutes, July 29, 1971; *Sudbury Star,* July 3, 1972.

12 Monahan memoirs, 304–7; Senate Minutes, June 30, 1971; Executive Minutes, February 22, 1972.

13 LUA, Levi interview with Monahan, May 5, 2004. See also Edward J. Monahan, "Duff-Berdahl Conference on University Government," *CAUT Bulletin* 16, 3 (February 1968): 54–62.

14 Monahan memoirs, 298; David M. Cameron, *The Northern Dilemma: Public Policy and Post-Secondary Education in Northern Ontario* (Toronto: Ontario Economic Council, 1978), 17–32; *Sudbury Star,* October 1, 1971, October 8, 1971; Executive Minutes, November 23, 1971, December 14, 1971; Senate Minutes, November 25, 1971; Board Minutes, January 21, 1972.

15 Howard Adelman, *The Holiversity: A Perspective on the Wright Report* (Toronto: new press, 1973), 9–10; Board Minutes, October 27, 1972, December 1, 1972; *Sudbury Star,* November 24, 1972; Board Minutes, March 16, 1973, September 21, 1973, December 7, 1973, January 18, 1974, March 15, 1974, October 25, 1974, December 6, 1974; Friedland, *The University of Toronto,*

581; *Laurentian University Gazette* (March 1975); *Sudbury Star*, October 23, 1975; AO, RG32, 1, 1, Acc.18006, box 389, Monahan to Hon. William Davis, February 2, 1976; *Sudbury Star*, February 18, 1976; Monahan memoirs, 323–6.

16 *Sudbury Star*, November 8, 1971; LUA, Levi interview with Monahan, May 5, 2004; ibid., F66, 5, Monahan memorandum to Senate, November 5, 1974; *Sudbury Star*, October 20, 1975; Laurentian University, Office of the Registrar, Senate Correspondence (hereafter Senate Correspondence), 1975–1976, Williamson to Jack Porter, December 15, 1975.

17 Executive Minutes, June 10, 1975; Board Minutes, September 19, 1975.

18 *Sudbury Star*, October 20, 1975; Senate Correspondence, 1975–1976, G.I. Clarke to the Senate executive, November 27, 1975; Senate Minutes, December 11, 1975; Board Minutes, January 16, 1976; LUA, F61, 2, Report of the Joint Committee of Review, April 6, 1976; Board Minutes, April 23, 1976.

19 Ibid., May 28, 1976; Senate Minutes, June 17, 1976; LUA, F65, 1, Report of the Joint Senate–Board Ad Hoc Committee to Assess and Make Recommendations to Simplify Academic Administration, May 10, 1977; Senate Minutes, May 19, 1977.

20 Senate Correspondence, 1975–1976, Monahan to J.-N. Desmarais, Chair, Board of Governors, November 5, 1975; Board Minutes, November 21, 1975; Senate Minutes, December 11, 1975; Executive Minutes, January 6, 1976; Edward J. Monahan to Matt Bray, December 1, 2008; Executive Minutes, March 19, 1976; Senate Minutes, March 25, 1976; Board Minutes, March 26, 1976.

21 LUA, PO63, V, 3, L. Wagner and B.-A. Gelin to Dr. P. Bruce-Lockhart, chair, committee of review, February 3, 1976; ibid., F61, 2, Report of the Joint Committee of Review, April 6, 1976; Monahan memoirs, 330–41.

22 LUA, F61, 2, Report of the Joint Committee of Review, April 6, 1976. See Edward J. Monahan, *Collective Autonomy: A History of the Council of Ontario Universities, 1962–2000*.

23 Board Minutes, April 23, 1976; Senate Briefs, June 1976–April 1977, Report of the Search Committee for the President by Dr. J.-N. Desmarais, December 12, 1976; Senate Minutes, December 9, 1976; Board Minutes, December 10, 1976.

24 Charles Levi notes on a meeting with Henry B.M. Best, January 16, 2004; *Northern Life*, November 30, 1977.

25 *Laurentian University Gazette*, June 1978, Council of Ontario Universities position paper, "The Present State of the Ontario University System"; ibid., "System on the Brink," October–November 1979; Senate Minutes, May 25, 1978; Board Minutes, May 26, 1978; Senate Briefs, Feb.–Oct. 1978, "Report of the Senate Budget and Short-Term Academic Planning Committee … 1978–1979 and Attached Minority Report," May 25, 1978.

26 AO, RG32, 1, 1, Acc.20958, "Laurentian, 1978/1979," Bette Stephenson to Annette Goddard, October 3, 1978; ibid., Acc.20909, Best to Stephenson, February 8, 1979.

27 Ibid., Acc.18925, "Laurentian 1979," "Laurentian – Possible Elimination of Four Departments," *University Relations*, June 6, 1979; *Sudbury Star*, June 6, 1979, June 14, 1979; AO, RG32, 1, 1, Acc.20959, Frith to Stephenson, June 20, 1979; ibid, Stephenson to Best, July 4, 1979; ibid., Acc.20216, Best to Stephenson, November 13, 1979; Senate Briefs, 1978–1979, Best to Secretary of Senate, November 7, 1979.

28 AO, RG4, Acc.18925, P.J. Wright, University Affairs Officer, to B.A. Wilson, Assistant Deputy Minister, MCU, "Visit to Laurentian University, August 15, 1979."

29 Senate Briefs, September 1978–December 1979, "Report of the Ad Hoc Committee of Senate and the Board of Governors on Budgeting and Financial Planning," November 6, 1979; Senate Minutes, November 15, 1979; Board Minutes, November 23, 1979; Senate Correspondence, 1981–1982, Jack Porter, secretary of Senate, to Garry Clarke, secretary of the Academic Planning Committee, March 24, 1982.

30 Senate Briefs, 1980–1981, Report of University Budget Committee, April 3, 1981; Board Minutes, June 5, 1981; Senate Briefs, 1980–1981, Report of University Budget Committee, May 11, 1982.

31 See chapter 19.

32 Board Minutes, May 25, 1979.

33 LUA, PO63, I, B, 6, Paul Copper, Dick James, Bob Whitehead, Tony Beswick, Bob Cameron and Jim Davies "On Certification," March 30, 1979; ibid, B, 1, "Why 'Y E S'? An Open Letter to the Faculty of Laurentian University re: Certification" by Roy Kari, Dieter Buse, Victor Clulow and Ashley Thomson, undated, *circa* April 1, 1979; Jones, et. al., "Academic Senate," 40.

34 LUA, F25, 1, "Negotiations 1979," G.I. Clarke, "The Role of the Laurentian Senate Under Collective Agreement with Faculty," September 13, 1979.

35 Ibid., "Negotiations, 1979–1980," Ashley Thomson and Louise Thirion-Nordstrom to all faculty, September 19, 1980; LUFA *Bulletin* 1, 1 (September 1981); Executive Minutes, September 20, 1977; LUA, F25, 1, "Negotiations 1979," G.I. Clarke, "The Role of the Laurentian Senate Under Collective Agreement with Faculty," September 13, 1979.

36 Three days before Algoma classes began, for example, Algoma's Laurence Brown, in an address to the Kiwanis Club of Sault Ste. Marie, decried Laurentian's 'colonial' attitude and called on the province to end the college's 'irksome' affiliation with Laurentian. See *Sudbury Star*, September 23, 1967, September 28, 1967. Executive Minutes, August 8, 1972; *Sudbury Star*, April 5, 1978; *Globe and Mail*, April 13, 1978. With regard to university-government relations, see Cameron, *The Northern Dilemma*, 17–32; Edward J. Monahan, "University-Government Relations in Ontario: The History of a Buffer Body, 1958–1996," *Minerva* 36, 4 (1998): 347–66; Monahan, *Collective Autonomy*, passim.

37 *Northern Life* (Sudbury), July 22, 1981; *Globe and Mail*, August 21, 1981; *Toronto Star*, August 20, 1981; *Laurentian University Gazette*, September 10, 1981; Board Minutes, June 5, 1981; A.N. Bourns, *A Proposal for Structural Change in the University System in Northeastern Ontario* (Toronto: Government of Ontario, 1981), 1; *Sault Star* (Sault Ste. Marie), November 28, 1981; LUA, I, 36, 3, "Parrott Commission," Bette Stephenson, MD, to Dr. Henry Best, October 29, 1982; *Laurentian University Gazette*, November 2, 1982, December 1, 1982.

38 H. Parrott, *Report of the Committee on University Education in Northeastern Ontario* (Toronto: Government of Ontario, 1983), 1–2; *Laurentian University Gazette*, October 20, 1983; *Sudbury Star*, November 2, 1983, November 4, 1983, November 16, 1983, November 17, 1983; Senate Minutes, November 3, 1983; *Northern Life*, November 8, 1983, November 23, 1983; *Laurentian University Gazette*, November 9, 1983; LUA, I36, 3, H.E. Brown, chairman, Board of Governors, Algoma University College, and Anthony Blackbourn, president and chairman of Senate, Nipissing University College, to Dr. Bette Stephenson, December 1, 1983; *Le Nord* (Hearst), November 9, 1983; *The Daily Nugget* (North Bay), October 20, 1983; *Sault Star*, October 22, 1983; *Laurentian University Gazette*, October 20, 1983; *Sudbury Star*, October 20, 1983; *Sault Star*, November 9, 1983, November 15, 1983.

39 Ibid., December 16, 1983; Executive Minutes, January 10, 1984; LUFA *Bulletin* 3, Special Issue (January 1984); Executive Minutes, July 26, 1984; *Laurentian University Gazette*, January 30, 1985; Executive Minutes, February 12, 1985; Board Minutes, February 22, 1985.

40 *Sault Star*, March 13, 1986; Executive Minutes, April 11, 1989; Board Minutes, October 13, 1989, October 5, 1990; Executive Minutes, November 10, 1992; Senate Minutes, November 19, 1992.

41 *Sudbury Star*, October 8, 1964; Executive Minutes, May 26, 1961; *Sudbury Star*, September 19, 1963, November 2, 1961, September 26, 1962; Ian Green, "Laurentian and the community," *Sudbury Star*, October 8, 1970.

42 Gwenda Hallsworth and Peter Hallsworth, "The 1960s," in Wallace and Thomson, eds, *Sudbury*, 236; Board Minutes, May 19, 1966, October 21, 1966; Executive Minutes, January 10, 1968, November 14, 1969.

43 Ibid., November 23, 1971; *Sudbury Star*, May 1, 1973, February 5, 1975, February 13, 1975, November 18, 1975, November 4, 1975, November 17, 1975.

44 LUA, Charles Levi interview with Ron Chrysler, January 20, 2005; *Laurentian University Gazette*, March 1978.

45 *Northern Life*, December 14, 2006, February 1978; Board Minutes, February 10, 1978.

46 Ibid., March 1, 1978; Oiva Saarinen, "Creating a Sustainable Community: The Sudbury Case Study," in Matt Bray and Ashley Thomson, eds, *At the End of the Shift: Mines and Single Industry Towns in Northern Ontario* (Toronto: Dundurn Press, 1992), 176.

47 Levi notes on a meeting with Henry B.M. Best, January 16, 2004.

48 *Laurentian University Gazette*, February–May 1979; Executive Minutes, April 9, 1974; *Northern Life*, January 14, 1981; *Sudbury Star*, May 13, 1983, August 12, 1983; *Laurentian University Gazette*, November 12, 1980.

49 Ibid., May 18, 1983.

50 LUA, F24, 4, "Laurentian University Report," March 24, 1980; *Northern Life*, April 18, 1981, April 22, 1981; LUA, PO63, V, 3, L. Cortis to O. Saarinen, May 5, 1981; *Laurentian University Gazette*, April 29, 1981; Board Minutes, May 21, 1981; *Sudbury Star*, June 2, 1981; *Northern Life*, June 3, 1981.

51 *Laurentian University Gazette*, March 9, 1983.

Chapter Five

1 *Laurentian University Gazette*, March 14, 1984; www.ibo.org/ibworld/sept07/sirjohndaniel.cfm.

2 LUA, Charles Levi interview with Ron Chrysler, January 20, 2005; Senate Briefs, May 1984–May 1985, Report of the President on the Budget Process, September 20, 1984; Senate Minutes, May 24, 1984, April 17, 1986.

3 Senate Briefs, May 1984–May 1985, Report of the President on the Position of Vice-President, Academic, August 31, 1984; ibid., John S. Daniel, Addendum to the Report of the Executive Committee to the September 1984 Meeting of Senate, September 13, 1984.

4 Senate Minutes, March 21, 1985; Board Minutes, April 12, 1985; Senate Briefs, May 1984–May 1985, John S. Daniel to Senate Executive, March 8, 1985; Executive Minutes, March 12, 1985; *Laurentian University Gazette*, March 13, 1985.

5 Board Minutes, October 18, 1985, October 5, 1990; Executive Minutes, March 27, 1980, May 14, 1985.

6 Board Minutes, April 12, 1985; Senate Minutes, January 16, 1986; Board Minutes, February 21, 1986; Board Minutes, October 13, 1989, December 16, 1994.

7 Executive Minutes, April 8, 1986, October 12, 1993; Board Minutes, April 17, 1998.

8 *Laurentian University Gazette*, June 19, 1985, May 28, 1986; Senate Briefs, October 1987–March 1989, "1988–89 Operating Budget Report," May 12, 1988; *Laurentian University Gazette*, December 13, 1989; ibid., March 25, 1987; Board Minutes, April 10, 1987, October 5, 1990; Senate Briefs, April 1991–April 1992, Report of the 1992–93 Budget committee, April 16, 1992.

9 See chapter 19 re: LUFA; *Northern Life*, September 27, 1989; *Sudbury Star*, September 27, 1989.

10 See chapter 4.

11 Executive Minutes, December 11, 1973; Board Minutes, October 1, 1976. *Northern Life*, October 20, 1984; Senate Minutes, January 18, 1979; Board Minutes, March 23, 1979, November 23, 1979; LUA, F35, 3, box 2, Minutes of the Meeting of the Fund Management Committee, November 16, 1981; Board Minutes, December 4, 1981; *Sudbury Star*, March 13, 1982; *Northern Life*, March 24, 1982; *Laurentian University Gazette*, March 24, 1982; *Northern Life*, February 23, 1983; Board Minutes, October 28, 1983, June 1, 1984; LUA, F35, 4, 3, Henry Best to Paul G. Desmarais, 28 June 1983; LUA, Charles Levi interview with Dr. Henry Best, January 16, 2004. See also Fred Lazar, "The National Economy," in R.B. Byers, ed., *Canadian Annual Review of Politics and Public Affairs, 1981* (Toronto: University of Toronto Press, 1984), 213–16.

12 LUA, PO63, IV, 22, Keyes D. Metcalfe to Father P.-E. Filion, chief librarian, February 9, 1966; ibid., A. Barnett, chair, Senate Library Committee, to J.R. Harrison, April 14, 1970; *Sudbury Star*, March 13, 1982; *Northern Life*, March 24, 1982; Board Minutes, April 16, 1982; LUA, 68, 1, "Dean of Science," Report by Margaret Beckman, Library Consultant, April 1971; Board Minutes, October 19, 1984.

13 Ibid., June 6, 1986, December 5, 1986; Carl Wallace, "The 1980s," in *Sudbury*, 278–9; Oiva Saarinen, "Creating a Sustainable Community: The Sudbury Case Study," in *At the End of the Shift*, 178.

14 *Laurentian University Gazette*, June 17, 1987; LUA, F35, 3, "Draft Proposal *Laurentian University Development Campaign*," undated, *circa* June 1987; Executive Minutes, September 9, 1986; Board Minutes, June 6, 1986, December 5, 1986; *Sudbury Star*, November 6, 1987; *Northern Life*, December 9, 1987; *Sudbury Star*, April 14, 1988; *Northern Life*, October 19, 1988; *Laurentian University Gazette*, December 14, 1988; *Sudbury Star*, May 7, 1989.

15 Board Minutes, June 5, 1987, October 13, 1987, July 4, 1988, February 16, 1990; *Laurentian University Gazette*, November 5, 1986, June 27, 1990; Board Minutes, March 14, 1989; Executive Minutes, February 13, 1990; Board Minutes, February 13, 1990, February 12, 1991, February 14, 1992, October 1, 1993.

16 Ibid., June 6, 1986, October 14, 1986, December 5, 1986; Executive Minutes, February 10, 1987; Senate Minutes, October 16, 1986. See also LUA, Charles Levi interview with Douglas Parker, February 23, 2005.

17 *Sudbury Star*, November 6, 1986; LUA, N34, 1, D.H. Parker to Alan Querney, March 13, 1988; Executive Minutes, October 13, 1987; Board Minutes, October 14, 1988; *Sudbury Star*, December 15, 1989; LUA, Levi interview with Douglas Parker, February 23, 2005.

18 Board Minutes, December 8, 1989; *Laurentian University Gazette*, December 16, 1989; Senate Briefs, May 1990–March 1991, Université Canadienne en France Academic Review, October 1990, passim, 59; Senate Minutes, November 15, 1990; Board Minutes, April 9, 1991.

19 Senate Briefs, May 1990–March 1991, Université Canadienne en France Academic Review, October 1990, 40; ibid., May 1992–December 1992, Report of the Academic Planning Committee to the Regular May 1992 Meeting of Senate; Executive Minutes, May 10, 1994; Board Minutes, December 15, 1995; Executive Minutes, April 9, 1996. See also LUA, Charles Levi interview with Ross Paul, February 18, 2005.

20 Executive Minutes, October 13, 1987; LUA, PO63, IV, 29, 1, Pierre Simoni, secretary, LUFA, to LUFA members, November 23, 1987; Senate Minutes, November 19, 1987; Board Minutes, December 4, 1987; ibid., July 4, 1988; www.col.org/colweb/site/pid/972.

21 *Laurentian University Gazette*, December 14, 1988.

22 LUA, PO63, IV, 29, 1, Schell to LUFA members, September 12, 1988; Senate Minutes, October 20, 1988; Board Minutes, December 2, 1988; *Laurentian University Gazette*, March 29, 1989.

23 Senate Briefs, May 1990–March 1991, Report of the Presidential Search Committee, January 28, 1991; Board Minutes, November 3, 1989; Senate Minutes, December 14, 1989; Executive Minutes, February 1, 1990, February 13, 1990; Board Minutes, February 16, 1990; Executive Minutes, April 17, 1990, June 27, 1990; Board Minutes, August 28, 1990; Senate Minutes, August 28, 1990; Executive Minutes, October 16, 1990; Board Minutes, January 28, 1991.

24 Executive Minutes, June 27, 1990; Board Minutes, August 28, 1990; Executive Minutes, August 27, 1990; LUA, PO63, IV, 29, 1, Lucien Cortis, president, LUFA, to A.A. Querney, chair, Board of Governors, August 28, 1990; Board Minutes, June 1, 1990, November 30, 1990.

25 *Laurentian University Gazette*, February 15, 1996.

26 Ibid., September 1997, April 23, 1993; Senate Minutes, January 28, 1990; Board Minutes, May 30, 1996.

27 Ibid., October 4, 1991; Senate Briefs, April 1991–April 1992, Report of the 1992–93 Budget committee, April 16, 1992; Board Minutes, December 4, 1992.

28 See chapter 20 for the general impact of the "Social Contract." *Laurentian University Gazette*, May 7, 1993, January 19, 1996; Executive Minutes, July 15, 1993; Board Minutes, June 10, 1994.

29 Executive Minutes, March 14, 1995; Board Minutes, February 16, 1996; *Laurentian University Gazette*, May 17, 1996; Board Minutes, December 15, 1995, April 19, 1996; *Laurentian University Gazette*, March 15, 1996; Senate Briefs, November 1995–November 1996, May 13, 1996, Proposed Budget, 1996–97.

30 *Laurentian University Gazette* (September 1997); LUA, Levi interview with Ron Chrysler, January 20, 2005.

31 Tom Booth, "The Evolution of University Government," *CAUT/ACPPU Bulletin Online* 55, 9 (November 2008); Jones, Goyan and Shanahan, "University Governance in Canadian Higher Education," 139; Monahan, *Collective Autonomy*, 164–75; http://communications.uwaterloo.ca/Gazette/1993; Board Minutes, October 4, 1991.

32 Executive Minutes, October 12, 1993; Board Minutes, December 3, 1993, April 12, 1994; Executive Minutes, December 13, 1994, March 14, 1995.

33 *Task Force on University Accountability: A Strengthened Framework* (Toronto: Government of Ontario, 1993), 8; Executive Minutes, March 14, 1995; Senate Minutes, September 18, 1997; Senate Briefs, November 1996–March 1998, "Laurentian University Accounts Committee," September 18, 1997 Meeting of Senate.

34 Ibid.

35 Senate Briefs, February 1999–June 2000, University Accounts Committee Summary Report, May 3, 1999; ibid., University Accounts Committee Summary Report 1999–2000, May 1, 2000; ibid., September 2000–April 2002, University Accounts Committee Preliminary Report to Senate, March 2001.

36 Board Minutes, February 18, 1994, December 14, 1994; Executive Minutes, December 10, 1996, February 11, 1997; Board Minutes, February 28, 1997; *Laurentian University Gazette*, November 20, 1992; Board Minutes, May 30, 1996, October 4, 1996.

37 Ibid., November 29, 1997; Executive Minutes, December 10, 1996, February 11, 1997; Senate Minutes, April 17, 1997; Board Minutes, April 18, 1997; Senate Minutes, May 15, 1997; *Laurentian University Gazette* (summer 2000).

38 LUA, Senate Briefs, May–December 1992, Anne-Marie Mawhiney, "Report to Senate Laurentian University Native Educational Council," September 1992; *Laurentian University Gazette*, March 5, 1993; Senate Minutes, November 18, 1993; Board Minutes, December 3, 1993.

39 *Laurentian University Gazette*, March 5, 1993; Senate Briefs, April–October 1995, "Laurentian University Native Education Council … Mandate and Terms of Reference," September 1, 1993; Senate Minutes, November 18, 1993; Board Minutes, December 3, 1993.

40 Executive Minutes, August 16, 1995, September 12, 1995; Senate Minutes, December 7, 1995; Board Minutes, December 15, 1995; Executive Minutes, July 16, 1997: Senate Minutes, September 18, 1997; *Laurentian University Gazette* (September 1997); Senate Minutes, December 11, 1997; *Laurentian University Gazette* (January 1998).

41 Board Minutes, October 10, 1997, December 5, 1997; *Laurentian University Gazette* (November 1997); Executive Minutes, November 11, 1997; Senate Minutes, February 12, 1998; Board Minutes, February 13, 1998.

42 *Laurentian University Gazette* (March 1998).

43 Executive Minutes, September 8, 1998; Senate Minutes, September 17, 1998; Senate Briefs, November 1996–March 1998, Laurentian University Budget Proposal, 1997–1998, May 22, 1997; Senate Minutes, September 18, 1997; Board Minutes, February 5, 1999; Senate Briefs, February 1999–June 2000, April 15, 1999; Board Minutes, May 5, 2000; Senate Briefs, September 2000–April 2002, Report of the University Accounts Committee, December 13, 2001.

44 Senate Minutes, September 17, 1998; Board Minutes, February 5, 1999; Executive Minutes, March 9, 1999, April 13, 1999.

45 Board Minutes, September 28, 2001; Ron Chrysler to Matt Bray, December 3, 2008.

46 Board Minutes, June 11, 1999, October 1, 1999; Board Minutes, December 3, 1999; Executive Minutes, February 8, 2000; Board Minutes, February 25, 2000; Senate Minutes, September 21, 2000, March 15, 2001; Executive Minutes, February 6, 2001.

47 Ibid., April 11, 2000, May 9, 2000, April 24, 2001.

48 Board Minutes, June 8, 2001, September 28, 2001, February 8, 2002.

49 Senate Minutes, December 18, 2001; *Laurentian University Gazette*, February 22, 2002; news.concordia.ca/recent_stories/012486.shtml, biography of Judith Woodsworth, plus "View Judith Woodsworth's C.V."; News@Concordia.ca, "Judith Woodsworth named new Concordia president and vice-chancellor," September 29, 2008.

50 Board Minutes, November 30, 2001, April 12, 2002; Senate Minutes, June 6, 2002; Board Minutes, November 29, 2002.

51 Ibid., February 7, 2003, November 28, 2003. http://www.laurentian.ca/Laurentian/Home/ Departments/Institutional+Research/Other/Enrolment/Academic+Load.htm? Laurentian_Lang=en-CA ; Board Minutes, February 6, 2004; Laurentian University Budget Report 2008–2009 presented to the Board of Governors, April 11, 2008, 3; Financial Statements of Laurentian University of Sudbury, Year ended April 30, 2003, and Year ended April 30, 2007. Because Laurentian changed the definition of "full-time status" in the autumn of 2004, it is impossible to compare precisely the pre- and post-double cohort data for categories such as full- and part-time students.

52 Senate Minutes, May 20, 2003; Budget Report 2008–2009 presented to the Board of Governors, April 11, 2008, 3; Board Minutes, October 3, 2003, June 11, 2004.

53 Executive Minutes, February 6, 2001; Laurentian University of Sudbury Budget Report 2008–2009 presented to the Board of Governors, April 11, 2008, 3–4. Because the Northern Ontario School of Medicine is an independent corporation, Laurentian is not responsible for either its operational or infrastructural costs, true also of the Sudbury Neutrino Observatory.

54 Laurentian University of Sudbury Consolidated Statement of Operations, 2007–2008, 2; Laurentian University 2007–2008, Schedule 1, Budget Estimates; Budget Report 2008–2009 presented to the Board of Governors, April 11, 2008, 7.

55 *Communiqué* (Laurentian University), January 28, 2008; *Northern Life*, October 27, 2008; *Industry Canada*, August 2008; Laurentian University, Public Affairs, press release, May 25, 2009.

56 See, for example, Elizabeth Church, "Universities looking outside academia for leaders," *Globe and Mail*, December 1, 2008.

Chapter Six

1 Board Minutes, May 7, 1960.

2 See *Laurentian University Calendar, 1960–1961*, 16.

3 Ibid., 13. (Translated from the original French.)

4 Senate Minutes, February 27, 1962.

5 Howard C. Clark, *Growth and Governance of Canadian Universities: An Insider's View* (Vancouver: University of British Columbia Press, 2005).

6 For more information, see Paul-André-Linteau, René Durocher, Jean-Claude Robert, François Ricard, *Histoire du Québec contemporain: Le Québec depuis 1930* (Montréal: Les Éditions du Boréal Express, 1986), 598–610; Claude Galarneau, *Les collèges classiques au Canada français* (Montréal: Fides, 1978); Gaétan Gervais, "L'enseignement supérieur en Ontario-français (1848–1965)," *Revue du Nouvel-Ontario* 7 (1985): 11–52; André Bertrand, *L'éducation classique au Collège du Sacré-Cœur* (Sudbury: La société historique du Nouvel-Ontario, *Documents historiques No. 86*, 1988).

7 Laurentian University, President's Report 1967–1968, 1.

8 Senate Minutes, September 19, 1983.

9 Clark, *Growth and Governance*, 35.

10 Senate Minutes, April 17, 1975 (Senate approved the appointments of the deans of Humanities, Social Sciences and Science but delayed the appointment of the dean of Professional Schools). The deans' appointments in 1975 were preceded by the appointment of vice-deans in the Faculty of Arts and Science (the dean of Science in 1970–1971 and the deans of Humanities and Social Sciences in 1971–1972, shortly after the disciplines in these three areas were grouped together). The vice-dean of Professional Schools was appointed in 1972.

11 Senate Correspondence, 1970–1971. The letter is signed by Pierre Bélanger, department of sociology, and dated November 26, 1970.

12 Georges Bélanger, "L'enseignement de la littérature et de la culture," *Revue du Nouvel-Ontario* 7 (1985): 54.

13 *Laurentian University Calendar, 1975–1976*, 27.

14 *Laurentian University Calendar, 1971–1972* (bilingual pamphlet inserted).

15 *Laurentian University Calendar, 1972–1973*, 21.

16 For more information on this topic, see Sally M. Weaver, *Making Canadian Indian Policy: The Hidden Agenda 1968–1970* (Toronto: University of Toronto Press, 1981), and Harold Cardinal, *The Unjust Society* (Edmonton: Hurtig, 1969).

17 See LUA, F44, 3, "Religious Studies 1962–1972," more specifically the document "Indian Studies at Laurentian University," dated May 15, 1969.

18 Ibid., H7, 2, "Senate."

19 Ibid., FG7, 3, "Administration 1972–1973."

20 Memorandum sent to the Program Committee, dated December 8, 1974. Senate Correspondence, January–May 1975.

21 J. Couture (Trent University) and S. Weaver (University of Waterloo), Report of the External Committee for the Appraisal of the Native Studies Programme at Laurentian University, November 14, 1975.

22 Report of the Ad Hoc Planning Committee on Native Studies Programme, Senate Briefs, June 1975–May 1976. The document is dated March 1976.

23 *Laurentian University Calendar, 1977–1978*, 73; Senate Minutes, December 5, 1974.

24 Senate Minutes, May 18, 1978; *Laurentian University Calendar, 1980–1981*, 83.

25 Senate Minutes, January 30, 1961.

26 Ibid., January 9, 1969.

27 *Laurentian University Calendar, 1978–1979*, 78; Senate Minutes, January 12, 1978.

28 Laurentian University of Sudbury, Ontario, Presentation to the Committee on University Affairs, October 20, 1969.

29 Matt Bray, Chair of History, Statement of Programme Objectives, May 25, 1977.

30 Executive Minutes, July 25, 1962.

31 Executive Minutes, June 26, 1963.

32 Also see two reports from the department's chair at the time, R.H. Farrant: "A Report with Predictive Estimates and Recommendations," October 1970, and "A Tentative History of Psychology in Laurentian University and Affiliated Colleges," speech given during the Psychology in the North symposium of the Third Regional Psychology Conference, held at Nipissing University College, North Bay, February 19, 1982.

33 LUA, Acc.F62, 2, "Dean's Office Box 40," Memorandum from Dean Bourbeau to President Bennett, April 6, 1962.

34 LUA, Acc.F62, 2, "Dean's Office Box," Correspondence from Dean Bourbeau to President Bennett, November 23, 1962.

35 Senate Minutes, December 16, 1971, Laurentian University Course Guide, 1972–1973, 21. In 1967, the psychology department chair wrote to President Mullins that: "I would therefore emphasize that Laurentian University should fairly soon set up in Anthropology since field studies of archaeological, anthropometric, linguistics and social aspects could well be conducted from this region," LUA, Acc.F62, 2, "Dean's Office Box 40."

36 *Laurentian University Calendar, 1972–1973*, 21.

37 S. McMullin, "Canadian Studies," thecanadianencyclopedia.com. The title of the Symons report is: "To Know Ourselves: The Report of the Commission on Canadian Studies" (Ottawa: Association of Universities and Colleges of Canada, 1975).

38 Senate Minutes, December 16, 1971.

39 LUA, G18, 1, "Dean, Social Sciences and Humanities. Canadian Studies," Letter from Edward Monahan to Matt Bray, dated July 11, 1975.

40 Ibid., Letter from Matt Bray to President Monahan, July 28, 1975.

41 *Laurentian University Calendar, 1977–1978*, 226; Senate Minutes, December 16, 1976.

42 LUA, PO63, IV, 28, Letter from W. Watson, dated June 26, 1969.

43 President's Report 1968–1969, 6.

44 Laurentian University of Sudbury, Presentation to the Committee on University Affairs, October 20, 1969, 2.

45 *Laurentian University Calendar, 1967–1968*, 17; Senate Minutes, March 31, 1966; Board Minutes, May 19, 1966.

46 *Laurentian University Calendar, 1968–1969*, 50; Senate Minutes, March 31, 1966; Board Minutes, May 19, 1966.

47 *Laurentian University Calendar, 1972–1973*, 22; Senate Minutes, December 16, 1971.

48 *Laurentian University Calendar, 1966–1967*, 22.

49 Its author, Dr. Philip Lapp, had received a mandate from the Government of Ontario to study the rationalization of the engineering programs and training in Ontario in 1969. He submitted his report in December 1970.

50 A.S. Tombalakian, "A Brief History of the Engineering School of Laurentian University," speech given by the past director of the school of engineering at its students' graduation banquet, March 11, 1995.

51 *Laurentian University Calendar, 1971–1972*, 23.

52 *Laurentian University Calendar, 1977–1978*, 73.

53 *Laurentian University Calendar, 1978–1979*, 33.

54 Senate Minutes, December 19, 1963.

55 In 1961, the Federal Government had established this Royal Commission of Inquiry. Recommendation 35(1) concerns the creation of a school at Laurentian.

56 Board Executive Minutes, April 28, 1965.

57 Senate Minutes, March 31, 1966; Board Minutes, May 19, 1966. The three schools – nursing, social work and physical education – were approved during this meeting.

58 Memorandum from Wendy Gerhard, dean of Professional Schools, to Vice-President Academic Frank Turner, February 3, 1975. The community reacted by creating a committee of nurses which presented a document to Senate requesting that the school of nursing remain open, but that changes be made at the administration level and within the program. See A Brief to the Senate of Laurentian University Re: the Kergin-Turner Report May 11, 1973 prepared by the Committee of Concerned Senior Nurses of Sudbury, in LUA, F70, 1, "Dean of Science."

59 Ibid., F67, 2, "Dean of Science," Acting president's opening statement in Laurentian University, Presentation to the Committee on University Affairs, December 14, 1970, 7.

60 *Laurentian University Calendar, 1975–1976*, 86; Senate Minutes, December 16, 1976; Board Minutes, May 25, 1973, September 21, 1973, March 15, 1974. An ad hoc committee for the integration of l'École normale with Laurentian University was set up in 1970; see Senate Committees and representations, annual report 1970–1971.

61 *Laurentian Gazette laurentienne* 1, 7 (April 1974): 1. It also states: "One of the propositions accepted by Senate was that the premises of l'École Normale be designated as a place of Francophone identification on campus ... It is also understood that the language of communication and the atmosphere on premises will be French." (Translated from the original French.)

62 *Laurentian University Calendar*, 1977–1978, 23; Senate Minutes, September 22, 1977.

63 Board Minutes, October 21, 1966.

64 LUA, 31, 22, B, "Senate, Academic Council-Science," Science Council Report to Senate of Council's meeting of June 16, 1971.

65 Ibid., for more information on this topic, see Brief History of the Biology Department, Memorandum from the dean of Science to the vice-president academic and research, May 5, 1977.

66 *Laurentian University Calendar, 1978–1979*, 82; Senate Minutes, September 22, 1977.

67 *Laurentian University Calendar, 1974–1975*, 27.

68 See, among others, *Laurentian University Calendar, 1976–1977*, 27.

69 Memorandum from D.H. Williamson to Dean R.J.A. Cloutier, May 23, 1968. The object of the memorandum was to raise the need of having graduate studies in geology, but it represents well the arguments put forth for the existence of a geology program, whether at the undergraduate or graduate level. It should be noted that the Jesuit Fathers, founders of Sacred Heart College and University of Sudbury, had recognized the validity of this argument when they had created a course in geology in 1958.

70 According to some authors, the story of this course extension service at the University of Sudbury is directly linked to the that of the conflicts between the mining business in the region and the unions, especially Mine, Mill. On this topic, see Mike Solski and John

Smaller, *Mine Mill: The History of the International Union of Mine, Mill and Smelter Workers in Canada Since 1895* (Ottawa: Steel Rail Publishing), 137–8.

71 *Laurentian University Calendar, 1960–1961*, 58. (Translated from the original French.)

72 LUA, F47, 2, Public Relations 1959–1961, Press Release October 14, 1960.

73 Anne-Marie Mawhiney and Ross Paul, "Women and Distance Education in Northeastern Ontario" in Margaret Kechnie and Marge Reitma-Street, eds, *Changing Lives: Women in Northern Ontario* (Toronto: Dundurn Press, 1996), 311–18.

74 *Laurentian University Calendar, 1974–1975*, 29.

75 For more information, see the Ontario Council on Graduate Studies' website (www.ocgs.cou.on.ca).

76 Senate Minutes, March 21, 1967, April 27, 1967. Two years earlier, a mathematics professor had asked the president when the university planned to inaugurate master's and doctoral programs in his discipline; the president had replied that he hoped the master's program could start in 1969–1970 and the PhD shortly after in 1970.

77 Senate Minutes, October 24, 1968, November 28, 1968, December 12, 1968.

78 Senate Minutes, December 18, 1972.

79 President's Report 1967–1968, 9.

80 Report to CUA, October 1970.

81 *Laurentian University Calendar, 1970–1971*, 22; Senate Minutes, September 25, 1969.

82 President's Report 1969–1970, 9, 11.

83 LUA, K66, 4, "Director, School of Graduate Studies 1968–1981," Letter to Dean Cloutier, November 11, 1968.

84 Ibid., K67, 3, Letter from the committee chair to Laurentian University director of graduate studies, October 12, 1971.

85 NAC, RG32, 1, 1, Acc.15129/4A, box 1: "Laurentian University Operating Grants 1971–1972," Letter dated March 8, 1971.

86 Ibid., Letters from the president, March 17, 1971, and from the minister, March 29, 1971.

87 Clark, *Growth and Governance*, 58–9. The author mentioned that his assessment of ACAP was not unanimous.

88 Senate Long Range Planning Committee, Five Year Plan for Graduate Studies 1972–1977, Board Minutes, January 21, 1972, and Senate Minutes, February 10, 1972.

89 *Laurentian University Calendar, 1972–1973*, 94; Senate Minutes, February 24, 1972. The English MA program was suspended in the 1980s following an external review of the program and based on the decision made by the director of graduate studies at the time.

90 *Laurentian University Calendar, 1972–1973*, 23.

91 LUA, F53, 2, "Graduate Studies Committee 1971–72," Letter from M.A. Preston, executive vice-president and director of graduate studies, to W. Watson, May 29, 1972.

92 Ibid., F53, 2, "Graduate Studies Committee September 1972," Memorandum from W.Y. Watson, February 21, 1973.

93 Academic Planning Committee, "Planning for Tomorrow." Report to Senate, May 1973.

94 School of Graduate Studies, "Five-Year Plan for Graduate Studies 1974–1979."

95 LUA, F53, 2, "LU Graduate Council from September 1974," Report from the Joint CUA–COU Subcommittee on goals and objectives for graduate development concerning the five-year plan of Laurentian University.

96 Ibid "Graduate Studies Planning Paper No. 2." This document signed by Edgar Wright, director of graduate studies, quotes the decision as follows: "ACAP could not recommend for Laurentian any programmes in addition to those in the approved five year plan which, we believe, will fully extend the university's resources."

97 *Laurentian University Graduate Calendar, 1975–1976*, 53; Senate Minutes, June 13, 1974.

98 Graduate Studies – A Situation Review, March 7, 1984, Senate Briefs, April 1983–April 1984.

99 *Laurentian University Graduate Calendar, 1974–1975*, 45.

100 *Laurentian University Graduate Calendar, 1980–1981*, 52; Senate Minutes, June 21, 1979.

101 *Laurentian University Graduate Calendar, 1997–1998*, 82; Senate Minutes, December 10, 1998.

102 Laurentian University, Brief to OCUA on Graduate Studies, Senate Briefs, June 1976–April 1977.

103 Brief Presented by Laurentian University to the Ontario Council on University Affairs, May 17, 1978.

104 Laurentian University, Presentation to the Committee on University Affairs, October 20, 1969, Appendix A, 2.

105 J.-E. Havel, *Les citoyens de Sudbury et la politique: Enquête sur l'information, le comportement politique et les partis politiques à Sudbury* (Sudbury: Presses de l'Université Laurentienne, 1966).

106 Laurentian University of Sudbury, President's Report 1966–1967, 64.

107 Edward J. Monahan, "Address to the Faculty of Laurentian University," 21-page photocopied document (signed by the author), dated September 13, 1974.

108 Senate Minutes, September 23, 1973. (Translated from the original French.)

109 For information on scientific policy development in Canada, see Gwendolyne Evans Pilkington, *Speaking With One Voice: Universities in Dialogue with Government* (Montreal: History of McGill Project, McGill University, 1983).

110 The brief presented by Laurentian University to the Ontario Council on University Affairs in 1978 contains a section analyzing the research issue at Laurentian and in small universities in Ontario in general. See the Brief Presented by Laurentian University to the Ontario Council on University Affairs, May 12, 1978, 1–23.

111 See *Senate Committee on Science Policy*, Volume II (better known as the "Lamontagne Report") (Ottawa: Government of Canada, 1972).

112 Laurentian University of Sudbury, President's Report 1966–1967, 97–102.

113 Board Minutes, March 6, 1981, April 12, 1985.

114 *Laurentian University Calendar, 1971–1972*, 153.

115 Donald Dennie and Annette Ribordy, "Les vingt-cinq ans de l'Institut," *Revue du Nouvel-Ontario* 25 (2001): 10. The founders of the Institute were: Benoît Cazabon, Gilles Comtois, Gaétan Gervais, Roger Breton, Donald Dennie and Lucien Michaud. Also see *Laurentian University Gazette* 5, 1, 2 (1977). (Translated from the original French.)

116 For CIMMER, see Board Minutes, May 31, 1985 and February 21, 1986, as well as *Northern Life*, July 1, 1984.

117 LUA, L4, 2, "Doyen des Sciences et de génie," A.E. Beswick, Future Direction for CIMMER, September 1986.

118 Ibid., 12, 3, Task Force on Academic Priorities Report, School of Graduate Studies and Research, April 1986.

Chapter Seven

1 LUA, 31, 22, B, "Senate – Academic Council – Sciences," Science academic council Minutes, March 7, 1980; Senate Minutes, March 20, 1980.

2 Report of the Presidential Advisory Committee on Engineering (PACE), "The Laurentian School of Engineering: Plans for the Future," January 27, 2000, Senate Briefs, February 1999–June 2000. The committee recommended that the doctoral program be estab-

lished jointly with University of Toronto and Queen's University. Laurentian opted for an independent program (see the section "Doctorate").

3 Senate Minutes, April 15, 2003.

4 LUA, 31, 22, B, Memorandum from the faculty dean to the vice-president academic and research, June 13, 1986.

5 Senate Minutes, February 11, 1999.

6 LUA, LU, L2, 1, Memorandum dated September 30, 1979, "Dean Science and Engineering."

7 Senate Minutes, January 19, 1984. The name of the mathematics department changed to department of mathematics and computer science in 1979.

8 Senate Minutes, December 10, 1981.

9 Ibid., June 21, 1990.

10 *Laurentian University Calendar, 1983–1984*, 79; Senate Minutes, December 10, 1981.

11 LUA, 31, 22, B, Memorandum from the dean of Science and Engineering to the vice-president academic and research, June 7, 1994.

12 Senate Minutes, June 20, 1996, June 20, 2002.

13 The type and number of options has varied since 1997. In English, the options have been biomedical, conservation and restoration ecology, wildlife and habitat ecology, forensic biology, zoology. In 2006, they numbered four: biomedical, conservation and restoration ecology, terrestrial and aquatic ecology, and zoology. In French, there were three options: biomédicale, écologie terrestre et aquatique, biologie intégrée. See *Laurentian University Calendars*, 2002–2004, 60–1; 2006, 34–5.

14 Senate Minutes, March 16, 2004.

15 *Laurentian University Calendar, 1985–1986*, 87.

16 *Laurentian University Calendar, 1981–1982*, 78–9; Senate Minutes, June 18, 1981.

17 *Laurentian University Calendar, 1980–1981*, 83; Senate Minutes, February 28, 1980.

18 *Laurentian University Calendar, 2000–2002*, 51; Senate Minutes, December 10, 1998.

19 *Laurentian University Calendar, 2002–2004*, 80; Senate Minutes, June 21, 2001. In 1981, the college's long-term planning committee had proposed the establishment of a school of communications to the Board of Regents that would have been bilingual and interdisciplinary. See LUA, F24, 4.

20 *Laurentian University Calendar, 2006*, 53–5; Senate Minutes, April 25, 2003.

21 Senate Minutes, December 14, 2004, January 18, 2005.

22 Ibid., June 20, 2006.

23 *Laurentian University Calendar, 1993–1994*, 40.

24 *Laurentian University Calendar, 1995–1996*, 46; Senate Minutes, February 11, 1991, April 20, 1995.

25 *Laurentian University Calendar, 2000–2002*, 51, 162; Senate Minutes, February 11, 1999.

26 *Laurentian University Calendar, 2000–2004*, 202–3; Senate Minutes, September 20, 2001.

27 Senate Minutes, January 16, 2007. This program received financing from the Consortium national de formation en santé.

28 *Laurentian University Calendar, 1981–1982*, 77, and 1986–1987, 82; Senate Minutes, February 26, 1981, February 13, 1986.

29 *Laurentian University Calendar, 1989–1990*, 190; Senate Minutes, January 16, 1986.

30 *Laurentian University Calendar, 1988–1989*, 261–5; Senate Minutes, October 15, 1987. This program was initially part of the tricultural structure of the school of social work but acquired its administrative independence in 2006 before requesting its own accreditation from the Canadian Association of Schools of Social Work in 2008.

31 *Laurentian University Calendar, 1986–1987*, 82, 89; Senate Minutes, January 16, 1986.

32 *Laurentian University Calendar, 1993–1994,* 39; Senate Minutes, June 18, 1992.

33 *Laurentian University Calendar, 2000–2002,* 69; Senate Minutes, June 17, 1999. During this meeting only the program's first-year courses were approved. At its June 20, 2000 meeting, Senate approved the program's last three years.

34 LUA, G18, 1, Dean, Social Sciences and Humanities, "Canadian Studies," Report of the Academic Planning Committee to the Regular November 1988 Meeting of Senate.

35 ACAPLAN Report – Senate Meeting – December 1988, in Senate Briefs, October 1987– March 1989. The report is signed by Charles H. Bélanger, committee chair.

36 Senate Minutes, February 14, 1991.

37 Senate Minutes, March 19, 1998. The resolution passed by Senate required this transfer to come into effect on July 1, 1998. See also Board Minutes, May 29, 1998.

38 For a brief history of the school and a description of its operations, see www.normed.ca. To understand the important steps in establishing the school, see Senate Minutes, February 10, 2000, December 13, 2001, March 18, 2003, March 18, 2004, April 20, 2004. See also Board Minutes, December 3, 1999, February 25, 2000, June 9, 2000. It is interesting to note that at its meeting on May 28, 1962, Jean-Noël Desmarais had suggested creating a Faculty of Medicine at Laurentian, something that obviously did not materialise immediately.

39 Acting president's opening statement, 1970, 9; also see the 1969 presidential annual report, 15–16.

40 LUA, LU G7, 2, "Dean of Science."

41 The first director of this health initiative was Geoff Tesson, who had also been dean of the Faculty of Social Sciences and vice-president academic and research.

42 Dr. Robert McKendry, "Physicians for Ontario. Too Many? Too Few? For 2000 and Beyond," Report of the Fact Finder on Physician Resources in Ontario, December 1999.

43 Senate Minutes, January 21, 2003, May 20, 2003.

44 Ibid.

45 See *Laurentian University Calendar, 1976,* 71–4; Senate Minutes, January 21, 2003.

46 Ibid., September 20, 2001.

47 *Laurentian University Calendar, 1973–1974,* 29.

48 *Laurentian University Calendar, 1987–1988,* 101.

49 *Laurentian University Calendar, 1987–1988,* 327. Primarily financial considerations forced the closure of this initiative in 1996. The Board of Governors discussed this matter many times (see Board Minutes, June 6, 1986, October 24, 1986) before deciding to do so. See Board Minutes, December 15, 1995. (Translated from the original French.)

50 See the College of Nurses of Ontario website (www.cno.org/reg/normemb/prog) for more information about the history of this new requirement and the cooperation between colleges and certain universities in Ontario; Board Minutes, December 8, 2000.

51 Senate Minutes, June 20, 2002.

52 The BSW program was developed to be offered online with federal government financing allocated by the Consortium national de formation en santé (CNFS) established in 2002.

53 LUA, K67, 3, Memorandum from D.H. Parker and E. Wright to F.J. Turner, April 28, 1983; ibid., letter from D.H. Parker to H.H. Yates, February 7, 1983.

54 Ibid., Memorandum from F.J. Turner to E. Wright, November 15, 1983.

55 *Laurentian University Graduate Calendar, 1995–1996,* 85; Senate Minutes, April 21, 1995.

56 *Laurentian University Graduate Calendar, 1988–1989,* 64.

57 *Laurentian University Graduate Calendar, 1986–1987,* 43; Senate Minutes, May 19, 1983; Board Minutes, April 15, 1983.

58 *Laurentian University Graduate Calendar, 1992–1993,* 90; Senate Minutes, January 21, 1988, March 16, 1989, April 20, 1989.

59 *Laurentian University Graduate Calendar, 1996–1997,* 108; Senate Minutes, September 15, 1994.

60 Ibid., March 18, 1993.

61 *Laurentian University Graduate Calendar, 1994–1995,* 78; Board Minutes, February 14, 1992.

62 *Laurentian University Graduate Calendar, 1995–1996,* 101–2; Senate Minutes, March 17, 1994.

63 Ibid., April 20, 1995. For some, this program represented the resumption of the master's in English that had been suspended in the 1980s.

64 *Laurentian University Graduate Calendar, 1996–1997,* 88.

65 See LUA, G17, 3, "Dean Humanities and Social Sciences," Memorandum from dean to faculty, May 20, 1990, and ibid., "Proposal for a Master's of Arts in Humanities at Laurentian University."

66 *Laurentian University Graduate Calendar, 2005–2006,* 102; Senate Minutes, December 13, 2001.

67 *Laurentian University Graduate Calendar, 2005–2006,* 129–30; Senate Minutes, December 9, 2003. This program's objective is to develop students' ability to share what is science and address questions raised by developments in the field of science. Students take this program simultaneously at Laurentian and Science North.

68 *Laurentian University Graduate Calendar, 2007–2008,* 76; Senate Minutes, June 20, 2006. This program prepares students for careers in research, teaching, and in the industry.

69 *Laurentian University Graduate Calendar, 2007–2008,* 96; Senate Minutes, June 20, 2006.

70 Board Minutes, April 15, 1988. Laurentian nonetheless established a doctoral program in clinical psychology in collaboration with University of Ottawa in 1995–1996 which was in effect until 2001.

71 *Laurentian University Graduate Calendar, 1992–1993,* 85–6.

72 Ibid., 2007–2008, 39–43; Senate Minutes, April 20, 2004.

73 Ibid., 2007–2008, 43–4; Senate Minutes, April 15, 2003.

74 *Laurentian University Graduate Calendar, 2007–2008,* 58–62; Senate Minutes, December 9, 2003.

75 *Laurentian University Graduate Calendar, 2007–2008,* 63–7; Senate Minutes, May 16, 2002.

76 *Laurentian University Graduate Calendar, 2007–2008,* 97–102; Senate Minutes, June 15, 2004.

77 *Laurentian University Graduate Calendar, 2007–2008,* 80–4; Senate Minutes, June 21, 2005.

78 LUA, G9, 1, "Science and Engineering," Letter of Agreement between Laurentian University and the University of Guelph concerning cooperation in graduate studies in the biological sciences, Draft Agreement, October 18, 1994.

79 LUA, G9, 1, Memorandum from ACAPLAN president to the director of the biology department, April 9, 1997.

80 *Laurentian University Graduate Calendar, 2007–2008,* 80. (Translated from the original French.)

81 *Northern Life,* July 11, 1984, 2.

82 Senate Minutes, January 19, 1989.

83 For more information on these centres, visit: EN: www.laurentian.ca then click on Research. FR: www.laurentienne.ca puis cliquer sur Recherche.

84 "L'exploration des réalités sociales canadiennes devient plus facile," *La clé Magazine de recherche de l'Université Laurentienne* (winter 2007): 8.

85 For a brief history of these institutes, see: http://www.cihr-irsc.ca.

86 See the report of the Task Force on Academic Priorities in 1986; in 1993, Senate approved a report called "Leadership and Opportunity for the North: Laurentian University Strategic Plan" (Senate Minutes, January 21, 1993); "Building on Excellence: A Strategic Plan for Laurentian University" (2003).

87 Senate Minutes, December 14, 2000.

88 Ibid., September 21, 2004.

89 See: www.chairs.gc.ca.

90 Jean Watters, president at the time, made the announcement at the Senate meeting. See Senate Minutes, April 20, 2000.

91 See the research website: www.laurentienne.ca/recherches/chaires. The other recipients of a research chair were: Gregory Baiden, natural sciences and engineering, research chair in mining robotics and automation; John Gunn, research chair in stressed aquatic systems; Balz Kamber, research chair in Precambrian geology; Aseem Kumar, research chair in biomolecular science; and Nancy Young, research chair in rural and northern children's health.

92 Senate Minutes, September 16, 2003.

93 Ibid.

94 Ibid., May 18, 2004, December 14, 2004.

95 Ibid., January 18, 2005. The first policy on conflicts of interest was adopted by Senate in 1993; see Senate Minutes, January 18, 1993.

96 Dieter K. Buse, director of graduate studies and research, The Research Record Laurentian University 1989–94: Productivity and Problems, Senate Minutes, January 17, 1996.

97 "Le premier mot," La clé, on the back of the title page.

98 La clé (winter 2008): 10. According to Associate Vice-President Research Liette Vasseur 85 per cent of research funding allocated by councils came from the NSERC.

99 Desmarais Library now offers access, for researchers and interested parties, to LUZONEUL, a website that provides free access to articles written by Laurentian professors, summarizing their research results. This initiative is part of a movement aiming to make research results published by researchers accessible and free of charge. See the Laurentian University Gazette (spring 2008): 1.

100 Brief Presented by Laurentian University of Sudbury to the Ontario Council on University Affairs, 12 May 1978, E-1.

101 Thomas Pocklington and Allan Tupper, No Place to Learn: Why Universities Aren't Working (Vancouver and Toronto: UBC Press, 2002), 100–11. The authors quote the Smith report: "Commission of Inquiry on Canadian University Education, Association of Universities and Colleges of Canada," Ottawa, 1991. Echos of this debate can be found in Clark, Growth and Governance of Canadian Universities; Murray G. Ross, The University: The Anatomy of Academe (New York: McGraw-Hill, 1976); Royal Society of Canada, Realizing the Potential: A Strategy for University Research in Canada (Ottawa: Royal Society of Canada, 1991).

Chapter Eight

1 I am indebted to Charles M. Levi, research consultant for the Laurentian University History Project, for creating meticulous research files, particularly on the 1968 to 1971 crisis in governance at Laurentian University. I also wish to thank my research assistant, Kaleigh Bradley, for skillfully combing through the volumes of student newspapers. "'Co-operation, goodwill, understanding' – school builds on these tenets," Sudbury Star, September

19, 1960; "Sudbury's university classes scattered across the city," *Sudbury Star*, November 4, 1960.

2 LUA, LU History Project File: Hagey Report, Charles Levi, Research Memo; Trevor MacDonald, "A Study of Laurentian University and the Full-Time Students," BA honours thesis (geography), Laurentian University, 1973.

3 "The downtown university," *Globe and Mail*, March 23, 1964.

4 LUA, Charles Levi interview with Kenneth Pryke, February 19, 2005.

5 "Spirit of unity is the aim," *Sudbury Star*, November 4, 1960.

6 Ibid.

7 City of Greater Sudbury Archives, Bob Keir fonds, photos: "Ojibway Indians take Extension Course through LU, March 7, 1962," 62-3-175 and 62-3-183.

8 LUA, LU History Project File: SGA/AGE, History of the Students' General Association: The Years 1960 until 1998, n.d.; "Will French-English be reconciled?"; "Constitution concerned with unity," *Lambda*, February 18, 1965.

9 Gérald M. Janneteau, "President's Message," *Laurentiana* (1963), 23. *Laurentiana* ceased publication between 1971 and 1982.

10 Catherine Gidney, *A Long Eclipse: The Liberal Protestant Establishment and the Canadian University, 1920–1970* (Montreal & Kingston: McGill-Queen's University Press, 2004), 26–47.

11 LUA, F48, 1, Extension Box 8, Minutes of Faculty Council, October 16, 1962. For a discussion of Fr. Bouvier's presidency, see the chapter by Matt Bray on university governance from 1960 to 1972.

12 *Sudbury Star*, May 16, 1962.

13 W.G. Fleming, *Post-secondary and Adult Education* (Toronto: University of Toronto Press, 1971), 389.

14 "Laurentian is a man's world in a four-to-one proportion!" *Sudbury Star*, September 30, 1966.

15 "Message of the President," *Laurentian Gazette*, December 15, 1960.

16 See, for example, *Lambda*, October 4, 1968; *Lambda*, January 17, 1969; *Le Lambda*, March 7, 1969.

17 "Results of the sex survey," *Lambda*, November–December 1963.

18 "Wide choice of activities offered students," *Sudbury Star*, February 28, 1963; LUA, Athletics Scrapbooks, I22, 2, Varsity Sports, 1981–1982, "What's in a name," n.d.

19 "The downtown university," *Globe and Mail*, March 23, 1964.

20 "Laurentian pays tribute to top athletes, choose nickname for school's sports teams," *Sudbury Star*, March 21, 1964; "Now is the time for all to offer good names for Laurentian teams," *Sudbury Star*, March 19, 1963; Robert Evans column, *Sudbury Star*, April 8, 1963; "Laurentian sport notes," *Sudbury Star*, April 2, 1965; LUA, Athletics Scrapbooks, I22, 2, Varsity Sports, 1981–1982, "What's in a name," n.d.

21 "Pool at Laurentian completed, can be used for competitions," *Sudbury Star*, March 15, 1972.

22 "Laurentian sport notes," *Sudbury Star*, November 1, 1963; LUA, Athletics Scrapbooks, I22, 1, Alumni Scrapbook, "Laurentian Sport Notes," n.d.

23 Laurentian Athletics Marketing and Communications Department, "Laurentian Athletics: Voyageurs and Lady Vees History," June 3, 2009; LUA, Athletic Scrapbooks, I23, 1, Voyageur High Lights, 1983–1984, "A Retrospective Look at Voyageur Soccer," n.d.; LUA, Athletic Scrapbooks, I22, 1, Varsity Sports, 1977–1978, "Soccer," n.d.

24 "Wide choice of activities offered students," *Sudbury Star*, February 28, 1963; "A U. of S. student's impression of Huntington," *Lambda*, December 14, 1962; "Dieu la sauve," *Lambda*, November 16, 1962.

25 Bob O'Riordan, "The new Laurentian," *Lambda*, January 1964.

26 LUA, LU History Project File: SGA/AGE, History of the Students' General Association: The Years 1960 until 1998, n.d.; "S.G.A. announce new policies and new décor for student lounges," *Lambda*, October 22, 1969.

27 "New Laurentian campus now overrun by frosh," *Lambda*, October 1964; "Laurentian enrolment up 60 per cent," *Sudbury Star*, October 23, 1965.

28 "Cafeteria prices not too high," *Lambda*, November 6, 1964.

29 "Tempest in the dining room over heavy meals, light lunches," *Sudbury Star*, March 25, 1966; "Laurentian students boycott dining hall," *Sudbury Star*, February 5, 1968. For the ongoing debates over the quality of food services, see, for example, "Changes in food services start this week," *Lambda*, February 6, 1973; "Petition for replacing Saga," *Lambda*, October 6, 1982; "Saga should be replaced," *Lambda*, March 6, 1986; "Students dying over rising price of grease at the cafeteria," *Lambda*, January 28, 1993.

30 "Frocked and feathered 'lowly frosh' in for week of misery at Laurentian," *Sudbury Star*, September 17, 1966.

31 "Laurentian queen crowning and kangaroo court," *Sudbury Star*, October 3, 1964; "Laurentian frosh play role of garbage collectors," *Sudbury Star*, September 21, 1965; "Shoe shine duty for Laurentian frosh," *Sudbury Star*, September 22, 1965; "Laurentian picks homecoming queen," *Sudbury Star*, November 5, 1966; "L.U. homecoming queen crowned!!!" *Lambda*, November 1966; "All freshmen beware this is antic week for Laurentian frosh," *Sudbury Star*, September 18, 1967; "It's dresses for all during frosh week," *Sudbury Star*, September 16, 1969; "Ku klux klangaroos kastigated?" *Lambda*, September 24, 1969.

32 "Welcomes 'frosh' class to Laurentian," *Sudbury Star*, September 7, 1969; "Residence rules offer diversity," *Lambda*, October 24, 1972.

33 LUA, LU History Project File: Student Affairs – Residence, Visiting Privileges in Men's and Women's Residences of Huntington College, n.d.

34 LUA, Huntington, V, 3, Buildings – Residences Women 1964–65.

35 "University ruling stays, new meeting March 27," *Sudbury Star*, March 13, 1969.

36 "Les cartes d'identité," *Lambda*, November 16, 1962; "La fondation de l'AECFNO," *Lambda*, March 1964; "Émission bilingue de L'U. Laurentienne à CKSO," *Le Lambda*, April 26, 1966.

37 Board Minutes, July 9, 1965, Report of the Special Committee.

38 "The Français-Anglais split at Laurentian," *Lambda*, December 14, 1962.

39 "J'accuse l'administration," *Le Lambda*, April 26, 1966; "In memoriam: le caractère bilinque de l'Université Laurentienne," *Le Lambda*, December 1967.

40 "Bilingualism's prospects are dim at Laurentian," *Lambda*, March 11, 1966; "Will French-English be reconciled?" *Lambda*, February 18, 1965.

41 "Laurentian students are ostriches," *Lambda*, February 18, 1965. A rare exception for this period is "Why are we in Vietnam?" *Lambda*, February 26, 1966.

42 "Dieu la sauve," *Lambda*, November 16, 1962.

43 LUA, 62, 1, Memos to Chairmen and Faculty, 1963–1968, J.D. Lamont to faculty, n.d.

44 "Nag's Head issue pushed," *Lambda*, October 27, 1967; "Students campaign for campus pub," *Sudbury Star*, October 27, 1967; "Over 500 march for pub," *Lambda*, November 3, 1967; "Nag's Head," *Lambda*, November 17, 1967.

45 Roberta Lexier, "'The Backdrop Against Which Everything Happened': English-Canadian Student Movements and Off-Campus Movements for Change," *History of Intellectual Cul-*

ture 7, 1 (2007): 1–18; Doug Owram, "Youth Radicalism in the Sixties," *Born at the Right Time: A History of the Baby Boom Generation* (Toronto: University of Toronto Press, 1996), 216–47; Catherine Gidney, "War and the Concept of Generation: The International Teach-Ins at the University of Toronto, 1965–1968," in Paul Stortz and E. Lisa Panayotidis, eds, *Universities and War: Histories of Academic Cultures and Conflict* (Toronto: University of Toronto Press, forthcoming).

46 In her examination of the governance issue in the student movements at the Regina Campus of the University of Saskatchewan, the University of Toronto, and Simon Fraser University, Roberta Lexier argues that faculty tended to support students' demands for participation but drew the line at equal representation. Lexier, "The Community of Scholars: The English-Canadian Student Movement and University Governance," in Marie Hammond-Callaghan and Matthew Hayday, eds, *Mobilizations, Protests and Engagements: Canadian Perspectives on Social Movements* (Halifax: Fernwood Publishing, 2008), 125–44.

47 LUA, F55, 1, Thorneloe University Students' Association, *The Thorne*, Etienne St-Aubin, "S.G.A. Presidential Report," n.d.

48 AO, RG32, 1, 1, Acc.13856, box M297, Laurentian University, Legislation, 1967, Memorandum from the SGA, March 21, 1968.

49 LUA, F55, 1, Thorneloe University Students' Association, *The Thorne*, "Presidential Interview," n.d.

50 Board Minutes, October 27, 1967; AO, RG32, 1, 1, Acc.13856, box M297, Laurentian University, Legislation, 1967, E.E. Stewart to W.C. Alcombrack, n.d.; AO, RG32, 1, 1, Acc.13856, box M297, Drafts of the Amended *Laurentian University of Sudbury Act*, October 5, 1967 and 1968; AO, RG32, 1, 1, Acc.13856, box M297, E.E. Stewart to Minister, March 22, 1968.

51 Arthur Marwick, *The Sixties: Cultural Revolution in Britain, France, Italy, and the United States, c.1958–c.1974* (Oxford: Oxford University Press, 1998), 584–675; Steve Hewitt, *Spying 101: The RCMP's Secret Activities at Canadian Universities, 1917–1997* (Toronto: University of Toronto Press, 2002), 146–52, 163–4; Hugh Johnston, *Radical Campus: Making Simon Fraser University* (Vancouver: Douglas & McIntyre, 2005), 282–92; James M. Pitsula, *New World Dawning: The Sixties at Regina Campus* (Regina: Canadian Plains Research Centre, 2008), 240–82; James M. Pitsula, *As One Who Serves: The Making of the University of Regina* (Montreal & Kingston: McGill-Queen's University Press, 2006), 318–28; Jean-Philippe Warren et Julien Massicotte, "La fermeture du departement de sociologie de l'Université de Moncton: histoire d'une crise politico-épistémologique," *Canadian Historical Review* 87, 3 (September 2006): 463–96; Joel Belliveau, "Moncton's Student Protest Wave of 1968: Local Issues, Global Currents and the Birth of Acadian Neo-Nationalism," paper presented at the Canadian Historical Association Annual Meeting, Vancouver, BC, June 2008; Cyril Levitt, *Children of Privilege: Student Revolt in the Sixties: A Study of Student Movements in Canada, the United States, and West Germany* (Toronto: University of Toronto Press, 1984), 72; François Ricard, *The Lyric Generation: The Life and Times of the Baby Boomers*, trans. Donald Winkler (Toronto: Stoddart, 1994), 111–27. Rebecca E. Klatch explores the theory that during periods of rapid social change, such as the sixties, separate and often antagonistic groups exist within the same generation. Rebecca E. Klatch, *A Generation Divided: The New Left, and New Right, and the 1960s* (Berkeley: University of California Press, 1999), 1–16.

52 Neil Compton, "Sir George Williams Loses Its Innocence," *Canadian Forum* (April 1969), reprinted in Tim and Julyan Reid, eds, *Student Power and the Canadian Campus* (Toronto: Peter Martin, 1969), 31–6; Hewitt, *Spying 101*, 163–4; Johnston, *Radical Campus*, 282–92; Pitsula, *As One Who Serves*, 318–28; Belliveau, "Moncton's Student Protest Wave of 1968."

53 "Ottawa U holds out," *Lambda*, November 15, 1968; "RCMP arrest SFU demonstrations," *Lambda*, November 29, 1968; "Censorship in Saskatchewan," *Lambda*, January 17, 1969; "Crise à Moncton!" *Le Lambda*, January 24, 1969.

54 Patricia Jasen has pointed out the contradiction inherent to the rhetoric of the student movement, which attempted to reconcile an emphasis on individual freedom with an ideology of collective social change. Patricia Jasen, "'In Pursuit of Human Values (or Laugh When You Say That)': The Student Critique of the Arts Curriculum in the 1960s," in Paul Axelrod and John G. Reid, eds, *Youth, University, and Canadian Society: Essays in the Social History of Higher Education* (Montreal & Kingston: McGill-Queen's University Press, 1989), 263.

55 *Lambda*, September 24, 1968.

56 "Laurentian 'student power,'" *Sudbury Star*, October 2, 1968.

57 LUA, LU History Project File: SGA/AGE, Wesley Cragg Papers, Etienne St-Aubin to Faculty, n.d.

58 "This university belongs to the student!" *Lambda*, November 15, 1968. In October 1968, the student newspaper at Saskatchewan's Regina campus, the *Carillon*, had printed the same inflammatory headline (without, of course, the subsequent reference to Mullins). Pitsula, *As One Who Serves*, 322.

59 "Mythe ou réalité?" *Le Lambda*, October 25, 1968; "Students request changes to restore 'lost bilingualism' at Laurentian," *Sudbury Star*, October 19, 1968.

60 Etienne St-Aubin, letter to the editor, *Lambda*, November 1, 1968.

61 LUA, LU History Project File: Bilingualism, Wesley Cragg Papers, Minutes of SGA Council, November 6, 1968.

62 "Victoire de l'exécutif de l'A.G.E. – 6 étudiants au sénat," *Le Lambda*, December 6, 1968; Laurentian University, Senate Minutes, v. 9, December 12, 1968.

63 "'The Quiet Revolution' – the S.G.A.L.U.," *Lambda*, February 28, 1969.

64 "President's brief runs into snag at Laurentian U.," *Sudbury Star*, October 18, 1969; "Teach-in today!" *Lambda*, October 20, 1969; "Laurentian head under fire from students, faculty," *Sudbury Star*, October 20, 1969; "Teach-in turns on over 1200," *Lambda*, October 22, 1969.

65 "Students, governors clash at Laurentian," *Sudbury Star*, October 31, 1969.

66 "Students get non-voting seats on board at Laurentian U.," *Sudbury Star*, November 1, 1969; "Students confront reluctant board," *Lambda*, November 5, 1969.

67 "Mullins to leave Laurentian," *Lambda*, March 19, 1970; "Laurentian's President Mullins ready to seek sabbatical leave," *Sudbury Star*, March 14, 1970.

68 Board Minutes, April 9, 1970.

69 "2-year leave for Laurentian head rejected," *Sudbury Star*, March 19, 1970; "Laurentian SGA calls meeting," *Sudbury Star*, March 31, 1970; "Senate and board clash over presidency," *Lambda*, March 31, 1970.

70 Ibid.

71 AO, RG32, 1, 1, Acc.18006, box M382, General Correspondence, 1970, Victor Cormier to Sirs, March 23, 1970.

72 "Laurentian Senate allied with students on sit-in," *Globe and Mail*, April 3, 1970; "Students' sit-in continues," *Sudbury Star*, April 2, 1970.

73 "Laurentian Senate allied with students on sit-in," *Globe and Mail*, April 3, 1970.

74 "Laurentian board, Senate agree to meet," *Globe and Mail*, April 6, 1970.

75 "Laurentian impasse continues; await governors' reply," *Sudbury Star*, April 3, 1970; "Laurentian governors will meet Senate, but sit-in continues," *Sudbury Star*, April 6, 1970; "Laurentian board, Senate agree to meet," *Globe and Mail*, April 6, 1970; "Laurentian Senate

discusses 'details' for joint meeting," *Sudbury Star*, April 7, 1970; "Laurentian future on the line," *Sudbury Star*, April 9, 1970; "Decision-making power increased in historic talks," *Sudbury Star*, April 10, 1970.

76 *Sudbury Star*, October 10, 1970. While local police did not intervene, it should be noted that the RCMP closely monitored student activities at Laurentian, a practice the force maintained on other Canadian campuses during this period. Clint MacNeil, "RCMP Surveillance of Laurentian University, 1962–1978," BA honours thesis (history), Laurentian University, 1998.

77 "Senate studies meeting results," *Sudbury Star*, April 10, 1970.

78 "Freshmen are welcomed to Laurentian," *Sudbury Star*, September 14, 1970.

79 Laurentian University, Board of Governors Minutes, September 25, 1970; Senate Minutes, September 28, 1970; "Senate censures B.O.G. executive committee," *Lambda*, September 24, 1970; "Support your Senate, back student demands, liberate your university," *Lambda* September 29, 1970.

80 *Sudbury Star*, October 1, 1970; October 6, 1970; "LU students picket at Queen's Park," *Lambda*, October 8, 1970; AO, RG3, 26, Office of the Premier, Robarts: Correspondence, box 426, file – Laurentian University, January–December 1969, Brief from SGA to Ontario Legislature, October 6, 1970.

81 Senate Minutes, October 8, 1970.

82 AO, RG32, 1, 1, Acc.18006, box M382, file – Laurentian University Faculty Association, 1970, Note of Senate Minutes, October 8, 1970; AO RG32, 1, 1, Acc.18006, box M382, file – Laurentian University Faculty Association, 1970, William Davis to J.G. Hagey, October 27, 1970.

83 UWL, Doris Lewis Rare Book Room, Office of the President, A79-0030, 231, J.G. Hagey, Memorandum to Laurentian University Board, Senate, Faculty, Staff and Students, November 3, 1970; LUA, I36, 3, Vice-President Executive, Laurentian University Faculty Association Consultation with Dr. J.G. Hagey, November 10, 1970; LUA, I36, 3, Vice-President Executive, Meeting of Dr. Hagey and Student General Association, November 11, 1970; Laurentian University, Senate Correspondence, 1970–1971, J.G. Hagey, Laurentian University of Sudbury, Report to Senate, November 19, 1970; UWL, Doris Lewis Rare Book Room, Office of the President, A79-0030/231, Report by Dr. J.G. Hagey to the Senate and to the Board of Governors, Laurentian University, December 10, 1970; LUA, F65, 1, J.G. Hagey, "Consultant's Report to Laurentian University;" Laurentian University, Senate Minutes, March 25, 1971.

84 "Dedication," *Slag* (1971), 156.

Chapter Nine

1 "Us – Them. We know who we are ... but who are they?" *Lambda*, September 29, 1970.

2 Gidney, *A Long Eclipse*, 112–24.

3 "*Lambda* editors niggers – damn right!" *Lambda*, February 9, 1968.

4 For an interesting discussion of the impact of counter-culture attitudes on undergraduate activities, see Charles Levi, "Sex, Drugs, Rock & Roll, and the University College Lit: The University of Toronto Festivals, 1965–69," *Historical Studies in Education* 18, 2 (2006): 163–90.

5 Board Minutes, May 31, 1968. One of the more arresting images from the *Lambda* issue of 1970 is an explicit, full-page drawing of a naked man and women having sex. *Lambda*, January 29, 1970.

6 "RCMP to probe drug smokers at Laurentian U," *Sudbury Star*, February 10, 1967. During the 1960s, the Yorkville district of Toronto became a centre for the youth counter-culture. See Stuart Henderson, "Toronto's Hippie Disease: End Days in the Yorkville Scene, August 1968," *Journal of the Canadian Historical Association*, New Series, 17, 1 (2006): 205–34.

7 "Don't bogart that joint my friend," *Lambda*, January 26, 1976.

8 Blair Neatby and Don McEown, *Creating Carleton: The Shaping of a University* (Montreal & Kingston: McGill-Queen's University Press, 2002), 186–8; "Asks Laurentian removal of student conduct rule," *Sudbury Star*, March 17, 1972.

9 "Sudbury University's eviction plans bring protest," *Sudbury Star*, March 16, 1972; "Threat of court eviction irks Laurentian Senate," *Sudbury Star*, March 17, 1972; "U. of S. is unfair to students, caused protest," *Lambda*, March 21, 1972.

10 LUA, F70, 1, Dean of Science, Report of the Executive Committee to Senate, February 14, 1974.

11 "Student Street, Married and Single Student," *Lambda*, September 25, 1973.

12 "Residence students gain new rights," *Lambda*, February 28, 1980.

13 "Ku klux klangaroos kastigated?" *Lambda*, September 24, 1969.

14 "Freshmen are welcomed to Laurentian," *Sudbury Star*, September 14, 1970. The great exception to this new policy are the initiation ceremonies sponsored by the Engineering Society, which still maintains its tradition of dying incoming students purple. See, for example, "Purple people everywhere!!!" *Lambda*, September 30, 1999.

15 "Mr and Ms Carnival," *Lambda*, January 30, 1973.

16 "We got it!!" *Lambda*, October 27, 1986.

17 "2 student senators resign posts," *Lambda*, November 9, 1971; "Committees require students," *Lambda*, October 24, 1972; "SGA/AGE welcome," *Lambda*, September 6, 1974.

18 "Report depicts dismal picture," *Sudbury Star*, October 20, 1975.

19 Alvin Finkel, *Our Lives: Canada after 1945* (Toronto: James Lorimer, 1997), 127–9.

20 LUA, Senate Correspondence, 1978–1979, Martin Purvis to Secretary of Senate, November 8, 1978; "Women's liberation," *Lambda*, November 1969; "Native students club," *Lambda*, November 20, 1973; "International students," *Lambda*, October 2, 1973.

21 "Council accepts executive budget," *Lambda*, October 3, 1972; "The shit has hit the fan," *Lambda*, December 5, 1972.

22 "Open letter," *Lambda*, October 23, 1973; "Acclamations cancel election at Laurentian," *Sudbury Star*, October 31, 1974; "Message du président de l'A.E.F.," *l'Orignal déchaîné*, September 14, 1987. For the creation of the flag, see Stéphanie St-Pierre, "Le drapeau franco-ontarien: 'Puissent ses couleurs nous rallier dans une nouvelle amitié et fraternité,' 1975–1977," in Guy Gaudreau, ed., *Le drapeau franco-ontarien* (Sudbury: Prise de parole, 2005), 13–42.

23 "Senate fucks Francophones," *Lambda*, November 20, 1973; "Que faire? Laisse choir," *Lambda*, November 16, 1976; "The university – pour qui?" *Lambda*, February 2, 1978; LUA, Senate Briefs, June 1975–May 1976, "Manifeste de l'A.E.F. au sujet du bilinguisme," n.d.

24 LUA, Senate Correspondence, 1978–1979, Secretary to Senate to Martin Purvis, November 8, 1978; "Un senator pour les francophones," *Lambda*, February 17, 1976; "SGA and AEF agree on pub renovations," *Lambda*, January 13, 1976.

25 "A.E.F. stalks third floor space," *Lambda*, December 6, 1978; "Students disrupt elevator use at Laurentian," *Sudbury Star*, February 15, 1979.

26 "Asking for the third floor is nothing short of foolish," *Lambda*, February 28, 1979.

27 "Rules out further student occupation of university floors," *Sudbury Star*, 17 February 1979; "AEF confronts admin for 3rd floor space," *Lambda*, February 28, 1979; "Occupation celebration: AEF wins 3rd floor," *Lambda*, April 4, 1979.

28 "Laurentian bilingualism cited as victor in issue," *Sudbury Star*, March 5, 1979.

29 "Pourquoi une université francophone?" *Réaction* (February 1980); "Money exists for northern French university," *Northern Life*, February 27, 1980; "A new French university," *Sault Star*, February 28, 1980; "French university groundwork being laid at Laurentian," *Sudbury Star*, July 16, 1980; "SGA defeats motion supporting Francophone university," *Lambda*, November 19, 1991.

30 Arthur J. Ray, *I Have Lived Here Since the World Began* (Toronto: Key Porter Books, 1996), 313–37.

31 City of Greater Sudbury Archives, Bob Keir fonds, photos: "Ojibway Indians take Extension Course through LU, March 7, 1962," 62, 3, 175 and 62, 3, 183; "Dr. Newbery: professor emeritus," *Sudbury Star*, May 31, 1979.

32 *Living and Learning: The Report of the Provincial Committee on Aims and Objectives of Education in the Schools of Ontario* (Hall-Dennis report) (Toronto: Ontario Department of Education, 1968), 111–13, 190; R.D. Gidney, *From Hope to Harris: The Reshaping of Ontario's Schools* (Toronto: University of Toronto Press, 1999), 151–2; "Laurentian site for Indian studies institute possible," *Sudbury Star*, June 12, 1968.

33 "Propose Indian studies department at Laurentian," *Sudbury Star*, May 13, 1968; "Will use tape recorders to preserve Indian culture," September 9, 1970.

34 "Indian-Eskimo studies may get large grant," *Lambda*, January 11, 1972; "Laurentian gets $17,000 for Amerindian studies," *Sudbury Star*, May 22, 1973.

35 "Native studies awarded $75,000," *Northern Life*, March 26, 1980.

36 "Native students club," *Lambda*, November 20, 1973; *Lambda*, March 23, 1975.

37 "Western co-eds woo the pill," *Lambda*, January 24, 1967.

38 "Women's liberation," *Lambda*, November 1969.

39 "Proposed women's centre endorsed," *Lambda*, March 23, 1982; "Sexual harassment can be handled," *Lambda*, September 29, 1982; Special Issue on International Women's Day, *Lambda*, March 8, 1984; "Who needs the women's centre? We do," *Lambda*, October 3, 1985; "Laurentian University women's centre," *Lambda*, July 28, 1994.

40 Anne Perdue, "Out and Proud," *U of T Magazine* (Summer 2009): 39–44; Gary Kinsman, *The Regulation of Desire: Homo and Hetero Sexualities* (Montreal: Black Rose Books, 1996).

41 "York holding a conference," *Lambda*, January 11, 1972.

42 "Gay liberation surfaces briefly at college campus," *Sudbury Star*, June 6, 1977.

43 "From the editor's pen," *Lambda*, March 9, 1983; "It's definitely not 'gai' Quebec," *Lambda*, March 3, 1983. For other articles dealing with gender issues, see, for example, "Time to face female facts," *Lambda*, January 25, 1983; "Ottawa women fight to destroy pornography," *Lambda*, March 30, 1983; "Male bias in student security hiring province-wide," *Lambda*, October 6, 1983.

44 "Confront homophobia," *Lambda*, February 14, 1985; Lesbian and Gay Issue, *Lambda*, February 13, 1986; "Le malheur d'etre gai," *l'Orignal déchaîné*, February 9, 1988.

45 "LU should keep open mind," *Lambda*, March 21, 1991; "Out and about," *Lambda*, November 25, 1993; "Stopping the madness: where to begin," *Lambda*, January 27, 1994; "Speaking out," *Lambda*, October 20, 1994; "Jeans Day Thursday, March 16th," *Lambda*, March 2, 1995.

46 LUA, LU History Project File: Student Issues, *Gay and Lesbian News*, November 23, 1995.

47 LUA, Senate Briefs, Summary of report on shortfall of registration, December 15, 1971; "Report depicts dismal picture," *Sudbury Star*, October 20, 1975; LUA, Appendix: Laurentian University Enrolment of full-time students, 1960–1985, in Gwenda Hallsworth, *Le beau risque du savoir: Un bref historique de l'Université Laurentienne / A venture into the realm of higher education: A brief history of Laurentian University*, 39.

48 "Laurentian students critical of five-year building plan," *Sudbury Star*, July 15, 1970.

49 "New campus shop," *Lambda*, September 1971; "Laurentian pub opens, permanency is urged," *Sudbury Star*, September 16, 1971.

50 "Pub loses $, store makes $," *Lambda*, December 14, 1971; "Council accepts executive budget," *Lambda*, October 3, 1972; "Students to get control of campus pub," *Sudbury Star*, January 13, 1975.

51 "Student Street," *Lambda*, October 2, 1973.

52 "Laurentian fund," *Lambda*, September 15, 1982; "The Laurentian farce fund," *Lambda*, December 5, 1985.

53 "Sees sports connecting link for community, university," *Sudbury Star*, March 11, 1971.

54 Laurentian Athletics Marketing and Communications Department, "Laurentian Athletics: Voyageurs and Lady Vees History," June 3, 2009.

55 "Soccer Vees win Canadian college championship," *Lambda*, November 16, 1972.

56 "Vees thank all," *Lambda*, November 17, 1981.

57 "All about the '95 hall inductees," *Lambda*, October 26, 1995.

58 "Laurentian – building a winning tradition," *Lambda*, February 23, 1982.

59 M. Ann Hall, "Creators of the Lost and Perfect Game? Gender, History, and Canadian Sport," in Philip White and Devin Young, eds, *Sport and Gender in Canada* (Don Mills: Oxford University Press, 1999), 5–23.

60 LUA, Athletic Scrapbooks, 124, 1, Women's Volleyball, 1967–1982, "Girls Sports," n.d.; LUA, Athletics Scrapbooks, 123, 1, "Laurentian Voyageur, 1988–1989," n.d.; Amanda N. Schweinbenz, "An Examination of the History of Women's Intercollegiate Athletics at Laurentian University," paper presented at the Canadian History of Education Association 15th Biennial Conference, Sudbury, Ontario, October 2008.

61 "Economic restraint blamed for lack of women athletes," *Sudbury Star*, March 7, 1972.

62 LUA, Athletic Scrapbooks, 123, 1, Laurentian Voyageur, 1988–1989, "Equality in athletics at Laurentian University," n.d.

63 Laurentian Athletics Marketing and Communications Department, "Laurentian Athletics: Voyageurs and Lady Vees History," June 3, 2009.

64 LUA, Athletic Scrapbooks, 122, 1, The Bronze Baby, 1975–1979, "The Bronze Baby," n.d.

65 "University replies to U of T claims," *Sudbury Star*, January 20, 1977.

66 "Laurentian women's team takes 4th basketball title," *Sudbury Star*, March 6, 1978.

67 Laurentian University, Senate Briefs, "Statement on Interuniversity Athletics, Laurentian University," June 1986.

68 "Pool at Laurentian completed, can be used for competitions," *Sudbury Star*, March 15, 1972; "Swim club celebrates milestone," *Northern Life*, April 28, 1983; LUA, Athletic Scrapbooks, 123, 1, "Varsity Sports, 1984–1985," "Baumann puts school first despite top athlete status," n.d.; LUA, Athletic Scrapbooks, 123, 1, "Varsity Hi-Lites, 1986–1987," "CIAU Record," n.d.

69 "World-famed athletes training here," *Sudbury Star*, July 13, 1976; "First-class track sold East Germans on using Sudbury for last-minute drills," *Globe and Mail*, July 21, 1976; "Summer Games start Friday," *Northern Life*, August 31, 1983; "Dream became reality," *Sudbury Star*, August 2, 1988; "CIAU '89," *Lambda*, March 3, 1989.

70 "Referendum results mediocre," *Lambda*, October 17, 1972; "Council kills trust fund," *Lambda*, December 12, 1972; "Withhold your fees," *Lambda*, January 9, 1973; "Laurentian sit-in blocks elevator," *Sudbury Star*, January 19, 1973; "Moratorium this Wednesday," *Lambda*, January 23, 1973; "Student rally to mobilize support for the boycott of classes," *Lambda*, January, 1976.

71 LUA, LU History Project File: Student Issues, Richard Hoffman to Laurentian Faculty, February 7, 1977.
72 "Students confront Parrott," *Sudbury Star*, October 5, 1977; "L.U. boycott most successful in Ontario," *Lambda*, February 15, 1977; "Editorial: We need NUS for many reasons," *Lambda*, October 11, 1978; "Councilor defends SGA price," *Lambda*, January 17, 1979; "Les étudiants "confrontent" les gouverneurs," *Réaction* (March–April 1980); "Second annual tower occupation," *Lambda*, March 13, 1980; "Second Francophone association joins OFS," *Lambda*, February 6, 1986.

Chapter Ten

1   "The student movement?" *Lambda*, September 22, 1986.
2   "SGA responds to criticism," *Lambda*, February 13, 1992.
3   "To every Laurentian student," *Lambda*, September 26, 1985; "Amnesty International," *Lambda*, October 19, 1987; "HIV and AIDS: Let's talk, before it's too late!" *Lambda*, October 13, 1989; "AIDS Awareness Week," *Lambda*, October 18, 1990; "Refugee sponsorship at Laurentian," *Lambda*, November 6, 1997. For a discussion of student apathy, see "Frankly, my dear, I don't give a damn!" *Lambda*, November 9, 1987.
4   "Profs on strike, education on hold," "Do it for yourself, support the strike," "Letters to the editor," *Lambda*, September 12, 1985.
5   "Students' opinion of the LUSA strike," *Lambda*, November, [date?] 1985; "SGA goes neutral," and "LUSA settles, dispute resolved," *Lambda*, November 28, 1985.
6   "LUFA strikes, students angry," *Lambda*, September 14, 1989; "Rally at Laurentian," *Lambda*, September 21, 1989; "Students rally again," *Lambda*, September 28, 1989.
7   "Laurentian library losing ground," *Lambda*, September 12, 1985; "Laurentian University launches construction of new computer and reading room," *Lambda*, July/August 2000.
8   "Campus centre not a priority: Daniel," *Lambda*, April 8, 1986; "The progress so far ...," *Lambda*, March 23, 1987; "Students vote in referendum to pay more for bigger centre," *Sudbury Star*, November 18, 1989; "The student centre," *Lambda*, August 3, 1993.
9   See Matt Bray, chapter 5, University Governance: The Modern Age, 1985 to the Present," pp. 77–97.
10 "Villefranche ... the scoop," *Lambda*, February 23, 1987; "Villefranche: No good for 99.77% of us," *Lambda*, March 2, 1987.
11 "UCF: Université Canadienne en France," *Lambda*, November 22, 1990. See also, "The case against UCF," *Lambda*, February 7, 1991; "Renewed calls for an end to UCF," *Lambda*, January 9, 1992.
12 "Laurentian lifestyle: A report of a survey conducted at Ontario universities," *Lambda*, November 10, 1988.
13 "National Alcohol Awareness Week," *Lambda*, October 21, 1999.
14 "Coordinator of student services appointed," *Lambda*, October 3, 1985; "Clubs and societies: Any ideas?" *Lambda*, December 5, 1985.
15 "Residence problems," *Lambda*, October [date?] 1985. See also, "Vandalism in residence," *Lambda*, January 13, 1989; "A quick break," *Lambda*, October 26, 1989.
16 "CAPE: Implementing it at Laurentian," *Lambda*, March 25, 1986; "CAPE: Setting the record straight," *Lambda*, September 22, 1986; "CAPE should return to drawing board," *Lambda*, December 1, 1986.
17 "Council on student life filling positions," *Lambda*, November 18, 1987; "Message: 'Drink responsibly,'" *Lambda*, October 28, 1993; "Blenkinsop trying to get council on student life

committees working," *Lambda*, February 11, 1988; "The student centre," *Lambda*, August 3, 1993.

18 "Bureaucratic shakeup leaves Paddy in the fray," *Lambda*, September 22, 1994; "New code of student conduct to be adopted by LU's student affairs," *Lambda*, September 11, 1997; "Notes from the file," *Lambda*, November 20, 1997.

19 "Smoke signals," *Lambda*, November 2, 2000.

20 "Nishnawbe news," *Lambda*, September 27, 1984.

21 "Native Students' Association hosts special events," *Lambda*, October 3, 1985; "SGA/AEF '87 elections," *Lambda*, March 16, 1987; "Need for a national Native students' association," *Lambda*, November 18, 1987; "Rebuilding Our Nations conference at LU," *Lambda*, November 15, 1990; "Native culture," *Lambda*, February 13, 1992.

22 "What is the Indian way? What do we want?" *Lambda*, October 1, 1992.

23 Laurentian University, Senate Briefs, "Report to Senate, Laurentian University Native Educational Council," September 1992; "Laurentian University Native Education Council (LUNEC) Mandate and Terms of Reference," September 1993.

24 "Native Studies Students' Association presents," *Lambda*, March 22, 1990; "Laurentian Native Studies Students' Association presents," *Lambda*, October 29, 1992; "Native Awareness Week," *Lambda*, October 5, 1995; "Native Students' Association orientation events," *Lambda*, Summer 1996; "Resistance and a common vision," *Lambda*, November 6, 1997; "Notes from the file," *Lambda*, January 15, 1998; "Native Awareness Week commencement," *Lambda*, November 4, 1999.

25 "Who is an Indian?" *Lambda*, October 26, 1995.

26 LUA, G7, 3, Science and Engineering Executive Council, Reid Keays to Science Chairmen, Director of School of Engineering, Vice-Deans, May 4, 1995; Laurentian University, Office of the Registrar, Statistical Report on Enrolment and Admissions, 1986–1998.

27 "To see ourselves – survey of Laurentian's first year students," *Lambda*, February 2, 1989.

28 See, for example, "OFS Week of Action," *Lambda*, March 11, 1988; "Students hit the streets across Canada," *Lambda*, February 5, 1998.

29 See, for example, "Constitutional and bylaw revisions" and "The bilingual week of action," *Lambda*, February 9, 1989.

30 LUA, LU History Project File: Student Organizations, Heather Bishop to Jack Porter, May 10, 1994; LUA, LU History Project File: Student Organizations, Jon Gonder to Members of Senate, January 16, 1995; "Students protest potential funding changes," *Laurentian University Gazette*, February 10, 1995.

31 "Student strike: Whoops or wow … whatever," *Lambda*, February 2, 1995.

32 "Cross country running team: Best in a decade," *Lambda*, October 10, 1991; "Yes Laurentian, you DO have a field hockey team," *Lambda*, November 19, 1991; "LU makes decisions on future of athletics programs," *Laurentian University Gazette*, May 7, 1993.

33 "LU's ski program dropped," *Sudbury Star*, September 21, 1989.

34 LUA, Athletic Scrapbooks, 123, 2, Voyageur, 1992–1993, "Advisory council report to address future of varsity sports at Laurentian," n.d.; "Investing in Varsity Athletics," *Laurentian University Gazette*, February 10, 1995; "The scandal at the athletic department: negligence and extreme prejudice," *Lambda*, February 11, 1993; "Restructuring of Laurentian University's department of interuniversity athletics," *Lambda*, July/August 2000. For criticism that the men's hockey team lacked support from students and received little coverage in the student newspapers, see, LUA, Athletic Scrapbooks, 123, 2, Voyageur Athletics, 1995–1996, "In need of hockey fans," n.d.; "Enough is enough," *Lambda*, November 19, 1992; "Hockey Vee fan," *Lambda*, December 10, 1992; "The reasons for the varsity sport cuts," *Lambda*, November 2, 2000.

35 LUA, Athletic Scrapbooks, 123, 2, Voyageur, 1991–1992, "Laurentian makes history by capturing both the OUAA and OUWAA Nordic ski titles," n.d.; "Laurentian's best kept secret," *Lambda*, September 12, 1991; Laurentian Athletics Marketing and Communications Department, "Laurentian Athletics: Voyageurs and Lady Vees History," June 3, 2009.

36 "Laurentian captures Wilson Cup by defeating McMaster," *Lambda*, March 16, 2000.

37 Letter to Peter and Co., *Lambda*, March 21, 1991.

38 Laurentian University, Office of the Registrar, Statistical Report on Enrolment and Admissions, 1986–1998; Facts and Figures, Institutional Research Office. 1999; Institutional Research Office, Datamart, 2000–2007.

39 Ontario Ministry of Training, Colleges and Universities, "2006–07 Multi-Year Accountability Agreement Report-Back For: Laurentian," 3.

40 "The student centre," *Lambda*, September 3, 1995.

Chapter Eleven

1 Gaétan Gervais, "L'enseignement supérieur en Ontario français (1848–1965)," *Revue du Nouvel-Ontario* 7 (1985): 43.

2 The battle for French-language instruction in the department of commerce at Laurentian, discussed in the second part of this article, is quite revealing on this point.

3 Board Minutes, September 10, 1960, 76.

4 Charles Dubé had been sent away to Gravelbourg, Saskatchewan, for having fought against a bilingual university. On the topic of the ACFEO, the Jesuits and Laurentian University, see Pierre Ouellette, "Éducation et économie, 1927–1965," in Guy Gaudreau, ed., *Bâtir sur le roc: De l'ACFÉO à l'ACFO du Grand Sudbury (1910–1987)* (Sudbury: Prise de parole, 1994), 80–8.

5 Donald Dennie, "Historique du bilinguisme à l'Université Laurentienne: 1960 à 1985," April 1986 (hereafter the Dennie report). See also his research notes: "Historique du bilinguisme à l'Université Laurentienne," *Revue du Nouvel-Ontario* 7 (1985): 115–18.

6 *Annuaire de l'Université Laurentienne*, 1964–1965, 18. (Quote translated in *Laurentian University Calendar*, 1964–1965, 18.)

7 Edward J. Monahan, Bilingualism at Laurentian University, September 1976, 5.

8 "Laurentian studies needs of declining French enrolment," *Sudbury Star*, November 3, 1969, 15.

9 See Senate Minutes, October 31, 1963.

10 Senate Minutes, March 24, 1966.

11 G.A. Bourbeau, Rapport de l'année 1962–1963, October 1963. (Quoted in English.)

12 We thank Alain Daoust, Chantal Beaulne and Shelley Duquette for going through the newspapers for this period for information about the activities of the ADELFNO. Alain Daoust, "Les années 1960"; Chantal Beaulne, "La bataille pour la francophonie sur le campus de la Laurentienne pendant les années 1960"; Shelley Duquette, "La première année de l'AEF"; unpublished texts written in the History 4165 course during the 1995–1996 academic year.

13 "Third annual conference of ADELFNO," *Sudbury Star*, December 10, 1965, 11.

14 Senate Minutes, November 26, 1964.

15 At first, Meakes proposed a 90-day delay, to which Campeau objected and proposed an amendment that was unanimously adopted. See the minutes of the meeting on May 20, 1965.

16 Board Minutes, May 20, 1965.

17 Board Minutes, November 19, 1965.

18 See Monahan, Bilingualism, 6.

19 Carole Ann Ranta, "Looking at Laurentian's bilingualism president forecasts greater demand," *Sudbury Star*, August 17, 1966, 16.

20 AO, Laurentian University General Correspondence, RG32, 1, 1, Acc.18006, box M377, Conrad Lavigne to Bill Davis, October 12, 1966. The archives show that the minister had received other letters to this effect, notably one from Jacques de Courville Nicol, president of the French section of Laurentian University's Student Association, who sent the minister a file indicating urgent action was needed, otherwise "Laurentian, the Bilingual University of the North, will have become an English University."

21 Ibid., AO, RG32, 1, 1, Acc.18006, box M377, Bill Davis to Conrad Lavigne, October 28, 1966.

22 "French enrolment low in the universities, but costly venture," *Sudbury Star*, May 25, 1966, 3.

23 Monahan, Bilingualism, 8.

24 *Sudbury Star*, October 19, 1968, 1 and 3.

25 "Meeting of the French Section of Laurentian University, Friday October 25th, 1968."

26 The other two were the Jesuit Gilles Garand, professor of religious studies, and Yvon Gauthier, professor of philosophy.

27 "Students request changes," 1.

28 In fact, the president had rounded up the total in his favour, because the percentage actually comes out to 27 per cent.

29 Board Minutes, November 29, 1968.

30 Senate Minutes, December 18, 1969.

31 This act might have had some bearing on Senate's March 1969 decision to the effect that correspondence with a Francophone member would be written in French "when possible."

32 One year later, the department would get a taste of its own medicine, when its students staged a sit-in to demand courses in Franco-Ontarian literature instead of works from France.

33 Manifesto of October 22, 1969.

34 Board Minutes, October 31, 1969.

35 Joint Committee on Bilingualism and Biculturalism Minutes, December 14, 1970. (Translated from the original French.)

36 "Quits Laurentian Senate, cites problem of language," *Sudbury Star*, September 24, 1971, 1 and 3.

37 Fernand Dorais, "Démission comme membre du Sénat," September 23, 1971. (Translated from the original French.)

38 Interview with André Girouard by Michèle Riou and Marie-Josée Beaudry in the winter of 1996, as part of the course HIST 4165FA.

39 Committee on Bilingualism Minutes, November 30, 1970. (Translated from the original French.)

40 Josée Bisson and Marko Roy, "Le réveil: la naissance d'une association étudiante francophone à l'Université Laurentienne," unpublished text written in the Histoire 4165 course, in 1996.

41 "La Maison française," *Réaction* 3, 1 (September 1973).

42 J.G. Hagey, Mémoire présenté à l'Université Laurentienne, March 1971, 23–4. (English translation drawn from J.G. Hagey, Consultant's Report to Laurentian University, March 1971.)

43 In fact, the president of the University of Sudbury, d'Auteuil Richard, appeared rather hesitant in reaction to this recommendation. See the *Sudbury Star* article dated March 24, 1971, entitled "Mixed reactions to French college idea," 3.

44 Only in March 1979 did the university agree to provide Francophone students with a physical space reserved for them on campus, namely rooms C305, C306 and C318, which are today classrooms. This was conceded after many requests and following the student occupation of the 11th floor a year earlier.

Chapter Twelve

1   See Michel Rodrigue, "1970–1975. Une nouvelle vision: la création collective," in Guy Gaudreau, ed., *Le Théâtre du Nouvel-Ontario, 20 ans* (Sudbury: TNO, 1991) 14.

2   Marie-Élisabeth Brunet, "La troupe universitaire présente un happening," *Le Voyageur*, January 21, 1970, 7; "Du théâtre pas comme les autres," *Le Voyageur*, January 28, 1970, 16.

3   Micheline Fournier-Thibault, *André Paiement (1950–1978): Avant tout un homme de son temps* (Sudbury: Prise de parole, 2004), 56.

4   Rodrigue, "1970–1975," 14. (Translated from the original French.)

5   Julie Lafrenière, "Des luttes au consensus, 1965–1982," in Guy Gaudreau, ed., *Bâtir sur le roc: De l'ACFÉO à l'ACFO du Grand Sudbury (1910–1987)* (Sudbury: Prise de parole, 1994), 119.

6   For more on the role of the federal government in this wave of socio-cultural engagement, see Valérie Malenfant, "La contribution des gouvernements fédéral et ontarien à la révolution culturelle: le cas du Nouvel-Ontario, 1969–1977," MA (history), Laurentian University, 2005, 191 pp.

7   See Michelle Boucher, "Animation socioculturelle à la Laurentienne," an unpublished text written in the Histoire 4165 course during the 1995–1996 academic year. See also Michel Bock, *Comment un peuple oublie son nom: La crise identitaire franco-ontarienne et la presse française de Sudbury (1960–1975)* (Sudbury: Prise de parole and Institut franco-ontarien, 2001), 58–63.

8   Dennie report, 12.

9   Laurent Alie, Thérèse Boutin, Fernand Dorais, Réjean Grenier, Yvan Rancourt and Gaston Tremblay, "Éditorial," *Réaction*, March 15, 1973, 6.

10 Interview with Yvan Rancourt in the winter of 1996.

11 Bock, *Comment un peuple*, 62. Boutin explained her decision in a letter she published in the student newspaper; see *Réaction* (October 1973): 12.

12 See Stéphanie St-Pierre, "Le drapeau franco-ontarien: 'Puissent ses couleurs nous rallier dans une nouvelle amitié et fraternité,' 1975–1977," in Guy Gaudreau, ed., *Le drapeau franco-ontarien* (Sudbury: Prise de parole, 2005), 32.

13 Laurent Alie, "Élection à l'association étudiante francophone," *Le Voyageur*, May 1, 1974, 7. (Translated from the original French.)

14 "Laurentian Francophones vote 'split,'" *Sudbury Star*, October 9, 1974, 3.

15 Stephen Nancoo, "Reaffirm bilingualism in Laurentian planning. New priorities outlined," *Sudbury Star*, April 3, 1973, 1.

16 "Special scholarship programs: bilingualism stressed in goals for Laurentian," *Sudbury Star*, June 5, 1973, 1.

17 See the article entitled "Culture limit at Laurentian is criticized," 1.

18 T.H.B. Symons, *Report of the Ministerial Commission on French-Language Secondary Education* (Toronto: 1972), 56.

19 Dennie report, 16. (Translated from the original French.)

20 See *Report of the Committee on University Affairs of Ontario for 1972–73 and 1973–74* (Toronto: Government of Ontario, 1974), 19.

21 Senate Minutes, March 21, 1974. (Translated from the original French.)

22 As the episode of the selection of the psychology department director in 1975 would indicate, this policy would soon be revealed as impracticable. The director at that time, Mr. Moroz, at the request of some Francophone colleagues, asked the Senate's secretary, Jack Porter, to clarify the practical effect of this policy that made him ineligible for the position he held. He kept his position nonetheless. See Mr. Moroz' letter to J. Porter, March 18, 1975.

23 Monahan, Bilingualism, 11.

24 This report, entitled "The Work of the Long-Term Academic Planning Committee During the Period January 23, 1975–April 8, 1975," bears the signatures of President Monahan, Vice-President Larouche and professors Buse, Kitching, Todd and Tombalakian.

25 Dennie report, 18–19.

26 Gaétan Gervais, "Pour une réforme des programmes en français à l'Université Laurentienne," 1976, 2. (English translation drawn from "For a Reform of the Programmes offered in French at Laurentian University," 1976, 2.)

27 J. Porter to B. Cazabon, Secretary of the Francophone Affairs Committee, April 20, 1976.

28 Dennie, "Historique du bilinguisme à l'Université Laurentienne," 116.

29 See vol. 3, 4.

30 "L'émergence de réalités nouvelles," *Revue du Nouvel-Ontario*, 8.

31 The exact title of this report was quite explicit as to its initial intentions: "Report of the Joint Senate–Board Committee to Assess and Make Recommendations to Simplify Academic Administration."

32 André Girouard, "Le CEF. Pourquoi?" document submitted to the Senate, written October 15, 1979, 2.

33 Motion presented by the Francophone Affairs committee at the Senate's meeting on September 22, 1977.

34 CEF Minutes, March 22, 1979, 1.

35 "Rapport du Conseil de l'enseignement en français," *Laurentian University Gazette* 6, 4 (December 1978): 2.

36 See *Annual Report Rapport Annuel, Laurentian University Université Laurentienne, 1980–1981*, 38.

37 "Le Sénat adopte un rapport de planification triennale," *Laurentian University Gazette* 10, 4 (May 1982): 1. (Translated from the original French.)

38 See André Girouard, "Document d'étude du CEF, no. 4," February 4, 1981.

39 See the CEF Minutes, March 11, 1980, 2. See also the CEF's Report to the Budget Committee on June 6, 1979.

40 Girouard, "Document d'étude du CEF, no. 4," 2. (Translated from the original French.)

41 Minutes of the Assembly of Francophone professors, May 5, 1986, 1.

42 See the 4th recommendation approved by the Senate at its meeting on October 1, 1981. (Translated from the original French.)

43 "Nouveau mandat confié au CEF," *Laurentian University Gazette*, November 12, 1981, 7. (Translated from the original French.)

44 "Le Sénat adopte un rapport de planification triennale," *Laurentian University Gazette*, May 5, 1982, 2. (Translated from the original French.)

45 Ibid.

46 Francophone Affairs Committee Minutes, December 3, 1974, 2.
47 See David Gillingham's memo to Jack Porter on December 6, 1982.
48 Dennie report, 21. (Translated from the original French.)
49 Memo from Henry Best to the Council's president, February 7, 1984. (Translated from the original French.)
50 Memo from André Lacroix, president of the Joint Committee on Bilingualism, to J. Porter, May 11, 1983.

Chapter Thirteen

1 Gaétan Gervais to Jack Porter, January 7, 1985.
2 Ad hoc Advisory Committee on French-Language Library Holdings, Report to the Senate, April 18, 1986.
3 See Joint Committee on Bilingualism, "Proposed plan work for 1986–1987," 1.
4 "Assistant vice-president appointed," *Laurentian University Gazette*, February 3, 1988, 3.
5 "L'évolution de l'enseignement en français: Extraits de l'allocution du Recteur au corps professoral sur l'état de l'union," *Laurentian University Gazette, Special Report*, December 14, 1988, 3. (Translated from the original French.)
6 Report from the vice-president academic and the assistant vice-president, Senate, April 19, 1990, 1.
7 Michael Dewson to John Daniel, February 17, 1989.
8 "Report on bicameralism from the vice-president, academic," Senate, June 17, 1993.
9 "Rapport du vice-recteur ... sur le modèle bicaméral," Senate, June 17, 1993, 4. (Translated from the original French.)
10 André Roberge, Ron Smith and Geoffrey Tesson, "Recommandations au recteur sur les modifications de la structure administrative," February 18, 1999, 5.
11 "La gestion de la francophonie laurentienne. Trois options," 1998, 4. (English translation from "Governance of the Laurentian Francophone Community. Three Options. Final report of the Special Committee on the Governance of the Laurentian Francophone Community (Excerpts)," March 1998.)
12 "Rapport du vice-recteur à l'enseignement et de la vice-rectrice adjointe," Senate, April 19, 1990, 4. (English translation from "Report from the Vice-President, Academic and the Assistant Vice-President," 4.)
13 "Rapport du vice-recteur à l'enseignement et à la recherche sur le modèle bicaméral," Senate meeting, June 17, 1993, 1. (English translation from "Report from the Vice-President, Academic concerning the bicameral model.")
14 "French university groundwork being laid at Laurentian," *Sudbury Star*, July 16, 1980, 3.
15 AO, Ministry of Colleges and Universities, Francophone and Native Affairs, RG 32, 1, 1, Acc.23300, RC 12, file 5020-4, B.A. Wilson to H.K. Fisher, "Study on French language education at the post-secondary level," July 2, 1980.
16 Ibid.,, MCU, University-General, RG 32, 1, 1, Acc.20216, RC 3, file 3030-5, C. Lacombe to B.A. Wilson, "Visit to Laurentian and Hearst," August 5, 1980,
17 See Volume 7, which contains 6 articles totalling 128 pages.
18 Hector-L. Bertrand, "Une université française publique à Sudbury" *Le Voyageur*, February 8, 1989, 4. (Translated from the original French.)
19 See Derek Nelson, "'Dialogue of the deaf' on bilingual policy," *Sudbury Star*, February 28, 1989, 4; Harold Carmichael, "More than 800 graduate from Cambrian College: Setting up

separate community colleges by race and religion not a good idea," *Sudbury Star*, May 29, 1989, 21; John Daniel, "Laurentian serves Francophones, Anglophones, Natives 'proudly,'" *Northen Life*, June 17, 1989, 4.

20 "Daniel lends support to bilingualism," *Sudbury Star*, February 10, 1989, 2.

21 John Daniel, "'Separatist forces' at work in Laurentian," *Sudbury Star*, March 25, 1989, 4.

22 Benoît Cazabon, "French university," *Sudbury Star*, August 10, 1989, 5.

23 "Laurentian president questions feasibility of French university," *Sudbury Star*, August 1, 1989, 3.

24 Hector-L. Bertrand, "Nous sommes toujours en faveur d'une université française," *Le Voyageur*, December 13, 1989, 4; see also his editorials on November 1, 1989 and February 28, 1990.

25 See "L'Université de l'Ontario français. Les pessimistes ont tort!" *Le Voyageur*, December 13, 1989, 12–13.

26 See page 17.

Chapter Fourteen

1 J.E. Havel, *Politics in Sudbury* (Sudbury, ON: Laurentian University Press, 1965), 5. According to this study, "the higher ratio of men to women is an indication that Sudbury attracts immigrants." The ratio in Alberta at the time was 107 men to 100 women, and in Saskatchewan, 108 men to 100 women.

2 *CAUT Handbook 1979*, Council Resolution (June 1961), 37.

3 This number was calculated from the listings in the 2008 LU campus telephone directory. Thanks to Kaleigh Bradley for her work on this.

4 For graduate students the ratio is 57 women to every 43 men. These statistics were provided by the LU Institutional Research Office, based on statistics compiled from 2000–2007: Institutional Research Office Datamart.

5 Pat Pickard and Wendy Jerome were featured in *Sudbury Star* as late as 1980 in this very manner.

6 "Wife of Laurentian president at best in prize-winning novel," *Sudbury Star*, December 16, 1961, 19.

7 "To receive guests," *Sudbury Star*, October 19, 1963; "Governors, wives tour site, Laurentian shows impressive progress," *Sudbury Star*, October 22, 1963, 3.

8 "Three have tea in library," *Sudbury Star*, May 23, 1963, 15.

9 Executive Minutes, April 15, 1964. In the end it was the IODE who supplied the university with its ceremonial mace.

10 "University Women's Club scholarships presented to four Sudbury students," *Sudbury Star*, September 20, 1964. Another women's group that made significant donations to the university in this period was the Imperial Order Daughters of the Empire. See for example, "Nickel chapter of IODE donates flag and flagpole to Laurentian," *Sudbury Star*, October 29, 1963, 12; and the Elizabeth Fry Chapter, IODE's contribution of $8,000 reported in "Gift to Laurentian," *Sudbury Star*, November 13, 1964, 3.

11 The university purchased the John Street residence in the fall of 1965. The house was described as "one of the few, if not the only home in Sudbury, which can provide facilities necessary to carry out the duties of the president's office, having large reception rooms essential for university meetings, separate dining areas and study space." "Merwin home and two others nearby are bought by Laurentian University," *Sudbury Star*, September 11, 1965, 3.

12 For more on Hartman's political career in Sudbury, see C.M. Wallace and Ashley Thomson, eds, *Sudbury: Rail Town to Regional Capital* (Toronto: Dundurn Press, 1993), 207, 221, 252.

13 *Sudbury Star*, June 12, 1964, 13: 6 women of 25 total graduates (from Huntington only); June 5, 1965, 5: 13 women of 49 total; and June 24, 1966 where 97 graduates appear, 29 of them women. In 1961 women made up 13 per cent of the student population. This number increased to 18 per cent in 1962 and then hovered around 24 per cent until 1968 and 1969 when it reached 27 per cent.

14 LUA, Huntington, V, 3, Buildings – Residences Women 1964–65.

15 "Students make survey of Sudbury. Most want women to stay at home," *Sudbury Star*, January 11, 1972.

16 Executive Minutes, April 28, 1967.

17 "Perhaps views changed by now," *Sudbury Star*, October 5, 1964, 5.

18 Ibid.

19 "Toronto paper sees Sudbury as mere 'forest clearing.' *Sudbury Star*, August 27, 1965, 5. The article was written in response to Andrew Osler, "Bilingual Laurentian blasted out of the wilderness," *Toronto Star*, August 25, 1965.

20 "Two women, three men gain Laurentian posts," *Sudbury Star*, October 1, 1968, 3.

21 LUA, PO63, V, 2C LUFA Minutes, October 10, 1968; ibid., April 3, 1969.

22 *Report of the Royal Commission on the Status of Women*, 1970, 263. For more on the Commission's position and recommendations on day care, see the report, chapter 4, "Women and the Family," 266–70, 272, 301.

23 Executive Minutes, March 25, 1971.

24 "Economic restraint blamed for lack of women athletes," *Sudbury Star*, March 7, 1972. For more on Hoffman and the context of women and sport in Canada, see M. Ann Hall, *The Girl and the Game: A History of Women's Sport in Canada* (Peterborough, ON: Broadview Press, 2002); and Helen Lenskyj, "Whose Sport? Whose Tradition? Canadian Women and Sport in the Twentieth Century," *International Journal of the History of Sport* 9, 1 (1992): 141–50.

Chapter Fifteen

1 LUA, PO63, IV, 44 "Laurentian University Faculty Association Committee on the Status of Women," February 22, 1973.

2 Mary Kinnear, "Disappointment in Discourse: Women University Professors at the University of Manitoba," *Historical Studies in Education* 4, 2 (1992): 269.

3 Ibid.

4 Laurentian University, "Presentation to the Committee on University Affairs," November 12, 1973 (Sudbury, ON), 7, "Status of Women."

5 "Report on Academic Women," University of Alberta, 1975, 2.

6 Presidential advisory committee on the status of women, "Status of Women Report" (Sudbury, ON: Laurentian University, 1979–80), 4.

7 Ibid., 6.

8 "Report on Academic Women," University of Alberta, 1975, 20.

9 "Men can discover new perspectives through women studies," [sic] *Sudbury Star*, April 3, 1978, 10.

10 The history department introduced a course on women in society in the fall of 1979. "L.U. introduces course on women in society," *Sudbury Star*, September 26, 1979, 4.

11 In 1989, a degree program in women's studies was introduced, demonstrating that the course offerings had developed significantly in scope and variety in several departments across the campus. The degree program depended on the cooperation of several departments, although Thorneloe, where the program was housed, consistently had at least two full-time faculty members in women's studies from 1989 on. For an academic treatment of the creating of women's studies programs in Canada, see Wendy Robbins, Margrit Eichler, Meg Luxton, and Francine Descarries, eds, *Minds of Our Own: Inventing Feminist Scholarship and Women's Studies in Canada and Quebec, 1966–1976* (Waterloo: Wilfrid Laurier University Press, 2008).

12 "Laurentian governors joined by three women," *Sudbury Star*, February 3, 1973, 3. The first woman to serve on the Board of Governors was Dr. Faustina Kelly Cook in the mid- to late-1960s.

13 *Sudbury Star*, February 3, 1973; "Status of Women Report," 1980, 6; and Board Minutes, June 1, 1984.

14 In its 1980 report, the presidential advisory committee on the status of women included the recommendation "That all three colleges – University of Sudbury, Thorneloe, and Huntington – as well as the Government of Ontario, be encouraged to appoint more women to the Board of Governors of Laurentian University." "Status of Women Report," 1980, 7.

15 See LUA, PO63, IV, 8, Correspondence around this question, October 15, 1974; October 29, 1974; and December 17, 1974.

16 "Status of Women Report," 1980, 6.

17 The average male salary was reported to be $35,433 while the average female salary was $29,801. *Sudbury Star*, February 6, 1982.

18 Senate Minutes, June 19, 1975; also "Status of Women Report," 1980, which includes quote.

19 "Report of the President's Committee on the Status of Women at Mount Allison University," June 17, 1975, "Preamble."

20 It is unclear what happened to the PAC between 1976 and 1979, but the mandate of the reactivated committee can be found in Board Minutes, December 10, 1980.

21 "Status of Women Report," 1980, 1.

22 Ibid.

23 Ibid., 4.

24 Ibid., 6.

25 Ibid., 7.

26 J.M. Porter, Secretary of Senate to P.E. Menard, Director of Personnel, "Memorandum," June 23, 1980. Senate Correspondence, 1980–1981.

27 LUFA *Bulletin*, 1, 7 (March 1982).

28 Parker's boss, Alan Ritchie, director of computer services, disputed the fact that he had threatened to dismiss Parker, but she recounted that her boss told her "that if she felt that strongly about the matter she should consider looking for another position and that he would help her if she wished." "Told to think about looking for another job: Secretary at Laurentian objects to serving coffee," *Sudbury Star*, March 7, 1981, 1.

29 Wilfred List, "A secretary is not a waitress, arbitrator rules in coffee case," *Globe and Mail*, July 31, 1981, 1.

30 Branco Rayakovich, quoted in "Told to think about looking for another job: Secretary at Laurentian objects to serving coffee," *Sudbury Star*, March 7, 1981, 1.

31 *Sudbury Star*, March 7, 1981; *Sudbury Star*, July 20, 1981; and *Globe and Mail*, July 31, 1981.

32　"Laurentian adopts harassment policy," *Northern Life*, July 7, 1982, 10.

33　Ibid.

34　For the full text of the sexual harassment policy adopted by Senate on May 20, 1982, see LUFA *Bulletin*, 2, 1 (September 1982) or Board Minutes, September 24, 1982.

35　LUA, PO63, IV, 40, Janet Sabourin, Chairperson, Presidential Advisory Committee on the Status of Women, to Dr. L. Wagner, President Laurentian University Faculty Association, April 6, 1984.

Chapter Sixteen

1　All of the statistics in this section were compiled by Andrea Levan, who was hired with funding from the Ministry of Colleges and Universities Ontario Women's Directorate to act as researcher for the Employment Equity Project Coordinators Margaret Kechnie and Patricia C. Hennessy. See "The Challenge for Laurentian: Employment Equity" (Sudbury, ON: Laurentian University, 1987), table 12, 49. It is unclear what the third position was exactly, but it was listed as "director," of which there were four: CIMMER, CEF, school of graduate studies, and library services.

2　Kechnie and Hennessy, "The Challenge for Laurentian," table 14, 51.

3　Ibid., table A3, 59.

4　Ibid., table A10, 63.

5　Board Minutes, December 13, 1985, cited in "The Challenge for Laurentian," 2.

6　Ibid.

7　Kechnie and Hennessy, "The Challenge for Laurentian," "Acknowledgements."

8　"Employment Equity." http://www.psacbc.com/archives/stewards-corner/stewards-dictionary. Accessed March 17, 2008.

9　For more on employment equity see http://www.chrc-ccdp.ca/employment_equity/default-en.asp

10　Kechnie and Hennessy, "The Challenge for Laurentian," 2.

11　Ibid., 15, Recommendation 1.1.

12　In fact, commerce had two tenured female faculty members at the time of the study. The list is a curious one, and could have been longer because other departments and programs with no tenured women at the time of the study could have been added including: philosophy, child development, engineering, geology, and physics and astronomy. Ibid., table 4, 43.

13　Ibid., 25–6.

14　Ibid., 27.

15　Ibid., 26, chart 5.

16　For an overview of the history of pay equity legislation in Canada (federal as well as the provinces) see: http://www.justice.gc.ca/eng/payeq-eqsal/1100.html

17　"Status of Women Report," 1980, 7.

18　For a more complete understanding of pay equity and the issues surrounding it, see: http://www.payequity.gov.on.ca/peo/english/overview.html

19　Laurentian University and Laurentian University Staff Association, *Joint Job Evaluation System Handbook*. Effective July 1, 1992, 1.

20　Laurentian University, "Pay Equity Plan," December 22, 1989. Approved by Branko Rayakovich, LU Director of Personnel, and Gisele Pageau, LUSU President.

21　"Campus sexism in spotlight following Montreal Massacre," *Sudbury Star*, December 27, 1989, 3.

22　See for example, Eileen Goltz and Pat Bailey, On behalf of the LUFA Board, to All LUFA Members, "Report on the Meeting of Laurentian University Women Faculty Held January 31, 1992," March 13, 1992. LUA, J50, 3, Strategic Plan "Teaching and Research."

23　"Status of Women Achievement Awards," *Laurentian University Gazette* (Summer 2001): 22.

24　http://142.51.14.1/Laurentian/Home/Departments/Status+Of+Women/Terms+Of+Reference

25　Doug Goldsack, Dean of Science and Engineering, to Chairmen of Science Departments, Director of School of Engineering, and Vice-Deans, March 6, 1992. LU, G8, 3, Science and Engineering "Advisory Committee on Engineering."

26　Ibid.

27　"LU 'insists' on women," *Sudbury Star*, June 19, 1993. It is clear that the university was making every reasonable effort to attract women to the school of engineering and to comply with the employment equity plan. The director of academic staff relations requested a special memorandum of agreement from LUFA agreeing to the appointment of a female faculty member who had not yet completed her PhD, but who was willing to enter into an agreement that would provide her with opportunity to teach for three years and then have two years of study leave to complete her doctoral studies. Hermann Falter to Wendy Jerome, LUFA President, February 16, 1993.

28　A. Farah, Director, School of Engineering to P. Cappon, Vice-President Academic, September 24, 1992.

Chapter Seventeen

1　See, for example, S.V. LaSelva, *Moral Foundations of Canadian Federalism* (Montreal & Kingston: McGill-Queen's University Press, 1996), 42–5.

2　Senate Minutes, October 24, 1960; LUA, P109, II, B, 1, 1, Ed Newbery to Ben Avery, August 29, 1961.

3　Ibid., I, 30, 4, "The Report of the Special Committee of the Board of Governors of Laurentian University, July 9, 1965," 26; AO, RG6-44, Ministry of Finance Policy Planning Division Subject Files, Laurentian University 1960–1966, D.L. James, Finance Committee, Laurentian, to John Robarts, Minister of Education, November 23, 1960; LUA, P109, I, 1, 1, Board of Regents Correspondence, Harold Bennett to Earl Lautenschlager, October 29, 1962; Board Minutes, January 18, 1963; Executive Minutes, April 24, 1963; Board Minutes, February 22, 1962; LUA, P109, II, B, 1, 2, Minutes of Huntington Senate, January 6, 1961; ibid., II, I, 4, 2, Newbery to Committee to advise the Architect, Laurentian, March 26, 1962.

4　Board Minutes, November 24, 1964; LUA, P109, III, A, 1, 1, Newbery to Claude de Mestrel, November 6, 1963 (emphasis in the original); ibid., III, A, 1, 2, Newbery to Rev. Foster Hilliard, November 11, 1963.

5　Ibid., I, 1, 1, Newbery to Donald Best, August 30, 1962; Executive Minutes, February 20, 1963; Board Minutes, July 30, 1963.

6　Ibid., December 9, 1963; LUA, I, 70, 4, Belisle to Avery, February 5, 1964; Board Minutes, March 11, 1964; Executive Minutes, March 18, 1964; LUA, P109, I, 1, 1, Newbery to Donald Best, February 13, 1964.

7　Ibid.

8　Board Minutes, November 24, 1964, January 22, 1965; *Sudbury Star*, May 22, 1965; LUA, I, 30, 4, Mullins presentation to the Special Committee, June 9, 1965, reprinted in "The Report of the Special Committee of the Board of Governors of Laurentian University," July 9, 1965, 23.

9   Ibid., "Synopsis of comments made at June 3rd Meeting," Minutes of the fourth meeting of the Special Committee of the Board, June 15, 1965.

10 Ibid., III, A, 1, 2, Newbery to John S. Bonnell, October 12, 1965; ibid., I, 30, 4, "The Report of the Special Committee of the Board of Governors of Laurentian University," July 9, 1965, 22, 4, 36–40; Board Minutes, July 9, 1965.

11 LUA, I, 30, 4, "The Report of the Special Committee of the Board of Governors of Laurentian University," July 9, 1965, 31; Board Minutes, May 19, 1966.

12 Executive Minutes, March 23, 1966; Board Minutes, May 19, 1966; Executive Minutes, June 22, 1966, August 12, 1966.

13 Board Minutes, May 25, 1967.

14 Ibid., October 18, 1968.

15 In 1961, for example, the NOUA had received pledges of more than $1.3 million to Huntington University, but four years later barely half had actually been subscribed. See LUA, P109, II, A, 2, 10, NOUA Financial Statements, February 22, 1961; ibid., II, B, 1, 1, D.P. Best to D.S. Holbrook, June 28, 1965; ibid., III, A, 1, 5, Newbery to H.J. Muehlamm, May 24, 1967; ibid., Newbery to Donald Best, May 29, 1967; ibid., F, 67, 3, Laurentian University, "Brief Regarding Laurentian University and Federated Colleges," May 1967.

16 Ibid., P109, III, A, 1, 6, Newbery to Rev. D. Graham Tipple, February 12, 1968; ibid., Newbery to Rev. R.C. Constant, South River, February 19, 1968; ibid., I, 1, 1, Staff Brief to R.T. Runciman, chair, Board of Regents, September 26, 1968; ibid., Runciman to Ladies and Gentlemen, September 30, 1968; ibid., Interim report of the Huntington University Committee for Revision and Renewal, undated, *circa* January 1969; Board Minutes, February 19, 1969; Executive Minutes, March 19, 1969, April 16, 1969; *Sudbury Star*, April 2, 1969.

17 Board Minutes, May 18, 1967; Executive Minutes, March 19, 1969; *Sudbury Star*, January 23, 1970.

18 Executive Minutes, April 16, 1969, December 10, 1969, January 23, 1970; LUA, 44, 3, F.A. Peake to G. Lafrenière, January 12, 1971.

19 Executive Minutes, August 8, 1972; LUA, F, 70, 1, Monahan to Members of Senate, February 13, 1974; ibid., "Draft Agreement between Laurentian University and the Federated Colleges," March 31, 1978.

20 Board Minutes, December 6, 1974.

21 Executive Minutes, November 21, 1978, January 30, 1979, May 16, 1979.

22 Senate Briefs, January 1993–January 1994, "Presidents' Commission on the Federated Universities," November 18, 1993, 1; Board Minutes, September 25, 1992, October 1, 1993; Executive Minutes, March 8, 1994; Board Minutes, April 22, 1994.

23 Andrii Krawchuk, President, University of Sudbury, "Responses to a request to the presidents of the federated universities on what they regard as essential qualifications for the position of President and Provost of Thorneloe University," undated, forwarded to Matt Bray, July 16, 2009.

Chapter Eighteen

1   Of the original 34 full-time faculty members, 24 were bilingual. Board Minutes, August 25, 1960, Appendix V.

2   Statistics supplied to the author by LUFA Office, July 2008.

3   For a sample of the form that was used for this arrangement, see LUA, PO63, II, A, 1.2 "Faculty/Salaries."

4   See Board Minutes, August 25, 1960, Appendix V; May 30, 1961, Appendix III; and May 28, 1962, Appendix III.

5 See Board Minutes, August 25, 1960, Appendix V; May 30, 1961, Appendix III; and May 28, 1962, Appendix III.

6 Clearly the constitution document went through several revisions in the early years. For two early versions, see LUA, PO63, I, A, 1, Constitution de l'association des professeurs de l'université laurentienne de Sudbury, adoptée 30 janvier 1961; and Constitution of the Laurentian University of Sudbury Faculty Association, Revised text, January 31, 1963.

7 LUA, PO63, III, 2, LUFA Financial Report, March 12, 1962.

8 D.D. Carter, "Collective Bargaining for University Faculty: A Legal Perspective," *Canadian Journal of Higher Education* 5, 1 (1975): 25–31; and Bernard Adell, "The Legal Framework of Faculty Collective Bargaining: Some Short Questions and Some Long Answers," *Canadian Journal of Higher Education* 5, 2 (1976): 57–75.

9 W.M. Sibley, "Modes of University Government," *Canadian Journal of Higher Education* 5, 1 (1976): 19–27.

10 Laurentian University Board of Governors Annual Report (hereafter Board Annual Report), May 30, 1961.

11 Board Minutes, November 24, 1964.

12 LUA, PO63, V, 2, b, Mullins to Faculty and Staff, October 7, 1965.

13 Executive Minutes, August 23, 1967.

14 Executive Minutes, June 21, 1967; "Laurentian·takes initiative to find housing for new staff," *Sudbury Star*, July 16, 1967, 2.

15 "Present the Laurentian side of Randolph Apartments issue," *Sudbury Star*, July 14, 1967, 2.

16 AO, RG3-26, Office of the Premier, Robarts: Correspondence, box 426, file "Laurentian University 1961–1965," file Laurentian University Jan–Dec 1967 Correspondence, Robarts, Davis, John R. Mason (Department of Economic and Development) and tenants of the Randolph Apartments.

17 AO, RG2-36, Robarts to Davis, July 12, 1967.

18 Ibid., Davis to Robarts, September 7, 1967.

19 Ibid., John R. Mason to Robarts, August 24, 1967.

20 Executive Minutes, May 12, 1972.

21 "Sudbury's university classes scattered across the city," *Sudbury Star*, November 4, 1960, 13. According to the same article, in addition to the full-time students, there were 429 taking evening classes toward degrees and 188 in the extension department studying mathematics and electricity.

22 "Total of 51 new teachers will be at Laurentian when classes resume," *Sudbury Star*, July 8, 1967, 3.

23 Ibid.

24 "High percentage of foreigners on Laurentian University staff," *Sudbury Star*, January 20, 1969, Z7.

25 LUA, PO63, IV, 13, 2, Havel, LUFA Vice-President, to Board of Governors.

26 LUA, PO63, IV, 13, 2, "Revised Regulation 64-1 (December 31, 1964) Policy on Appointments, Tenure, Promotion, Teaching Load and Leave." Professor Berg wrote to President Mullins on January 11, 1965 stating that LUFA had approved the document with one minor amendment, replacing the word "permanent" with "full-time" in a couple of places in the document.

27 LUA, PO63, IV, 13, 2, "Revised University Regulation 64-1 (December 31, 1964)."

28 Michiel Horn points out that the University of Toronto adopted a set of rules for dealing with appointments, promotions and tenure in 1967. At the time, he says, "Other governing boards were doing the same kind of thing." Michiel Horn, *Academic Freedom in Canada: A History* (Toronto: University of Toronto Press, 1999), 305.

29 LUA, PO63, IV, 13, 2, "Revised University Regulation 64-1 (December 31, 1964)."

30 LUA, PO63, II, A, 1, 1, "Faculty Employment Policy in Laurentian University of Sudbury, S.G. Mullins, President, November 1963."

31 LUA, PO63, IV, 13, 2, "Revised University Regulation 64-1 (December 31, 1964)," 6.

32 LUA, PO65, II, A, 1, 1, "A Report [of] The Committee on Salary, Pensions and Fringe Benefits, Faculty Association of Laurentian University of Sudbury," October 1965. The committee members were: J. Chung (chairman), economics; C. Botton, mathematics; P. Matton, S.J., biology; A. Queen, chemistry; J. Willes, business administration; and R. Winter, economics.

33 Ibid., table I, 13.

34 Ibid., 3.

35 LUA, PO63, IV, 39, 1, G.I. Clarke to F.B. Lavoie, July 31, 1970.

36 "Laurentian teachers threaten strike over salary dispute," *Sudbury Star*, September 15, 1970, 1.

37 "Suggest plan to end recess at Laurentian," *Sudbury Star*, October 3, 1970, 3.

38 "Senate 'recess' at Laurentian slices attendance," *Sudbury Star*, October 2, 1970, 3.

39 Ibid.

40 "Laurentian in 'serious financial situation,' Senate is warned," *Sudbury Star*, November 27, 1970, 1.

41 "Laurentian 'referee' advises board, Senate to reform procedures," *Sudbury Star*, March 23, 1971, 1, 3.

42 LUA, F, 60, 3, "Press Releases," February 2, 1971.

Chapter Nineteen

1 B.L. Adell and D.D. Carter, *Collective Bargaining for University Faculty in Canada* (Kingston, ON: The Industrial Relations Centre, Queen's University, 1972), 3.

2 D. Owen Carrigan, "Collective Bargaining in Canadian Universities," *International Journal of Institutional Management in Higher Education* 1, 1 (May 1977): 19.

3 LUA, PO63, II, A, 1, 1, Gaucher, President, LUFA, to CAUT, January 19, 1963. The LUFA president wrote to invite CAUT to enquire into the non-renewal of the contract of Professor Leo Pare, philosophy department. More than fifteen years later, similar issues around contracts were still being discussed. National Archives of Canada, CAUT Papers, File: Laurentian – General, Ted Bartley, CAUT Collective Bargaining Officer to Roland Penner, President CAUT, July 12, 1979. Bartley advised Penner that at Laurentian, "it seems virtually all new appointments are now of a limited-term nature ... Moreover, several who were recommended for probationary appointments by the Senate this past Spring fear that they will only be receiving term appointments, but do not even know that as yet. Roy Kari tells me that ... things are generally being run on a very ad hoc basis."

4 The case of Leandre Page, a professor of French caused great furor in the summer of 1970 when Page's colleague discovered that he was "alleged to have compiled a long criminal record in Europe before his arrival in Canada in 1965." It turned out that Page had fabricated his academic credentials; as he appealed a deportation order, he finally offered his resignation to the university on August 4, 1970. A series of articles in the *Sudbury Star* covered the case. See, for example, "Laurentian professor fights extradition over alleged record," August 7, 1970, 1; "Laurentian Senate meeting over French professor issue," August 11, 1970, 3; "Resignation of professor is accepted," August 12, 1970, 1, 3.

5 The case of Dr. Artin Tombalakian made headlines several times as a 20-month legal battle ensued after Henry Best removed Tombalakian from the position of director of the school of engineering in March 1978. The professor refused to acknowledge the president's decision, and Best charged him with "unprofessional behaviour and persistent neglect of duties [which] threatened the School's opportunity to gain accreditation for [its] new degree programs." "Bitter Tombalakian arbitration hearings begin," *Sudbury Star*, September 19, 1979, 4. After Best attempted to dismiss Tombalakian from the university, the case went to arbitration and a settlement was reported on December 1, 1979. According to the *Sudbury Star*, "all allegations have been withdrawn" and the university paid Tombalakian's legal expenses. "Hatchet buried on Laurentian legal hassle," *Sudbury Star*, December 1, 1979, 3.

6 Memories of such decisions and faculty protest against them are shared by members such as Graeme Mount, who recounted his work on a committee considering the question in an email to the author.

7 AO, RG 32, 1, 1, Acc.1800 G, box RCM 386, file 3030-5-4, "Universities – General – Laurentian Staff Problems 1974," Bud Germa, MPP Sudbury, to the Honourable James Auld, July 22, 1974.

8 Carrigan, "Collective Bargaining in Canadian Universities," 19.

9 Ibid., 19.

10 LUA, F25, 1, "Negotiations 1979," G.I. Clarke, "The Role of the Laurentian Senate Under Collective Agreement with Faculty," September 13, 1979.

11 Carter, "Collective Bargaining for University Faculty: A Legal Perspective," *Canadian Journal of Higher Education* 5, 1 (1975): 25.

12 LUFA Minutes, May 19, 1976.

13 LUA, PO63, I, B, 1 "An open letter on Faculty Certification," November 17, 1976. The signatories were 48 faculty members, including Wes Cragg and Hermann Falter, who would take a very different stance on this question two years hence when they served on the LUFA executive.

14 "An Open Letter on Faculty Certification."

15 Canadian Association of University Teachers, *CAUT Handbook* (Ottawa: CAUT, 1979), 31–5.

16 Ibid, 31.

17 Wes Cragg and Hermann Falter were among the 48 who had signed the 1976 document opposing certification.

18 LUA, PO63, V, 2e, Roy Kari to Members of LUFA, October 10, 1978, "Re: The organization of the special meeting at 7:00 p.m. on October 13, 1978."

19 LUA, PO63, I, B, 3, Kari to Faculty, November 13, 1978.

20 LUA, PO63, I, B, 3, Thomson to Faculty, November 30, 1978. Recalling this period, Ashley Thomson told the author that because of the thorough campaign effort which LUFA conducted, he "knew every voter and how he/she would vote. The outcome was never in doubt."

21 *CAUT Handbook* (1979), vi.

22 Howard C. Clark, *Growth and Governance of Canadian Universities: An Insider's View* (Vancouver: UBC Press, 2003), 181.

23 Carrigan, "Collective Bargaining," 18.

24 Savage to The Faculty at Laurentian University, October 30, 1979.

25 Best to The Faculty at Laurentian University, November 12, 1979.

26 Ibid. Ashley Thomson, who assumed the role of chief negotiator for LUFA part way through the process, recalls that there were some lighter moments during the negotiations including this memory: "One day we were negotiating in the Arts Building when the Snowbirds flew by. Frank Turner, [LU vice-president academic at the time] suggested that we adjourn

to the top of the Parker Building where we could really appreciate their performance and we did. Does that sound really adversarial?"

27 This document was extremely important because it covered a range of issues. In a memo to the LUFA membership written just a few weeks before the collective agreement was ratified, Ashley Thomson gave an encouraging update reporting that "the Association and Board negotiators have come to agreement on most of the core articles in the new contract." He went on to list eleven different articles which had already been signed off, including a statement about the rights and responsibilities of faculty, a formal mechanism for annual evaluation, a mechanism whereby faculty could have access to their own personnel files, professional allowance, and "grievance procedures that will allow members to take disputes to neutral outside arbitration." LUFA 25, 1, Laurentian University, 2, Personnel, "Negotiations 1979–1980," Ashley Thomson to All Faculty Members, "Re: Negotiations," September 19, 1980.

Chapter Twenty

1 "Profs on strike, education on hold," *Lambda*, September 12, 1985, 1.
2 Mike Dewson, Laurentian Chief Negotiator, cited in ibid.
3 "Laurentian students to support teachers," *Sudbury Star*, September 6, 1985, 3; "Laurentian profs go out on strike," *Sudbury Star*, September 9, 1985, 1.
4 File: LUFA-Viz. Richard Carrière, LUFA Secretary, to LUFA Members, August 26, 1985. The memo contained two attachments: "Signed Off Articles" and "Monetary Proposals."
5 *Lambda*, September 12, 1985, 1.
6 Ibid.
7 "University profs accept pact with reluctance," *Sudbury Star*, September 14, 1985, 1.
8 "Laurentian pact okayed, classes resumed today," *Sudbury Star*, September 16, 1985, 1.
9 Editorial: "Laurentian dispute," *Sudbury Star*, September 18, 1985, 4.
10 "Laurentian pact okayed, classes resumed today," *Sudbury Star*, September 16, 1985, 1.
11 Editorial: "Laurentian turmoil turned off students," *Sudbury Star*, May 14, 1986, 4.
12 Dr. Bernadette Schell, President, and Dr. Pierre Simon, Secretary, LUFA to Dr. B. Lynch, Chairman, Executive Committee, Board of Governors, November 23, 1987. File: LUFA-Viz.
13 Ibid.
14 Ibid.
15 "President says enrolment jeopardized by strike," *Sudbury Star*, September 14, 1989, 3. Compared to statistics supplied by the Institutional Research office, those numbers seem inflated since the official record was 6,672 total students that fall.
16 "LU contract talks resume today: Professors seek students' support," *Sudbury Star*, September 6, 1989, 3.
17 "Laurentian University professors on strike," *Sudbury Star*, September 11, 1989, 1.
18 "Some students head home as Laurentian profs go out," *Sudbury Star*, September 12, 1989, 5.
19 "Native students concerned strike will affect funds," *Sudbury Star*, September 29, 1989, 3.
20 Ibid.
21 "Laurentian, faculty resume talks today," *Sudbury Star*, September 29, 1989, 1.
22 "Laurentian professors vote 77 per cent to accept contract," *Sudbury Star*, October 3, 1989, 3.
23 Ibid.
24 "Daniel's decision to resign from Laurentian tough because he enjoyed time in Sudbury," *Northern Life*, November 5, 1989, 3.

25 Ibid.
26 Bob Rae, *From Protest to Power: Personal Reflections on a Life in Politics* (Toronto: Penguin Books Canada, 1996), 197.
27 Ibid., 204.
28 Peter A. Baskerville, *Ontario: Image, Identity, and Power* (Toronto: Oxford University Press, 2002), 226.
29 J.-C. Cachon, Vice-President of LUFA, "To the editor," *Bulletin* (Spring 1994): 3.
30 Roy Kari, ibid., 5.
31 Ibid.
32 Senate Briefs, Feb 1994–March 1995, Wendy Jerome, President LUFA to Jack Porter, Secretary of Senate, re: Rae Days, May 2, 1994.
33 LUFA-Viz, B. Rayakovich, Director of Personnel to All Employees Affected by Social Contract Deductions, February 8, 1996.
34 Source: Graphs created by Eric Larocque, based on data supplied by Laurentian Office of Institutional Research, 2008.
35 Laurentian University Public Affairs, Press Release, November 28, 2007.
36 Ibid.

Conclusion

1 Cited in Jones, Goyan and Shanahan, "University Governance in Canadian Higher Education," 137–8.
2 Ibid., 138.
3 "Strong public support urged for Laurentian U.," *Northern Ontario Register*, December 1, 1962.
4 "'Separatist forces' at work in Laurentian," *Sudbury Star*, March 25, 1989.
5 "Bilingual Laurentian blasted out of the wilderness," *Toronto Daily Star*, August 25, 1965.

A NOTE ON SOURCES

The Laurentian University Archives were the single most important source for this institutional history, a remarkable fact given that before the mid-1990s they did not exist. Over the next decade and a half, archivist Marthe Brown and her staff assembled the wide range of collections relating to all facets of academic and administrative life upon which we have relied heavily. Valuable, too, were other non-archival records such as minutes and correspondence of Senate, the Board of Governors and the board executive committee, scrapbooks and photographs located in various departments and offices, and campus newspapers and journals such as *Lambda, le Lambda, l'Orignal déchaîné* and the *Laurentian University Gazette.*

Newspapers also provided critical information and insights from local (the *Sudbury Star, Le Voyageur, Northern Life*), regional (the *Sault Star,* the *North Bay Nugget*) and provincial (*Le Droit, Globe and Mail, Toronto Daily Star*) perspectives. Other useful sources were the Archives of Ontario, particularly RG-2, Ministry of Education, RG-32, Ministry of Colleges and Universities, RG-6, Ministry of Finance, and RG-3, the papers of various premiers, and records in the National Archives of Canada. A series of interviews by researcher Charles Levi provided colour and feel for life at Laurentian, especially during its early years. Lastly, we have drawn on an abundance of secondary sources, a selection of which is cited in the bibliography.

BIBLIOGRAPHY

Adell, B.L. "The Legal Framework of Faculty Collective Bargaining: Some Short Questions and Some Long Answers." *Canadian Journal of Higher Education* 5, 2 (1976): 57–75

Adell, B.L., and D.D. Carter. *Collective Bargaining for University Faculty in Canada.* Kingston, Ontario: The Industrial Relations Centre, Queen's University, 1972

Adelman, Howard. *The Holiversity: A Perspective on the Wright Report.* Toronto: new press 1973

Aiken, Gordon. *Looking Out On the 20th Century*, vol. 2. Orillia, ON: RO Publications 1993

Aitken, Brian. "Huntington, Silas." In *Dictionary of Canadian Biography*, vol. 13, 1901 to 1910. Toronto: University of Toronto Press 1994

Axelrod, Paul. *Scholars and Dollars: Politics, Economics, and the Universities of Ontario 1945–1980.* Toronto: University of Toronto Press 1982

Baskerville, Peter A. *Ontario: Image, Identity, and Power.* Toronto: Oxford University Press 2002

Bertrand, André. *L'éducation classique au Collège du Sacré-Cœur.* Sudbury: Société historique du Nouvel-Ontario 1988

Bock, Michel. *Comment un peuple oublie son nom: La crise identitaire franco-ontarienne et la presse française de Sudbury (1960–1975).* Sudbury: Prise de parole et Institut franco-ontarien 2001

Bourns, A.N. *A Proposal for Structural Change in the University System in Northeastern Ontario.* Toronto: Government of Ontario 1981

Braun, H.S. *A Northern Vision: The Development of Lakehead University.* Thunder Bay: Lakehead University Press 1987

Cameron, David M. *The Northern Dilemma: Public Policy and Post-Secondary Education in Northern Ontario.* Toronto: Ontario Economic Council 1978

Cameron, Peter. "The Duff-Berdahl Report. Will the Patient Live?" *CAUT Bulletin* 15, 2 (1966): 47–52

Cardinal, Harold. *The Unjust Society.* Edmonton: Hurtig 1969

Carrigan, D. Owen. "Collective Bargaining in Canadian Universities." *International Journal of Institutional Management in Higher Education* 1, 1 (May 1977): 17–31.

Carter, D.D. "Collective Bargaining for University Faculty: A Legal Perspective." *Canadian Journal of Higher Education* 5, 1 (1975): 25–31

Clark, Howard C. *Growth and Governance of Canadian Universities. An Insider's View.* Vancouver: UBC Press 2003

Dennie, Donald, and Annette Ribordy. "Les vingt-cinq ans de l'Institut." *Revue du Nouvel-Ontario* 25 (2001): 9–44

Fleming, W.G. *Post-secondary and Adult Education*. Toronto: University of Toronto Press 1971

Foot, David. *Boom, Bust & Echo*. Toronto: Macfarlane Walker and Ross 1996

Fournier-Thibault, Micheline. *André Paiement (1950–1978): Avant tout un homme de son temps*. Sudbury: Prise de parole 2004

Galarneau, Claude. *Les collèges classiques au Canada français (1620–1970)*. Montréal: Fides 1978

Gaudreau, Guy, and Michel Verrette. "Évolution des effectifs étudiants au Collège de Saint-Boniface, 1885–1967." *Cahiers franco-canadiens de l'Ouest* 6, 1 (1994): 87–109

Gervais, Gaétan. "L'enseignement supérieur en Ontario français (1848–1965)." *Revue du Nouvel-Ontario* 7 (1985): 11–52

Gidney, Catherine. *A Long Eclipse: The Liberal Protestant Establishment and the Canadian University, 1920–1970*. Montreal & Kingston: McGill-Queen's University Press 2004

– "War and the Concept of Generation: The International Teach-Ins at the University of Toronto, 1965–1968." In Paul Stortz and E. Lisa Panayotidis, eds, *Universities and War: Histories of Academic Cultures and Conflict*. Toronto: University of Toronto Press forthcoming

Gidney, R.D. *From Hope to Harris: The Reshaping of Ontario's Schools*. Toronto: University of Toronto Press 1999

Graham, Roger. *Old Man Ontario: Leslie M. Frost*. Toronto: University of Toronto Press 1990

Hall, M. Ann. "Creators of the Lost and Perfect Game? Gender, History, and Canadian Sport." In Philip White and Devin Young, eds, *Sport and Gender in Canada*. Don Mills: Oxford University Press 1999

– *The Girl and the Game: A History of Women's Sport in Canada*. Peterborough, ON: Broadview Press 2002

Hallsworth, Gwenda. *Le beau risque du savoir: Un bref historique de l'Université Laurentienne / A venture into the realm of higher education: A brief history of Laurentian University*. Sudbury, ON: Laurentian University 1985

Havel, J.E. *Politics in Sudbury*. Sudbury, ON: Laurentian University Press 1965

Henderson, Stuart. "Toronto's Hippie Disease: End Days in the Yorkville Scene, August 1968." *Journal of the Canadian Historical Association*, New Series, 17, 1 (2006): 205–34

Hewitt, Steve. *Spying 101: The RCMP's Secret Activities at Canadian Universities, 1917–1997*. Toronto: University of Toronto Press 2002

Horn, Michiel. *Academic Freedom in Canada: A History*. Toronto: University of Toronto Press 1999

– "Unionization and the Canadian University: Historical and Personal Observations." *Interchange* 25, 1 (1994): 39–48

Jasen, Patricia. "'In Pursuit of Human Values (or Laugh When You Say That)': The Student Critique of the Arts Curriculum in the 1960s." In Paul Axelrod and John G. Reid, eds, *Youth, University and Canadian Society: Essays in the Social History of Higher Education*. Montreal & Kingston: McGill-Queen's University Press 1989

Idylwylde's First Fifty Years 1922–1972. Toronto: Canadian Yearbook Services 1972

Johnston, Hugh. *Radical Campus: Making Simon Fraser University*. Vancouver: Douglas & McIntyre 2005

Jones, Glen A., Paul Goyan and Theresa Shanahan. "The Academic Senate and University Governance in Canada." *Canadian Journal of Higher Education* 34, 2 (2004): 35–48

- "University Governance in Canadian Higher Education." *Tertiary Education and Management* 7, 2 (2001): 135–48
Kettle, John. *The Big Generation.* Toronto: McClelland & Stewart 1980
Kinnear, Mary. "Disappointment in Discourse: Women University Professors at the University of Manitoba." *Historical Studies in Education* 4, 2 (1992): 269–87
Kinsman, Gary. *The Regulation of Desire: Homo and Hetero Sexualities.* Montreal: Black Rose Books 1996
Klatch, Rebecca E. *A Generation Divided: The New Left, and New Right, and the 1960s.* Berkeley: University of California Press 1999
Kostash, Myrna. *Long Way from Home: The Story of the Sixties Generation in Canada.* Toronto: Lorimer Press 1980
Lafrenière, Julie. "Des luttes au consensus, 1965–1982." In Guy Gaudreau, ed., *Bâtir sur le roc: De l'ACFÉO à l'ACFO du Grand Sudbury (1910–1987).* Sudbury: Prise de parole 1994
LaSelva, S.V. *Moral Foundations of Canadian Federalism.* Montreal & Kingston: McGill-Queen's University Press 1996
Lenskyj, Helen. "Who's Sport? Who's Tradition? Canadian Women and Sport in the Twentieth Century." *International Journal of the History of Sport* 9, 1 (1992): 141–50
Levi, Charles. "Sex, Drugs, Rock & Roll, and the University College Lit: The University of Toronto Festivals, 1965–69." *Historical Studies in Education* 18, 2 (2006): 163–90
Levitt, Cyril. *Children of Privilege: Student Revolt in the Sixties: A Study of Student Movements in Canada, the US and West Germany.* Toronto: University of Toronto Press 1984
Lexier, Roberta. "'The Backdrop Against Which Everything Happened': English-Canadian Student Movements and Off-Campus Movements for Change." *History of Intellectual Culture* 7, 1 (2007)
- "The Community of Scholars: The English-Canadian Student Movement and University Governance." In Marie Hammond-Callaghan and Matthew Hayday, eds, *Mobilizations, Protests and Engagements: Canadian Perspectives on Social Movements.* Halifax: Fernwood Publishing 2008
Living and Learning: The Report of the Provincial Committee on Aims and Objectives of Education in the Schools of Ontario (Hall-Dennis Report). Toronto: Ontario Department of Education 1968
Marwick, Arthur. *The Sixties: Cultural Revolution in Britain, France, Italy, and the United States, c.1958–c.1974.* Oxford: Oxford University Press 1998
Mawhiney, Anne-Marie, and Ross Paul. "Women and Distance Education in Northeastern Ontario." In Margaret Kechnie and Marge Reitsma-Street, eds, *Changing Lives: Women in Northern Ontario.* Toronto & Oxford: Dundurn Press 1996
Monahan, Edward J. *Collective Autonomy: A History of the Council of Ontario Universities, 1962–2000.* Waterloo: Wilfrid Laurier University Press 2004)
- "Duff-Berdahl Conference on University Government." *CAUT Bulletin* 16, 3 (February 1968): 54–62
- "University-Government Relations in Ontario: The History of a Buffer Body, 1958–1996." *Minerva* 36, 4 (1998): 347–66
Neatby, H.B., and Don McEown. *Creating Carleton: The Shaping of a University.* Montreal & Kingston: McGill-Queen's University Press 2002
Ouellette, Pierre. "Éducation et économie, 1927–1965." In Guy Gaudreau, ed., *Bâtir sur le roc.* Sudbury: Prise de parole and SHNO 1994
Owram, Douglas. *Born at the Right Time.* Toronto: University of Toronto Press 1996

Pilkington, Gwendolyne Evans. *Speaking With One Voice: Universities in Dialogue with Government*. Montreal: History of McGill Project, McGill University, 1983

Pitsula, James M. *As One Who Serves: The Making of the University of Regina*. Montreal & Kingston: McGill-Queen's University Press 2006

- *New World Dawning: The Sixties at Regina Campus*. Regina: Canadian Plains Research Centre 2008

Plante, Albert. *Vingt-cinq ans de vie française: Le Collège de Sudbury*. Montreal: 1938

Pocklington, Tom, and Allan Topper. *No Place to Learn: Why Universities Aren't Working*. Vancouver: UBC Press 2002

Rae, Bob. *From Protest to Power: Personal Reflections on a Life in Politics*. Toronto: Penguin Books Canada 1996

Ray, Arthur J. *I Have Lived Here Since the World Began*. Toronto: Key Porter Books 1996

Raymond, Alphonse. "Origines universitaires à Sudbury." *Laurentian University Review* 3, 4 (1971): 68–72

- *1914–1978. Mes souvenirs recueillis*. Trans. and annotated by Huguette Parent, s.c.o. Ottawa: Centre franco-ontarien de ressources pédagogiques 1996

Realizing the Potential: A Strategy for University Research in Canada. Ottawa: Royal Society of Canada 1991

Reid, Tim, and Julyan Reid. *Student Power and the Canadian Campus*. Toronto: Peter Martin Associates 1969

Ricard, François. *The Lyric Generation: The Life and Times of the Baby Boomers*. Trans. Donald Winkler. Toronto: Stoddart 1994

Riopel, Pierre A. "La fondation de l'École normale de Sudbury (1957–1963)." *Revue du Nouvel-Ontario* 33 (2008): 97–132

Robbins, Wendy, Margrit Eichler, Meg Luxton, and Francine Descarries, eds. *Minds of Our Own: Inventing Feminist Scholarship and Women's Studies in Canada and Quebec, 1966–1976*. Waterloo: Wilfrid Laurier University Press 2008

Rodrigue, Michel. "1970–1975. Une nouvelle vision: la création collective." In Guy Gaudreau, ed., *Le Théâtre du Nouvel-Ontario, 20 ans*. Sudbury: TNO 1991

Ross, Murray G. *The University: The Anatomy of Academe*. New York: McGraw-Hill 1976

Rowat, Donald C. "The Duff-Berdahl Report." *CAUT Bulletin* 14, 4 (1966): 23–30

Saarinen, Oiva. "Creating a Sustainable Community: The Sudbury Case Study." In Matt Bray and Ashley Thomson, eds, *At the End of the Shift: Mines and Single Industry Towns in Northern Ontario*. Toronto & Oxford: Dundurn Press 1992

Sheffield, Edward F. "The Post-War Surge in Post-Secondary Education, 1945–1969." In J. Donald Wilson, Robert M. Stamp, and Louis-Philippe Audet, eds, *Canadian Education: A History*. Scarborough: Prentice-Hall of Canada 1970

Sibley, W.M. "Modes of University Government." *Canadian Journal of Higher Education* 5, 1 (1976): 19–27

Solski, Mike, and John Smaller. *Mine Mill: The History of the International Union of Mine, Mill and Smelter Workers in Canada Since 1895*. Ottawa: Steel Rail Publishing 1985

St-Pierre, Stéphanie. "Le drapeau franco-ontarien: 'Puissent ses couleurs nous rallier dans une nouvelle amitié et fraternité,' 1975–1977." In Guy Gaudreau, ed., *Le drapeau franco-ontarien*. Sudbury: Prise de parole 2005

Symons, T.H.B. *Report of the Ministerial Commission on French-Language Secondary Education*. Toronto: Government of Ontario 1972

Toupin, Robert. "Le rôle des jésuites dans l'enseignement classique et universitaire de la région de Sudbury." *Laurentian University Review* 3, 4 (1971): 73–77

Waite, P.B. *The Lives of Dalhousie University,* vol. 2, *1925–1980 The Old College Transformed.* Montreal & Kingston: McGill-Queen's University Press 1998

Wallace, C.M. and Ashley Thomson, eds. *Sudbury: Rail Town to Regional Capital.* Toronto & Oxford: Dundurn Press 1993

Warren, Jean-Philippe, and Julien Massicotte. "La fermeture du departement de sociologie de l'Université de Moncton: histoire d'une crise politico-épistémologique." *Canadian Historical Review* 87, 3 (September 2006): 463–96

Weaver, Sally M. *Making Canadian Indian Policy: The Hidden Agenda 1968–1970.* Toronto: University of Toronto Press 1981

Whalley, George, ed. *A Place of Liberty: Essays on the Government of Canadian Universities.* Toronto: Clarke-Irwin 1964

INDEX

107–8, 110, 118, 119, 133; études de la santé,
133; geography, 105, 107–8, 110, 116, 131–2;
gerontology, 289; history, 15, 38, 76, 99,
105, 107, 110, 134, 141, 162, 220, 244, 275,
311; labour and trade union studies, 133;
law and justice, 110, 133; political science, 105, 107–8, 110, 125, 133, 186, 193, 198;
psychology, 107–10, 115, 133; sociology, 12,
103, 105, 107–10, 133, 216, 224, 258, 260;
sports psychology, 133
– Sciences: astronomy, 127, 133; behavioural neuroscience, 133; biochemistry,
115, 131, 144, 149; biology, 73–4, 99, 109,
111, 115, 125, 131–2, 134, 275; chemistry, 93,
99, 115–16, 131–3, 144, 149, 248, 275; computer science, 116, 131, 133, 137, 143, 191,
275; earth sciences (geology), 45, 67, 108,
113, 116–17, 122–3, 131–2, 146, 248; forensic science, 132, 134; liberal science, 133;
mathematics, 5, 7, 99, 115–16, 131, 133, 156,
275; physics, 99, 109, 116, 131–3, 148, 241
Adam, Dyane, 235–7, 239–40, 246
Advisory Committee on Academic
Programmes (ACAP), 120–3
affiliated colleges: Algoma University
College, 70–2, 139, 141; Collège universitaire de Hearst, 13, 70–1, 139–41, 232, 242;
Nipissing University College, 70–2, 115,
137, 139, 141
Albert, Hugues, 9, 59, 62, 217, 221, 266
Allaire, Chrysologue, 59
Allaire, Gratien, 93, 239–41
alumni, 9, 58, 89, 97, 188, 322
Andrew, Jack, 242
animal facility, 127
architecture, 137
Arteca, Gustavo, 149
articulation agreements, 133, 320, 327
Ashby, Connor, 48
Assembly of Francophone professors, 224,
228, 230, 234, 236–8, 243
Association canadienne-française de
l'éducation en Ontario (ACFEO and
ACFO): provincial, 9–11, 14–15, 24–5, 203;
Sudbury, 203, 227, 232
Association des étudiants canadiens-
français du nord-Ontario, 163

Association des étudiants de langue fran-
çaise du Nord de l'Ontario (ADELFNO),
207, 219
Association of Universities and Colleges of
Canada (AUCC), 43, 92, 152, 303
Assumption College (Windsor), 4, 10
Athabasca University, 77, 85
athletics, 158, 159, 183, 185–6, 197–8, 256, 326
(see also students: athletics)
Auld, James, 304
Avery, Benjamin, 13, 33, 36, 39

Banting, Sir Frederick, 66
Baskerville, Peter A., 318
Baumann, Alex, 75, 186, 193, 310
Baxter, Jean. 257, 267, 270
Beaton, William, 9
Bélanger, Charles, 79, 83–5, 129, 146, 234–5,
240, 315, 328
Bélanger, Georges, 103, 241
Bélanger, Pierre, 103, 216–17
Bélisle, Rhéal, 12, 37, 284
Bell, W.J., 72
Bennett, Elizabeth M. Granger, 252
Bennett, Harold, 23–7, 30, 33, 36–40, 109,
282–3, 286
Berdahl, Robert, 43
Berger, Jacques, 228
Bernard, Roger, 241
Bernier, Leo, 67
Bertrand, André, 7–8
Bertrand, Hector-L., 242
Bertrim, Thomas, 206
Best, Charles, 66
Best, Henry B.M., 152, 230, 232, 267, 269,
307; administrative challenges, 67–70,
75–6; affiliate relations, 70–2, 12, 24;
appointment and biography, 66–7, 76;
community relations, 72–5; fundraising,
80–1
biculturalism, xiii, 24, 30, 67, 163, 207, 211,
214, 221
Bideau, Michel, 209
bilingualism, 24–5, 30, 36, 79, 83, 90, 114,
138, 203–5, 239, 242–3, 247–8, 265 (see
also students); administrative personnel, 40, 61–2, 66, 77, 201, 206–7, 222–4;

Hinde, Mary, 163, 255
Hoffman, Abby, 185, 259
Hope commission, 10
Horn, Michiel, 43
Howarth, Thomas, 39
Huntington, Rev. Silas, 20
Huntington University, 156, 160, 179, 282, 284, 287–9, 324; federation relations, 35–6, 42, 99, 324 (*see also* chapter 17); founding, 18–20, 25, 27–9; programs, 35–6, 99, 104–6, 133, 135, 287–9; residence, 163, 192, 213, 255, 283, 285
Hurtubise, J.-Raoul, 9–19

Ibero-American University of Mexico, 35
Imperial Order Daughters of the Empire, 254
institutes/research centres: Centre for Excellence in Mining Innovation (CEMI), 146; Centre for Research in Human Development (CRHD), 147; Centre for Research in Occupational Safety and Health (CROSH), 149; Centre for Research in Social Justice and Policy (CRSJP), 149; Centre for Rural and Northern Health (CRaNHR), 147; Centre in Mining and Mineral Exploration Research (CIMMER), 128–9; Centre in Mining Materials Research (CIMMR), 146–7; Cooperative Freshwater Ecology Unit (CFEU), 146; Elliot Lake Research Field Station (ELRFS), 147; Geomechanics Research Centre (GRC), 129, 147; Institut franco-ontarien (IFO), 127–8, 146–7, 227; Institute for Research in Fine Particles, 127; Institute for Sport Marketing (ISM), 148; Institute of Astronomy, 116; Institute of Northern Ontario Research and Development (INORD), 147; Laurentian University Mining Automation Laboratory (LUMAL), 148; Mineral Exploration Research Centre (MERC), 129, 148; Mining Innovation, Rehabilitation, Applied Research Corporation (MIRARCO), 148; Northern Health Human Resources Research Unit, 147; Sudbury Cardio-Thoracic Foundation,

127; Sudbury Neutrino Observatory (SNO), 132, 148
interdisciplinary studies, 66, 122–3, 128, 133, 142–3
International Council for Distance Education, 77
International Students' Organization, 176
International Union of Mine, Mill and Smelter Workers, 13, 16, 22, 162, 302

James, Donald, 42
Jensen, Christian, 40
Jerome, Wendy, 319
John Street residence, 73, 254

Kaiser, Peter, 147
Kari, Roy, 307–8, 318
Keays, Reid, 132
Kechnie, Margaret, 266, 273–4
Kinnear, Mary, 261
Kinoshameg, Stella, 179
Knox, Sandy, 185, 197
Krawchuk, Andrii, 290

Lacombe, Claude, 242
Lacroix, Maureen, 251, 274
Lafrenière, Gérard, 9
Lakehead University, 56, 135, 137, 147, 280, 312, 315–16, 325
Lalement University, 29
Lallier, Raymond, 241
Larouche, Laurent, 59
Laurentian University Accounts Committee, 88
Laurentian University Alumni Association, 58
Laurentian University of Sudbury Act, 12, 29–30, 33, 35–6, 39, 44, 87, 166, 286, 288, 305;
Laurentian University [of Sudbury] Faculty Association (LU[S]FA), 52, 70, 75, 83–4, 97, 261, 265, 269, 271, 321; certification, 69–70, 267, 303–9, 311–12, 323, 327; collective agreement, 69–70, 78, 87, 239, 267, 305, 307, 309–11; committee on the status of women, 260; creation, 37, 293–4; employment policy, 298–9; faculty housing, 295–7; faculty representation on

Northeastern University Committee
(NEUC), 16, 19–21, 25–7
Northern Ontario University Association
(NOUA), 19–26, 28, 105, 283
Nurmi, Carl, 46, 53, 60, 76

Oblates, 6, 10–11, 15
Official Languages Act, 30, 211
Ontario Council of Graduate Studies
(OCGS), 118–21, 141–2, 143
Ontario Council of University Faculty
Associations (OCUFA), 54–5, 260
Ontario Economic Council, 70
Ontario Federation of Students (OFS), 180,
187–8, 196
Ontario Intercollegiate Athletic
Association (OIAA), 159–60, 183–4
Ontario Labour Relations Act, 304, 308
Ontario Ministry of Colleges and
Universities, 58, 67–8, 71–2, 82, 89, 95–6,
120, 202, 230, 235, 242, 263, 274, 288, 304
Ontario Ministry of Community and
Social Services, 265
Ontario Ministry of Northern Affairs, 67
Ontario-Quebec Women's Conference of
Intercollegiate Athletics (OQWCIA), 185
Ontario Task Force on Learning
Technology, 92
Ontario Task Force on University
Accountability, 87–8
Ontario University Athletic Association
(OUAA), 183–4, 197
Ontario Women's Intercollegiate Athletic
Conference (OWIAA), 185–6, 197
Ordre de Jacques-Cartier, 9
Ottawa Teachers' College, 7
Ouellette, Denise, 251
Ouellette, Pierre, 9
Oxford University, 77

Page, Léandre, 209
Paiement, André, 216
Palmer, Thomas, 28
Paquette, Robert, 216
Parker, Doris, 269–71, 280
Parker, Douglas, xi, 82, 92, 150, 324
Parker, Ralph D., 13, 22–6, 29, 33, 34, 36,
40, 286

Parrott, Harry, 71, 188, 231–2, 289
Parti québécois, 227
Paul, Linda, 280
Paul, Ross H., 83–4, 93, 118; appointment
and biography, 85, 90; presidency, 86–7,
89–90
Pauling, Linus, 73
Peel, Bruce, 195
Peltier, Jacques, 37, 118
Perron, Ronald, 9
Peterson, David, 72, 80–2
Pickard, Patricia, 185–6, 256
Plante, Albert, 9
Plaunt, W.B., 75
Pong, Ray, 147
Popovich, Sonya, 267
Porter, Chief Justice Dana, 29–30
Porter, Jack, 122, 196, 227
Porter, Janice, 279
Powell, Mary, 280
presidential advisory committee on
appointments, 34
presidential advisory committee on con-
sultative structures and procedures,
44–6, 167
presidential advisory committee on engin-
eering (PACE), 130–1
presidential searches, 1960, 34; 1963, 40;
1972, 61–2; 1977, 66; 1984, 77; 1991, 85;
1998, 90; 2001, 93; 2009, 96
Prise de parole, 217–18, 328
Pryke, Kenneth, 37, 118

Querney, Alan, 82

Rabin, Cedric, 118
Rae, Bob, 72, 86–7, 196, 317–19, 327
Rancourt, Yvan, 217
Raymond, Fr. Alphonse, 10–12, 14–15, 17, 22
Reed, Lloyd, 84–5, 143
Regimbal, Maurice, 157–9, 183, 192
Regulation XVII, 5
Reid, Paul, 75
Reid, Stewart, 37
Reid, Weir, 302
Renaud, Normand, 244
Research, Development and Creativity
Council, 150

research funding, 96, 126–7, 146, 151
Revue du Nouvel-Ontario, 128, 227, 240, 242
Robarts, John, 51, 208, 286, 296–7
Roberge, André, 92–3, 241, 324
Rock, Allan, 97
Royal Commission on Bilingualism and
    Biculturalism, 20, 30, 163, 207
Russell, Peter, 195

Sabourin, Janet, 217
Sabourin, Pascal, 9, 228
Sacred Heart College (Collège Sacré
    Coeur), 3, 10, 12–13, 15, 37, 157; academic
    programs, 5–7; affiliations (University
    of Ottawa, Laval University), 6, 20;
    bilingualism, 4–5; charter, 10–11; faculty,
    7–8; founding, 3–4; funding, 8; origin of
    students, 8
Saint-Aubin, Judge Albert, 203
San Francisco State University, 43
Savage, Donald C., 311
Sawyer, Patrice, 324
Schell, Bernadette, 267, 314
Schumpeter, Joseph, 34
Scollard, Bishop David J., 4
Scott, Frank, 43
Senate, 52, 90, 130, 228, 237–8, 323; aca-
    demic planning, 43, 46–8, 50, 60, 70, 78,
    94–5, 101, 106, 114, 118–22, 132–5, 137, 144,
    149–50, 219, 224, 228–9, 258, 289, 325;
    'academic recesses,' 49–50, 54–5, 170–1,
    301–2, 312; bicameralism, 92, 226–7, 232,
    235, 237–9, 241; bilingualism, 177, 207,
    211–12, 221–3, 226–7, 230–1, 235, 238, 241
    (*see also* bilingualism, and Board of
    Governors, bilingualism committee);
    budgetary questions, 47, 50, 60–1, 64,
    67–70, 78, 88, 96; composition, 34, 44–5,
    273; governance conflict (1967–1970),
    44–50, 53–6, 166–72, 301; language of
    debate, 212; representation on Board of
    Governors, 43, 46–7, 50, 58; research,
    126, 129, 146; role, 34, 43–5, 53, 56–7,
    59–60, 63–5, 69–70, 77, 79, 83, 87–8, 114,
    175–7, 187, 193, 229–30, 261, 268, 270, 305,
    307, 323–4; selection of senior academic
    administrators, 59–61, 78–80
Shea, William, 46–52

Sibley, W.M., 294, 303, 311
Silverton, Susan, 96, 251
Simoni, Pierre, 314
Sinclair, Carolyn, 251
Sir George Williams University, 167
Smith, James, 290
Smith, Ronald, 241
Smith, Stuart, 152
"Social contract," 86–7, 195–6, 312, 317–19,
    327
Social Sciences and Humanities Research
    Council (SSHRC), 127–9, 150–1
Société des universitaires de langue fran-
    çaise de l'Ontario (SULFO), 243–4
Société historique du Nouvel-Ontario, 35
Society of Jesus (Jesuit Order), 3–7, 9–10,
    12–15, 24–5, 37, 99, 157, 206–7, 209, 212,
    287
Sopha, Elmer, 44
Sorbara, Gregory, 72, 82
Speigel, Sara, 265
Spencer, Sister Leona, 265
St-Aubin, Étienne, 44, 167–8
St. Francis Xavier University, 62
St. Jerome's College (Waterloo), 19
Steedman, Mercedes, 280
Stelter, Gilbert, 47–8
Stephenson, Bette, 67, 71
Stewart, E.E., 55
Students: Association des étudiant(e)s
    francophones (AEF), 58, 176–8, 188,
    190–1, 193, 196, 218–21, 224, 226–7, 241;
    Association of Gays and Lesbians of
    Laurentian (Pride@LU), 181; Association
    of Laurentian Part-time Students
    (ALPS), 176–7, 188, 191, 193; athletics,
    74–5, 86, 158–60, 183, 184–7, 197–8, 256,
    259, 326; bilingualism (*see* bilingualism,
    and Board of Governors, bilingualism
    committee); court of discipline, 44,
    157, 163, 166; drinking, 157, 166, 192–4;
    enrolment, 38, 41, 44, 51, 63, 67, 69, 73,
    75, 80, 86, 91, 94–5, 137, 155, 157, 161, 181,
    190, 199, 244–5, 273, 291, 303–4, 307, 315,
    317, 319–20; double cohort, 94–5, 143,
    199, 320, 327–8; Extension Students'
    General Association (ESGA), 46, 169;
    extracurricular activities, 156–8, 171–5,

284, 286; continuing education, 11, 13, 117; creation of Laurentian, 12, 15–17, 19–20, 22, 24–9, 99–100, 107, 117, 325; denominationalism, 5–6, 14, 17–18; federation relations, 35–6, 42, 99 (*see also* chapter 17); founding, 9, 11–13, 20; Franco-Ontarian flag, 199, 218–20, 248; president, 5, 8, 10, 12, 14, 17, 35, 157, 241, 283, 290; provincial funding, 10, 14, 17–18; residence, 163, 175, 192, 213; role in creation of Laurentian, 25–6, 29–30, 35–6; Séminaire de Hearst affiliation, 13, 70, 139; workers' movements, 13, 22

University of Toronto, 7, 11, 20, 23, 25, 33, 39, 40, 62, 65, 73, 93, 99, 112, 180, 186, 252, 282, 295

University of Waterloo, 17

University of Western Ontario, Huron College, 93

University of Windsor, 17, 90

University of Wisconsin, 41

University Women's Club of Sudbury, 253, 329

Valiquette, Josée, 7

Vallillee, Gerald, 52

Vanstone, Sue, 279

Vasseur, Liette, 150, 251, 321

Vaughan, Rev. Harold, 25–8, 30

Vegetation Enhancement Technical Advisory Committee (VETAC), 73–4

Vethamany-Globus, Swani, 280

Vickery, Norman, 186

Villanova University, 62

Vincent, Gaston, 11, 13, 24–5

Wadge, Norman, 62

Wagner, Lloyd, 269, 271, 307

Wallace, Donald, 302

Wallace, James, 95

Watson, Wynn, 52

Watters, Jean R. (president, 1998–2001), appointment and biography, 90–1, 93; presidency, 91–2; resignation, 92–3

Weaver, Mary, 64–5, 228

Whalen, Mary, 75

Wilfred Laurier University, 59

Williams, Lorna, 267

Williamson, Douglas, 64, 73, 116, 224

Wilson, B.A., 242

Wilson, Tuzo, 73

women, administrators, 251–2, 261–2, 265–8, 270, 272–3, 277–8; affirmative action, 259; attitudes toward, 255–67, 264, 266, 268–71, 274; Board of Governors chairs, 251, 272, 274; Board of Governors members, 33, 58, 265, 267–8, 273; employment equity, 254, 266, 269, 273, 275, 279–80, 329; 1987 employment equity report, 274–5; equality for, 251, 262, 269, 272–3; faculty, 250–1, 256, 260–2, 266, 273, 278, 281; Francophones, compared to, 267; LEAF breakfasts, 278; Montreal Massacre, 278; PAC Celebrate Women Event, 278; PAC 1980 report, 263, 266–9, 275–7; pay equity, 254, 266, 269, 270, 273, 275–8, 280, 329; pension plan, 257–8; presidential advisory committee on the status of, 180, 264, 267, 270–1, 278; Royal Commission on the Status of, 257, 260–1; salary levels, 262, 265–6, 304; sexual harassment, 180, 192, 270, 272, 277, 280, 329; staff, 252–3, 257–8, 261–2, 265–9, 270, 272–3, 276–8; students, 157–8, 180, 199, 251–2, 254–6, 266–8, 273, 278–81; supporting university, 251–3, 278; women's centre, 180

Woodsworth, Judith Weisz, 133, 136, 241, 251, 321; appointment and biography, 93; presidency, 93–6; resignation, 96

Wright, Peter, 68, 70, 222

Wright, Archbishop W.L., 24–6, 30, 286

Xavier University, 62

York University, 67

Zaborszky, Dorothy, 265–7

Zorbas, Greg, 8, 9

ILLUSTRATION CREDITS

6   Sacred Heart College. City of Greater Sudbury Historical Database, MK0203EN.
11 Alphonse Raymond. Photo courtesy of the University of Sudbury.
14 President Émile Bouvier, the University of Sudbury, 1961. City of Greater Sudbury Archives, Bob Kier Fonds, 61-411.
16 University of Sudbury Convocation, 1960. *Laurentiana*, 1961.
18 Earl S. Lautenslager, 1960. City of Greater Sudbury Archives, Bob Kier Fonds, 60-367.
22 Ralph D. Parker. *Laurentiana*, 1961–1963.
27 Official entrance of the Laurentian University downtown campus in the Empire Block on Elgin Street, 1960. Laurentian University Archives, Public Affairs Photographs, CD2-DC3.
29 Signing the *Laurentian University Act of Incorporation*, March 28, 1960. *Laurentiana*, 1961–1963.
35 Huntington University on Larch St., *circa* 1961. City of Greater Sudbury Archives, Bob Kier Fonds, 60-464.
41 Stanley G. Mullins. Laurentian University Archives, Public Affairs Photographs, CD4-PR54q.
50 Construction of the Laurentian University Great Hall, 1963. Laurentian University Archives, Public Affairs Photographs, CD2-CO23.
60 Laurentian University Museum and Arts Centre. Laurentian University Archives, Public Affairs Photographs, CD1-LM26.
62 Edward J. Monahan. Laurentian University Archives, Public Affairs Photographs, CD4-PR53.
65 Landscape of the campus. Laurentian University Archives, Public Affairs Photographs, CD2-AE6.
68 Henry B.M. Best. Laurentian University, Instructional Media.
74 Laurentian and the re-vegetation of the Sudbury Basin. Photograph courtesy of Peter Beckett.
78 John S. Daniel. Laurentian University Archives, Public Affairs Photographs, CD4-PR38.
85 Ross H. Paul. Laurentian University, Instructional Media.
91 Jean R. Watters. Laurentian University, Instructional Media.
94 Judith W. Woodsworth. Laurentian University, Instructional Media.
97 Dominic Giroux. Laurentian University, Instructional Media.

187 Upcoming Varsity Events, 1978. Laurentian University Archives, Public Affairs Photographs, CD2-SL95.
188 Exam in gym. Laurentian University Archives, Public Affairs Photographs, CD6-TL236.
190 Laissez-nous notre bibliothèque, *circa* 1989. Laurentian University Archives, Public Affairs Photographs, CD4-SG14.
192 Cartoon of female security officer, 1983. Ollie Simpkins, *Northern Life*, October 12, 1983.
194 City transit bus. Laurentian University Archives, Public Affairs Photographs, CD2-SL124.
196 Career day. Laurentian University Archives, Public Affairs Photographs, CD6-UE4.
198 Model parliament. Photograph courtesy of Megan Yeadon.
199 The Voyageur mascot. Photograph courtesy of Laurentian Athletics. Photograph by John Sabourin, Action Event Photos.
205 President Mullins confers a degree at an outdoor convocation in the mid-1960s. Laurentian University Archives, Public Affairs Photographs, CD3-GR147.
206 André Girouard. Laurentian University Archives, Public Affairs Photographs, CD4-IG47.
210 University of Sudbury, 1967. Photograph courtesy of the University of Sudbury, A-135.
213 A student sing-song. Laurentian University Archives, Public Affairs Photographs, CD4-AF9.
220 Raising the Franco-Ontarian flag, 1975. *Sudbury Star*, September 26, 1975. *Sudbury Star* file photograph.
222 A typical day in the bowling alley. Laurentian University Afchives, Public Affairs Photographs, 164.3-P324. Photograph by Karl Sommerer.
228 French department professors Jacques Berger and Pascal Sabourin browse the *Revue du Nouvel-Ontario* and other Francophone journals. Laurentian University Archives, Public Affairs Photographs, CD2-SL175.
229 Two students read the Francophone student newspaper *Réaction* in the early 1980s. Laurentian University Archives, Public Affairs Photographs, CD4-AF8.
232 President Best proposes a toast to Laurentian's Francophone community. Laurentian University Archives, Public Affairs Photographs, CD4-AF11.
236 Dyane Adam. Laurentian University Archives, Public Affairs Photographs, CD1-WS2.
240 Official launch of an issue of *Revue du Nouvel-Ontario, circa* 1984. Laurentian University Archives, Public Affairs Photographs, CD1-LI165.
243 The official opening of the J.N. Desmarais Library by Paul Desmarais in June, 1990. Laurentian University Archives, Public Affairs Photographs, CD5-SE404.
248 Michel Dupuis and Gaétan Gervais at the ceremony honouring the 30th Anniversary of the Franco-Ontarian flag, 2005. Photograph courtesy of Guy Gaudreau.
253 IODE members donate university mace. *Sudbury Star*, May 19, 1966. *Sudbury Star* file photograph.
255 Huntington University students, 1960. City of Greater Sudbury Archives, Bob Kier Fonds, 60-728.
256 Sandy Knox, Human Kinetics and Pat Pickard, Athletics. *Sudbury Star*, January 17, 1982. *Sudbury Star* file photograph.

258 University staff reviewing filing system. Laurentian University Archives, Public Affairs Photographs, CD6-TL176.

261 Johanne Rioux and the Instructional Media team provide technology and communications support to faculty, staff and students. Laurentian University Archives, Public Affairs Photographs, CD6-UE337.

263 Women studying in University College residence. Laurentian University Archives, Public Affairs Photographs, CD2-RL64.

264 Nursing students. Laurentian University Archives, Public Affairs Photographs, CD1-NU4.

266 Dorothy Zaborszky and Margaret Kechnie. Laurentian University Archives, Public Affairs Photographs, CD5-SE887.

269 Laurentian students, *circa* 1960s. Laurentian University Archives, Public Affairs Photographs, CD2-SL3.

270 Staff and administration sign agreement. Laurentian University Archives, Public Affairs Photographs, CD4-LS2.

274 Maureen Lacroix. Laurentian University, Board of Governors. Photograph by Mike Dupont of Dupont Photography.

275 LUSU strategy session. Laurentian University Archives, Public Affairs Photographs, CD4-LS1.

277 Campus safety measures. Laurentian University Archives, Public Affairs Photographs, CD5-CE812.

279 University women's centre opened, 1994. Laurentian University Archives, Public Affairs Photographs, CD1-WC4.

283 The University of Sudbury. Laurentian University Archives, Public Affairs Photographs, CD2-US6.

285 Huntington University during its later construction phase. Laurentian University Archives, Public Affairs Photographs, CD2-HU6.

287 St. Mark's Chapel at Thorneloe University. Laurentian University Archives, Public Affairs Photographs, CD2-TH31.

289 *Northern Life*'s perceptive and witty take on the Parrott Commission recommendation about renaming Laurentian "Champlain University." Ollie Simpkins, *Northern Life*, October 26, 1983.

294 Indigenous learners take extension course, 1962. City of Greater Sudbury Archives, Bob Kier Fonds, 62-3-175.

296 Randolph apartment building. Photograph courtesy of Rob Ambrose.

298 Early teaching technology. Laurentian University Archives, Public Affairs Photographs, CD6-TL165.

301 Brian Kaye, Fine Particle Research Lab. City of Greater Sudbury Archives, Bob Kier Fonds, 69-10-9.

305 Arts building classroom. Laurentian University Archives, Public Affairs Photographs, CD6-TL222.

306 Garry Clarke, LUFA president. Laurentian University Archives, Public Affairs Photographs, CD6-UE 326.

309 Signing the collective agreement, 1980. Laurentian University Archives, Public Affairs Photographs, CD4-LU3.

310 Swim coach Jeno Tihanyi and Olympic gold medalist Alex Baumann. Laurentian University Archives, Public Affairs Photographs, CD4-IB64.

313 Professors on strike, 1985. *Lambda*, September 12, 1985.

315   LUFA bargaining session. Laurentian University Archives, Public Affairs Photographs, CD4-LU2.

317   Students protest 1989 faculty strike. *Sudbury Star*, September 27, 1989. *Sudbury Star* file photograph.

318   Department heads' retreat, late 1980s. Laurentian University Archives, Public Affairs Photographs, CD6-UE245.

322   Sheila Cote-Meek. Laurentian University, Instructional Media.

Colour Insert

Plate 1   Alphonse Raymond building, 1976. Photograph courtesy of Richard Everitt.

Plate 2   Aerial view of the campus athletic facilities. Laurentian University Archives, Public Affairs Photographs, CD2-AE42.

Plate 3   Brenda Wallace Reading Room. Laurentian University, Instructional Media, Brenda Wallace.

Plate 4   J.N. Desmarais Library in winter. Laurentian University, Instructional Media.

Plate 5   Northern Ontario School of Medicine. Laurentian University, Instructional Media.

Plate 6   Laurentian beach. Laurentian University, Instructional Media.

Plate 7   Tipi in Founders' Square. Laurentian University, Instructional Media.

Plate 8   School of Education building. Laurentian University, Instructional Media.

Plate 9   Science buildings at dusk. Laurentian University, Instructional Media.

Plate 10   Campus in winter. Laurentian University, Instructional Media.

Plate 11   Laurentian campus from Bell Park. Laurentian University, Instructional Media.

Plate 12   Snowy rooftop view from the student residences, 1976. Photograph courtesy of Richard Everitt.

Cover

Front   Aeriel view of Laurentian University. Laurentian University, Instructional Media. Photograph by AirScapes.

Back   Laurentian University crest. Laurentian University, Board of Governors